T0335723

Analysis and Applications of Lattice Boltzmann Simulations

Pedro Valero-Lara
Barcelona Supercomputing Center (BSC), Spain

A volume in the Advances
in Computer and Electrical
Engineering (ACEE) Book Series

Published in the United States of America by
  IGI Global
  Engineering Science Reference (an imprint of IGI Global)
  701 E. Chocolate Avenue
  Hershey PA, USA 17033
  Tel: 717-533-8845
  Fax: 717-533-8661
  E-mail: cust@igi-global.com
  Web site: http://www.igi-global.com

Library of Congress Cataloging-in-Publication Data

Names: Valero-Lara, Pedro, 1985- editor.
Title: Analysis and applications of Lattice-Boltzmann simulations / Pedro
  Valero-Lara, editor.
Description: Hershey, PA : Engineering Science Reference, [2018] | Includes
  bibliographical references.
Identifiers: LCCN 2017032863| ISBN 9781522547600 (hardcover) | ISBN
  9781522547617 (ebook)
Subjects: LCSH: Mathematical models. | Computer science--Mathematics. |
  Lattice Boltzmann methods.
Classification: LCC TA343 .A53 2018 | DDC 620.1/064--dc23 LC record available at https://lccn.
loc.gov/2017032863

This book is published in the IGI Global book series Advances in Computer and Electrical Engineering (ACEE) (ISSN: 2327-039X; eISSN: 2327-0403)

British Cataloguing in Publication Data
A Cataloguing in Publication record for this book is available from the British Library.

All work contributed to this book is new, previously-unpublished material.
The views expressed in this book are those of the authors, but not necessarily of the publisher.

For electronic access to this publication, please contact: eresources@igi-global.com.

Advances in Computer and Electrical Engineering (ACEE) Book Series

ISSN:2327-039X
EISSN:2327-0403

Editor-in-Chief: Srikanta Patnaik, SOA University, India

MISSION

The fields of computer engineering and electrical engineering encompass a broad range of interdisciplinary topics allowing for expansive research developments across multiple fields. Research in these areas continues to develop and become increasingly important as computer and electrical systems have become an integral part of everyday life.

The **Advances in Computer and Electrical Engineering (ACEE) Book Series** aims to publish research on diverse topics pertaining to computer engineering and electrical engineering. **ACEE** encourages scholarly discourse on the latest applications, tools, and methodologies being implemented in the field for the design and development of computer and electrical systems.

COVERAGE

- Computer Architecture
- Analog Electronics
- Circuit Analysis
- Computer Hardware
- Optical Electronics
- VLSI Design
- Microprocessor Design
- Power Electronics
- Applied Electromagnetics
- Algorithms

IGI Global is currently accepting manuscripts for publication within this series. To submit a proposal for a volume in this series, please contact our Acquisition Editors at Acquisitions@igi-global.com or visit: http://www.igi-global.com/publish/.

Titles in this Series

For a list of additional titles in this series, please visit:
https://www.igi-global.com/book-series/advances-computer-electrical-engineering/73675

Free and Open Source Software in Modern Data Science and Business Intelligence...
K.G. Srinivasa (CBP Government Engineering College, India) Ganesh Chandra Deka (M.
S. Ramaiah Institute of Technology, India) and Krishnaraj P.M. (M. S. Ramaiah Institute
of Technology, India)
Engineering Science Reference • ©2018 • 189pp • H/C (ISBN: 9781522537076) • US $190.00

Design Parameters of Electrical Network Grounding Systems
Osama El-Sayed Gouda (Cairo University, Egypt)
Engineering Science Reference • ©2018 • 316pp • H/C (ISBN: 9781522538530) • US $235.00

Design and Use of Virtualization Technology in Cloud Computing
Prashanta Kumar Das (Government Industrial Training Institute Dhansiri, India) and Ganesh
Chandra Deka (Government of India, India)
Engineering Science Reference • ©2018 • 315pp • H/C (ISBN: 9781522527855) • US $235.00

Smart Grid Test Bed Using OPNET and Power Line Communication
Jun-Ho Huh (Catholic University of Pusan, South Korea)
Engineering Science Reference • ©2018 • 425pp • H/C (ISBN: 9781522527763) • US $225.00

Transport of Information-Carriers in Semiconductors and Nanodevices
Muhammad El-Saba (Ain-Shams University, Egypt)
Engineering Science Reference • ©2017 • 677pp • H/C (ISBN: 9781522523123) • US $225.00

Accelerating the Discovery of New Dielectric Properties in Polymer Insulation
Boxue Du (Tianjin University, China)
Engineering Science Reference • ©2017 • 388pp • H/C (ISBN: 9781522523093) • US $210.00

Handbook of Research on Nanoelectronic Sensor Modeling and Applications
Mohammad Taghi Ahmadi (Urmia University, Iran) Razali Ismail (Universiti Teknologi
Malaysia, Malaysia) and Sohail Anwar (Penn State University, USA)
Engineering Science Reference • ©2017 • 579pp • H/C (ISBN: 9781522507369) • US $245.00

For an entire list of titles in this series, please visit:
https://www.igi-global.com/book-series/advances-computer-electrical-engineering/73675

701 East Chocolate Avenue, Hershey, PA 17033, USA
Tel: 717-533-8845 x100 • Fax: 717-533-8661
E-Mail: cust@igi-global.com • www.igi-global.com

Table of Contents

Detailed Table of Contents

Pedro Valero-Lara, Barcelona Supercomputing Center (BSC), Spain

The use of lattice Boltzmann method (LBM) has been extended to numerous fields of scientific and industrial interest due to its inherent characteristics, which make this methodology a very efficient and fast method for fluid simulations. In this chapter, the numerical formulation behind LBM is presented in detail. However, the main motivation of this chapter is the introduction to those aspects regarding the programmability of this method. The authors present different implementations, data layout, and strategies to efficiently implement LBM. The performance achieved by each of the techniques is analyzed in detail, over some of the currently used computer platforms. They pay particular attention to those techniques that attempt to reduce the memory requirement of their method, which is one of the most important weak-points when implementing and computing LBM.

Claudio Schepke, Federal University of Pampa, Brazil
João V. F. Lima, Federal University of Santa Maria, Brazil
Matheus S. Serpa, Federal University of Rio Grande do Sul, Brazil

Currently NVIDIA GPUs and Intel Xeon Phi accelerators are alternatives of computational architectures to provide high performance. This chapter investigates the performance impact of these architectures on the lattice Boltzmann method. This method is an alternative to simulate fluid flows iteratively using discrete representations. It can be adopted for a large number of flows simulations using simple operation rules. In the experiments, it was considered a three-dimensional version of the method, with 19 discrete directions of propagation (D3Q19).

Performance evaluation compare three modern GPUs: K20M, K80, and Titan X; and two architectures of Xeon Phi: Knights Corner (KNC) and Knights Landing (KNL). Titan X provides the fastest execution time of all hardware considered. The results show that GPUs offer better processing time for the application. A KNL cache implementation presents the best results for Xeon Phi architectures and the new Xeon Phi (KNL) is two times faster than the previous model (KNC).

Chapter 3

*Enrico Calore, University of Ferrara, Italy & National Institute for
Nuclear Physics, Italy*
*Alessandro Gabbana, University of Ferrara, Italy & National Institute
for Nuclear Physics, Italy*
*Sebastiano Fabio Schifano, University of Ferrara, Italy & National
Institute for Nuclear Physics, Italy*
*Raffaele Tripiccione, University of Ferrara, Italy & National Institute for
Nuclear Physics, Italy*

GPUs deliver higher performance than traditional processors, offering remarkable energy efficiency, and are quickly becoming very popular processors for HPC applications. Still, writing efficient and scalable programs for GPUs is not an easy task as codes must adapt to increasingly parallel architecture features. In this chapter, the authors describe in full detail design and implementation strategies for lattice Boltzmann (LB) codes able to meet these goals. Most of the discussion uses a state-of-the art thermal lattice Boltzmann method in 2D, but all lessons learned in this particular case can be immediately extended to most LB and other scientific applications. The authors describe the structure of the code, discussing in detail several key design choices that were guided by theoretical models of performance and experimental benchmarks, having in mind both single-GPU codes and massively parallel implementations on commodity clusters of GPUs. The authors then present and analyze performances on several recent GPU architectures, including data on energy optimization.

Chapter 4

Pedro Valero-Lara, Barcelona Supercomputing Center (BSC), Spain

The use of mesh refinement in CFD is an efficient and widely used methodology to minimize the computational cost by solving those regions of high geometrical complexity with a finer grid. The author focuses on studying two methods, one based on multi-domain and one based on irregular meshing, to deal with mesh refinement over LBM simulations. The numerical formulation is presented in detail.

Two approaches, homogeneous GPU and heterogeneous CPU+GPU, on each of the refinement methods are studied. Obviously, the use of the two architectures, CPU and GPU, to compute the same problem involves more important challenges with respect to the homogeneous counterpart. These strategies are described in detail paying particular attention to the differences among both methodologies in terms of programmability, memory management, and performance.

Chapter 5

This chapter presents the challenges and techniques in the efficient LBM implementations for sparse geometries. The first part contains a review of applications requiring support for sparse geometries including industry, geology, and life sciences. For each category, a short description of a geometry characteristic and the typical LBM extensions are provided. The second part describes implementations for single-core and parallel computers. Four main methods allowing for the reduction of memory usage and computational complexity are presented: hierarchical grids, tiles, and two techniques based on the indirect addressing (the fluid index array and the connectivity matrix). For parallel implementations, the advantages and disadvantages of the different methods of domain decomposition and workload balancing are discussed.

Chapter 6

This chapter develops a meshless formulation of lattice Boltzmann method for simulation of fluid flows within complex and irregular geometries. The meshless feature of proposed technique will improve the accuracy of standard lattice Boltzmann method within complicated fluid domains. Discretization of such domains itself may introduce significant numerical errors into the solution. Specifically, in phase transition or moving boundary problems, discretization of the domain is a time-consuming and complex process. In these problems, at each time step, the computational domain may change its shape and need to be re-meshed accordingly for the purpose of accuracy and stability of the solution. The author proposes to combine lattice Boltzmann method with a Galerkin meshfree technique popularly known as element-free Galerkin method in this chapter to remove the difficulties associated with traditional grid-based methods.

In this chapter, a brief discussion about the application of lattice Boltzmann method on complex flow characteristics over circular structures is presented. A two-dimensional computational simulation is performed to study the fluid flow characteristics by employing the lattice Boltzmann method (LBM) with respect to Bhatnagar-Gross-Krook (BGK) collision model to simulate the interaction of fluid flow over the circular cylinders at different spacing conditions. From the results, it is observed that there is no significant interaction between the wakes for the transverse spacing's ratio higher than six times the cylinder diameter. For smaller transverse spacing ratios, the fluid flow regimes were recognized with presence of vortices. Apart from that, the drag coefficient signals are revealed as chaotic, quasi-periodic, and synchronized regimes, which were observed from the results of vortex shedding frequencies and fluid structure interaction frequencies. The strength of the latter frequency depends on spacing between the cylinders; in addition, the frequency observed from the fluid structure interaction is also associated with respect to the change in narrow and wide wakes behind the surface of the cylinder. Further, the St and mean Cd are observed to be increasing with respect to decrease in the transverse spacing ratio.

This chapter presents several partitioned algorithms to couple lattice Boltzmann method (LBM) and finite element method (FEM) for numerical simulation of transient fluid-structure interaction (FSI) problems with large interface motion. Partitioned coupling strategies allow one to solve separately the fluid and solid subdomains using adapted or optimized numerical schemes, which provides a considerable flexibility for FSI simulation, especially for more realistic and industrial applications. However, partitioned coupling procedures often encounter numerical instabilities due to the fact that the time integrations of the two subdomains are usually carried out in a staggered way. As a consequence, the energy transfer across the fluid-solid interface is usually not correctly simulated, which means numerical energy injection or dissipation might occur at the interface with partitioned methods. The focus of the present chapter is given to the energy conservation property of different partitioned coupling strategies for FSI simulation.

Chapter 9

Iñaki Zabala, SENER Ingeniería y Sistemas S.A., Spain
Jesús M. Blanco, Universidad del País Vasco, Spain

Shallow water conditions are produced in coastal and river areas and allow the simplification of fluid solving by integrating in height to the fluid equations, discarding vertical flow so a 3D problem is solved with a set of 2D equations. Usually the boundary conditions defined by the surface pressure are discarded, as it is considered that the difference in atmospheric pressure in simulation domain is irrelevant in most hydraulic and coastal engineering scenarios. However, anticyclones and depressions produce noticeable pressure gradients that may affect the consequences of phenomena like tides and tsunamis. This chapter demonstrates how to remove this weakness from the LBM-SW by incorporating pressure into the LBM for this kind of scenario in a consistent manner. Other small-scale effects like buoyancy may be solved using this approach.

Chapter 10

Iñaki Zabala, SENER Ingeniería y Sistemas S.A., Spain
Jesús M. Blanco, Universidad del País Vasco, Spain

The lattice Boltzmann method (LBM) is a novel approach for simulating convection-diffusion problems. It can be easily parallelized and hence can be used to simulate fluid flow in multi-core computers using parallel computing. LES (large eddy simulation) is widely used in simulating turbulent flows because of its lower computational needs compared to others such as direct numerical simulation (DNS), where the Kolmogorov scales need to be solved. The aim of this chapter consists of introducing the reader to the treatment of turbulence in fluid dynamics through an LES approach applied to LBM. This allows increasing the robustness of LBM with lower computational costs without increasing the mesh density in a prohibitive way. It is applied to a standard D2Q9 structure using a unified formulation.

Preface

Computational Fluid Dynamics (CFD) is a set of numerical methods applied to obtain approximate solutions of problems of fluid dynamics and heat transfer. According to this definition, CFD is not a science by itself, but a way to apply the methods of one discipline (numerical analysis) to another (heat and mass transfer). The physics of any fluid flow is governed by the fundamental principles, which can be expressed in terms of equations. CFD is, in part, the art of replacing the governing equations of the fluid flow with a discrete series of numbers, and advancing these expressions in space and time to achieve, numerically, a description of the flow field. Some problems allow the immediate solution of the flow field without advancing in time or space, and others involve integral equations or statistical distributions rather than partial differential equations. In any case, all problems involve the manipulation, and the solution of discrete systems. The final result of CFD is indeed a collection of numbers, in contrast to an analytical solution. However, in the long run the objective of most engineering analyses is a quantitative description of the problem, i.e., numbers. Obviously, High Performance Computing (HPC) is the instrument which has allowed the advance of fluid simulations. CFD solutions require the repetitive management of millions of numbers. Therefore, the advances and its applications to problems of increasing detail and sophistication are intimately related to advances in computer hardware, particularly in regard to storage and execution speed. This is why one of the strongest forces driving the development of HPC during the 80's and the 90's came from the CFD community. Indeed, CFD continues to be one of the major drivers for advances in HPC.

Throughout most of the twentieth century the study and practice of fluid dynamics (indeed, all of physical science and engineering) involved the use of pure theory and pure experiment (Anderson, Menter, Dick, Degrez, & Vierendeels, 2013). However, CFD has become so important that nowadays it can be viewed as a new third dimension in fluid dynamics. From 1687, with the publication of Issac Newton's Principia, to the mid-1960's, fluid mechanics advanced through a combination of experiments and theoretical analysis, which always required the use of simplified models to obtain solutions of the governing equations (Wendt, & Anderson, 2008).

These solutions have the distinct advantage of immediately identifying some of the fundamental parameters of a given problem, and explicitly demonstrating how the problems are influenced by the variation of these parameters. On the other hand, they present a disadvantage of not including all the required physics of the flow. The advent of computing in the 60's allowed CFD to mitigate these problems. With its ability to handle the governing equations in "full" form, and to include detailed physical phenomena such as chemical reactions, CFD became a popular tool in engineering analyses. Now, CFD supports and complements both pure experiment and pure theory. CFD and supercomputers will remain a third dimension in fluid dynamics, of equal importance to experiment and theory. They have taken a permanent place in all aspects of fluid dynamics, from basic research to engineering design.

HISTORICAL PERPECTIVE: CFD AS A TOOL

Perhaps, the first major example of CFD was the work of Kopal (1947), who in 1947 compiled massive tables of supersonic flow over sharp cones by numerically solving the governing differential equations. The computing was carried out on a primitive digital computer at Massachusetts Institute of Technology (Wendt, & Anderson, 2008). The first generation of CFD solutions appeared during the 1950's and early 1960's, spurred by the simultaneous advent of computers and the need to solve the high velocity, high temperature re-entry body problem. High temperatures necessitated the inclusion of vibrational energies and chemical reactions in flow problems. Such physical phenomena generally cannot be solved analytically, even for simple geometries. Therefore, numerical solutions of the governing equations on computer systems became absolute necessary. In 1970, the existing computers and algorithms restricted all practical solutions basically to two-dimensional flows. The real world of fluid is mainly a three-dimensional world. The storage and speed capacity of computer at that time were not sufficient to manage three-dimensional practical fashion. Nevertheless, the story changed drastically in 1990. Today, three-dimensional solvers are abundant, although it is necessary a great deal of human and computer resources to successfully carry out such applications. They are increasing in importance within industry and government facilities. Modern CFD complemets the use of wind tunnel testing and pure experiments, to study and validate physics problems. This is related to the rapid decrease in the cost of computations compared to the cost of real experiments. As a result, the calculation of the physics characteristics via application of CFD is becoming economically cheaper than measuring the same characteristics by other means. CFD offers the opportunity to obtain detailed flow field information, some of which is either difficult or impossible to be measured. Overall, inherent in the above discussion is the assumption that CFD results are accurate as well as cost effective. It is important to highlight that the results of CFD are only as valid as the physical models incorporated in the governing equations and boundary conditions, and therefore are subject to error, especially for complex experiments. Additionally, truncation error associated with the particular algorithm used to obtain a numerical solution, as well as round-off errors, both combine to compromise the accuracy of CFD results. Despite these drawbacks, the results of CFD are amazingly accurate for a very large number of applications. Indeed, it is possible to find a large number of problems which can be adequately handle by CFD: Supersonic flows, turbulent flows, combustion, solid-fluid interaction, blood flows are just a few examples. In many areas of applications, the basic methodologies are well established and have been implemented into commercial software packages. Nevertheless, it is still necessary to develop advance CFD methods for complex flow problems.

THE LATTICE BOLTZMANN METHOD

The current state-of-the-art methods for simulating the transport equations (heat, mass, and momentum) are based on the use of macroscopic partial differential equations. On the other extreme, we can view the medium from a microscopic viewpoint where small particles (molecule, atom) collide with each other (molecular dynamic). In this scale the inter-particle forces must be identified, which requires one to know the location, velocity, and trajectory of every particle. However, there is no definition of viscosity, heat capacity, temperature, pressure, etc. These methods are extremely expensive computationally (Mohamad, 2011). However, it is possible to use statistical mechanics as a translator between the molecular world and the microscopic world, avoiding the management of every individual particle, while obtaining the important macroscopic effects by combining the advantages of both macroscopic and microscopic approaches with manageable computer resources. This is the main idea of the Boltzmann equation and the mesoscopic scale (Mohamad, 2011).

In the last few decades the study of the relationship among Navier-Stokes equations and the Boltzmann equation has become an important research field (Chapman, & Cowling, 1991; Sone, 2002; Marié, Ricot, & Sagaut, 2009). The Boltzmann equation presents some relevant capabilities for modeling gas flows. However, numerical methods based on Navier-Stokes are more efficient, such that these methods are preferred for flow simulations. The first attempts towards a simplified approach of the Boltzmann equation, such as the lattice-gas automata (Frisch, Hasslacher, & Pomeau, 1986; Doolen, 1990), introduced a new approach for simulating fluid flow in an efficient way. Today, these new solvers (Higuera, & Jiménez, 1989; Higuera, Succi, & Benzi, 1989) have become a real alternative to classical fluid-flow approaches based on Navier-Stokes. Lattice Boltzmann methods (LBM) combine those characteristics developed to solve the Boltzmann equation over a finite number of microscopic speeds. LBM presents some lattice-symmetry properties which allows the conservation of the macroscopic moments (He, & Luo, 1997). The standard lattice Boltzmann method (Qian, D'Humières, & Lallemand, 1992) is an explicit-time-step solver for incompressible flows. It divides each temporal iteration into two steps, one for propagation-advection and one for collision step which represents inter-particle interactions, achieving a first order in time and second order in space scheme.

Multiple studies have compared the efficiency of LBM with other methods (Axner, Hoekstra, Jeays, Lawford, Hose, & Sloot, 2000; Kollmannsberger, Geller, Dster, Tlke, Sorer, Krafczyk, & Rank, 2009; Kandhai, Vidal, Hoekstra, Hoefsloot, Iedema, & Sloot, 1998; Rapaka, Mansi, Georgescu, Pop, Wright, Kamen, & Comaniciu, 2012). They show that LBM can achieve a similar numerical accuracy over a large number of applications as compared to the other methods. As it is shown in this book, this kind of solvers have been used in multiple applications successfully. Due to particular features of LBM, it has been adapted to numerous parallel architectures, such as multicore processors (Pohl, Kowarchik, Wilke, Rüde, & Iglberger, 2003), manycore accelerators (Rinaldi, Dari, Vnere, & Clausse, 2012; Bernaschi, Fatica, Melchionna, Succi, & Kaxiras, 2010; Alexandrov, Lees, Krzhizhanovskaya, Dongarra, Sloot, Crimi, Mantovani, Pivanti, Schifano, & Tripiccione, 2013) and distributed-memory clusters (Obrecht, Kuznik, Tourancheau, & Roux, 2013; Januszewski & Kostur, 2014). Given the growing popularity of LBM, multiple tools have recently arisen, consolidating this method into both academia and industry.

TARGET AUDIENCE

This book aims to not only serve the interest of traditional CFD users, students, academics, researchers, and engineers, but also non-expert users with an interest in both, Computational Fluid Dynamics and High-Performance Computing. Our target is to bridge the gap between the theory of complex CFD formulations, problems and applications based on LBM, and the programming of these problems on HPC platforms. For sake of clarity, the computational methods described in this book are described mainly using simple two-dimensional examples, so that the different interpretations and models of the LBM can be appreciated without being overwhelmed. Indeed, as the audience can note, the necessary extension for three-dimensional simulations is straight forward using LBM formulation. Furthermore, some examples are also described using three-dimensional domains.

The main important focus of this book is the LBM. It is not necessary to have any previous knowledge about this methodology, as this is deeply described. However, it is recommendable to have certain experience and knowledge about CFD. It important to highlight, the this book could be particularly interesting for those that want to accelerate their CFD simulations using LBM. This book can be also particularly interesting for those readers that want to learn how to implement LBM codes on the current parallel and HPC platforms.

This book concentrates on the "big three" problems for CFD simulations: mesh refinement, solid-fluid interaction and turbulent flows. It was decided to focus on these three problems, as they are the most extended used in the community and these need to be efficiently solved to be able to address the numerous problems, not only numerical but also computational, problems that are found in multiple scientific and industrial applications.

THE CHALLENGES

The Computational Fluid Dynamics (CFD) community has always explored new numerical approaches to leverage emerging computing platforms in its never-ending quest for faster and more accurate simulations. The widespread usage of multi-core and heterogeneous architectures, which we have experienced over the last few years, has created new challenges and opportunities for performance optimization in advanced CFD solvers. The LBM has become a real alternative due to its intrinsic and particular characteristics. However, this methodology is still in need of being proven on those more complex scenarios. In this sense, this book tries to address some of these challenges and opportunities. One of our focus is the programming of LBM solvers on emerging parallel platforms found in current HPC systems. While the computing community is building tools and libraries to ease the use of such systems, its effective use still requires a deep knowledge of low-level programming and a good understanding of the underlying hardware. On the other hand, this book explores the effectiveness of LBM on a large variety of problems, such as mesh refinement, turbulent flows, solid-fluid interaction among others. These problems are widely known into the CFD community. Finally, multiple different applications are explored and analyzed through the chapters, which proves the efficiency of this method.

ORGANIZATION OF THE BOOK

The book is organized into 10 chapters. A brief description of each of the chapters follows:

Chapter 1: Programming and Computing Lattice Boltzmann Method

The main motivation of this chapter is the introduction to those aspects regarding the programmability of LBM. It is presented and discussed different implementations, data layout, strategies to efficiently implement LBM. The performance achieved by each of the techniques is analyzed in detail, over some of the most currently used computer platforms. We pay particular attention to those techniques that attempt to reduce the memory requirement of this method, which is one of the most important constraints when implementing and computing LBM.

Chapter 2: Challenges on Porting Lattice-Boltzmann Method on Accelerators – NVIDIA Graphic Processing Unites and Intel Xeon Phi

This chapter investigates the performance and programming impact of the NVIDIA GPUs and Intel Xeon Phi accelerators on the LBM.

Chapter 3: Design and Optimizations of Lattice Boltzmann Methods for Massively Parallel GPU-Based Clusters

In this chapter the authors describe in full detail the design and implementation of LBM codes on heterogeneous clusters. Most of the discussion is focused on a state-of-the art example based on thermal Lattice Boltzmann method in 2D, but all lessons learned in this particular case can be immediately extended to other LBM based applications.

Chapter 4: Mesh Refinement for LBM Simulations on Cartesian Meshes

The use of mesh refinement in CFD is an efficient and widely used methodology to minimize the computational cost by solving those regions of high geometrical complexity with a finer grid. This Chapter focuses on studying two methods, one based on Multi-Domain and one based on Irregular meshing, to deal with mesh refinement using LBM simulations. The differences among both methodologies in terms of programmability, memory management, and performance are deeply analyzed.

Chapter 5: Lattice-Boltzmann Method for Sparse Geometries – Theory and Implementation

This chapter presents the challenges and techniques for efficient LBM implementation on sparse geometries. The first part contains a review of applications requiring support for sparse geometries including industry, geology and life sciences. The second part describes the implementations for single-core and parallel computers.

Chapter 6: A Meshfree-Based Lattice Boltzmann Approach for Simulation of Fluid Flows Within Complex Geometries – Application of Meshfree methods for LBM Simulations

This chapter describes how to develop a mesh-less formulation based on LBM for fluid simulations in complex and irregular geometries. Mesh-less techniques can improve the accuracy of standard LBM on complex fluid domains, specifically, in the transition phase or moving boundary problems. The author proposes the combination of LBM and Element free Galerkin Method to mitigate the difficulties associated with traditional grid-based methods.

Chapter 7: Wake Interaction Using Lattice Boltzmann Method

This Chapter presents a deeply discussion about the application of LBM on complex flow characteristics over circular structures.

Chapter 8: Fluid-Structure Interaction Using Lattice Boltzmann Method Coupled With Finite Element Method

In this chapter the authors present several partitioned algorithms to couple LBM and Finite Element Method for numerical simulation of transient Fluid-Structure interaction (FSI) problems. Partitioned coupling strategies allow to solve separately the fluid and solid sub-domains using adapted or optimized numerical schemes. The focus of this chapter is the energy conservation property of different partitioned coupling strategies for FSI simulations.

Chapter 9: Lattice Boltzmann Shallow Water Simulation With Surface Pressure

Shallow water conditions are produced in coastal and river areas and allow to simplify fluid solving by integrating in height the fluid equations, thus discarding vertical flow, so a 3D problem is solved with a set of 2D equations. Usually the boundary conditions defined by the surface pressure are discarded. However anticyclones and depressions produce noticeable pressure gradients that may affect the consequences of phenomena like tides and tsunamis. This chapter focuses on how to remove this weakness from the LBM-SW by incorporating the pressure into the LBM for this kind of scenarios in a consistent manner.

Chapter 10: Large Eddy Simulation Turbulence Model Applied to the Lattice Boltzmann Method

Large Eddy Simulation is widely used in simulating turbulent flows because of its lower computational needs compared to others, such as Direct Numerical Simulation. The aim of this chapter consists of introducing the reader to the treatment of turbulence in fluid dynamics, through a LES approach, applied to LBM.

Pedro Valero-Lara
Barcelona Supercomputing Center (BSC), Spain

ACKNOWLEDGMENT

The editor thanks the support of the following funding: The Spanish Government through Programa Severo Ochoa (SEV-2011-0067), the Spanish Ministerio de Economia y Competitividad under contract Computacion de Altas Prestaciones VII (TIN2015-65316-P), and the Departament d'Innovacio, Universitats i Empresa de la Generalitat de Catalunya, under project MPEXPAR: Models de Programacio i Entorns d'Execucio Paral·lels (2014-SGR-1051).

REFERENCES

Alexandrov, V., Lees, M., Krzhizhanovskaya, V., Dongarra, J., Sloot, P., Crimi, G., ... Tripiccione, R. (2013). Early Experience on Porting and Running a Lattice Boltzmann Code on the Xeon-phi Co-Processor. *Procedia Computer Science*, *18*, 551–560. doi:10.1016/j.procs.2013.05.219

Anderson, J. D., Menter, F. R., Dick, E., Degrez, G., & Vierendeels, J. (2013). *Introduction to Computational Fluid Dynamics*. von Karman Institute for Fluid Dynamics.

Axner, L., Hoekstra, A., Jeays, A., Lawford, P., Hose, P., & Sloot, P. (2000). Simulations of time harmonic blood flow in the mesenteric artery: Comparing finite element and lattice boltzmann methods. *Biomedical Engineering Online*. PMID:19799782

Chapman, S., & Cowling, T. G. (1991). *The mathematical theory of non-uniform gases*. Cambridge University Press.

Doolen, G. (1990). *Lattice gas methods for partial differential equations*. Addison-Wesley.

Frisch, U., Hasslacher, B., & Pomeau, Y. (1986). Lattice-gas automata for the navier-stokes equation. *Physical Review Letters*, *56*(14), 1505–1508. doi:10.1103/PhysRevLett.56.1505 PMID:10032689

He, X., & Luo, L.-S. (1997). A priori derivation of the lattice boltzmann equation. *Physical Review E: Statistical Physics, Plasmas, Fluids, and Related Interdisciplinary Topics*, *55*(6), 6333–6336. doi:10.1103/PhysRevE.55.R6333

Higuera, F. J., & Jiménez, J. (1989). Boltzmann approach to lattice gas simulations. *Europhysics Letters*, *9*(7), 663–668. doi:10.1209/0295-5075/9/7/009

Higuera, F. J., Succi, S., & Benzi, R. (1989). Lattice gas dynamics with enhanced collisions. *Europhysics Letters*, *9*(4), 345–349. doi:10.1209/0295-5075/9/4/008

Januszewski, M., & Kostur, M. (2014). Sailfish: A flexible multi-GPU implementation of the lattice Boltzmann method. *Computer Physics Communications*, *185*(9), 2350–2368. doi:10.1016/j.cpc.2014.04.018

Kandhai, D., Vidal, D., Hoekstra, A., Hoefsloot, H., Iedema, P., & Sloot, P. (1998). A comparison between lattice-boltzmann and finite-element simulations of fluid flow in static mixer reactors. *International Journal of Modern Physics C*, *09*(08), 1123–1128. doi:10.1142/S0129183198001035

Kollmannsberger S., Geller S., Dster A., Tlke J., Sorger C., Krafczyk M., Rank E. (2009). *Fixed-grid fluid-structure interaction in two dimensions based on a partitioned lattice Boltzmann and p-fem approach.* Academic Press.

Kopal, Z. (1947). *Tables of supersonic flow around cones.* Cambridge University Press.

Marié, S., Ricot, D., & Sagaut, P. (2009). Comparison between lattice boltzmann method and navier-stokes high order schemes for computational aeroacoustics. *Journal of Computational Physics, 228*(4), 1056–1070. doi:10.1016/j.jcp.2008.10.021

Mohamad, A. A. (2011). *The lattice Boltzmann method–Fundamental and engineering applications with computer codes.* Springer.

Obrecht, C., Kuznik, F., Tourancheau, B., & Roux, J. (2013). Scalable lattice boltzmann solvers for CUDA GPU clusters. *Parallel Computing, 39*(6-7), 259–270. doi:10.1016/j.parco.2013.04.001

Pohl, T., Kowarchik, M., Wilke, J., Rüde, U., & Iglberger, K. (2003). Optimization and profiling of the cache performance of parallel lattice boltzmann codes. *Parallel Processing Letters, 13*(4), 549–560. doi:10.1142/S0129626403001501

Qian, Y. H., D'Humières, D., & Lallemand, P. (1992). Lattice bgk models for navier-stokes equation. *Europhysics Letters*, 17.

Rapaka, S., Mansi, T., Georgescu, B., Pop, M., Wright, G. A., Kamen, A., & Comaniciu, D. (2012). Lbm-ep: Lattice-boltzmann method for fast cardiac electrophysiology simulation from 3d images. In *Proceedings of the Medical Image Computing and Computer-Assisted Intervention* (pp. 33–40). Academic Press. doi:10.1007/978-3-642-33418-4_5

Rinaldi, P. R., Dari, E. A., Vénere, M. J., & Clausse, A. (2012). A Lattice-Boltzmann solver for 3D fluid simulation on GPU. *Simulation Modelling Practice and Theory, 25*, 163–171. doi:10.1016/j.simpat.2012.03.004

Sone, Y. (2002). *Kinetic theory and fluid dynamics.* Birkhäuser. doi:10.1007/978-1-4612-0061-1

Wendt, J. F., & Anderson, J. D. (2008). *Computational Fluid Dynamics: An Introduction.* Springer.

Chapter 1
Programming and Computing Lattice Boltzmann Method

Pedro Valero-Lara
Barcelona Supercomputing Center (BSC), Spain

ABSTRACT

The use of lattice Boltzmann method (LBM) has been extended to numerous fields of scientific and industrial interest due to its inherent characteristics, which make this methodology a very efficient and fast method for fluid simulations. In this chapter, the numerical formulation behind LBM is presented in detail. However, the main motivation of this chapter is the introduction to those aspects regarding the programmability of this method. The authors present different implementations, data layout, and strategies to efficiently implement LBM. The performance achieved by each of the techniques is analyzed in detail, over some of the currently used computer platforms. They pay particular attention to those techniques that attempt to reduce the memory requirement of their method, which is one of the most important weakpoints when implementing and computing LBM.

INTRODUCTION

Advanced strategies for the efficient implementation of computationally intensive numerical methods have a strong interest in the industrial and academic community. We could define Computational Fluid Dynamics (CFD) as a set of numerical methods applied to obtain approximate solutions of problems of fluid dynamics and heat transfer (Zikanov, 2010). Today, the Lattice-Boltzmann method (LBM) is one of the most popular methodologies in CFD, and its use is extended to a high number of different CFD applications. Furthermore, the advantage of using LBM

DOI: 10.4018/978-1-5225-4760-0.ch001

has been consistently confirmed by many authors (Bernaschi, Fatica, Melchionna, Succi, & Kaxiras, 2010) (Rinaldi, Dari, Vnere, & Clausse, 2012) (Zhou, Mo, Wu, & Zhao, 2012) (Feichtinger, Habich, Kstler, Rude, & Aoki, 2015) (Alexandrov, Lees, Krzhizhanovskaya, Dongarra, Sloot, Crimi, Mantovani, Pivanti, Schifano, & Tripiccione, 2013) for a large variety of problems and computing platforms. Unlike other methodologies, which can be inefficient or difficult to implement (Valero-Lara, Pinelli, Favier, & Prieto-Matías, 2012) (Valero-Lara, Pinelli, & Prieto-Matías, 2014), LBM is well suited for parallel computing (Succi, 2001). However, there are important details about the programmability that have to be analyze in detail. These details are sometimes difficult to find in the literature. It is because of this, that this chapter attempts to cover those important details about the programming and computing of LBM that help to the community to understand those strategies, which can help to achieve a good performance. As many other methods, LBM can be adapted or implemented in very different ways. Here, it is introduced some of the most popular approaches to deal with LBM, and what are the advantages and disadvantages of each of them. We pay particular attention to the different implementations, data layouts, parallel granularities that can be exploited on those simulations based on LBM.

The scientific community in its never-ending road of larger and more efficient computational resources is in need of more efficient implementations that can adapt efficiently on the current parallel platforms. Despite this method is particularly amenable to be efficiently parallelized, it is in need of a considerable memory capacity, which is the consequence of a dramatic fall in performance when dealing with large simulations. In the second part of this chapter, it is presented some initiatives to minimize such demand of memory, which allows us to execute bigger simulations on the same platform without additional memory transfers/copies, keeping a high performance.

LATTICE-BOLTZMANN METHOD

Background

Most of the current methods for simulating the transport equations (heat, mass, and momentum) are based on the use of macroscopic partial differential equations (Wendt, & Anderson, 2008) (Anderson, Menter, Dick, Degrez, & Vierendeels, 2013) (Anderson, 1995) (Swarztrauber, 1974). On the other extreme, we can view the medium from a microscopic viewpoint where small particles (molecule and atom) collide with each other (molecular dynamic) (Mohamad, 2011). In this scale, the inter-particle forces must be identified, which requires to know the location, velocity, and trajectory of every particle. However, there is no definition of viscosity, heat capacity, temperature, pressure, etc. These methods are extremely expensive computationally (Mohamad, 2011). However, it is possible to use statistical mechanisms as a translator between the molecular world and the microscopic world, avoiding the management of every individual particle, while obtaining the important macroscopic effects by combining the advantages of both macroscopic and microscopic approaches with manageable computer resources. This is the main idea of the Boltzmann equation and the mesoscopic scale (Mohamad, 2011). Multiple studies have compared the efficiency of LBM with respect to other 'classic' methods based on Navier-Stokes (Kollmannsberger, Geller, Dster, Tlke, Sorer, Krafczyk, & Rank, 2009) (Kandhai, Videl, Hoekstra, Hoefsloot, Iedema, & Sloot, 1998). They show that LBM can achieve an equivalent numerical accuracy over a large number of applications. In particular, LBM has been used to simulate high Reynolds turbulent flows over Direct Numerical and Large Eddy simulations (Malaspinas, & Sagaut, 2012). Another challenging applications where LBM has proved to be quite successful concerns aeroacoustics problems (Marié, Ricot, & Sagaut, 2009) or bio-engineering applications (Bernaschi, Fatica, Melchionna, Succi, & Kaxiras, 2010). Also, LBM has been efficiently integrated with other methods such as the Immersed Boundary Method (Peskin, 2002) (Valero-Lara, 2014) for Fluid-Solid Interaction problems (Valero-Lara, Igual, Prieto-Matías, Pinelli, & Favier, 2015) (Favier, Revell, & Pinelli, 2014) (Valero-Lara, Pinelli, Prieto-Matías, 2014).

Lattice Boltzmann Method Formulation

Lattice-Boltzmann method combines some features developed to solve the Boltzmann equation over a finite number of microscopic speeds. LBM presents lattice-symmetry characteristics which allow to respect the conservation of the macroscopic moments (He, & Luo, 1997). The standard LBM (Qian, Humires, & Lallemand, 1992) is an explicit solver for incompressible flows. It divides each temporal iteration into two steps, one for propagation-advection and one for collision (inter-particle interactions), achieving a first order in time and second order in space scheme. Lattice-Boltzmann method describes the fluid behaviour at mesoscopic level. At this level, the fluid is modelled by a distribution function of the microscopic particle (f). Similarly to the Boltzmann equation, LBM solves the particle speed distribution by discretizing the speed space over a discrete finite number of possible speeds. The distribution function evolves according to the following equation:

$$\frac{\partial f}{\partial t} + e \nabla f = \wp$$

where f is the particle distribution function, e is the discrete space of speeds and $\wp$ is the collision operator. By discretizing the distribution function f in space, in time, and in speed ($e = e_i$) we obtain $f_i(x,t)$, which describes the probability of finding a particle located at x at time t with speed e_i. $e\nabla f$ can be discretized as:

$$e\nabla f = e_i \nabla f_i = \frac{f_i(x + e_i dt, t + dt) - f_i(x, t + dt)}{dt}$$

In this way, the particles can move only along the links of a regular lattice (Figure 1) defined by the discrete speeds

$$(e_0 = c(0,0); e_i = c(\pm 1, 0), c(0, \pm 1), i = 1, ..., 4; e_i = c(\pm 1, \pm 1, i = 5, ..., 8) \text{ with } c = dx / dt)$$

so that the synchronous particle displacements $dx_i = e_i dt$ never takes the fluid particles away from the lattice. In this work, we consider the standard two-dimensional 9-speed lattice D2Q9 (He, & Luo, 1997).

Figure 1. The standard two-dimensional 9-speed lattice (D2Q9)

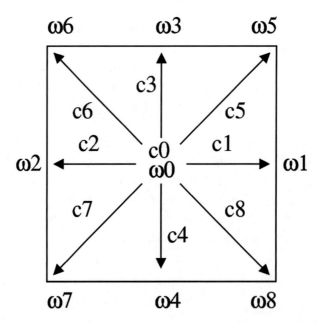

The operator $\wp$ describes the changes suffered by the collision of the microscopic particles, which affect the distribution function (f). To calculate the collision operator, we consider the BGK (Bhatnagar-Gross-Krook) formulation (Gross, Bhatnagar, & Krook, 1954) which relies upon a unique relaxation time, t, toward the equilibrium distribution f_i^{eq}:

$$\wp = \frac{-1}{t} f_i \left(x,t \right) - f_i^{eq} \left(x,t \right)$$

The equilibrium function $f_i^{eq} \left(x,t \right)$ can be obtained by Taylor series expansion of the Maxwell- Boltzmann equilibrium distribution (Qian, Humires, & Lallemand, 1992):

$$f_i^{eq} = pw_i \left[1 + \frac{e_i \times u}{c_s^2} + \frac{\left(e_i \times u \right)^2}{2c_s^4} - \frac{u^2}{2c_s^2} \right]$$

where c_s is the speed of sound ($c_s = 1 / \sqrt{3}$) and the weight coefficients w_i are

$$w_0 = 4 / 9, w_i = 1 / 9, i = 1,...,4; w_i = 1 / 36, i = 5,...,8$$

based on the current normalization. Through the use of the collision operator and substituting the term $\partial f_i / \partial t$ with a first order temporal discretization, the discrete Boltzmann equation can be written as:

$$\frac{f_i \left(x,t + dt \right) - f_i \left(x,t \right)}{dt} + \frac{f_i \left(x + e_i dt, t + dt \right) - f_i \left(x,t + dt \right)}{dt} = -\frac{1}{t} \left(f_i \left(x,t \right) - f_i^{eq} \left(x,t \right) \right)$$

which can be compactly written as:

$$f_i \left(x + e_i dt, t + dt \right) - f_i \left(x,t \right) = -\frac{dt}{t} \left(f_i \left(x,t \right) - f_i^{eq} \left(x,t \right) \right)$$

The macroscopic velocity u must satisfy a Mach number requirement $\left(u \right) / c_s \approx M \ll 1$. This stands as the equivalent of the Courant Friedrichs Lewy (CFL) number (CFL number arises in those schemes based on explicit time computer simulations. As a consequence, this number must be less than a certain time to achieve coherent results) for classical Navier Stokes solvers.

As mentioned earlier, the above equation is typically advanced in time in two stages, the collision and the streaming stages (Valero-Lara, 2014). Given $f_i(x,t)$ compute:

$$p = \sum_i f_i(x,t)$$

and

$$pu = \sum_i e_i f_i(x,t)$$

Collision stage:

$$f_i^{tmp}(x,t+dt) = f_i(x,t) - \frac{dt}{t}\left(f(x,t) - f_i^{eq}(x,t)\right)$$

Streaming stage:

$$f_i(x + e_i dt, t + dt) = f_i^{tmp}(x,t+dt)$$

IMPLEMENTATION OF LATTICE BOLTZMANN METHOD (LBM)

LBM Update

One important issue about the implementation of LBM is how to implement a single LBM update. Conceptually, a discrete time step consists of a local collision operation followed by a streaming operation that propagates the new information to the neighbor lattice nodes. However, most implementations do not apply those operations as separate steps. Instead, they usually fuse in a single loop nest (that iterates over the entire domain), the application of both operations to improve temporal locality (Wellein, Zeiser, Hager, & Donath, 2006) (Habich, Feichtinger, Kstler, Hager, & Wellein, 2013).

This fused loop can be implemented in different ways. In the pull scheme introduced in (Wellein, Zeiser, Hager, & Donath, 2006), the body of the loop performs the streaming operation before collision, i.e. the distribution functions are gathered (pulled) from the neighbors before computing the collision. Listing 1 shows a sketch of this implementation.

Other implementations (Bernaschi, Fatica, Melchionna, Succi, & Kaxiras, 2010) (Zhou, Mo, Wu, & Zhao, 2012) (Januszewski, & Kostur, 2014) (Schnherr, Kucher, Geier, Stiebler, Freudiger, & Krafczyk, 2011) have used the traditional implementation sketched in Listing 2, which performs the collision operation before the streaming. It is known as the "push" scheme (Wellein, Zeiser, Hager, & Donath, 2006) since it loads the distribution function from the current lattice point and then it "pushes" (scatters) the updated values to its neighbors.

Listing 1. Pseudo-code for LBM-pull approach

1. **Pull** $(f_1, \ f_2, \ w, c_x, c_y)$
2. $x, \ y, \ x_{stream}, \ y_{stream}$ x and y are the coordinates for a particular lattice node
3. $local_{ux}, \ local_{uy}, \ local_p, \ local_f[9], \ f_{eq}, \ cu$
4. for i = 1 → 9 do
5. $\quad x_{stream} = x - c_x[i]$
6. $\quad y_{stream} = y - c_u[i]$
7. $\quad local_f[i] = f_1[x_{stream}][y_{stream}][i]$
8. end for
9. for i = 1 → 9 do
10. $\quad local_p \ += \ local_f[i]$
11. $\quad local_{ux} \ += \ c_x[i] * local_f[i]$
12. $\quad local_{uy} \ += \ c_y[i] * local_f[i]$
13. end for
14. $local_{ux} = local_{ux} \ / \ local_A$
15. $local_{uy} = local_{uy} \ / \ local_A$
16. for i = 1 → 9 do
17. $\quad cu = c_x[i] local_{ux} + c_y[i] local_{uy}$
18. $\quad f^{eq} = w[i] \rho \left(1 + 3(cu) + (cu)^2 - 1,5 \times \left(local_{ux} \right)^2 + local_{uy} \right)^2$
19. $\quad f_2[x][y][i] = local_f[i] \left(1 - \frac{1}{t} \right) + f^{eq} \frac{1}{t}$
20. end for

Listing 2. Pseudo-code for LBM-push approach

```
1.  Push ( f₁ , f₂ , w , cₓ , c_y )
2.  x, y, x_stream , y_stream    x and y are the coordinates for a
        particular lattice node
3.  local_ux , local_uy , local_p , local_f[9] , f_eq , cu
4.  for i = 1 → 9 do
```

5. $local_f[i] = f_1[x][y][i]$

6. $local_p\ \texttt{+=}\ local_f[i]$

7. $local_{ux}\ \texttt{+=}\ c_x[i] * local_f[i]$

8. $local_{uy}\ \texttt{+=}\ c_y[i] * local_f[i]$

```
9.  end for
```

10. $local_{ux} = local_{ux} / local_p$

11. $local_{uy} = local_{uy} / local_p$

```
12. for i = 1 → 9 do
```

13. $cu = c_x[i] local_{ux} + c_y[i] local_{uy}$

14. $f^{eq} = w[i]\rho\left(1 + 3(cu) + (cu)^2 - 1,5 \times \left(local_{ux}\right)^2 + local_{uy}\right)^2$

15. $local_f[i] = local_f[i]\left(1 - \dfrac{1}{t}\right) + f^{eq}\dfrac{1}{t}$

```
16. end for
17. for i = 1 → 9 do
```

18. $x_{stream} = x + c_x[i]$

19. $y_{stream} = y + c_u[i]$

20. $f_2[x_{stream}][y_{stream}][i] = local_f[i]$

```
21. end for
```

LBM Granularity

Parallelism is abundant in the LBM update and can be exploited in different ways. On throughput oriented architectures, such as current GPUs, the lattice nodes can be distributed across cores using a fine-grained distribution. As shown in Figure 2, using an 1D Grid of 1D block of threads, each thread can perform the LBM update of a single lattice node. On multi-core processors, cache locality is a major performance issue and it is better to distribute the lattice nodes across cores using a 1D coarse-grained distribution (Figure 3). The cache coherence protocol keeps the boundaries between sub-domains updated.

Figure 2. Coarse-grained distribution of the lattice nodes

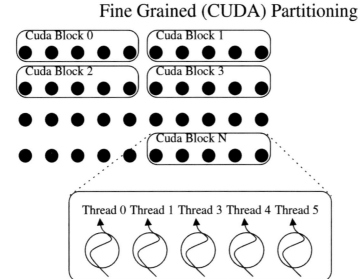

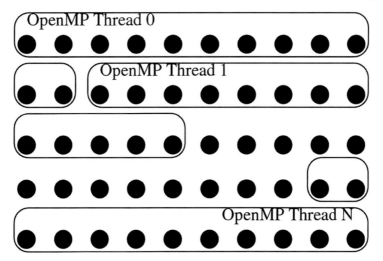

Figure 3. Fine-grained distribution of the lattice nodes

LBM Data Layout and Memory Management

Since LBM is a memory-bound algorithm, another important problem is to maximize data locality. Many groups have considered this issue and have introduced several data layouts and code transformations that are able to improve locality on different architectures (Favier, Revell, & Pinelli, 2014) (Bailey, Myre, Walsh, Lilja, & Saar, 2009) (Habich, Feichtinger, Kstler, Hager, & Wellein, 2013) (Wittmann, Zeiser, Hager, & Wellein, 2013) (Januszewski, & Kostur, 2014) (Shet, Sorathiya, Krithivasan, Deshpande, Kaul, Sherlekar, & Ansumali, 2013). Here we briefly describe the strategies used on LBM. Different data structures have been proposed to store the discrete distribution functions f_i in memory:

- **AoS:** This data structure stores all the discrete distribution functions f_i of a given lattice point in adjacent memory positions (see Figure 4). This way, it optimizes locality when computing the collision operation (Shet, Sorathiya, Krithivasan, Deshpande, Kaul, Sherlekar, & Ansumali, 2013). However, it does not provide good performance on GPU architectures since it leads to poor bandwidth utilization (Bernaschi, Fatica, Melchionna, Succi, & Kaxiras, 2010) (Rinaldi, Dari, Vnere, & Clausse, 2012) (Januszewski, & Kostur, 2014).

- **SoA:** In this alternative data structure, the discrete distribution functions f_i for a particular velocity direction are stored sequentially in the same array (see Figure 5). Since each thread handles the update of a single lattice node, consecutive threads access adjacent memory locations with the SoA layout (Bernaschi, Fatica, Melchionna, Succi, & Kaxiras, 2010) (Rinaldi, Dari, Vnere, & Clausse, 2012) (Januszewski, & Kostur, 2014). This way, they can be combined (coalesced) into a single memory transaction, which is very appropiate for throughput oriented architectures and it is not possible using the AoS counterpart.

- **SoAoS:** We have also explored a hybrid data structure, denoted as SoAoS in (Shet, Sorathiya, Krithivasan, Deshpande, Kaul, Sherlekar, & Ansumali, 2013). As SoA, it also allows coalesced memory transactions on hardware accelerators, such as GPUs. However, instead of storing the discrete distribution functions f_i for a particular velocity direction in a single sequential array, it distributes them across different blocks of a certain block size (see Figure 6). This size is a tunable parameter that trades off between spatial and temporal locality.

Apart from the data layout, the memory management of the different implementations may also differ in the number of lattices that are used internally. We have used a two-lattice implementation, which is denoted as the AB scheme in (Bailey, Myre, Walsh, Lilja, & Saar, 2009) (Januszewski, & Kostur, 2014). Essentially, AB holds the data of two successive time steps (f_1 and f_2) and the simulation alternates between reading from f_1 and writing to f_2, and vice versa. Other proposals, such as the AA data layout in (Bailey, Myre, Walsh, Lilja, & Saar, 2009) (Januszewski, & Kostur, 2014), are able to use a single copy of the distributions arrays and reduce the memory footprint. Some previous works have shown that those single lattice schemes outperform the AB scheme on multi-core processors (AA achieved the best results in (Wittmann, Zeiser, Hager, & Wellein, 2013)). However, on GPUs the performance benefits of these schemes are less clear. In fact, a recent work has shown that both schemes get similar performance on GPUs (Januszewski, & Kostur, 2014) or the AB scheme is typically a little faster on the latest GPUs. We discuss about this in the next sections.

Figure 4. AoS data layout

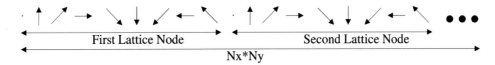

Figure 5. SoA data layout

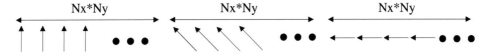

Figure 6. SoAoS data layout

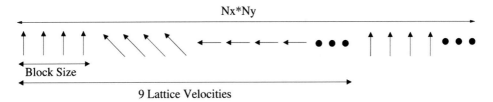

Table 1. Main features of the platforms used

Platform	2 x Intel Xeon E5520 (2.26 GHz)	4 x NVIDIA Kepler K20c
Cores	8	2496
On-Chip Memory	L1 32KB (per core)	SM 16/48 KB (per MP)
	L2 512 KB (unified)	L1 48/16 KB (per MP)
	L3 20 MB (unified)	L2 768 KB (unified)
Memory	64 GB DDR3	5GB GDDR5
Bandwidth	51.2 GB/s	208 GB/s

LBM Data Layout and Memory Management

To critically evaluate the performance of the different strategies presented, we have considered next a number of tests executed on one heterogeneous platforms, whose main characteristics are summarized in the next Table:

On the GPU, the on-chip memory hierarchy has been configured as 16 KB shared memory and 48 KB L1, since our codes do not benefit from a higher amount of shared memory on the investigated tests. Simulations have been performed using double precision, and we have used the conventional MFLUPS metric (millions of fluid lattice updates per second) to assess the performance.

Figure 7 shows the performance of the pull scheme and the use two lattices (AB scheme) with the SoA data layout. As a reference we also show the performance of the Sailfish software package (Januszewski, & Kostur, 2014), which includes a LBM solver based on the push scheme, and the following estimation of the ideal MFLUPS (Shet, Sorathiya, Krithivasan, Deshpande, Kaul, Sherlekar, & Ansumali, 2013):

$$MFLUPS_{ideal} = \frac{B \times 10^9}{10^6 \times n \times 6 \times 8}$$

where $B \times 10^9$ is the memory bandwidth (GB/s), n depends on LBM model (DxQn), for our framework $n = 9$, D2Q9. The factor 6 is for the memory accesses, three read and write operations in the spreading step and three read and write operations in the collision step, and the factor 8 is for double precision (8 bytes).

Figures 8 shows the performance on an Intel Xeon server. Although on multi-core processor it is natural to use the AoS data layout, SoA and SoAoS (with a block size of 32 elements) turn to be the most efficient data layouts. The main reason behind these unexpected results lies on the vector capabilities of modern processors. The compiler has been able to vectorize the main loops of the LBM update and both

Figure 7. Performance of the LBM update on the NVIDIA Kepler GPU

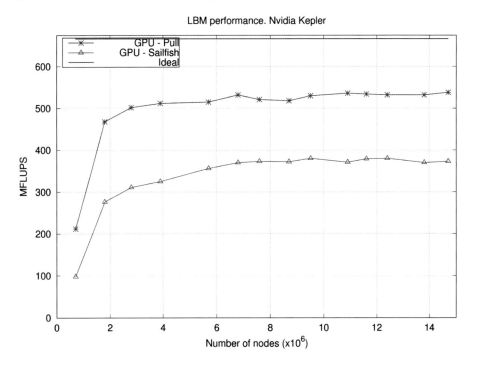

Figure 8. Performance of the LBM update on the Intel Xeon multi-core processor

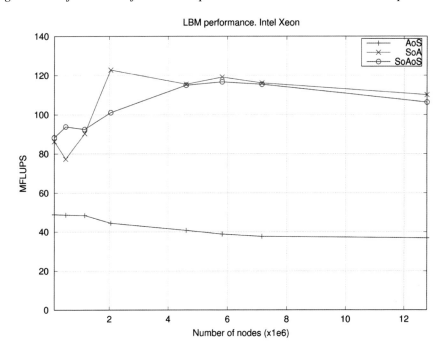

Figure 9. Scalability of the LBM update on an Intel Xeon multi-core processor

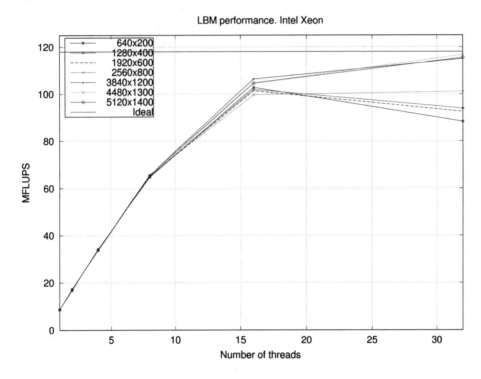

the AoS and SoAoS layouts allow a better exploitation of vectorization. Figure 9 shows the scalability on this solver. The observed speedup factors over the sequential implementation almost peak with 16 threads, but the application scales relatively well since its performance is limited by the memory bandwidth.

REDUCING MEMORY REQUIREMENTS ON LBM

The benefit of using LBM on parallel computers is consistently confirmed in many works (Bernaschi, Fatica, Melchionna, Succi, & Kaxiras, 2010) (Rinaldi, Dari, Vnere, & Clausse, 2012), for a large number of different problems and computing platforms. However, The demand of computational resources from scientific community is constantly increasing in order to simulate more and more complex scenarios. One of the most important challenges to deal with such scenarios is the large memory capacity that the scientific applications need. Multiple works have explored new techniques to reduce the impact of some applications on memory capacity (Yang W., Li K., Mo Z., & Li K., 2015) (Li K., Yang W., & Li K., 2016). Although LBM is amenable to be efficiently parallelized, it is in need of a high memory capacity. In LBM-Ghost, we propose the use of ghost-cells to minimize the memory requirements. The implementation of LBM-Ghost is in needs of non-trivial optimizations in comparison to the state-of-the-art implementations, which make difficult its implementation. On the other hand, LBM-swap is based on (Jonas, 2007), which is much easier to implement. It basically consists of swapping the lattice-speed after the two main LBM steps.

LBM-Ghost

This section explains how we have adapted the use of ghost cells to LBM to reduce the memory requirements for GPU-based implementations. Although, the ghost cells are usually used for communication in distributed memory systems (Valero-Lara, & Jansson, 2015), we use this strategy to reduce memory requirements and avoid race conditions among the set of fluid blocks. To minimize the number of ghost cells, the biggest possible size of block must be used. This depends on the architecture to be used. The use of ghost cells consists of replicating the borders of all immediate neighbors blocks, in our case fluid blocks. These ghost cells are not updated locally, but provide stencil values when updating the borders of local blocks. Every ghost cell is a duplicate of a piece of memory located in neighbors nodes. To clarify, Figure 10 illustrates a simple scheme for our interpretation of the ghost cell strategy applied to LBM (LBM-Ghost).

In LBM-streaming operation (Figure 11), some of the lattice-speed in each ghost cell are used by adjacent fluid (lattice) elements located in neighbors fluid blocks. Depending on the position of the fluid units, a different pattern needs to be computed for the LBM-streaming operation. For instance, if one fluid element is located in one of the corners of the fluid block, this requires to take 5 lattice-speed from 3 different ghost cells. However, if it is in other position of the boundary, it has to take 3 lattice-speed from one ghost cell (Figure 11).

The information of the ghost cells have to be updated once per time step. The updating is computing via a second kernel before computing LBM. This kernel moves some lattice-speed from lattice units to ghost cells. This kernel can computed by as many threads as ghost cells (fine grained). To optimize memory management and minimize divergence, continuous fluid blocks compute each of the updating cases. To clarify Figure 12 shows the differences between each of the cases regarding the location. Similarly to the LBM-streaming, a different number of memory movements are necessary depending on the position of the ghost cells. In particular, if one ghost cell is located in one of the ghost cell rows or columns (Vertical and Horizontal cases in Figure 12), this needs to take 6 lattice-speed from 2 different fluid units (3 lattice-speed per fluid unit). However, if one ghost cell is positioned in one of

Figure 10. A simple scheme for our LBM approach composed by four fluid blocks (CUDA blocks) composed by ghost-cells (dark-gray background), boundary (light-gray background), and fluid (white-background) units

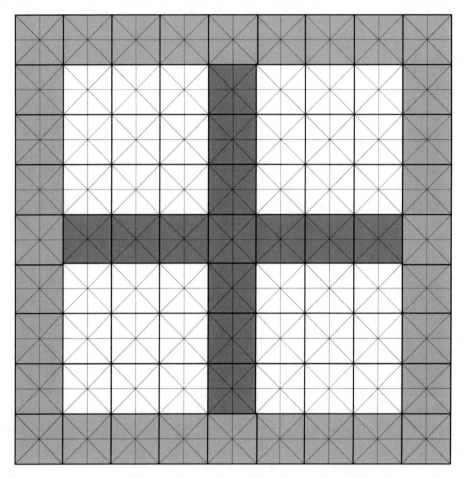

the corners (Corner case in Figure 12), then this ghost cell requires 4 lattice-speed from 4 fluid units.

Unlike the LBM-Standard implementation (pull approach), the fluid blocks need to be synchronized before computing collision. This is possible using syncthreads() (see Listing 3). The synchronizations and ghost cells make possible the absence of race conditions.

It is well known that the memory management has an impressive impact on performance, in particular on those parallel computers that suffer from a high latency such as, GPUs or Xeon Phi (Valero-Lara, Igual, Prieto-Matías, Pinelli, & Favier, 2015). Furthermore, LBM is a memory-bound algorithm, so that, another

Figure 11. Streaming operation from ghost cells to fluid units

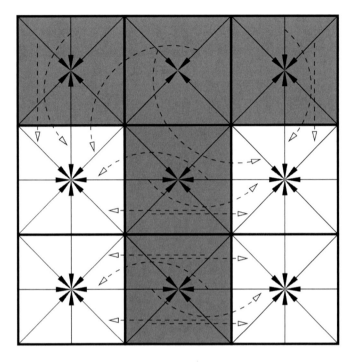

Streaming Operation

Figure 12. Update operation from fluid units (white background) to ghost cells (gray background), depending on ghost cells position

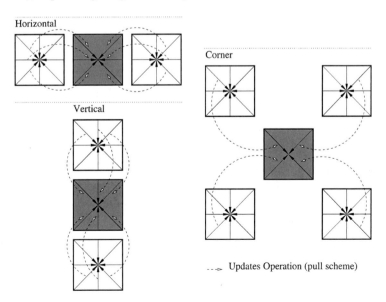

Listing 3. Pseudo-code for pull-ghost approach

1. **Pull-Ghost** (f_1 , f_2 , w , c_x , c_y)

2. x, y, x_{stream} , y_{stream} x and y are the coordinates for a particular lattice node

3. $local_{ux}$, $local_{uy}$, $local_p$, $local_f[9]$, f_{eq} , cu

4. for i = 1 → 9 do

5. $\qquad x_{stream}$ = x − $c_x[i]$

6. $\qquad y_{stream}$ = y − $c_u[i]$

7. $\qquad local_f[i]$ = $f_1[x_{stream}][y_{stream}][i]$

8. end for

9. for i = 1 → 9 do

10. $\qquad local_p$ += $local_f[i]$

11. $\qquad local_{ux}$ += $c_x[i] * local_f[i]$

12. $\qquad local_{uy}$ += $c_y[i] * local_f[i]$

13. end for

14. $local_{ux} = local_{ux} / local_\rho$

15. $local_{uy} = local_{uy} / local_\rho$

16. syncthreads()

17. for i = 1 → 9 do

18. $\qquad cu = c_x[i]local_{ux} + c_y[i]local_{uy}$

19. $\qquad f^{eq} = w[i]\rho\left(1 + 3(cu) + (cu)^2 - 1,5 \times \left(local_{ux}\right)^2 + local_{uy}\right)^2$

20. $\qquad f_2[x][y][i] = local_f[i]\left(1 - \dfrac{1}{t}\right) + f^{eq}\dfrac{1}{t}$

21. end for

important optimization problem is to maximize data locality. The previous thread-data distribution shown in Figure 3 does not exploit coalescence (contiguous threads access to continuous memory locations), when dealing with ghost cells, so we have to use a new memory mapping which fits better our particular data structure. We follow the same aforementioned strategy (SoA), adapting it to this approach. Instead of mapping every lattice-speed in consecutive memory locations for the whole simulation domain (Figures 4, 5 and 6), we map the set of lattice-speed of every bi-dimensional fluid block in consecutive memory locations, as graphically illustrated by Figure 13.

Figure 13. Memory mapping for the 1 lattice + ghost approach

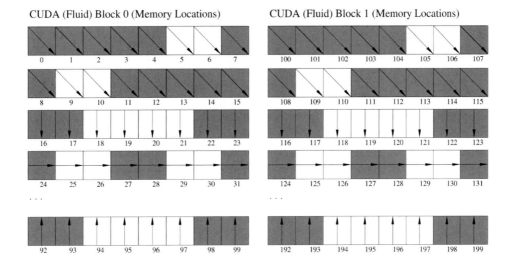

CUDA (Fluid) Block & Memory Mapping (wise−row order)

CUDA (Fluid) Block 0 (Memory Locations)

CUDA (Fluid) Block 1 (Memory Locations)

LBM-Swap

In this section, we explore other strategy to minimize the memory requirements for LBM simulations. Unlike the previous strategy, this approach (LBM-swap) does not need more memory (ghost cells) or change the data layout. This makes much easier the implementation and the integration with the CPU for heterogeneous implementations (Valero-Lara, Igual, Prieto-Matías, Pinelli, & Favier, 2015) (Valero-Lara, 2014a) (Valero-Lara, 2014b) (Valero-Lara, Pinelli, & Prieto-Matías, 2014) (Valero-Lara, 2014c) (Valero-Lara, & Jansson, 2017) . The LBM-swap algorithm only needs one

Listing 4. Swap implementation

```
1. Swap(a, b)
2. tmp = a
3. a = b
4. b = tmp
```

lattice-speed data space. For sake of clarity and make easier the understanding in the rest of this section, let's define the opposite relation as follow:

$$c_{opposite(i)} = -c_i$$

The LBM-swap consists of swapping the lattice-speed after computing the two-main LBM steps, collide and streaming. In this way we avoid race conditions among neighbor lattice. The swap function can be implemented as Listing 4 describes.

Basically, this approach is based in the next property:

$$f_i\left(x + e_i dt, t + dt\right) \leftarrow f_{opposite(i)}\left(x, t\right)$$

which is symmetric and then it can be reverted by using the previous property

$$f_{opposite(i)}\left(x, t\right) \leftarrow f_i\left(x + e_i dt, t + dt\right)$$

As the LBM-Ghost, here we need two kernels, one LBM-collision and one for LBM-streaming. It is necessary a strong point of synchronism among both steps to guarantee the absence of race conditions among them. This is because of the use of one lattice (AA scheme) instead of 2-lattice (AB scheme). In each kernel we may have as many threads as number of lattice (fluid) nodes. We use the same thread and memory mapping used for the LBM- approach (Figures 2 and 3).

Listing 5 describes the first kernel of the LBM-Swap. As shown, apart of using one lattice-space (AA scheme), the only difference with respect to the LBM-Standad consists of computing a swap operation after LBM-collision on all lattice nodes.

The second kernel is implemented as Listing 6 describes. Basically it consists of computing stream and swap.

For sake of clarity, Figure 14 graphically illustrates the swapping carried out in both LBM steps, collision (top) and streaming (bottom):

Listing 5. LBM-swap, kernel collision

```
1. Collision-Swap ( f_1 , w , c_x , c_y )
2. x, y
3. local_ux , local_uy , local_p , local_f [9] , f_eq , cu
4. for i = 1 → 9 do
```
$$5. \quad local_f[i] \quad += \quad f[i][x][y]$$
$$6. \qquad local_p \quad += \quad local_f[i]$$
$$7. \qquad local_{ux} \quad += \quad c_x[i] * local_f[i]$$
$$8. \qquad local_{uy} \quad += \quad c_y[i] * local_f[i]$$
```
9. end for
```
$$10.\ local_{ux} = local_{ux} / local_A$$
$$11.\ local_{uy} = local_{uy} / local_A$$
```
12. for i = 1 → 9 do
```
$$13. \quad cu = c_x[i] local_{ux} + c_y[i] local_{uy}$$
$$14. \quad f^{eq} = w[i]\rho\left(1 + 3(cu) + (cu)^2 - 1,5 \times \left(local_{ux}\right)^2 + local_{uy}\right)^2$$
$$15. \quad f_1[x][y][i] = local_f[i]\left(1 - \frac{1}{t}\right) + f^{eq}\frac{1}{t}$$
```
16. end for
17. for i = 1 → 4 do
```
$$18.\ swap\left(f_1[i][x][y] , \ f_1[i+4][x][y] \right)$$
```
19. end for
```

Listing 6. LBM_swap, kernel stream

```
1. Stream-Swap ( f_1 , c_x , c_y )
```
2. x, y, x_{stream} , y_{stream} x and y are the coordinates for a particular lattice node
```
3. for i = 1 → 4 do
```
$$4. \qquad x_{stream} \quad = x + c_x[i]$$
$$5. \qquad y_{stream} \quad = y + c_u[i]$$
$$6.\ swap\left(f_1[i+4][x][y] , \ f_1[i][x][y] \right)$$
```
7. end for
```

Performance Analysis

Big fluid domains (from 45 millions of nodes) can not be fully stored in global memory of our GPU (Table 1), which forces us to execute our problem in two-steps, when using LBM-Standard, requiring additional memory transfers. In this case, several sub-domains must be transfered from GPU to CPU and vice-versa every temporal iteration, causing a big fall in performance. Otherwise, the LBM-Ghost is able to achieve a better performance when dealing with big problems. Although this approach is in need of 2 kernels, instead of 1 as in the LBM-Standard, the time required by the new kernel (Ghost in Figure 15), which is in charge of updating the information in the ghost elements, does not cause a significant overhead. Indeed the time consumed is less than 2% with respect to the total consumed time.

The reduction achieved by LBM-Ghost represents about the 55% of the memory consumed by the LBM-Standard. On the other hand, the LBM-Swap is in need of the lowest memory requirements with respect to the other two implementations, needing the half of the memory required by the LBM-Standard and about a 5% less than the

Figure 14. Swap operation in LBM-collision (top) and in the LBM-stream (bottom)

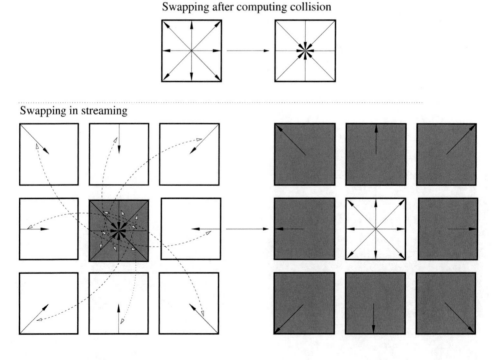

Swapping after computing collision

Swapping in streaming

- - -▷ Swap Operation

Figure 15. Execution time for the LBM-Ghost approach

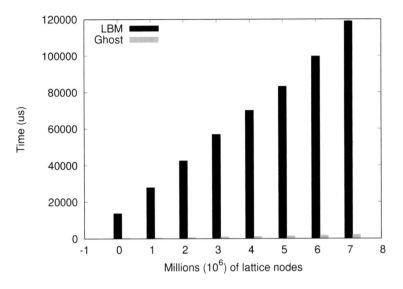

Figure 16. MFLUPS reached by each of the approaches

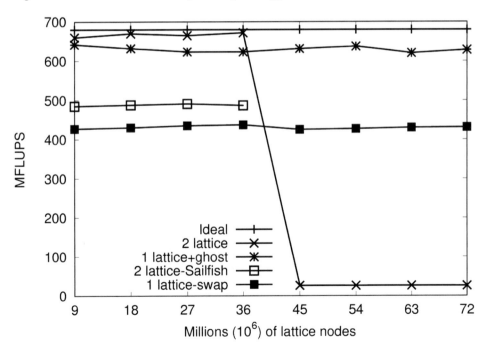

LBM-Ghost. Using both approaches, bigger simulations can be computed without additional and computationally expensive memory transfers. Figure 16 illustrates the MFLUPS achieved by all the implementations tested and an estimation for the ideal MFLUPS for our platform. The LBM-Standard approach is close to ideal performance for "small" problems (until 36 millions of fluid units), being the LBM-Ghost almost a 10% slower, due to a more complex implementation The LBM-swap is positioned as the slowest implementation tested. This implementation is about a 30% and 40% slower than the LBM-Ghost and LBM-Standard respectively. This is mainly because of the swap operation carried out at the end of the collision-kernel (Listings 5 and 6).

However, when bigger domains are considered (from 45 to 72 millions of fluid units), the LBM-Standard turns out to be very inefficient, causing an important fall in performance. In contract, the performance achieved by the other two approaches, LBM-Ghost and LBM-Swap, keeps constant for the rest of tests. Also, as reference, we included the performance achieved by the GPU based implementation provided in the sailfish package (Januszewski, & Kostur, 2014), which is slower than LBM-Standard and LBM-Ghost and faster than LBM-Swap for small simulations.

Figure 17 illustrates the speedup, in terms of MFLUPS, achieved by the LBM-Ghost and LBM-Swap implementations over the LBM-Standard. Both approaches (LBM-Ghost and LBM-Swap) are slower than the LBM-Standard counterpart when executing simulations equal or smaller than 36 millions of fluid units, however the LBM-Standard turns to be the slowest when dealing with bigger domains. The LBM-Ghost is able to achieve a peak speedup equal to 25, while the peak speedup achieved by the LBM-Swap is about 16.

Figure 17. Speedup achieved by the LBM-Ghost and LBM-Swap on the LBM-Standard

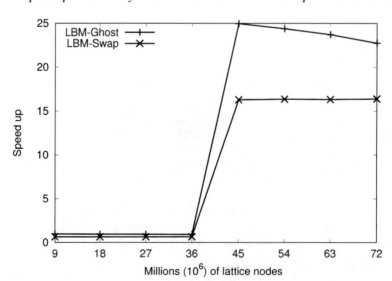

Remarks

Although the LBM-Ghost achieves a high performance when dealing with big simulations, it makes use of non-trivial optimizations, which makes difficult its implementation. Otherwise, the LBM-Swap is straight-forward. It basically consists of swapping the lattice-units of each fluid node after computing LBM-collision and LBM-streaming. Also, it is important to note the LBM-Ghost is in need of a different data-layout which may suppose additional overheads regarding pre/post-processing to adapt the standard data-layout to/from the particular data-layout used by this approach. On the other hand, the LBM-Swap is not in need of a different data layout with respect to the LBM-Standard, so that no pre/post-processing is needed.

REFERENCES

Alexandrov, V., Lees, M., Krzhizhanovskaya, V., Dongarra, J., Sloot, P., Crimi, G., ... Tripiccione, R. (2013). Early Experience on Porting and Running a Lattice Boltzmann Code on the Xeon-phi Co-Processor. *Procedia Computer Science*, *18*, 551–560. doi:10.1016/j.procs.2013.05.219

Anderson, J. D. (1995). *Computational fluid dynamics - the basics with applications*. McGraw-Hill.

Anderson, J. D., Menter, F. R., Dick, E., Degrez, G., & Vierendeels, J. (2013). *Introduction to computational fluid dynamics*. Von Karman Institute for Fluid Dynamics.

Bailey, P., Myre, J., Walsh, S., Lilja, D., & Saar, M. (2009). Accelerating lattice Boltzmann fluid flow simulations using graphics processors. In *Proceedings of International Conference on Parallel Processing* (pp. 550-557). Academic Press. doi:10.1109/ICPP.2009.38

Bernaschi, M., Fatica, M., Melchiona, S., Succi, S., & Kaxiras, E. (2010). A flexible high- performance lattice boltzmann gpu code for the simulations of fluid flows in complex geometries. *Concurrency Computa.: Pract. Exper.*, *22*(1), 1–14. doi:10.1002/cpe.1466

Fakhari, A., & Lee, T. (2014). Finite-difference lattice boltzmann method with a block-structured adaptive-mesh-refinement technique. *Physical Review*, *89*(033310). PMID:24730970

Favier, J., Revell, A., & Pinelli, A. (2014). A Lattice Boltzmann–Immersed Boundary method to simulate the fluid interaction with moving and slender flexible object. *Journal of Computational Physics, 261*(0), 145–161. doi:10.1016/j.jcp.2013.12.052

Habich, J., Feichtinger, C., Kstler, H., Hager, G., & Wellein, G. (2013). Performance engineering for the lattice Boltzmann method on GPGPUs: Architectural requirements and performance results. *Computers & Fluids, 80*(0), 276–282. doi:10.1016/j.compfluid.2012.02.013

He, X., & Luo, L. S. (1997). A priori derivation of the lattice boltzmann equation. *Physical Review, 55*.

Januszewski, M., & Kostur, M. (2014). Sailfish: A flexible multi-GPU implementation of the lattice Boltzmann method. *Computer Physics Communications, 185*(9), 2350–2368. doi:10.1016/j.cpc.2014.04.018

Jonas, L. (2007). *How to implement your ddqq dynamics with only q variables per node (instead of 2q). (Technical report)*. Tufts University.

Kandhai, D., Vidal, D. J. E., Hoekstra, A. G., Hoefsloot, H., Iedema, P., & Sloot, P. M. A. (1998). A comparison between lattice-boltzmann and finite-element simulations of fluid flow in static mixer reactors. *International Journal of Modern Physics, 09*(08), 1123–1128. doi:10.1142/S0129183198001035

Kollmannsberger, S., Geller, S., Dster, A., Tlke, J., Sorger, C., Krafczyk, M., & Rank, E. (2009). Fixed-grid fluid-structure interaction in two dimensions based on a partitioned lattice boltzmann and p-fem approach. *International Journal for Numerical Methods in Engineering, 79*(7), 817–845. doi:10.1002/nme.2581

Lagrava, D., Malaspinas, O., Latt, J., & Chopard, B. (2012). Advances in multi-domain lattice boltzmann grid refinement. *Journal of Computational Physics, 231*(14), 4808–4822. doi:10.1016/j.jcp.2012.03.015

Li, K., Yang, W., & Li, K. (2016). A hybrid parallel solving algorithm on gpu for quasi-tridiagonal system of linear equations. *IEEE Transactions on Parallel and Distributed Systems, 27*(10), 2795–2808. doi:10.1109/TPDS.2016.2516988

Malaspinas, O., & Sagaut, P. (2012). Consistent subgrid scale modelling for lattice boltzmann methods. *Journal of Fluid Mechanics, 700*, 514–542. doi:10.1017/jfm.2012.155

Marié, S., Ricot, D., & Sagaut, P. (2009). Comparison between lattice boltzmann method and navier-stokes high order schemes for computational aeroacoustics. *Journal of Computational Physics, 228*(4), 1056–1070. doi:10.1016/j.jcp.2008.10.021

Mohamad, A. A. (2011). *The lattice Boltzmann method–fundamental and engineering applications with computer codes*. Springer.

Pohl, T., Kowarchik, M., Wilke, J., Rüde, U., & Iglberger, K. (2003). Optimization and profiling of the cache performance of parallel lattice boltzmann codes. *Parallel Processing Letters*, *13*(4), 549–560. doi:10.1142/S0129626403001501

Qian, Y. H., D'Humires, D., & Lallemand, P. (1992). Lattice bgk models for navier-stokes equation. *Europhysics Letters*, *17*(6), 479–484. doi:10.1209/0295-5075/17/6/001

Rinaldi, P. R., Dari, E. A., Vénere, M. J., & Clausse, A. (2012). A Lattice-Boltzmann solver for 3D fluid simulation on GPU. *Simulation Modelling Practice and Theory*, *25*, 163–171. doi:10.1016/j.simpat.2012.03.004

Schnherr, M., Kucher, K., Geier, M., Stiebler, M., Freudiger, S., & Krafczyk, M. (2011). Multi-thread implementations of the lattice boltzmann method on non-uniform grids for CPUs and GPUs. *Computers & Mathematics with Applications (Oxford, England)*, *61*(12), 3730–3743. doi:10.1016/j.camwa.2011.04.012

Shet A. G., Siddharth K., Sorathiya S. H., Deshpande A. M., Sher-lekar S. D., Kaul B., & Ansumali S. (2013). On Vectorization for Lattice Based Simulations. *International Journal of Modern Physics*.

Succi, S. (2001). *The lattice Boltzmann equation: For fluid dynamics and beyond*. New York: Oxford university press.

Swarztrauber, P. N. (1974). A direct Method for the Discrete Solution of Separable Elliptic Equations. *SIAM Journal on Numerical Analysis*, *11*(6), 1136–1150. doi:10.1137/0711086

Valero-Lara, P. (2014a). Accelerating solid-fluid interaction based on the immersed boundary method on multicore and GPU architectures. *The Journal of Supercomputing*, *70*(2), 799–815. doi:10.1007/s11227-014-1262-2

Valero-Lara, P. (2014b). A fast multi-domain lattice-boltzmann solver on heterogeneous (multicore-gpu) architectures. In *Proceedings of 14th International Conference Computational and Mathematical Methods in Science and Engineering* (pp. 1239-1250). Academic Press.

Valero-Lara, P. (2014c). A fast multi-domain lattice-boltzmann solver on heterogeneous (multicore-gpu) architectures. In *Proceedings of 14th International Conference Computational and Mathematical Methods in Science and Engineering* (pp. 1239-1250). Academic Press.

Valero-Lara, P., Igual, F. D., Prieto-Matías, M., Pinelli, A., & Favier, J. (2015). Accelerating fluid–solid simulations (Lattice-Boltzmann & Immersed-Boundary) on heterogeneous architectures. *Journal of Computational Science*, *39*(67), 259–270.

Valero-Lara, P., & Jansson, J. (2015). LBM-HPC An open-source tool for fluid simulations. case study: Unified parallel C (UPC-PGAS). In *2015 IEEE International Conference on Cluster Computing* (pp 318-321). IEEE. doi:10.1109/CLUSTER.2015.52

Valero-Lara, P., & Jansson, J. (2017). Heterogeneous cpu+gpu approaches for mesh refinement over lattice- boltzmann simulations. *Concurrency and Computation*, *29*(7), e3919. doi:10.1002/cpe.3919

Valero-Lara, P., Pinelli, A., Favier, J., & Prieto-Matías, M. (2012). Block Tridiagonal Solvers on Heterogeneous Architectures. In *Proceedings of 10th IEEE International Symposium on Parallel and Distributed Processing with Applications Workshop* (pp. 609-616). IEEE.

Valero-Lara, P., Pinelli, A., & Prieto-Matías, M. (2014). Fast finite difference Poisson solvers on heterogeneous architectures. *Computer Physics Communications*, *185*(4), 1265–1272. doi:10.1016/j.cpc.2013.12.026

Valero-Lara, P., Pinelli, A., & Prieto-Matías, M. (2014). Accelerating Solid-fluid Interaction using Lattice-boltzmann and Immersed Boundary Coupled Simulations on Heterogeneous Platforms. In *Proceedings of the International Conference on Computational Science* (pp. 50-61). Academic Press. doi:10.1016/j.procs.2014.05.005

Wellein, G., Zeiser, T., Hager, G., & Donath, S. (2006). On the single processor performance of simple lattice boltzmann kernels. *Computers & Fluids*, *35*(8-9), 910–919. doi:10.1016/j.compfluid.2005.02.008

Wendt, J. F., & Anderson, J. D. (2008). *Computational fluid dynamics: An introduction*. Springer.

Wittmann, M., Zeiser, T., Hager, G., & Wellein, G. (2013). Comparison of different propagation steps for lattice Boltzmann methods. *Computers & Mathematics with Applications (Oxford, England)*, *65*(6), 924–935. doi:10.1016/j.camwa.2012.05.002

Yang, W., Li, K., Mo, Z., & Li, K. (2015). Performance optimization using partitioned spmv on gpus and multicore cpus. *IEEE Transactions on Computers*, *64*(9), 2623–2636. doi:10.1109/TC.2014.2366731

Zhou, H., Mo, G., Wu, F., Zhao, J., Rui, M., & Cen, K. (2012). GPU implementation of lattice boltzmann method for flows with curved boundaries. *Computer Methods in Applied Mechanics and Engineering*, *225228*(0), 65–73. doi:10.1016/j. cma.2012.03.011

O. Zikanov (Ed.). (2010). *Essential computational fluid dynamics*. John Wiley & Sons.

KEY TERMS AND DEFINITIONS

AoS: Array of structures, a typical data layout used to exploit cache memories.

CPU: A computer architecture composed by large cache memories. It is also known as low latency-oriented processors.

GPU: A computer architecture composed by a large number of cores and small cache memories. It is also known as throughput-oriented processors.

Heterogeneous: Those systems where more than one kind of processor, typically CPUs and GPUs coexist. These systems attempt to gain performance by adding the different computer architectures for specialized processing capabilities.

Multicore: A single computational component composed by two or more independent processing units (cores). Each of the units integrates its own arithmetic-logic and control units. All cores can access to a shared memory integrated. It is also known as low latency-oriented processors.

Reynold (Re) Number: A dimensionless quantity used in fluid mechanics to predict flow patterns in fluid flow simulations.

SoA: Structure of arrays, a typical data layout used to exploit vectorization.

SoAoS: Structure of array of structures, a combination of the two aforementioned data layouts that attempts to exploit both vectorization and cache memories efficiently.

Thread: In computer science, a thread is known as a sequence of instructions. On a parallel processor, such as multicore or manycore, multiple threads can be executed simultaneously.

Viscosity: A quantity used to measure the "diffusion" of momentum in the direction of flow.

Chapter 2
Challenges on Porting Lattice Boltzmann Method on Accelerators:
NVIDIA Graphic Processing Units and Intel Xeon Phi

Claudio Schepke
Federal University of Pampa, Brazil

João V. F. Lima
Federal University of Santa Maria, Brazil

Matheus S. Serpa
Federal University of Rio Grande do Sul, Brazil

ABSTRACT

Currently NVIDIA GPUs and Intel Xeon Phi accelerators are alternatives of computational architectures to provide high performance. This chapter investigates the performance impact of these architectures on the lattice Boltzmann method. This method is an alternative to simulate fluid flows iteratively using discrete representations. It can be adopted for a large number of flows simulations using simple operation rules. In the experiments, it was considered a three-dimensional version of the method, with 19 discrete directions of propagation (D3Q19). Performance evaluation compare three modern GPUs: K20M, K80, and Titan X; and two architectures of Xeon Phi: Knights Corner (KNC) and Knights Landing (KNL). Titan X provides the fastest execution time of all hardware considered. The results show that GPUs offer better processing time for the application. A KNL cache implementation presents the best results for Xeon Phi architectures and the new Xeon Phi (KNL) is two times faster than the previous model (KNC).

DOI: 10.4018/978-1-5225-4760-0.ch002

INTRODUCTION

High performance computing has been responsible for a scientific revolution. Using computers, problems that could not be solved, or demanded too much time to be solved, became available to the scientific community. The evolution of computer architectures improved the computational power, increasing the range of problems that could be dealt. The adoption of integrated circuits, pipelines, increased frequency of operation, out-of-order execution, and branch prediction are an important part of the technologies introduced up to the end of the 20th century. Recently, the concern about energy consumption has been growing, with the goal of achieving computation at the exascale level in a sustainable way. However, the aforementioned technologies alone do not allow the achievement of exascale computing, due to the high energy cost of increasing frequency and pipeline stages, as well as the fact that we are at the limits of exploration the instruction level parallelism.

In order to solve such problems, multicore and accelerators architectures have been introduced in recent years. The main feature of multicore and accelerators is the presence of several processing cores operating concurrently, in which the application has to be programmed by separating it into several tasks that communicate with each other. Concerning the use of accelerators in HPC architectures, its main characteristic is the presence of different environments in the same system, each with its own specialized architecture for a type of task. A typical HPC system is normally composed by a generic processor, responsible of managing the system, and several accelerators present in the system to perform the computation of certain kind of tasks.

The usage of accelerators poses several challenges for HPC. Applications need to be coded considering the particularities and constraints of each environment, as well as considering their distinct architectural characteristics. For example, in the memory hierarchy, the presence of several cache memory levels, some shared and others private, as well as whether the memory banks are centralized or distributed, introduce non-uniform access times, which impact the performance. In addition, in accelerators, the number of functional units may vary between different hardware versions, and the instruction set itself may not be the same. All these aspects influence on the performance of applications and need to be considered in the application code.

This chapter covers recent challenges of parallel programming for the Lattice-Boltzmann Method (LBM) (Schepke, Maillard, & Navaux, 2009). LBM is the current backbone for fluid flow through porous media. It has been extensively applied for Soil Filtration and Fuel Cells for the last five years. LBM is an iterative numerical method to model and to simulate fluid dynamics properties, where space, time and velocity are discrete. The method enables the computational modeling of a large variety of problems, including fluid with multi-components, in one or more phases, with irregular boundary conditions and in complex geometries (Valero-Lara, 2014) (Valero-Lara, & Jansson, 2016). The LBM has been used for simulations of blood vessels, flow of oil in porous rocks with water emulsions, and turbulent flows (Nita, Itu, Suciu, & Suciu, 2013) (Obrecht, Kuznik, Tourancheau, & Roux, 2011).

The LBM is a numerical approach for simulation of fluid flows that take benefits of the fact that it can be used for specific flow conditions, to be naturally discrete and to be parallelized. In terms of development, the fluid flow modeling begins discrete, that is, the domain representation does not need to be discretized after. This model simplifies coding because both method and algorithm are the same. At last, because the operations of the method are local, each lattice element can be computed in parallel. So, a parallel version of the algorithm should be straightforward.

Computational methods, such as LBM, should be continuously ported to the newest HPC hardware available to maintain competitiveness. Parallel programming strategies are considered for operations over each lattice element and it neighbor elements. To execute parallel simulations, state-of-art HPC architectures are employed, generating accurate and faster results at each generation. The software must evolve to support the features of each design to keep performance scaling. Furthermore, it is important to understand the software impact in order to improve performance.

The last decade has seen a trend of building systems with dedicated devices and accelerators, which produce a good return regarding FLOPs/Watt (Uribe-Parides, Valero-Lara, Arias, Sánchez, & Cazorla, 2011). Among the available HPC alternatives, chip manufacturers have dedicated efforts to provide tens to hundreds of processing units working at low frequencies, such as the Intel Xeon Phi coprocessors and NVIDIA GPUs. Even traditional multicore processors, such as the Intel Xeon family, are including dozens of cores in NUMA systems.

Several challenges must be addressed to better support these manycore systems and thus achieve high performance. One of the most important aspects to be considered is the memory hierarchy, composed of several cache layers and memory controllers, that has a significant impact in performance. Likewise, the cache memory behavior plays a key role in the performance. Current multicore and manycore architectures support vectorization, which allows several operations per instruction, and can boost the performance by several times. Furthermore, such manycore systems are heavily dependent on load balancing, due to the large number of cores. An application must address these challenges to take advantage of the new architectures.

This work presents an approximation to correlate the hardware impact using a 3D (D3Q19) Lattice-Boltzmann Method simulation running on new architectures. The next sections describe the related work, accelerator platforms and their programming model, parallel implementations of the LBM, experimental results, and the conclusion.

THE LATTICE BOLTZMANN METHOD

Most problems of Fluid Dynamics are described by the Euler and Navier-Stokes equations (Chung, 2010). Through the study of the liquid and gas properties, it is possible to determine different kinds of physical phenomena like tsunami effects, weather forecast, aerodynamics, aeroacoustics and thermal management.

The evolution of computational systems make possible to solve these problems in an efficient way through new simulation techniques. Therewith, some methods and algorithms were developed for numerical simulations. Usually, the domain of a fluid dynamic problem is discretized, generating a collection of linear equations that are solved through numerical methods. Alternative methods like the Lattice Boltzmann Method (LBM) improve and simplify these steps (Randles, Kale, Hammond, Gropp, & Kaxiras, 2013).

The LBM is considered a discrete representation of the Boltzmann equation, the base of kinetic theory of gases. This method uses real values for the diffusion of the physical properties, making it different of Lattice Gas Automata. Therefore LBM can be considered an evolution of the Lattice Gas Automata once it does consider the motion of a set of particles and because it uses real values instead of logical values. These features of Lattice Gas Automata make relatively easy the development and solution of a problem, but limited due the way of this method determines the physical properties of a fluid. As a consequence of these limitations, the Lattice Gas Automata changed, evolving into the Lattice Boltzmann Method (Chen, & Doolen, 1998).

The Lattice Boltzmann Equation (LBE) can be developed from a kinetic equation of the distribution function of particles, in terms of relaxation and propagation functions, as presented, respectively, below.

$$f_i^{new}\left(x,t\right) - f_i\left(x,t\right) = \Omega\left(f_i\left(x,t\right)\right), \left(i = 1,...,d\right). \tag{1}$$

$$f_i\left(x+e, t+1\right) = f_i^{new}\left(x,t\right), \left(i = 1,...,d\right). \tag{2}$$

where f_i is the distribution function of the particle velocity in each one of the d lattice directions $\left(i = 1,...,d\right)$, e is the space variation of x when the discrete time t changes to $t+1$ and Ω is a relaxation operator defined in equation 4. Joining equation 1 with equation 2 one gets:

$$f_i\left(x + e, t + 1\right) = f_i\left(x, t\right) + \Omega\left(f_i\left(x, t\right)\right). \tag{3}$$

In the LBM, instead of considering all the collisions among the particles, a relaxation operator model called Lattice Bhatnagar-Gross-Krook (BGK) is used (Flekkøy, 1993).

This relaxation operator is defined according to the mass and momentum conservation laws and is given by:

$$\Omega\left(f_i\left(x, t\right)\right) = -\frac{1}{\tau} f_i\left(x, t\right) - f_q^{eq}\left(\rho, u\right). \tag{4}$$

In this equation, t represents a relaxation time scale, that controls the rate of equilibrium approximation, $f_q^{eq}\left(\rho, u\right)$ is the equilibrium distribution function and ρ and u are macroscopic values for density and velocity.

The equation 5 defines the equilibrium distribution function $f_q^{eq}\left(\rho, u\right)$, where the value of w_i depends on the lattice geometry, e_i is the discrete velocity for each lattice direction and $c = \Delta x / \Delta t$

$$f_q^{eq}\left(\rho, u\right) = \rho w_i \left[1 + \frac{3e_1 u}{c^2} + \frac{9\left(e_i u\right)^2}{2c^4} - \frac{3u^2}{2c^2}\right]. \tag{5}$$

The macroscopic values of density ρ and momentum ρu can be calculated from f, respectively as:

$$\rho = \sum_{i=1}^{d} f_i\left(x, t\right) = \sum_{i=1}^{d} f_i^{eq}\left(x, t\right), \tag{6}$$

$$\rho u = \sum_{i=1}^{d} e_i f_i\left(x, t\right) = \sum_{i=1}^{d} e_i^{eq} f_i\left(x, t\right). \tag{7}$$

In this method, the behavior of the particles that composes a fluid is represented by a structure known by lattice. A lattice, also called of grid, consists on a discrete model characterized for a mesh, having several cells or points. These points represent the particles of a fluid, being that the update of these occurs concurrently in intervals of the discrete time.

In the literature, it is possible to find several models of lattice (Chen, & Doolen, 1998). This work used a model known as D3Q19, being this nomenclature assigned due to the three-dimensional space and the nine possibilities of discrete displacement of the physical properties. In this model, each physical property can be moved to six cardinal directions, twelve diagonals or keep up static in a point represented in Figure 1. Therefore, there are situations that more than one physical property will flow to the same position in the lattice. These situations are called collisions and have its effect described through a relaxation operator.

The algorithm of the method is presented in Figure 2. It is essentially a loop over four operations. First, physical properties are applied and an equilibrium function are called. Next, the relaxation operator emules the shock amount the particles. In the propagation, the physical properties are redirect for neighbor lattice points. At the end, the bounce back simulates the collision over barriers. Listing 1 to Listing 4 present pseudocodes for each part of the iterative simulation. For each operation, all elements of the lattice are visited. The difference in each method is the processing of local and/or neighbor elements.

In addition to propagation and relaxation operations, it is necessary to manage the boundary conditions. In this work, the mechanism known as Bounce Back (reflexive barriers) is used to deal with the limits of the flow. In case of collision,

Figure 1. D3Q19 lattice model

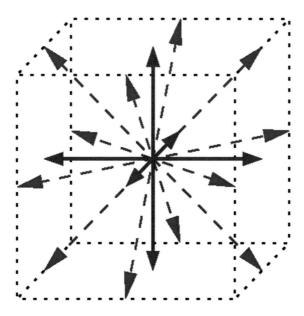

Listing 1. Redistribution pseudocode

```
1.          redistribute(lattice, accel, density){
2.          for(1 to MAX_DIM_X)
3.            for(1 to MAX_DIM_Y)
4.              for(1 to MAX_DIM_Z)
5.                if(lattice[x][y][z].obs == FALSE)
6.                  add_acceleration(lattice[x][y][z], accel, density);
7.          }
```

Listing 2. Propagation pseudocode

```
1.          propagate(lattice) {
2.            for(1 to MAX_DIM_X)
3.              for(1 to MAX_DIM_Y)
4.                for(1 to MAX_DIM_Z)
5.                  if(lattice[x][y][z].obs == FALSE)
6.                    forward_neighbors(lattice[x][y][z]);
7.            }
```

Listing 3. Bounceback pseudocode

```
1.          bounceback(lattice) {
2.            for(1 to MAX_DIM_X)
3.              for(1 to MAX_DIM_Y)
4.                for(1 to MAX_DIM_Z)
5.                  if(lattice[x][y][z].obs == TRUE)
6.                    invert_direction(lattice[x][y][z]);
7.            }
```

Listing 4. Relaxation pseudocode

```
1.          relaxation(lattice, relaxation_factor) {
2.            for(1 to MAX_DIM_X)
3.              for(1 to MAX_DIM_Y)
4.                for(1 to MAX_DIM_Z)
5.                  if(lattice[x][y][z].obs == FALSE)
6.                    apply_relaxation(lattice[x][y][z], relaxation_factor);
7.            }
```

Figure 2. Algorithm of the Lattice Boltzmann Method

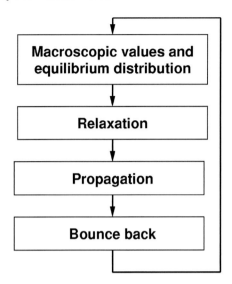

the directions of the velocity vectors are inverted. This condition ensures that the fluid does not surpass the lattice.

From a computational point of view, the operations of LBM are essentially local, and the algorithm parallelization becomes a possible alternative to reduce the execution time. Therefore, multicore and manycore systems are evaluated, to indicate the best approach for fluid dynamic applications, like LBM (Tölke, 2010) (Crimi, Mantovani, Pivanti, Schifano, & Tripiccione, 2013) (Habich, Feichtinger, Kstler, Hager, & Wellein, 2013) (Kraus, Pivanti, Schifano, Tripiccione, & Zanella, 2013).

ACCELERATORS

In the last years, microprocessors have followed two different design approaches (Kirk, & Hwu, 2012). The multicore approach maximizes the execution speed of sequential programs. A multicore microprocessor has dozens of out-of-order multiple issue processor cores, implementing the full x86 instruction set. On the other hand, the accelerator approach emphasis on the execution throughput of parallel programs. Accelerators have a large number of heavily multithreaded, in-order, single-instruction cores. The hardware takes advantage of the massive number of threads to find work to do when some of them are in a stall on memory accesses. Besides, accelerators have been enhanced with Arithmetic Logical Units (ALU) for floating-point operations such as fused multiply-add (FMA) from NVIDIA GPUs and Vector Processing Unit (VPU) from Intel coprocessors. Figure 3 illustrates the differences of design between multicore (left) and accelerator (right) microprocessors.

Regarding the parallel interfaces, the authors employ CUDA on GPUs and standard OpenMP pragmas on Intel Xeon Phi coprocessors.

Intel Xeon Phi

The Intel Xeon Phi is a many-core accelerator. The Knights Corner (KNC) version is a coprocessor which incorporate up to 61 x86 cores supporting 4-way Simultaneous Multithreading (SMT) (Lima, Broquedis, Gautier, & Raffin, 2013). The architecture employs x86 cores with many more hardware threads on a dual-slot PCI Express card with a lightweight Linux distribution. It also includes 16GB of GDDR5 memory and each core is clocked at 1.238 GHz. The cores are based on a modified version of the Pentium released in 1995. Each core of Intel® Xeon Phi™ is equipped with 512 KB L2 cache locally with access to all other L2 caches, making L2 cache size over 30 MB (Jeffers, & Reinders, 2013).

The Knights Landing (KNL) architecture is a processor version that is organized in tiles and has a distributed tag directory. Each tile contains two cores, with private L1 caches and a shared L2 cache. The cores in KNL implement an out-of-order pipeline and can execute 4 threads in parallel using simultaneous multithreading (SMT) (Sodani, Gramunt, Corbal, Kim, Vinod, Chinthamani, Hutsell, Agarwal, & Liu, 2016). The architecture, besides DDR4 memory, includes an on-package high-bandwidth memory (HBM) based on MCDRAM, which can work as a cache to the DDR4 memory. Table 1 summarizes maximum capacity, bandwidth, and latency on MCDRAM and DDR4 (Reinders, Jeffers, & Sodani, 2016).

Figure 3. Design differences between a multicore (left) and an accelerator (right) microprocessor. The multicore layout is based on a basic model from recent microprocessors, and the accelerator layout is similar to a GPU architecture representation.

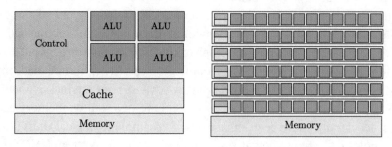

Table 1. Memory capacity, bandwidth, and capacity of Intel Xeon Phi KNL architecture

	Capacity	Bandwidth	Idle Latency
MCDRAM	Up to 16GB	Up to 450GB/s	Approx. 150ns
DDR4	Up to 384GB	Up to 90GB/s	Approx. 125ns

Figure 4 illustrates the three memory modes of KNL architecture. In cache mode, the MCDRAM is used as a Last Level Cache (LLC) located between L2 cache and the addressable memory. The addressable memory from DDR4 may be used by the user for explicit memory allocation, while MCRAM is not visible. In flat mode the entire MCDRAM is addressable and may be used by the user through explicit memory allocation. The MCDRAM portion of the addressable memory is exposed as a separate NUMA node without cores, and another NUMA node contains all the cores and DDR4 memory. Last, the hybrid mode uses a portion of the MCDRAM as addressable memory and the rest as cache. The cache portion acts as in cache mode memory, and the addressable memory portion acts as in flat mode.

The three memory modes have advantages and drawbacks:

- Cache mode does not require modifications in code, but it may have lower performance in cases of frequent cache misses to DDR4.
- Flat mode may offer better performance than cache mode; however, it requires code and execution environment modifications.
- Hybrid mode includes benefits from both flat mode and cache mode, but it restricts the available memory sizes of each.

Figure 4. Three modes for the MCDRAM usage in the Intel Xeon Phi KNL architecture and their relation with DDR4 memory
Source: Reinders, Jeffers, & Sondani, 2016.

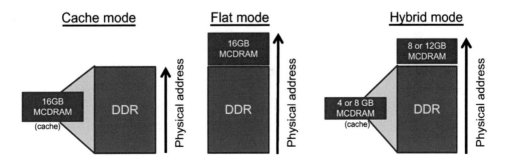

NVIDIA GPUs

Graphics Processing Unit (GPU) is a widespread class of accelerator. Over the past few years, GPUs have evolved from a fixed function special-purpose processor to a general-purpose architecture. In the early 2000s, GPU was a fixed-function processor, build around the graphics pipeline, composed mainly of two hardware units: the vertex units to compute geometrical transformations, and the fragment units to process pixels. This fixed-function pipeline lacked of generality and restricted GPU programming to graphics applications. The efforts at this time for general purpose computation, in conjunction with advances in microprocessor design, resulted in unified shader models. All programmable units in the pipeline shared an array of processing units, in which featured the same instruction set.

The programming model of modern GPUs follows a SIMD model with many processing units in parallel applying the same instruction. Each unit operates on integer or floating-point data with a general-purpose instruction set, and can read or write data from a shared global memory. This programming model allows branches in the code but not without performance loss. GPUs devote a large fraction of resources to computation. Supporting different execution paths on each unit requires a substantial amount of control hardware. Today's GPUs group units into blocks, and they are processed in parallel. If some units branch to different directions within a block, the hardware computes both sides of the branch for all units in the block. The size of a block is known as the "branch granularity'' (Owens, Houston, Luebke, Green, Stone, & Phillips, 2008).

In the context of General-Purpose Computing on the GPU (GPGPU), programming for GPUs were not trivial since applications still had to be programmed using graphics APIs. General-purpose programming APIs has been conceived to express applications in a familiar programming language. Examples of such APIs are NVIDIA's CUDA and OpenCL.

The architecture of a NVIDIA GPU is composed of streaming-processor (SP) cores organized as an array of streaming multiprocessors (SM). The number of SP cores and SMs can vary from one generation to other. Each SM has a number of SPs that share control logic and instruction cache. In addition, each SP core contains a scalar multiply-add (MAD) unit and floating-point multipliers. A low-latency interconnect network between the SPs and the shared-memory banks provides shared-memory access.

The SM hardware efficiently executes hundreds of threads in parallel while running several different programs. Each SM thread has its own thread execution state and can execute an independent code path. Concurrent threads of computing programs can synchronize at a barrier with a single SM instruction. The SM uses the single-instruction, multiple-thread (SIMT) processor architecture. The SMs SIMT multithreaded instruction unit creates, manages, schedules, and executes threads in groups of 32 parallel threads called *warps*.

Since the G80 architecture, each SM manages a pool of warps. Individual threads composing a SIMT warp are of the same type and start together at the same program address, but they are otherwise free to branch and execute independently. At each instruction issue time, the SIMT instruction unit selects a warp that is ready to execute and issues the next instruction to that warp of active thread. A SIMT instruction is broadcasted synchronously to a warp of active parallel threads; individual threads can be inactive due to independent branching or prediction. A SIMT computes full efficiency and performance when all 32 threads of a warp take the same execution path. If threads of a warp diverge via a data-dependent conditional branch, the warp serially executes each branch path taken, disabling threads that are not on that path. Branch divergence only occurs within a warp; different warps execute independently. Figure 5 illustrates an example of branch divergence on the first warp.

Programming Models

In this Section, the authors briefly describe the two programming models to implement the parallel version of the LBM 3D on GPUs and Intel Xeon Phi: OpenMP and NVIDIA CUDA.

OpenMP

OpenMP is a standard API for shared-memory parallel programming. It consists of a set of compiler directives, library routines, and environment variables for building multithreaded parallel applications (Chapman, Jost, & Van Der Pas, 2008). A main concept of OpenMP is incremental parallelism through the addition of *parallel regions*. The programmer adds parallel directives to the sequential code. In parallel regions, the program forks additional threads to form a team of threads. The threads execute in parallel across a region of code and, at the end, wait until the full team reaches this point and then join back together.

Figure 5. GPU branch divergence example on the first warp

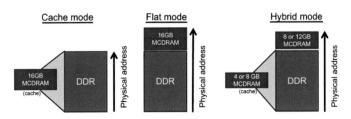

A parallel region does not distribute the work by itself, being necessary the use of *work-sharing* directives to specify how the work is to be shared among the executing threads. Probably, the most common work-sharing directive is the for loop. Version 4.0 of OpenMP introduced dynamic task creation through task construct, which specifies an unit of parallel work as an *explicit task*, and synchronization by taskwait construct. The code block below shows an example of the for loop directive to sum two vectors.

In addition, OpenMP specifies data-sharing clauses to describe data access by all concurrent threads such as shared (shared by all threads) and private (local to each thread).

NVIDIA CUDA

The Compute Unified Device Architecture (CUDA) is a general-purpose parallel programming model for NVIDIA GPUs. A CUDA program consists of one or more phases that are executed on either the host (CPU) or a GPU device in a fork-join strategy like OpenMP parallel regions. The phases that exhibit little or no data parallelism are implemented in the host code, while whose phases rich in data parallelism are implemented in the device code. The NVIDIA C Compiler nvcc separates both phases at compile time. The host code is ordinary C/C++ code, while the device code is an extended ANSI C with keywords for labeling data-parallel functions, called *kernels*, and their associated data structures.

The GPU parallelism is expressed by a hierarchy of thread groups. A *CUDA thread* is a lightweight unit of execution that is identified using a thread index that can be one-dimensional up to three-dimensional forming a *thread block*. There is a limit to the number of threads per block; however, a kernel can be executed by multiple equally-shaped thread blocks. Blocks are organized into a one-dimensional up to three-dimensional *grid* of thread blocks.

In CUDA, the host and devices have separate address spaces. The host allocates GPU memory with cudaMalloc() calls and transfers data to and from the GPU using cudaMemcpy calls. The GPU address space has three memory levels:

Listing 5. Example of parallel for coding

```
1.        #pragma omp parallel for
2.        for(i = 0; i < N; i++) {
3.          a[i] = a[i] + b[i];
4.        }
```

- **Local Memory:** Read-write and private to each thread;
- **Shared Memory:** Read-write and shared per-block thread;
- **Global Memory:** Read-write and accessible to all threads.

It also offers a subset of the texturing hardware that the GPU uses for graphics to access texture and surface memory.

The code below demonstrates an simple CUDA program with one thread and one thread block. GPU entry functions are annotated with __global__ attribute, and the compiler calls the function with <<<>>> annotation.

CUDA supports a number of features such as asynchronous execution, concurrency with streams, event monitoring, unified virtual address space (UVA), and multi-device support.

PARALLEL IMPLEMENTATIONS

This section presents implementation aspects of the LBM D3Q19 model over both accelerators NVIDIA GPUs and Intel Xeon Phi. The programming models are the NVIDIA CUDA (Nickolls, Buck, Garland, & Skadron, 2008) architecture and the OpenMP (Chapman, Jost, & Van Der Pas, 2008) interface, respectively used for GPU and Coprocessor.

OpenMP

The code in Listing 7shows the main loop of the LBM 3D OpenMP version. It iterates over all phases for a number of time steps in the simulation. This version is similar to the serial version and uses the same data structures.

Listing 6. Example of kernel CUDA code and its call in a main function

```
1.       __global__ void mykernel(void) {
2.
3.       }
4.       int main(void)
5.       {
6.        mykernel<<<1,1>>>();
7.        printf("Hello World!\n");
8.        return 0;
9.       }
```

To illustrate the implementation of computing kernels, the code below has a summarized version of the redistribute phase implementation using OpenMP. It uses the for directive with the collapse directive to distribute iterations of three loops instead of only the outer loop on x dimension (Listing 8).

The memory layout of this version is a Structure of Array (SoA) approach along with a two-lattice algorithm (Mattila, Hyväluoma, Timonen, & Rossi, 2008) (Valero-Lara, Igual, Prieto-Matías, Pinelli, & Favier, 2015).

NVIDIA CUDA

The code in Listing 9 shows the main loop of the LBM 3D CUDA version. It iterates over all phases for a number of time steps in the simulation. This version differs from the serial and OpenMP version since it has CUDA annotations to launch the computing kernel. In addition, the CUDA implementation requires the data transfer of the entire lattice to and from the GPU memory, which is done before and after the main loop.

Listing 7. Iterative step of LBM

```
1.          for (t= 0; t < Tmax; t++) {
2.              Redistribute(&lattice);
3.              Propagate(&lattice);
4.              Boundary(&lattice);
5.              Relaxation(&lattice);
6.          }
```

Listing 8. Example of omp parallel for applied in a LBM operation

```
1.          void redistribute(s_lattice *l) {
2.          int x, y, z, n;
3.          #pragma omp parallel for collapse(3) private(x, y, z)
4.          for (x = 0; x < l->lx; x++) {
5.            for (y = 0; y < l->ly; y++) {
6.              for (z = 0; z < l->lz; z++) {
7.                // rest of the code
8.              }
9.            }
10.         }
11.         // rest of the code
12.         }
```

To illustrate the implementation of computing kernels, Listing 10 shows a summarized version of the redistribute phase implementation using CUDA. Since CUDA threads are grouped in 3D blocks, each thread computes a single lattice point using its thread and block coordinates. The built-in variables blockIdx and threadIdx describe the block and thread index respectively.

Similarly, this version has a Structure of Array (SoA) memory layout along with a two-lattice algorithm (Mattila, Hyväluoma, Timonen, & Rossi, 2008) (Valero-Lara, Igual, Prieto-Matías, Pinelli, & Favier, 2015).

EXPERIMENTAL RESULTS

Platform and Environment

All experiments have been conducted on five accelerator architectures: three NVIDIA GPUs and two Intel Xeon Phi coprocessors:

- **NVIDIA Tesla K20m:** Kepler architecture with 2496 CUDA cores, running at 706 MHz. Each Streaming Multiprocessor (SMX) has a configurable on-chip memory that can be configured as 48/32/16 KB shared memory with 16/32/48 KB of L1 cache. They also have a faster 48 KB read-only cache, a

Listing 9. CUDA kernel calls of operations of the LBM implementation

```
1.        for(t= 0; t < Tmax; t++) {
2.            Redistribute<<<gridSize, blockSize>>>(...);
3.            Propagate<<<gridSize, blockSize>>>(...);
4.            Boundary<<<gridSize, blockSize>>>(...);
5.            Relaxation<<<gridSize, blockSize>>>(...);
6.        }
```

Listing 10. Example of index accessing for each element of the lattice in CUDA

```
1.        __global__ void redistribute(...)
2.        {
3.          int x = blockIdx.x * blockDim.x + threadIdx.x;
4.          int y = blockIdx.y * blockDim.y + threadIdx.y;
5.          int z = blockIdx.z * blockDim.z + threadIdx.z;
6.          // rest of the code.
7.        }
```

1280 KB shared L2 cache and 5 GB global memory. Summarizing, the entire GPU has a register file of 6656 KB, an L1 / shared memory of 1664 KB and a read-only memory of 624 KB.

- **NVIDIA Tesla K80:** Kepler architecture with 2496 CUDA cores, running at 560 MHz. Each Streaming Multiprocessor (SMX) has a 128 KB of L1/ shared cache. They also have a faster 48 KB read-only cache, a 1280 KB shared L2 cache and 12 GB global memory. Summarizing, the entire GPU has a register file of 6656 KB, an L1 / shared memory of 1664 KB and a read-only memory of 624 KB.

- **NVIDIA GTX Titan X:** Kepler architecture with 3072 CUDA cores, running at 1.0 GHz. Each Maxwell Streaming Multiprocessor (SM) has an L1 / read-only memory of 48 KB. They also have a shared memory of 96 KB, a 3072 KB shared L2 cache and 12 GB global memory. Summarizing, the entire GPU has a register file of 12228 KB, an L1 / read-only memory of 1152 KB and a shared memory of 2304 KB.

- **Intel Xeon Phi Knights Corner (KNC):** This is an Intel Xeon Phi 3120P architecture, which has 57 cores with 4-way SMT running at 1.1 GHz, total of 228 threads, 6 GB GDDR of internal memory. Each core has a private L1 (32 KB) and L2 cache (28.5 MB).

- **Intel Xeon Phi Knights Landing (KNL):** Intel Xeon Phi 7250 architecture, 68 cores with 4-way SMT running at 1.4 GHz, total of 272 threads, 32 KB of L1 private cache for instructions and 32KB L1 for data, 34 MB of L2 cache, 16GB HBM that can be LLC in cache mode, 96GB DDR4 RAM of system memory.

The proposal of this chapter is to evaluate these architectures using different sizes of lattices. In this way, it is possible to understand how different aspects of the memory hierarchy and floating-point units influence on the performance of applications. Such a study can also serve as a basis for developers of other parallel applications to optimize their applications.

Performance Results

The LBM was executed using different lattice sizes, considering the maximal memory capacity of GPUs and coprocessors. Each result is a mean of at least 5 executions with 99% confidence interval with Student's t-distribution represented on the graphs by a vertical black line around the mean values. In addition, all experiments were in double precision floating-point operations.

Figure 6 presents performance results on the Intel Xeon Phi coprocessors KNC and KNL. KNL clearly outperformed KNC for all lattice configurations, and the KNL cache mode achieved better performance results over the KNL flat mode. KNL cache mode was up to 65% better than KNC at lattice size 240x240x240. Regarding at KNL modes, KNL cache mode had up to 19.31% better performance than KNL flat mode at lattice size 256x256x256. However, our results show that KNL standard deviation was higher than KNC. The observed standard deviation was up to 79.25s (8.3%) on cache mode and 80.93s (6.9%) on flat mode. The authors note that it was not possible to run experiments with stencil size of 256x256x256 on the KNC due to its memory card size and the high memory footprint of the application.

Figure 7 shows performance results on the NVIDIA GPUs Tesla K20m, Tesla K80, and GTX Titan X. The Titan X outperformed other GPUs in all lattice configurations, and the K20m had slightly better performance than K80. The Titan X was up to 45.56% better than the K80 at lattice size 256x256x256 and 59.86% better than the K20m at lattice size 240x240x240. Titan X is faster than the others GPUs due to the high number of resource such as CUDA cores, clock, register file, L2 and shared memories. The standard deviation was under 8% for all GPU experiments. The authors note that it was not possible to run experiments with stencil size of 256x256x256 on the K20m due to its memory card size and the high memory footprint of the application.

Figure 8 presents a comparison between the GTX Titan X GPU and the KNL cache mode Xeon Phi. The Titan X GPU was up to 71.46% better than the KNL

Figure 6. Performance results on the Intel Xeon Phi coprocessors KNC and KNL

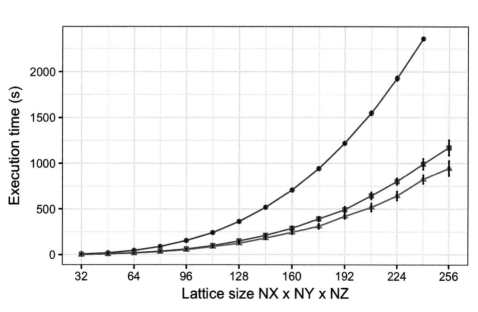

Figure 7. Performance results on the NVIDIA GPUs Tesla K20m, Tesla K80, and GTX Titan X

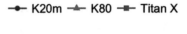

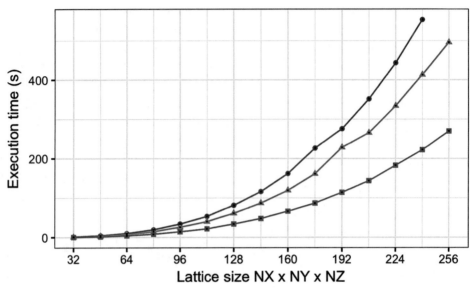

cache mode at lattice size 256x256x256. Moreover, the authors note that the KNL cache mode results had significant variation at this lattice size.

The experimental results suggest that GPUs are less sensitive to high memory footprints than Intel Xeon Phi coprocessors. The three GPU architectures had better performance results than both Intel Xeon Phi coprocessors. Since the LBM D3Q19 implementation is memory bound, it stresses significantly the memory system and requires a high bandwidth memory architecture.

A disadvantage of GPUs is the CUDA programming model that demands major modifications in the application code. For instance, the LBM D3Q19 described in this chapter has the same steps but the implementation has major modifications regarding the original serial version. Nevertheless, the Intel Xeon Phi KNC and KNL architectures support widely used programming models OpenMP and MPI. Basically, the parallel code for Intel Xeon Phi has the serial code plus pragma annotations.

A question to consider on accelerator experiments is the memory footprint of an application. The Intel Xeon Phi KNL in cache mode is able to launch lattice sizes bigger than 256x256x256 since the application resides in the system memory with high capacity and the on-chip memory turns into a last-level cache between the L2 cache and on-platform DDR4 memory. The KNL cache mode manages all

Figure 8. Comparison of performance results between the NVIDIA GTX Titan X and Intel Xeon Phi KNL

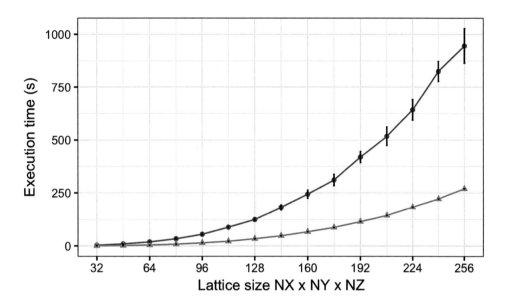

data transfers and is transparent to the application. On the other hand, GPUs does not have a similar cache strategy to launch applications that do not fit on-chip memory. CUDA offers a unified memory feature in which the system migrates data allocated memory between host and device. This feature seems to work at software level, instead of hardware, and does not allow memory allocations greater than the available device memory.

CONCLUSION

The LBM has been selected as benchmark for evaluating HPC systems. Since the appearance of the GPGPU notion, graphics cards are evaluated using the method to prove the real processing capacity of the architecture. Operations over lattices involves local computation on each node and data from neighbor nodes. Many other applications have the same computational stencil operations such as image processing and some numerical methods. In this way, the LBM will continue to be used to evaluate emerging architectures.

In this work, the authors presented the implementation and experimental analysis of the 3D (D3Q19) Lattice-Boltzmann Method simulation over accelerator platforms. The authors evaluated the LBM 3D implementations on CUDA and OpenMP over three NVIDIA GPUs and two Intel Xeon Phi accelerators respectively.

The experimental results in this work suggests that GPUs are more efficient for high footprint, memory bound applications such as the LBM 3D simulation. However, GPUs have two main disadvantages that are their on-chip memory size and proprietary programming model. The Intel Xeon Phi KNL showed performance improvements over KNC architecture, and allow to execute lattice size configurations that do not fit the on-chip memory.

REFERENCES

Chapman, B., Jost, G., & Van Der Pas, R. (2008). *Portable Shared Memory Parallel Programming* (Vol. 10). MIT Press.

Chen, S., & Doolen, C. D. (1998). Lattice Boltzmann Method for Fluid Flows. *Annual Review of Fluid Mechanics*, *30*(1), 329–364. doi:10.1146/annurev.fluid.30.1.329

Chung, T. J. (2010). *Computational Fluid Dynamics*. Cambridge, MA: Cambridge University Press. doi:10.1017/CBO9780511780066

Crimi, G., Mantovani, F., Pivanti, M., Schifano, S., & Tripiccione, R. (2013). Early Experience on Porting and Running a Lattice Boltzmann Code on the Xeon-phi Co-Processor. *Procedia Computer Science*, *18*(x0), 551–560. doi:10.1016/j.procs.2013.05.219

Flekkøy, E. G. (1993). Lattice Bhatnagar-Gross-Krook models for miscible fluids. *Physical Review E: Statistical Physics, Plasmas, Fluids, and Related Interdisciplinary Topics*, *47*(6), 4247–4257. doi:10.1103/PhysRevE.47.4247 PMID:9960501

Habich, J., Feichtinger, C., Kstler, H., Hager, G., & Wellein, G. (2013). Performance Engineering for the Lattice Boltzmann Method on GPGPUs: Architectural Requirements and Performance Results. *Computers & Fluids*, *80*(0), 276–282. doi:10.1016/j.compfluid.2012.02.013

Jeffers, J., & Reinders, J. (2013). *Intel Xeon Phi Coprocessor High Performance Programming*. San Francisco, CA: Morgan Kaufmann.

Kraus, J., Pivanti, M., Schifano, S., Tripiccione, R., & Zanella, M. (2013). Benchmarking GPUs with a Parallel Lattice-Boltzmann Code. In *Proceeding of the 25th SBAC-PAD* (pp. 160-167). Porto de Galinhas, Brazil: IEEE. doi:10.1109/SBAC-PAD.2013.37

Lima, J. V. F., Broquedis, F., Gautier, T., & Raffin, B. (2013). Preliminary Experiments with XKaapi on Intel Xeon Phi Coprocessor. In *Proceedings of the 25th SBAC-PAD*. Porto de Galinhas, Brazil: IEEE. doi:10.1109/SBAC-PAD.2013.28

Mattila, K., Hyväluoma, J., Timonen, J., & Rossi, T. (2008). Comparison of implementations of the lattice-Boltzmann method. *Computers & Mathematics with Applications (Oxford, England), 55*(7), 1514–1524. doi:10.1016/j.camwa.2007.08.001

Nickolls, J., Buck, I., Garland, M., & Skadron, K. (2008). Scalable Parallel Programming with CUDA. *Queue, 6*(2), 40–53. doi:10.1145/1365490.1365500

Nita, C., Itu, L., Suciu, C., & Suciu, C. (2013). GPU Accelerated Blood Flow Computation Using the Lattice Boltzmann Method. In *Proceedings of the IEEE 2013 HPEC* (pp. 1-6). IEEE. doi:10.1109/HPEC.2013.6670324

Obrecht, C., Kuznik, F., Tourancheau, B., & Roux, J.-J. (2011). A New Approach to the Lattice Boltzmann Method for Graphics Processing Units. *Computers & Mathematics with Applications (Oxford, England), 61*(12), 3628–3638. doi:10.1016/j.camwa.2010.01.054

Owens, J. D., Houston, M., Luebke, D., Green, S., Stone, J. E., & Phillips, J. C. (2008). GPU Computing. *Proceedings of the IEEE, 96*(5), 879–899. doi:10.1109/JPROC.2008.917757

Randles, A. P., Kale, V., Hammond, J., Gropp, W., & Kaxiras, E. (2013). Performance Analysis of the Lattice Boltzmann Model beyond Navier-Stokes. In *IEEE 27th International Symposium on Parallel & Distributed Processing* (pp. 1063-1074). Boston: IEEE.

Reinders, J., Jeffers, J., & Sodani, A. (2016). *Intel Xeon Phi Processor High Performance Programming, Knights Landing Edition*. Cambridge, MA: Morgan Kaufmann.

Schepke, C., Maillard, N., & Navaux, P. O. A. (2009). Parallel Lattice Boltzmann Method with Blocked Partitioning. *International Journal of Parallel Programming, 37*(6), 593–611. doi:10.1007/s10766-009-0113-x

Sodani, A., Gramunt, R., Corbal, J., Kim, H., Vinod, K., Chinthamani, S., ... Liu, Y. (2016). Knights Landing: Second-Generation Intel Xeon Phi Product. *IEEE Micro, 36*(2), 34–46. doi:10.1109/MM.2016.25

Succi, S. (2001). *The Lattice Boltzmann Equation for Fluid Dynamics and Beyond.* New York: Oxford University Press.

Tölke, J. (2010). Implementation of a Lattice Boltzmann kernel Using the Compute Unified Device Architecture Developed by nVIDIA. *Computing and Visualization in Science, 13*(1), 29–39. doi:10.1007/s00791-008-0120-2

Uribe-Paredes, R., Valero-Lara, P., Arias, E., Sánchez, J. L., & Cazorla, D. (2011). A GPU-Based Implementation for Range Queries on Spaghettis Data Structure. In *International Conference on Computational Science and Its Applications - ICCSA 2011* (pp. 615-629). Springer. doi:10.1007/978-3-642-21928-3_45

Valero-Lara, P. (2014). Accelerating solid-fluid interaction based on the immersed boundary method on multicore and GPU architectures. *The Journal of Supercomputing, 70*(2), 799–815. doi:10.1007/s11227-014-1262-2

Valero-Lara, P., Igual, F. D., Prieto-Matías, M., Pinelli, A., & Favier, J. (2015). Accelerating fluid-solid simulations (Lattice-Boltzmann & Immersed-Boundary) on heterogeneous architectures. *Journal of Computational Science, 10,* 249–261. doi:10.1016/j.jocs.2015.07.002

Valero-Lara, P., & Jansson, J. (2017). Heterogeneous CPU+GPU approaches for mesh refinement over Lattice-Boltzmann simulations. *Concurrency and Computation, 29*(7), e3919. doi:10.1002/cpe.3919

KEY TERMS AND DEFINITIONS

Exascale Computing: A challenge to achieve one exaFLOPS, that is a billion calculations per second. The first exascale machine would appear in 2018, 10 years after the first petascale computer system.

Fuel Cell: An electrochemical cell that converts a chemical energy from a fuel into electricity through an electrochemical reaction of hydrogen-containing fuel with oxygen or another oxidizing agent.

GPGPU: General-purpose computing on graphics processing units is the use of a graphics processing unit (GPU), which typically handles computation only for computer graphics, to perform computation in applications traditionally handled by the central processing unit (CPU).

HPC: High performance computing is based on the clustering concept, where multiple processors, connected through various physical and logical media, operate together, as if they were a single machine. This technique greatly reduces processing times, allowing scientists and researchers to deal with problems on larger scales, which would not be possible by the methods of conventional computing.

Hybrid: Those systems where more than one kind of processors, typically CPUs, GPUs, and coprocessors coexist. These systems attempt to improve the performance by adding different computer architectures for specialized processing capabilities.

Manycore: Computer architecture composed of a large number of cores and small cache memories. It is also known as throughput-oriented processors.

Multicore: A single hardware component composed by two or more independent processing units (cores). Each of the units integrates its own arithmetic-logic (ALU) and control units. The cores may access an integrated shared memory (cache). It is also known as low-latency-oriented processors.

NUMA: Non-uniform memory access is a kind of memory design, where the memory access time depends on the memory location relative to the processor. Under NUMA, a processor can access a local fast memory and a non-local memory from another processor or memory shared between processors.

SIMD: Single instruction multiple data, in Flynn's taxonomy, refers to one particular kind of processor, which is composed of multiple processing elements that commonly share the same control unit and can perform the same operation on different data simultaneously.

Soil Filtration: An application area of LBM where different soil compositions are evaluated. The soil is a structure of porous or distribution of different materials or phases (composition media). Physical properties, including multi-phase flow and solute transport, are studied.

Thread: A set of instructions in an execution flow. Multiple threads can be executed simultaneously on a parallel processor, such as multicore or manycore (Simultaneous MultiThreading – SMT).

Chapter 3
Design and Optimizations of Lattice Boltzmann Methods for Massively Parallel GPU–Based Clusters

Enrico Calore
University of Ferrara, Italy & National Institute for Nuclear Physics, Italy

Alessandro Gabbana
University of Ferrara, Italy & National Institute for Nuclear Physics, Italy

Sebastiano Fabio Schifano
University of Ferrara, Italy & National Institute for Nuclear Physics, Italy

Raffaele Tripiccione
University of Ferrara, Italy & National Institute for Nuclear Physics, Italy

ABSTRACT

GPUs deliver higher performance than traditional processors, offering remarkable energy efficiency, and are quickly becoming very popular processors for HPC applications. Still, writing efficient and scalable programs for GPUs is not an easy task as codes must adapt to increasingly parallel architecture features. In this chapter, the authors describe in full detail design and implementation strategies for lattice Boltzmann (LB) codes able to meet these goals. Most of the discussion uses a state-of-the art thermal lattice Boltzmann method in 2D, but all lessons learned in this particular case can be immediately extended to most LB and other scientific applications. The authors describe the structure of the code, discussing in detail several key design choices that were guided by theoretical models of performance and experimental benchmarks, having in mind both single-GPU codes and massively parallel implementations on commodity clusters of GPUs. The authors then present and analyze performances on several recent GPU architectures, including data on energy optimization.

DOI: 10.4018/978-1-5225-4760-0.ch003

INTRODUCTION AND BACKGROUND

The Lattice Boltzmann Method (LBM) is widely used in computational fluid-dynamics, to describe fluid flows. This class of applications, discrete in time and momenta, and living on a discrete and regular grid of points, offers a large amount of available parallelism, making LBM an ideal target for recent multi- and many-core processor-based clusters. LBM is an interesting simulation tool, not only in basic sciences but also for engineering and industrial applications. It is also popular in the energy sector, and is widely used in the oil&gas industry to model porous, multi-phase or otherwise complex flows, in order to better understand the dynamics of oil and shale-gas reservoirs and to maximize their yield. Recent developments have also started to tackle relativistic fluid dynamics, further extending the potential application domain not only to astrophysics problems or elementary particle physics applications, but also to the study of exotic materials, graphene for instance, were the peculiar behavior of the electrons moving in the material lattice can be treated within a formalism similar to relativistic hydrodynamics.

High Performance Computing (HPC) has seen in recent years an increasingly large role played by Graphics Processing Units (GPUs), offering significantly larger performance than traditional processors. In GPUs many slim processing units perform in parallel thousands of operations on a correspondingly large number of operands. This architectural structure nicely adapts to algorithms with a large amount of available parallelism, as in these cases it is possible to identify and concurrently schedule many operations on data items that have no dependencies among them. This is very often the case for so-called stencil codes typically used to model systems defined on regular lattices. They process data elements associated to each lattice site applying some regular sequence of mathematical operations to data belonging to a fixed pattern of neighboring cells. General implementation and optimization of stencils on GPUs has been extensively studied by many authors, (Holewinski, Pouchet, & Sadayappan, 2012), (Maruyama & Aoki, 2014), (Vizitiu, Itu, Lazar, & Suciu, 2014), (Vizitiu, Itu, Niţă, & Suciu, 2014). This approach is appropriate for several computational *Grand Challenge* applications, such as Lattice QCD (LQCD) and LBM, for which a large effort has gone in the past in porting and optimizing codes and libraries for both custom and commodity HPC computing systems (Bernard at al., 2002; Bilardi, Pietracaprina, Pucci, Schifano & Tripiccione, 2005). More recently many efforts have been focused on GPUs (Bernaschi, Fatica, Melchionna, Succi, & Kaxiras, 2010; Bonati et al., 2017; Bonati, Cossu, D'Elia, & Incardona, 2012; Pedro Valero-Lara, 2014; Pedro Valero-Lara et al., 2015; Januszewski & Kostur, 2014; Tölke, 2008). These efforts have allowed to obtain significant performance levels, at least on one or just a small number of GPUs (Bailey, Myre, Walsh, Lilja,

& Saar, 2009; Biferale et al., 2012; Biferale et al., 2010; Rinaldi, Dari, Vénere, & Clausse, 2012), (Jonas Tölke, 2008; Xian & Takayuki, 2011).

Most of these works are written in CUDA (Peter Bailey, Myre, Walsh, Lilja, & Saar, 2009; Herdman et al., 2012; Kraus, Pivanti, Schifano, Tripiccione, & Zanella, 2013; Tölke & Krafczyk, 2008) or OpenCL (Calore, Schifano, & Tripiccione, 2014a). However, as diversified HPC architectures emerge, it is becoming more and more important to have robust methodologies to port and maintain codes for several architectures. This need has sparked the development of frameworks based on directives where compilers generate offload-functions for accelerators, following "hints" provided by programmers as annotations to the original C, C++ or Fortran codes (Reyes, López, Fumero, & Sande, 2013; Wienke, Springer, Terboven, & Mey, 2012). Examples along this direction are OpenACC (OpenACC, 2016) and OpenMP (OpenMP, 2016). Other proposals, such as the Hybrid Multi-Core Parallel Programming model (HMPP) proposed by CAPS, hiCUDA (Han & Abdelrahman, 2011), OpenMPC (Lee & Eigenmann, 2010) and OmpSs (Ayguadé et al., 2010) follow the same line. OpenACC is considered today one of the most promising approaches (Claudio Bonati et al., 2015); its structure is in many ways similar to OpenMP (Wienke, Terboven, Beyer, & Müller, 2014): both frameworks are directive based, but while OpenMP is more *prescriptive* OpenACC is more *descriptive*. Within OpenACC the programmer only specifies that a certain loop should run in parallel on the accelerator and leaves the exact mapping to the compiler. This approach gives more freedom to the compiler and the associated runtime support, offering, at least in principle, larger scope for performance portability. So far very few OpenACC implementations of LBM codes have been described in literature: (Kraus, Schlottke, Adinetz, & Pleiter, 2014) focuses on accelerating via OpenACC a part of a large CFD application optimized for CPU; recently Blair, Albing, Grund, & Jocksch (2015) have described an implementation of a MPI Lattice Boltzmann code with OpenACC but portability of code and performances across different architectures has not been addressed, while the scalability of OpenACC codes on GPU clusters has been rarely addressed (Hart, Ansaloni, & Gray, 2012; Obrecht, Kuznik, Tourancheau, & Roux, 2013).

In the last few years, we have conducted a large and systematic analysis of several properties of convective turbulence, using as our computational tool a massively parallel GPU-based LBM code. After an early development, and in parallel with physics simulations, our codes have undergone a systematic process of further refinements, both at the algorithmic and implementation level, improving optimization strategies, adapting to new GPU generations and exploiting faster and faster GPU-to-GPU communications strategies.

In this chapter we describe in full details the computational aspects of this work, discussing several problems, and the corresponding solutions, related to the design of the code, the optimization strategies appropriate to boost performances on just one GPU, and the possible approaches to obtain a good scaling behavior of the code on large GPU clusters. In other words, what we plan to present in this contribution is not just an efficient code but rather a sound optimization approach to GPUs programming, able to exploit a large fraction of the peak computing power of state-of-the-art GPUs. This is a multi-faceted effort, that covers several related aspects, that we describe in detail, assessing the corresponding contribution to performance. In more details, we plan to consider: i) memory layouts and data-structures and the role that they play in order to maximize vector computing and to support an efficient flow of data from memory and/or an effective use of caches; ii) programming methodologies; here we provide two different implementations, one fully host-driven, and one using both GPUs and CPUs; iii) performance scaling of codes on large GPU-cluster using standard MPI communication techniques; iv) portability across several architectures using the OpenACC directive driven programming framework; v) energy-awareness, describing how to monitor the energy consumption of LBM simulations, interesting per-se and as a basis of a software-based approach to energy cost reduction.

Our analysis is largely based on a specific and computationally relevant LBM, but our results provide useful guidance to adapt and optimize other LBM codes, or even a wider class of stencil-based computational applications for GPU-based computing systems.

In conclusion, this chapter describes in detail the strategies to be adopted to implement efficient GPU-based LBM applications and also review their power consumption in detail.

AN OVERVIEW OF LATTICE BOLTZMANN METHOD

Lattice Boltzmann Method, see (Succi, 2001) for a systematic introduction, stems from lattice-gas models, based on boolean variables, that were introduced as computer friendly solvers for fluid dynamics so long ago that floating-point computing was still an esoteric technique (Frisch et al., 1986). LBM followed in the late eighties of the previous century as (floating-point) ensemble averages for the populations were introduced and it was appreciated that the collisional operator could be linearized while still retaining hydrodynamic behavior (McNamara & Zanetti, 1988). The following step saw the collisional operator replaced by a relaxation-time term (Chen, Chen, Martinez, & Matthaeus, 1991) linked LBM to the Bhatnagar, Gross, Krook approach (Bhatnagar, Gross, & Krook, 1954) to the (proper) Boltzmann equation. It then became clear that increasingly complex LBM could be designed, able to recover higher and higher moments of the pseudo-particle distribution function;

the natural development along this line was the development of thermal LBM (Alexander, Chen, & Sterling, 1993), that used higher-order approximations for the equilibrium distribution function (Y. Chen, Ohashi, & Akiyama, 1994). All these attempts were made more systematic by directly linking LBM to an underlying Boltzmann equation (He & Luo, 1997) through a systematic expansion in orthogonal polynomials (Shan, 2016). Today, LBM has been extended to treat more complex flows, such as magneto-hydrodynamics, quantum models, combustion, multi-phase flows, while relativistic flows are starting to be solidly developed (Mendoza, Boghosian, Herrmann, & Succi, 2010).

At the conceptual level, LBM is a general class of algorithms able to capture the physics of complex flows, that have been systematically improved over the years to include more and more accurate details and kinematical regimes. All these theoretical improvements have not changed the basic features of the corresponding algorithms, that can be easily implemented on modern computer architectures, as they feature a very regular algorithmic flow and offer a huge amount of exploitable parallelism. A further advantage of most LBM codes is that it is easy to enforce a variety of boundary conditions even on irregular integration domains.

LBM in principle provide a numerical solution to the kinetic Boltzmann equation

$$\partial_t f + \boldsymbol{v} \cdot \nabla f = \Omega\big(f\big),$$

that describes the evolution of the probability function $f\big(\boldsymbol{x}, \boldsymbol{v}\big)$ that a fluid particle at position $\boldsymbol{x}$ has velocity $\boldsymbol{v}$. The collision term $\Omega\big(f\big)$ is assumed to follow the well-known Bathnagar, Gross, Krook (BGK) ansatz,

$$\Omega\big(f\big) = -\frac{1}{\tau}\big(f - f^{(0)}\big); f^{(0)}\big(\boldsymbol{v}, \boldsymbol{u}, \rho, T\big) = \frac{\rho}{(2\pi T)^{D/2}} e^{-(\boldsymbol{v}-\boldsymbol{u})^2/2T},$$

with τ a relaxation time towards the local equilibrium distribution $f^{(0)}$ in D spatial dimensions, that also depends on the local density ρ and temperature T and on the bulk fluid velocity $\boldsymbol{u}$. The lattice (and time)-discrete counterpart of Equation 1 is

$$f_i\big(\boldsymbol{x} + \boldsymbol{c}_i\Delta t, t + \Delta t\big) - f_i\big(\boldsymbol{x}, t\big) = -\frac{\Delta t}{\tau}\Big[f_i\big(\boldsymbol{x}, t\big) - f_i^{(0)}\Big],$$

written in terms of a finite set of N pseudo-particle *populations* $f_l, \{l = 1 \cdots N\}$, each streaming at each time step to a destination lattice site connected to the start site by a velocity vector c_l. Macroscopic quantities depend on the values of the f_l,

$$\rho = \sum_l f_l; \rho u = \sum_l f_l c_l; D\rho T \sum_l (c_l - u)^2.$$

The rationale of Equation 3 is that one samples f on a finite number of velocity values c_l; mathematically, these values are the abscissas of a Gauss-Hermite quadrature (with corresponding weights w_l) that ensures that all moments of the distribution function up to some prescribed order M are correctly evaluated.

$$\int f(v) v^M d^M v = \sum_l w_l v_l^M f_l.$$

One moves from the kinetic level of Equation 1 to the hydrodynamical level through a Chapman-Enskog expansion, in which only a limited number of moments of f appear; for instance, the momentum flux and the heat flux are respectively the second and third moments of f. For the Navier-Stokes approximation, moments up to the third and fourth one are necessary to ensure that the transport of momentum and heat in the discrete kinetic equation is the same as in the continuum.

Summing up, LBM is defined by the set of c_l velocities that ensure the correctness of Equation 5 up to the desired M. LBM in d dimensions with N populations is usually referred to as DdQN; in the following we will use very often a recently developed D2Q37 method (L. Biferale et al., 2013a), (Ripesi, Biferale, Schifano, & Tripiccione, 2014), (M. Sbragaglia et al., 2009), (A. Scagliarini, Biferale, Sbragaglia, Sugiyama, & Toschi, 2010) at the fourth order describing an ideal gas (equation of state $p = \rho T$) whose thermo-hydrodynamical equations are (i, j are spatial indexes and summation on the same indexes is implied):

$$\partial_t \rho + \partial_i \left(\rho u_i\right) = 0$$

$$\rho \partial_t u_i + \rho u_j \partial_j u_i = \rho g_i + \partial_j \sigma_{ji}$$

$$\rho \partial_t e + \rho u_j \partial_j e = \sigma_{ij} \partial_j u_i + k\Delta e,$$

written in terms of the stress tensor (σ_{ij}, containing shear and bulk viscosities), thermal conductivity k, the ideal gas internal energy ($e = T$) and an external forcing field g.

LBM codes are typical HPC applications, with large lattices often employed in an attempt to resolve fine details of the flow, but they have a remarkably simple structure. A typical code takes an initial assignment of populations describing an initial condition at $t = 0$ on some spatial domain and iterates Equation 3 for all sites on the lattice and for as many time steps are required. One enforces boundary conditions at the edges of the integration volume by assigning appropriate values at and close to the boundaries.

Let us rewrite Equation 3 as follows:

$$f_i\left(\boldsymbol{y}, t + \Delta t\right) = f_i\left(\boldsymbol{y} - \boldsymbol{c}_i\Delta t, t\right) - \frac{\Delta t}{\tau}\left[f_i\left(\boldsymbol{y} - \boldsymbol{c}_i\Delta t, t\right) - f_i^{(0)}\right]$$

One sees immediately that processing at each time step implies first a so called *propagation* phase, in which populations drift from lattice site to lattice site as dictated by their corresponding velocities. On arrival at site $\boldsymbol{y}$ populations interact and adjust their values; this step is usually referred to as the *collision* phase.

LBM algorithms have a huge degree of easily identified parallelism; Equation 9 clearly shows that, during propagation, for each site on the lattice, data must be gathered independently from nearby sites; this a typical example of stencil computation, based on a possibly complex but regular address structures. The following step, collision, performs all mathematical steps needed to compute the right-hand side of Equation 9; this step may be mathematically complex, but it can be performed independently on all lattice sites, as there is no data dependency among different sites.

The two kernels described above are the only compute critical sections of any LBM code; the only additional processing steps are the evaluation of the boundary conditions, that happens after propagation and before collision, but only applies to boundary sites and a set of measurement routines, that depend on the specific simulations setup but are usually invoked after a large number of time steps are completed.

GPGPU ARCHITECTURES AND PROGRAMMING

In the following sections we present results obtained using three generations of NVIDIA GPU architectures, Fermi, Kepler and Pascal, running our codes respectively on C2050/C2070, K20X/K40/K80 and P100 GPU boards. GPUs adopt a multi-core design of processing units, called SM (Streaming Multiprocessors) on Fermi and SMX on the more recent Kepler and Pascal architectures as they have enhanced capabilities. These GPUs have a varying number of compute units, 32 for Fermi, 192 for Kepler and 64 for Pascal, called CUDA-cores in NVIDIA jargon; those units execute at each clock-cycle multiple warps, i.e. groups of 32 operations, called CUDA-threads, which proceed in Single Instructions Multiple Threads (SIMT) fashion. At variance with CPU threads, context switches among active CUDA-threads are very fast, as these architectures maintain many thread states. Typically, one CUDA-thread processes one element of the data-set of the application. This helps exploit available parallelism of the algorithm and hides latencies by switching between threads waiting for data coming from memory and threads ready to run. This structure has remained stable across all three generations. Several enhancements are available in the more recent *Kepler* and *Pascal* architecture that have 256 32-bit registers addressable by each CUDA-thread (a 4× increase over *Fermi*) and each SMX has 65536 registers (a 2× increase). *Kepler* and *Pascal* GPUs are also able to increase their clock frequency beyond the nominal value (this is usually referred to as *GPUBoost*), if power and thermal constraints allow to do so.

Within each generation, minor differences occur. The C2050 and C2070 boards based on the *Fermi* architecture differ in the amount of available global memory. The K20, K40 and K80 are boards based on *Kepler* processors. The K40 processor has more global memory than the K20 and slightly improves memory bandwidth and floating-point throughput, while the K80 has two enhanced *Kepler* GPUs with more registers and shared memory than K20/K40 and extended GPUBoost features. Today the only board based on the *Pascal* processor is the P100.

The Tesla C2050 system has a peak performance of 1 Tflops in single-precision (SP), and ≈500 Gflops in double-precision (DP); on the *Kepler* K20 and K40, the peak SP (DP) performance is ≈5 Tflops (≈1.5Tflops), while on the K80 the aggregate SP (DP) performance of the two GPUs is ≈5.2 Tflops (≈1.9 Tflops). The P100 delivers up to ≈10.5 Tflops (SP) and ≈5.3 (DP).

Fast access to memory strongly correlates with performance: peak bandwidth is 144 GB/s for the C2050 and C2070 processors, and 250 and 288 GB/s respectively for the K20X and the K40; on the K80, the aggregate peak is 480 GB/s, increased to 732 GB/s on the P100. The memory system has an error detection and correction system (ECC) to increase reliability when running large codes. We have always used this feature, even if it slightly reduces available memory and bandwidth (e.g. on the Tesla C2050 available memory is reduced by ≈12% and we measure a typical bandwidth cost ≈20-25%). The next generation NVIDIA GPU architecture Volta further increases the computing throughput to 7.5 Tflops DP, and the memory bandwidth to 900 GB/s, a factor 1.4× and 1.2× w.r.t. the Pascal architecture. At this point in time, Volta processors are not yet available. For a more complete description, see (NVIDIA Fermi, 2009), (NVIDIA Kepler GK110, 2012), (NVIDIA Pascal P100, 2016), (NVIDIA Volta V100, 2017); Table 1 summarizes just a few relevant parameters.

The native language for NVIDIA GPUs is CUDA together with OpenCL. Both languages have a very similar programming model but use a slight different terminology; for instance, on OpenCL the CUDA-thread is called work-item, the CUDA-block work-group, and the CUDA-kernel is a device program. A CUDA or OpenCL program consists of one or more functions that run either on the host, a standard CPU, or on a GPU. Functions that exhibits no (or limited) parallelism run on the host, while those exhibiting a large degree of data parallelism can go onto the GPU. The program is a modified C (or C++, Fortran) program including keyword extensions defining data parallel functions called *kernels* or *device programs*. Kernel functions typically translate into a large number of threads, i.e. a large number of independent operations processing independent data items. Threads are grouped into blocks which in turn form the execution *grid*. The grid can be configured as a 1-, 2- or 3-dimensional array of blocks, each block is itself a 1-, 2- or 3-dimensional array of threads, running on the same SM, and sharing data on a fast shared memory. When all threads complete their execution, the corresponding grid terminates. Since threads run in parallel with host CPU threads, it is possible to overlap in time processing on the host and on the accelerator.

Table 1. Selected hardware features of the GPU systems considered in this paper: The C2050 and C2070 are based on the Fermi architecture, while the K20X, K40 and K80 follow the Kepler architecture.

	C2050/ C2070	C2050 / C2070	K20X	K40	K80	P100
GPU	GF100	GF100	GK110	GK110B	GK210 ×2	P100
Number of SMs	16	16	14	15	13 ×2	56
Number of CUDA-cores	448	448	2688	2880	2496 ×2	3584
Base clock frequency (MHz)	1.15	1.15	735	745	562	1328
Base DP performance (Gflops)	515	515	1310	1430	935 ×2	4755
Boosted clock frequency (MHz)	--	--	--	875	875	1480
Boosted DP performance(Gflops)	--	--	--	1660	1455 ×2	5300
Total available memory (GB)	3 / 6	3 / 6	6	12	12 ×2	16
Memory bus width (bit)	384	384	384	384	384×2	4096
Peak mem. BW (ECC-off) (GB/s)	144	144	250	288	240 ×2	732
Max Power (Watt)	215	215	235	235	300	300

New programming approaches are now emerging, mainly based on directives, moving the coding abstraction layer at a higher level. These approaches should make code development easier on heterogeneous computing systems (OpenACC, 2016), simplifying the porting of existing codes on different architectures. OpenACC is one of such programming models, increasingly used by several scientific communities. OpenACC is based on *pragma* directives that help the compiler to identify those parts of the code that can be implemented as *parallel functions* and offloaded on the accelerator or divided among CPU cores. The actual construction of the parallel code is left to the compiler, making, at least in principle, the same code portable without modifications across different architectures and possibly offering more opportunities for performance portability. Listing 1 shows an example of the *saxpy* operation of the *Basic Linear Algebra Subprogram* (BLAS) set coded in OpenACC. The *pragma acc kernels* clause identifies the code fragment running on the accelerator, while *pragma acc loop...* specifies that the iterations of the for-loop should execute in parallel.

The OpenACC standard defines many such directives, allowing a fine tuning of applications. As an example, the number of threads launched by each device function and their grouping can be tuned by the *vector*, *worker* and *gang* directives, in a similar fashion as setting the number of *work-items* and *work-groups* in CUDA. Data transfers between host and device memories are automatically generated, and occur on entering and exiting the annotated code regions. Specific data directives help to optimize data transfers, e.g. overlapping transfers and computation. For example, in *Listing 1* the clause *copyin(ptr)* copies the array pointed by *ptr* from host onto accelerator memory before entering the following code region; *copy(ptr)* copies it back to the host memory after leaving the code region. An asynchronous directive *async* instructs the compiler to generate asynchronous data transfers or device function executions; a corresponding clause (i.e. *#pragma wait(queue)*) instructs to wait for completion.

Listing 1. Sample OpenACC code computing a saxpy function on vectors x and y. The pragma clauses control data transfers between host and accelerator and identify the code regions to be run on the accelerator.

```
#pragma acc data copyin(x), copy(y) {
  #pragma acc kernels present(x) present(y) async(1)
  #pragma acc loop vector(256)
  for (int i = 0; i < N; ++i)
    y[i] = a*x[i] + y[i];
  #pragma wait(1);
}
```

OpenACC is similar to the OpenMP (Open Multi-Processing) framework widely used to manage parallel codes on multi-core CPUs (Wienke et al., 2014); both frameworks are directive based, but OpenACC targets accelerators in general, while at this stage OpenMP targets mainly multi-core CPUs; the OpenMP standard has introduced directives to manage also accelerators, but currently, compiler support is still limited. Regular C/C++ or Fortran code, already developed and tested on traditional CPU architectures, can be annotated with OpenACC pragma directives (e.g. parallel or kernels clauses) to instruct the compiler to transform loop iterations into distinct threads, belonging to one or more functions to run on an accelerator. With the above features, OpenACC is particularly well suited for developing scientific HPC codes for several reasons: it is highly hardware agnostic, allowing to target several architectures, GPUs and CPUs, allowing to develop and maintain one single code version; the programming overhead to offload code regions to accelerators is limited to few pragma lines, in contrast to CUDA and OpenCL verbosity; the code annotated with OpenACC pragmas can still be compiled and run as plain C code, ignoring pragma directives.

OPTIMIZATION STRATEGIES: I. DATA LAYOUT

This and the following sections discuss in detail several different aspects related to the development of GPU-optimized codes of LBM algorithms; we start with a discussion on the role played by data structures.

A major initial implementation decision in the design of a new code is the choice of the most appropriate data structures, as this choice has a strong impact on computing performances while changes at a later stage of the development cycle are almost impossible. For several decades, the use of cache-based processors with no (or very limited) support of vector instructions, has suggested to organize data for LBM codes as *Array of Structures* (*AoS*). This is a two-level structure: the inner level hosts population values associated to each lattice site stored in memory at consecutive addresses; the outer level stores the lattice-sites in an array one after the other. This memory layout keeps population data at each lattice site at addresses close to each other, helping cache-based CPUs to improve performance.

As underlined in the section *GPGPU Architectures and Programming*, for GPUs it is important to exploit data-parallelism, otherwise performances are heavily limited. This implies that two or more sites should be processed concurrently, fetching, processing and storing in parallel the corresponding data-items. For example, we consider the case of the *propagate* kernel, and in particular the movement of a population with index p_i at lattice-sites s_n and s_{n+1}. A parallel implementation of this operation can be done through the use of SIMD instructions supported by several modern processors. This requires to fetch population p_i for both sites s_n and s_{n+1} from memory using a vector register of the processor, and then store back the register in memory at appropriate locations. Using the *AoS* organization populations p_i of sites s_n and s_{n+1} are not stored close in memory, and this translates in fetching data items stored at not unit-strided memory location, see Figure 1. Standard memory installed on commodity processors does not support in hardware this operation, since they are designed to read burst of data stored at consecutive memory addresses. On recent processors, reads of not-unit-strided data can be done through *gather* instructions, but they are expensive in terms of execution time, since they require to collect data-items one-at-time with one memory access for each of them.

To parallelize the fetching, processing and storing of two data-population of two lattice-sites, it is then necessary to have in memory at consecutive addresses population p_i of sites s_n and s_{n+1}. This suggest to adopt a different memory layout, where the inner level is an array storing population p_i for all lattice-sites, and the outer level is the structure hosting the arrays of all populations. This organization is called *Structure of Array (SoA)*; using the *SoA* organization, population p_i of two (or more) consecutive sites can be processed in parallel, loading them onto a vector register of the processor. For this reason, the *SoA* data-organization is a better choice on GPUs. Figure 2 quantifies the impact of these two structures on performance for the *propagate* and *collide* kernels, showing that *SoA* has a very large performance gain ($\approx 10\times$) for *propagate* and a smaller but still significant gain for *collide*, with a much softer dependence on the number of threads or blocks.

A further refinement has to do with the choice between the *pull* or *push* schemes for the *propagate* kernel. In the first case populations are moved from a set of neighbor sites onto one site, while in the latter case populations are pushed from one site towards

Figure 1. Graphical representation of the AoS and SoA layout, using as an example the D2Q37 stencil

The notation $f_i[j]$ is used to refer to the i-th population of the j-th grid point. Top figure shows the AoS format, where all populations of a given lattice site are stored in memory at consecutive addresses; bottom figure shows the SoA format, where populations of same index i but belonging to different lattice sites are stored consecutively in memory.

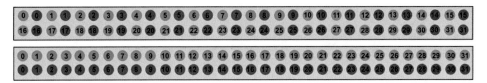

Figure 2. Execution time of propagate and collide running on an NVIDIA P100, using AoS and SoA data-structure for the D2Q37 (top) on a lattice 1024 × 2048 and for a D3Q19 (bottom) on a lattice 192 × 192 × 192.

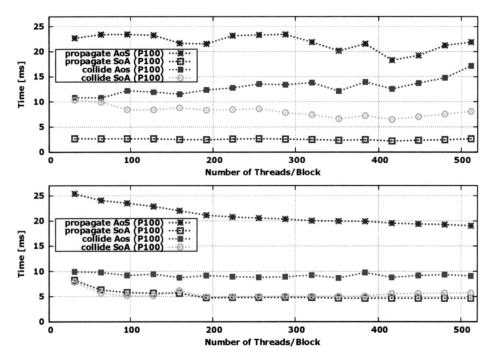

a set of neighbor sites, according to the LBM used. *push* generates aligned-reads of population values from memory, but write-back to neighbors is misaligned since values have to be stored at non-consecutive addresses. *pull* reverses the situation, as in this case reads are misaligned and writes are aligned. In both cases, misaligned memory operations are needed, and these may introduce time overheads possibly causing performance losses. Figure 3 shows the effective bandwidth of a memory copy benchmark using misaligned-reads and aligned-writes (mraw) or vice-versa (armw). This benchmark copies data elements from one array to another. In either cases reads (writes) are misaligned by 1 to 32 words. One sees that the effects of misalignment s are small, with the combination of *mraw* slightly better than *armw*. On other architectures like cache-based CPUs, the impact of misaligned operation is larger, and more complex data organization may be required (E. Calore, Gabbana, Schifano, & Tripiccione, 2017c).

Figure 3. Memory performance (ECC enabled) of misaligned-read-aligned-write (mraw) and aligned-write-misaligned-read (armw) accesses on the C2050 (GF100), K40 (GK110B), and P100 systems.

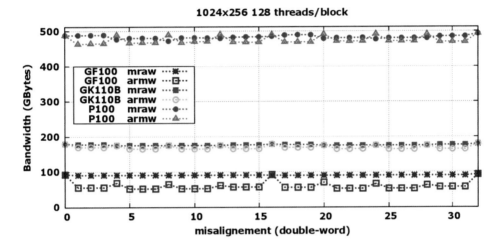

OPTIMIZATION STRATEGIES: II. SINGLE GPU

In our GPU implementation, two copies of the lattice are kept in memory. The choice of having two copies allows to easily map one GPU thread per lattice site, and to process all threads in parallel. This is required by the *propagate* kernel which needs to access neighbors' data before it gets updated, and for this reason this kernel reads input form one copy of the lattice and writes output to the other one. For the *collide* kernel this is not necessary since each lattice site can be updated *in-situ*, and this kernel can read and write data from and to the same lattice copy. The remainder of this section and the following assumes that lattice data is stored using column-major ordering and two copies are kept in memory. Each kernel reads from one copy and writes to the other. To make the computation of *propagate* uniform for all lattice sites, and avoid thread divergences while processing sites close to the borders, which have a bad impact on performance, the lattice is surrounded by halo- columns and rows, as shown in Figure 4.

More in detail, when considering a physical lattice of size $L_x \times L_y$, a grid of $N_x \times N_y$ lattice points is allocated in memory, where $N_x = H_x + L_x + H_x$, and $N_y = H_y + L_y + H_y$. For example, for the D2Q37 the *propagate* kernel accesses neighbors at distance up to three, so a frame of 3 points is set with $H_x, H_y = 3$. This requires that halos are updated before *propagate* starts, with appropriate data taking into account boundary conditions. For example, for a fully periodic boundary

Figure 4. Left: Allocation of lattice data in global memory; green regions are the halo frames; the white area is the physical lattice. Right: sketchy view of the mapping of the lattice on CUDA thread-blocks and block-grids

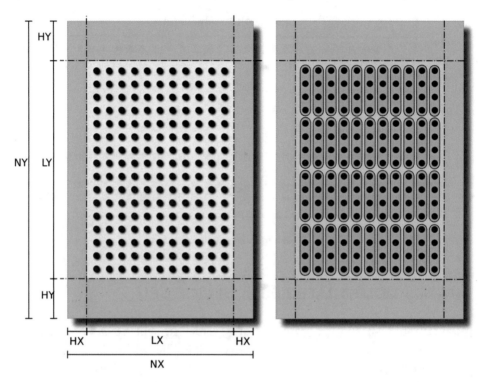

conditions, the halos are updated with copies of three inner rows and columns of the lattice as shown in the following picture. In the y direction it can be more convenient to set the frame H_y to keep data aligned to multiples of the size of each cache line (128 bytes, in our case). For this reason, H_y is set to 16 lattice points corresponding to 128 Bytes.

The execution of the code starts on the host, and, considering the case of D2Q37, at each iteration four main steps are performed as shown below:

```
for (istep=0; istep < MAXSTEPS; istep++) {
  pbc();
  propagate()
  bc()
  collide()
}
```

first the *pbc* kernel is executed to update y-halo columns, and then three kernels, *propagate*, *bc* and *collide*, perform the computational tasks. Each kernel is implemented as a separate CUDA function.

For a single-GPU implementation, the *pbc* kernel is a device-to-device copy operation performed by calling one memory-copy function of the CUDA library cudaMemCpy; it moves data from the three right-most columns of the lattice to the left-halo columns, and vice-versa. Using the CUDA function library cudaMemcpyAsync allows to execute the update of the right and left halos asynchronously overlapping in time the two operations.

The propagate kernel moves populations of each site according to a specific pattern associated to the LBM used; the pattern used in the D2Q37 model is given as an example in Figure 5.

We adopt the *pull* scheme (that is, mraw accesses) as it is slightly more efficient, as discussed earlier. The *pull* scheme is also a good option for CPU architectures specially because it allows to use *non-temporal* stream storing and thus saving time (Mantovani, Pivanti, Schifano, & Tripiccione, 2013b). For our D2Q37 model, each CUDA block is configured as a unidimensional array of N_THREAD threads, processing data allocated at successive locations in memory, while the grid of blocks is a bi-dimensional array of (L_y/N_THREAD L_x) blocks as shown in Figure 4, right. The performance of this obviously memory-bound kernel depends strongly on available memory bandwidth. As shown in Figure 2 the effective bandwidth

Figure 5. Left: Velocity vectors for populations in the D2Q37 model, associated to the lattice hop that they perform in the propagate phase; Right: each population is identified by an arbitrary label

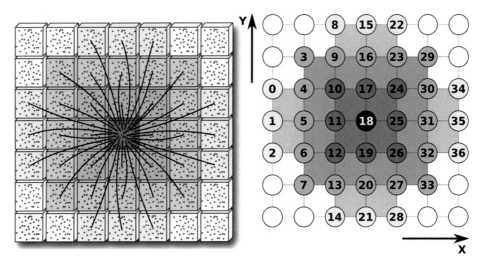

attained with ECC enabled, as a function of the number of threads per block is substantially constant for a number of threads per block larger than 64. With ECC enabled, on the P100 system, the bandwidth measured ranges from 464 GB/s using 32 threads per block to a maximum value of 568 GB/s using 416 threads per block corresponding respectively to 63% and 77% of the raw peak bandwidth available.

For the D2Q37 model the bc kernel computes boundary conditions, and it applies only to lattice-sites with coordinates $y = 0, 1, 2$ and $y = L_y - 1, L_y - 2, L_y - 3$. In this case the layout of each CUDA block is the same of that used to compute the propagate kernel, and the code uses if statements to disable threads not involved in the computation. This causes thread divergence, but the computational load of the bc kernel is negligible compared to all other steps and inefficiencies in this kernel have a small overall impact.

The collide kernel computes the collisional operator of populations gathered by the propagate step. For each time step, each thread reads the populations of each lattice site, performs all needed mathematical operations and stores the resulting populations. For this kernel the use of two lattice copies prv and nxt is not necessary because the update can be done *in situ*. For this kernels reading and writing of population data is always properly aligned enabling memory coalescing. In the case of D2Q37 the CUDA block is configured in the same way as for propagate, see Figure 4 right, and the N_THREADS/block parameter should again be tuned for performance. For the D2Q37 model, collide is a strongly compute bound kernel. This is shown in Table 2, collecting the output of the NVIDIA nvprof execution profiler running on the P100 board.

After optimizations and compilation, the collide kernel executes approximately 6400 double-precision mathematical operations for each lattice site, but only ≈42% are executed as *Fused-Multiply-Add* (FMA), reaching a GPU utilization of approximately 50%. Taking into account that *collide* kernel loads and stores a total

Table 2. Output of the NVIDIA nvprof profiler for collide on a lattice of 1024×8192 sites. The table shows the number of ADD, MUL and FMA (fused Multiply-Add) operations, the total number of floating-point operations per site and the fraction of cycles in which the ALU is used (ALU Utilization).

	K80	P100
FLOPS (Double Add)	2,824,314,768	2,824,314,768
FLOPS (Double Mul)	6,106,851,696	6,106,851,696
FLOPS (Double FMA)	2.2461e+10	2.2461e+10
FLOPS per site	6,420	6,420
ALU Utilization	High (48%)	Mid(50%)

of 2×37 double-precision items per lattice site, data from the table translates into an arithmetic intensity of ≈11Flops/byte, confirming that this kernel is limited by arithmetic throughput, rather than memory bandwidth. The kernel also needs several constants which are kept stored in the constant memory of the device. The code uses data prefetch to hide memory accesses and on *Kepler* and *Pascal* all loops accessing the thread-private prefetch array have been unrolled via the #pragma unroll directive. This allows the compiler to keep the elements of the prefetch array in registers and make use of the larger register file available on these GPUs.

We end this section comparing the performance delivered by GPUs with that of other recent processors; this is done in Table 3, where we compare performance figures on GPUs systems with those of implementations of the same code developed and optimized for multi-core Intel systems.

We consider a dual-E5-2630 V3 system, with two eight-core Haswell V3 processors. For this type of architectures, we have optimized the code parallelizing the execution over all available cores and using SIMD instructions within the cores; for details, see (Mantovani et al., 2013b; Mantovani, Pivanti, Schifano, & Tripiccione, 2013a) and (Bortolotti et al., 2014; Crimi, Mantovani, Pivanti, Schifano, & Tripiccione, 2013).

Table 3. Performance comparison of the propagate and collide kernels running on several systems: a dual eight-core E5-2630 2.4 GHz (Intel Haswell V3) processor, and a more recent dual E5-2697 v4 (Intel Broadwell v4), and three NVIDIA GPUs, K40, K80 and P100. ε is the effective performance w.r.t. peak performance. For collide we also measure performance in Million Lattice Updates per Second (MLUPS).

	Dual E5-2630 v3	Dual E5-2697 v4	Tesla K40	Tesla K80	P100
propagate (GB/s)	88	102	187	261	410
ε_p	75%	66%	65%	54%	56%
collide (GF/s)	222	635	696	1544	2622
ε_c	36%	55%	42%	53%	47%
MLUPS	29	61	107	220	405

OPTIMIZATION STRATEGIES: III. MULTI-GPU

In this section we describe the design and implementation of our code for a large multi-GPU cluster. We consider a general purpose commodity cluster where nodes have two or more GPU installed, and are interconnected through high speed networks such as InfiniBand. This means that communications among GPUs needs to be optimized according to their physical allocation and may require different coding solutions. We divide this section in three parts: we first summarize some simple theoretical models of performance that have guided our parallelization strategies; we then review the programming environment and tools available to support GPU-to-GPU communication, and finally we present details of our implementation.

Modelling the Impact of Communications

Designing a parallel multi-processor LBM code is in principle straightforward. One just maps regular tiles of the physical lattice on the processors; the processing load is balanced among processing elements if all domains have the same size; finally, tile-to-tile communication patterns are regular and predictable and only involve (logically) nearest-neighbor processors. Still, node-to-node communications are an unavoidable overhead that may become an important bottleneck as the number of nodes increases. The amount of data to be moved is roughly proportional to the surface of each computational domain, while computing scales as the domain volume, so, in order to ensure better scaling figures, one should i) identify the domain decomposition that minimizes the surface-over-volume ratio, and ii) overlap communications with parts of the computation that have no dependency with data incoming from neighbor nodes.

For a lattice with N points in D dimensions (i.e., with linear size $L \approx N^{1/D}$) one maps regular tiles onto N_p processors, and each tile contains points associated to all coordinate values in $D - d$ dimensions and an equal number of coordinate values in the remaining d dimensions ($d \leq D$). Considering the surface-over-volume ratio (S / V):

$$S / V \approx dN_p^{1/d},$$

one easily find that in principle $d = D$ ($d = 2$ for the case of D2Q37) should have the best asynptotic scaling performance.

Things are more complex in practice, as multi-dimensional lattices are stored in memory as uni-dimensional arrays, and communications of data elements at different borders of the lattice may require different strategies of communications with widely different bandwidths. This depends on data memory layout which defines how elements are stored at non-contiguous addresses, usually at fixed distance (*stride*) from each other. For memory-contiguous data words, a node-to-node communication involves a stream of data items from memory elements to the network interface, and then at destination from the network interface again to contiguous memory cells. However, data from sparse memory location has to be first gathered into a contiguous buffer, then transmitted and finally scattered to memory cells at sparse addresses. These access patterns may be much slower than for contiguous memory cells, so effective bandwidths may be widely different.

Consider a 2D lattice of $L_x \times L_y$ sites partitioned on N_p processing elements, with each processor handling a tile of $\left(L_x / n_x \right) \times \left(L_y / n_y \right)$ sites ($n_x \times n_y = N_p$). Assume that transfers in the X and Y directions have bandwidths B_x and B_y. A simple analysis, see (E. Calore, Gabbana, Kraus, Schifano, & Tripiccione, 2016b), shows that the tiling which optimizes communication time is given by

$$n_x = \sqrt{N_p} R, n_y = \sqrt{N_p} / R,$$

with $R = \sqrt{\dfrac{L_x B_y}{L_y B_x}}$ a factor taking into account the aspect-ratio of the lattice and the mismatch of the bandwidth values.

Since the processing time of each processor T_P grows as the number of lattice sites handled, an upper bound to total processing time T is the sum of communication time and processing time $T_P = \beta N / N_p$.

One notes at this point that for each tile, all lattice points belonging to the bulk (i.e., away from the tile boundary by more than 3 lattice points for the D2Q37 model) have no dependency from data of other nodes. This suggests to overlap bulk processing and data transfer. For a 1-D tiling, the estimated processing times (see again E. Calore et al., 2016b) is then

$$T = \beta \frac{N}{N_p} \left\{ \max \left(1 - 6 L_y N_p / N, \frac{2 S L_y}{\beta B_y} N_p / N \right) + 6 L_y N_p / N \right\}.$$

Going to 2-D tiling we need to gather not contiguous data in GPU memory to transfer few large data chunks and achieve an efficient node-to-node communication, otherwise we could avoid non contiguous data gathering, but would need to use multiple small and less efficient node-to-node transfers. Details of this will be explained in a later section. One is then forced to perform a communication step for non-contiguous data first (in the Y direction in our case), followed by overlapped bulk computation and communication of contiguous buffers and finally by computation of border data. The corresponding estimate, that for simplicity we write only for square lattices and for the not necessarily optimal case $n_x = n_y = \sqrt{N_p}$, is:

$$T = \beta \frac{N}{N_p} \left\{ \max\left[\left(1 - 12\sqrt{N_p / N}\right), \frac{2S}{\beta B_y} \sqrt{N_p / N} \right] + \frac{2S}{\beta B_x} \sqrt{N_p / N} + 12\sqrt{N_p / N} \right\}.$$

Extracting accurate predictions from Equation 12 to Equation 13 is made more difficult by the fact that communications bandwidths depend on the transfer direction (as already remarked) and *also* on buffers size. In spite of all these caveats, even these simple-minded models provide useful guidance. We compare measured results and predictions in Figure 6 for one typical lattice size, using measured bandwidth values that we discuss later (shown later, see Figure 10, where several important details of this measurement are discussed). In conclusion, two main lessons emerge from our models: i) overlapping communication and computation has a strong impact on performance; if we do so, to the extent made possible by system features, one can expect limited violations to scaling on reasonably-sized lattices and on a fairly large number of GPUs, and, ii) contrary to naive expectation, a 1-D tiling of the lattice may have good performances up to a reasonably large number of processors.

Figure 6. Violation of linear scaling (linear scaling is equal to 1) predicted by our performance model (Equation 13) on a lattice of 1940×1940 sites, using experimentally measured single-node processing performance and node-to-node bandwidths for contiguous and non-contiguous data buffers. In 2D we use the possibly not-optimal choice $n_x = n_y$.

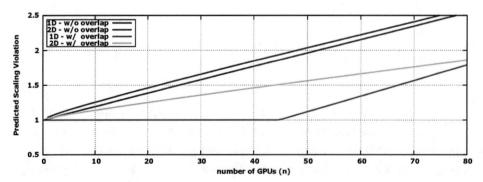

Based on this overall picture, several parallel versions of the code can be designed and compared. In the following we describe and compare two different implementations, using 1-D and 2-D tilings.

Communication Strategies for Multi-GPU Applications

In this sub-section we briefly overview communications strategies relevant for multi-GPU programs. The goal is to make code development and management easier and communications more efficient.

Large GPU clusters are widely heterogeneous computing systems with varying number of GPUs connected to the same CPU, but in virtually all cases today GPUs are directly connected to their host through a PCIe interface, which has reasonably high bandwidth (several GBytes/sec) but also long startup latency ($\geq 1\mu$ sec). The network interface is also connected to one of the CPUs via PCIe. The complexity of this structure implies that what, at application level, is a plain GPU-to-GPU communication may involve different routes, different communication strategies, and correspondingly different performances. We discuss here two key aspects of the problem, namely i) a programming environment able to specify in a unified way all different communication patterns and, ii) the ensemble of run-time support features that help maximize effective communication bandwidth for any possible pair of communication end-points.

Concerning the first point, a reasonable approach is to use the standard MPI communication libraries currently supporting also GPUs; we then associate one MPI process to each GPU, so MPI libraries are able to automatically handle the transfer of data buffers from GPU to GPU in the most appropriate way. Transferred buffers must be allocated at contiguous locations on memory; however, transfers of non-contiguous buffers can also be handled automatically by MPI, using the derived vector data type: the vector data type describes how data buffers are placed in memory; the library automatically packs data into a contiguous buffer, performs the MPI communication and then unpacks data at destination. Note that in regular MPI versions, i.e. without GPU support, these buffers had to be allocated on the host CPU, so each data transfer has to be preceded and followed by an explicit data move from/to GPU and its host. CUDA-aware MPI (Jiri Kraus, 2013) improves on this, allowing to specify buffers allocated on the GPU memory as arguments of the MPI operations, making codes terser and more readable; *Listing 2* compares the CUDA definitions of a function that performs a bi-directional remote memory-copy of a buffer allocated on the memory of two GPUs, using regular MPI and CUDA-aware MPI.

Listing 2. Definition of two CUDA-codes for a bi-directional memory-copy of buffers allocated on two GPUs; the first case is a regular MPI implementation requiring to move explicitly data from GPU to host and vice-versa; the latter case uses CUDA-aware MPI allowing to call directly the MPI_Sendrecv with pointers to buffers in GPU memory as source and destination parameters.

```
#ifdef MPI_REGULAR
cudaMemcpy (sndbuf_h, sndbuf_d, N, cudaMemcpyDeviceToHost);
MPI_Sendrecv(
   sndbuf_h, N, MPI_DATATYPE, nxt, 0,
   rcvbuf_h, N, MPI_DATATYPE, prv, 0,
   MPI_COMM_WORLD; MPI_STATUS_IGNORE);
cudaMemcpy (rcvbuf_d, rcvbuf_h, N, cudaMemcpyHostToDevice);
#endif

#ifdef CUDA_AWARE_MPI
MPI_Sendrecv(
   sndbuf_d, N, MPI_DATATYPE, nxt, 0,
   rcvbuf_d, N, MPI_DATATYPE, prv, 0,
   MPI_COMM_WORLD; MPI_STATUS_IGNORE);
#endif
```

Using this approach to specify the communication patterns needed by our program, we must now make sure that all possible steps are taken to reduce the latency time of each communication, as this has a critical impact on the scaling performance of the complete code. This is done by enabling a variety of features, available in the low-level communication libraries; here we describe the most relevant points.

For GPUs attached to the same host-CPU, CUDA-IPC (Inter-Process Communications) moves data directly across GPUs without staging on CPU-memory. This makes communication faster. GPUs attached to different CPUs of the same node communicate through CPU-memory staging; here pipelining helps to reduce the communication latency. For GPUs belonging to different nodes, GPUDirect RDMA moves short data packets from the GPU to the network interface without any involvement of the host CPU. For longer data packets due to PCIe architectural bottlenecks, RDMA becomes less effective, see (Davide Rossetti, 2014). In this case, GPUDirect simplifies the operation by sharing a common staging region between the GPU and the network interface.

1-D Tiling

We divide a lattice of size $L_x \times L_y$ on N_p GPUs tiling along just one dimension. In our case, since lattice is allocated by column-major order, we split the lattice along the X dimension and then each GPU allocates a *sub-lattice* of size $L_x / N_p \times L_y$, see Figure 7.

This tiling implies a virtual ordering of the GPUs along a ring, so each GPU is connected with a previous and a next GPU; at the beginning of each time-step, GPUs must exchange data, since cells close to the right and left edges of the sub-grid of each GPU needs data allocated on the logically previous and next GPUs, see again Figure 7.

For processing, the lattice is divided in three regions: two regions of size $3 \times Ly$ include the three leftmost and the three rightmost column-borders, while another region includes the central part of the lattice that we call the bulk. Processing the left and right regions can start only after the left and right halos have been updated, while processing on the bulk can start immediately and overlaps with the update of halos. Each MPI process executes a code structured as in *Listing 3*: it runs a CUDA-stream executing in sequence the propagate, bc and collide kernels on the bulk region. In parallel, the host-PC executes the pbc_c (_c stands for contiguous) function which performs MPI communications to update left and right halos with neighbor GPUs in the ring. After all data transfers are complete, two additional CUDA-streams start propagate, bc and collide, operating on the left and right border regions. Figure 8 shows the timeline execution of the code. We directly see that an efficient implementation of pbc helps to enlarge the scaling window of the program; as we partition the lattice onto a larger and larger number of processors, the combined execution times of propagate, bc and collide reduces accordingly, while the execution time of pbc remains approximately constant. Eventually, pbc takes longer than the computational kernels, and performance scaling is badly hampered. There is no way to escape this situation asymptotically, but an efficient implementation of pbc_c

Figure 7. 1-D tiling of a lattice on N_p GPUs virtually ordered along a ring

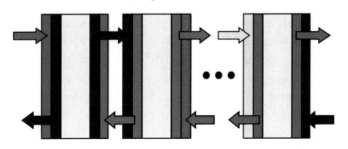

Listing 3. Sample code and timeline of a multi-GPU code executed by each MPI-process using the 1-d tiling of the lattice. Communications are performed by pbc and use CUDA-aware MPI; this step is then translated into CUDA device-to-device memory copies since this example refers to GPUs allocated on the same host; communication overlaps with the execution of the propagate, bc and collide kernels on the bulk of the lattice. After MPI communications have completed, the computational kernels acting on the right and left edges of the lattice can start; they do so as soon as GPU resources become available.

```
// Computing propagate over lattice bulk
prop_Bulk    <<< dimGridB, dimBlockB, 0, stream[0] >>> (...);
bc_Bulk      <<< dimGridB, dimBlockB, 0, stream[0] >>> (...);
collide_Bulk <<< dimGridB, dimBlockB, 0, stream[0] >>> (...);
// Update halos
pbc_c();
// Computing propagate on left columns
prop_L    <<< dimGridLR, dimBlockLR, 0, stream[1] >>> (...);
collide_L <<< dimGridB, dimBlockB, 0, stream[1] >>> (...);
// Computing propagate on right columns
prop_R    <<< dimGridLR, dimBlockLR, 0, stream[2] >>> (...);
collide_R <<< dimGridLR, dimBlockLR, 0, stream[2] >>> (...);
```

Figure 8. Timeline execution of the code in Listing 3, obtained using the NVIDIA profiler

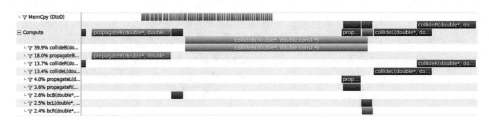

delays the onset of this behavior. We have found that the implementation of pbc_c through a sequence of CUDA-aware MPI operations gives good results; in our case, 26 populations must be moved for each for each boundary site, corresponding to 52 MPI operations. If the lattice is large enough in the Y direction (e.g., ≥ 512 points) the overheads associated to separate MPI operations are negligible. For smaller lattices it may be useful to pack data in a contiguous buffer and perform just one larger MPI transfer. We discuss this further optimization in the next section, where we also consider the fusion of propagate and collide into just one CUDA kernel.

2-D Tiling

Code organization using a 2-D tiling is slightly more complex. We split the lattice on a grid of $n_x \times n_y$ GPUs, virtually arranged at the edges of a 2D mesh. Each GPUs needs data allocated on eight neighbor GPUs, see Figure 9-left.

All needed data transfers (from adjacent and from diagonal neighbor nodes) can be done performing a sequence (see again Figure 9-center and right) in which first all nodes exchange data along one of the two directions, not including halo elements; when this is completed a further step in the orthogonal direction is started, including this time also halo elements.

One of the two communications steps implies non-contiguous data elements. As discussed in an earlier section, communications of non contiguous buffers is automatically handled by MPI using the vector derived data type. The corresponding standard library gathers all data elements into an intermediate buffer, starts a transfer operation for the intermediate buffer and finally scatters received data items to their final destination. We tested two well-known CUDA-aware MPI libraries, OpenMPI and MVAPICH2. Results were unsatisfactory for two reasons: i) OpenMPI has large overheads because of the many calls involved in the copy of all data items into the intermediate MPI buffer on the host; ii) MVAPICH2 does not use *persistent* intermediate MPI buffers, that are allocated and de-allocated on the GPU at each time step, and the corresponding overhead in doing that is obviously not justified in our case, as persistent allocation can be easily used in our program. We have overcome these issues developing a custom communication library that uses persistent send and receive buffers, allocated once on the GPUs at program initialization. Every time a communication of non contiguous buffers is needed, function pbc_nc (_nc stands for non-contiguous) starts the pack kernel to gather non-contiguous data into a contiguous buffer allocated on the GPU. When this is

Figure 9. 2-D tiling of the lattice on N_p GPUs. Left: diagram of the tiles and of the corresponding halos; Right: communication patterns to update halos belonging to a given tile

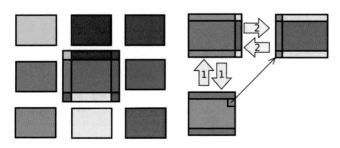

done, an MPI communication is started, followed by a final scatter of the received data. See (E. Calore et al., 2016b) for a detailed description and for sample codes.

Figure 10 reflects the global result of this optimization effort, showing the effective bi-directional bandwidth measured in the update of memory-contiguous and non contiguous halos as a function of the corresponding lattice size. This test involves two K80 boards attached to two different host-CPUs interconnected through InfiniBand network. We see that, as expected, non-contiguous halos have a reduced effective bandwidth, but the difference between the two cases is not too large. Data shown in Figure 10 has been used in the scaling prediction models that we have discussed before.

For the processing steps of the algorithm, the lattice is divided in five regions, see *Figure 9*-right: two regions of $3L_y$ sites, including the three leftmost and the three rightmost columns, two regions of size $3L_x$ including the three topmost and lowermost rows and the central part of the lattice including all bulk sites. The code in Listing 4 shows how we schedule operations. We first exchange the (non-contiguous) top and bottom halos; when this operation has completed, we start processing the lattice bulk on a GPU stream, and in parallel we update the contiguous left and right halos. After all halos have been updated, we start separate GPU streams processing the left, right, top and bottom borders.

With this scheduling it is easy to merge propagate and collide for all points on which bc kernel does not apply, belonging to the bulk, left and right regions. On the other hand, top and bottom borders must be processed by a sequence of propagate, bc and collide kernels. Figure 11 shows the corresponding execution timeline as recorded by the NVIDIA profiler, while the final organization of the code including these improvements is shown in Listing 5.

Figure 10. Measured effective bi-directional bandwidth to update contiguous and non contiguous halos as a function of the size of the lattice tile. The test has been done on two K80 systems on two remote nodes, interconnected by an InfiniBand FDR network and GPUDirect RDMA enabled.

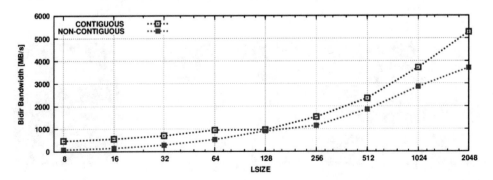

Listing 4. Scheduling of operations for the code using 2-D tiles

```
// Update non-contiguous halos
pbc_nc()

// Computing over bulk
prop_Bulk     <<< .dimGridB, dimBlockB, 0, stream[0] >>> (...)
collide_Bulk  <<< dimGridB, dimBlockB, 0, stream[0] >>> (...);

// Update contiguous halos
pbc_c()

// Computing propagate on left columns of the lattice
prop_L     <<< dimGridLR, dimBlockLR, 0, stream[1] >>> (...);
collide_L  <<< dimGridLR, dimBlockLR, 0, stream[1] >>> (...);

// Computing propagate on right columns of the lattice
prop_R     <<< dimGridLR, dimBlockLR, 0, stream[2] >>> (...);
collide_R  <<< dimGridLR, dimBlockLR, 0, stream[2] >>> (...);

// Computing propagate on top rows of the lattice
prop_T     <<< dimGridTB, dimBlockTB, 0, stream[3] >>> (...);
bc_T       <<< dimGridTB, dimBlockTB, 0, stream[3] >>> (...);
collide_T  <<< dimGridTB, dimBlockTB, 0, stream[3] >>> (...);

// Computing propagate on bottom rows of the lattice
prop_B     <<< dimGridTB, dimBlockTB, 0, stream[4] >>> (...);
bc_B       <<< dimGridTB, dimBlockTB, 0, stream[4] >>> (...);
collide_B  <<< dimGridTB, dimBlockTB, 0, stream[4] >>> (...);
```

The update of non-contiguous halos ca not overlap (see caption for details) with other data-processing operation, because: i) MPI communications along Y must be done before starting those along X, in order to update also halos with data coming from diagonal neighbor sites, ii) the corresponding pack and unpack kernels must be executed before GPU resources become busy in processing the sites of the lattice bulk. On the other hand, the update of contiguous halos fully overlaps with processing of the bulk region. Finally, unpack of received data for contiguous halos, and the processing of the 4 border regions starts as soon as GPU resources are freed by the kernel processing the bulk regions.

Figure 11. Execution timeline of the code using a 2-D tiling, as shown by the NVIDIA profiler. In this example, we first execute update of non-contiguous halos starting first the pack_bot kernel, and after MPI communication (MemCpy DtoD in the figure) we launch the unpack_top kernel. These operations cannot overlap with other data-processing. After we start the pack_left and pack_right to pack data to update contiguous halos, and in parallel we execute the propagateCollideBulk kernel to process all sites belonging to lattice bulk. As soon as propagateCollideBulk kernel frees GPU resources, unpack_left and unpack_right kernels are executed to update contiguous halos, followed by the processing of the 4 border regions.

Listing 5. Overall organization of the code for a 2-D tiling of the lattice, fusing the propagate and collide kernels in one step. The code first update non contiguous halos calling function pbc_nc. After this is fully completed, starts pack of left and right borders on two GPU streams, and in parallel starts execution of propagateCollideBulk kernel processing lattice bulk. As MPI operations complete, data are unpacked on left and right halos, and we start processing of left, right, top and bottom borders. For left and right borders, we apply kernels propagateCollideL and propagateCollideR computing propagate and collide phases in one step. For top and bottom borders, we apply in sequence propagate, bc and collide kernels is the GPU is associated to a tile at top and bottom region of the lattice. Otherwise we only run propagateCollideT and propagateCollideB.

```
// update non-contiguous halos
pbc_nc(f2_soa_d);

// pack right/left borders
pack_right <<< ..., stream[1] >>> (...);
pack_left  <<< ..., stream[2] >>> (...);

// run propagateAndCollide over Bulk
```

continued on following page

Listing 5. Continued

```
propagateCollideBulk <<< ..., stream[0] >>> (...);

// wait end of pack right borders
cudaStreamSynchronize(stream[1]);
// perform MPI operations
MPI_Sendrecv();

// wait end of pack left borders
cudaStreamSynchronize(stream[2]);
MPI_Sendrecv();

// unpack right/left halos
unpack_left  <<< ..., stream[1] >>> (...);
unpack_right <<< ..., stream[2] >>> (...);

// wait end of unpack right/left halos
// (required before starting processing left, right, top and
bottom borders)
cudaStreamSynchronize(stream[1]);
cudaStreamSynchronize(stream[2]);

// process left/right borders
propagateCollideL <<< ..., stream[1] >>> (...);
propagateCollideR <<< ..., stream[2] >>> (...);

// process top/bottom borders
if (uppermost-rank){
  propagateT <<< ..., stream[3] >>> (...);
  bcT        <<< ..., stream[3] >>> (...);
  collideT   <<< ..., stream[3] >>> (...);
} else {
  propagateCollideT <<< ..., stream[3] >>> (...);
}

if (lowermost-rank){
```

continued on following page

Listing 5. Continued

```
  propagateB  <<< ..., stream[4] >>> (...);
  bcB         <<< ..., stream[4] >>> (...);
  collideB    <<< ..., stream[4] >>> (...);
} else {
  propagateCollideB <<< ..., stream[4] >>> (...);
}

cudaDeviceSynchronize();
```

Results

We first examine results for just one (or two) GPUs: Table 4 collects performance results of the full production-ready code running on one host with one or two GPUs on a lattice of 1024×8192 points; the main computational load is associated to the propagate and collide kernels, as expected.

Table 4. Performance of our full production-ready code, measured on a lattice of 1024×8192 sites. We show the execution time of each phase of the code, the performance of the propagate and collide kernels, the effective performance of the complete code (Global P), and the MLUPS (Million Lattice Updates per second) metric. The clock frequencies for the SMs of the K40 and K80 boards are set at the "boosted" values of 875 MHz.

	GF100	2 × GF100	GK110B	2 × GK110B	GK210	2 × GK210	P100	2 × P100
T_{Prop} (ms)	60.6	30.9	25.8	12.2	32.3	19	12.1	6.2
T_{Bc} (ms)	6.5	3.6	2.8	1.4	1.4	0.8	0.2	0.1
T_{Coll} (ms)	276	158	78	39	71.1	38.1	20.7	10.6
Propagate (GB/s)	81	155	187	376	155	261	410	800
Collide (GF/s)	197	344	696	1388	764	1544	2622	5121
Global P. (GF/s)	158	281	506	1010	519	988	1686	3340
MLUPS	24	43	78	156	80	153	260	516

Memory bandwidth (relevant for propagate) is close to 55 of the theoretical peak for the C2050 accelerator; it reaches 65 of peak for the K40 and the K80. The *Kepler* processor is more efficient from the point of view of floating-point throughput, as measured by the FP performance of the collide kernel, reaching 43 versus 38 for the C2050 board; the K80 board exploits its larger register file and shared memory to reach 53 of peak. On a dual-K40 system and on a K80 board using both GPUs, the collide kernel largely breaks the sustained double precision 1 Tflops performance barrier; also the global performance figures of the full code, which take into account all execution phases, are satisfactory: we measure an efficiency of respectively 31 and 34 of the raw peak floating-point throughput.

We now move to consider scaling results for multi-GPU codes. Following our introductory discussion, we expect that, contrary to expectation, an 1D tiling of the lattice may be as efficient or even more efficient than a 2D tiling up to relatively large number of GPUs. We settle the question experimentally, measuring the performance of the codes described in the previous sections on several medium-size to large lattices, using all possible tilings consistent with the number of available GPUs. Our tests have been run on a GPU cluster installed at the NVIDIA Technology Center. Each node is a dual socket 10-core Ivy Bridge E5-2690 v2 processor running at 3.00GHz, with 4 K80 GPUs. Nodes are interconnected with an InfiniBand FDR network, and up to 32 GPUs are available.

Figure 12 presents a sample subset of our results, plotting $n \times T(n)$ (in arbitrary units) on a lattice of 3600×3600 points for almost all possible 1-D and 2-D tilings of the lattice on n GPUs.

This quantity is constant if the program enjoys perfect scaling, so it is a direct measurement of departure from scaling. Scaling violations are less than 10% up to 32 GPUs, and some tiling choices are clearly more efficient than others; as predicted by our model, the 1D tiling enjoys good scaling up to a reasonably large (24 in this case) number of GPUs.

From this data (and from equivalent data for other lattice sizes) one derives the relative speed up and the effective tiling-optimized performance as a function of n; this is shown in Figure 13, that wraps up our results.

Performance increases smoothly for all lattices and number of GPUs: performance is not ideal but the bottom line of this analysis is that our codes run efficiently on up to at least 32 GPUs for physics relevant lattice sizes, with a sustained performance in the range of tens of Tflops.

Figure 12. Benchmark results on a lattice of 3600×3600 sites. For a varying number of GPUs (n) we plot (in arbitrary units) $n \times T(n)$ for all possible 1-D and 2-D decompositions of the lattice ($T(n)$ is the wall-clock execution time); this product stays constant if the code enjoys perfect scalability.

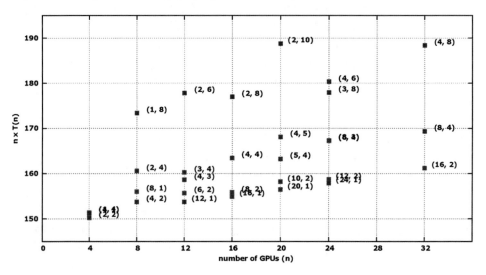

Figure 13. Aggregate performance of the code for the best lattice tiling as a function of the number of GPUs, for several lattice sizes. Results are shown as speedup values (left) or effective sustained performance (Tflops, right).

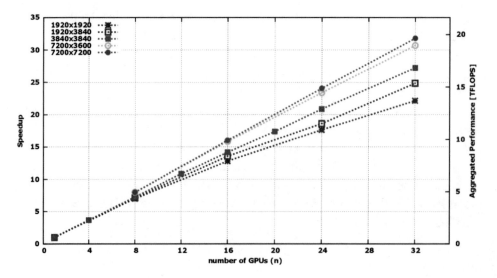

OPTIMIZATION STRATEGIES: IV. PORTABILITY

In this section we describe the strategies we have adopted to write an OpenACC version of our LBM code suitable for compilation and execution on NVIDIA GPUs as well as on other architectures. The details of this work are described in Calore et al. (2016b).

The OpenACC code follows many of implementation strategies we have presented in previous sections. In this case we have adopted the 1D-splitting, which is simpler to implement and has simpler inter-node communication requirements. We use MPI to control node-parallelism, and one MPI rank is associated to each GPU. Data is stored in memory as Structure-of-Array (*SoA*), and the lattice is copied on the accelerator memory at the beginning of the loop over time steps; all three kernels of the algorithm, *propagate*, *bc* and *collide,* run in sequence on the accelerator. As lattice data is stored in the *SoA* format, pbc exchanges 37 buffers, each of 3 columns, with its left and right neighbors, executing a loop over the 37 populations, and performing two MPI send-receive operations at each iteration, respectively for the left and the right halo (see Listing 6).

We exploit *CUDA-aware* MPI features, available in the OpenMPI library, and use data pointers referencing GPU-memory buffers as source and destination, making the code more compact and readable. In OpenACC this is controlled by the #pragma acc host_data use_device(p) clause, that maps a GPU memory pointer p into host space, so it can be used as an argument of the MPI send and receive functions. Also, communications between GPUs are optimized in the library and implemented according to physical location of buffers and the capabilities of the devices involved, also enabling *GPUDirect* peer-to-peer and *RDMA* features.

Coming now to the main kernels of the algorithm, Listing 7 shows the code of the propagate function.

We split *bc* in two kernels, processing the upper and lower boundaries. They run in parallel since there is no data dependencies among them. We have not further optimized this step because its computational cost is small compared to the other phases of the code.

The *collide* kernel sweeps all lattice sites and computes the collisional function. The code has two outer loops over the two dimensions of the lattice, and several inner loops to compute temporary values. We have annotated the outer loops as we did for *propagate*, making each thread to process one lattice site. Inner loops are computed serially by the thread associated to each site.

Performance wise, *pbc* is the most critical step of the multi-GPU code, since it involves node-to-node communications that can badly affect performance and scaling. We organize the code so node-to-node communications are (fully or partially) overlapped with the execution of other segments of the code. Generally speaking,

Listing 6. Scheduling of operations started at each time step; processing of the lattice bulk run asynchronously on the accelerator, and overlap with communications executed by the host.

```
// processing of lattice-bulk
propagateBulk(f2, f1); // async execution on queue (1)
bcBulk(f2, f1);        // async execution on queue (1)
collideInBulk(f2, f1); // async execution on queue (1)

// execution of pbc step
#pragma acc host_data use_device(f2) {
  for (pp = 0; pp < 37; pp++) {
    MPI_Sendrecv (&(f2[...]), 3*NY, ...);
    MPI_Sendrecv (&(f2[...]), 3*NY, ...);
  }
}

// processing of the three leftmost columns
propagateL(f2, f1);    // async execution on queue (2)
bcL(f2, f1);           // async execution on queue (2)
collideL(f1, f2);      // async execution on queue (2)

// processing of the three rightmost columns
propagateR(f2, f1);    // async execution on queue (3)
bcR(f2, f1);           // async execution on queue (3)
collideR(f1, f2);      // async execution on queue (3)
```

propagate, *bc* and *collide* must execute one after the other, and they cannot start before *pbc* has completed. As this dependency does not apply to all sites of the lattice outside the three leftmost and rightmost border columns processing of the *bulk* of the lattice can proceed in parallel with the execution of pbc, while the sites on the three leftmost and rightmost columns are processed only after pbc has completed.

OpenACC abstracts concurrent execution using queues: function definitions flagged by the #pragma acc async(n) directive enqueue the corresponding kernels *asynchronously* on queue n, leaving the host free to perform other tasks concurrently. In our case, this happens for propagateBulk, bcBulk and collideBulk, which start on queue 1 (see *Listing 6*), while the host concurrently executes the MPI transfers of pbc. After communications complete, the host starts three more kernels on two different queues (2 and 3) to process the right and left borders, so they execute in parallel if

Listing 7. OpenACC pragmas in the body of the propagate function; pragmas before the loops instruct the compiler to generate corresponding accelerator kernels and to configure the grid of threads and blocks.

```
inline void propagate (
  const data_t* restrict prv, data_t* restrict nxt) {
  int ix, iy, site_i;

  #pragma acc kernels present(prv) present(nxt)
  #pragma acc loop gang independent
  for (ix=HX; ix < (HX+SIZEX); ix++) {
    #pragma acc loop vector independent
    for (iy=HY; iy<(HY+SIZEY); iy++) {
      site_i = (ix*NY) + iy;
      nxt[        site_i] = prv[        site_i-3*NY+1];
      nxt[NX*NY+site_i] = prv[NX*NY+site_i-3*NY   ];
      ....
    }
  }

}
```

sufficient resources on the accelerator are available. This structure allows to overlap pbc with all other steps of the code, most importantly with collideBulk, which is the most time consuming kernel, giving more opportunities to hide communication overheads when running on a large number of nodes.

Figure 14 shows the profiling of one time step on one GPU on a lattice of 1080×2048 points split across 24 GPUs. MPI communications started by pbc are internal (MemCopy DtoD), moving data between GPUs on the same PCIe Root

Figure 14. Profiling of a single time step; in this example, pbc (yellow line marked as "MPI") and the kernels processing the bulk of the lattice (blue line marked as "Bulk") fully overlap

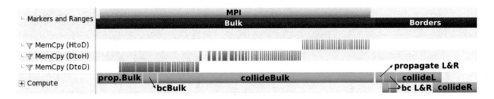

Complex, or external (MemCopy DtoH and HtoD) moving data requiring a staging on the host memory (e.g. to/from a GPU on another compute node).

As expected, both types of GPU-to-GPU communications fully overlap with propagate, bc and collide on the bulk.

Results

Table 5 summarizes performance figures of codes on a reference lattice of 1920×2048 sites run on three NVIDIA systems, the K40, K80 and P100 boards, comparing our OpenACC code with an implementation of the same algorithm written in CUDA (Biferale et al., 2013), (Jiri Kraus et al., 2013) and optimized for Fermi and Kepler architectures. The codes executed on the K80 system runs two MPI ranks, each using one GPU of the same accelerator board.

The first line of Table 5 refers to the execution of propagate, and for this kernel we show the execution time, the effective bandwidth, and the efficiency ε_p computed

Table 5. Performance comparison of OpenACC code with CUDA version running on NVIDIA Tesla K40, K80 and P100 GPU accelerator cards; all codes run on a lattice size of 1920×2048 points. The last two rows show the wall-clock execution time and the corresponding MLUPS (Millions Lattice UPdate per Second) for the full code.

	K40		K80		P100
Code Version	CUDA	OACC	CUDA	OACC	CUDA
T_{Prop} [msec]	13.78	13.91	7.60	7.51	5.11
GB/s	169	167	306	310	456
ε_p	59%	58%	64%	65%	62%
T_{Bc} [msec]	4.42	2.76	1.11	0.71	0.39
$T_{Collide}$ [msec]	39.86	78.65	16.80	36.39	10.5
MLUPS	99	50	234	108	373
ε_c	45%	23%	52%	24%	46%
T_{WC} /iter [msec]	58.07	96.57	26.84	44.61	16.03
MLUPS	68	41	147	88	245

w.r.t. the peak memory bandwidth of each system; the table then lists execution times of the bc function, showing that this routine has limited (although non negligible) impact on performance. For the collide kernel, we show the execution time and the efficiency ε_c as a fraction of peak performance. Efficiency is computed using as number of double-precision operations for each lattice-site either the number measured by the profiler through the hardware counters available on the processor or the number of floating-point instructions of the corresponding assembly code. Finally, the last two lines at bottom show the wall-clock execution time (WcT) and the corresponding *Millions Lattice UPdate per Second* (MLUPS), counting the number of sites handled per second, of the full production-ready code. For propagate, which is strongly memory bound, the CUDA and OpenACC versions run at 60% of peak on all GPU boards, and in this case OpenACC is very competitive with the CUDA version of the code. For the collide kernel, which is the most computationally intensive part of the application, the OpenACC code has an efficiency of 25% on K40 and K80 systems, while the CUDA version doubles this figure, running at 45% of peak on the K40 and 52% on the K80 thanks to the higher number of available registers. On P100 board the efficiency is lower delivering the same performance of a K80 board.

Our analysis of the performance gap between OpenACC and CUDA codes for the collide kernel shows that this is due to a different way in which Hermite coefficients are stored. OpenACC stores them in the standard global-memory, while the CUDA code store them in the constant-cache and this make saves registers that can be used to unrolls all inner loops of the collide routine improving performance significantly (E. Calore et al., 2016b). Looking at the overall MLUPS delivered of the full code on each system, we have that performances of OpenACC code are approximately 40% lower with respect to the CUDA code.

OpenACC implementation is able to target also other class of processors. We have considered three different target computing systems supported by the PGI OpenACC compiler: an *x*86 commodity multi-core processor, and two accelerators, an NVIDIA K80 and an AMD FirePro S9150 GPU. Table 6 collects our final comparison results. For *x*86 CPUs we show results of two multi-thread codes compiled with the Intel compiler version 15: one uses intrinsics functions (Mantovani et al., 2013a), (Mantovani et al., 2013b) to exploit vectorization, while the latter (E. Calore, Demo, Schifano, & Tripiccione, 2016a) uses OpenMP directives; both use OpenMP to handle multicore parallelization. For NVIDIA GPUs we consider the CUDA code, while for AMD GPUs we have used GCC and OpenCL (E. Calore et al., 2014a), (E. Calore, Schifano, & Tripiccione, 2014b).

Our experience with OpenACC is very positive from the point of view of code portability and programmability. The effort to port existing codes to OpenACC

Table 6. Performance comparison of various programming frameworks on three different platforms. MLUPS stands for Mega-Lattice Updates per Second; the performance in GFLOPs is obtained assuming that each lattice points uses 6500 floating-point operations; Total performance (Tot perf.) is evaluated on a program that invokes in sequence propagate and collide.

	E5-2630 v3			Hawaii XT		P100	
compiler	ICC 15	ICC 15	PGI 15.10	GCC	PGI 15.10	*NVCC 8.0*	PGI 17.5
model	Intrinsics	OMP	OACC	OCL	OACC	CUDA	OACC
T_{Prop} [GB/s]	38	32	32	232	216	456	485
ε_p	65%	54%	54%	73%	70%	62%	66%
T_{Coll} [MLUPS]	14	11	12	76	54	372	108
T_{Coll} [GFLOPs]	92	71	78	494	351	2421	703
ε_c	28%	22%	24%	19%	14%	46%	13%
Tot perf. [MLUPS]	11.5	9.2	9.8	63.7	47	247	90

is reasonably limited and easy to handle; we started from an existing C version and marked through *directives* regions of code to offload and run on accelerators, instructing the compiler to identify and exploit available parallelism.

Trying to provide a global assessment of the performance portability offered by the PGI OpenACC compiler, we first remark that it is able to produce very efficient code for the propagate kernel exploiting a large fraction of the memory bandwidth offered by all processors; this is substantiated by the reported figures for ε_p, i.e., by the sustained memory bandwidth w.r.t. peak memory bandwidth, reported in Table 6. For the compute intensive collide kernels, OpenACC comes at the cost of a non negligible performance gap for GPUs where, considering in this case ε_c measuring the actual floating point performance, we see a performance drop of a factor 2×; on CPUs and AMD GPU we get the same level of performance compared respectively with C and OpenCL code versions. As a global assessment, the last line of Table 6 shows an effective performance metric for the whole code assuming to execute propagate and collide in sequence; this gives a lower-bound of performances of the program since the two routines can often (actually depends on routines to be run between the two) be merged in one single step. Our figures show that OpenACC is indeed able to support code portability at the price of a performance drop lower than 50%, and with reasonable expectations of further improvements in the future. As an unexpected aside, we also show that the PGI compiler is remarkably efficient for multi-core $x86$ CPUs.

OPTIMIZATION STRATEGIES: V. HETEROGENEOUS IMPLEMENTATIONS

In this section we describe a fully heterogeneous implementation, concurrently executing portions of code both on GPUs and on their host CPU processors. We first provide the general details of the implementation, describing how the workload partitioning between host and accelerator can be realized in a portable and efficient way. Next, we define a performance model which is then used to evaluate the achieved performances.

Implementation Description

In previous sections we have relied on a host-driven approach, in which the host offloads all compute-intensive sections of the code onto the GPU. In section *OPTIMIZATION STRATEGIES: II. ONE GPU* we have been focusing in the optimization of the relevant kernels to be executed on the GPU, while the role of the host CPUs has yet been confined to handling only inter-node communications. Aiming to improve the usage of the computational resources available at a node level, a natural step forward is represented by executing the most relevant kernels in a concurrent and balanced way on both host and accelerator. In the following we will limit ourselves to describe and evaluate the implementation of the D2Q37 model, although extensions to other models, such as the previously mentioned D3Q19, are straightforward.

We assume a multi-node implementation making use of the MPI library in which each MPI-process manages one accelerator. The MPI-process runs on the host CPU; part of the lattice domain is processed on the host itself, and part is offloaded and processed by the accelerator. For simplicity we consider a 1D domain decomposition with the lattice partitioned among the MPI-processes along one direction, the X-direction in our example. Within each MPI-process each partition is further divided between host and accelerator. It is convenient to define three regions, namely left border, bulk, and right border, as shown in Figure 15. The right and left borders consist of M columns each and are allocated on the host memory, while the remaining SIZEX - $2M$ reside on the accelerator memory. Since the D2Q37 stencil involves interactions with neighboring sites at distance up to 3, each region is

Figure 15. Logic partitioning of the lattice domain among host and accelerator. The central (dark-green) region is allocated on the accelerator, side (orange and gray) regions on the host. Checkerboard textures flag lattice regions involved in MPI communications with neighbor nodes.

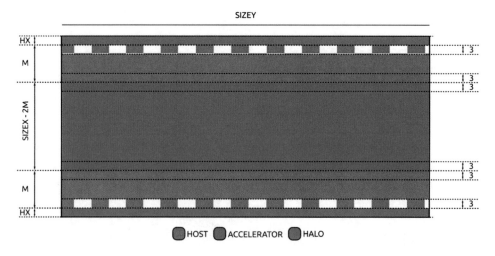

extended by a three columns halo. Each halo stores a copy of lattice sites of the adjacent region either allocated on the host, on the accelerator, or on the neighbor MPI-process.

Each MPI-process performs a loop over time steps, and at each iteration it launches in sequence on the accelerator the propagate, bc and collide kernels, processing the bulk region. In order to allow the CPU to operate in overlapped mode, kernels are launched asynchronously on the same logical execution queue to ensure in-order execution. After launching the kernels on the accelerator, the host first exchanges halos with adjacent MPI-processes and then starts processing its left and right borders applying the same sequence of kernels. After the processing of borders completes, the host updates the halo regions shared with the accelerator; this step moves data between host and accelerator. The control-flow of the code executed by the MPI-process is shown in Figure 16, where the bc kernel applies the physical boundary conditions at the three uppermost and lowermost rows of the lattice.

In Listing 8 we show an example using *OpenACC* directives. This implementation is described in more detail in (E. Calore et al., 2016b), (E. Calore et al., 2017c). Here each kernel takes as parameters the first and the last columns to be updated in order to specify which portion of the lattice has to be processed, alongside an integer value specifying the *OpenACC* queue to be used, enabling asynchronous execution. Another approach that could be used to express the control flow depicted in Figure 16 would consist in employing *OpenMP 4.5* directives. We conclude this

Figure 16. Control flow executed by each MPI-process; the schedule executed on the accelerator is on the upper band, while the one executed by the host is on the lower band. Execution on the accelerator runs on two concurrent queues; synchronization-points are marked with red lines

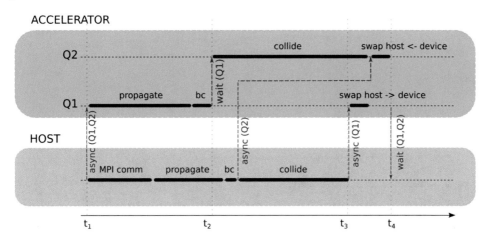

Listing 8. Example of implementation of the heterogeneous code using OpenACC

```
// Accelerator
//------------------------------------
propagateGPU(f1, f2,       HX + M, HX + SIZEX - M, Q1); // f1 <-- f2
bcGPU       (f1, f2, param, HX + M, HX + SIZEX - M, Q1); // f1 <-- f1,f2


#pragma acc wait(Q1) async(Q2)


collideGPU  (f2, f1, param, HX + M, HX + SIZEX - M, Q2); // f2 <-- f1


// MPI Comm
//------------------------------------
MPI_Irecv(rcvbufL, BORDER_DIM, MPI_DOUBLE, mpi_rankL, tag[1], MPI_COMM_
WORLD, &reqs[2]);
MPI_Irecv(rcvbufR, BORDER_DIM, MPI_DOUBLE, mpi_rankR, tag[0], MPI_COMM_
WORLD, &reqs[3]);


MPI_Isend(sndbufL, BORDER_DIM, MPI_DOUBLE, mpi_rankL, tag[0], MPI_COMM_
```

continued on following page

Listing 8. Continued

```
WORLD, &reqs[0]);
MPI_Isend(sndbufR, BORDER_DIM, MPI_DOUBLE, mpi_rankR, tag[1], MPI_COMM_
WORLD, &reqs[1]);

MPI_Waitall(4, reqs, MPI_STATUS_IGNORE);

// Host: Propagate
//------------------------------------
propagateCPU(f1, f2, HX          , HX          + M, SYNC); // f1 <-- f2
propagateCPU(f1, f2, HX + SIZEX - M, HX + SIZEX  , SYNC); // f1 <-- f2

// Host: BC
//------------------------------------
bcCPU(f1, f2, param, HX          , HX          + M, SYNC); // f1 <-- f1,f2
bcCPU(f1, f2, param, HX + SIZEX - M, HX + SIZEX  , SYNC); // f1 <-- f1,f2

// Host <--- Accelerator
//------------------------------------
#pragma acc update host(f2[LHOST_HALO_OFFSET:BORDER_DIM]) async(Q2)
#pragma acc update host(f2[RHOST_HALO_OFFSET:BORDER_DIM]) async(Q2)

// Host: Collide
//------------------------------------
collideCPU(f2, f1, param, HX          , HX          + M, SYNC); // f2 <-- f1
collideCPU(f2, f1, param, HX + SIZEX - M, HX + SIZEX  , SYNC); // f2 <-- f1

// Host ---> Accelerator
//------------------------------------
#pragma acc update device(f2[LDEV_HALO_OFFSET:BORDER_DIM]) wait(Q1)
async(Q3)
#pragma acc update device(f2[RDEV_HALO_OFFSET:BORDER_DIM]) wait(Q1)
async(Q4)

// Sync
//------------------------------------
#pragma acc wait
```

Figure 17. Performance of the heterogeneous code (measured in MLUPS, see the text for definition) for three different platforms, as a function of the fraction of lattice sites ($2M / LX$) mapped on the Haswell (HSW) host CPU. P100 is the NVIDIA Pascal GPU, K80 is the NVIDIA Tesla GPU and Hawaii is the AMD GPU; dots are measured values, dashed lines are the prediction of the performance model

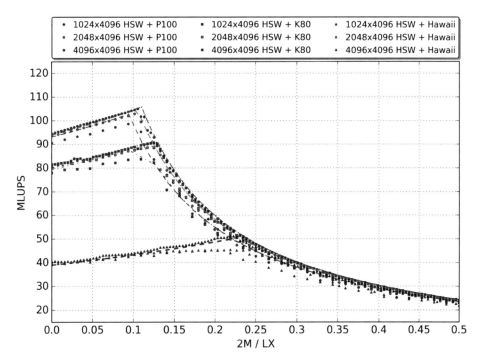

section with a remark on the optimization of the code for the CPU side. While we have thoroughly discussed GPU optimizations in previous sections, it is clear that maximizing performances on the host is crucial for benefiting from a heterogeneous implementation. In general, the two crucial performance-factors on modern processors are the optimization of data-accesses and the exploitation of the vector unit. In LBM codes both aspects are closely related to the data-layout adopted (Calore et al., 2016a; Shet et al., 2013a; Shet et al., 2013b; Wittmann, Zeiser, Hager, & Wellein, 2011). In general the data-layout giving best performances may differ between host and accelerator. Therefore, in a heterogeneous implementation one would need to either sacrifice performances (either on the host or the accelerator side), or introduce costing conversions from a layout to the other. A third approach consists in adopting hybrid data structures, which will be the preferred choice in the following. Although a detailed description of these data structures goes beyond the scope of this chapter, the interested reader is referred to (Calore et al., 2016a; Calore et al., 2017c) for further information.

Performance Modeling

Hosts and accelerators have different peak (and sustained) performance, so a careful workload balancing between the two concurrent processors is necessary. A simple model describing the execution time T_{exe} of the above described heterogeneous implementation is given by following set of equations:

$$T_{exe} = \max\left(T_{acc}, T_{host} + T_{mpi}\right) + T_{swap}$$

$$T_{acc} = \left(LX - 2M\right)LY\tau_d$$

$$T_{host} = \left(2M\right)LY\tau_h$$

$$T_{mpi} = \tau_c,$$

where T_{acc} and T_{host} are the execution times of the accelerator and host respectively, T_{swap} is the time required to exchange data between host and accelerator at the end of each iteration, and T_{mpi} is the time to move data between two MPI-processes in a multi-accelerator implementation. Since T_{swap} is independent of M, T_{exe} is minimal for a value M for which the following equation holds:

$$T_{acc}\left(M\right) = T_{host}\left(M\right) + T_{mpi}\left(M\right).$$

For a given problem size, one can estimate approximate values for τ_d, $\ddot{A}_h$, $\ddot{A}_c$ and plug them in Equation 18 to derive M, an estimate of the value of M that minimizes time to solution.

Results

We consider an implementation based on *OpenACC* directives (Calore et al., 2016b) for the GPU side, allowing us to execute the code both on NVIDIA and AMD GPUs. We use the PGI 17.5 compiler for targeting NVIDIA architectures, while PGI 16.5 is used to compile the code for AMD. *OpenMP* directives are used to expose vectorization and parallelize codes for CPUs, compiled using Intel compiler ICC v17.0. Codes for the accelerator and the host are then linked in one single executable.

We consider three different platforms, all sharing the same host processor, an 8-core Intel Xeon E5-2630v3 CPU based on the *Haswell* micro-architecture, but with different attached accelerator, namely an NVIDIA P100 GPU, a NVIDIA K80 and an AMD Hawaii GPU. In Figure 17 we show the performance obtained for three different lattice sizes as a function of $2M / LX$, the fraction of lattice sites that we map on the host CPU; dots refer to measured values, while lines are the performances as predicted from the model in Equation 14. For the NVIDIA K80 we use two MPI processes, since the K80 consists of two GK210 cards. The model predicts performances with good accuracy, in particular it estimates with good precision the workload distribution between host and device for which the execution time reaches its minimum. As expected, for values of $M < M^*$ and $M > M^*$ performances decrease because the workload is unbalanced either on the accelerator or on the host side; results at $2M / LX = 0$ correspond to earlier implementations in which critical kernels are fully offloaded to accelerators; for the platforms we have considered executing kernels concurrently on host and accelerators leads to a performance increase of approximately 10-20%. Finally, as M becomes much larger than M^*, all lines in the plot fall on top of each other, as in this limit the host CPU handles the largest part of the overall computation.

One can make use of the performance model to develop an auto-tuning strategy to determine beforehand the value M^* that optimizes the workload distribution. Besides that, one can also use the model to evaluate how performances are affected when either the host CPU or the accelerator is replaced by a different processor; in particular, one may ask what happens if announced but not yet available processors or accelerators are adopted. One such exercise replaces the host processor that we have used for our previous tests with the new Intel multicore Xeon E5-2697v4, based on the latest *Broadwell* micro-architecture. To this use we run the code on a *Broadwell* processor with no attached accelerators and measure the host-related performance parameters used in Equation 14; next we use the model to forecast the performances of a would-be machine whose nodes combine Broadwell hosts with either P100 or K80 accelerators.

Results are shown in Figure 18 where we compare the measured performance on the present hardware (dots) with the predictions of our model (dashed lines). One can observe that, for both accelerators, performances would improve by approximately 10-15%, when perfectly balancing the workload between host and accelerator. Observe that the model predictions overlap with measured data when $2M / LX$ values tends to zero; this is expected, since in this case the fraction of lattice sites mapped on the host-CPU tends to zero and the execution time is dominated by the accelerator. A similar analysis might be performed, for instance, to assess the overall performance gains to be expected when next generation GPUs become available.

Figure 18. Performance predictions (dashed-lines) for a would-be system using as host the recently-released Broadwell (BRD) CPU compared with measured data on a Haswell (HSW) CPU (dots). Measurements refer to three different lattice sizes.

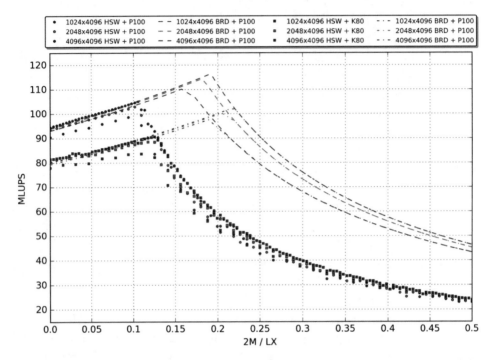

ENERGY-AWARE LBM COMPUTING

Energy consumption is quickly becoming one of the critical issues in modern HPC systems. HPC facilities are already considering the option to account users for energy on top of total node usage time. In this context, application developers are starting to consider energy costs as part of a more general optimization strategy that is not limited to just performance optimization.

Recent papers discuss hardware approaches to energy efficiency (Etinski, Corbalán, Labarta, & Valero, 2012), and also energy-specific software optimizations (Anzt, Haugen, Kurzak, Luszczek, & Dongarra, 2015). In GPU systems, the largest fraction of the overall power consumption is no more ascribable to CPUs (Coplin & Burtscher, 2016), (Ge et al., 2013), so even small savings per accelerator translate into a not negligible saving at the cluster level.

In this section we present an overview of the energy profile of the LBM codes that we have discussed in the previous section, focusing mainly on the impact of data layout on energy costs. Energy optimizations, for any code, is obviously only possible if energy costs can be accurately measured. For this reason, we start this section with a quick overview on this subject, also introducing the library, developed in (E. Calore et al., 2017b), that we have used in our tests.

Measuring Energy Consumption

The most common metric for energy efficiency of a generic workload is usually taken to be *energy-to-solution*, E_s, defined in term of another performance-critical parameter *time-to-solution*, T_s and of the average power (P_{avg}) consumption while computing the workload:

$$E_s = T_s \times P_{avg} .$$

The rationale behind energy optimization is that one would like to reduce E_s while not affecting (or only marginally affecting) T_s, so the quest is for a code that executes efficiently on the target processor (hence it reduces T_s) but does not increase too much P_{avg}. An interesting remark here is that one may write $P_{avg} = P_{Static} + P_{Dynamic}$, as the sum of P_{Static} which is a background energy consumption, independent of what the processor actually does, and $P_{Dynamic}$, that we loosely define as the additional power required by the processor to run the code. From this equation one derives the interesting fact that reducing T_s has in any case the advantage of reducing the contribution of P_{Static} to E_s.

Most recent processor architectures have energy counters, containing measured samples of power, or energy values already computed over an interval. Although we can not yet speak of a standardization between different architectures, an existing library, the PAPI library (Weaver et al., 2012), can be used to read those counters on both Intel CPUs and NVIDIA GPUs, using a common API which is quite stable also across different models and generations. On top of the PAPI library, we developed a custom wrapper library (E. Calore, 2016), available for download as Free Software (E. Calore, 2016), to manage data acquisition from hardware registers, allowing to easily instrument codes to directly start and stop measurements. Our library also allows to place markers in the data stream so we can accurately correlate the running kernel functions and the acquired energy measurement. An instrumented code sample is reported in Listing 9 showing an example of its possible usage.

Listing 9. Usage example of the custom wrapper library exploiting PAPI

```
#include "papi-read.h"

int main() {

  // Sampling Frequency in Hertz
  float acquisition_frequency = 10.0f;

  // Initialize specifying which PAPI Components to read.
  PAPI_reader_Init("output.log", acquisition_frequency, "rapl nvml");

  // Start to read PAPI components, storing data in memory
  PAPI_reader_Start();

  { // Function to be profiled
    PAPI_reader_Marker(); // Place a marker where needed
    do_something();
    PAPI_reader_Marker(); // Place a marker where needed
    do_something_else();
    PAPI_reader_Marker(); // Place a marker where needed
  }

  // Stop reading PAPI components
  PAPI_reader_Stop();

  // Start again if needed or otherwise close.

  // Only at this point acquired data is dumped to file:
  PAPI_reader_Close();

}
```

Analysis of Energy Data

We have used the library described above to profile a benchmark embedding different single GPU implementations of the LBM described in the section *OPTIMIZATION STRATEGIES: II. ONE GPU*. This benchmark performs several iterations of different implementations of the two most important functions of a LBM simulation (i.e. propagate and collide). In particular, we report the results for the benchmark performing in sequence several iterations of each of 4 different kernel functions: the propagate and collide kernel functions with *AoS* data layout and then the same kernels adopting the *SoA* data layout. The function used to apply Boundary conditions heavily depends on the details of the specific simulation and having often a marginal computational cost in typical simulations (of the order of 1-2%), so we neglect this computational phase in our energy analysis.

To evaluate the *energy-to-solution* metric for the different implementations, we measured their execution time, while monitoring the power consumption of the processors executing them. As shown in the previous section, just the average power consumption would be enough, but to study the energy behavior of the different software components we decided to sample the instantaneous power consumption with the finer resolution we could obtain, without introducing a significant measuring overhead.

Figure 19 shows a plot of our typical raw data, showing the measured power consumption, sampled at 10Hz on one of the 2 GPUs of an NVIDIA K80 board at the requested GPU frequency of 875MHz. We can clearly identify 4 different phases corresponding to each kernel function. The first two phases are the *AoS* implementations, while the last two are the *SoA* ones.

Figure 19. Power consumption while executing 1000 iterations of the propagate function, followed by 1000 iterations of the collide function using the AoS data layout and then again, using the SoA data layout; kernels are executed on one of the two GPUs of an NVIDIA K80 accelerator at a requested GPU clock frequency of 875MHz; as power exceeds the designed TDP (150W), frequency is automatically reduced to limit the power consumption; power is sampled at 10Hz granularity

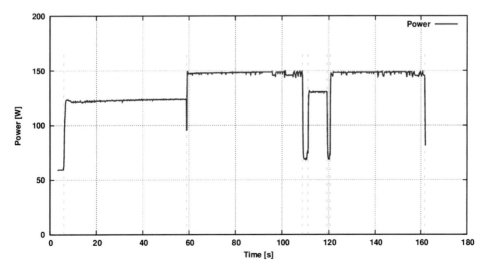

Looking at the raw data in *Figure 19*, we clearly see that concerning the propagate function, the use of the *SoA* data layout, instead of *AoS*, slightly increase the average power consumption P_{avg}, but sharply decreases T_s. The collide function on the other side when using the *SoA* data layout, instead of *AoS*, slightly decrease P_{avg} and T_s too. In the case of collide, for both the data layouts, we can also notice the appearance of some ripples which are associated to the automatic DVFS (Dynamic Voltage and Frequency Scaling) governor of the GPU trying to adjust the clock frequency to keep the P_{avg} under the 150 Watt TDP (Thermal Design Power).

Results

From the raw data reported in Figure 19 we integrate the power consumption over the execution time T_s for each kernel function, to obtain the corresponding energy consumption E_s. The energy can later be normalized by the lattice sites in order to obtain a lattice independent metric.

Figure 20 shows our results for two NVIDIA GPUs, one Kepler GK210 (out of the two contained in an NVIDIA K80 board) and one Pascal P100.

From Figure 20 we can see that the P100 is about 3 times more energy-efficient than the K80 and that for both the NVIDIA architectures the *SoA* data layout gives to the propagate function a factor 6 improvement in energy-efficiency w.r.t. to the *AoS* layout. Also for the collide kernel there is a slight improvement, but being a strongly compute-bound function the data layout does not affect much performances neither energy-efficiency.

Figure 20. Energy consumption of Propagate and Collide functions (D2Q37 model) in nano-Joules per lattice sites for different architectures and memory layouts

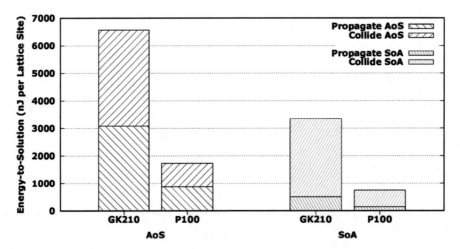

Summarizing the results of this section, we just state that, in our application domain, accurate programming is able to increase at the same time computing performance and energy efficiency; this statement is definitely true for GPUs, while it has to be taken with some caveats for other computing architectures.

CONCLUSION

In this chapter we have discussed several topics relevant to an efficient implementation of LBM code, and more generally scientific codes based on stencils, for GPUs:

- Data-structures used to store the application domain are crucial to fully use GPU computing power. In this case the *SoA* organization is the most suitable to exploit data-parallelism, letting the code run efficiently on GPUs. In the section *OPTIMIZATION STRATEGIES: I. DATA LAYOUT* we have carefully assessed the impact of *AoS* and *SoA* implementations on the two computationally critical kernels of typical LBM applications, *propagate* and *collide* for a bi- and three-dimensional case;
- Codes able to scale over a large number of GPUs require efficient MPI communications; GPU-Direct and RDMA help to set up low-latency communications. Moreover, the identification of the best domain splitting is not trivial. In section *OPTIMIZATION STRATEGIES: II. ONE GPU* we have described a LBM application for a single GPU, while in section *OPTIMIZATION STRATEGIES: III. MULTI GPUs* we have analyzed a theoretical model for a 1D- and 2D-splitting of the lattice domain that can be used to compare the corresponding communication time for a multi-GPU implementation. We have also made several benchmarks and provided several codes examples using standard MPI libraries which developers can use as a base for multi-GPU implementations;
- The portability of codes and of performances are becoming critical for several scientific communities. In this direction frameworks such as OpenACC are very useful and effective. In section *OPTIMIZATION STRATEGIES: IV. PORTABILITY* we discussed how to design and implement LBM codes using OpenACC and made an extensive comparison of performances between CUDA, as native language for NVIDIA GPUs, and OpenACC. We have also provided some results on code and performance portability across several different architectures, comparing multi-core Intel CPUs and NVIDIA and AMD GPUs;
- Several implementations of applications for GPUs confine the host CPU to the role of a driver; in section *OPTIMIZATION STRATEGIES: V.*

HETEROGENEOUS IMPLEMENTATIONS we have discussed how to design an efficient implementation that exploit both the computing resources of the host processor and accelerators;

- GPUs are very energy-efficient processors; monitoring their power consumption is the starting point to design specific software optimizations further increasing energy efficiency. In section *ENERGY-AWARE LBM COMPUTING* we have assessed the impact of data structures on energy-efficiency, and provided useful examples that developers can use to monitor energy consumption of their own codes.

As a very final remark, GPUs are today among the most competitive processors for HPC applications, but their efficient use still requires careful and informed programming. We believe that our detailed examples provide a set of best-practices that will prove useful for the LBM and other scientific communities.

ACKNOWLEDGMENT

This work has been done in the framework of the COKA and COSA projects of INFN, and of the PRIN2015 project of MIUR. We would like to thank CINECA and Jülich Supercomputing Center (JSC) for access to their HPC systems. AG has been supported by the EU Horizon 2020 research and innovation programme under the Marie Sklodowska-Curie grant agreement No 642069. The COKA cluster, is funded by University of Ferrara and INFN.

REFERENCES

Alexander, F. J., Chen, S., & Sterling, J. D. (1993). Lattice Boltzmann Thermohydrodynamics. *Physical Review E: Statistical Physics, Plasmas, Fluids, and Related Interdisciplinary Topics*, *47*(4), R2249–R2252. doi:10.1103/PhysRevE.47. R2249 PMID:9960345

Anzt, H., Haugen, B., Kurzak, J., Luszczek, P., & Dongarra, J. (2015). Experiences in autotuning matrix multiplication for energy minimization on GPUs. *Concurrency and Computation*, *27*(17), 5096–5113. doi:10.1002/cpe.3516

Ayguadé, E., Badia, R. M., Bellens, P., Cabrera, D., Duran, A., Ferrer, R., & Quintana-Ortí, E. S. (2010). Extending OpenMP to Survive the Heterogeneous Multi-Core Era. *International Journal of Parallel Programming*, *38*(5-6), 440–459. doi:10.1007/s10766-010-0135-4

Bailey, P., Myre, J., Walsh, S. D. C., Lilja, D. J., & Saar, M. O. (2009). *Accelerating Lattice Boltzmann fluid flow simulations using graphics processors. In 2009 international conference on parallel processing* (pp. 550–557)., doi:10.1109/ICPP.2009.38

Bernard, C., Christ, N., Gottlieb, S., Jansen, K., Kenway, R., Lippert, T., ... Wittig, H. (2002). Panel discussion on the cost of dynamical quark simulations. *Nuclear Physics B - Proceedings Supplement*, *106*(Supplement C), 199–205. doi:10.1016/S0920-5632(01)01664-4

Bernaschi, M., Fatica, M., Melchionna, S., Succi, S., & Kaxiras, E. (2010). A flexible high-performance Lattice Boltzmann GPU code for the simulations of fluid flows in complex geometries. *Concurrency and Computation*, *22*(1), 1–14. doi:10.1002/cpe.1466

Bhatnagar, P. L., Gross, E. P., & Krook, M. (1954). A model for collision processes in gases. I. Small amplitude processes in charged and neutral one-component systems. *Physical Review Letters*, *94*(3), 511–525. doi:10.1103/PhysRev.94.511

Biferale, L., Mantovani, F., Pivanti, M., Pozzati, F., Sbragaglia, M., Scagliarini, A., & Tripiccione, R. (2012). A Multi-GPU implementation of a D2Q37 Lattice Boltzmann code. In R. Wyrzykowski, J. Dongarra, K. Karczewski, & J. Waśniewski (Eds.), *Parallel processing and applied mathematics: 9th international conference, PPAM 2011, Torun, Poland, September 11-14, 2011. revised selected papers, part i* (pp. 640-650). Berlin: Springer Berlin Heidelberg. doi:10.1007/978-3-642-31464-3_65

Biferale, L., Mantovani, F., Pivanti, M., Pozzati, F., Sbragaglia, M., Scagliarini, A., & Tripiccione, R. (2013). An optimized D2Q37 Lattice Boltzmann code on GP-GPUs. *Computers & Fluids*, *80*, 55–62. doi:10.1016/j.compfluid.2012.06.003

Biferale, L., Mantovani, F., Pivanti, M., Sbragaglia, M., Scagliarini, A., Schifano, S. F., & Tripiccione, R. (2010). Lattice Boltzmann fluid-dynamics on the QPACE supercomputer. *Procedia Computer Science*, *1*(1), 1075–1082. doi:10.1016/j.procs.2010.04.119

Bilardi, G., Pietracaprina, A., Pucci, G., Schifano, F., & Tripiccione, R. (2005). The potential of on-chip multiprocessing for QCD machines. *Lecture Notes in Computer Science*, *3769*, 386–397. doi:10.1007/11602569_41

Blair, S., Albing, C., Grund, A., & Jocksch, A. (2015). Accelerating an MPI Lattice Boltzmann code using OpenACC. In *Proceedings of the second workshop on accelerator programming using directives* (pp. 3:1-3:9). New York: ACM. doi:10.1145/2832105.2832111

Bonati, C., Calore, E., Coscetti, S., D'Elia, M., Mesiti, M., Negro, F., & Tripiccione, R. (2015). Development of scientific software for HPC architectures using OpenACC: The case of LQCD. In The 2015 international workshop on software engineering for high performance computing in science (sE4HPCS) (pp. 9-15). Academic Press. doi:10.1109/SE4HPCS.2015.9

Bonati, C., Coscetti, S., D'Elia, M., Mesiti, M., Negro, F., Calore, E., & Tripiccione, R. (2017). Design and optimization of a portable LQCD monte carlo code using OpenACC. *International Journal of Modern Physics C, 28*(5), 1750063. doi:10.1142/S0129183117500632

Bonati, C., Cossu, G., D'Elia, M., & Incardona, P. (2012). QCD simulations with staggered fermions on GPUs. *Computer Physics Communications, 183*(4), 853–863. doi:10.1016/j.cpc.2011.12.011

Bortolotti, G., Caberletti, M., Crimi, G., Ferraro, A., Giacomini, F., Manzali, M., & Zanella, M. (2014). Computing on Knights and Kepler architectures. *Journal of Physics: Conference Series, 513*(5), 052032. doi:10.1088/1742-6596/513/5/052032

Calore, E. (2016). *PAPI-power-reader*. Retrieved from https://baltig.infn.it/COKA/PAPI-power-reader

Calore, E., Demo, N., Schifano, S. F., & Tripiccione, R. (2016a). Experience on vectorizing Lattice Boltzmann kernels for multi- and many-core architectures. In *Parallel processing and applied mathematics: 11th international conference, PPAM 2015, Krakow, Poland, September 6-9, 2015. revised selected papers, part i* (pp. 53-62). Cham: Springer International Publishing. doi:10.1007/978-3-319-32149-3_6

Calore, E., Gabbana, A., Kraus, J., Schifano, S. F., & Tripiccione, R. (2016b). Performance and portability of accelerated Lattice Boltzmann applications with OpenACC. *Concurrency and Computation, 28*(12), 3485–3502. doi:10.1002/cpe.3862

Calore, E., Gabbana, A., Schifano, S. F., & Tripiccione, R. (2017a). *Early experience on using Knights Landing processors for Lattice Boltzmann applications*. (in press)

Calore, E., Gabbana, A., Schifano, S. F., & Tripiccione, R. (2017b). Evaluation of DVFS techniques on modern HPC processors and accelerators for energy-aware applications. *Concurrency and Computation, 29*(12), e4143. doi:10.1002/cpe.4143

Calore, E., Gabbana, A., Schifano, S. F., & Tripiccione, R. (2017c). Optimization of Lattice Boltzmann simulations on heterogeneous computers. *International Journal of High Performance Computing Applications*, 1–16. doi:10.1177/1094342017703771

Calore, E., Schifano, S. F., & Tripiccione, R. (2014a). A Portable OpenCL Lattice Boltzmann Code for Multi-and Many-core Processor Architectures. *Procedia Computer Science*, *29*, 40–49. doi:10.1016/j.procs.2014.05.004

Calore, E., Schifano, S. F., & Tripiccione, R. (2014b). On portability, performance and scalability of an MPI OpenCL Lattice Boltzmann code. In L. Lopes, J. Žilinskas, A. Costan, R. G. Cascella, G. Kecskemeti, E. Jeannot, & M. Alexander (Eds.), *Euro-par 2014: Parallel processing workshops: Euro-par 2014 international workshops, Porto, Portugal, August 25-26, 2014, revised selected papers, part II* (pp. 438-449). Cham: Springer International Publishing. doi:10.1007/978-3-319-14313-2_37

Chen, S., Chen, H., Martnez, D., & Matthaeus, W. (1991). Lattice Boltzmann model for simulation of magnetohydrodynamics. *Physical Review Letters*, *67*(27), 3776–3779. doi:10.1103/PhysRevLett.67.3776 PMID:10044823

Chen, Y., Ohashi, H., & Akiyama, M. (1994). Thermal lattice Bhatnagar-Gross-Krook model without nonlinear deviations in macrodynamic equations. *Physical Review E: Statistical Physics, Plasmas, Fluids, and Related Interdisciplinary Topics*, *50*(4), 2776–2783. doi:10.1103/PhysRevE.50.2776 PMID:9962315

Coplin, J., & Burtscher, M. (2016). Energy, Power, and Performance Characterization of GPGPU Benchmark Programs. *12th IEEE Workshop on High-Performance, Power-Aware Computing (HPPAC'16)*. doi:10.1109/IPDPSW.2016.164

Crimi, G., Mantovani, F., Pivanti, M., Schifano, S. F., & Tripiccione, R. (2013). Early Experience on Porting and Running a Lattice Boltzmann Code on the Xeon-phi Co-Processor. *Procedia Computer Science*, *18*, 551–560. doi:10.1016/j.procs.2013.05.219

Davide Rossetti. (2014). *Benchmarking GPUDirect RDMA on modern server platforms*. Retrieved from http://devblogs.nvidia.com/parallelforall/benchmarking-gpudirect-rdma-on-modern-server-platforms

Etinski, M., Corbalán, J., Labarta, J., & Valero, M. (2012). Understanding the future of energy-performance trade-off via DVFS in HPC environments. *Journal of Parallel and Distributed Computing*, *72*(4), 579–590. doi:10.1016/j.jpdc.2012.01.006

Frisch, U., d' Humieres, D., Hasslacher, B., Lallemand, P., Pomeau, Y., & Rivet, J. (1986). *Lattice gas hydrodynamics in two and three dimensions*. Retrieved from http://www.osti.gov/scitech/servlets/purl/6063731

Ge, R., Vogt, R., Majumder, J., Alam, A., Burtscher, M., & Zong, Z. (2013). Effects of Dynamic Voltage and Frequency Scaling on a K20 GPU. In *Proceedings of the 2013 42nd international conference on parallel processing* (pp. 826-833). Washington, DC: IEEE Computer Society. doi:10.1109/ICPP.2013.98

Han, T., & Abdelrahman, T. (2011). hiCUDA: High-Level GPGPU Programming. *Parallel and Distributed Systems. IEEE Transactions on*, *22*(1), 78–90. doi:10.1109/TPDS.2010.62

Hart, A., Ansaloni, R., & Gray, A. (2012). Porting and scaling OpenACC applications on massively-parallel, GPU-accelerated supercomputers. *The European Physical Journal. Special Topics*, *210*(1), 5–16. doi:10.1140/epjst/e2012-01634-y

He, X., & Luo, L.-S. (1997). Theory of the Lattice Boltzmann method: From the Boltzmann equation to the Lattice Boltzmann equation. *Physical Review E: Statistical Physics, Plasmas, Fluids, and Related Interdisciplinary Topics*, *56*(6), 6811–6817. doi:10.1103/PhysRevE.56.6811

Herdman, J., Gaudin, W., McIntosh-Smith, S., Boulton, M., Beckingsale, D., Mallinson, A., & Jarvis, S. A. (2012). Accelerating hydrocodes with OpenACC, OpenCL and CUDA. In High Performance Computing, Networking, Storage and Analysis (SCC), 2012 SC Companion: (pp. 465-471). IEEE. doi:10.1109/SC.Companion.2012.66

Holewinski, J., Pouchet, L.-N., & Sadayappan, P. (2012). High-performance code generation for stencil computations on GPU architectures. In *Proceedings of the 26th aCM international conference on supercomputing* (pp. 311-320). New York: ACM. doi:10.1145/2304576.2304619

Januszewski, M., & Kostur, M. (2014). Sailfish: A flexible multi-GPU implementation of the Lattice Boltzmann method. *Computer Physics Communications*, *185*(9), 2350–2368. doi:10.1016/j.cpc.2014.04.018

Jiri Kraus. (2013). *An introduction to CUDA-aware MPI*. Retrieved from http://developer.nvidia.com/content/introduction-cuda-aware-mpi

Kraus, J., Pivanti, M., Schifano, S. F., Tripiccione, R., & Zanella, M. (2013). Benchmarking GPUs with a parallel Lattice-Boltzmann code. In *Computer Architecture and High Performance Computing (SBAC-PAD), 25th International Symposium on* (pp. 160-167). IEEE. doi:10.1109/SBAC-PAD.2013.37

Kraus, J., Schlottke, M., Adinetz, A., & Pleiter, D. (2014). Accelerating a C++ CFD code with OpenACC. In *Accelerator programming using directives (WACCPD), 2014 first workshop on* (pp. 47-54). Academic Press. doi:10.1109/WACCPD.2014.11

Lee, S., & Eigenmann, R. (2010). OpenMPC: Extended OpenMP Programming and Tuning for GPUs. In *Proceedings of the 2010 ACM/IEEE International Conference for High Performance Computing, Networking, Storage and Analysis* (pp. 1-11). Washington, DC: IEEE Computer Society. doi:10.1109/SC.2010.36

Mantovani, F., Pivanti, M., Schifano, S. F., & Tripiccione, R. (2013a). Exploiting parallelism in many-core architectures: Lattice Boltzmann models as a test case. *Journal of Physics: Conference Series, 454*(1). doi:10.1088/1742-6596/454/1/012015

Mantovani, F., Pivanti, M., Schifano, S. F., & Tripiccione, R. (2013b). Performance issues on many-core processors: A D2Q37 Lattice Boltzmann scheme as a test-case. *Computers & Fluids, 88*, 743–752. doi:10.1016/j.compfluid.2013.05.014

Maruyama, N., & Aoki, T. (2014). Optimizing stencil computations for NVIDIA kepler GPUs. In *International workshop on high-performance stencil computations* (pp. 1-7). Vienna, Austria: Academic Press.

McNamara, G. R., & Zanetti, G. (1988). Use of the Boltzmann equation to simulate lattice-gas automata. *Physical Review Letters, 61*(20), 2332–2335. doi:10.1103/PhysRevLett.61.2332 PMID:10039085

Mendoza, M., Boghosian, B. M., Herrmann, H. J., & Succi, S. (2010). Fast lattice Boltzmann solver for relativistic hydrodynamics. *Physical Review Letters, 105*(1), 014502. doi:10.1103/PhysRevLett.105.014502 PMID:20867451

NVIDIA Fermi. (2009). Retrieved from http://www.nvidia.com/content/PDF/fermi_white_papers/NVIDIA_Fermi_Compute_Architecture_Whitepaper.pdf

NVIDIA Kepler GK110. (2012). Retrieved from http://www.nvidia.com/content/PDF/kepler/NVIDIA-Kepler-GK110-Architecture-Whitepaper.pdf

NVIDIA Pascal P100. (2016). Retrieved from https://images.nvidia.com/content/pdf/tesla/whitepaper/pascal-architecture-whitepaper.pdf

NVIDIA Volta V100. (2017). Retrieved from https://images.nvidia.com/content/volta-architecture/pdf/Volta-Architecture-Whitepaper-v1.0.pdf

Obrecht, C., Kuznik, F., Tourancheau, B., & Roux, J.-J. (2013). Scalable lattice Boltzmann solvers for CUDA GPU clusters. *Parallel Computing, 39*(6-7), 259–270. doi:10.1016/j.parco.2013.04.001

OpenMP. (2016). *OpenMP application program interface version 4.0*. Retrieved from http://www.openmp.org/mp-documents/OpenMP4.0.0.pdf

OpenACC. (2016). *OpenACC directives for accelerators*. Retrieved from http://www.openacc-standard.org

Reyes, R., López, I., Fumero, J. J., & de Sande, F. (2013). A preliminary evaluation of OpenACC implementations. *The Journal of Supercomputing, 65*(3), 1063–1075. doi:10.1007/s11227-012-0853-z

Rinaldi, P., Dari, E., Vénere, M., & Clausse, A. (2012). A Lattice-Boltzmann solver for 3D fluid simulation on GPU. *Simulation Modelling Practice and Theory, 25*, 163–171. doi:10.1016/j.simpat.2012.03.004

Ripesi, P., Biferale, L., Schifano, S. F., & Tripiccione, R. (2014). Evolution of a double-front Rayleigh-Taylor system using a graphics-processing-unit-based high-resolution thermal Lattice Boltzmann model. *Phys. Rev. E, 89*(4), 043022. doi:10.1103/PhysRevE.89.043022 PMID:24827347

Sbragaglia, M., Benzi, R., Biferale, L., Chen, H., Shan, X., & Succi, S. (2009). Lattice Boltzmann method with self-consistent thermo-hydrodynamic equilibria. *Journal of Fluid Mechanics, 628*, 299–309. doi:10.1017/S002211200900665X

Scagliarini, A., Biferale, L., Sbragaglia, M., Sugiyama, K., & Toschi, F. (2010). Lattice Boltzmann methods for thermal flows: Continuum limit and applications to compressible Rayleigh-Taylor systems. *Physics of Fluids, 22*(5), 055101. doi:10.1063/1.3392774

Shan, X. (2016). The mathematical structure of the lattices of the Lattice Boltzmann method. *Journal of Computational Science, 17*, 475–481. doi:10.1016/j.jocs.2016.03.002

Shet, A. G., Siddharth, K., Sorathiya, S. H., Deshpande, A. M., Sherlekar, S. D., Kaul, B., & Ansumali, S. (2013a). On vectorization for lattice based simulations. *International Journal of Modern Physics C, 24*(12), 1340011. doi:10.1142/S0129183113400111

Shet, A. G., Sorathiya, S. H., Krithivasan, S., Deshpande, A. M., Kaul, B., Sherlekar, S. D., & Ansumali, S. (2013b). Data structure and movement for lattice-based simulations. *Phys. Rev. E, 88*(1), 013314. doi:10.1103/PhysRevE.88.013314 PMID:23944590

Succi, S. (2001). *The Lattice-Boltzmann Equation*. Oxford, UK: Oxford University Press.

Tölke, J. (2008). Implementation of a Lattice Boltzmann kernel using the compute unified device architecture developed by NVIDIA. *Computing and Visualization in Science, 13*(1), 29–39. doi:10.1007/s00791-008-0120-2

Tölke, J., & Krafczyk, M. (2008). TeraFLOP Computing on a Desktop PC with GPUs for 3D CFD. *International Journal of Computational Fluid Dynamics, 22*(7), 443–456. doi:10.1080/10618560802238275

Valero-Lara, P. (2014). Accelerating solid-fluid interaction based on the immersed boundary method on multicore and GPU architectures. *The Journal of Supercomputing, 70*(2), 799–815. doi:10.1007/s11227-014-1262-2

Valero-Lara, P., Igual, F. D., Prieto-Matías, M., Pinelli, A., & Favier, J. (2015). Accelerating fluid-solid simulations (Lattice-Boltzmann & Immersed-Boundary) on heterogeneous architectures. *Journal of Computational Science, 10*, 249–261. doi:10.1016/j.jocs.2015.07.002

Vizitiu, A., Itu, L., Lazar, L., & Suciu, C. (2014). Double precision stencil computations on kepler GPUs. In *System theory, control and computing (iCSTCC), 2014 18th international conference* (pp. 123-127). Academic Press. doi:10.1109/ICSTCC.2014.6982402

Vizitiu, A., Itu, L., Niţă, C., & Suciu, C. (2014). Optimized three-dimensional stencil computation on fermi and kepler GPUs. In *High performance extreme computing conference (HPEC), 2014* (pp. 1–6). IEEE. doi:10.1109/HPEC.2014.7040968

Weaver, V., Johnson, M., Kasichayanula, K., Ralph, J., Luszczek, P., Terpstra, D., & Moore, S. (2012). Measuring energy and power with PAPI. In *Parallel processing workshops (iCPPW), 2012 41st international conference on* (pp. 262-268). Academic Press. doi:10.1109/ICPPW.2012.39

Wienke, S., Springer, P., Terboven, C., & an Mey, D. (2012). OpenACC-first experiences with real-world applications. In Euro-Par 2012 Parallel Processing (pp. 859-870). Springer Berlin Heidelberg. doi:10.1007/978-3-642-32820-6_85

Wienke, S., Terboven, C., Beyer, J. C., & Müller, M. S. (2014). A pattern-based comparison of OpenACC and OpenMP for accelerator computing. In F. Silva, I. Dutra, & V. Santos Costa (Eds.), *Euro-par 2014 parallel processing: 20th international conference, Porto, Portugal, August 25-29, 2014. proceedings* (pp. 812-823). Cham: Springer International Publishing. doi:10.1007/978-3-319-09873-9_68

Wittmann, M., Zeiser, T., Hager, G., & Wellein, G. (2011). *Comparison of different propagation steps for the lattice Boltzmann method.* CoRR, abs/1111.0922

Xian, W., & Takayuki, A. (2011). Multi-GPU performance of incompressible flow computation by lattice Boltzmann method on GPU cluster. *Parallel Computing, 37*(9), 521–535. doi:10.1016/j.parco.2011.02.007

KEY TERMS AND DEFINITIONS

CFD: Computational fluid dynamics is a branch of fluid mechanics that uses numerical analysis and data structures to solve and analyze problems that involve fluid flows.

CUDA: Compute unified device architecture is a parallel computing platform and application programming interface (API) model that allows GPGPU on NVIDIA GPUs. The CUDA platform is designed to work with programming languages such as C, C++, and Fortran.

Directive-Based Programming: A language construct that specifies how a compiler should process its input. In general directives are processed by a preprocessor to specify the compiler behavior.

GPGPU: General-purpose computing on graphics processing units is the use of a graphics processing unit (GPU) to perform computation in applications traditionally handled by the CPU/multicore processors.

Heterogeneous Computing: Those systems where more than one kind of processors, typically CPUs and GPUs coexist.

HPC: High-performance computing is the use of parallel processing in order to solve large problems in science, engineering, or business.

LBM: Lattice-Boltzmann method is a class of CFD methods for fluid simulation.

MPI: Message passing interface is a portable message-passing standard which defines the syntax and semantics of a library routines allowing for portable message-passing programs in C, C++, and Fortran.

Multicore: A single computational component composed by two or more independent processing units (cores) each coming with its own arithmetic-logic and control units.

OpenACC: A directive-based programming standard for parallel computing developed with the aim to simplify parallel programming of heterogeneous CPU/GPU systems. The programmer can annotate C, C++, and Fortran source code to identify the areas that should be accelerated using compiler directives and additional functions.

OpenMP: An application programming interface (API) that supports multi-platform shared memory multiprocessing programming in C, C++, and Fortran, offering a simple and flexible interface for developing parallel applications.

SIMD: Single instruction multiple data is a class of parallel processors composed of multiple processing elements that can perform the same operation on different data simultaneously.

Chapter 4
Mesh Refinement for LBM Simulations on Cartesian Meshes

Pedro Valero-Lara
Barcelona Supercomputing Center (BSC), Spain

ABSTRACT

The use of mesh refinement in CFD is an efficient and widely used methodology to minimize the computational cost by solving those regions of high geometrical complexity with a finer grid. The author focuses on studying two methods, one based on multi-domain and one based on irregular meshing, to deal with mesh refinement over LBM simulations. The numerical formulation is presented in detail. Two approaches, homogeneous GPU and heterogeneous CPU+GPU, on each of the refinement methods are studied. Obviously, the use of the two architectures, CPU and GPU, to compute the same problem involves more important challenges with respect to the homogeneous counterpart. These strategies are described in detail paying particular attention to the differences among both methodologies in terms of programmability, memory management, and performance.

INTRODUCTION

Advanced strategies for the efficient implementation of computationally intensive numerical methods have a strong interest in the industrial and academic community. We could define Computational Fluid Dynamics (CFD) as a set of numerical methods applied to obtain approximate solutions of problems of fluid dynamics and heat transfer (Zikanov, 2010). The CFD community has always explored new ways to

DOI: 10.4018/978-1-5225-4760-0.ch004

take advantage of high-performance computing systems in its never-ending quest for faster and more accurate simulations. The emergence of Graphics Processing Units (GPUs) has been an important advance in this field and it has created new challenges and opportunities for increasing performance in multiple CFD solvers. Many CFD applications and software packages have already been ported and redesigned to exploit GPUs. These developments have often involved major changes because some classical solvers may turned out to be inefficient or difficult to tune (Valero-Lara, Pinelli, Favier, & Prieto-Matías, 2012) (Valero-Lara, Pinelli, & Prieto-Matías, 2014). Fortunately, other solvers are particularly well suited for GPU acceleration and are able to achieve significant performance improvements. The Lattice Boltzmann method (LBM) (Succi, 2001) is one of those examples thanks to its inherently data-parallel nature. Certainly, the computing stages of LBM are amenable to fine grain parallelization in an almost straightforward way.

This fundamental advantage of LBM has been consistently confirmed by many authors (Bernaschi, Fatica, Melchionna, Succi, & Kaxiras, 2010) (Rinaldi, Dari, Vnere, & Clausse, 2012) (Zhou, Mo, Wu, & Zhao, 2012) (Feichtinger, Habich, Kstler, Rude, & Aoki, 2015), for a large variety of problems and computing platforms. For instance, in (Pohl, Kowarchik, Wilke, Rüde, & Iglgerger, 2003) is proposed a set of possible memory access patterns to maximize the temporal locality optimizing the cache performance over multicore architectures. Also in (Rinaldi, Dari, Vnere, & Clausse, 2012) is modified the standard ordering of the LBM steps to reduce the number of memory accesses. Lattice-Boltzmann method has been ported on multiple parallel architectures, such as multicore processors (Pohl, Kowarchik, Wilke, Rüde, & Iglgerger, 2003), manycore accelerators (Bernaschi, Fatica, Melchionna, Succi, & Kaxiras, 2010) (Rinaldi, Dari, Vnere, & Clausse, 2012) (Alexandrov, Lees, Krzhizhanovskaya, Dongarra, Sloot, Crimi, Mantovani, Pivanti, Schifano, & Tripiccione, 2013) (Valero-Lara, Igual, Prieto-Matías, Pinelli, & Favier, 2015) and distributed-memory clusters (Januszewski, & Kostur, 2014). Given the growing popularity of LBM, multiple tools (Januszewski, & Kostur, 2014) have been developed recently, consolidating this method in academia and industry. In particular, in this work, we have considered LBM-HPC framework (Valero-Lara, 2016) as our reference software tool. Lattice-Boltzmann method is an efficient and fast method; however, the usage of Cartesian grids is expensive. Although scientific problems exist for which a homogeneous description of the domain is a reasonable choice, it is usually desirable to solve regions of high geometrical complexity with a

finer grid to minimize the computational cost. Several refinement techniques have been implemented for LBM-based solvers, such as Adaptive-Mesh-Refinement (AMR) (Fakhari, & Lee, 2014), Multi-Grid (Scnherr, Kucher, Geier, Stiebler, Freudiger, & Krafczyk, 2011), Irregular meshing (Valero-Lara, 2014), and Multi-Domain (Lagrava, Malaspinas, Latt, & Chopard, 2012). Each of these techniques exhibit its own advantages and disadvantages. For AMR and Multi-Grid, the coarse grid is present all over the simulation domain. In the Multi-Domain refinement, the regions where refined patches are inserted are taken off the coarse grid. The Multi-Domain method exhibits better performances and higher memory savings and a more complex grid coupling with respect to the other approaches. Nevertheless, those approaches based on AMR represents the most complex scenario for data management, due mainly to its dynamic data structure, while the Multi-Grid approaches are easier to implement. All these approaches require to use synchronization points as there exists a data dependency among the different refined levels, such that those refined regions must be computed at least several times per time-step. All this degrades the performance and makes difficult the implementation on parallel processors. To address these shortcomings and reduce the complexity of the previous refinements approaches, recently in (Valero-Lara, & Jansson, 2015) (Valero-Lara, & Jansson, 2017) is presented a new approach based on Irregular meshing. This idea has been previously considered in other methods (Yoon, Yang, & Choi, 2010). This new methodology reduces the overhead related with communication and synchronization among the different refined levels; however, it requires a higher number of fluid elements to carry out the same test cases (simulations). In this work, we have focused on two approaches, Multi-domain and Irregular meshing. We have chosen the Multi-Domain approach in order to have better performance and higher memory savings. However, the coupling between grids is more complex. The Irregular meshing approach was also studied as it presents a simple coupling between grids. Nevertheless, it requires a higher number of fluid units over the same scenarios. Thus, we can discover what are the features more amenable of each of the methodologies on our heterogeneous platform. Not many works extend the parallel efficiency of LBM to cases involving refinement techniques. A very recent work that covers a subject closely related with the present contribution is (Schnherr, Kucher, Geier, Stiebler, Freudiger, & Krafczyk, 2011), where a new and efficient 2D implementation of LBM method for multi-grid flows is presented. Here, we focus on two different approaches coupled with LBM; one based on multi-domain introduced in (Lagrava, Malaspinas, Latt, & Chopard, 2012), and one based on Irregular meshing presented in (Valero-Lara, & Jansson 2015) (Valero-Lara, & Jansson, 2017). These methodologies have been analyzed deeply and validated in several numerical scenarios (Valero-Lara, & Jansson 2015) (Valero-Lara, & Jansson, 2017) (Lagrava, Malaspinas, Latt, & Chopard, 2012) (Valero-Lara, 2014), so we focus on the implementation techniques adopted to keep the solver highly efficient on CPU+GPU heterogeneous platforms. Also, this work includes a comparative study (in terms of performance and numerical accuracy) among two different refinement methods for LBM simulations. We study deeply the GPU implementation of both approaches as well as its porting to heterogeneous CPU+GPU platforms.

LATTICE-BOLTZMANN METHOD

Background

Most of the current methods for simulating the transport equations (heat, mass, and momentum) are based on the use of macroscopic partial differential equations (Wendt, & Anderson, 2008) (Anderson, Menter, Dick, Degrez, & Vierendeels, 2013) (Anderson, 1995) (Swarztrauber, 1974). On the other extreme, we can view the medium from a microscopic viewpoint where small particles (molecule and atom) collide with each other (molecular dynamic) (Mohamad, 2011). In this scale, the inter-particle forces must be identified, which requires to know the location, velocity, and trajectory of every particle. However, there is no definition of viscosity, heat capacity, temperature, pressure, etc. These methods are extremely expensive computationally (Mohamad, 2011). However, it is possible to use statistical mechanisms as a translator between the molecular world and the microscopic world, avoiding the management of every individual particle, while obtaining the important macroscopic effects by combining the advantages of both macroscopic and microscopic approaches with manageable computer resources. This is the main idea of the Boltzmann equation and the mesoscopic scale (Mohamad, 2011). Multiple studies have compared the efficiency of LBM with respect to other 'classic' methods based on Navier-Stokes (Kollmannsberger, Geller, Dster, Tlke, Sorer, Krafczyk, & Rank, 2009) (Kandhai, Videl, Hoekstra, Hoefsloot, Iedema, & Sloot, 1998). They show that LBM can achieve an equivalent numerical accuracy over a large number of applications. In particular, LBM has been used to simulate high Reynolds turbulent flows over Direct Numerical and Large Eddy simulations (Malaspinas, & Sagaut, 2012). Another challenging applications where LBM has proved to be quite successful concerns aeroacoustics problems (Marié, Ricot, & Sagaut, 2009) or bio-engineering applications (Bernaschi, Fatica, Melchionna, Succi, & Kaxiras, 2010). Also, LBM has been efficiently integrated with other methods such as the Immersed Boundary Method (Peskin, 2002) (Valero-Lara, 2014) for Fluid-Solid Interaction problems (Valero-Lara, Igual, Prieto-Matías, Pinelli, & Favier, 2015) (Favier, Revell, & Pinelli, 2014) (Valero-Lara, Pinelli, Prieto-Matías, 2014).

Lattice Boltzmann Method Formulation

Lattice-Boltzmann method combines some features developed to solve the Boltzmann equation over a finite number of microscopic speeds. LBM presents lattice-symmetry characteristics which allow to respect the conservation of the macroscopic moments (He, & Luo, 1997). The standard LBM (Qian, Humires, & Lallemand, 1992) is an explicit solver for incompressible flows. It divides each temporal iteration into two steps, one for propagation-advection and one for collision (inter-particle interactions), achieving a first order in time and second order in space scheme. Lattice-Boltzmann method describes the fluid behaviour at mesoscopic level. At this level, the fluid is modelled by a distribution function of the microscopic particle (f). Similarly to the Boltzmann equation, LBM solves the particle speed distribution by discretizing the speed space over a discrete finite number of possible speeds. The distribution function evolves according to the following equation:

$$\frac{\partial f}{\partial t} + e\nabla f = \wp$$

where f is the particle distribution function, e is the discrete space of speeds and $\wp$ is the collision operator. By discretizing the distribution function f in space, in time, and in speed ($e = e_i$) we obtain $f_i(x,t)$, which describes the probability of finding a particle located at x at time t with speed e_i. $e\nabla f$ can be discretized as:

$$e\nabla f = e_i\nabla f_i = \frac{f_i\left(x + e_i dt, t + dt\right) - f_i\left(x, t + dt\right)}{dt}$$

In this way, the particles can move only along the links of a regular lattice (Figure 1) defined by the discrete speeds

$$(e_0 = c(0,0); e_i = c(\pm 1, 0), c(0, \pm 1), i = 1,...,4; e_i = c(\pm 1, \pm 1, i = 5,...,8)) \text{ with } c = dx / dt)$$

so that the synchronous particle displacements $dx_i = e_i dt$ never takes the fluid particles away from the lattice. In this work, we consider the standard two-dimensional 9-speed lattice D2Q9 (He, & Luo, 1997).

The operator $\wp$ describes the changes suffered by the collision of the microscopic particles, which affect the distribution function (f). To calculate the collision operator, we consider the BGK (Bhatnagar-Gross-Krook) formulation (Gross, Bhatnagar, & Krook, 1954) which relies upon a unique relaxation time, t, toward the equilibrium distribution f_i^{eq}:

$$\wp = \frac{-1}{t} f_i(x,t) - f_i^{eq}(x,t)$$

Figure 1. The standard two-dimensional 9-speed lattice (D2Q9)

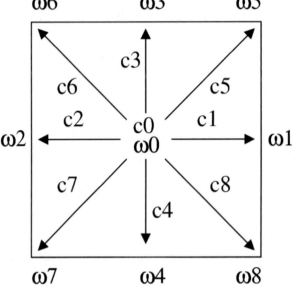

The equilibrium function $f_i^{eq}(x,t)$ can be obtained by Taylor series expansion of the Maxwell- Boltzmann equilibrium distribution (Qian, Humires, & Lallemand, 1992):

$$f_i^{eq} = pw_i \left[1 + \frac{e_i \times u}{c_s^2} + \frac{\left(e_i \times u\right)^2}{2c_s^4} - \frac{u^2}{2c_s^2} \right]$$

where c_s is the speed of sound ($c_s = 1/\sqrt{3}$) and the weight coefficients w_i are

$$w_0 = 4/9, w_i = 1/9, i = 1,...,4; w_i = 1/36, i = 5,...,8$$

based on the current normalization. Through the use of the collision operator and substituting the term $\partial f_i / \partial t$ with a first order temporal discretization, the discrete Boltzmann equation can be written as:

$$\frac{f_i\left(x,t+dt\right)-f_i\left(x,t\right)}{dt} + \frac{f_i\left(x+e_i dt,t+dt\right)-f_i\left(x,t+dt\right)}{dt} = -\frac{1}{t}\left(f_i\left(x,t\right)-f_i^{eq}\left(x,t\right)\right)$$

which can be compactly written as:

$$f_i\left(x + e_i dt, t + dt\right) - f_i\left(x, t\right) = -\frac{dt}{t}\left(f_i\left(x, t\right) - f_i^{eq}\left(x, t\right)\right)$$

The macroscopic velocity u must satisfy a Mach number requirement $\left(u\right)/c_s \approx M \ll 1$. This stands as the equivalent of the Courant Friedrichs Lewy (CFL) number (CFL number arises in those schemes based on explicit time computer simulations. As a consequence, this number must be less than a certain time to achieve coherent results) for classical Navier Stokes solvers.

As mentioned earlier, the above equation is typically advanced in time in two stages, the collision and the streaming stages (Valero-Lara, 2014). Given $f_i\left(x, t\right)$ compute:

$$p = \sum f_i\left(x, t\right)$$

and

$$pu = \sum e_i f_i\left(x, t\right)$$

Collision stage:

$$f_i^{tmp}\left(x, t + dt\right) = f_i\left(x, t\right) - \frac{dt}{t}\left(f\left(x, t\right) - f_i^{eq}\left(x, t\right)\right)$$

Streaming stage:

$$f_i\left(x + e_i dt, t + dt\right) = f_i^{tmp}\left(x, t + dt\right)$$

Lattice Boltzmann Implementation

Lattice-Boltzmann method exhibits a high degree of parallelism and is amenable to fine granularity (one thread per lattice node), because the solving of every lattice point is totally independent with respect to the others. To compute streaming in parallel, we need two different distribution functions (f_1 and f_2 in Listing 1).

Listing 1. Pseudo-code for LBM-pull approach

```
1.  Pull ( f₁ , f₂ , w , cₓ , c_y )

2.  x, y, x_stream , y_stream   x and y are the coordinates for a
    particular lattice node

3.  local_ux , local_uy , local_p , local_f [9] , f_eq , cu

4.  for i = 1 → 9 do

5.      x_stream  = x - cₓ[i]

6.      y_stream  = y - c_u[i]

7.      local_f[i] = f₁[x_stream][y_stream][i]

8.  end for

9.  for i = 1 → 9 do

10.     local_p  += local_f[i]

11.     local_ux  += cₓ[i] * local_f[i]

12.     local_uy  += c_y[i] * local_f[i]

13. end for
```

14. $local_{ux} = local_{ux} \, / \, local_{\rho}$

15. $local_{uy} = local_{uy} \, / \, local_{\rho}$

```
16. for i = 1 → 9 do
```

17. $cu = c_x[i] \, local_{ux} + c_y[i] \, local_{uy}$

18. $f^{eq} = w[i]\rho\left(1 + 3(cu) + (cu)^2 - 1{,}5 \times \left(local_{ux}\right)^2 + local_{uy}\right)^2$

19. $f_2[x][y][i] = local_f[i]\left(1 - \dfrac{1}{t}\right) + f^{eq}\dfrac{1}{t}$

```
20. end for
```

Depending on the ordering of the major LBM steps (collision and streaming), two different strategies arise: The classical approach is known as push method and performs collision before streaming. On the contrary, the pull approach performs the same major steps but in the opposite order (streaming-collision). These differences have important consequences in terms of performance (Valero-Lara, Igual, Prieto-Matías, Pinelli, & Favier, 2015). The push approach (collide-stream strategy) has been used in numerous works (Bernaschi, Fatica, Melchionna, Succi, & Kaxiras, 2010) (Zhou, Mo, Wu, & Zhao, 2012) (Schnherr, Kucher, Geier, Stiebler, Freudiger,

& Krafczyk, 2011). In general, the push method divides the LBM steps into two steps. The first one computes collision and streaming and the second one solves macroscopic variables (velocities and density). This can hinder the implementation of the algorithm on parallel architectures and imposes a greater pressure on memory (Valero-Lara, Igual, Prieto-Matías, Pinelli, & Favier, 2015). On the other hand, the pull approach, introduced in (Wellein, Zeiser, Hager, & Donath, 2006), has been recently consider in (Valero-Lara, Pinelli, & Prieto-Matías, 2014). This is an efficient approach based on a single-loop strategy; Each lattice node can be independently computed by performing one complete time step of LBM (a schematic sketch of this LBM implementation is given in Listing 1). Basically, this strategy fuses in a single loop (that iterates over the entire domain), the application of both operations to improve temporal locality. Furthermore it does not need any synchronization among the major LBM steps. Also, it eases pressure on memory with respect to the push approach, as the macroscopic level can be completely computed on top regions of memory hierarchy. Memory management plays a crucial role in LBM implementation.

Figure 2. SoA data layout to store the discrete distribution functions f_i in memory

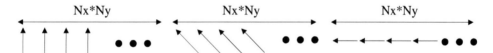

Figure 3. Fine-grained distribution of the lattice nodes

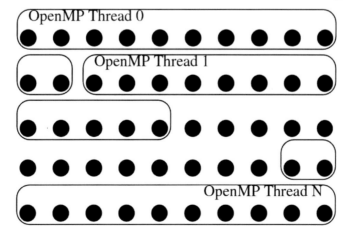

Figure 4. Coarse-grained distributions of the lattice nodes

Fine Grained (CUDA) Partitioning

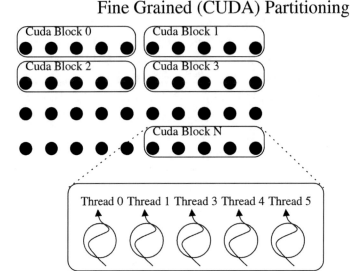

The information of the fluid domain should be stored in memory in such way that reduces the number of memory accesses and keeps the implementation highly efficient by taking advantages of vector units. In this work, we consider a coalescing memory access pattern by using a Structure of Array (SoA) approach. This strategy has proven to be very efficient in multicore and GPUs architectures (Valero-Lara, Pinelli, & Prieto-Matías, 2014). The discrete distribution functions f_i is stored sequentially in the same array (Figure 2). This way, consecutive threads access adjacent memory locations. Parallelism is abundant in the LBM update and can be exploited in different ways. The parallelization of LBM over multicore is very transparent from programmer point of view by using OpenMP pragmas before loops to orchestrate the distribution of the workload over the set of threads (coarse grain). On multi-core processors, cache locality is a major performance issue, so we distribute the lattice nodes across cores using a 1D coarse-grained distribution (Figure 3). The parallelization of LBM over GPUs consists of using a single kernel. We use a 1D Grid of 1D CUDA Block, in which each CUDA-thread performs a complete LBM update on a single lattice node. Lattice nodes are distributed across GPU cores using a fine-grained distribution (Figure 4).

Table 1. Main features of the platforms used

Platform	2 x Intel Xeon E5520 (2.26 GHz)	4 x NVIDIA Kepler K20c
Cores	8	2496
On-Chip Memory	L1 32KB (per core)	SM 16/48 KB (per MP)
	L2 512 KB (unified)	L1 48/16 KB (per MP)
	L3 20 MB (unified)	L2 768 KB (unified)
Memory	64 GB DDR3	5GB GDDR5
Bandwidth	51.2 GB/s	208 GB/s

Performance Analysis

Before discussing the performance of the approaches for mesh refinement, it is important to deter- mine the maximum performance that we can attain. We can estimate an upper limit by omitting the overhead related with the special processing of mesh refinement. For a complete overview of the platforms considered, see the next Table:

Figure 5 shows the performance of this benchmark on a Kepler GPU (K20c). As a reference, we also show the performance of the Sailfish software package (Januszewski, & Kostur, 2014), which includes a LBM solver based on the push scheme, and the following estimation of the ideal millions of fluid lattice updates per second (MFLUPS) (Shet, Sorathiya, Krithivasan, Deshpande, Kaul, Sherlekar, & Ansumali, 2013):

$$MFLUPS_{ideal} = \frac{B \times 10^9}{10^6 \times n \times 6 \times 8}$$

where $B \times 10^9$ is the memory bandwidth (GB/s), n depends on LBM model (DxQn), for our framework $n = 9$, D2Q9. The factor 6 is for the memory accesses, three read and write operations in the spreading step and three read and write operations in the collision step, and the factor 8 is for double precision (8 bytes). Given the features of our GPU, the ideal MFLUPS achieved is close to 580. As graphically illustrated (Figure 5), the pull approach is closer to the ideal performance than the other approaches. From these results, we have opted to use the pull scheduling in our solvers.

Figure 5. Performance of the LBM update on the NVIDIA Kepler GPU

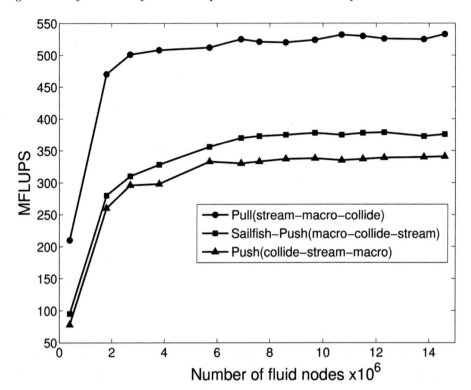

MULTI-DOMAIN MESHING

When using multi-resolution approaches (Lagrava, Malaspinas, Latt, & Chopard, 2012), a communication between the grids is needed. In the case of multi-domain methods, the communication is performed on the boundaries connecting the grids. The coupling is made in two directions: from coarse to fine and from fine to coarse grids. On the boundaries of each refinement level, after a 'collide-and-stream' operation there will be some missing information (some populations f_i are unknown on the coarse and on the fine grids) that one needs to reconstruct. For the sake of clarity, let us call C the ensemble of coarse sites and F the ensemble of all fine sites. Let us now define $x_{f\to c}$ the fine sites that are contained in F and C where the coupling from fine to coarse is performed and $x_{c\to f}$ all the sites contained in F and C where the coupling goes from coarse to fine. Let us also define

$$x^c_{f\to c} = \left\{ x \in x_{f\to c} \right\} \wedge x \notin F \,,$$

$$x^c_{c \to f} = \left\{ x \in x_{c \to f} \right\} \wedge x \notin F$$

and

$$x^c_{f \to c} = \left\{ x \in x_{f \to c} \right\} \wedge x \notin x^c_{c \to f}.$$

The coupling proposed in this work requires the grids to overlap themselves by a domain of at least one coarse cell width, as Figure 6 illustrates.

In LBM a regular Cartesian grid is used. Therefore, an abrupt transition occurs when refining the computational domain. This change of scales induces a need for a rescaling of the physical quantities between the grids. In the following, we will work in lattice units, the c subscript stands for coarse grid units, while f for fine grid units. To clarify, we chose to refine the grids by a factor of two. Thus defining dx_c and dx_f the spacial discretization of the coarse and fine grids, respectively, one has the following relation between them (Lagrava, Malaspinas, Latt, & Chopard, 2012):

$$dx_f = dx_c / 2$$

The temporal loop in the fine grid must do twice the iterations of the coarse grid. Another consequence of the convective scaling, is that the velocity and the pressure

Figure 6. Example of a multi-domain meshing

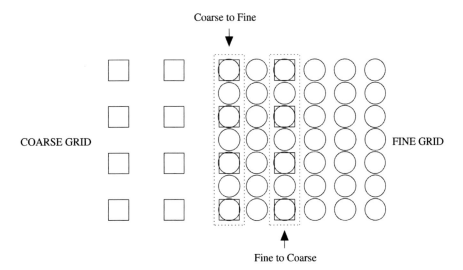

in lattice units are continuous fields on the grid transition, while the relaxation time t must be rescaled (Lagrava, Malaspinas, Latt, & Chopard, 2012).

$$t_f = 2t_c / 4 - t_c$$

The rescaling of the distribution function f_i now needs to be discussed. Each $f_{i,n}$ can be written as (Lagrava, Malaspinas, Latt, & Chopard, 2012):

$$f_{i,n} = f_i^{eq}\left(p_n, u_n\right) + f_{i,n}^{noneq}\left(\nabla u\right)$$

$f_{i,n}$ does not need any rescaling (Lagrava, Malaspinas, Latt, & Chopard, 2012), as it only depends on p and u and both are continuous between the grids. On the other hand, the non-equilibrium part $f_{i,n}^{noneq} = f_{i,f} - f_{i,n}^{eq}$ is proportional to the gradient of the velocity, it is therefore necessary to rescale it when it is moved between grids with different resolutions (Lagrava, Malaspinas, Latt, & Chopard, 2012).

$$f_{i,n}^{noneq} = \frac{2t_f}{t_c} f_{i,f}^{npneq}$$

We are now going to discuss in more detail the actual coupling procedure between the coarse and fine grids. In the $F \rightarrow C$ boundary, the fine grid has more sites than the coarse one. The necessary steps are: restrict the values, rescale them and copy them to the coarse grid. The proposed coupling is over the sites marked as $x_{f \rightarrow c}$. It is expressed by the following equation:

$$f_{i,c}\left(x_{f \rightarrow c}^c, t\right) = f_i^{eq}\left(p_f\left(X_{f \rightarrow c}^c, t\right), u_f\left(x_{f \rightarrow f^c}, t\right)\right) + \frac{2t_f}{t_c} \overline{f_{i,f}^{noneq}}\left(x_{f \rightarrow c}^c, t\right)$$

where $p_f = \sum f_{i,f}$ and $u_f = \sum e_i f_{i,f}$ and is the result of applying the restriction to the incoming fine grid values. We carry out only a filter on the non-equilibrium part of the populations f_i^{noneq} averaging over all the q lattice directions, thus obtaining the following restriction:

$$\overline{f_{i,f}^{noneq}}\left(x_{f \rightarrow c}^c, t\right) = \frac{1}{q} \sum f_{i,f}^{noneq}\left(x_{f \rightarrow c}^c + e_i, t\right)$$

The coupling over the $C \to F$ boundary ($x_{c \to f}$) is given by two different operations. If a point has a corresponding coarse site in $x_{c \to f}$ (i.e., if a computational node has both a coarse and a fine site, or in a mathematical notation if $x_f \in \to x^c_{c \to f}$) then

$$f_{i,f}\left(x^c_{cf}\right) = f^{eq}_i\left(p_c\left(x^c_{c \to f}\right), u_c\left(x^c_{c \to f}\right)\right) + \frac{t_c}{2t_f} f^{noneq}_{i,c}\left(x^c_{c \to f}\right)$$

where $p_c = \sum f_{i,c}$ and $u_c = \sum e_i f_{i,c}$ and $f^{noneq}_{i,c}$ are computed from the populations of the coarse grid. However, if the fine site does not correspond to a coarse site in $x_{c \to f}$:

$$f_{i,f}\left(x^f_{cf}\right) = f^{eq}_i\left(\overline{p_c}, \overline{u_c}\right) + \frac{t_c}{2t_f} \overline{f^{noneq}_{i,c}}$$

where $\overline{p_c}$, $\overline{u_c}$ and $\overline{f^{noneq}_{i,c}}$ are interpolated from the values where the fine and coarse sites are coincident. Next, we present a detailed version of the coupling algorithm that we implemented:

1. A 'collide-and-stream' operation is performed on the coarse grid bringing it to time $t + dt_c$. At this point the populations in $x_{f \to c}$ that were supposed to be streamed from the fine grid are unknown.
2. A 'collide-and-stream' cycle is performed on the fine grid bringing it at time $t + dt_c / 2$. The grid lacks information in $x_{c \to f}$.
3. $C \to F$ communication. One then performs a double interpolation, one in time and one in space. First the values of $\overline{p_c}$, $\overline{u_c}$ and $f^{noneq}_{i,c}$ of the coarse sites in $x_{c \to f}$ are interpolated at time $t + dt_c / 2$. Then, the values of the fine sites $p_c\left(t + dt / 2\right)$, $u_c\left(t + dt / 2\right)$ and $f^{noneq}_{i,c}\left(t + dt / 2\right)$ are interpolated in space.
4. A second 'collide-and-stream' operation is performed on the fine grid, bringing it to time $t + dt_c$. At this point, we have the information from the coarse grid to complete the fine grid in $x_{c \to f}$.
5. $F \to C$ communication. All the populations of the coarse grid in $x_{c \to f}$ are replaced according to $f_{i,c}\left(x^c_{f \to c}, t\right)$ and $\overline{f^{noneq}_{i,f}}\left(x^c_{f \to c}, t\right)$.

Figure 7. Data dependencies among the major steps of the multi-domain meshing

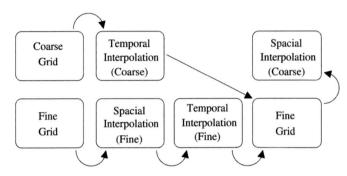

To take advantage of the maximum parallel potential of the multi-domain method, we analyze the data dependencies regarding the major steps. Some steps are independent among them, so can be computed in parallel. These data dependencies can be visualized through a state graph (Figure 7).

Implementation

Next, we introduce the main characteristics and steps about the homogeneous GPU implementation of the Multi-Domain meshing. First, the coarse grid is computed in one kernel. The number of threads is equal to the number of lattice nodes of the coarse grid. Then, a second Stream-Collide step is carried out on the nodes of the fine grid. After that, the next step consists of computing the coarse to fine communication. In particular this step is carried out on both set of points, coarse and fine, located in the coarse to fine region of the fine grid (Figure 6). This step is divided into three different interpolation operations: temporal interpolation on coarse points, spacial and temporal interpolations on fine points. The first kernel corresponds to the computation of $\overline{f_{i,c}}\left(x^c_{f \to c}, t\right)$. The next two interpolations correspond, first, to the elements $\overline{p_c}$, $\overline{u_c}$ and $\overline{f^{noneq}_{i,c}}$ (spacial-interpolation), and, second (temporal-interpolation), to the computation of $f_{i,f}\left(x^c_{c \to f}\right)$. The two first interpolations are independent between them, and so, we use a single kernel. The third interpolation is carried out by a separate kernel. After computing the first communication step, the fine grid is completed for a second Stream-Collide step. Finally, the $F \to C$ communication is carried out on the points of the coarse grid of the fine to coarse region ($f_{i,c}\left(x^c_{f \to c}, t\right)$) in a separate kernel. We have used the Dynamic Parallelism CUDA extension to implement our homogeneous GPU approach. Dynamic Parallelism enables a CUDA kernel to create and synchronize

Figure 8. Grid geometry for multi-domain meshing

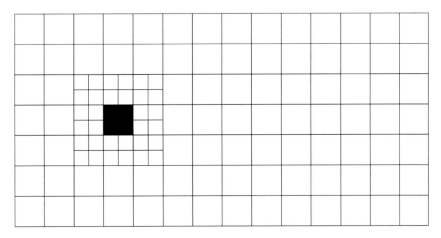

new nested work. It avoids the use of CPU for synchronizing the different steps for computing multiple kernels on the same GPU.

In the following, we present our heterogeneous scheduler as an alternative to the homogeneous counterpart. It takes advantages of both, the data independence among some steps (Figure 8) and the coupling of non balanced features of our method with our non homogeneous system. Our strategy is based on a temporal segmentation of the major steps. To clarify, Figure 9 graphically illustrates the proposed strategy. The execution of the temporal interpolation on the coarse points of the coarse to fine region ($f_{i,f}\left(x^c_{cf}\right)$) can be overlapped with the first LBM step of the fine grid, since the output of this interpolation is required by the temporal interpolation on fine points of the same region ($f_{i,f}\left(x^c_{cf}\right)$), which has to be computed after the first fine-LBM step. The fine to coarse communication step is lightly modified with respect the homogeneous GPU approach. In particular, it is implemented by a single OpenMP-pragmas/CUDA-kernel which computes, first, the spacial interpolation on fine points, and then, the temporal interpolation on the same points ($f_{i,f}\left(x^c_{cf}\right)$).

Additionally, it is possible to compute a prediction operation for the next coarse-LBM step, while all the previous steps on fine grid are being computed. However, it is necessary to compute a Stream-Collide step on points which lack information concerning coarse points of the fine to coarse region.

Although, this step is not overlapped with others, it does not suppose an important overhead, as it is only carried out on the points located in the fine to coarse region of the coarse grid. The heterogeneous approach requires more memory transfers with respect to the homogeneous GPU counterpart. In particular, the boundary

Figure 9. Heterogeneous CPU+GPU pipeline for multi-domain meshing

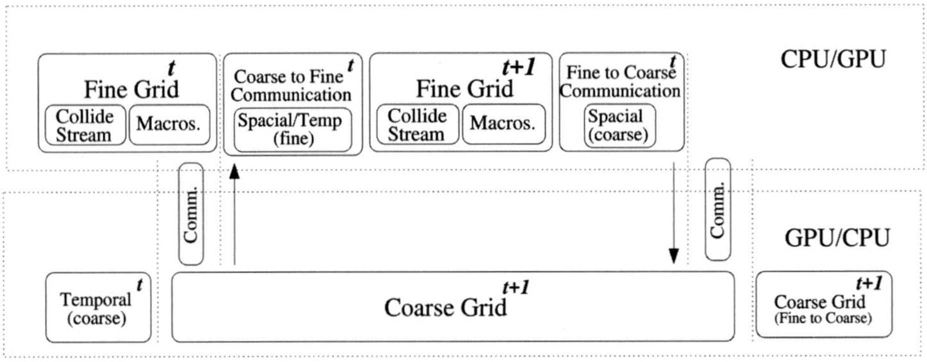

regions among grids have to be transfered from(to) both memories, main (CPU) and global (GPU). As Figure 9 shows, after computing the interpolation on the boundary region the missing information is transfered from (to) both grids. The first transfer is performed after computing the temporal interpolation (Temporal interpolation (coarse) in Figure 9). However the transfer of the points from the coarse grid located in the coarse to fine region is mostly overlapped with execution of Stream-Collide over the fine grid without causing additional overheads. After spacial interpolation ($f_{i,c}\left(x^c_{f\to c}, t\right)$ and Spacial(coarse) in Figure 9), the points from the fine grid located in the coarse locations (fine to coarse region) are transfered. This communication can be overlapped with the LBM execution over the coarse grid. These transfers involve a very small portion of the grid. Two different heterogeneous approaches arise (Figure 9), Top-GPU, in which GPU computes the top pipeline (Figure 9) and CPU the bottom one, and Top-CPU, in which CPU computes the top pipeline and the GPU the bottom one.

IRREGULAR MESHING

This section describes the numerical development behind the Irregular meshing applied over LBM (Valero-Lara, Igual, Prieto-Matías, Pinelli, & Favier, 2015). Essentially, it consists of using multiples relaxation frequencies ($d = 1 / t$) into the same lattice unit. To clarify Figures 8 and 10 illustrate a case of classical simulation (fluid-solid interaction) for uniform and Irregular grid refinement. The rescaling of physical quantities is inspired by the work described in (Lagrava, Malaspinas, Latt, & Chopard, 2012). To keep the discussion simple, we chose to refine the grid by a factor of two, as in the previous subsection. dx_c and dx_f are the spacial discretization of the coarse and fine grid respectively, so it follows that: $dx_f = dx_c / 2$.

Figure 10. Grid geometry for irregular meshing

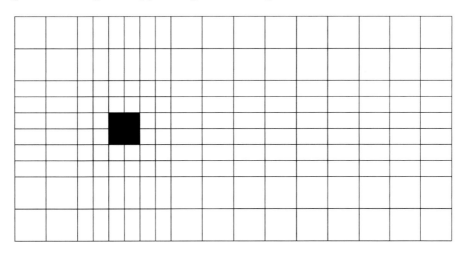

Given the aforementioned relation, the rescaling of the relaxation time now needs to be discussed. Let the Reynolds number be: $\text{Re}_n = U_n L_n / v_n$, where n refers to fine (f) or coarse (c) domain, U, L, v are the characteristic velocity, the characteristic length-scale and the viscosity, respectively. U_n and L_n are given by: $U_n = U dt_n / dx_n$ and $L_n = L / dx_n$. Forcing the Reynolds number to be independent of the grid, one obtains:

$$\text{Re}_c = \text{Re}_f \rightarrow \frac{ULdt_c}{dx_c^2 v_c} = \frac{ULdt_f}{dx_f^2 v_f}$$

Recalling that $dx_f = dx_C / 2$, the rescaling of the viscosity can be seen as:

$$v_f = \frac{dx_c}{dx_f} v_c$$

By using the relation between the relaxation frequency and viscosity: $v = c_s^2 \left(1/d - 1/2 \right)$ (Lagrava, Malaspinas, Latt, & Chopard, 2012), d_f can be written as:

$$d_f = \frac{2d_c}{4 - d_c}$$

Figure 11. Kind of refined lattices for the irregular approach. d_c, d_f *and* d_r *denoted in the figure as c, f and r respectively*

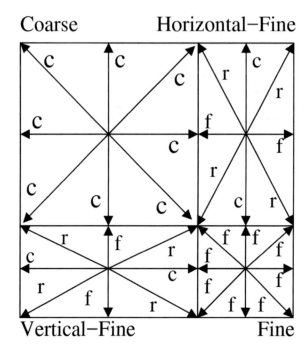

The rescaling process introduced earlier can be applied over a Nonuniform Staggered Cartesian Grid by following the scheme illustrated in Figure 11.

Depending on the lattice speed to be refined, one of the three different d factors (d_c, d_f, and d_r) is considered. Both, d_c and d_f, have been described previously. d_r is computed as arithmetic average of the other two d factors ($d_r = \left(d_c + d_f\right)/2$). This process only affects collision.

Next, we present the coupling algorithm. It consists of a simple communication from/to the different refined levels, which affects only streaming. In essence, an adaptation to the local relaxation factor is performed before computing the streaming step over those lattice functions (f_i), which need to be communicated among the different levels (boundary regions). To visualize the differences among this method with respect to standard LBM, the major steps are now detailed: Given $f_i\left(x,t\right)$ compute:

$$p = \sum f_i\left(x,t\right) \text{ and}$$

$$pu = \sum_i e_i f_i \left(x, t \right)$$

Collision stage:

$$f_i^{tmp} \left(x, t + dt \right) = f_i \left(x, t \right) - d_{ref} \left(f_i \left(x, t \right) - f_i^{eq} \left(x, t \right) \right); ref \rightarrow c, r, f$$

Depending on the lattice speed (i) and the refinement level associated to this, just one of the factors (d_c , d_r or d_f) is considered. Streaming stage: If target (f_i^t) and source (f_i^s) lattice speed share the same refinement level do:

$$f_i \left(x + c_i dt, t + dt \right) = f_i^{tmp} \left(x, t + dt \right)$$

Otherwise do:

$$f_i^t \left(x + c_i dt, t + dt \right) = f_i^s - d_{ref}^t \left(f_i^s - f_i^{eq_s} \right); ref \rightarrow c, r, f$$

For the sake of simplicity, we show the transformations between lattice unit according to the simple geometry illustrated by Figure 10. The enumeration is in agreement with respect to Figure 1.

$$f_2^c = f_2^{f(hor.)} - d_c \left(f_2^{f(hor.)} - f_2^{eq_{f(hor.)}} \right)$$

$$f_6^c = f_6^f - d_c \left(f_6^f - f_6^{eq_f} \right)$$

$$f_3^c = f_3^{f(ver.)} - d_c \left(f_3^{f(ver.)} - f_3^{eq_{f(ver)}} \right)$$

$$f_1^{f(hor.)} = f_1^c - d_f \left(f_1^c - f_1^{eq_c} \right)$$

$$f_4^{f(ver.)} = f_4^c - d_f \left(f_4^c - f_4^{eq_c} \right)$$

$$f_8^f = f_8^c - d_f \left(f_8^c - f_8^{eq_c} \right)$$

The previous case can be easily generalized for the rest of streaming cases. Unlike other refinement approaches, LBM is computed on every fluid node only once per time step. Also, it is not necessary to have additional overlapping regions between the different refined levels and complex communication (interpolation) from/to each of the levels.

Implementation

Homogeneous GPU code is quite similar to normal (no refinement) LBM implementation. Essentially, the only difference is only found in the computing of the streaming step on those regions located in the boundaries among different levels of refinement. This special processing does not affect considerably on the final performance with respect to those processes carried out in the other regions. These additional operations are computed accessing top-regions of the hierarchy of memory, so it does not require more accesses to main (CPU) or global (GPU) memory.

As in the previous grid refinement approach, the CPU+GPU collaboration can also allows us to achieve a higher performance. Given the differences found among both approaches, we opted to use a different implementation that simplifies code development. Figure 12 graphically illustrates the new partitioning. We do not pay a particular attention to different levels of refinement. In fact, the workload distribution is carried out as though our fluid field were uniform (without any level of refinement). Essentially, it consists on splitting the computational domain into two sub-domains. Every time step, it is necessary to exchange the boundaries

Figure 12. Heterogeneous CPU+GPU pipeline for irregular meshing

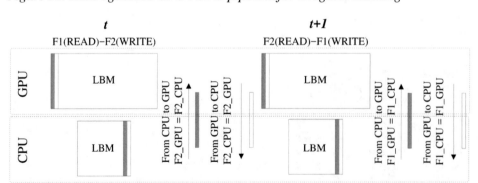

between both sub-domains. To reduce the penalty of such data transfers, we update the boundaries between sub-domains at the beginning of each time step. With this transformation, it is possible to exchange those boundaries with asynchronous operations that are overlapped with the update of the rest of the sub-domain. In our target simulations, the CPU sub-domain is much smaller that the GPU counterpart. To improve performance, the size of both sub-domains is adjusted to balance the loads between both processors.

NUMERICAL VALIDATION

To validate the grid refinement approaches previously presented, we carry out a widely known and extended test scenario, which consists of simulating a flow past a square cylinder. Three different LBM implementations are compared: no refinement, where no refined fluid domain is considered, multi-domain meshing and irregular meshing. The finest domain is located around the square cylinder. In the irregular approach, two additional refined regions are necessary, one located in the top-bottom around the main refined region, and another located in left-right of the cylinder. Figures 8 and 10 graphically illustrate the different grid geometries with respect to multi-domain and irregular approaches. For the cylinder diameter D, the grid flow is set as $21D \times 14D$.

Table 2. Comparison between the numerical results obtained by this work and other previous studies

Reference	C_D	Reference	C_D	Reference	C_D
Simulation:		Experimental:		This work:	
(Verstappen, & Veldman, 1997)	2,09	(Lyn, & Rodi, 1994)	2,1	No refinement	2,48
(Pourquie, Breuer, & Rodi, 1997)	2,2			Multi-Domain Meshing	2,02
(Murakami, & Mochida, 1995)	2,05			Irregular Meshing	2,01
(Wang, & Vanka, 1997)	2,03				
(Nozama, & Kawamura, 1997)	2,62				
(Kawashima, & Kawamura, 1997)	2,72				

Figure 13. Streamlines for flow past a square cylinder at Re = 100

Several Reynolds numbers (50, 100, 150 and 200) have been tested for the same configuration. In LBM the Reynolds number ($\mathrm{Re} = UL\,/\,v$) is related to the relaxation time t as: $t = \left[(2 \times UL)\,/\,\mathrm{Re}\right] + 0,5$ (Marié, Ricot, & Sagaut, 2009). When the Reynolds number is lower than 100, there is no vortex structure formed during the evolution, i.e., the flow field is laminar and steady. In contrast, for a Reynolds number of 100, the symmetric rectangular zones disappear and an asymmetric pattern is formed. The vorticity is shed behind the circular cylinder, and vortex structures are formed downstream. This phenomenon is well-capture by both approaches. This phenomenon is graphically illustrated in Figure 13.

One important dimensionless number is studied, the drag ($C_D = F_D\,/\,0,5pU^2D$) coefficient. F_D corresponds to the resistance force of the square cylinder to the fluid in the streamwise direction, p is the density of the fluid, and U is the velocity of inflow. In order to verify the numerical results, the coefficients were calculated and compared with the results of previous studies:

PERFORMANCE EVALUATION

Multi-Domain Meshing

Taking into account the high number of case- study with particular requirements in terms of size of the fine domains over the size of coarse domain/s, we have carried out several synthetic cases, which are composed by 4 different ratios, which simulates several real scenarios of academia and industrial interest; $fine_{size}\,/\,coarse_{size}$ for one refined-level ($0,25; 0,5; 1; 2$), and

$$(fine_{size}^{2^{nd}level}\,/\,fine_{size}^{1^{st}level}; fine_{size}^{1^{st}level}\,/\,coarse_{size})$$

for two refined-levels

$$(\,(0,1;0,25),(0,25;0,5),(0,5;1),(1;2)\,).$$

A ratio equals 0,25 means that the coarse domain is 4 times bigger than fine domain, and a ratio equals 2 means that the fine grid is 2 times bigger than the coarse domain. Three implementations are studied, one homogeneous GPU and two heterogeneous Multicore-GPU, Top-GPU and Top-Multicore, previously introduced. Figure 14 and 15 graphically illustrate the performance achieved in terms of MFLUPS. A larger fine domain exhibits a much lower performance, as fine grids are computed twice (first refined level) or four times (second refined level) per time step. Better results are reached for smaller fine domains.

The Top-Multicore approach reaches a good performance for small fine domains, achieving a good balancing for ratios equal to 0,25 and $(0,1;0,25)$. However, worse gains are achieved in the rest of experiments. A different trend arises for the Top-GPU approach. This load distribution is very beneficial for greather fine grids. For balanced domains (1 and (1; 2)), the heterogeneous Top-GPU implementation is approximately 30% and 15% faster over the homogeneous GPU counterpart for one

Figure 14. One refined level performance, in terms of MFLUPS, achieved by the three approaches, homogeneous GPU, heterogeneous Top-Multocore and heterogeneous Top-GPU

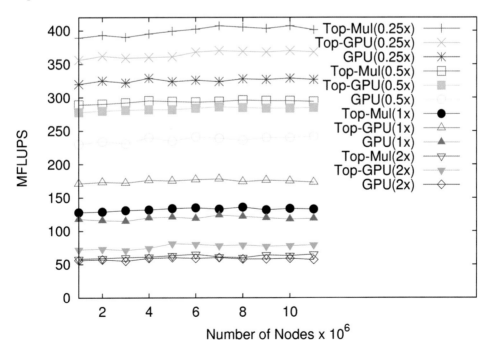

refined level and two refined levels respectively. The difference among the regions of both grids has an important impact in performance, which degrades or increases the whole performance, so that both heterogeneous implementations, Top-Multicore and Top-GPU, present a better performance with respect to the other depending on this ratio. Figure 16 and 17 graphically illustrate the gain of both heterogeneous approaches over the homogeneous GPU, for each ratio. The dealing of multiple domains over GPU degrades the benefit of using the Top-GPU approach. This reduces the benefit of using our heterogeneous approach, at least in those case-study with greater fine grids. Despite the overheads aforementioned, our heterogeneous implementation is able to outperform the homogeneous counterpart in all cases evaluated.

Irregular Meshing

Next, we evaluate the two different approaches, homogeneous GPU and heterogeneous CPU+GPU, for the Irregular meshing. As expected, a fall in performance is reached by increasing the size of the refined region (Figure 18). However, this fall is not so abrupt as in the previous approach. Increasing the size of the refined sub-domain, we also increase the size of those regions which are in need of a special processing. These regions are located in the boundaries among the different sub-domains, full-refined, partial-refined and non-refined. Unlike the previous subsection, here, even considering a big refined region, is reachable high MFLUPS ratios, so the influence of the size of refined region is not so important. The use of CPU helps us to outperform the performance achieved by the homogeneous GPU implementation. In particular, it is achieved an extra benefit of around 20, in terms of % (Figure 19). Unlike the Multi-Domain approach, the contribution of the CPU is exactly the same in every case and does not vary a lot regarding the size of the refined sub-domain.

Multi-Domain Meshing Against Irregular Meshing

In this section, we focused on presenting the main differences found among our two methodologies, Multi-Domain Mesing and Irregular Meshing. Essentially, the differences can be divided into three different subjects, memory requirements, performance, and programmability.

We start to analyze the differences in term of memory requirements. As graphically illustrated in Figure 10, the Irregular approach is in need of a more number of lattice nodes with respect to the Multi-Domain approach. This is due to sub-domains around the full-refined sub-domain. The Irregular approach uses 'partial' refinement on

Figure 15. Two refined levels performance, in terms of MFLUPS, achieved by the three approaches, homogeneous GPU, heterogeneous Top-Multocore and heterogeneous Top-GPU

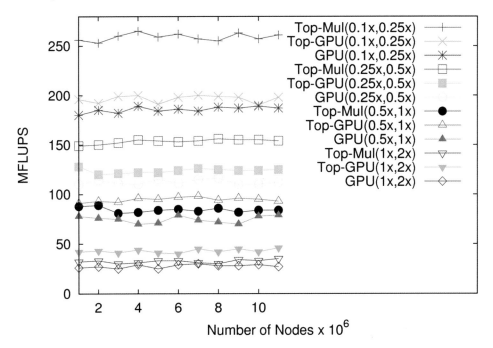

these sub-domains. For the ratios considered in this work $(0,25; 0,5; 1; 2)$, the additional lattice nodes (in terms of %) required by the

Irregular approach with respect the Multi-Domain counterpart corresponds to

$$0,25 \rightarrow 36; 0,5 \rightarrow 43; 1 \rightarrow 50; 2 \rightarrow 48.$$

As far as we can see in Figure 18, the percentage of additional lattice nodes has an important influence over the performance for the Irregular implementation. Next, we analyze the performance reached by both approaches. It is clear that the Irregular approach obtains higher MFLUPS ratios (Figure 18) than the Multi-Domain approach (Figures 14 and 15) for the same number of lattice nodes. Also, it is remarkable that the extra benefit of using a heterogeneous CPU+GPU implementation is greater in the Multi-Domain approach than in the Irregular approach, as an average benefit around 20, in terms of %, is reached by the last approach (Figure 19) against the peak benefit of around 30 reached by the Multi-Domain counterpart (Figures 16 and 17). This is basically due to that in the Multi-Domain approach, the CPU-GPU

Figure 16. One refined level gain, in terms of percentage, of each of the both heterogeneous implementations, Top-Multicore and Top-GPU, against the homogeneous GPU implementation

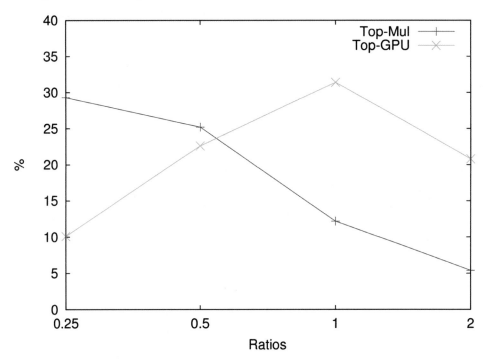

communication is mostly overlapped with CPU/GPU execution. As we have explained earlier, the Irregular approach is in need of a higher number of lattice nodes with respect the Multi-Domain approach for the same case-study (simulation). In this sense and for the sake of clarity, we have included an additional study which compares both approaches for the same case-study. For this purpose, we have run several tests for a Multi-Domain fluid composed by 6×10^6 lattice nodes using different refinement ratios ($0,25;0,5;1;2$). The size for the Irregular fluid changes according the ratio to be dealt.

In this study, we have considered the heterogeneous CPU+GPU implementation for both approaches (Figures 9 and 12). In particular, for the Multi-Domain implementation, we have used the most beneficial approach according the ratio. This means that for ratios 0,25 and 0,5, we used the Top-CPU approach, and the Top-GPU approach for the rest of tests. Figure 20 graphically illustrates the time consumed by both implementations for the same case-study. The Multi-Domain implementation (Top-CPU) turns out to be lightly faster than the Irregular implementation for a ratio equals 0,25. However, the Irregular implementation is proven to be the fastest

Figure 17. Two refined levels performance, in terms of MFLUPS, achieved by the three approaches, homogeneous GPU, heterogeneous Top-Multocore and heterogeneous Top-GPU

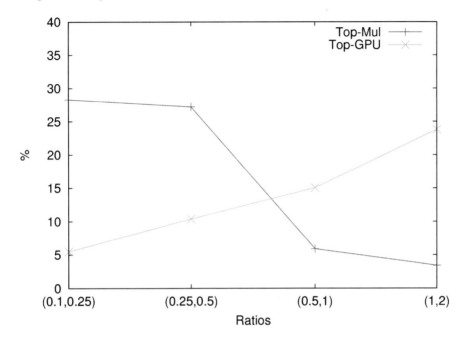

Figure 18. Performance, in terms of MFLUPS, achieved by the two approaches, homogeneous GPU and heterogeneous CPU+GPU

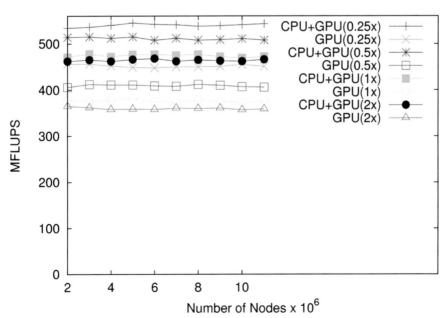

143

Figure 19. Gain, in terms of percentage, of the heterogeneous CPU+GPU implementation against the homogeneous GPU implementation

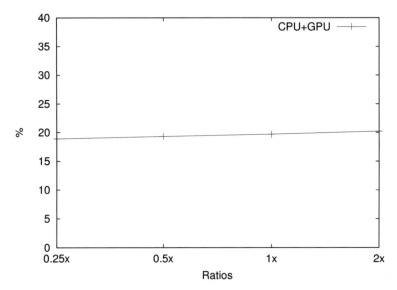

implementation for the rest of tests, even being in need of a higher number of lattice nodes. The bigger the ratio, bigger the benefit of using the Irregular implementation (Figure 21). The results obtained in this study can be extrapolated to other case-study.

Finally, we analyze the effort of implementing each of the approaches studied in this work. While, the Multi-Domain implementation is composed by seven different operations and two memory transfers among CPU and GPU, the Irregular implementation is composed by one operation to be executed on both architectures, CPU and GPU, and one memory transfer. Also, two different approaches arise in the Multi-Domain implementation, Top-CPU and Top-GPU. The programmers must take into account the ratio to be dealt in order to select what is the best choice among the two previous approaches. By contrast the Irregular implementation is quite similar to a normal LBM implementation. Essentially, the differences are found in those regions located in the boundaries among full-refined, partial-refined, and non-refined sub-domains, where a special processing must be carried out. We basically implement this additional processing to address with Irregular meshing just adding some if-else statements. Also, this processing only affects to streaming step and is not in need of a higher number of accesses to main (CPU) or global (GPU) memory, which is the main bottleneck in this kind of applications. Also, the communication among both, CPU and GPU, is considerably easier to implement. In conclusion, the Irregular implementation turns out to be considerably easier to implement and more transparent from a programmer point of view.

CONCLUSION

We have studied two different methods, Multi-Domain and Irregular, to deal with mesh refinement over LBM simulations. The numerical accuracy of these methods is in agreement with other studies/methods of the literature (state-of-the-art). Before focusing on mesh refinement methods, we presented different LBM implementations to determine the maximum performance that we can reach, concluding that the performance reached by the pull-SoA approach is situated closest to ideal performance with respect to others. Using this approach to implement LBM, we proposed and developed two implementations (homogeneous GPU and heterogeneous CPU+GPU) on each methodologies. Each method/implementation presents its own advantages and disadvantages with respect to the other. In general, the Multi-Domain method/implementation requires a lower number of lattice nodes. It allows us to execute bigger simulations over the same platform. However, the Irregular method/implementation is considerably much easier to implement. We have proven that the Irregular implementation is much faster than the Multi-Domain implementation for the same case-study, except for those simulations with a very small refined region, in which the performance reached by both approaches is equivalent. The Irregular implementation is able to execute problems with a big refined region 4.5x faster than the Multi-Domain counterpart. As conclusion, the Irregular meshing not only

Figure 20. Execution time consumed by both approaches for different ratios

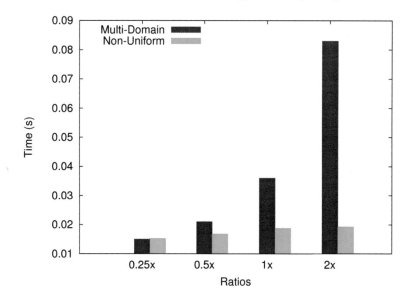

Figure 21. Speedup reached by both approaches for different ratios

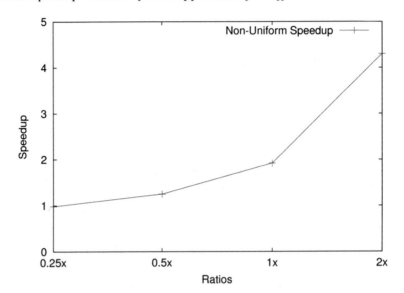

offers a high MFLUPS ratio, even on simulations with big refined sud-domains, but also it is an affordable methodology to implement mesh refinement on LBM.

REFERENCES

Alexandrov, V., Lees, M., Krzhizhanovskaya, V., Dongarra, J., Sloot, P., Crimi, G., ... Tripiccione, R. (2013). Early Experience on Porting and Running a Lattice Boltzmann Code on the Xeon-phi Co-Processor. *Procedia Computer Science*, *18*, 551–560. doi:10.1016/j.procs.2013.05.219

Anderson, J. D. (1995). *Computational fluid dynamics - the basics with applications*. McGraw-Hill.

Anderson, J. D., Menter, F. R., Dick, E., Degrez, G., & Vierendeels, J. (2013). *Introduction to computational fluid dynamics*. Von Karman Institute for Fluid Dynamics.

Bernaschi, M., Fatica, M., Melchiona, S., Succi, S., & Kaxiras, E. (2010). A flexible high- performance lattice boltzmann gpu code for the simulations of fluid flows in complex geometries. *Concurrency Computa.: Pract. Exper.*, *22*(1), 1–14. doi:10.1002/cpe.1466

Fakhari, A., & Lee, T. (2014). Finite-difference lattice boltzmann method with a block-structured adaptive-mesh-refinement technique. *Physical Review*, *89*(033310). PMID:24730970

Favier, J., Revell, A., & Pinelli, A. (2014). A Lattice Boltzmann–Immersed Boundary method to simulate the fluid interaction with moving and slender flexible object. *Journal of Computational Physics*, *261*(0), 145–161. doi:10.1016/j.jcp.2013.12.052

Feichtinger, C., Habich, J., Kstler, H., Rude, U., & Aoki, T. (2015). Performance modeling and analysis of heterogeneous lattice boltzmann simulations on cpugpu clusters. *Parallel Computing*, *46*(0), 1–13. doi:10.1016/j.parco.2014.12.003

Gross, E., Bhatnagar, P., & Krook, M. (1954). A model for collision processes in gases. I: Small amplitude processes in charged and neutral one-component system. *Physical Review*, *94*(3), 511–525. doi:10.1103/PhysRev.94.511

He, X., & Luo, L. S. (1997). A priori derivation of the lattice boltzmann equation. *Physical Review*, 55.

Januszewski, M., & Kostur, M. (2014). Sailfish: A flexible multi-GPU implementation of the lattice Boltzmann method. *Computer Physics Communications*, *185*(9), 2350–2368. doi:10.1016/j.cpc.2014.04.018

Kandhai, D., Vidal, D. J. E., Hoekstra, A. G., Hoefsloot, H., Iedema, P., & Sloot, P. M. A. (1998). A comparison between lattice-boltzmann and finite-element simulations of fluid flow in static mixer reactors. *International Journal of Modern Physics*, *09*(08), 1123–1128. doi:10.1142/S0129183198001035

Kawashima, N., & Kawamura, H. (1997). Numerical analysis of les of flow past a long square cylinder. In *Direct and Large-Eddy Simulation II*. Springer. doi:10.1007/978-94-011-5624-0_40

Kollmannsberger, S., Geller, S., Dster, A., Tlke, J., Sorger, C., Krafczyk, M., & Rank, E. (2009). Fixed-grid fluid-structure interaction in two dimensions based on a partitioned lattice boltzmann and p-fem approach. *International Journal for Numerical Methods in Engineering*, *79*(7), 817–845. doi:10.1002/nme.2581

Lagrava, D., Malaspinas, O., Latt, J., & Chopard, B. (2012). Advances in multi-domain lattice boltzmann grid refinement. *Journal of Computational Physics*, *231*(14), 4808–4822. doi:10.1016/j.jcp.2012.03.015

Lyn, D. A., & Rodi, W. (1994). The flapping shear layer formed by flow separation from the forward corner of a square cylinder. *Journal of Fluid Mechanics*, *5*(267), 353–376. doi:10.1017/S0022112094001217

Malaspinas, O., & Sagaut, P. (2012). Consistent subgrid scale modelling for lattice boltzmann methods. *Journal of Fluid Mechanics*, *700*, 514–542. doi:10.1017/jfm.2012.155

Marié, S., Ricot, D., & Sagaut, P. (2009). Comparison between lattice boltzmann method and navier-stokes high order schemes for computational aeroacoustics. *Journal of Computational Physics*, *228*(4), 1056–1070. doi:10.1016/j.jcp.2008.10.021

Mohamad, A. A. (2011). *The lattice boltzmann method–fundamental and engineering applications with computer codes*. Springer.

Murakami, S., & Mochida, A. (1995). On turbulent vortex shedding flow past 2d square cylinder predicted by CFD. *Journal of Wind Engineering and Industrial Aerodynamics*, *54-55*(0), 191–211. doi:10.1016/0167-6105(94)00043-D

Nozawa, K., & Tamura, T. (1997). Les of flow past a square cylinder using embedded meshes. In *Direct and Large-Eddy Simulation II*. Springer. doi:10.1007/978-94-011-5624-0_39

Peskin, C. S. (2002). The immersed boundary method. *Acta Numerica*, *11*, 479–517. doi:10.1017/S0962492902000077

Pohl, T., Kowarchik, M., Wilke, J., Rüde, U., & Iglberger, K. (2003). Optimization and profiling of the cache performance of parallel lattice boltzmann codes. *Parallel Processing Letters*, *13*(4), 549–560. doi:10.1142/S0129626403001501

Pourquie, M., Breuer, M., & Rodi, W. (1997). Computed test case: Square cylinder. In *Direct and Large-Eddy Simulation II*. Springer. doi:10.1007/978-94-011-5624-0_34

Qian, Y. H., D'Humires, D., & Lallemand, P. (1992). Lattice bgk models for navier-stokes equation. *Europhysics Letters*, *17*(6), 479–484. doi:10.1209/0295-5075/17/6/001

Rinaldi, P. R., Dari, E. A., Vénere, M. J., & Clausse, A. (2012). A Lattice-Boltzmann solver for 3D fluid simulation on GPU. *Simulation Modelling Practice and Theory*, *25*, 163–171. doi:10.1016/j.simpat.2012.03.004

Schnherr, M., Kucher, K., Geier, M., Stiebler, M., Freudiger, S., & Krafczyk, M. (2011). Multi-thread implementations of the lattice boltzmann method on non-uniform grids for CPUs and GPUs. *Computers & Mathematics with Applications (Oxford, England)*, *61*(12), 3730–3743. doi:10.1016/j.camwa.2011.04.012

Shet A. G., Siddharth K., Sorathiya S. H., Deshpande A. M., Sher-lekar S. D., Kaul B., & Ansumali S. (2013). On Vectorization for Lattice Based Simulations. *International Journal of Modern Physics*.

Succi, S. (2001). *The lattice Boltzmann equation: for fluid dynamics and beyond.* New York: Oxford university press.

Swarztrauber, P. N. (1974). A direct Method for the Discrete Solution of Separable Elliptic Equations. *SIAM Journal on Numerical Analysis*, *11*(6), 1136–1150. doi:10.1137/0711086

Valero-Lara, P. (2014). Accelerating solid-fluid interaction based on the immersed boundary method on multicore and GPU architectures. *The Journal of Supercomputing*, *70*(2), 799–815. doi:10.1007/s11227-014-1262-2

Valero-Lara, P., Igual, F. D., Prieto-Matías, M., Pinelli, A., & Favier, J. (2015). Accelerating fluid–solid simulations (Lattice-Boltzmann & Immersed-Boundary) on heterogeneous architectures. *Journal of Computational Science*, *39*(67), 259–270.

Valero-Lara, P., & Jansson, J. (2015). A non-uniform staggered cartesian grid approach for lattice-boltzmann method. *Procedia Computer Science*, *51*, 296–305. doi:10.1016/j.procs.2015.05.245

Valero-Lara, P., & Jansson, J. (2017). Heterogeneous CPU+GPU approaches for mesh refinement over Lattice-Boltzmann simulations. *Concurrency and Computation*, *29*(7), e3919. doi:10.1002/cpe.3919

Valero-Lara, P., Pinelli, A., Favier, J., & Prieto-Matías, M. (2012). Block Tridiagonal Solvers on Heterogeneous Architectures. In *Proceedings of 10th IEEE International Symposium on Parallel and Distributed Processing with Applications Workshop* (pp. 609-616). IEEE.

Valero-Lara, P., Pinelli, A., & Prieto-Matías, M. (2014). Fast finite difference Poisson solvers on heterogeneous architectures. *Computer Physics Communications*, *185*(4), 1265–1272. doi:10.1016/j.cpc.2013.12.026

Valero-Lara, P., Pinelli, A., & Prieto-Matías, M. (2014). Accelerating Solid-fluid Interaction using Lattice-boltzmann and Immersed Boundary Coupled Simulations on Heterogeneous Platforms. In *Proceedings of the International Conference on Computational Science* (pp. 50-61). Academic Press. doi:10.1016/j.procs.2014.05.005

Verstappen, R. W. C. P., & Veldman, A. E. P. (1997). Fourth-order dns of flow past a square cylinder: First results. In *Direct and Large-Eddy Simulation II*. Springer. doi:10.1007/978-94-011-5624-0_35

Wang, G., & Vanka, S. P. (1997). Les of flow over a square cylinder. In *Direct and Large-Eddy Simulation II*. Springer. doi:10.1007/978-94-011-5624-0_37

Wellein, G., Zeiser, T., Hager, G., & Donath, S. (2006). On the single processor performance of simple lattice boltzmann kernels. *Computers & Fluids*, *35*(89), 910–919. doi:10.1016/j.compfluid.2005.02.008

Wendt, J. F., & Anderson, J. D. (2008). *Computational fluid dynamics: An introduction.* Springer.

Wu Z., Xu Z., Kim O., & Alber M. (2014). Three-dimensional multi-scale model of deformable platelets adhesion to vessel wall in blood flow. Philosophical Transactions of the Royal Society of London A: Mathematical. *Physical and Engineering Sciences, 372*(2021).

Yoon, D. H., Yang, K. S., & Choi, C. B. (1994). Flow past a square cylinder with an angle of incidence. *Physics of Fluids*, *22*(4).

Zhou, H., Mo, G., Wu, F., Zhao, J., Rui, M., & Cen, K. (2012). GPU implementation of lattice boltzmann method for flows with curved boundaries. *Computer Methods in Applied Mechanics and Engineering*, *225228*(0), 65–73. doi:10.1016/j.cma.2012.03.011

O. Zikanov (Ed.). (2010). *Essential computational fluid dynamics.* John Wiley & Sons.

KEY TERMS AND DEFINITIONS

CPU: A computer architecture composed by large cache memories. It is also known as low latency-oriented processors.

Drag Coefficient: A dimensionless quantity used to compute the resistance (drag) of an object in a fluid environment. This coefficient indicates aerodynamic of an object or of a particular surface area.

GPU: A computer architecture composed by a large number of cores and small cache memories. It is also known as throughput-oriented processors.

Heterogeneous: Those systems where more than one kind of processor, typically CPUs and GPUs coexist. These systems attempt to gain performance by adding the different computer architectures for specialized processing capabilities.

Multicore: A single computational component composed of two or more independent processing units (cores). Each of the units integrates its own arithmetic-logic and control units. All cores can access an integrated shared memory. It is also known as low-latency oriented processors.

Reynold (Re) Number: A dimensionless quantity used in fluid mechanics to predict flow patterns in fluid flow simulations.

SoA: Structure of array, a typical data layout used to exploit vectorization.

Thread: In computer science, a thread is known as a sequence of instructions. On a parallel processor, such as multicore or manycore, multiple threads can be executed simultaneously.

Viscosity: A quantity used to measure the "diffusion" of momentum in the direction of flow.

Chapter 5
Lattice Boltzmann Method for Sparse Geometries:
Theory and Implementation

Tadeusz Tomczak
Wrocław University of Science and Technology, Poland

ABSTRACT

This chapter presents the challenges and techniques in the efficient LBM implementations for sparse geometries. The first part contains a review of applications requiring support for sparse geometries including industry, geology, and life sciences. For each category, a short description of a geometry characteristic and the typical LBM extensions are provided. The second part describes implementations for single-core and parallel computers. Four main methods allowing for the reduction of memory usage and computational complexity are presented: hierarchical grids, tiles, and two techniques based on the indirect addressing (the fluid index array and the connectivity matrix). For parallel implementations, the advantages and disadvantages of the different methods of domain decomposition and workload balancing are discussed.

INTRODUCTION

One of the features of many LBM implementations is the use of uniform grids for the computational domain. This, connected with the spatial and temporal locality of the Boltzmann transport equation, allows for the use of simple data structures (multidimensional matrices), an automated mesh preparation even for complex geometries, and for trivial parallelization of computations. Unfortunately, the uniform

DOI: 10.4018/978-1-5225-4760-0.ch005

grid requires special techniques to correctly and efficiently handle geometries with borders of complex shape or with many areas without fluid (sparse geometries), especially on parallel machines. Since many real geometries belong to both the above-mentioned classes, these issues are especially important considering that even current desktop systems are based on processors performing computations in a parallel, single-instruction-multiple-data (SIMD) way.

Two main issues must be treated to efficiently simulate sparse geometries: a proper boundary conditions treatment for complex shapes and an efficiency of implementation (memory usage, performance and scalability on multiprocessor machines). This work concerns primarily the later issue, especially in the context of the geometry impact. In fact, almost all LBM implementations specialised for sparse, complex geometries focus primarily on decreasing the performance penalties and an additional memory usage caused by storing and processing of solid nodes.

One of the main geometry parameters affecting performance is a geometry porosity defined as

$$\varphi = \frac{fluid\_volume}{total\_volume}.$$ (1)

In practice, due to the space discretization, the porosity is computed as a ratio of the number of fluid LBM nodes to the total number of nodes. In addition to porosity, also its complementary coefficient, solidity, equal to

$$s = \frac{solid\_volume}{total\_volume},$$ (2)

may be useful. Notice, that both $\varphi, s \in \langle 0,1 \rangle$ and $\varphi + s = 1$.

The range of porosity values of real sparse geometries can vary greatly (see Fig. 1). The porosity of engineering materials is usually below 70% and in many cases can be much lower; for example, the typical porosity of hydrocarbon-bearing sandstones is between 5% and 35% (O'Connor & Fredrich, 1999). In medical geometries (vascular systems) the porosity may be even as low as 0.3% (Godenschwager, Schornbaum, Bauer, Köstler, & Rüde, 2013).

Besides porosity, many other parameters can be found for a sparse geometry including permeability, dispersion, tortuosity, percolation and surface/volume ratio to name a few. Nevertheless, their impact on implementation performance or memory usage is not known yet.

The geometry porosity may be used to decide whether an implementation specialised for sparse geometries should give higher performance, but it may be

Figure 1. Examples of geometries with different porosity: cavity 3D benchmark (left, $\varphi = 1$), Berea sandstone from (Dong, 2008) (center, $\varphi = 0.2$), and aorta with coarctation from (Nita, Itu, & Suciu, 2013) (right, $\varphi = 0.09$); only non-solid nodes are shown

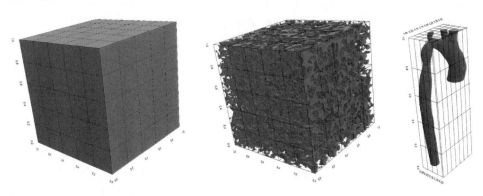

difficult to give a clear distinction. Additionally, other factors must be considered as well. Classical LBM implementations with multidimensional matrices used to represent the domain may be a reasonable solution, especially for geometries with high porosity or when a low code complexity is much more important than performance or memory usage. Moreover, some techniques used to increase performance for sparse geometries, especially those based on indirect addressing, introduce an overhead about 100% per fluid node compared to the classical implementation. Thus, when the porosity is above 50% then the specialised implementation may give the lower performance and higher memory usage than the simple, classical version. On the other side, many widely available LBM implementations optimised for sparse geometries offer a wide variety of functionalities, thus their use may be justified even for dense geometries, where a performance penalty is likely to be observed. Moreover, techniques based on multidimensional, hierarchical grids may be equally successful for both dense and sparse geometries.

This chapter presents both the challenges faced in various LBM applications requiring simulations for geometries with a large number of solid nodes and the techniques used in the high-performance LBM implementations optimised for sparse geometries. The first section "Applications" shows typical problems solved using LBM simulations in sparse geometries and contains short characteristic of geometries occurring in each application area. Separate subsections are devoted to artificially generated geometries, packed beds, geology and oil industry, fuel cells, life sciences, and other various applications. The second section "Implementation Techniques" demonstrates techniques for efficient implementation on single-core and parallel computers. Subsection "Data Structures" presents four methods allowing for the reduction of memory usage and computational complexity: the connectivity matrix, the fluid index array, hierarchical grids, and tiles. Subsection "Domain Partitioning and Workload Balancing" discusses advantages and disadvantages of domain decomposition and workload balancing methods used in parallel implementations. Section "Conclusion" concludes the chapter.

APPLICATIONS

Below, the commonly occurring applications of LBM simulations for sparse geometries are presented. For each of the described classes, a short information about both physical models and characteristic of geometry is provided. Notice that even distant areas of applications use similar techniques and geometries. This is especially visible for artificial geometries, which are widely used in many real cases.

Artificial Geometries

Artificially generated porous geometries were used as the first examples showing potential advantages of LBM in simulations for complex geometries. They are also a good approximation of real geometries met in different applications. Notice that many of the presented models of sparse media use some placement of rectangular or circular obstacles.

Flow simulations in porous media were first done for lattice gas automatons. (Balasubramanian, Hayot, & Saam, 1987) used a hexagonal lattice-gas model with randomly placed scatterers and showed that the Darcy's law was obtained. Also, the state-of-the-art (Rothman, 1988) paper presented the good accordance with Darcy's law of the cellular automaton simulation results for a manually constructed complex 2D geometry. LBM simulations of a flow through a 3D porous medium were presented in (Succi, Foti, & Higuera, 1989). The geometry was a random sequence of elementary blocks of four units in size distributed in a way that no free pore smaller than 4 x 4 lattice units in cross-section can appear. Additionally, the authors reported that to reproduce the fluid behaviour with sufficient accuracy, even channels as small as 4×4 lattice units are sufficient. Permeability calculations based on LBM flow simulations in three-dimensional porous geometries were presented in (Cancelliere, Chang, Foti, Rothman, & Succi, 1990). The geometries were constructed by the random positioning of penetrable spheres of equal radii. LBM simulations of non-Newtonian fluid flows through 2D porous media with rectangular obstacles (a network of channels) were analysed in (Aharonov & Rothman, 1993), (Boek, Chin, & Coveney, 2003) and (Sullivan, Gladden, & Johns, 2006b). (Adrover & Giona, 1996) used 2D LBM to calculate permeability of the deterministic fractals and fractal percolation lattices. These results were extended in (Singh & Mohanty,

2000) to exponentially correlated 3D porous media generated by a stochastic process. Several simulation results for the tortuosity, effective porosity and permeability of a 2D porous medium were shown in (Koponen, Kataja, & Timonen, 1997) and (Koponen, Kataja, Timonen, & Kandhai, 1998). The medium was created by either regularly or randomly placing rectangles of equal size with unrestricted overlap. Additionally, in (Koponen, Kataja, Timonen, & Kandhai, 1998), the flow through a large random 3D fibre web constructed using the growth algorithm (structures closely resembling those of paper and nonwoven fabrics) was analysed as well. (Bernsdorf, Durst, & Schäfer, 1999) compared accuracy and performance of the lattice Boltzmann automata to the finite volume method (FVM) for channels with the different sets of regularly placed square obstacles. Simulations of dispersion in the random sphere packings generated with a hard-sphere Monte Carlo technique were presented in (Maier, Kroll, Bernard, Howington, Peters, & Davis, 2000). (Martys & Hagedorn, 2002) analysed permeability as a function of the distance between two parallel planes. Authors reported correct results even when the distance was only one node because LBM accurately calculates the net flux rate of a fluid. The parallel Monte Carlo algorithm was used in (Schure, Maier, Kroll, & Davis, 2002) to build a geometric model of a liquid chromatographic column. Simulations of the three-dimensional reacting flow were shown in (Freund, Zeiser, Huber, Klemm, Brenner, Durst, & Emig, 2003), where the authors used a two-step algorithm (raining and compressing) to synthetically generate packing of spherical particles. Two-phase flow through the geometry of the randomly arranged spheres from (Yang, Miller, & Turcoliver, 1996) was presented in (Pan, Hilpert, & Miller, 2004). (Geller, Krafczyk, Tölke, Turek, & Hron, 2006) compared accuracy and computational efficiency of LBM and the finite element method (FEM) for simulations of incompressible laminar flow through a channel filled with regularly placed cylindrical obstacles. (Yoshino, Hotta, Hirozane, & Endo, 2007) presented the non-Newtonian fluid flows in a three-dimensional porous structure built from rectangular bodies. Authors used LBM extended with the determination of shear-dependent viscosity of the fluid by using a variable parameter related to the local shear rate. Two-dimensional LBM simulations of flow through randomly placed rectangular obstacles with free overlapping were presented in (Nabovati & Sousa, 2007) and (Nabovati & Sousa, 2008). Detailed performance analysis of LBM simulations of flow through a porous medium with low porosity on vector supercomputer NEC SX8 and PC cluster were shown in (Axner, Bernsdorf, Zeiser, Lammers, Linxweiler, & Hoekstra, 2008). (Nabovati, Llewellin, & Sousa, 2009) studied fluid flow and computed permeability values for two geometries: a two-dimensional hexagonal array of infinite, parallel cylinders, and for a three-dimensional structure of the randomly oriented, straight, cylindrical fibres of constant diameter placed with free overlapping (the fibre overlapping allowed to model the full range of porosities). LBM simulations for the Darcy and non-Darcy flow regimes in the 2D channel filled with randomly placed cylinders were shown in (Chai, Shi, Lu, & Guo, 2010). (Vidal, Roy, & Bertrand, 2010a) used the large porous hexagonal packing of cylinders and a random packing of polydisperse spheres to analyse the performance of a fast implementation of BGK LBM. (Nejat, Abdollahi, & Vahidkhah, 2011) applied a second order non-Newtonian Power-Law LBM to simulate 2D non-Newtonian flows (such as mud flow) over confined cylindrical objects. Such flow fields happen in the support structures, polymer processing operations, applications of thin cylinders and wires as measurement probes and sensors, and in tubular heat exchangers. (Ohta, Nakamura, Yoshida, & Matsukuma, 2011) presented LBM simulations for the 2D flow of the Bingham and the Casson viscoplastic fluids through complex flow channels including rectangular and circular obstacles. (Hasert, Masilamani, Zimny, Klimach, Qi, Bernsdorf, & Roller, 2014) used the woven spacer structure in a channel as an easily scalable geometry for performance analysis. (Nabovati & Sousa, 2015) investigated the fluid flow and the permeability of 3D sphere packs with three different arrangements (with and without free overlapping).

Packed Beds

Packed beds, due to a simple construction and use, are utilised in many industrial and scientific applications. Typical examples are separation and purification processes or catalytic reactors. Pore-scale LBM simulations of flow through packed bed reconstructions were one of the first examples of LBM applications for real sparse geometries. An important characteristic of these geometries is an ease of reconstruction or an artificial generation due to simple and relatively large shapes used as obstacles (spheres or cylinders with dimensions measured even in millimetres).

(Maier, Kroll, Kutsovsky, Davis, & Bernard, 1998) simulated viscous fluid flow through a column with glass beads and compared the results with velocity distributions obtained from nuclear magnetic resonance spectroscopy. Similar experiments were performed in (Manz, Gladden, & Warren, 1999) where authors used magnetic resonance imaging (MRI) to obtain reconstructions of random packings of spheres with diameters 1 mm, 0.5 mm and 0.1 mm. LBM flow simulation through a 3D reconstruction of a fixed-bed reactor was described in (Yuen, Sederman, Sani, Alexander, & Gladden, 2003), (Sullivan, Gladden, & Johns, 2006a) and (Sullivan, Gladden, & Johns, 2006b) (for non-Newtonian fluids). The reactor was built as an acidic ion exchange resin (Amberlyst 15) catalyst in the form of small beads of diameter 600-850 µm packed within a 10 mm diameter column The authors demonstrated an excellent agreement between simulated and experimentally determined flow fields. (Sullivan, Sederman, Johns, & Gladden, 2007) compared the non-Newtonian fluids flow simulation with experimental data for the MRI 3D reconstruction of random packings of 5 mm diameter glass ballotini contained within a cylindrical glass column with an internal diameter of 46 mm. In (Sullivan, Sani, Johns, & Gladden, 2005) the reconstructions of two packing beds, a packing of 100 μm glass ballotini and the catalyst from (Yuen, Sederman, Sani, Alexander, & Gladden, 2003), were used to present LBM modifications allowing for low values of diffusivity.

In addition to the works mentioned above, there are also known many theoretical studies based on artificially generated geometries. Some examples were presented in the previous section.

Geology and Oil Industry

The flow simulations through geological materials also were among the first LBM simulations for sparse geometries. The common feature of these applications is the use of rock models as a porous media. Artificial generation of such geometries often requires fractals or stochastic algorithms, although for soil and sandstones the approximations with randomly placed spheres are met. Oilfield industry focuses on non-Newtonian flows, for example for the needs of recovery of hydrocarbons from oil reservoirs, whereas geological applications consider rather mineral dissolution and precipitation. Sandstone flows may be also useful for methods of carbon dioxide capture and storage.

(Bernsdorf, Durst, & Schäfer, 1999) showed that lattice Boltzmann simulations of sparse geometries give the same accuracy as FVM for flow through a 2D reconstruction of a digitised electron microscope picture of a sedimentary layer of the Northern sea shore. Additionally, the authors observed that for increasing geometry complexity the LBM performance was higher than FVM, even for a simple LBM implementation without optimisations considering geometry sparsity. Single-phase flow simulations and the permeability calculations for a 3D reconstruction of Berea sandstone were presented in (O'Connor & Fredrich, 1999). (Knutson, Werth, & Valocchi, 2001) simulated water flow and solute transport from distributed nonaqueous phase liquid blobs in a two-dimensional porous medium. (Martys & Hagedorn, 2002) analysed flows through the Fontainebleau sandstones and cement-based materials. Simulations of reactive species through porous media were conducted and verified with laboratory experiments (dissolution of geologically realistic rocks) by (O'Brien, Bean, & McDermott, 2002) and (O'Brien, Bean, & McDermott, 2003). (Boek & Venturoli, 2010) presented permeability calculations based on LBM flow simulation through 2D Berea sandstone and 3D Bentheimer sandstones. Two- (water-oil) and three-phase flows through the 3D model of Berea sandstone were analysed in (Li, Zhang, Wang, & Ge, 2013).

Fuel Cells

An important virtue of LBM is an ease of extension with multiphase flows (allowing to simulate gas-liquid interactions) and with electrochemical reactions. This, connected with the simple and robust handling of complex shapes met in porous media, caused that LBM was often used in fuel cell simulations. LBM applications focused on modelling transport through porous media being parts of a cell (electrodes and/or electrolyte). The results were then used to calculate media parameters (permeability) or cell parameters.

Two main types of fuel cells were usually considered: the proton exchange membrane fuel cell (PEMFC) and the solid oxide fuel cell (SOFC). PEMFC contains the thin, porous electrodes separated by a membrane electrolyte assembly (MEA). MEA consists of the gas diffusion layer (GDL), catalyst layer and proton exchange membrane (PEM), usually in the form of woven material. GDL is a porous medium generally made of carbon cloth or paper and permits gas to be transported to the catalyst layer. Solid oxide fuel cell consists of porous electrodes separated by an electrolyte. The structure of porous materials from SOFC differs from woven materials used in PEMFC - usually some ceramic is used. For example, the common SOFC anode material is the two-phase nickel and yttria stabilised zirconia (Ni-YSZ) porous cermet.

PEMFC

(Wang & Afsharpoya, 2006) used LBM to simulate two flow problems related to PEMFC: the 3D viscous flow through a section of serpentine channels and the flow through porous media for which multiple time and length scales exist. In (Park, Matsubara, & Li, 2007) and (Park & Li, 2008) the three-dimensional LBM model was used to investigate the effect of fibre tow orientation on the effective permeability of the porous GDL. Authors reported a good agreement of simulation results with analytical calculations. (Niu, Munekata, Hyodo, & Suga, 2007) used a multiphase, multiple-relaxation-time (MRT) lattice Boltzmann model to study the water-gas transport process in GDL. The results included absolute and relative permeability calculations and an analysis of the pressure drop, wettability and viscosity ratio impact on the relative permeability. (Koido, Furusawa, & Moriyama, 2008) combined the two-phase LBM with single-phase LBM and predicted the capillary pressure and relative permeability of both liquid water and air as a function of the saturation of a carbon-fibre paper GDL. Also (Inoue, Yoshimoto, Matsukuma, & Minemoto, 2008) calculated the GDL permeability on the basis of LBM gas flow simulations, though due to the small calculation area and low-resolution mesh a certain amount of error was observed. MRT-LBM simulations of a single phase, 3D micro-scale flow of liquid transport in the nonwoven carbon paper GDL were shown in (Hao & Cheng, 2009). (Hao & Cheng, 2010) used results of the free energy multiphase LBM simulations to thoroughly examine an impact of different factors on the relative permeability of the carbon paper GDL. (Gao, Zhang, Rama, Chen, Ostadi, & Jiang, 2013) used MRT-LBM for numerical investigations of the impact of a hydrophobicity on a water intrusion in hydrogen fuel cell GDL. (Han & Meng, 2013) presented LBM simulations of liquid water transport in randomly generated, two-dimensional models of porous materials used in PEMFC.

SOFC

(Joshi, Grew, Peracchio, & Chiu, 2007) presented modelling of the multi-component gas transport (H_2, N_2, H_2O) in the SOFC anode using the two-dimensional LBM. (Asinari, Quaglia, Spakovsky, & Kasula, 2007) used the LBM-based model to show the spatial distribution of the mass fluxes for the reactants and the products of the electrochemical reactions in a thin, 50 μm anode of Ni-YSZ cermet for a high-temperature electrolyte supported SOFC. (Suzue, Shikazono, & Kasagi, 2008) used results of LBM simulations to obtain the polarisation resistance and its sintering temperature dependence of the SOFC anode. The calculations of anodic overpotential were done by coupling the mass and charge transfer and the electrochemical reaction, the anode was reconstructed using a stochastic technique. Authors reported the good agreement with the literature data. (Grew, Joshi, Peracchio, & Chiu, 2010) developed and validated the two-dimensional, LBM-based model to study the pore-scale transport phenomena in a porous Ni-YSZ cermet anode of SOFC. The model allowed also to analyse an electrochemical oxidation of gas phase hydrogen and water. In (Grew, Peracchio, & Chiu, 2010) LBM was extended for the consideration of the charge transfer processes in the Ni and YSZ regions and used to identify the resistive losses due to Joule heating. (Iwai et al., 2010) compared LBM-based calculations of tortuosity for reconstructed Ni-YSZ anode with the random walk calculations and reported differences smaller than 3%. Three-dimensional LBM numerical simulations for SOFC anode polarisation in Ni-YSZ microstructures were presented in (Kanno, Shikazono, Takagi, Matsuzaki, & Kasagi, 2011). The microstructures were reconstructed by a focused ion beam scanning electron microscope. (Shikazono, Kanno, Matsuzaki, Teshima, Sumino, & Kasagi, 2010) simulated Ni-YSZ anode overpotentials by solving gaseous, ionic, and electronic transport equations by LBM with electrochemical reaction at the three-phase boundary (TPB). (Matsuzaki, Shikazono, & Kasagi, 2011) used the three-dimensional LBM to solve coupled transport equations for the electron, oxide ion and gas species with charge transfer at gas/solid interface. The results were used to predict the overpotential of mixed ionic and electronic conducting cathode, $La_{0.6}Sr_{0.4}Co_{0.2}Fe_{0.8}O_{3-\delta}$ (LSCF6428).

Biology and Medicine

One of the widely recognised LBM applications in medicine is a blood flow simulation. Many researchers showed a good applicability of LBM to real cases due to a simple, automated mesh generation on the base of tomographic medical data, easy parallelization that allows to simulate large domains (for example large parts of a circulatory system), and an ability to combine LBM with other techniques allowing for biochemical or cell movement simulations. However, compared with the previous areas of application, the blood flow simulations have specific hindrances. The first important difference is a large heterogeneity of vascular geometries – other geometries analysed so far are practically homogeneous. This causes that the blood flow simulations often need to handle very large geometries required to correctly simulate a selected fragment of the circular system, whereas for previous applications usually only some part of a domain could be simulated without impact on results quality. An additional difficulty is that for patient-specific treatment planning the simulations should be interactive. This requirement, combined with the large geometry size, causes that medical simulations often require excellent scalability allowing to efficiently utilize the largest supercomputers.

(Hirabayashi, Ohta, Rüfenacht, & Chopard, 2003) analysed an impact of stent implantation on a flow reduction in an artificial two-dimensional model of a vessel deformed by an aneurysm. (Artoli, Kandhai, Hoefsloot, Hoekstra, & Sloot, 2004) validated LBM-BGK as a tool for patient treatment planning by interactive geometry changes of a simplified 2D model of a symmetric aorta bifurcation. Three-dimensional flow study was presented in (Artoli, Hoekstra, & Sloot, 2003) and (Artoli, Hoekstra, & Sloot, 2006), where a bifurcation region of a human abdominal aorta with parts of the left and right iliac arteries were reconstructed from a magnetic resonance angiography (MRA). Authors reported that an important LBM advantage was an ability to directly obtain shear stress, what avoids approximation errors caused by a non-circular lumen. (Axner, Bernsdorf, Zeiser, Lammers, Linxweiler, & Hoekstra, 2008) analysed the performance of human abdominal aorta simulations on NEC SX8 vector computer and a PC cluster. (Mazzeo & Coveney, 2008) presented simulations of the patient-specific intracranial vasculature systems with up to 7.7 million fluid nodes obtained from the medical MRA datasets. A 2.5% porosity model of a real intracranial vessel with a large saccular aneurysm was used in (Stürmer, Götz, Richter, Dörfler, & Rüde, 2009) for performance evaluation. (Axner, Hoekstra, Jeays, Lawford, Hose, & Sloot, 2009) validated the LBM for time-harmonic flows in the abdominal aorta and one of the major abdominal branches, the superior mesenteric artery.

(Bernaschi, Fatica, Melchionna, Succi, & Kaxiras, 2010) employed the simulation of the blood flow with the presence of white cells in a human coronary artery model containing about 4×10^6 fluid cells (porosity about 4%) for the performance analysis of the multi-GPU LBM implementation. Large-scale simulations of the blood flow (about 10^9 fluid nodes and up to 300×10^6 suspended bodies) were presented in (Peters, Melchionna, Kaxiras, Lätt, Sircar, Bernaschi, Bison, & Succi, 2010), (Bernaschi, Matsuoka, Bisson, Fatica, Endo, & Melchionna, 2011), (Bisson, Bernaschi, Melchionna, Succi, & Kaxiras, 2012), (Bernaschi, Bisson, Fatica, Melchionna, & Succi, 2013), and (Godenschwager, Schornbaum, Bauer, Köstler, & Rüde, 2013). Authors used the geometry derived from the computed tomography angiography (CTA) scan of human coronary arteries and other vessels supplying blood to the heart muscle. (Groen, Hetherington, Carver, Nash, Bernabeu, & Coveney, 2013) used vascular network geometries with almost 10^8 fluid nodes for benchmarking HemeLB software from (Mazzeo & Coveney, 2008). GPU simulations on Keppler architecture of a blood flow in a patient-specific geometry of aorta with coarctation were presented in (Nita, Itu, & Suciu, 2013). (Zimny, Chopard, Malaspinas, Lorenz, Jain, Roller, & Bernsdorf, 2013) simulated the thrombus formation in the aneurysm bulge. (Groen et al., 2015) used bifurcation and aneurysm geometries to investigate how to improve load balance of HemeLB software using specialized decomposition strategies.

An interesting LBM application in biology, not connected directly with haematology, was presented in (Kobel, Valero, Latt, Renaud, & Lutolf, 2010) where flow simulations through microfluidic single cell traps were used to optimise its efficiency. (Krause, Gengenbach, & Heuveline, 2011) and (Fietz, Krause, Schulz, Sanders, & Heuveline, 2012) simulated the expiration in a human lung geometry containing up to almost 60×10^6 fluid nodes. In (Bernaschi, Bisson, Fatica, & Melchionna, 2013) the large simulation (about 10^{10} nodes) of protein suspension in crowding conditions were presented.

Various Applications

This section contains examples which do not directly fit into one of the areas mentioned above, but which also benefit from LBM ability to efficiently handle complex flow simulations in sparse geometries. Examples are different simulations in ceramic foams (heat transfer, reaction catalysis, flow stabilisation, filtration) or soil percolation.

Simulations of a three-dimensional fluid flow through a static mixer geometry designed in Sulzer company showed that in many cases LBM uses less memory and computational power to provide the same accuracy as FEM, even without special techniques to treat sparse geometries (Kandhai, Vidal, Hoekstra, Hoefsloot, Iedema, & Sloot, 1999). A model for solute transport in 3D variably saturated porous medium was described and verified by simulation in an unsaturated heterogeneous soil in (Zhang, Bengough, Deeks, Crawford, & Young, 2002). (Zhang & Ren, 2003) used LBM to model the transport of agrochemicals (pesticides, herbicides) in soils and showed good agreement of simulation with experimental results of the leaching of atrazine through soil columns in the laboratory. Three-dimensional pore-scale modelling of soil hydraulic conductivity was reported in (Zhang, Deeks, Bengough, Crawford, & Young, 2005). Performance analysis of LBM simulations for sparse geometries (exhaust system and metal foams) using dense data structures (multidimensional arrays) on three different machines (vector computer NEC SX6, supercomputer Hitachi SR8000 with fast interconnection network and RISC CPUs, and SGI Altix machine as an example of the "commodity-of-the-shelf" hardware) was presented in (Pohl, Deserno, Thürey, Rüde, Lammers, Wellein, & Zeiser, 2004). Authors observed that the network with a high bandwidth and a low latency is crucial to achieve a good scalability up to hundreds of processors. (Stahl, Chopard, & Latt, 2010) investigated the effect of melting on the flow of an invading buoyant non-wetting fluid in a porous medium. (Hasert, Bernsdorf, & Roller, 2011) studied air flow through a porous medium to validate the LBM at Reynolds numbers beyond the limit of Darcy's law for the needs of simulations of the noise emission of a pneumatic device with a porous medium acting as a silencer. Comparison of the LBM-based computations of pressure drop across Al_2O_3 VUKOPAR A ceramic filters (10 ppi, 20 ppi, and 30 ppi nominal pore densities) with experimental results was presented in (Regulski, Szumbarski, Łaniewski-Wołłk, Gumowski, Skibiński, Wichrowski, & Wejrzanowski, 2015).

IMPLEMENTATION TECHNIQUES

An efficient implementation for sparse geometry has to find a balance between achieved performance, memory usage, and code reusability and complexity. The additional complications are the different geometry characteristics of real geometries used in different applications. For example, porous media found in fuel cells, the oil industry and packed beds have usually more "randomly" placed fluid nodes, whereas blood vessels simulations can use relatively large channels filled with fluid separated with large solid areas.

Data Structures

In the simplest approach, the simulations for sparse geometries may be done using code optimised for the dense ones. The main advantage of dense LBM implementation is a simple data structure (multi-dimensional matrices) which allows for the simple access to neighbour nodes. This method allows to use a wide variety of advanced implementation techniques resulting in minimised memory usage and maximised performance. Many valuable results presented above have been achieved using LBM implementations without specific optimisations for sparse geometries. The state-of-the-art efficient LBM implementations for dense geometries can be found in (Valero-Lara, Igual, Prieto-Matias, Pinelli, & Favier, 2015), (Valero-Lara, 2016) and references.

Unfortunately, the use of full matrices requires storage of all data for all nodes (fluid and solid). For geometries with a low porosity, this may significantly (order of magnitude, when $\varphi \approx 0.1$) increase memory usage (see Fig. 2). Also, the memory bandwidth usage, and the performance as a consequence, can suffer. Theoretically, the bandwidth overhead for the full matrix representation can be reduced to negligible values through skipping of operations for solid nodes after checking a type of node. However, since modern machines transfer data from memory in burst transactions (usually containing between 32 and 256 bytes), the interlacing of fluid and solid nodes data results in an additional bandwidth usage, when no special memory layouts are used. Additionally, the neighbouring of solid and fluid nodes may hurt performance on parallel machines processing data in SIMD way, because the operations for solid nodes are wasted. To avoid these issues, many authors developed specialised techniques allowing to reduce memory and performance penalties resulting from geometry sparsity.

To minimise memory usage for geometries with the low porosity, the storage of data for solid nodes should be avoided. Placing in memory data only for fluid nodes results in a loss of association between the memory location and the geometry position, which was present in the classical implementations based on full, multi-dimensional matrices. To allow for localisation of neighbour node data during the propagation stage, many authors used some form of indirect addressing that allows computing memory addresses of neighbour node data. Two general forms of indirect addressing are used, the connectivity matrix and the fluid index array. Performance comparison for CPU implementations of these methods can be found in (Mattila, Hyväluoma, Timonen, & Rossi, 2008). There are also known solutions, where explicit indirect addressing is replaced with data structures (hierarchical grids or space partitioning trees).

Connectivity Matrix

In the first method based on indirect addressing, named the connectivity list (CL) or connectivity matrix (CM) and implemented in the parallel lattice gas library PELABS (Parallel Environment for LAttice Based Simulations) presented in (Dupuis & Chopard, 1999), the fluid nodes are stored in a 1-dimensional array and each node contains an additional list of indices of all neighbours. It is also convenient, but not required, to store coordinates for each fluid node to simplify postprocessing. This method is characterised by a simple lattice traversal, constant overhead (for each fluid node the same amount of additional data is used) and a simple domain partitioning for parallel machines. In the implementation from (Dupuis & Chopard, 1999) the Metis library (Karypis & Kumar, 1998) was used to find the domain partitioning formulated as the graph partitioning problem.

An adaptation of the technique from (Dupuis & Chopard, 1999) to LBM implementation was presented by (Schulz, Krafczyk, Tölke, & Rank, 2002). First, authors sorted the 1-dimensional array of node values by node type to optimise collision computations - nodes of the same type were placed in consecutive memory locations. Then, two methods were used to avoid the incorrect order of node updates during propagation stage. The former used a single copy of probability distribution functions (PDF) and two lists of source and target indices, what required two indirect addressing operations. In the latter, the two copies of PDF and a single precomputed list of indices of target memory locations reduced the number of indirect addressing operations to one, but at the cost of almost doubled memory usage.

Another LBM implementation using indices to neighbour nodes was presented in (Pan, Prins, & Miller, 2004), where two copies of PDF and complex indices (up to 7 bytes each) containing neighbour node type, index and processor index (for multiprocessor computations) were used. In (Donath, Zeiser, Hager, Habich, & Wellein, 2005) an analysis of different optimisation techniques for general purpose CPU (cache blocking, loop splitting to avoid register spilling, and different memory layouts, also based on space-filling curves) was presented for the CM method.

The CM scheme was successfully applied in MUPHY, a multi-physics/scale code based upon the combination of microscopic Molecular Dynamics (MD) with a hydro-kinetic LBM (Bernaschi, Melchionna, Succi, Fyta, Kaxiras, & Sircar, 2009). Also, the International Lattice Boltzmann Development Consortium (ILBDC) solver uses this addressing scheme. The detailed ILBDC performance analysis for a wide variety of parallel machines (NEC SX8 vector processor, Cray XT4 massively parallel processing (MPP) system, IBM BlueGene L/P supercomputer and the commodity cluster) were reported in (Zeiser, Hager, & Wellein, 2009b) and (Zeiser, Hager, & Wellein, 2009a). In (Wittmann, Zeiser, Hager, & Wellein, 2013b) the single node performance of CPU implementations for different propagation methods including two grids, compressed grid (Pohl, Kowarschik, Wilke, Iglberger, & Rüde, 2003), swap algorithm (Mattila, Hyväluoma, Rossi, Aspnäs, & Westerholm, 2007), A-A pattern (Bailey, Myre, Walsh, Lilja, & Saar, 2009), and esoteric twist (Schönherr, Geier, & Krafczyk, 2011) was analyzed. Detailed information about building sparse implementation can be found in (Wittmann, Zeiser, Hager, & Wellein, 2013a). Optimised implementations based on CM can be also found in (Vidal, Roy, & Bertrand, 2010b).

(Astorino, Sagredo, & Quarteroni, 2012) presented a combination of the direct addressing and the connectivity matrix, where the indirect addressing is used only for boundary nodes. This method potentially can accelerate simulations with moving solids, since only the small part of the connectivity matrix (referring only to boundary nodes) has to be reconstructed every time-step. However, a full memory storage for all nodes (fluid and solid) is required.

One of the shortcomings of the CM technique is a relatively large overhead required to store indices to all neighbours. In real cases, the number of nodes (millions or more) requires using of 4-byte indices. Since a separate index is required per each lattice link but one, the number of indices is almost equal to the number of the probability distribution functions. Depending on the format used to represent PDF, CM requires about an additional 50% memory for double precision PDF and about 100% more memory for single precision PDF. Additionally, all these indices must be read from memory causing about 25% (50%) additional memory traffic for double precision (single precision) PDF. The highest reported performance for the highly optimized implementation based on CM described in (Huang, Shi, Guo, & Chai, 2015) utilizes less than 50% of theoretical memory bandwidth, whereas the fast implementation for dense geometries from (Januszewski & Kostur, 2014) achieves up to 80% for the same machine, lattice and computational models.

Fluid Index Array

The second method of indirect addressing, the fluid index array (FIA), uses a single multi-dimensional, dense matrix that for each lattice node contains either a pointer to the node data, for a fluid node, or a NULL value, for a solid node, (Martys & Hagedorn, 2002). Modification of this method was presented in (Mattila, Hyväluoma, Timonen, & Rossi, 2008), where pointers were replaced with indices and an additional array containing locations and lengths of segments containing only fluid nodes was used. The FIA method avoids a large amount of additional data per each fluid node but requires storage of the single pointer per each node in geometry. For very sparse geometries this may result in a large overhead, especially when a small amount of data per fluid node is required (for example in 2D lattices and single precision PDF representations). An additional issue is a necessity to use the indirect addressing not only for the neighbour nodes but also for the currently processed node.

The GPU implementation using FIA can be found in (Nita, Itu, & Suciu, 2013). Two versions of FIA, with two and a single copy of PDF data, were implemented in Sailfish package as well (Januszewski & Kostur, 2014).

Hierarchical Grids

In addition to the methods based on indirect addressing, the lattice sparsity can be tackled using multi-level, hierarchical grids. Hierarchical grids were designed for local grid refinement allowing to increase an accuracy without a significant increase in computational complexity by increasing grid resolution only in small parts of the domain (Filippova & Hänel, 1998). State-of-the-art implementations for dense geometries are presented in (Valero-Lara & Jansson, 2015), (Valero-Lara & Jansson, 2017) and references.

For sparse geometries, the use of hierarchical grids allows minimising the memory wasted to store data for solid nodes - although some data is still stored, it is only done on coarse grid levels resulting in "packing" of neighbour solid nodes into single blocks. The advantage of this approach is the same code used for simulations for dense and sparse geometries.

Analysis of performance and accuracy of the LBM simulations for sparse geometries handled using quadtree/octree based hierarchical grid was presented in (Geller, Krafczyk, Tölke, Turek, & Hron, 2006). HemeLB simulator presented in (Mazzeo & Coveney, 2008) used the two-level hierarchical grid, where each coarse-resolution block contained 8^3 fine-resolution nodes. According to authors themselves, this was the good tradeoff between code complexity, performance and sparsity overheads. To increase the performance of transformation between indices from different grid levels, the look-up tables were applied. The performance results for a machine with tenths of thousands of CPU cores were reported in (Groen, Hetherington, Carver, Nash, Bernabeu, & Coveney, 2013). Multi-layer grid refinement is also supported by Palabos (Parmigiani, Huber, Bachmann, & Chopard, 2011), one of the widely recognised LBM implementations.

Multi-block approach with the removal of empty blocks and different resolution subgrids was used in the OpenLB software showing good performance of real sparse geometry simulations on hundreds of processor cores (Fietz, Krause, Schulz, Sanders, & Heuveline, 2012). Also the Musubi framework was based on a similar approach, a distributed octree with local mesh refinement, and showed an excellent CPU performance on clusters with thousands of nodes (Hasert, Masilamani, Zimny, Klimach, Qi, Bernsdorf, & Roller, 2014).

Tiles

The geometry sparsity can also be handled using a technique similar to hierarchical grids, but without transformations between different levels of resolutions. In (Stürmer, Götz, Richter, Dörfler, & Rüde, 2009) the sparse domain was decoupled into patches containing 8^3 nodes each and all patches containing only solid nodes were removed. Such data structure with two copies of PDF allowed to efficiently map operations to the single-instruction-multiple-data (SIMD) units of IBM Cell processor. This technique evolved into patch-and-block concept used in the widely applicable Lattice-Boltzmann from Erlangen (WaLBerla) software (Feichtinger, Donath, Köstler, Götz, & Rüde, 2011) that allows simulating complex scenarios on large parallel machines. Excellent performance results for geometry with 10^{12} fluid cells and porosity 0.3% on up to 2^{17} processor cores were shown in (Godenschwager, Schornbaum, Bauer, Köstler, & Rüde, 2013) - almost 70% of the total machine memory bandwidth was utilised. The sparse domain decomposition into disjoint, cubical subdomains with ghost cells was also used in (Krause, Gengenbach, & Heuveline, 2011), though the subdomain size was rather large (50^3 nodes).

Similar domain decomposition into small cubic tiles, an equivalent of patches from (Stürmer, Götz, Richter, Dörfler, & Rüde, 2009), was analysed by (Tomczak & Szafran, 2016) and (Tomczak & Szafran, 2017) in GPU implementations. Two versions were considered - the two-dimensional with a single copy of PDF, 16^2 nodes per tile and ghost buffers at tile edges, and the three-dimensional with two copies of PDF data and 4^3 nodes per tile. The detailed analysis showed that this method may give the best performance, but tiles must contain only a very small amount of solid nodes. Also, for 3D lattices, the ghost cells were found inefficient due to complex code with synchronisation issues and a large overhead caused by a small tile size required to obtain a good tile filling with fluid nodes. Performance comparison of different LBM implementations is shown in Fig. 2.

Domain Partitioning and Workload Balancing

The presented data structures allow to efficiently use resources (computational power and memory) per single fluid node. However, even with the use of the techniques mentioned above, the number of nodes in real simulations often impose the use of large multi-processor clusters due to the required domain size, resolution, or both. Good utilisation of such clusters requires not only a high single-node performance but also the uniform workload distribution and the minimalization of communication between processors.

Since the computations for a single LBM node are relatively simple and require the communication only with the closest neighbours, the standard parallel LBM

Figure 2. Estimated memory usage and performance limits of five LBM implementations (dense LBM, CM, FIA, and two versions of tiles) and three geometries from Fig. 1; the values are normalized to idealized implementation that stores and process only minimal data set for non-solid nodes; performance limits ignore impact of burst memory transactions

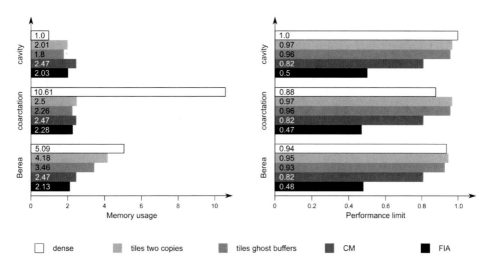

implementations divide the domain into subdomains and distribute these subdomains to cluster nodes. For dense geometries the natural domain partitioning uses cuboid subdomains (or slices for geometries with dominating one axis dimension) due to a simple implementation and a low communication caused by a high ratio of cuboid volume to the wall area (Amati, Succi, & Piva, 1997), (Desplat, Pagonabarraga, & Bladon, 2001). Unfortunately, such uniform partitioning of sparse geometries can result in a very unbalanced load of cluster computational nodes. Thus, the specialised domain partitioning algorithms are usually used in parallel LBM implementations.

In (Kandhai, Koponen, Hoekstra, Kataja, Timonen, & Sloot, 1998) the orthogonal recursive bisection (ORB) algorithm was used due to its simplicity. The comparison of orthogonal recursive bisection to rectilinear decomposition was presented in (Pan, Prins, & Miller, 2004). Though the rectilinear decomposition was simple to implement and offered simple communication pattern, the authors observed better workload balance and parallel efficiency for ORB due to a small impact of communication between subdomains on performance.

(Dupuis & Chopard, 1999) formulated the sparse domain partitioning problem as finding the subsets such that the number of cells with a neighbour in a different subset is minimised. By using the connectivity matrix, the authors brought the domain partitioning to the graph partitioning problem where the number of cut edges is minimal. Notice, that in this implementation the numbers of neighbour nodes per subdomain are not equal. Since this problem is NP-complete, the heuristic multilevel *k*-way algorithm implemented in the Metis library (Karypis & Kumar, 1998) was used. The real implementation results showed that the proposed technique gives better performance on systems with up to 8 processors when the geometry porosity is about 50% or less. (Schulz, Krafczyk, Tölke, & Rank, 2002) also used the Metis library and achieved parallel efficiency up to 90% by overlapping the collision and propagation of the subdomains inner nodes with communication between subdomains. The MUPHY software achieved parallel efficiency above 84% for a system with up to 32 GPUs (Bisson, Bernaschi, Melchionna, Succi, & Kaxiras, 2012) using domain decomposition done by graph partitioning libraries Metis and SCOTCH (Chevalier & Pellegrini, 2008). An excellent performance and scalability on CPU (up to hundreds of thousands of processors) and GPU (up to 18 000 GPUs) was shown in (Peters, Melchionna, Kaxiras, Lätt, Sircar, Bernaschi, Bison, & Succi, 2010), (Bernaschi, Matsuoka, Bisson, Fatica, Endo, & Melchionna, 2011) and (Bernaschi, Bisson, Fatica, & Melchionna, 2013). The performance evaluation of implemented in OpenLB software the load balancer employing KaFFPa framework (Sanders & Schulz, 2011) for systems with up to 512 cores was presented in (Fietz, Krause, Schulz, Sanders, & Heuveline, 2012).

(Axner, Bernsdorf, Zeiser, Lammers, Linxweiler, & Hoekstra, 2008) used the performance prediction model based on the fractional communication overheads to analyse the parallel scalability of the sparse LBM implementation. Theoretical and experimental analysis of two different domain partitioning algorithms implemented in the Metis library, the multilevel *k*-way and the multilevel recursive bisection (RB), showed that for simple geometries the multilevel RB gives more even amount of communication per domain, while for complex geometries the combination of both methods gives an optimal solution. The authors also observed, that for a large number of processors the partitioning quality has a significant impact on performance.

Despite the good decomposition quality, the main disadvantages of the multilevel decomposition methods are large memory requirements and high computational complexity, especially for large geometries. As reported in (Peters, Melchionna, Kaxiras, Lätt, Sircar, Bernaschi, Bison, & Succi, 2010), even the parallel version of Metis library was unable to partition the geometry with 10^9 nodes due to memory requirements and the PT-SCOTCH partitioning tool (Chevalier & Pellegrini, 2008) had to be used on the reduced geometry. Also, the communication patterns resulting from partitioning are complex due to irregular borders between subdomains. Thus, a different domain decomposition method was presented in (Wang, Zhang, Bengough, & Crawford, 2005). Authors first divided the linearized array of fluid cells into equally sized fragments and then recovered boundary nodes using simple rules. The main advantages of this method are a very simple single pass implementation without searching and sorting of nodes, and a simple communication pattern. Unfortunately, the produced decomposition is similar to the slice-based partitioning what results in the large communication overhead if subdomains are small (Vidal, Roy, & Bertrand, 2010b) - in the worst case each node requires communication with the neighbour subdomains. This issue was addressed in (Zeiser, Hager, & Wellein, 2009b) and (Zeiser, Hager, & Wellein, 2009a) where the fluid cell numbering in the linearized array was done according to different space-filling curves. The authors also measured the LBM implementation performance on different hardware showing about 15% impact of node ordering for NEC SX8 vector processor. (Wittmann, Zeiser, Hager, & Wellein, 2013a) reported superior performance of domain partitioning based on lexicographic ordering compared to PT-SCOTCH and Metis, but for achieving high performance of LBM simulation the blocking factor for lexicographic ordering had to be carefully selected based on many factors.

Another partitioning algorithm with linear computational and memory complexity and low communication overhead was presented in (Mazzeo & Coveney, 2008) where an optimised implementation based on graph growing partitioning was applied. In (Bernaschi, Matsuoka, Bisson, Fatica, Endo, & Melchionna, 2011) the authors found that an optimal way of partitioning the geometry with about 10^9 nodes is a combining of the SCOTCH-based coarse partitioning followed by the graph growing scheme.

An efficient and simple domain decomposition method was implemented in WaLBerla, where the domain was divided into rectangular patches equally distributed among cluster nodes. Through the removal of blocks containing no fluid nodes and efficient communication between patches on the same cluster node, an excellent scalability for hundreds of processors was achieved (Feichtinger, Götz, Donath, Iglberger, & Rüde, 2009). The optimised distribution of blocks to the computational nodes for geometry with about 2×10^{12} nodes was found using Metis library as presented in (Godenschwager, Schornbaum, Bauer, Köstler, & Rüde, 2013).

(Hasert, Masilamani, Zimny, Klimach, Qi, Bernsdorf, & Roller, 2014) presented the load balancing by a distribution of neighbouring octree leaves to computational nodes. The leaves were traversed in an order defined by a space-filling curve giving a fair degree of locality. The authors reported small imbalance of communication with minor impact on performance.

The computational performance of current supercomputers should approach 1 EFLOPS soon (in June 2017 the first machine on the TOP500 list achieves about 100 PFLOPS (Strohmaier, 2006)). Preparing LBM implementations to exascale computing requires solving new problems, for example, a reliability of computations, load balancing and scalability on massively parallel heterogeneous machines with 10^6 cores, and energy efficient execution. Thus, despite lack of hardware, active research in this field has been done in the last few years. (Chen et al., 2012) discussed challenges at exascale pre- and post-processing of data in HemeLB software. (Groen et al., 2015) found that load imbalance of cluster nodes can be significantly reduced by weighted decomposition with weights assigned to lattice vertices, although at the cost of communication overhead. (Schornbaum & Rüde, 2016) presented a combination of techniques (volume-based refinement, load balancing algorithms, data structures and communication patterns) designed to ensure applicability for current petascale and future exascale computers.

CONCLUSION

The presented material has shown that LBM is a viable option for simulations of fluid flow through sparse geometries. Thanks to the simple mesh generation based on uniform grids, easy parallelization that allows simulating large domains, robust boundary conditions for complex shapes, and the ability to extend it and combine with other techniques, the LBM has been successfully used in many industrial and scientific applications requiring sparse geometries.

Though LBM implementation may use the simple, multidimensional matrices for domain representation, such approach results in the extensive memory usage and the large performance penalty for geometries with low porosity. Hence, many specialised techniques have been developed to efficiently handle sparse geometries on both single- and multi-processor computers. The memory usage and computational complexity can be decreased using either indirect addressing (the connectivity matrix or the fluid index array) or techniques based on domain partitioning into smaller blocks (hierarchical grids or tiles). All these ideas can be adapted to parallel machines by using graph partitioning methods and space-filling curves for the domain decomposition. Many large, mature software implementations based on all these concepts are under active development and they offer good performance and scalability. In fact, currently the decision which implementation is the best option for given application can be made mainly based on offered features, for example, implemented models or licensing. When a specialised implementation needs to be prepared from scratch, it seems that methods based on domain partitioning into smaller blocks may potentially offer the best performance due to a lack of overhead caused by indirect addressing, but a detailed analysis should be done for each case.

REFERENCES

Adrover, A., & Giona, M. (1996). A predictive model for permeability of correlated porous media. *The Chemical Engineering Journal and the Biochemical Engineering Journal, 64*(1), 7–19. doi:10.1016/S0923-0467(96)03084-9

Aharonov, E., & Rothman, D. H. (1993). Non-Newtonian flow (through porous media): A lattice-Boltzmann method. *Geophysical Research Letters, 20*(8), 679–682. doi:10.1029/93GL00473

Amati, G., Succi, S., & Piva, R. (1997). Massively parallel lattice-Boltzmann simulation of turbulent channel flow. *International Journal of Modern Physics C, 08*(04), 869–877. doi:10.1142/S0129183197000746

Artoli, A., Hoekstra, A., & Sloot, P. (2006). Mesoscopic simulations of systolic flow in the human abdominal aorta. *Journal of Biomechanics, 39*(5), 873–884. doi:10.1016/j.jbiomech.2005.01.033 PMID:16488226

Artoli, A., Kandhai, D., Hoefsloot, H., Hoekstra, A., & Sloot, P. (2004). Lattice BGK simulations of flow in a symmetric bifurcation. *Future Generation Computer Systems, 20*(6), 909–916. doi:10.1016/j.future.2003.12.002

Artoli, A. M., Hoekstra, A. G., & Sloot, P. M. A. (2003). Simulation of a systolic cycle in a realistic artery with the lattice Boltzmann BGK method. *International Journal of Modern Physics B, 17*(1-2), 95-98.

Asinari, P., Quaglia, M. C., von Spakovsky, M. R., & Kasula, B. V. (2007). Direct numerical calculation of the kinematic tortuosity of reactive mixture flow in the anode layer of solid oxide fuel cells by the lattice Boltzmann method. *Journal of Power Sources, 170*(2), 359–375. doi:10.1016/j.jpowsour.2007.03.074

Astorino, M., Sagredo, J., & Quarteroni, A. (2012). A modular lattice Boltzmann solver for GPU computing processors. *SeMA Journal, 59*(1), 53–78. doi:10.1007/BF03322610

Axner, L., Bernsdorf, J., Zeiser, T., Lammers, P., Linxweiler, J., & Hoekstra, A. (2008). Performance evaluation of a parallel sparse lattice Boltzmann solver. *Journal of Computational Physics, 227*(10), 4895–4911. doi:10.1016/j.jcp.2008.01.013

Axner, L., Hoekstra, A. G., Jeays, A., Lawford, P., Hose, R., & Sloot, P. M. (2009). Simulations of time harmonic blood flow in the mesenteric artery: Comparing finite element and lattice Boltzmann methods. *Biomedical Engineering Online, 8*(1), 23. doi:10.1186/1475-925X-8-23 PMID:19799782

Bailey, P., Myre, J., Walsh, S., Lilja, D., & Saar, M. (2009, Sept). Accelerating lattice Boltzmann fluid flow simulations using graphics processors. In ICPP'09 international conference on parallel processing (pp. 550-557). Academic Press. doi:10.1109/ICPP.2009.38

Balasubramanian, K., Hayot, F., & Saam, W. F. (1987). Darcy's law from lattice-gas hydrodynamics. *Physical Review A.*, *36*(5), 2248–2253. doi:10.1103/PhysRevA.36.2248 PMID:9899116

Bernaschi, M., Bisson, M., Fatica, M., & Melchionna, S. (2013). 20 petaflops simulation of proteins suspensions in crowding conditions. In *SC'13 - International conference for high performance computing, networking, storage and analysis* (pp. 1-11). Academic Press.

Bernaschi, M., Bisson, M., Fatica, M., Melchionna, S., & Succi, S. (2013). Petaflop hydrokinetic simulations of complex flows on massive GPU clusters. *Computer Physics Communications*, *184*(2), 329–341. doi:10.1016/j.cpc.2012.09.016

Bernaschi, M., Fatica, M., Melchionna, S., Succi, S., & Kaxiras, E. (2010, January). A flexible high-performance lattice Boltzmann GPU code for the simulations of fluid flows in complex geometries. *Concurr. Comput.: Pract. Exper.*, *22*(1), 1–14. doi:10.1002/cpe.1466

Bernaschi, M., Matsuoka, S., Bisson, M., Fatica, M., Endo, T., & Melchionna, S. (2011, Nov). Petaflop biofluidics simulations on a two million-core system. In *SC'11 International conference for high performance computing, networking, storage and analysis* (pp. 1-12). Academic Press. doi:10.1145/2063384.2063389

Bernaschi, M., Melchionna, S., Succi, S., Fyta, M., Kaxiras, E., & Sircar, J. (2009). Muphy: A parallel MUlti PHYsics/scale code for high performance bio-fluidic simulations. *Computer Physics Communications*, *180*(9), 1495–1502. doi:10.1016/j.cpc.2009.04.001

Bernsdorf, J., Durst, F., & Schäfer, M. (1999). Comparison of cellular automata and finite volume techniques for simulation of incompressible flows in complex geometries. *International Journal for Numerical Methods in Fluids*, *29*(3), 251–264. doi:10.1002/(SICI)1097-0363(19990215)29:3<251::AID-FLD783>3.0.CO;2-L

Bisson, M., Bernaschi, M., Melchionna, S., Succi, S., & Kaxiras, E. (2012). Multiscale hemodynamics using GPU clusters. *Communications in Computational Physics*, *11*(1), 48–64. doi:10.4208/cicp.210910.250311a

Boek, E. S., Chin, J., & Coveney, P. V. (2003). Lattice Boltzmann simulation of the flow of non-Newtonian fluids in porous media. *International Journal of Modern Physics B, 17*(1-2), 99-102.

Boek, E. S., & Venturoli, M. (2010). Lattice-Boltzmann studies of fluid flow in porous media with realistic rock geometries. *Computers & Mathematics with Applications (Oxford, England), 59*(7), 2305–2314. doi:10.1016/j.camwa.2009.08.063

Cancelliere, A., Chang, C., Foti, E., Rothman, D. H., & Succi, S. (1990). The permeability of a random medium: Comparison of simulation with theory. *Physics of Fluids. A, Fluid Dynamics, 2*(12), 2085–2088. doi:10.1063/1.857793

Chai, Z., Shi, B., Lu, J., & Guo, Z. (2010). Non-Darcy flow in disordered porous media: A lattice Boltzmann study. *Computers & Fluids, 39*(10), 2069–2077. doi:10.1016/j.compfluid.2010.07.012

Chen, F., Flatken, M., Basermann, A., Gerndt, A., Hetheringthon, J., Krüger, T., et al. (2012). Enabling in situ pre- and post-processing for exascale hemodynamic simulations - A co-design study with the sparse geometry lattice-Boltzmann code HemeLB. *2012 SC companion: High performance computing, networking storage and analysis*, 662-668.

Chevalier, C., & Pellegrini, F. (2008). PT-SCOTCH: A tool for efficient parallel graph ordering. *Parallel Computing, 34*(6-8), 318–331. doi:10.1016/j.parco.2007.12.001

Desplat, J.-C., Pagonabarraga, I., & Bladon, P. (2001). Ludwig: A parallel lattice-Boltzmann code for complex fluids. *Computer Physics Communications, 134*(3), 273–290. doi:10.1016/S0010-4655(00)00205-8

Donath, S., Zeiser, T., Hager, G., Habich, J., & Wellein, G. (2005). Optimizing performance of the lattice Boltzmann method for complex structures on cache-based architectures. In Proceedings Simulationstechnique ASIM (pp. 728-735). Academic Press.

Dong, H. (2008). *Micro-CT imaging and pore network extraction* (Doctoral dissertation). Department of Earth Science and Engineering, Imperial College London.

Dupuis, A., & Chopard, B. (1999). Lattice gas: An efficient and reusable parallel library based on a graph partitioning technique. In P. Sloot, M. Bubak, A. Hoekstra, & B. Hertzberger (Eds.), *High-performance computing and networking: 7th International conference, HPCN Europe 1999, Amsterdam, The Netherlands* (pp. 319-328). Berlin: Springer Berlin Heidelberg.

Feichtinger, C., Donath, S., Köstler, H., Götz, J., & Rüde, U. (2011). WaLBerla: HPC software design for computational engineering simulations. *Journal of Computational Science, 2*(2), 105–112. doi:10.1016/j.jocs.2011.01.004

Feichtinger, C., Götz, J., Donath, S., Iglberger, K., & Rüde, U. (2009). WaLBerla: Exploiting massively parallel systems for lattice Boltzmann simulations. In R. Trobec, M. Vajtersic, & P. Zinterhof (Eds.), *Parallel computing: Numerics, applications, and trends* (pp. 241–260). London: Springer London. doi:10.1007/978-1-84882-409-6_8

Fietz, J., Krause, M. J., Schulz, C., Sanders, P., & Heuveline, V. (2012). Optimized hybrid parallel lattice Boltzmann fluid flow simulations on complex geometries. In C. Kaklamanis, T. Papatheodorou, & P. G. Spirakis (Eds.), *Euro-Par 2012 parallel processing: 18th International conference, Euro-Par 2012, Rhodes Island, Greece* (pp. 818-829). Berlin: Springer Berlin Heidelberg. doi:10.1007/978-3-642-32820-6_81

Filippova, O., & Hänel, D. (1998). Grid refinement for lattice-BGK models. *Journal of Computational Physics, 147*(1), 219–228. doi:10.1006/jcph.1998.6089

Freund, H., Zeiser, T., Huber, F., Klemm, E., Brenner, G., Durst, F., & Emig, G. (2003). Numerical simulations of single phase reacting flows in randomly packed fixed-bed reactors and experimental validation. *Chemical Engineering Science, 58*(3-6), 903–910. doi:10.1016/S0009-2509(02)00622-X

Gao, Y., Zhang, X., Rama, P., Chen, R., Ostadi, H., & Jiang, K. (2013). Lattice Boltzmann simulation of water and gas flow in porous gas diffusion layers in fuel cells reconstructed from micro-tomography. *Computers & Mathematics with Applications (Oxford, England), 65*(6), 891–900. doi:10.1016/j.camwa.2012.08.006

Geller, S., Krafczyk, M., Tölke, J., Turek, S., & Hron, J. (2006). Benchmark computations based on lattice-Boltzmann, finite element and finite volume methods for laminar flows. *Computers & Fluids, 35*(8-9), 888–897. doi:10.1016/j.compfluid.2005.08.009

Godenschwager, C., Schornbaum, F., Bauer, M., Köstler, H., & Rüde, U. (2013). A framework for hybrid parallel flow simulations with a trillion cells in complex geometries. In *Proceedings of the international conference on high performance computing, networking, storage and analysis* (pp. 35:1-35:12). New York: ACM. doi:10.1145/2503210.2503273

Grew, K. N., Joshi, A. S., Peracchio, A. A., & Chiu, W. K. (2010). Pore-scale investigation of mass transport and electrochemistry in a solid oxide fuel cell anode. *Journal of Power Sources, 195*(8), 2331–2345. doi:10.1016/j.jpowsour.2009.10.067

Grew, K. N., Peracchio, A. A., & Chiu, W. K. (2010). Characterization and analysis methods for the examination of the heterogeneous solid oxide fuel cell electrode microstructure: Part 2. Quantitative measurement of the microstructure and contributions to transport losses. *Journal of Power Sources*, *195*(24), 7943–7958. doi:10.1016/j.jpowsour.2010.07.006

Groen, D., Chacra, D. A., Nash, R. W., Jaros, J., Bernabeu, M. O., & Coveney, P. V. (2015). Weighted decomposition in high-performance lattice-Boltzmann simulations: Are some lattice sites more equal than others? In S. Markidis & E. Laure (Eds.), *Solving software challenges for exascale: International Conference on Exascale Applications and Software, EASC 2014, Stockholm, Sweden, April 2-3, 2014, revised selected papers* (pp. 28-38). Cham: Springer International Publishing. doi:10.1007/978-3-319-15976-8_2

Groen, D., Hetherington, J., Carver, H. B., Nash, R. W., Bernabeu, M. O., & Coveney, P. V. (2013). Analysing and modelling the performance of the HemeLB lattice-Boltzmann simulation environment. *Journal of Computational Science*, *4*(5), 412–422. doi:10.1016/j.jocs.2013.03.002

Han, B., & Meng, H. (2013). Numerical studies of interfacial phenomena in liquid water transport in polymer electrolyte membrane fuel cells using the lattice Boltzmann method. *International Journal of Hydrogen Energy*, *38*(12), 5053–5059. doi:10.1016/j.ijhydene.2013.02.055

Hao, L., & Cheng, P. (2009). Lattice Boltzmann simulations of anisotropic permeabilities in carbon paper gas diffusion layers. *Journal of Power Sources*, *186*(1), 104–114. doi:10.1016/j.jpowsour.2008.09.086

Hao, L., & Cheng, P. (2010). Pore-scale simulations on relative permeabilities of porous media by lattice Boltzmann method. *International Journal of Heat and Mass Transfer*, *53*(9-10), 1908–1913. doi:10.1016/j.ijheatmasstransfer.2009.12.066

Hasert, M., Bernsdorf, J., & Roller, S. (2011). Lattice Boltzmann simulation of non-Darcy flow in porous media. *Procedia Computer Science*, *4*, 1048–1057. doi:10.1016/j.procs.2011.04.111

Hasert, M., Masilamani, K., Zimny, S., Klimach, H., Qi, J., Bernsdorf, J., & Roller, S. (2014). Complex fluid simulations with the parallel tree-based lattice Boltzmann solver Musubi. *Journal of Computational Science*, *5*(5), 784–794. doi:10.1016/j.jocs.2013.11.001

Hirabayashi, M., Ohta, M., Rüfenacht, D. A., & Chopard, B. (2003). Characterization of flow reduction properties in an aneurysm due to a stent. *Phys. Rev. E*, *68*(2), 021918. doi:10.1103/PhysRevE.68.021918 PMID:14525017

Huang, C., Shi, B., Guo, Z., & Chai, Z. (2015). Multi-GPU based lattice Boltzmann method for hemodynamic simulation in patient-specific cerebral aneurysm. *Communications in Computational Physics*, *17*(04), 960–974. doi:10.4208/cicp.2014. m342

Inoue, G., Yoshimoto, T., Matsukuma, Y., & Minemoto, M. (2008). Development of simulated gas diffusion layer of polymer electrolyte fuel cells and evaluation of its structure. *Journal of Power Sources*, *175*(1), 145–158. doi:10.1016/j. jpowsour.2007.09.014

Iwai, H., Shikazono, N., Matsui, T., Teshima, H., Kishimoto, M., Kishida, R., ... Yoshida, H. (2010). Quantification of SOFC anode microstructure based on dual beam FIB-SEM technique. *Journal of Power Sources*, *195*(4), 955–961. doi:10.1016/j. jpowsour.2009.09.005

Januszewski, M., & Kostur, M. (2014). Sailfish: A flexible multi-GPU implementation of the lattice Boltzmann method. *Computer Physics Communications*, *185*(9), 2350–2368. doi:10.1016/j.cpc.2014.04.018

Joshi, A. S., Grew, K. N., Peracchio, A. A., & Chiu, W. K. (2007). Lattice Boltzmann modeling of 2D gas transport in a solid oxide fuel cell anode. *Journal of Power Sources*, *164*(2), 631–638. doi:10.1016/j.jpowsour.2006.10.101

Kandhai, D., Koponen, A., Hoekstra, A., Kataja, M., Timonen, J., & Sloot, P. (1998). Lattice-Boltzmann hydrodynamics on parallel systems. *Computer Physics Communications*, *111*(1), 14–26. doi:10.1016/S0010-4655(98)00025-3

Kandhai, D., Vidal, D.-E., Hoekstra, A., Hoefsloot, H., Iedema, P., & Sloot, P. (1999). Lattice-Boltzmann and finite element simulations of fluid flow in a SMRX static mixer reactor. *International Journal for Numerical Methods in Fluids*, *31*(6), 1019–1033. doi:10.1002/(SICI)1097-0363(19991130)31:6<1019::AID-FLD915>3.0.CO;2-I

Kanno, D., Shikazono, N., Takagi, N., Matsuzaki, K., & Kasagi, N. (2011). Evaluation of SOFC anode polarization simulation using three-dimensional microstructures reconstructed by FIB tomography. *Electrochimica Acta*, *56*(11), 4015–4021. doi:10.1016/j.electacta.2011.02.010

Karypis, G., & Kumar, V. (1998). A fast and high quality multilevel scheme for partitioning irregular graphs. *SIAM Journal on Scientific Computing*, *20*(1), 359–392. doi:10.1137/S1064827595287997

Knutson, C. E., Werth, C. J., & Valocchi, A. J. (2001). Pore-scale modeling of dissolution from variably distributed nonaqueous phase liquid blobs. *Water Resources Research*, *37*(12), 2951–2963. doi:10.1029/2001WR000587

Kobel, S., Valero, A., Latt, J., Renaud, P., & Lutolf, M. (2010). Optimization of microfluidic single cell trapping for long-term on-chip culture. *Lab on a Chip*, *10*(7), 857–863. doi:10.1039/b918055a PMID:20300672

Koido, T., Furusawa, T., & Moriyama, K. (2008). An approach to modeling two-phase transport in the gas diffusion layer of a proton exchange membrane fuel cell. *Journal of Power Sources*, *175*(1), 127–136. doi:10.1016/j.jpowsour.2007.09.029

Koponen, A., Kataja, M., & Timonen, J. (1997). Permeability and effective porosity of porous media. *Physical Review E: Statistical Physics, Plasmas, Fluids, and Related Interdisciplinary Topics*, *56*(3), 3319–3325. doi:10.1103/PhysRevE.56.3319

Koponen, A., Kataja, M., Timonen, J., & Kandhai, D. (1998). Simulations of single-fluid flow in porous media. *International Journal of Modern Physics C*, *09*(08), 1505–1521. doi:10.1142/S0129183198001369

Krause, M. J., Gengenbach, T., & Heuveline, V. (2011). Hybrid parallel simulations of fluid flows in complex geometries: Application to the human lungs. In M. R. Guarracino & ... (Eds.), *Euro-Par 2010 Parallel processing workshops* (pp. 209–216). Berlin: Springer Berlin Heidelberg. doi:10.1007/978-3-642-21878-1_26

Li, X., Zhang, Y., Wang, X., & Ge, W. (2013). GPU-based numerical simulation of multi-phase flow in porous media using multiple-relaxation-time lattice Boltzmann method. *Chemical Engineering Science*, *102*, 209–219. doi:10.1016/j.ces.2013.06.037

Maier, R. S., Kroll, D. M., Bernard, R. S., Howington, S. E., Peters, J. F., & Davis, H. T. (2000). Pore-scale simulation of dispersion. *Physics of Fluids*, *12*(8), 2065–2079. doi:10.1063/1.870452

Maier, R. S., Kroll, D. M., Kutsovsky, Y. E., Davis, H. T., & Bernard, R. S. (1998). Simulation of flow through bead packs using the lattice Boltzmann method. *Physics of Fluids*, *10*(1), 60–74. doi:10.1063/1.869550

Manz, B., Gladden, L. F., & Warren, P. B. (1999). Flow and dispersion in porous media: Lattice-Boltzmann and NMR studies. *AIChE Journal. American Institute of Chemical Engineers*, *45*(9), 1845–1854. doi:10.1002/aic.690450902

Martys, N. S., & Hagedorn, J. G. (2002). Multiscale modeling of fluid transport in heterogeneous materials using discrete Boltzmann methods. *Materials and Structures*, *35*(10), 650–658. doi:10.1007/BF02480358

Matsuzaki, K., Shikazono, N., & Kasagi, N. (2011). Three-dimensional numerical analysis of mixed ionic and electronic conducting cathode reconstructed by focused ion beam scanning electron microscope. *Journal of Power Sources, 196*(6), 3073–3082. doi:10.1016/j.jpowsour.2010.11.142

Mattila, K., Hyväluoma, J., Rossi, T., Aspnäs, M., & Westerholm, J. (2007). An efficient swap algorithm for the lattice Boltzmann method. *Computer Physics Communications, 176*(3), 200–210. doi:10.1016/j.cpc.2006.09.005

Mattila, K., Hyväluoma, J., Timonen, J., & Rossi, T. (2008). Comparison of implementations of the lattice-Boltzmann method. *Computers & Mathematics with Applications (Oxford, England), 55*(7), 1514–1524. doi:10.1016/j.camwa.2007.08.001

Mazzeo, M., & Coveney, P. (2008). HemeLB: A high performance parallel lattice-Boltzmann code for large scale fluid flow in complex geometries. *Computer Physics Communications, 178*(12), 894–914. doi:10.1016/j.cpc.2008.02.013

Nabovati, A., Llewellin, E. W., & Sousa, A. C. (2009). A general model for the permeability of fibrous porous media based on fluid flow simulations using the lattice Boltzmann method. *Composites. Part A, Applied Science and Manufacturing, 40*(6-7), 860–869. doi:10.1016/j.compositesa.2009.04.009

Nabovati, A., & Sousa, A. C. (2015). LBM mesoscale modeling of porous media. *International Journal on Heat and Mass Transfer - Theory and Applications, 3*(4).

Nabovati, A., & Sousa, A. C. M. (2007). Fluid flow simulation in random porous media at pore level using lattice Boltzmann method. In F. G. Zhuang & J. C. Li (Eds.), *New trends in fluid mechanics research: Proceedings of the fifth international conference on fluid mechanics* (pp. 518-521). Berlin: Springer Berlin Heidelberg. doi:10.1007/978-3-540-75995-9_172

Nabovati, A., & Sousa, A. C. M. (2008). Fluid flow simulation at open–porous medium interface using the lattice Boltzmann method. *International Journal for Numerical Methods in Fluids, 56*(8), 1449–1456. doi:10.1002/fld.1614

Nejat, A., Abdollahi, V., & Vahidkhah, K. (2011). Lattice Boltzmann simulation of non-Newtonian flows past confined cylinders. *Journal of Non-Newtonian Fluid Mechanics, 166*(12-13), 689–697. doi:10.1016/j.jnnfm.2011.03.006

Nita, C., Itu, L., & Suciu, C. (2013, Sept). GPU accelerated blood flow computation using the lattice Boltzmann method. In *High performance extreme computing conference* (pp. 1–6). HPEC. doi:10.1109/HPEC.2013.6670324

Niu, X.-D., Munekata, T., Hyodo, S.-A., & Suga, K. (2007). An investigation of water-gas transport processes in the gas-diffusion-layer of a PEM fuel cell by a multiphase multiple-relaxation-time lattice Boltzmann model. *Journal of Power Sources, 172*(2), 542–552. doi:10.1016/j.jpowsour.2007.05.081

O'Brien, G., Bean, C., & McDermott, F. (2002). A comparison of published experimental data with a coupled lattice Boltzmann-analytic advection-diffusion method for reactive transport in porous media. *Journal of Hydrology (Amsterdam), 268*(1-4), 143–157. doi:10.1016/S0022-1694(02)00173-7

O'Brien, G., Bean, C., & McDermott, F. (2003). Numerical investigations of passive and reactive flow through generic single fractures with heterogeneous permeability. *Earth and Planetary Science Letters, 213*(3-4), 271–284. doi:10.1016/S0012-821X(03)00342-X

O'Connor, R., & Fredrich, J. (1999). Microscale flow modelling in geologic materials. *Physics and Chemistry of the Earth. Part A: Solid Earth and Geodesy, 24*(7), 611–616. doi:10.1016/S1464-1895(99)00088-5

Ohta, M., Nakamura, T., Yoshida, Y., & Matsukuma, Y. (2011). Lattice Boltzmann simulations of viscoplastic fluid flows through complex flow channels. *Journal of Non-Newtonian Fluid Mechanics, 166*(7–8), 404–412. doi:10.1016/j.jnnfm.2011.01.011

Pan, C., Hilpert, M., & Miller, C. T. (2004). Lattice-Boltzmann simulation of two-phase flow in porous media. *Water Resources Research, 40*(1). doi:10.1029/2003WR002120

Pan, C., Prins, J. F., & Miller, C. T. (2004). A high-performance lattice Boltzmann implementation to model flow in porous media. *Computer Physics Communications, 158*(2), 89–105. doi:10.1016/j.cpc.2003.12.003

Park, J., & Li, X. (2008). Multi-phase micro-scale flow simulation in the electrodes of a PEM fuel cell by lattice Boltzmann method. *Journal of Power Sources, 178*(1), 248–257. doi:10.1016/j.jpowsour.2007.12.008

Park, J., Matsubara, M., & Li, X. (2007). Application of lattice Boltzmann method to a micro-scale flow simulation in the porous electrode of a PEM fuel cell. *Journal of Power Sources, 173*(1), 404–414. doi:10.1016/j.jpowsour.2007.04.021

Parmigiani, A., Huber, C., Bachmann, O., & Chopard, B. (2011). Pore-scale mass and reactant transport in multiphase porous media flows. *Journal of Fluid Mechanics, 686*, 40–76. doi:10.1017/jfm.2011.268

Peters, A., Melchionna, S., Kaxiras, E., Lätt, J., Sircar, J., Bernaschi, M., ... Succi, S. (2010. Multiscale simulation of cardiovascular flows on the IBM BlueGene/P: Full heart-circulation system at red-blood cell resolution. In *2010 ACM/IEEE International conference for high performance computing, networking, storage and analysis* (pp. 1-10). IEEE. doi:10.1109/SC.2010.33

Pohl, T., Deserno, F., Thurey, N., Rüde, U., Lammers, P., Wellein, G., & Zeiser, T. (2004). Performance evaluation of parallel large-scale lattice Boltzmann applications on three supercomputing architectures. In *Supercomputing, 2004. Proceedings of the ACM/IEEE SC2004 conference* (pp. 21-21). IEEE. doi:10.1109/SC.2004.37

Pohl, T., Kowarschik, M., Wilke, J., Iglberger, K., & Rüde, U. (2003). Optimization and profiling of the cache performance of parallel lattice Boltzmann codes. *Parallel Processing Letters, 13*(04), 549–560. doi:10.1142/S0129626403001501

Regulski, W., Szumbarski, J., Łaniewski-Wołłk, L., Gumowski, K., Skibiński, J., Wichrowski, M., & Wejrzanowski, T. (2015). Pressure drop in flow across ceramic foams - a numerical and experimental study. *Chemical Engineering Science, 137*, 320–337. doi:10.1016/j.ces.2015.06.043

Rong, L., Dong, K., & Yu, A. (2014). Lattice-Boltzmann simulation of fluid flow through packed beds of spheres: Effect of particle size distribution. *Chemical Engineering Science, 116*, 508–523. doi:10.1016/j.ces.2014.05.025

Rothman, D. H. (1988). Cellular-automaton fluids: A model for flow in porous media. *Geophysics, 53*(4), 509–518. doi:10.1190/1.1442482

Sanders, P., & Schulz, C. (2011). Engineering multilevel graph partitioning algorithms. In C. Demetrescu & M. M. Halldorsson (Eds.), *Algorithms - ESA 2011: 19th Annual European symposium, Saarbrücken, Germany* (pp. 469–480). Berlin: Springer Berlin Heidelberg.

Schönherr, M., Geier, M., & Krafczyk, M. (2011). 3D GPGPU LBM implementation on non-uniform grids. *International conference on parallel computational fluid dynamics ParCFD*.

Schornbaum, F., & Rüde, U. (2016). Massively parallel algorithms for the lattice Boltzmann method on nonuniform grids. *SIAM Journal on Scientific Computing, 38*(2), C96–C126. doi:10.1137/15M1035240

Schulz, M., Krafczyk, M., Tölke, J., & Rank, E. (2002). Parallelization strategies and efficiency of CFD computations in complex geometries using lattice Boltzmann methods on high-performance computers. In M. Breuer, F. Durst, & C. Zenger (Eds.), *High Performance Scientific and Engineering Computing: Proceedings of the 3rd International FORTWIHR Conference on HPSEC, Erlangen* (pp. 115-122). Berlin: Springer Berlin Heidelberg. doi:10.1007/978-3-642-55919-8_13

Schure, M. R., Maier, R. S., Kroll, D. M., & Davis, H. T. (2002). Simulation of packed-bed chromatography utilizing high-resolution flow fields: Comparison with models. *Analytical Chemistry*, *74*(23), 6006–6016. doi:10.1021/ac0204101 PMID:12498196

Shikazono, N., Kanno, D., Matsuzaki, K., Teshima, H., Sumino, S., & Kasagi, N. (2010). Numerical assessment of SOFC anode polarization based on three-dimensional model microstructure reconstructed from FIB-SEM images. *Journal of the Electrochemical Society*, *157*(5), B665–B672. doi:10.1149/1.3330568

Singh, M., & Mohanty, K. (2000). Permeability of spatially correlated porous media. *Chemical Engineering Science*, *55*(22), 5393–5403. doi:10.1016/S0009-2509(00)00157-3

Stahl, B., Chopard, B., & Latt, J. (2010). Measurements of wall shear stress with the lattice Boltzmann method and staircase approximation of boundaries. *Computers & Fluids*, *39*(9), 1625–1633. doi:10.1016/j.compfluid.2010.05.015

Straka, R. (2016). Numerical simulation of heat transfer in packed beds by two population thermal lattice Boltzmann method. *Mechanics & Industry*, *17*(2), 203. doi:10.1051/meca/2015071

Strohmaier, E. (2006). Top500 supercomputer. In *Proceedings of the 2006 ACM/IEEE conference on supercomputing*. New York: ACM.

Stürmer, M., Götz, J., Richter, G., Dörfler, A., & Rüde, U. (2009). Fluid flow simulation on the Cell broadband engine using the lattice Boltzmann method. *Computers & Mathematics with Applications (Oxford, England)*, *58*(5), 1062–1070. doi:10.1016/j.camwa.2009.04.006

Succi, S., Foti, E., & Higuera, F. (1989). Three-dimensional flows in complex geometries with the lattice Boltzmann method. *EPL*, *10*(5), 433–438. doi:10.1209/0295-5075/10/5/008

Sullivan, S., Gladden, L., & Johns, M. (2006). Simulation of power-law fluid flow through porous media using lattice Bboltzmann techniques. *Journal of Non-Newtonian Fluid Mechanics*, *133*(2–3), 91–98. doi:10.1016/j.jnnfm.2005.11.003

Sullivan, S., Sani, F., Johns, M., & Gladden, L. (2005). Simulation of packed bed reactors using lattice Boltzmann methods. *Chemical Engineering Science, 60*(12), 3405–3418. doi:10.1016/j.ces.2005.01.038

Sullivan, S., Sederman, A., Johns, M., & Gladden, L. (2007). Verification of shear-thinning LB simulations in complex geometries. *Journal of Non-Newtonian Fluid Mechanics, 143*(2-3), 59–63. doi:10.1016/j.jnnfm.2006.12.008

Sullivan, S. P., Gladden, L. F., & Johns, M. L. (2006). 3D chemical reactor LB simulations. *Mathematics and Computers in Simulation, 72*(2-6), 206–211. doi:10.1016/j.matcom.2006.05.023

Suzue, Y., Shikazono, N., & Kasagi, N. (2008). Micro modeling of solid oxide fuel cell anode based on stochastic reconstruction. *Journal of Power Sources, 184*(1), 52–59. doi:10.1016/j.jpowsour.2008.06.029

Tomczak, T., & Szafran, R. G. (2016). *Memory layout in GPU implementation of lattice Boltzmann method for sparse 3D geometries.* CoRR, abs/1611.02445

Tomczak, T., & Szafran, R. G. (2017). *Sparse geometries handling in lattice-Boltzmann method implementation for graphic processors.* CoRR, abs/1703.08015

Valero-Lara, P. (2016). Leveraging the performance of LBM-HPC for Large sizes on GPUs using ghost cells. In J. Carretero, J. Garcia-Blas, R. Ko, P. Mueller, & K. Nakano (Eds.), Lecture Notes in Computer Science: Vol. 10048. *Algorithms and Architectures for Parallel Processing. ICA3PP 2016* (pp. 417–430). Cham: Springer. doi:10.1007/978-3-319-49583-5_31

Valero-Lara, P., Igual, F. D., Prieto-Matías, M., Pinelli, A., & Favier, J. (2015). Accelerating fluid-solid simulations (lattice-Boltzmann & immersed-boundary) on heterogeneous architectures. *Journal of Computational Science, 10*, 249–261. doi:10.1016/j.jocs.2015.07.002

Valero-Lara, P., & Jansson, J. (2015). A non-uniform staggered Cartesian grid approach for lattice-Boltzmann method. *Procedia Computer Science, 51*, 296–305. doi:10.1016/j.procs.2015.05.245

Valero-Lara, P., & Jansson, J. (2017). Heterogeneous CPU+GPU approaches for mesh refinement over lattice-Boltzmann simulations. *Concurrency and Computation: Practice and Experience, 29*(7).

Vidal, D., Roy, R., & Bertrand, F. (2010a). On improving the performance of large parallel lattice Boltzmann flow simulations in heterogeneous porous media. *Computers & Fluids, 39*(2), 324–337. doi:10.1016/j.compfluid.2009.09.011

Vidal, D., Roy, R., & Bertrand, F. (2010b). A parallel workload balanced and memory efficient lattice-Boltzmann algorithm with single unit BGK relaxation time for laminar Newtonian flows. *Computers & Fluids, 39*(8), 1411–1423. doi:10.1016/j.compfluid.2010.04.011

Wang, J., Zhang, X., Bengough, A. G., & Crawford, J. W. (2005). Domain-decomposition method for parallel lattice Boltzmann simulation of incompressible flow in porous media. *Phys. Rev. E, 72*(1), 016706. doi:10.1103/PhysRevE.72.016706 PMID:16090133

Wang, L.-P., & Afsharpoya, B. (2006). Modeling fluid flow in fuel cells using the lattice-Boltzmann approach. *Mathematics and Computers in Simulation, 72*(2-6), 242–248. doi:10.1016/j.matcom.2006.05.038

Wittmann, M., Zeiser, T., Hager, G., & Wellein, G. (2013a). Comparison of different propagation steps for lattice Boltzmann methods. *Computers & Mathematics with Applications (Oxford, England), 65*(6), 924–935. doi:10.1016/j.camwa.2012.05.002

Wittmann, M., Zeiser, T., Hager, G., & Wellein, G. (2013b). Domain decomposition and locality optimization for large-scale lattice Boltzmann simulations. *Computers & Fluids, 80*, 283–289. doi:10.1016/j.compfluid.2012.02.007

Yang, A., Miller, C. T., & Turcoliver, L. D. (1996). Simulation of correlated and uncorrelated packing of random size spheres. *Physical Review E: Statistical Physics, Plasmas, Fluids, and Related Interdisciplinary Topics, 53*(2), 1516–1524. doi:10.1103/PhysRevE.53.1516 PMID:9964415

Yoshino, M., Hotta, Y., Hirozane, T., & Endo, M. (2007). A numerical method for incompressible non-Newtonian fluid flows based on the lattice Boltzmann method. *Journal of Non-Newtonian Fluid Mechanics, 147*(1–2), 69–78. doi:10.1016/j.jnnfm.2007.07.007

Yuen, E., Sederman, A., Sani, F., Alexander, P., & Gladden, L. (2003). Correlations between local conversion and hydrodynamics in a 3-D fixed-bed esterification process: An MRI and lattice-Boltzmann study. *Chemical Engineering Science, 58*(3-6), 613–619. doi:10.1016/S0009-2509(02)00586-9

Zeiser, T., Hager, G., & Wellein, G. (2009a). Benchmark analysis and application results for lattice Boltzmann simulations on NEC SX vector and Intel Nehalem systems. *Parallel Processing Letters, 19*(04), 491–511. doi:10.1142/S0129626409000389

Zeiser, T., Hager, G., & Wellein, G. (2009b). Vector computers in a world of commodity clusters, massively parallel systems and many-core many-threaded CPUs: Recent experience based on an advanced lattice Boltzmann flow solver. In W. E. Nagel, D. B. Kröner, & M. M. Resch (Eds.), *High performance computing in science and engineering: Transactions of the high performance computing center, Stuttgart (HLRS)* (pp. 333–347). Berlin: Springer Berlin Heidelberg. doi:10.1007/978-3-540-88303-6_24

Zhang, X., Bengough, A. G., Deeks, L. K., Crawford, J. W., & Young, I. M. (2002). A novel three-dimensional lattice Boltzmann model for solute transport in variably saturated porous media. *Water Resources Research, 38*(9), 6-1-6-10.

Zhang, X., Deeks, L. K., Bengough, A. G., Crawford, J. W., & Young, I. M. (2005). Determination of soil hydraulic conductivity with the lattice Boltzmann method and soil thin-section technique. *Journal of Hydrology (Amsterdam), 306*(1-4), 59–70. doi:10.1016/j.jhydrol.2004.08.039

Zhang, X., & Ren, L. (2003). Lattice Boltzmann model for agrochemical transport in soils. *Journal of Contaminant Hydrology, 67*(1-4), 27–42. doi:10.1016/S0169-7722(03)00086-X PMID:14607468

Zimny, S., Chopard, B., Malaspinas, O., Lorenz, E., Jain, K., Roller, S., & Bernsdorf, J. (2013). A multiscale approach for the coupled simulation of blood flow and thrombus formation in intracranial aneurysms. *Procedia Computer Science, 18*, 1006–1015. doi:10.1016/j.procs.2013.05.266

KEY TERMS AND DEFINITIONS

Burst Memory Transfer: A single memory transaction (read or write) consisting one request with address and a response containing 2^b neighbour bytes at aligned address. Burst transfers are used to decrease the overhead caused by high memory latency resulting from a complex communication protocol and a low memory clock frequency.

CPU: Central processing unit, a computer element that performs arithmetic, logical, control, and communication operations by executing instructions from memory. Due to a large gap between CPU and memory speed, the modern CPUs use large cache memories and parallel, speculative, and out-of-order execution of instructions. Current multicore processors can run more than 10 instructions per one clock cycle in each core.

GPU: Graphics processing unit, a computer element specialised in generation and manipulation of images. Modern GPUs are in fact versatile, programmable general-purpose coprocessors with up to ten times more computational power than CPU and a few times higher memory bandwidth. Masking of memory latency in GPUs is done by a fast, hardware instruction switching between tenths of thousands of simultaneously running instructions.

Graph Partitioning Problem: The problem of finding subgraphs with specific properties, for example, the equal number of vertices per subgraph and the minimal number of edges connecting subgraphs. Uniform graph partitioning is the NP-complete problem.

NP-Complete Problem: In computer science the problem for which there is no algorithm allowing to find the solution in polynomial time, although any solution can be verified in polynomial time.

Octree: The tree data structure where each node contains eight children. Octrees are often used for 3D space partitioning into cubes – each cube is divided into eight smaller cubes with two times shorter sides. For 2D space, the square-based quadtrees can be used.

SIMD: Single instruction multiple data, according to Flynn's taxonomy, a class of parallel computers that simultaneously perform the same operation on multiple data elements. Almost every modern processor is equipped with SIMD unit operating on both integer and floating point numbers, for x86 architecture examples are SSE and AVX instructions.

Vector Processor: A processor with implemented operations on one-dimensional data arrays called vectors. Vector processors offer a large memory bandwidth required to avoid stalls during execution of instructions.

Chapter 6

A Meshfree–Based Lattice Boltzmann Approach for Simulation of Fluid Flows Within Complex Geometries:
Application of Meshfree Methods for LBM Simulations

Sonam Tanwar
University of Delhi, India

ABSTRACT

This chapter develops a meshless formulation of lattice Boltzmann method for simulation of fluid flows within complex and irregular geometries. The meshless feature of proposed technique will improve the accuracy of standard lattice Boltzmann method within complicated fluid domains. Discretization of such domains itself may introduce significant numerical errors into the solution. Specifically, in phase transition or moving boundary problems, discretization of the domain is a time-consuming and complex process. In these problems, at each time step, the computational domain may change its shape and need to be re-meshed accordingly for the purpose of accuracy and stability of the solution. The author proposes to combine lattice Boltzmann method with a Galerkin meshfree technique popularly known as element-free Galerkin method in this chapter to remove the difficulties associated with traditional grid-based methods.

DOI: 10.4018/978-1-5225-4760-0.ch006

INTRODUCTION

Lattice Boltzmann method (LBM), originated from Ludwig Boltzmann's kinetic theory of gases has emerged as a promising tool for fluid flow simulations besides the classical Navier-Stokes equations solvers (Begum, & Basit, 2008), (Guo et al., 2000), (Ubertini et al., 2003). The discrete Boltzmann equation is a velocity discrete form of the Boltzmann transport equation based upon microscopic model and mesoscopic kinetic theory of gases/fluids. The basic difference between standard Lattice Boltzmann method and Navier-Stokes model is that LBM is not limited to the continuum approach. Further, with a proper choice of collision operator, Navier-Stokes model can be recovered from LBM. Lattice Boltzmann method due to their simple formulation, easy implementation and substantial potential of parallel processing are suitable for flow simulations within complex/ irregular geometries (Musavia & Ashrafizaadeh, 2016), flow within porous media (Pan et al., 2006), fluid-structure interaction (FSI) problems (Kwon, 2006) and multi-phase flow problems (Kupershtokh, 2014), (Shan, & Chen, 1993).

Initially, Lattice Boltzmann method was considered to be a direct extension of Lattice Gas automata (LGA) (McNamara, & Zanetti, 1988). Later, it was shown (McNamara et al., 1995), (Sterling, & Chen, 1996) that the lattice Boltzmann equation is a special discretization of the discrete Boltzmann equation along characteristics where streaming equation becomes the exact solution of the linear advection equation. Streaming equation is commonly known as perfect shift.

However, it becomes difficult to deal with irregularly shaped geometries or curved boundaries with uniform grid structure of standard lattice Boltzmann method (Bao et al., 2008), (Chun, & Ladd, 2007), (Pan et al., 2006). This restriction is the consequence of the fact that standard lattice Boltzmann method involves discretization of velocity space and physical space coupled on a lattice (He & Luo, 1997). There have been several studies in the literature to address this drawback of the lattice Boltzmann method. There are two major approaches to extend Lattice Boltzmann method over non-uniform or unstructured grids so that it can be applied to complex problems. One is Interpolation-supplemented LBM (ISLBM), proposed by He and his colleagues (He et al., 1996). In this method, interpolation is applied at every time step in order to obtain the distribution function at the grid point. It increases the computational time and makes it computationally inefficient, especially for three-dimensional problems. The other scheme is based on the solution of a differential Lattice Boltzmann equation. The differential Lattice Boltzmann equation can further be solved by the finite volume algorithm. Succi and co-workers (Benzi et al., 1992) (Nannelli, 1992) were apparently the first to extend the technique over irregular lattice geometries by suggesting a finite volume formulation for the lattice Boltzmann equation. It was shown by Chen (Chen, 1998), that finite volume based LBM can exactly obey the conservation laws. Many authors Filippova and Hanel (Filippova, & Hanel, 1998), Dupuis and Chopard (Dupuis, & Chopard, 2003) suggested grid refinement techniques for lattice Boltzmann simulations. Although, grid-refinement algorithms may increase the efficiency of the lattice Boltzmann method, particularly in simulating strongly anisotropic flows, (e.g., high Reynolds number boundary layer flows), but still the basic problem of restriction to the uniform Cartesian grid system for standard lattice Boltzmann method remains unfixed.

The simple solution is that for the Boltzmann equation, the velocity space and the physical space can be discretized independently. Different approaches for discretization of the discrete Boltzmann equation in physical space such as finite difference, finite element, finite volume formulation of LBM have been proposed so that the technique could be extended to non-uniform or unstructured grid. It leads to Finite-Difference-LBM (Bardow et al., 2006), (Cao et al., 1997), (Mei & Shyy, 1998), (Sofonea, & Sekerka, 2003), Finite Volume-LBM (Patil, & Lakshmisha, 2009), (Stiebler et al., 2006), (Ubertini et al., 2003), (Xe et al., 1999), Finite Element-LBM (Lee, & Lin, 2001), (Lee, & Lin, 2003), (Li et al., 2005) and Discontinuous Galerkin-LBM (Begum, & Basit, 2008), (Duster et al., 2006), (Shi et al., 2003) methods.

In this chapter, mesh free formulation of standard lattice Boltzmann method has been proposed. The advantage of using mesh free formulation over grid based methods (FD, FEM, FVM) is the efficiency of mesh free discretization within complex or irregular domains. However, grid based formulations of standard LBM are capable of simulating geometrically complex flows, yet the accuracy of method highly depends upon quality of the mesh chosen. Mesh improvement in complex geometries is itself a costly and time consuming affair. Further flow simulation problems which require re-meshing during the solution process such as phase transition problems could be computationally expensive prohibitively and could produce results with unacceptable numerical errors. Meshfree methods are answer to these difficulties of grid based discretization. These methods involve only a set of nodes scattered arbitrarily within the problem domain as well as on the boundaries for discretization purpose without any fixed connectivity, which makes insertion or deletion of the nodes during the process quite flexible. Practically, nodal distribution depends upon the problem under consideration, part of the domain with larger gradients need higher nodal density for the purpose of accuracy. However, within regular and simple geometries, even uniform nodal distribution yields good results. Thus, noting all the basic advantages of a meshless formulation, for space discretization of lattice Boltzmann method a mesh free technique known as 'Element free Galerkin method' has been utilized in this chapter.

BACKGROUND

Lattice Boltzmann method owes its origin from cellular automata and lattice gas automata, it is based upon fundamental principal that gases/fluids consist of large number of small particles/molecules moving with random motions. During their random motions, particles stream and collide with each other which provide exchange of momentum and energy respectively. Boltzmann transport equation successfully models this phenomenon, as follows

$$\frac{\partial f_i}{\partial t} + \vec{e_i} \cdot \nabla f_i = \Omega_i \tag{1}$$

where $f_i\left(\vec{x}, t\right)$ denotes microscopic particle distribution function, $\vec{e_i}$ denotes microscopic particle velocity, and Ω_i is the collision operator along direction 'i'. Lattice Boltzmann equations are obtained via special discretization of Boltzmann transport equation by reducing the number of particles in original gas/fluid dynamics and confining them to the nodes of a lattice.

There are several lattice models available such as D2Q4, D2Q5, D2Q7 and D2Q9 as shown in Figure 1. (In general for a DmQn model 'm' refers to the dimension and 'n' is the number of velocity vectors). Although, D2Q9 model is computationally more expensive than other models available but it has been successfully employed to simulate two-dimensional fluid flows. It has been observed that D2Q4, D2Q5 models are inappropriate to recover the important non-linear convective terms of Navier-Stokes model due to lack of lattice symmetry (Chen & Doolen, 1998), (Succi, 2001).

Figure 1. Different two-dimensional lattice models (a) D2Q4 (b) D2Q5 (c) D2Q7 (d) D2Q9

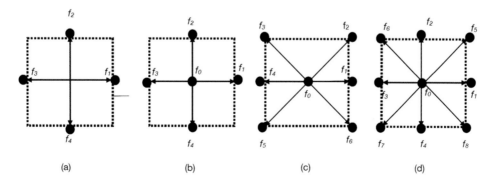

In a two-dimensional D2Q9 lattice, the microscopic velocities $\vec{e}_i$ $\left(i=0,1,2,...,8\right)$ of a particle, restricted to stream in possible 9 directions (as shown in Figure 2), are defined as follows;

$$\vec{e}_i = \begin{cases} \left(0,0\right) & i=0 \\ c\left(\cos\left\{\left(i-1\right)\pi/2\right\},\sin\left\{\left(i-1\right)\pi/2\right\}\right) & i=1,2,...,4 \\ c\left(\sqrt{2}\cos\left\{\left(i-1\right)\pi/2+\pi/4\right\},\sqrt{2}\sin\left\{\left(i-1\right)\pi/2+\pi/4\right\}\right) & i=5,6,...,8 \end{cases}$$

(2)

where $c=\Delta x/\Delta t$ represents the lattice speed, Δx is the lattice spacing and Δt is the time increment, usually both Δx and Δt are set to unity.

Collision operator, which in general is a complex non-linear integral, is obtained via linearising the collision term around its local equilibrium and according to Bhatnagar Gross Krook (BGK) (Bhatnagar et al., 1954), the collision operator Ω is defined as follows;

$$\Omega_i = -\frac{1}{\tau}\left(f_i - f_i^{eq}\right)$$

(3)

In equation (3), τ is the rate of relaxation towards local equilibrium, f_i^{eq} denotes the local equilibrium distribution function in direction 'i'. The rate of relaxation τ

Figure 2. Illustration of nine velocity vectors for D2Q9 lattice model

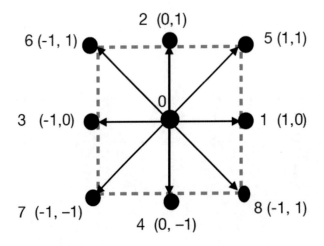

in equation (3) is assumed to be constant along all directions and this scheme is known as single time relaxation scheme (SRT). Further, collision operator defined in equation (3) is equivalent to viscous term in classical Navier-Stokes model and Navier-Stokes equations can be obtained from discrete from of Lattice Boltzmann equation via Chapman-Enskog expansion (Frish et al., 1986). The comparison between basic structure of Navier-Stokes equation and Lattice Boltzmann equation is depicted in Table 1.

The fluid kinematic viscosity ν for D2Q9 lattice model is related to single relaxation time τ by;

$$\nu = \frac{\left(2\tau - 1\right)\left(\Delta x\right)^2}{6\Delta t} \qquad (4)$$

In absence of any external forces, after substituting collision operator from BGK (Bhatnagar Gross Krook) model in equation (1), general lattice Boltzmann equation for a typical lattice node is given as follows;

$$\frac{\partial f}{\partial t} + \vec{e}.\nabla f = -\frac{1}{\tau}\left(f - f^{eq}\right) \qquad (5)$$

In D2Q9 lattice model, a node is free to stream in nine possible directions, therefore for a specific direction, discrete from of lattice Boltzmann equation would be;

Table 1. Comparison between basic structures of Navier-Stokes equation and Lattice-Boltzmann equations

Navier-Stokes equation	Lattice Boltzmann equation
$\rho\left(\dfrac{\partial \boldsymbol{u}}{\partial t} + \left(\boldsymbol{u}.\nabla\boldsymbol{u}\right)\boldsymbol{u}\right) = -\nabla p + \mu\nabla^2\boldsymbol{u}$	$\dfrac{\partial f}{\partial t} + \vec{e}.\nabla f = -\dfrac{1}{\tau}\left(f - f^{eq}\right)$
Navier-Stokes equations are based upon continuum approach.	LBM is based upon microscopic models and mesoscopic kinetic equations.
Navier-Stokes equations are second order PDE.	Lattice Boltzmann equations are first order PDE.
Non-linear in nature due to presence of convective term $\left(\boldsymbol{u}.\nabla\boldsymbol{u}\right)$, which makes analytical solution difficult to obtain.	Lattice Boltzmann equation avoids convective term; convection is simply turned into advection.
Macroscopic quantities (velocity, momentum density etc) are obtained directly.	Unknown variable is distribution function f in Lattice Boltzmann equation, later during the process; these quantities are obtained with the help of distribution function.

$$\frac{\partial f_i}{\partial t} + \vec{e_i} . \nabla f_i = -\frac{1}{\tau}\left(f_i - f_i^{eq}\right) \; for \; i = 0,1,...,8 \tag{6}$$

The equilibrium distribution function f^{eq} defined in equation (5) is obtained from Maxwell-Boltzmann distribution function for low Mach number (Mach number $M = u / c_s$, c_s is the speed of sound and u is the macroscopic velocity). While deriving equilibrium distribution function f^{eq} from Maxwell distribution function, the expansion is kept upto second order only to match with the order of Navier-Stokes equations;

$$f_i^{eq} = \rho w_i \left[1 + \frac{3u.\vec{e_i}}{c^2} + \frac{\left(9u.\vec{e_i}\right)^2}{2c^4} - \frac{3u.u}{2c^2} \right] \tag{7}$$

In this equation (7), ρ is the macroscopic fluid density and u is the vector of macroscopic fluid velocities. For any practical situation, these are the most significant quantities of interest. In Navier-Stokes model these macroscopic quantities (density, velocity, and pressure) are obtained directly, while in LBM equation (6), the unknown field variable is distribution function $f(\vec{x},t)$ and macroscopic quantities such as density, velocity are obtained by evaluating hydrodynamic moments of distribution function f (Yu et al., 2003). In discretised velocity space, the fluid density ρ and velocity vector u for a D2Q9 lattice model are expressed as follows;

$$\rho = \sum_{i=0}^{8} f_i \tag{8}$$

$$u = \frac{1}{\rho}\sum_{i=0}^{8} \vec{e_i} f_i \tag{9}$$

In addition, the weighting parameter defined in equation (7), for each velocity direction in D2Q9 model is given as follows;

$$w_i = \begin{cases} 4/9 & i = 0 \\ 1/9 & i = 1, 2, 3, 4 \\ 1/36 & i = 5, 6, 7, 8 \end{cases} \qquad (10)$$

The normalization condition for weights is $\sum_{i=0}^{8} w_i = 1$

Imposition of Boundary Conditions in Lattice-Boltzmann Method

Imposition of boundary conditions is a complex issue to deal with in Lattice Boltzmann method, as in a fluid flow simulation problem boundary conditions are usually prescribed over macroscopic quantities such as pressure, density, velocity, stress etc. However in lattice Boltzmann method, the advection equation (6), is obtained in terms of microscopic distribution function. Thus, prescribed boundary conditions of macroscopic flow variables need to be translated in terms of microscopic distribution function. There are several approaches available in literature for translating the hydro-dynamical conditions to the conditions of distribution function f_i such as bounce-back boundary conditions (Shi et al., 2003), Zou-He velocity and pressure boundary conditions (Zuo & He, 1997), Equilibrium boundary conditions etc. with different order of accuracy and stability. Bounce-back boundary conditions are generally used to simulate no-slip velocity boundary conditions. Bounce-back means that when a fluid particle reaches the boundary node of a lattice, it will scatter back to the fluid along with its incoming direction, i.e. incoming directions of the distribution function are reversed after encountering a boundary node. Although, this approach is easy to implement and provides decent accuracy, but in case of complex or curvilinear geometries, this approach requires some special modifications. On the other hand, Zou-He velocity and pressure boundary conditions are suitable to model flows with prescribed velocities, pressure or density on the boundaries. This type of boundary condition depends upon the orientation of the boundary; hence this approach is also difficult to be generalized for complex geometries. Equilibrium boundary conditions (EBC) are easiest and simplest type of boundary conditions which are based on the assumption that boundary values of f_i are equal to the values of f_i^{eq} along the boundary. f_i^{eq} can be easily calculated from the prescribed values of ρ, u on the boundary. The EBC can be applied without any troubles on arbitrary curvilinear boundaries also. The only physical restriction on the application of EBC to the hydrodynamical problem is that it can be applied only in a regime of low wall-shear flow, because in EBC shear stress near the wall is neglected (Mohamad & Succi, 2009). It has been observed that the usage of EBC for the problem of backward facing-step flow at Reynolds number $\text{Re} \approx 500$ ($\text{Re} = UL / \nu, U$ is velocity, L is the length and ν is the kinematic viscosity) can produce accurate results in comparison with the case of non equilibrium BC, which take into account existence of shear stress near the wall (Mohamad & Succi, 2009). Thus, in present chapter, author has used Equilibrium boundary condition (EBC) approach for imposition of boundary conditions of hydrodynamic variables.

MESHFREE FORMULATION OF LATTICE-BOLTZMANN EQUATION

In traditional form of solution for standard Lattice Boltzmann equation equation (6) the computations are confined on a lattice, which can be characterized as a structured mesh with regular grid. A brief outline about the solution procedure of traditional Lattice Boltzmann method is presented in the form of a flow chart in Figure 3.

However, fluid flow simulations within complex geometries, e.g. blood flow problems within arteries, multiphase flows, fluid-structure interaction problems, phase transition problems etc. require unstructured meshes for space discretization to obtain numerical efficiency and accuracy. Meshfree methods are next generation techniques for solution of space discretization related problems (unstructured meshes) with quite accuracy and consistency. These methods do not require any mesh for discretization purpose, they use just a set of nodes arbitrarily scattered in the problem

Figure 3. Schematic process of LBM algorithm

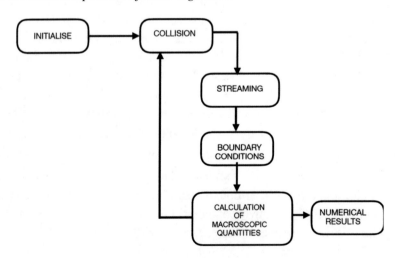

domain without any fixed connectivity. It gives maximum flexibility for insertion or deletion of nodes even during the process of simulation, if there is a need of high or low resolution grid in computational domain without re-discretizing the whole problem domain. A particular example comparing mesh free discretization and grid based discretization (FEM) is shown in Figure 4, Figure 5 and Figure 6 for the purpose of clarity. In this example, the computational domain is a square enclosure with a solid circular cylinder inside it. It could be easily observed from Figure 4, that meshfree discretization which is obtained by deleting nodes within circular domain from regular nodal distribution, is quite easier as compared to FEM discretization.

This chapter discusses Element free Galerkin (a popular mesh free technique) formulation of Lattice Boltzmann method in detail, but before that a brief introduction about Element Free Method (EFGM) is required for clear understanding of the process for the reader. Complete details of EFGM are provided in the Appendix at the end of the chapter.

Figure 4. FEM discretization of an enclosure with a solid circular cylinder inside

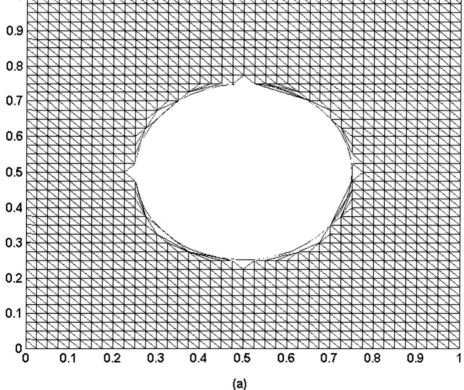

(a)

Figure 5. Complete nodal discretization of enclosure

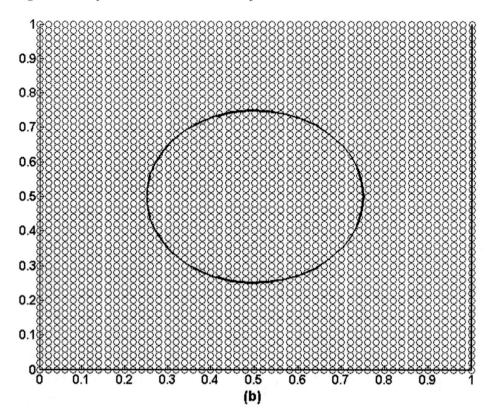

(b)

EFGM Formulation of Lattice Boltzmann Equation

In EFGM formulation computational domain is discretized with the help of the arbitrarily scattered nodes. The nodal density and their distribution depend upon computational geometry or the complexity of the fluid flow problem under consideration. Then Element Free Galerkin model of Lattice Boltzmann equation (6), is obtained by substituting Moving Least Square (MLS) approximation for the unknown field variable i.e. distribution function $f(\vec{x}, t)$ over the computational domain Ω as;

$$f_i^h(X) = \sum_{I=1}^{n} \Phi_I(X) f_{iI} = \Phi(X) f_i \tag{11}$$

Figure 6. Meshfree discretization of an enclosure with a solid circular cylinder inside

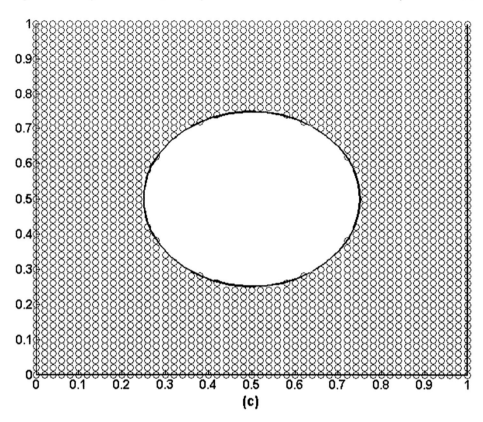

(c)

MLS shape functions $\Phi(X)$ are defined in Appendix-1 in equation (1.15), 'n' denotes the number of nodes that are included in the support domain of an evaluation point *X*. The size and shape of the support domain (circular, rectangular) may be different for different points as per the problem requirement.

Weighted Residual Form of the Lattice Boltzmann Equation

The discrete form equation of EFG based lattice Boltzmann method is obtained by multiplying the equation (6) by a test function 'w' and integrating it over the entire problem domain, which results in,

$$\int_{\Omega} w \left[\frac{\partial f_i}{\partial t} + \vec{e}_i . \nabla f_i + \frac{1}{\tau} \left(f_i - f_i^{eq} \right) \right] d\Omega = 0 \, for \, i = 0, 1, ..., 8 \qquad (12)$$

Imposition of Essential Boundary Conditions With Penalty Method

The MLS shape functions as defined in Appendix-1, are unable to satisfy the kronecker delta property in contrast to Finite element shape functions. Thus, special measures have to be taken in Element free Galerkin method for imposition of essential boundary conditions (different approaches discussed in Appendix-1). In this chapter, the author has chosen to employ Penalty method for boundary condition imposition due to its easy implementation and modest accuracy.

After applying penalty method, for imposition of Equilibrium boundary conditions (i.e. $f_i = f_i^{eq}$ at the boundary nodes of computational domain), the weighted integral form (12) reduces to;

$$\int_{\Omega} w \left[\frac{\partial f_i}{\partial t} + \vec{e}_i \cdot \nabla f_i + \frac{1}{\tau} \left(f_i - f_i^{eq} \right) \right] d\Omega + \int_{\Gamma} \bar{\alpha} \left(f_i - f_i^{eq} \right) d\Gamma = 0 \, for \, i = 0,1,...,8$$

(13)

In this equation (13), $\bar{\alpha}$ is the penalty parameter to penalise the difference between the true value of field variable and the approximated value at the boundary nodes. Ideally, $\bar{\alpha}$ should be infinity, but usually, a high value within the range of 10^{6-10} may serve the purpose. Ω denotes the computational domain and symbol " reflects boundaries of the computational domain, which could be either straight, curvilinear or any type of complex boundary.

In Galerkin form, the test function or weight function w are replaced by approximation function only. Hence, in EFGM also, the test function w is replaced by MLS approximation/shape functions $\Phi_I (I = 1,2,...,N)$ to obtain the expression of stiffness matrices. Here, N refers to the total nodes in whole computational domain. The nodes which are included in the support domain of an evaluation or quadrature point, have non-zero values for MLS shape functions (obtained from equation 1.15) and for the nodes outside the support domain, MLS shape functions are simply prescribed zero value. It makes size of stiffness matrix corresponding to each evaluation point fixed i.e. $N \times N$ and stiffens matrix becomes a sparse matrix. After substituting w by $\Phi_I (I = 1,2,...,N)$ and the unknown field variable f_i by MLS approximation, given in (11), into equation (13), the system of equations can be defined as follows;

$$M \left\{ \frac{\partial f_i}{\partial t} \right\} + K f_i = \left[G \right], i = 0,1,2,...,8$$

(14)

where matrices,

$$M_{IJ} = \int_\Omega \Phi_I \Phi_J d\Omega, K_{IJ} = \int_\Omega \left[\vec{e_i}\Phi_I \left(\frac{\partial \Phi_J}{\partial x} + \frac{\partial \Phi_J}{\partial y} \right) + \frac{1}{\tau}\Phi_I\Phi_J \right]d\Omega + \int_\Gamma \bar{\alpha}\Phi_I\Phi_J d\Gamma$$

$$G_I = \int_\Omega \frac{1}{\tau}\Phi_I f_i^{eq} d\Omega + \int_\Gamma \bar{\alpha}\Phi_I f_i^{eq}d\Gamma, I,J = 1,2,...,N$$

After developing matrix equation (as given in (14)), of first order time derivative, the expression is integrated over time numerically. There are various numerical time integration techniques available in literature such as forward differencing, backward differencing, Runge-Kutta, Crank-Nickolson scheme, predictor corrector scheme etc. With unconditionally stable Crank-Nickolson scheme, equation (14), at $(p+1)^{th}$ time step can be written as;

$$[\hat{K}]_{p+1}[f_i]_{p+1} = [\overline{K}]_p[f_i]_p + [G]_{p,p+1}$$

where

$$[\hat{K}]_{p+1} = [M] + \frac{\Delta t}{2}[K]_{p+1}, [\overline{K}] = [M] - \frac{\Delta t}{2}[K]_p \qquad (15)$$

$$[G]_{p,p+1} = \frac{\Delta t}{2}[G_p + G_{p+1}]$$

Thus, to obtain microscopic particle distribution function $f_i(\vec{x},t)$ corresponding to each microscopic particle velocity $\vec{e_i}(i = 0,1,...,8)$, equation (15) is solved iteratively over defined time step " t with given initial and boundary conditions. Once, these microscopic quantities (f_i) are obtained corresponding to every node of computational domain, macroscopic fluid velocity **u**, fluid density ρ etc. are obtained for each node from equation (8)-(9). The complete process of EFGM based Lattice Boltzmann method may be represented with the help of a flow chart, given in Figure 7. Also, implementation details of EFGM for fluid flow simulations are provided in (Singh & Bhargava, 2014), (Singh & Bhargava, 2015), (Singh et al., 2007).

Figure 7. Schematic process for EFGM based LBM

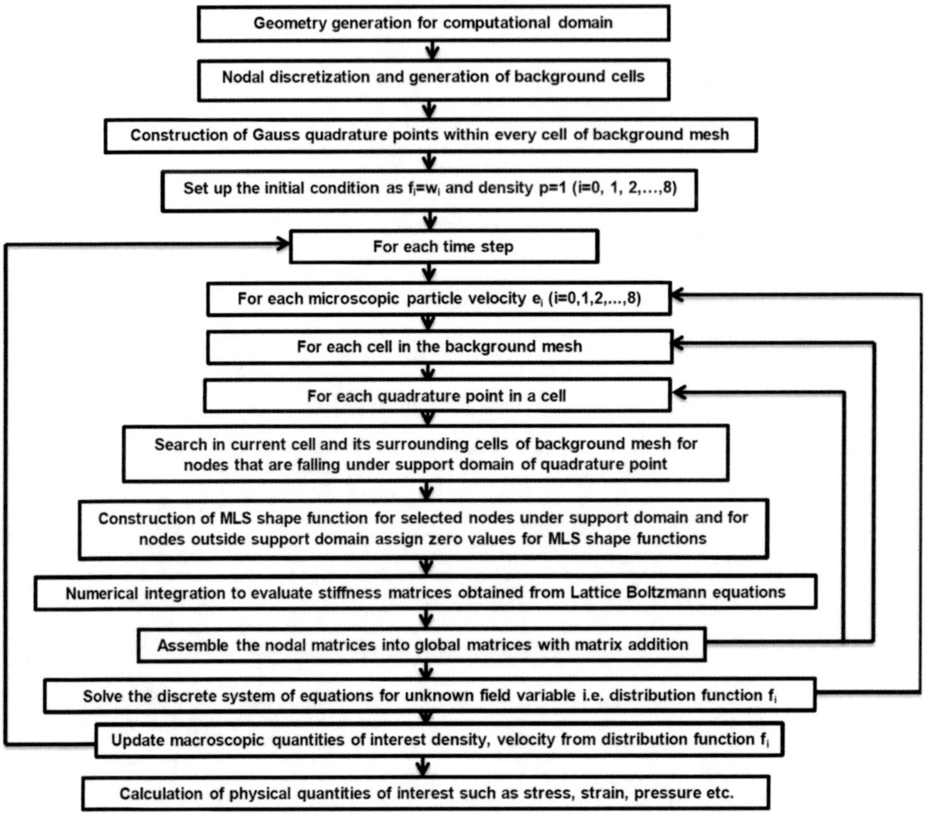

Geometry generation for computational domain
Nodal discretization and generation of background cells
Construction of Gauss quadrature points within every cell of background mesh
Set up the initial condition as $f_i=w_i$ and density p=1 (i=0, 1, 2,...,8)
For each time step
For each microscopic particle velocity e_i (i=0,1,2,...,8)
For each cell in the background mesh
For each quadrature point in a cell
Search in current cell and its surrounding cells of background mesh for nodes that are falling under support domain of quadrature point
Construction of MLS shape function for selected nodes under support domain and for nodes outside support domain assign zero values for MLS shape functions
Numerical integration to evaluate stiffness matrices obtained from Lattice Boltzmann equations
Assemble the nodal matrices into global matrices with matrix addition
Solve the discrete system of equations for unknown field variable i.e. distribution function f_i
Update macroscopic quantities of interest density, velocity from distribution function f_i
Calculation of physical quantities of interest such as stress, strain, pressure etc.

TEST PROBLEM FOR VALIDATION OF METHODOLOGY PROPOSED

Planar Flow Past a Circular Cylinder

To validate the accuracy and efficiency of the methodology discussed above, a flow problem which requires unstructured mesh for purpose of discretization has been considered. This problem investigates flow between two circular cylinders of radii r_0 and R, (Dennis & Cheng, 1970), (Mei & Shyy,1998). The velocity components u_x and u_y over the boundary of circular cylinder with radius r_0 are prescribed zero values, while on the cylinder with radius R, the velocity components are defined as;

$$u_x = U_0 \neq 0, u_y = 0$$

The computational domain of the problem stated above becomes circular and for accuracy of the numerical simulations, a coarse unstructured mesh is required. We have proposed to utilize meshless based LBM to remove the discretization based difficulties. In previously obtained results (Krivovichev, 2014), the computational domain was discretized with finite element unstructured mesh utilizing 2889 grid nodes. However, in present simulation, the computational domain was discretized using 1500 arbitrary scattered nodes without any connectivity. The FEM & EFGM discretization of the domain are shown in Figure 8 and Figure 9.

Figure 8. FEM discretization of computational domain with unstructured mesh Krivovichev, 2014.

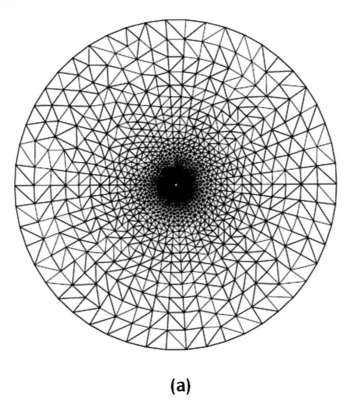

(a)

Figure 9. EFGM discretization of computational domain

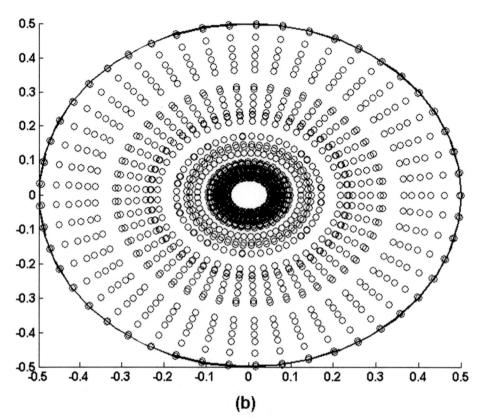

(b)

Parameters of Simulation

Physical Parameters of the Problem

The following physical parameters are used for numerical simulation of above stated problem;

$$r_0 = 0.05\,m, R = 0.5\,m, U_0 = 0.01\,m\,/\,s$$

For computation of Reynolds number $\mathrm{Re}, (\mathrm{Re} = UL\,/\,\nu)$ velocity $U = U_0$ and length $L = 2r_0$. Time interval of 0 to 200s has been considered.

Parameters for Numerical Technique

1. **Lattice:** D2Q9 lattice model has been considered with microscopic velocities $\vec{e}_i \left(i = 0, 1, 2, ..., 8 \right)$ defined in equation (2). The macroscopic quantities ρ, u and weighting parameters w_i are already defined in equation (8)-(10).

2. **MLS Shape Functions and Weight Functions:** The approximation of the unknown field variable i.e. particle distribution function $f_i \left(\vec{x}, t \right)$ in equation (12), is done with MLS shape functions and linear polynomial basis functions defined in Appendix-1 (equation (1.15) and (1.8)).

In present simulation, cubic spline weight functions as defined in Appendix-1 (equation (1.2)) have been used.

3. **Background Cells and Quadrature Points:** Ideally, Element free Galerkin method is not completely mesh free, as background cells are required for the purpose of numerical integration in this approach. For present simulation, element quadrature approach, defined in section 1.8 of Appendix-1 has been used. In each background cell, 2×2 Gauss quadrature points are considered for the purpose of numerical integration as well as for the selection of nodes while constructing MLS shape functions.

4. **Support Domain:** The concept of support domain has been utilized in present numerical simulation. The shape of the support domain for each quadrature point is considered to be rectangular with following size in x and y-direction;

Size of support domain in x-direction $d_{mxI} = d_{max} C_{xI}$

Size of support domain in y-direction $d_{myI} = d_{max} C_{yI}$

where d_{max} is a scaling parameter and C_{xI}, C_{yI} are the distances to nearest neighbours in x and y-direction respectively. Since, in the present simulation nodal distribution is irregular, therefore the size of the support domain may be different for different quadrature points depending upon C_{xI}, C_{yI}. The scaling parameter d_{max} has been fixed as 1.2.

NUMERICAL RESULTS

As a result of numerical computations, the macroscopic velocity components u_x, u_y are obtained within whole computational domain and a dimensionless drag coefficient C_D defined as

$$C_D = (1 / \rho r_0 U_0^2) \int_D S_{x\alpha} n_\alpha dS$$

(where D is the circle with radius r_0; n_x, n_y are components of normal to D and S_{xx}, S_{xy} are the components of stress tensor), is evaluated.

In present simulation, the drag coefficient C_D is calculated up to $\text{Re} < \text{Re}_c \approx 50$. Also, essential boundary conditions are satisfied by the method of Equilibrium boundary conditions, which yields good results for this range of Reynolds number. Obtained results are presented in Table 2 and a comparison is shown with previously obtained results.

Parallel Processing of LBM and EFGM for Computational Efficiency

Both Lattice Boltzmann and Element free Galerkin method are powerful and significant alternatives for computational fluid dynamics due to their ease of implementation for computer simulations. The only drawback of Element free Galerkin method is its high computational time requirement as compared to grid based methods (FEM, FDM). The computational time in Element free Galerkin method increases due to many factors such as selection of nodes for construction of MLS shape functions corresponding to each evaluation or quadrature point, construction of shape function

Table 2. Comparison of results for the validation of study

C_D	$\text{Re} = 10$	$\text{Re} = 20$	$\text{Re} = 40$
Dennis & Cheng results	2.846	2.045	1.522
FEM based LBM (Krivovichev, 2014)	2.437	2.051	1.526
Present EFG based LBM	2.687	2.036	1.531

during the process in contrast to predetermined Finite element shape functions, imposition of boundary conditions as they are not automatically satisfied, large size of stiffness matrices etc. Further, in Lattice Boltzmann simulations, the code needs to run over time steps due to unsteady nature of Lattice Boltzmann equations. Therefore, reduction of computational time becomes essential requirement for mesh free based Lattice Boltzmann simulations within complex geometries and three dimensional flows.

The advantageous feature of both LBM and EFGM is that both are local in nature which makes them highly compatible for parallel processing. In EFGM, the construction of stiffness matrices corresponding to each evaluation or quadrature point is an independent process. The construction of stiffness at different evaluation points does not affect each other, as there is no connectivity between nodes. Once all the stiffness matrices are evaluated, their assembly requires merely matrix addition. Thus the task of stiffness matrices construction could be distributed over different processing units. Many-core processors, such as graphic processing units (GPUs), are promising platforms for intrinsic parallel algorithms. EFGM based LBM simulation may be carried out on a GPU cluster with many nodes, each having multiple Fermi GPUs. Asynchronous execution with CUDA (Compute Unified Device Architecture) stream functions, Open MPI and non-blocking MPI communication may be incorporated to improve efficiency (Xiong et al., 2012).

SUMMARY

This chapter proposes mesh free implementation of lattice Boltzmann simulations, which could have high potential for simulation of flow within complex, irregular geometries, flow through porous medium, fluid structure interaction problems, blood flow simulation through arteries etc. Another mesh free method; Meshless local Petrov Galerkin method (MLPG) could also be synced with Lattice Boltzmann method (Musavi & Ashrafizaadeh, 2016) as both of these methods EFGM and MLPG are quite similar in their approaches and yield good results for fluid flow simulations. Also, hybrid approaches such as FEM/EFGM, Boundary element method (BEM), Smooth particle Hydrodynamic (SPH) may be a good alternative to deal with complex domains or three-dimensional flows.

REFERENCES

Bao, J., Yuan, P., & Schaefer, L. (2008). A mass conserving boundary condition for the lattice Boltzmann equation method. *Journal of Computational Physics*, *227*(18), 8472–8487. doi:10.1016/j.jcp.2008.06.003

Bardow, A., Karlin, I., & Gusev, A. (2006). General characteristic-based algorithm for off-lattice Boltzmann simulations. *Europhysics Letters*, *75*(3), 434–440. doi:10.1209/epl/i2006-10138-1

Begum, R., & Basit, M. A. (2008). Lattice Boltzmann Method and its Applications to Fluid Flow Problems. *European Journal of Science & Research*, *22*, 216–231.

Belytschko, T., Lu, Y. Y., & Gu, L. (1994). Element-free galerkin methods. *International Journal for Numerical Methods in Engineering*, *37*(2), 229–256. doi:10.1002/nme.1620370205

Benzi, R., Succi, S., & Vergassola, M. (1992). The lattice Boltzmann equation: Theory and applications. *Physics Reports*, *222*(3), 145–197. doi:10.1016/0370-1573(92)90090-M

Bhatnagar, P. L., Gross, E. P., & Krook, M. (1954). A Model for Collision Processes in Gases. I. Small Amplitude Processes in Charged and Neutral One-Component Systems. *Physical Review*, *94*(3), 511–525. doi:10.1103/PhysRev.94.511

Cao, N., Chen, S., Jin, S., & Martinez, D. (1997). Physical symmetry and lattice symmetry in the lattice Boltzmann method. *Physical Review. E*, *55*(1), R21–R24. doi:10.1103/PhysRevE.55.R21

Chen, H. (1998). Volumetric formulation of the lattice Boltzmann method for fluid dynamics: Basic concept. *Physical Review. E*, *58*(3), 3955–3963. doi:10.1103/PhysRevE.58.3955

Chen, S., & Doolen, G. (1998). Lattice Boltzmann method for fluid flows. *Annual Review of Fluid Mechanics*, *30*(1), 329–364. doi:10.1146/annurev.fluid.30.1.329

Chun, B., & Ladd, A. (2007). Interpolated boundary condition for lattice Boltzmann sim- ulations of flows in narrow gaps. *Physical Review. E*, *75*(6), 066705. doi:10.1103/PhysRevE.75.066705 PMID:17677387

Dennis, S. C. R., & Chang, G. Z. (1970). Numerical solutions for steady flow past a circular cylinder at Reynolds numbers up to 100. *Journal of Fluid Mechanics*, *42*(3), 471–489. doi:10.1017/S0022112070001428

Dupuis, A., & Chopard, B. (2003). Theory and applications of an alternative lattice Boltzmann grid refinement algorithm. *Physical Review. E, 67*(6), 066707. doi:10.1103/PhysRevE.67.066707 PMID:16241380

Duster, A., Demkowicz, L., & Rank, E. (2006). High order finite elements applied to the discrete Boltzmann equations. *International Journal for Numerical Methods in Engineering, 67*(8), 1094–1121. doi:10.1002/nme.1657

Filippova, O., & Ḧanel, D. (1998). Grid refinement for lattice-BGK models. *Journal of Computational Physics, 147*(1), 219–228. doi:10.1006/jcph.1998.6089

Frish, U., Hasslacher, B., & Pomeau, Y. (1986). Lattice gas automata for the Navier-Stokes equation. *Physical Review Letters, 56*(14), 1505–1508. doi:10.1103/PhysRevLett.56.1505 PMID:10032689

Guo, Z., Shi, B., & Wang, N. (2000). Lattice BGK Model for Incompressible Navier-Stokes Equation. *Journal of Computational Physics, 165*(1), 288–306. doi:10.1006/jcph.2000.6616

He, X., & Luo, L. S. (1997). Theory of the lattice Boltzmann method: From the Boltzmann equation to the lattice Boltzmann equation. *Physical Review. E, 56*(6), 6811–6817. doi:10.1103/PhysRevE.56.6811

He, X., Luo, L. S., & Dembo, M. (1996). Some progress in lattice Boltzmann method. Part I. Nonuniform mesh grids. *Journal of Computational Physics, 129*(2), 357–363. doi:10.1006/jcph.1996.0255

Krivovichev, G. V. (2014). On the Finite-Element-Based Lattice Boltzmann Scheme. *Applied Mathematical Sciences, 8*(33), 1605–1620. doi:10.12988/ams.2014.4138

Kupershtokh, A. L. (2014). Three-dimensional LBE simulations of a decay of liquid dielectrics with a solute gas into the system of gas-vapor channels under the action of strong electric fields. *Computers & Mathematics with Applications (Oxford, England), 67*(2), 340–349. doi:10.1016/j.camwa.2013.08.030

Kwon, Y. W. (2006). Development of coupling technique for LBM and FEM for FSI application. *Engineering Computations, 23*(8), 860–875. doi:10.1108/02644400610707766

Lee, T., & Lin, C. L. (2001). A characteristic Galerkin method for discrete Boltzmann equation. *Journal of Computational Physics, 171*(1), 336–356. doi:10.1006/jcph.2001.6791

Lee, T., & Lin, C. L. (2003). An Eulerian description of the streaming process in the lattice Boltzmann equation. *Journal of Computational Physics, 185*(2), 445–471. doi:10.1016/S0021-9991(02)00065-7

Li, Y., LeBoeuf, E. J., & Basu, P. K. (2005). Least-squares finite-element scheme for the lattice Boltzmann method on an unstructured mesh. *Physical Review. E, 72*(4), 046711. doi:10.1103/PhysRevE.72.046711 PMID:16383571

Liu, G. R. (2003). *Meshfree methods-moving beyond the finite element method.* London: CRC press.

Lu, Y. Y., Belytschko, T., & Gu, L. (1994). A new implementation of element free galerkin methods. *Computer Methods in Applied Mechanics and Engineering, 113*(3-4), 397–414. doi:10.1016/0045-7825(94)90056-6

McNamara, G. R., Garcia, A. L., & Alder, B. J. (1995). Stabilisation of thermal lattice Boltzmann models. *Journal of Statistical Physics, 81*(1-2), 395–408. doi:10.1007/BF02179986

McNamara, G. R., & Zanetti, G. (1988). Use of the Boltzmann Equation to Simulate Lattice-Gas Automata. *Physical Review Letters, 61*(20), 2332–2335. doi:10.1103/PhysRevLett.61.2332 PMID:10039085

Mei, R., & Shyy, W. (1998). On the Finite Difference-Based Lattice Boltzmann Method in Curvilinear Coordinates. *Journal of Computational Physics, 143*(2), 426–448. doi:10.1006/jcph.1998.5984

Mei, R., & Shyy, W. (1998). On the finite difference–based lattice Boltzmann method in curvilinear coordinates. *Journal of Computational Physics, 143*(2), 426–448. doi:10.1006/jcph.1998.5984

Min, M., & Lee, T. (2011). A spectral-element discontinuous Galerkin lattice Boltzmann method for nearly incompressible flows. *Journal of Computational Physics, 230*(1), 245–259. doi:10.1016/j.jcp.2010.09.024

Mohamad, A. A., & Succi, S. (2009). A note on equilibrium boundary conditions in lattice Boltzmann fluid dynamic simulations. *The European Physical Journal. Special Topics, 171*(1), 213–221. doi:10.1140/epjst/e2009-01031-9

Musavi, S. H., & Ashrafizaadeh, M. (2016). A mesh-free lattice Boltzmann solver for flows in complex geometries. *International Journal of Heat and Fluid Flow, 59*, 10–19. doi:10.1016/j.ijheatfluidflow.2016.01.006

Nannelli, F., & Succi, S. (1992). The lattice Boltzmann equation on irregular lattices. *Journal of Statistical Physics, 68*(3-4), 401–407. doi:10.1007/BF01341755

Pan, C., Luo, L.-S., & Miller, C. T. (2006). An evaluation of lattice Boltzmann schemes for porous medium flow simulation. *Computers & Fluids*, *35*(8), 898–909. doi:10.1016/j.compfluid.2005.03.008

Patil, D. V., & Lakshmisha, K. (2009). Finite volume TVD formulation of lattice Boltzmann simulation on unstructured mesh. *Journal of Computational Physics*, *228*(14), 5262–5279. doi:10.1016/j.jcp.2009.04.008

Shan, X., & Chen, H. (1993). Lattice Boltzmann model for simulating flows with multiple phases and components. *Physical Review. E*, *47*(3), 1815–1819. doi:10.1103/PhysRevE.47.1815 PMID:9960203

Shi, X. I, Lin, J., & Yu, Z. (2003). Discontinuous Galerkin spectral element lattice Boltzmann method on triangular element. *International Journal for Numerical Methods in Fluids*, *42*(11), 1249–1261. doi:10.1002/fld.594

Singh, A., Singh, I. V., & Prakash, R. (2007). Numerical analysis of fluid squeezed between two parallel plates by meshless method. *Computers & Fluids*, *36*(9), 1460–1480. doi:10.1016/j.compfluid.2006.12.005

Singh, S. & Bhargava, R. (2014). Simulation of phase transition during cryosurgical treatment of a tumor tissue loaded with nano-particles using meshfree approach. *ASME Journal of Heat Transfer, 136*(12). DOI: .10.1115/1.4028730

Singh, S., & Bhargava, R. (2015). Numerical simulation of a phase transition problem with natural convection using hybrid FEM / EFGM technique. *International Journal of Numerical Methods for Heat & Fluid Flow*, *25*(3), 570–592. doi:10.1108/HFF-06-2013-0201

Sofonea, V., & Sekerka, R. F. (2003). Viscosity of finite difference lattice Boltzmann models. *Journal of Computational Physics*, *184*(2), 422–434. doi:10.1016/S0021-9991(02)00026-8

Sterling, J. D., & Chen, S. (1996). Stability Analysis of Lattice Boltzmann Methods. *Journal of Computational Physics*, *123*(1), 196–206. doi:10.1006/jcph.1996.0016

Stiebler, M., Tolke, J., & Krafczyk, M. (2006). An upwind discretization scheme for the finite volume lattice boltzamnn method. *Computers & Fluids*, *35*(8-9), 814–819. doi:10.1016/j.compfluid.2005.09.002

Succi, S. (2001). *The lattice Boltzmann Equation for Fluid Dynamics and Beyond*. Oxford University Press.

Sukop, M., & Thorne, D. T. (2006). *Lattice Boltzmann Modeling: an introduction for geoscientists and engineers* (1st ed.). Springer Verlag.

Ubertini, S., Bella, G., & Succi, S. (2003). Lattice Boltzmann method on unstructured grids: Further developments. *Physical Review. E*, *68*(1), 016701. doi:10.1103/PhysRevE.68.016701 PMID:12935281

Xi, H., Peng, G., & Chou, S. H. (1999). Finite-volume lattice Boltzmann method. *Physical Review. E*, *59*(5), 6202–6205. doi:10.1103/PhysRevE.59.6202 PMID:11969609

Xiong, Q., Li, B., Xu, J., Fang, X. J., Wang, X. W., Wang, L. M., ... Ge, W. (2012). Efficient parallel implementation of the lattice Boltzmann method on large clusters of graphic processing units. *Chinese Science Bulletin*, *57*(7), 707–715. doi:10.1007/s11434-011-4908-y

Yu, D., Mei, R., Luo, L., & Shyy, W. (2003). Viscous flow computations with the method of lattice Boltzmann equation. *Progress in Aerospace Sciences*, *39*(5), 329–367. doi:10.1016/S0376-0421(03)00003-4

Zhu, T., & Atluri, S. N. (1998). A modified collocation method and a penalty formulation for enforcing the essential boundary conditions in element free Galerkin method. *Computational Mechanics*, *21*(3), 211–222. doi:10.1007/s004660050296

Zienkiewicz, O. C. (1989). *The finite element method, 4th edlition*. London: Mc.Graw-Hill.

Zou, Q., & He, X. (1997). Pressure and velocity boundary conditions for the lattice Boltzmann. *Journal of Physics of Fluids*, *9*(6), 1591–1598. doi:10.1063/1.869307

KEY TERMS AND DEFINITIONS

Nodal Density: The density of nodes within computational domain; part of the domain where large gradients are expected should have higher nodal density to capture the changes accurately as compared to the rest of the domain.

Quadrature Points: Gauss quadrature points generated within each background cell for the purpose of numerical integration; their order depends upon the order of integrand and total number of nodes in computational domain.

Shape/Interpolation Functions: Functions that provide an approximation for the unknown field variables, preferably polynomials of first or second order.

Stiffness Matrix: A square matrix obtained by weighted residual form of the given differential equation, representing a system of linear equations whose solution provides an approximation solution of the differential equation.

APPENDIX

Element-Free Galerkin Method (EFGM)

In element free Galerkin method, the unknown field variable is approximated via interpolation or shape functions and unknown nodal variables. Shape functions are constructed using moving least square approximation and discretized system equations are developed using Galerkin weak form as in the case of Finite Element method.

The detailed procedure of MLS shape function construction requires a brief idea of some of the key concepts, which are given below;

Support Domain

The support domain of a point X (need not to be necessarily a node) determines the nodes that will be used for approximating the field variable at point X. The field variable 'u' at any point $X = (x; y; z)$, is interpolated with the help of only those nodes which are falling under the support domain of the point X.

$$u\left(X\right) = \sum_{I=1}^{n} \Phi_i u_i \qquad (1.1)$$

where 'n' is the number of nodes, included in the support domain of point X and u_I is the nodal field variable at node I. Support domains may have different shape and size for different points, as shown in Figure 10. The idea of support domain is useful, when the nodal density does not change drastically in the problem domain.

Influence Domain

Influence domain of a node refers to a domain upon which a node exerts an influence. It is defined for each node of the problem domain, in contrast to support domain, which is defined for a point of interest; that does not necessarily have to be a node. It may be different from node to node to represent the area of influence of the node.

The idea of influence domain is used for selection of nodes for interpolation or for constructing shape functions. For construction of shape functions at a point X, only those nodes are used whose influence domain covers the point X. As shown in Figure 11, node 1, 2, and 3 have circular influence domain with radii r_1, r_2, r_3 and the influence domain of nodes 1 and 2 cover the point X. Therefore, while constructing shape shape function at point X only node 1 and node 2 will be utilized, not node 3, even though node 3 may be closer to point X in comparison to node 1 and 2. The concept of influence domain is useful for non-regularly distributed nodes.

Figure 10. Rectangular and circular support domains

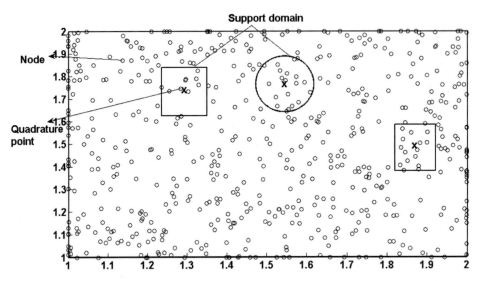

Figure 11. Influence domains of different nodes

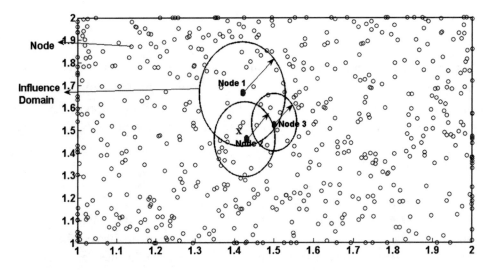

Choice of Weight Functions

Construction of MLS shape function requires weight functions. They play a significant role and resulting approximation $u^h(X)$ in EFGM and other meshless methods is affected by the choice of weight function. The weight functions are used to provide weightings for the residuals at different nodes included in the support domain of a point X. Therefore, only over a small neighborhood or support domain of a point, the value of the weight functions is non-zero and outside the support domain; weight function takes zero value. The smoothness and continuity of the shape function depends upon the smoothness and continuity of the weight function $W(X, X_I)$ shown in Figure 12. If weight function is C_1 continuous then shape function will also have C_1 continuity. A weight function must satisfy the following conditions;

1. It must be positive, continuous and differentiable in the support domain.
2. It must be zero outside the support domain to ensure a local compact support in order to get a banded system matrix.
3. Weight function must be a monotonically decreasing function so that the nodes which are closer to the point where the field variable is to be approximated get more weightage as compared to far away nodes.

Different weight functions (Liu, 2003) in terms of normalized radius, r are given as follows;

Figure 12. Plot of weight function and corresponding shape functions

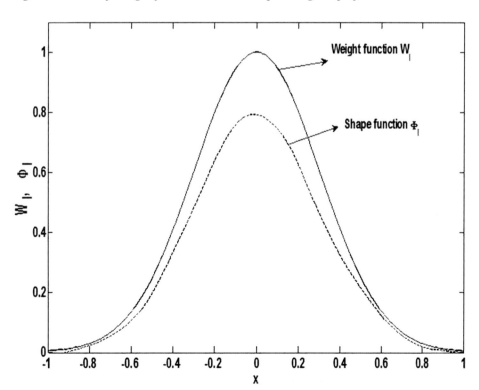

Cubic Spline Weight Function (W_1)

$$W\left(X - X_I\right) = W\left(\bar{r}\right) = \begin{cases} \dfrac{2}{3} - 4\bar{r}^2 + 4\bar{r}^3 & \bar{r} <= \dfrac{1}{2} \\ \dfrac{4}{3} - 4\bar{r} + 4\bar{r}^2 + \dfrac{4}{3}\bar{r}^3 & \dfrac{1}{2} < \bar{r} <= 1 \\ 0 & \bar{r} > 1 \end{cases} \qquad (1.2)$$

Quartic Spline Weight Function $\left(W_2\right)$

$$W\left(X - X_I\right) = W\left(\bar{r}\right) = \begin{cases} 1 - 6\bar{r}^2 + 8\bar{r}^3 - 3\bar{r}^4 & \bar{r} <= 1 \\ 0 & \bar{r} > 1 \end{cases} \qquad (1.3)$$

Exponential Weight Function $\left(W_3\right)$

$$W\left(X - X_I\right) = W\left(\bar{r}\right) = \begin{cases} e^{\left(\dfrac{\bar{r}}{\alpha}\right)^2} & \bar{r} <= 1 \\ 0 & \bar{r} > 1 \end{cases} \qquad (1.4)$$

where α is a constant, commonly chosen as 0.3.

New Quartic Weight Function (W_4)

$$W(X - X_I) = W(\bar{r}) = \begin{cases} \dfrac{2}{3} - \dfrac{9}{2}\bar{r}^2 + \dfrac{19}{3}\bar{r}^3 - \dfrac{5}{2}\bar{r}^4 & \bar{r} <= 1 \\ 0 & \bar{r} > 1 \end{cases} \qquad (1.5)$$

In all these weight functions, $\bar{r} = \dfrac{\|X - X_I\|}{d_{mI}}$, $\|X - X_I\|$ is the distance from an evaluation point X to node X_I, d_{mI} is related to the size of support domain and it is calculated as $d_{mI} = d_{max}C_I$, where d_{max} is a scaling parameter. C_I is the distance to nearest neighbour from evaluation point. The scaling parameter d_{max} is the only parameter to control the size of the support domain d_{mI}. In case of a uniform nodal distribution as the distance between nearest neighbor and evaluation point always remains fixed.

The support domains may be circular, rectangular or both, but, rectangular support domains are more common. In 2D space, for rectangular support domain, the weight function at any point is calculated as;

$$W\left(\bar{r}\right) = W\left(\bar{r}_x\right)W\left(\bar{r}_y\right) \text{ where } \bar{r}_x = \frac{\left|X - X_I\right|}{d_{mI}}, \bar{r}_y = \frac{\left|Y - Y_I\right|}{d_{mI}}$$

While in circular support domain,

$$\bar{r} = \frac{\left\|\boldsymbol{X} - \boldsymbol{X}_I\right\|}{d_{mI}} \text{ where } \left\|X - \boldsymbol{X}_I\right\| = \sqrt{(x - x_I)^2 + (y - y_I)^2}$$

Moving Least Square (MLS) Approximation

In element free Galerkin method, the field variable at a point of interest within the problem domain is approximated using MLS approximation. MLS approximation requires only a set of nodes for its construction and only three components namely a compact support weight function associated with each node, a polynomial basis function and a set of coefficients that depend upon nodal locations.

Using MLS approximation, the approximation for a field variable $u\left(X\right)$ at a point X, denoted by $u^h\left(X\right)$ can be written as (Zhu & Atluri, 1998);

$$u^h(X) = \sum_{j=1}^{m} p_j(X)a_j(X) = p^T(X)a(X) \tag{1.6}$$

where $p\left(\boldsymbol{X}\right)$ is a vector of complete basis function (usually polynomials) that consists most often monomials of lowest orders to ensure minimum completeness and 'm' is the number of terms in polynomial basis functions.

In I-D space; $p^T\left(\boldsymbol{X}\right) = \left\{1, x, x^2, x^3, ..., x^m\right\}$ \hfill (1.7)

In 2-D space; $p^T(X) = p^T(x,y) = \left\{1, x, y, xy, x^2, y^2, ..., x^m, y^m\right\}$ (1.8)

In 3-D space; $p^T(X) = p^T(x,y,z) = \left\{1, x, y, z, xy, yz, zx, x^2, y^2, z^2, ..., x^m, y^m, z^m\right\}$ (1.9)

The unknown coefficients $a(X)$ are obtained by minimizing a functional of weighted residual which is constructed using approximated values

$$u^h(X_1), u^h(X_2), ..., u^h(X_n)$$

of the field function 'u' and the nodal values $u_1, u_2, ..., u_n$ at the nodes $X_1, X_2, ..., X_n$; included in the support domain of point X. The weighted residual function denoted by L(X) is written in the following quadratic form;

$$L(X) = \sum_{I=1}^{n} W(X - X_I)\left[u^h(X_I) - u_I\right]^2$$ (1.10)

The minimization of weighted residual L(X) w.r.t a(X) requires;

$$\frac{\partial L}{\partial a} = 0$$ (1.11)

This results in the following set of linear equations:

$$A(X)a(X) = B(X)u \Rightarrow a(X) = A^{-1}(X)B(X)u$$

where the weighted moment matrix A(X) and matrix B(X) are given as follows;

$$A(X) = \sum_{I=1}^{n} W(X - X_I)p(X_I)p^T(X_I)$$ (1.12)

$$B(X) = \left[W(X - X_1)p(X_1), W(X - X_2)p(X_2), ..., W(X - X_n)p(X_n)\right]$$ (1.13)

Substituting these values of A(X) and B(X) from equation (1.12) and (1.13), in equation (1.6), the MLS approximant is obtained as;

$$u^h(X) = \sum_{I=1}^{n} \Phi_I(X)u_I = \Phi^T(X)u \tag{1.14}$$

where $\Phi^T\left(\boldsymbol{X}\right) = \left[\Phi_1\left(\boldsymbol{X}\right), \Phi_2\left(\boldsymbol{X}\right), ..., \Phi_n\left(\boldsymbol{X}\right)\right], u^T = \left[u_1, u_2, ..., u_n\right]$

The required MLS shape functions $\Phi(X)$ is defined as;

$$\Phi_I(X) = \sum_{j=1}^{m} p_j(X)(A^{-1}(X)B(X))_{jI} = p^T A^{-1} B_I \tag{1.15}$$

In equation (1.15), 'm' is the number of terms in the polynomial basis function $p(X)$ and it is observed that in order to prevent the singularity of weighted moment matrix A, 'm' must be much smaller than the number of nodes 'n' included in the support domain at a particular point of interest for construction of MLS shape functions i.e. n >> m. Therefore, it is required that minimum value of $d_{max} > 1$, so that n > m. Also, maximum value of d_{max} should ensure the local character of MLS approximation. Therefore, size of support domain should be sufficiently large to ensure non-singular stiffness matrix, but even too large support domain may lead to high computational expense due to involvement of large number of nodes for construction of shape functions at each point.

Enforcement of Essential Boundary Conditions

However, MLS approximation functions used in EFGM satisfy the partition of unity condition, i.e. $\sum_{I=1}^{n} \Phi_I = 1$, but they do not satisfy kronecker delta function property i.e. $\Phi_I\left(\boldsymbol{X_J}\right) \neq \delta_{IJ}$. It makes imposition of boundary condition in EFGM, a difficult task. Many numerical techniques have been proposed to enforce the essential boundary conditions in EFGM, such as Lagrange Multiplier and Penalty approach.

Lagrange Multiplier Approach

Belytschko et al. (Belytschko et al., 1994) proposed Lagrange multiplier method for this purpose. Although, this technique is numerically quite accurate, it requires extra computational time. In this approach, besides calculation of unknown field variables in the domain, Lagrange multipliers at the boundary nodes also require to be calculated and it leads to a significant increment in total number of nodal unknowns in the discretized system equations. Also, in Lagrange multiplier method, the bandedness of the stiffness matrix is distorted. Further, a modified variational approach was proposed by Lu et al. (Lu et al., 1994), in which Lagrange multipliers were replaced by their physical meaning. It resulted in a set of banded system equations, but the obtained numerical results are found to be less accurate as compared to Lagrange multiplier approach.

Penalty Approach

Further, Zhu and Atluri (Zhu & Atluri, 1998) introduced penalty approach for imposition of boundary conditions in EFGM. Penalty approach is quite easy in implementation and it produces stiffness matrices of same order that conventional FEM produces for the same number of nodes. Also, the symmetry, bandedness and positive definite properties of the system matrix are also preserved in penalty approach. In penalty approach, the proper selection of penalty parameter is very important. Penalty parameter is introduced to penalize the difference between the field variable of MLS approximation and the prescribed nodal value on the essential boundary. Theoretically, penalty factor must be infinite, but it is not possible in practical numerical analysis. Therefore, in general, a large penalty factor which could enforce the boundary condition properly is sufficient. Some criteria has also been proposed by G.R. Liu (Liu, 2003) for selection of penalty parameter $\bar{\alpha}$.

$$\bar{\alpha} = 1.0 \times 10^{4-13} \times \max \text{ (diagonal element in the stiffness matrix)}$$

Although, results obtained with penalty approach may be less accurate, but other advantages make the penalty approach more efficient and attractive as compared to Lagrange multiplier method.

Numerical Integration in EFGM

In element free Galerkin method, the computation of stiffness matrices requires numerical integration scheme such as Gauss quadrature scheme and for purpose of numerical integration, a background mesh of proper density needs to be designed. The accuracy of the obtained approximation depends upon the number of integration points or gauss quadrature points and the density of background mesh used. It has been observed that for good results, the cell density of background mesh and the number of gauss points have to be in balance, i.e. a too fine background mesh without enough gauss points or too many gauss points with a coarse background mesh, may not provide accurate results. The proper number of quadrature points may be decided using benchmark problems and it is observed that for good accuracy $n_Q \gg n_t$ where n_Q is the number of total quadrature points in problem domain and n_t is total number of nodes in problem domain. This concept is based on Zienkiewicz results (Zienkiewicz, 1989), which states that for non-singularity of stiffness matrix, the number of independent relations provided by all integration points must be higher than the number of unknowns in problem domain.

The background mesh for numerical integration may be generated in two ways, first is element quadrature in which vertices of background mesh are often used as the initial array of nodes for the EFGM model. However, additional nodes may be added anywhere in the computational domain. This scheme is particularly useful in problem involving the discontinuous domain. The second integration technique, which is often called cell quadrature, uses a background grid of cells independent of the domain. In this method, at each integration point, it is necessary to check whether Gauss point is inside or outside the domain, and if Gauss point lies inside the domain then only it is included for integration otherwise not. This technique is not widely used because it does not yield accurate results along curved and angled boundaries. However, this approach gives good results for regular domains. Figure 13 and Figure 14 illustrate both the approaches of numerical integration namely Element quadrature and Cell quadrature.

Figure 13. Numerical integration with element quadrature

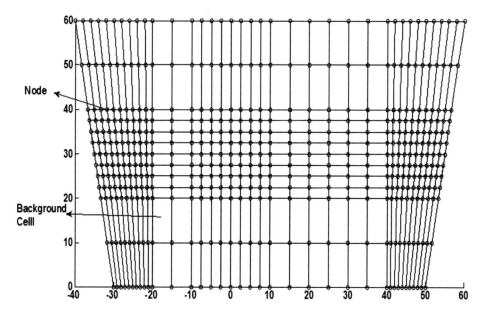

Figure 14. Numerical integration with cell quadrature

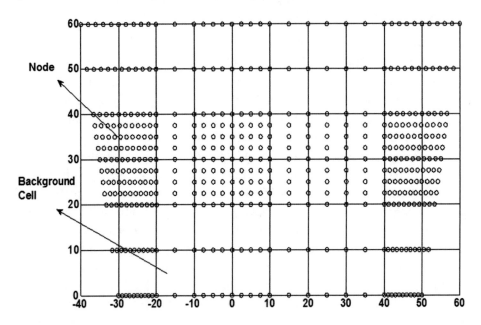

Chapter 7
Wake Interaction Using Lattice Boltzmann Method

K. Karthik Selva Kumar
National Institute of Technology, India

L. A. Kumaraswamidhas
Indian Institute of Technology (ISM), India

ABSTRACT

In this chapter, a brief discussion about the application of lattice Boltzmann method on complex flow characteristics over circular structures is presented. A two-dimensional computational simulation is performed to study the fluid flow characteristics by employing the lattice Boltzmann method (LBM) with respect to Bhatnagar-Gross-Krook (BGK) collision model to simulate the interaction of fluid flow over the circular cylinders at different spacing conditions. From the results, it is observed that there is no significant interaction between the wakes for the transverse spacing's ratio higher than six times the cylinder diameter. For smaller transverse spacing ratios, the fluid flow regimes were recognized with presence of vortices. Apart from that, the drag coefficient signals are revealed as chaotic, quasi-periodic, and synchronized regimes, which were observed from the results of vortex shedding frequencies and fluid structure interaction frequencies. The strength of the latter frequency depends on spacing between the cylinders; in addition, the frequency observed from the fluid structure interaction is also associated with respect to the change in narrow and wide wakes behind the surface of the cylinder. Further, the St and mean Cd are observed to be increasing with respect to decrease in the transverse spacing ratio.

DOI: 10.4018/978-1-5225-4760-0.ch007

INTRODUCTION

Fluids, such as air and water, are frequently met in our daily life. Physically, all fluids are composed of a large set of atoms or molecules that collide with one another and move randomly. Interactions among molecules in a fluid are usually much weaker than those in a solid, and a fluid can deform continuously under a small applied shear stress. Usually, the microscopic dynamics of the fluid molecules is very complicated and demonstrates strong in homogeneity and fluctuations. On the other hand, the macroscopic dynamics of the fluid, which is the average result of the motion of molecules, is homogeneous and continuous. Therefore, it can be expected that mathematical models for fluid dynamics will be strongly dependent on the length and time scales at which the fluid is observed. Generally, the motion of a fluid can be described by three types of mathematical models according to the observed scales, i.e. microscopic models at molecular scale, kinetic theories at mesoscopic scale, and continuum models at macroscopic scale. The lattice Boltzmann method (LBM) has found applications in fields as diverse as quantum mechanics and image processing, it has historically been and predominantly remains a computational fluid dynamics method. This is also the spirit of this book in which we largely develop and apply the LBM for solving fluid mechanics phenomena.

The fluid flow around cylindrical structures give rise to numerous complex flow phenomena at subcritical Reynolds numbers. Vortex-induced vibration (VIV) has been a dynamic research area in the field of computational and experimental fluid dynamics. The fluid flow past a bluff-body resulting in the development of oscillating forces on the structures contained by a narrow frequency band, further the oscillation frequency of the fluid flow coincides with the resonance frequencies of cylindrical structure; resulting of increased vibrations amplitude excitation. The vibration induced by the fluid flow can be classified according to the nature of the fluid structure interaction, as shown in the following Table 1. The present study is about the Flow Induced Vibration due to the external flow of fluid over the bluff bodies i.e. circular cylinders. Basically, interaction between the fluids and the structures is more of a complex phenomenon to study. (Shiels, Leonard, & Roshko, 2001) established that the induced vibration in an elastically constrained 2-D circular cylinder has become a significant problem in studying the interaction between the fluids and structures. (Grucelski, & Pozorski, 2013) employed a single relaxation time variant of LBM approach for the simulation of two-dimensional viscous fluid flow past the circular cylinder all along in the porous medium. Investigation performed at a Reynolds number (Re=2.5 x 104) to understand the flopping and quasi static for two circular cylinders at different spacing condition (Agarwal, Djenidi, & Antonia, 2006). It shows that at T/d≥4.0, the cylinders wakes were not interacting after a significant spacing in the downstream. Further (Kim,

& Durbin, 1988), observed only a flopping, when performed the investigation at Re=2200 and 6200 for the transverse spacing ratio of T/d=0.75. (Sumner, Wong, Price, & Paidoussis, 1999) examined the vortices field behind the test cylinders by employing the particle image velocimetry. Most of the studies presented above, as a function of time the drag and lift coefficients were taken into consideration for verifying the observed numerical results along with experimental studies. Besides, by employing the schlieren technique for the dependence of the vortex formation region along with the coanda effect on the gap flow, it is observed that the Strouhal number is increasing with decrease in the spacing ratios from T/d=1.5 to 0.2. An investigation to analyze the flow regimes of two, three and four cylinder by placing normal to the fluid flow at different spacing ratios, it is identified the presence of multiple peaks in the power spectra regime corresponding to the respective Strouhal number (Guillaume, & LaRue, 1999). Apart from that an anti-phase flopping is observed behind the two and a quasi-static flow behavior is observed behind three and two cylinders respectively. To reduce the vortices behind the two and three test cylinders during the fluid flow. A detailed phase average based analysis of data observed through hot wire anemometer (Zhou, So, Liu, & Zhang, 2000). Whereas (Sreenivasan, 1985) observed the various chaotic flow pattern behind the circular cylinder for low Reynolds numbers. This annotation leads to discover that whether the chaotic attractor of a low-dimensional may possibly explain the turbulent flow dynamics for instance wakes boundary layers and mixing layers. (Karthik Selva Kumar, & Kumaraswamidhas, 2015) has performed the experimental and numerical investigation on fluid flow characteristics over the elastically mounted bluff bodies (Circular and square cylinders) at different orientation. Besides that (Van Atta, & Gharib, 1987), acknowledged that aero-elastic property could also take part in developing chaotic flow behavior. In view of moving cylinders, (Olinger, & Sreenivasan, 1988) premeditated the nonlinear dynamics of an oscillating cylinder in the wake at low Reynolds numbers for the case of forced oscillations. (Pedro, Francisco, Manuel, Alfredo, & Favier, 2015) proposed a numerical method based on the Lattice-Boltzmann (LBM) and Immersed Boundary (IB) methods to deal with the problems related to fluid-structure interactions and its implementation on heterogeneous platforms based on data-parallel accelerators. Further the parallelization of these methods and depicted the number of optimizations, primarily focusing on enhancing the memory management and decreasing the cost of host accelerator communication.

In the current study, a numerical analysis has done by employing Lattice Boltzmann Method along with a BGK collision model for single relaxation time to identify the fluid flow characteristics and vibration excitation in the circular cylinders arranged in side by side configuration at Re=250 for different spacing ratios. Whereas, the pragmatic results of various flow regimes and vorticity dynamics are briefly discussed in the results and discussion section. Besides that, the key conclusions from the observed results were summarized in the conclusion section. Subsequently the Numerical modeling of the current study, i.e., the classification of the fluids and structure models, is introduced in Computational analysis Section.

LATTICE BOLTZMANN METHOD (LBM) FOR FLUID STRUCTURE INTERACTION PROBLEMS

The aim of the computational study is to predict the vibration response of the side-by-side circular cylinders arranged in different spacing condition. The schematic representation of circular cylinders arranged in side by side configuration is shown in Figure 1. In turn, LBM is employed in the current study to simulate the interaction of fluid flow with circular cylinders at different transverse spacing ratios. In which $\vec{c}_i$ represent the unitary velocity along the direction i of a D2Q9 lattice, the D represent the space dimensions and Q as the number of particles in the computational node adopted for the study.

the unitary cell is a square developed by quad, $\left|\vec{c}_i\right|=1.0$, in turn the principal direction by the quad, $\left|\vec{c}_i\right|=\sqrt{2.0}$, diagonals and by single $\left|\vec{c}_i\right|=0$. Let $N_i(\vec{X},t)$ designates the particle dispensation in the 'i' direction of the plot $\vec{X}$, at the time t. the Lattice Boltzmann equation with respect to Bhatnagar-Gross-Krook (BGK) collision model is written as

Figure 1. (a) Computational node with eight moving particles (representing 1-8) along with a single particle at rest (0). (b) Numerical model of circular cylinders in cross-flow

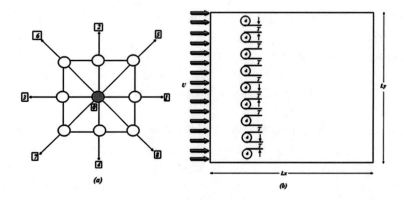

$$N_i(\vec{X} + \vec{c}_i, t+1) - N_i(\vec{X}, t) = \frac{N_i^{eq}(\vec{X}, t) - N_i(\vec{X}, t)}{\tau},$$

The relaxation time related to fluid kinematics viscosity is represented as τ and the $N_i^{eq}(\vec{X}, t)$ is an equilibrium distribution that can be contemplate as a D2Q9 Gaussian quadrature of Maxwell-Boltzmann continuous distribution function (He, & Luo, 1997) is given as

$$N_i^{eq}(\vec{X}, t) = w_i \rho \left\{ 1 + \frac{c_i . u}{c_s^2} + \frac{(c_i . u)^2}{2c_s^4} - \frac{u^2}{2c_s^2} \right\},$$

$w_i = 1/9$ of the principal axis particle, i=1,2,3,4; $w_i = 1/36$ of the diagonals particles, i=5,6,7,8; and $w_0 = 4/9$ for the rest of the particle respectively. For the D2Q9 lattice $c_s^2 = (1/\sqrt{3})^2$ is the square for the LB sound velocity. In each time step, the velocity flow field $\vec{u}(\vec{X}, t)$ and the pressure $\vec{P}(\vec{X}, t)$ respectively are deliberated by employing

$$\rho \vec{u} = \sum_i N_i \vec{c}_i,$$

$$P = c_s^2 \sum_i N_i = c_s^2 \rho$$

In order to extending the results up to an infinite number of cylinders, in this case a recurrent boundary condition is applied on the lateral sides of the cylinders. A bounce–back condition is employed for simulating the flow adherence at the boundaries of the solids, in which by imposing that

$$N_i(X_b, t+1) = N_{-i}(\vec{X}_b, t)$$

for all the b-area at the fluid domain closest to the solid-boundaries also for all the domain in the direction 'i'. A rough surface developed with respect to the discreteness of the considered discrete circles, which is needed to enlarge the simulation domain until the results observed from simulation become insentient to the effects of discreteness. To overcome the stability related problems occurring in other methods during the simulation, as per the demonstration (He, & Luo, 1997). Lattice Boltzmann equation is considered to be a special form of discrete Boltzmann continuous equation. According to that, some attempt has been taken in consideration for the lattice Boltzmann simulations, to implement the irregular lattices and/or varying the mesh size. For varying the mesh size an interpolation is required, which results in the increase of stability related problems. The present study is restricted to uniform D2Q9 lattice. The D represents the cylinder diameter, where $\nu = (0.5)/3$ is the LB kinematic viscosity in D2Q9 lattice. The complete force exerted by the fluid on the surface of square cylinders having the surface boundary Γ is deliberated as,

$$\vec{F} = \sum_{\Gamma}\sum_{i}\left[N_{-i}\left(\vec{X}_{\Gamma}, t^{+}\right) + N_{i}\left(\vec{X}_{\Gamma}, t^{-}\right)\right]\vec{c}_{i},$$

By deliberating the momentum variation at each area $\vec{X}_{\Gamma}$ in the fluid domain adjacent to the boundary surface, taking into account of the particles $N_{i}(\vec{X}_{\Gamma}, t^{-})$ in the direction of 'i' indicating the surface, prior to the propagation, which be bounce back in the '–i' direction, besides propagation, $N_{-i}(\vec{X}_{\Gamma}, t^{+})$. The code employed in this study is validated by comparing the results of single circular cylinder with results of previous studies. By employing a parabolic velocity inlet profile the variation in St with respect to the Re is plotted in the Figure 2.

$$St = fd / U$$

Figure 2. Variation in St with respect to the Re

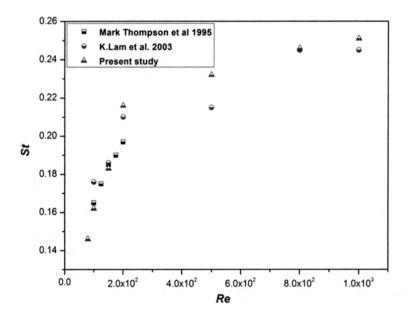

In turn, in this case the drag and the lift forces are in x and y direction with respect to $\vec{F}$, the flow pattern is proportional with respect to main flow (x) direction, the lift force is found to be zero. Normally, it is happened with respect to the immersed cylinders at smaller Reynolds number. Whenever Reynolds number increases, the vortex shedding behind the bluff bodies produces an oscillating lift and amplitude similar to the frequency of the vortices developed, the average Drag Cd and Lift coefficient Cl is deliberated with respect the time average as

$$C_d(t) = \frac{F(t)}{(1/2)\rho U^2 d}$$

"f" represent the vortex shedding frequency, Whereas the observed drag and lift coefficient Cd, Cl of single cylinder and the Fourier spectrum with respect to the lift coefficient Cl were shown in the Figure 3. In turn the observed results were found to be in good agreement with the results of previous studies, which shows the reliability of the code employed along with the spatial and temporal resolutions. Besides the spatial ability is tested by changing the number of respective grid points (12, 24 & 48) delineate the cylinders, also comparing the St Values for different Re in the Table 1. Regarding the 12 grid points the computational domain consists of 500 x 300 points along the longitudinal and transverse directions, gaining a blockage ratio of 0.17. It is apparent that the difference in the St between the three resolution for a range of Re is found to be less (<5%) and further the drag coefficient respectively between the grid points of 24 and 48. From the result, it is observed that at the convergence has taken place at the grid having 24 points, whereas the maximum vibration excitation of the single cylinder were observed as A/d=0.291.

Ensuing test with circular cylinders in the cross flow satisfied with the observed results, the Variation in the Drag and Lift coefficient at Re = 250 due to the influence of spatial resolution for a single circular cylinder along with the validation is presented in the Table 2. Initially, it was identified that the variation in the results between the 12 and 24 grid points are found to be small, which suggests that the 24 grid points might be suitable for the computation. The maximum value observed for the normalized u' (longitudinal velocity component) and v'(transverse velocity component, in the flip flop regime of 26% and 37% for the 12 points grid, in turn for the 24 grid points the flip flop regime is observed to be 27% and 38%. Besides, the test on lift and drag coefficient shows a converged result within 2.01%. Certainly upon increasing the resolution to 48 grid points for all the phenomena discussed in this article shows an excellent agreement with the observed value of *St* from the above test results, the ability of producing better results on a 24 grid points is proved for all the ensuing computations.

Figure 3. (a) Cd, Cl of single cylinder (b) Fourier spectrum of Cl

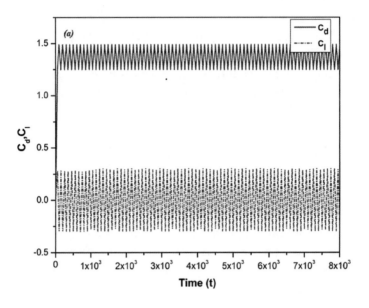

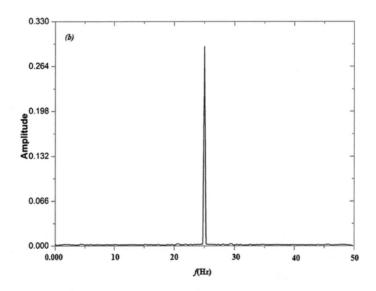

SOLUTIONS AND RECOMMENDATIONS

The simulations have been done at different transverse spacing ratios for a range of $0.1 \leq T/d \leq 6.0$. The results observed for the spacing ratios $T/d = 5\&6$ there is no significant interaction between the fluids and structures. It is deduced by investigating the mean, rms and wake. In the present study, it is observed that there

Table 1. Variation in the Strouhal number at different Re due to the influence of spatial resolution for a single circular cylinder

Reynolds Number	St		
	12 Points	24 Points	48 Points
1000	0.255(0.5%)	0.257(0.5%)	0.257
500	0.221(0.6%)	0.222(0.6%)	0.222
250	0.201(0.6%)	0.200(0.5%)	0.200
200	0.187(0.6%)	0.179(0.5%)	0.179
100	0.168(0.6%)	0.167(0.6%)	0.167

Table 2. Variation in the Drag and Lift coefficient at Re = 250 due to the influence of spatial resolution for a single circular cylinder

	12 Points	24 Points	Experimental (Laurence, et.al. 2007)	Computational (Laurence, et.al. 2007)
Cd	1.377(1.2%)	1.383	1.11	1.01
Cl	0.381(1.0%)	0.386	0.29	0.28

is no significant effects in flow pattern at $4< T/d \leq 6$. In turn, a complicated flow pattern/ wakes behind the cylinders are observed for $T/d \leq 4.0$, which were briefly discussed in the following section.

Synchronized Flow Pattern at 3.0≥T/d≥4.0

The flow pattern observed at T/d=3.0 & 4.0, shows that, the vortices shed occur behind the cylinders having unique and constant frequency along with a definite relationship of phases with the vortex shedding at the neighboring cylinders. At T/d=3.0 & 4.0 Figure 4 (a&b), the vortex shedding is observed to be almost in the pattern of in-phase due to the vortices of the cylinders in respect to the shedding occurred in the cylinders at the same stream. For this case, the observed vortices were found to be separated throughout the computational area, which is due to the less interaction between the cylinders at higher spacing ratio. The observed results of in-phase flow pattern are well supported with respect to the time series analysis of lift coefficients Cl of adjoining cylinders. In the Figure 5, a sinusoidal pattern of lift and drag coefficients were observed, it shows that amplitude of Cl is found to be constant, whereas the amplitude of Cl1 and Cl2 is observed to be 0.194. The Fourier spectrum observed for the Cl is observed to be half of the Cd which shows a consistent relationship with single cylinder. From the Figure 6 (a&b) it reveals

Figure 4. Synchronized flow regime at (a) T/d=3.0 & (b) T/d=4.0

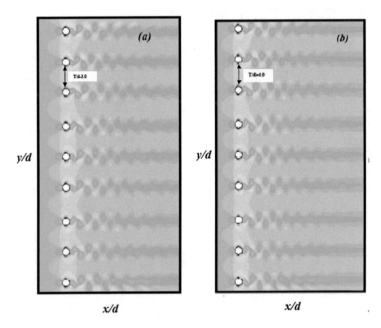

Figure 5. Drag and Lift coefficient for (a) T/d=3.0, (b) T/d=4.0

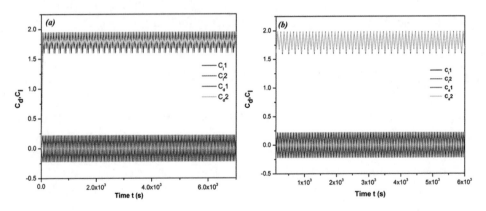

that the vibration excitation of the cylinder 1 and cylinder 2 at T/4=3.0, were the vibration excitation/amplitude ratio of the test cylinders as A/d=0.178 & 0.181 respectively. Subsequently from the Figure 6(c&d) the observed amplitude ratio for the test cylinder at T/d=4.0 as 0.176 & 0.177. Whereas at this spacing condition the observed amplitude ratio is found to be minimum; the decrease in the vibration excitation of the test cylinders were mainly due to increase in spacing conditions, and also observed that there is no significant interaction between the vortices.

Figure 6. Vibration excitation (a) at T/d=3.0 for Cylinder 1, (b) at T/d=3.0 for Cylinder 2, (c) at T/d=4.0 for cylinder 1, (d) at T/d=4.0 for cylinder 2

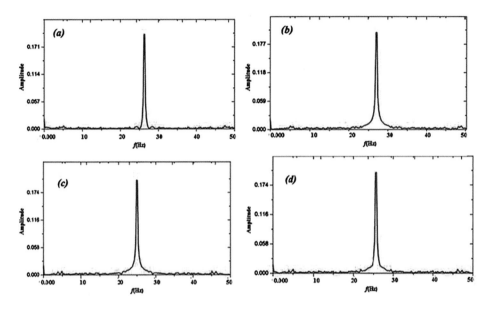

Quasi Periodic Flow Pattern - a, 2.0≤T/d<3.0

For T/d=2.0, the vortices become clearly detectable in the Figure 7. However, the vortices are found to be merging with each other. There is a definite phase relationship between the vortices shedding between the test cylinders. In turn, a closer look shows that, the observed time period at consecutive shedding were not constant. The drag and lift coefficient of a test cylinder is plotted in the Figure 8. Which is mismatched with the sinusoidal variation in drag and lift signals observed for a single cylinder. The presence of primary (vortex-shedding) and secondary (inflection) frequency in the Cl; leads to the vibration excitation of the test cylinders. The drag coefficient reveals a higher lawless flow pattern than the lift force coefficient. This reveals that the exciting behavior of the drag and lift force coefficients become detached for the circular cylinders, due to the irregular flow pattern and the shedding of vortices resulting in the vibration excitation of the circular cylinders C1&C2 as A/d=0.216 & 0.222 in Figure 9. Subsequently, the similar excitation patter is occurs in the in the row of adjacent cylinders.

Figure 7. Quasi periodic flow regime at T/d=2.0

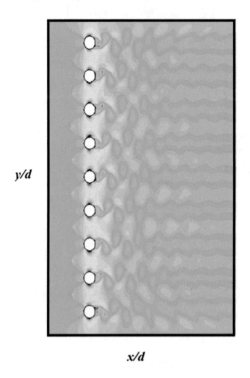

Figure 8. Drag and Lift coefficient for (a) T/d=2.0

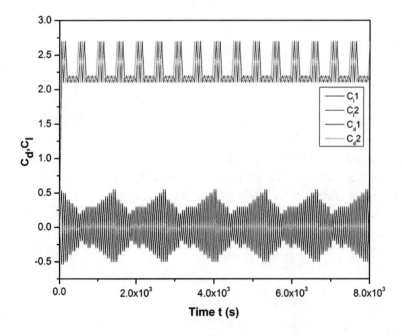

Figure 9. Vibration excitation (a) at T/d=2.0 for Cylinder 1, (b) at T/d=2.0 for Cylinder 2

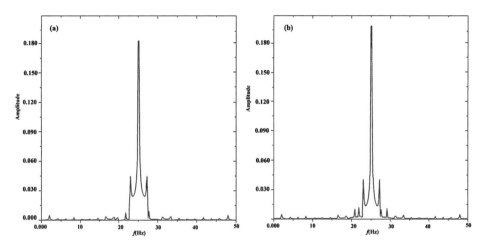

Quasi Periodic Flow Pattern – b, 1.0≤T/d<2.0

Figure 10 with T/d=1.0 and 1.5 reveals that despite the fact that the vortices immediately downstream of the cylinders are evident, further the vortices moved in the downstream were merge with each other. Whereas the downstream distance around which the merging of vortices in the present flow regime were found to be

Figure 10. Quasi Periodic Flow regime – b at (a) T/d=1.0, (b) T/d=1.5

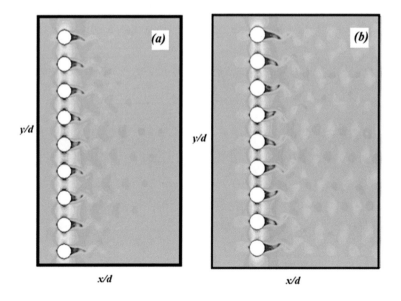

smaller than the previous flow regime; the vortices were be likely to lose their identity utterly upon merging in the present regime implausible the previous flow regime. In addition the immediate vorticity contours show that observed vortex shedding is neither in in-phase nor in anti phase. However, the time series of the respective drag and lift force coefficient doesn't reveal a prevalence of any of these two modes. A linear stochastic approximation for two cylinders at T/d=0.7 for the Reynolds number of 73 shows the presence of both in-phase and anti-phase shedding (Agarwal, Djenidi, & Antonia, 2006), though, it is difficult to distinguish these essential modes without employing the special data-analyzing techniques. The drag force coefficient reveals a higher disordered pattern than the lift force coefficient. This reveals that the exciting behavior of the drag and lift force coefficients become decoupled for the circular cylinders. Besides that the vortex shedding period observed for the drag force coefficient become irregular. Unlike the previous regimes, the secondary cycle period of the present flow regime is found to be irregular.

This shows that the successive cylinders are roughly in anti-phase with respect to the secondary frequency, which means that, when a large wake is observed behind the one test cylinder, such a narrow wake is observed behind the adjacent cylinders. The variation in the drag and lift force coefficient with respect to time series for T/d=1.0&1.5 is represented in the Figure 11(a&b). Whereas the vibration excitation/amplitude ratio of the test cylinders C1 & C2 were as A/d=0.257 & 0.249 at T/d=1.0 and A/d=0.253&0.258 at T/d= 1.5 respectively in the Figure 12.

Chaotic Flow Pattern, T/d < 1.0

From the Figure 13, reveals a chaotic flow pattern behind the test cylinders at different spacing ratios, especially at T/d=0.1 the flow regime contains an irregular wake pattern behind the test cylinders. Apart from that, a similar flow pattern was

Figure 11. Drag and Lift coefficient for (a) T/d=1.0, (b) T/d=1.5

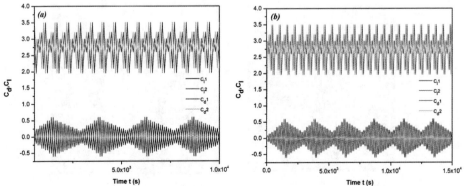

Figure 12. Vibration excitation (a) at T/d=1.0 for Cylinder 1, (b) at T/d=1.0 for Cylinder 2, (c) at T/d=1.5 for cylinder 1, (d) at T/d=1.5 for cylinder 2

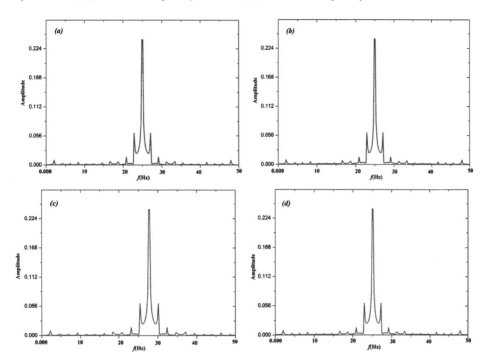

Figure 13. Chaotic flow regime at (a) T/d=0.1

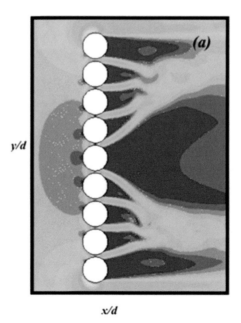

observed which were just appeared to be like a jet flow. The observed results of flow pattern and wake behind the cylinder are found to be very wide and also consistent with the results of experimental analysis performed (Cheng, & Morreti, 1988). According to the observation, the present result also having the vortex formation in a narrow wake (Ishigai, & Nishikawa, 1975). Further the flow pattern is agreeing with observation of (Bradshaw, 1965) for circular cylinders at Re=1500 for similar spacing conditions. From the observation it reveals that the flow at similar spacing between the test cylinders the merging of jets was observed. The variation in the drag and lift force coefficient with respect to time series for T/d=0.1 is represented in the Figure 14. Whereas from the observed result; the vibration excitation of the test cylinders is represented in the Figure 15 (a&b), the maximum vibration excitation in the cylinders were found to be A/d=0.746 & 0.752 respectively at T/d=0.1, whereas at this regime the flow is found to be irregular and resulting in higher vibration excitation were observed.

Figure 14. Drag and Lift coefficient for T/d=0.1

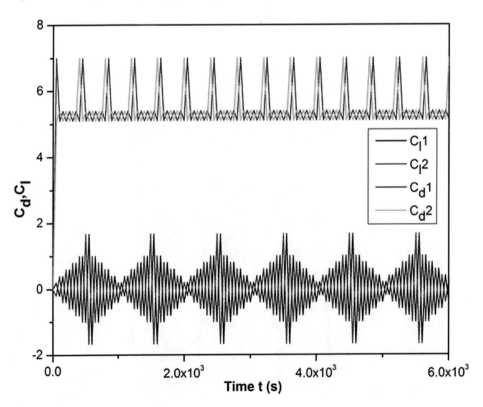

Figure 15. Vibration excitation at T/d=0.1 (a) Cylinder 1 (b) Cylinder 2

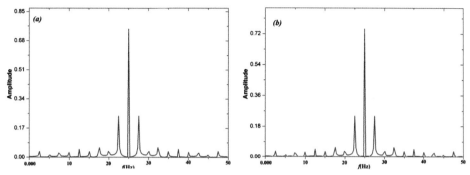

Summary of Various Flow Regimes

In the preceding section, various flow patterns at different spacing conditions were briefly discussed. The delineation of the flow pattern is basically depends on either signal or vorticity of the drag coefficient. In the present study, it shows the presence of four different flow regimes namely (i) synchronized flow pattern, (ii) quasi static flow pattern-I, (iii) quasi static flow pattern-II and (iv) chaotic flow pattern. For synchronized flow pattern, the interaction between the vortices of any cylinder with the vortices of the adjacent cylinders having a definite phase relationship. The vortex shedding of primary cycle is more or less similar to the initial shedding at any cylinder. However, the period of vortex shedding were found to be in dissimilar pattern for the consecutive flow regimes. The primary cycle can be clearly identified at quasi static flow regime-I, in turn the phase observed between the secondary cycles were found to be constant for the both quasi static flow regimes. Whereas the shedding observed for single cylinder is related with respect to the spacing condition of the shear layers and its thickness. Besides, the cylinders at cross flow direction were occasionally designed as an oscillator, in turn the vortex shedding was considered to be vibration/oscillation developed.

Distinction in the Fundamental Parameters With Respect to Spacing Ratios

The dissimilarity in the flow parameters such as shedding frequency, phase difference and mean drag coefficient among shedding of vortices, with respect to spacing ratios have been briefly discussed in this section. Whereas the mean drag coefficient and Strouhal number (St) endow with more information regarding the interaction fluid flow at various regimes, in turn the position of the each cylinders were identified with respect to the phase difference. As far as it is observed from the Figure 16 (a) the mean drag coefficient (Cd) is increases with the decrease in transverse spacing ratio T/d. Further the slope got decreased, when it reaches T/d≥3. Whereas the highest mean drag coefficient observed in this case were found to 20 times higher than the isolated/ single cylinder. Besides, at T/d>6 the drag coefficient is assumed to be 1.738. Apart from that the cylinders at higher spacing ratios reveals a behavior of single cylinder. Whereas the relationship between the drag coefficient and spacing ratios has been defined as;

$$C_d = (1.473 - 1.28\xi) + 6.57\xi^2; \xi = \left| \frac{1}{\left(T/d\right)^{0.66}} \right|$$

Figure 16. (a) Variation in the mead drag coefficient Cd with respect to transverse spacing ratio (b) Variation in Strouhal number with respect to transverse spacing ratio and (c) Variation in the Phase difference between the adjacent cylinders.

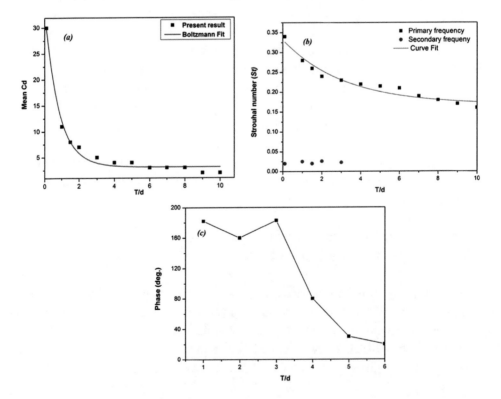

Subsequently, when the transverse spacing T/d= ∞; the equation above is employed to identify the mean drag coefficient of the isolated cylinder. Whereas the above equation has a similar functional type as that of mean drag coefficient with the Reynolds number (Re) is replaced with the transverse spacing ratio (T/d) with a exponent of 0.66 instead of 0.5. Further the Strouhal number (St) is calculated for different spacing ratios were plotted in the Figure 16. Whereas the vortex shedding frequencies the vortex shedding frequency is calculated by taking the half inverse time difference between the peak signal observed for the drag coefficient; in the time series analysis the drag coefficient doesn't reveal any pattern, so with the help of spectral analysis the dominant frequencies were identified from the drag signal. The Figure 16 reveals that the shedding frequencies were decreases with the increases in the transverse spacing ratio. The relation between the Strouhal number and transverse spacing ratio is defined as;

$$St = 0.128 + \frac{0.21}{\left(T/d\right)}$$

It is apparent that the velocity of the fluid flow through the gap between the cylinders was increasing with respect to the decline in the spacing ratios (T/d). Presumptuous that the indifference in the vortices observed at a fixed distance behind the cylinder surface, the higher stream wise velocity leads to a reduced time for detachment; therefore, the shedding frequency is found to be increasing. Figure 16 (C) reveals the difference in the phase variation of vortex shedding occurs between the adjacent cylinders with respect to the different spacing ratio of various flow regimes, such as synchronized flow, quasi static flow I & II, and Chaotic regime. Whereas the phase difference is deliberated by investigating the time signal of the lift force coefficient from the adjacent cylinders, in turn only spacings the vortex shedding from the adjacent cylinders were found to be invariant with respect to the time. Form the observed mean drag coefficient, flow pattern and Strouhal number the interaction between the cylinders were found to be ceases at different spacing ratios. Further at T/d>4.0, shows that there is no significant interaction between the cylinders were observed at higher spacing ratios.

Vorticity Dynamics

As per the results, the observed instantaneous vorticity field shows interesting flow patterns. Whereas in this section, it reveals that the persistence of the flow pattern developed at the downstream end of the cylinders, ought to be governed by the orientation of the velocity from the adjacent vortices on a given vortex; similarly it should apply to stretch the vortices in the cross flow direction. The movements of the vortices at synchronized and quasi-static flow regimes were analyzed using vorticity dynamics in this chapter.

Synchronized and Quasi-Static Flow-A

When Considering the vortex pattern 1 in Figure 17 in view of the fact that the time period for shedding of successive vortices is found to be constant for $T/d \geq 3.0$ and the standard convective velocity from the centre of the vortex 6 to the centre of the vortex 1is nearly identical; therefore, the vortices 6 and 10 must be in middle from the vortex. Further, it can be seen from the Figure 17 the vortex strength is in the order of constant for $x/d > 4$; therefore, the strength of the vortices 6 and 10 should be approximately same. Whereas the induced velocity in the cross-direction results in a formation of vortex at the centre; which is just about suppressed by the adjacent vortices. Based on the above facts, it shows that if the developed vortices being in a constant frequency, which will result in the termination of each other vortices.

Quasi Static Flow Regime-B

Regarding quasi static flow regime, the vortices were found to be stretched in the transverse direction finally it is merged in the downstream. Whereas, the formation of vortices in combined form tend to extend in the cross wise direction with respect to distance of the downstream, further it is observed that a considerable progress

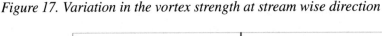

Figure 17. Variation in the vortex strength at stream wise direction

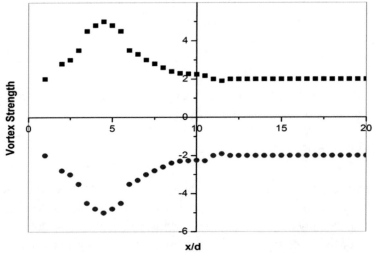

of fluid particles across the spacing in the centerline. (Williamson, 1996) observed that in the flow regimes, four different regions can be identified while travelling in downstream, due to merging of vortices developed from adjacent cylinders. Further closest to the test cylinders in the similar region, it is observed that two parallel in-phase vortex streets are developed. Whereas, before transformation of two separate wakes in to a combined binary vortex streets, the two separate wakes are followed by a transitory region. At last the binary vortex streets were combined together and become a single vortex. Form the current simulation it supports the existence of different regions with respect to large number of test cylinders in the fluid flow direction. Further the Figure 18 reveals that the difference in the sinusoidal variation implying that the higher primary cycle of one cylinder corresponds to the smaller primary cycle of the adjacent cylinder.

Secondary Frequency (Structure Interaction)

The secondary (cylinder structures interaction) frequency and its effects on flow characteristics are breifly discussed in this section; and bringing on the subject of the pertinent observation from the different literatures. Basically the secondary frequency is developed due to the presence of relatively narrow wakes behind one of the test cylinders and a relatively wide wake behind the adjacent cylinder; as an exchange in the arrangement of narrow and wide wakes with the time duration for

Figure 18. Variaton in the primary shedding period of adjacent cylinders a function with respect to primary cycle number, over a secondary cycle

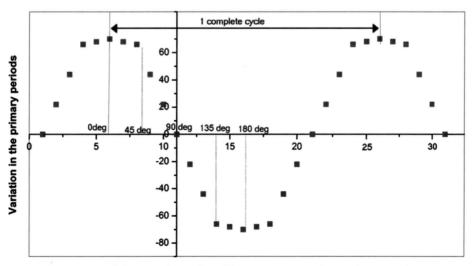

Primary cycle number with respect to secondary cycle

completing the cycle. Several important factors with respect to secondary frequency have to be discussed; as an evident a change in the primary periodic cycle over a secondary periodic cycle occurs at T/d=2.0. Whereas considering this data along with the phase information in Figure 16 (c) can be employed for identifying the primary shedding cycle period of the test cylinders. Figure 18 shows the variation in the primary periods of the adjacent cylinders as a function of primary periodic cycle number over the secondary cycle. The variation is sinusoidal; implying that for a higher primary cycle of one test cylinder corresponds to shorter primary periodic cycle of the adjacent cylinders and vice versa.

This dissimilarity leads to the pattern of short and long wakes for longer phase correlating with the shorter edge. Figure 19 (a) revels that a smaller longitudinal position is correlated with a smaller lateral position referred as a shorter and narrower wake and conversely as a long and wide wake. In turn the vortices equivalent to the largest wakes are moving faster than the shorter narrow wakes counterparts. Further the vortices moved into the downstream, the vortices equivalent to the largest wakes moves still in higher lateral position. The data observed from this section is supported by Figure 18. From the picture observed that the until additional widening or narrowing is impossible, besides that the wide wakes starts to become narrow and the narrow wakes become widen in vice versa. Whereas the secondary period with respect to the time interval; in which a narrow wake behind one of the test cylinder becomes wide and then became narrow. Further for strengthening the results observed, the positions of the vortices are followed over the secondary cycle. Each curve in the Figure 19 (b) representing the different position of the vortex centers after each vortex primary vortex shedding cycle. From the observation it is identified that the position of the vortices centers does not coincides with each

Figure 19. The position of the vortices centres, shedding from the test cylinders C1, C2 and C3 (a) reveals a short and narrow wake behind the test cylinder C2 and relatively wide and largest wakes behind the adjacent cylinders. (b) The end of a primary cycle over a secondary cycle

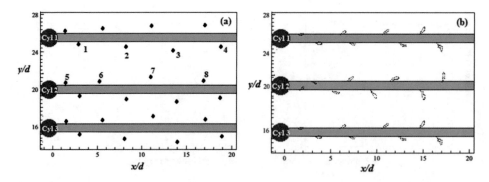

other. Further it is observed to be just behind the cylinders (x/d ≤6), the wakes are primarily transit between smaller and largest wakes, due to the vortex positions scan a straight line parallel in the stream wise direction. Consequently, the position of the vortex centres scans a line situated in an angle with respect to the coordinates in stream wise direction; which represents the presence of shorter and longer wakes. For the additional credibility for the proposal on the origin of secondary frequency is observed by investigating both pressure field and vorticity at the similar instant. Whereas, relatively a higher-pressure field in the downstream is observed due to the presence of largest wakes behind the test cylinders.

There are several factors have to be discussed in regards of the secondary frequency, the initial factor, secondary frequency found to be makes a gradually more dominant contribution for the drag force coefficient with the decreasing in the spacing ratio. For example, at T/d=3.0; there is no apparent component of the secondary frequency with respect to drag force coefficient. Whereas, the amplitude of the drag force coefficient is brought about by primary shedding cycle. Because of the relationship and proportionality between the secondary frequencies with respect to cylinder spacing, it is suggested to consider the secondary frequency as new component brought about due to the interaction between the wakes generated. Therefore, the secondary frequency is also can be regarded as the frequency developed due to the interaction between the cylinders. Further it is observed that the secondary frequency is affecting the primary frequencies, as seen by the variation in the primary cycle over the secondary cycle. Besides that, for smaller spacing ratios, the cycle-cycle variation in the shedding period becomes higher. In other terms, the vortex shedding was found to be irregular and further leads to chaotic regime as observed for T/d=0.1. Therefore, all the regimes were developed as interplay between the primary and secondary cycles; the primary cycle is considered to be vital in the synchronized flow regime. As soon as the primary and secondary cycle having comparable magnitude the subsequent frequencies will led to quasi static flow regimes. In additional on the quasi static flow regime-I, the primary cycle is found to be stronger than the secondary frequency; whereas it is observed that the secondary frequency is found to be dominating in the quasi static flow regime-b. At last the secondary frequency overcomes the primary resulting in a chaotic flow regime.

CONCLUSION

By employing 2-D Lattice Boltzmann method at different spacing conditions (0.1≤T/d≤ 6), a numerical analysis has been carried out for studying the fluid flow characteristics around the circular cylinders arranged in side-by-side configuration at Re=250. The objective of the present study is to understand the fluid flow characteristics and the induced vibration excitation amplitude in the test cylinders. According to the variation in the shedding period and mean C_d with respect to the gaping ratios, for the results it is observed that when T/d.≤4.0, the wakes behind the cylinders interacts, resulting in different flow patterns. For larger gaping ratios, the interactions between the wakes were found to be having minor significance. The shedding frequency and mean C_d are about 8% higher than the isolated cylinder at higher spacing ratios; in turn it is drastically decreases with respect to the reduction in the gaping ratios. The variation in the vortex shedding with respect to the gaping/ spacing ratios expose that the vortex shedding is mostly affected with respect to the arrangement of test cylinders and its spacing conditions. Besides that, it is also observed that the synchronized vortex shedding is developed for T/d≥3.0, whereas the shedding of vortices from any test cylinder is in a steady frequency and having a definite relationship with vortex shedding of the adjacent cylinders. Accordingly, there is only one frequency related to the shedding cycle. At T/d≤ 2.0, the vortex shedding occurs in one cylinder reveals a explicit relationship with the vortex shedding from adjacent cylinders, in turn the vortex shedding period were observed to be inconsistent. Whereas the time signal analogous with respect to the secondary frequency is supposed to be relatively having narrow and wide wakes; and also observed that the secondary frequency play a dominating role with respect to C_d and its role is found to be increasing with respect to decrease in spacing ratios. Comparatively the squat vortex shedding period and higher drag coefficients were correspond to a diminutive wake; in turn higher vortex shedding periods and squat drag coefficient correspond to a greater wake. Consecutively the adjacent cylinders were in an anti-phase in the midst of secondary frequency. Whereas quasi static flow II is observed at 1.0 ≤T/d≤ 1.5 in which there is no unambiguous pattern of shedding from the cylinder as well as the shedding occurs from the adjacent cylinders. Further, in this regime due to the effects of drag coefficient a secondary cycle is identified; in which it is observed that the vortex shedding frequency on the drag force coefficient is found to be smaller for smaller spacing ratios (T/d). For T/d<1, the flow is become chaotic; (i.e.) there is no similarity in the fluid flow pattern. From the results it is identified that the variation in the flow regime is because of fluid structure interaction and the vortex shedding frequencies. The different fluid flow pattern observed in the various flow regimes were primarily based on the interaction of vortices. At T/d≥3.0, the vortices are observed to be different and evidently clear without significant tangential spread. For T/d=<2.0, the fluid flow in the centerline in the gaping is found to be minimum; whereas after flow past the test cylinders, the vortices were stretched in the transverse direction and finally it starts to merge with the adjacent vortices and became a single vortex in the downstream.

Significant Summary of the Observed Results Are as Follows:

- **Transverse Spacing Ratio (T/d) ≥5.0:** No significant interaction between the vortices
- **3.0<T/d≤4.0 (Synchronized):** Along with a phase lag there is an in-phase interaction between the fluid and structures.
- **2.0≤T/d<3.0(Quasi Periodic Flow Pattern – a):** Tangential movement of vortices causes the development of secondary frequency.
- **1.0≤T/d<2.0 (Quasi Periodic Flow Pattern – b):** Significant tangential movement of vortices.
- **T/d < 1.0 (Chaotic Flow Pattern):** The primary frequency is overwhelmed by the secondary frequency.

REFERENCES

Agarwal, A., Djenidi, L., & Antonia, R. A. (2006). Investigation of flow around of a pair of side-by-side square cylinders using the lattice Boltzmann method. *Computers & Fluids*, *35*(10), 1093–1107. doi:10.1016/j.compfluid.2005.05.008

Bearman, P. W., & Wadcock, A. J. (1973). The interaction between a pair of circular cylinders normal to a stream. *Journal of Fluid Mechanics*, *61*(03), 499–511. doi:10.1017/S0022112073000832

Cheng, M., & Morreti, M. (1988). Experimental study of the flow field downstream of a single tube row. *Experimental Thermal and Fluid Science*, *1*(1), 69–74. doi:10.1016/0894-1777(88)90049-0

Grucelski, A., & Pozorski, J. (2013). Lattice Boltzmann Simulations of flow past a circular cylinder and in a simple porous media. *Computers & Fluids*, *71*, 406–416. doi:10.1016/j.compfluid.2012.11.006

Guillaume, D. W., & LaRue, J. C. (1999). Investigation of the flopping regime with two-, three- and four-cylinder arrays. *Experiments in Fluids*, *27*(2), 145–156. doi:10.1007/s003480050339

He, X., & Luo, L. S. (1997). Theory of lattice Boltzmann method: From the Boltzmann equation to the lattice Boltzmann equation. *Physical Review. E*, *56*(6), 6811–6817. doi:10.1103/PhysRevE.56.6811

Ishigai, S., & Nishikawa, E. (1975). Experimental study of structure of gas flow in tube banks with tube axes normal to flow. Part II: On the structure of gas flow in single-column, single-row, and double-rows tube banks. *Bulletin of Japan Society of Mechanical Engineering*, *18*(119), 528–535. doi:10.1299/jsme1958.18.528

Karthik Selva Kumar, K., & Kumaraswamidhas, L. A. (2014). Numerical Study on Fluid Flow Characteristics Over the Side-By-Side Square Cylinders at Different Spacing Ratio. *International Review of Mechanical Engineering*, 8(5), 962–969. doi:10.15866/ireme.v8i5.3709

Karthik Selva Kumar, K., & Kumaraswamidhas, L. A. (2015a). Experimental investigation on flow induced vibration excitation in the elastically mounted circular cylinder in cylinder arrays. *Fluid Dynamics Research*, 47(1), 015508. doi:10.1088/0169-5983/47/1/015508

Karthik Selva Kumar, K., & Kumaraswamidhas, L. A. (2015b). Experimental investigation on flow induced vibration excitation in the elastically mounted square cylinders. *Journal of Vibroengineering*, 17, 468–477.

Karthik Selva Kumar, K., & Kumaraswamidhas, L. A. (2015c). Experimental and Numerical Investigation on Flow Induced Vibration Excitation in Engineering Structures: A Review. *International Journal of Applied Engineering Research*, 10(15), 35971–35991.

Khan, W. A., Culham, J. R., & Yovanovich, M. M. (2005). Fluid Flow Around and Heat Transfer from an Infinite Circular Cylinder, *ASME. Journal of Heat Transfer*, 127(7), 785–790. doi:10.1115/1.1924629

Kim, H. J., & Durbin, P. A. (1988). Investigation of the flow between a pair of circular cylinders in the flopping regime. *Journal of Fluid Mechanics*, 196(-1), 431–448. doi:10.1017/S0022112088002769

Laurence, S. J., Deiterding, R., & Hornung, H. G. (2007). Proximal bodies in hypersonic flows. *Journal of Fluid Mechanics*, 590, 209–237. doi:10.1017/S0022112007007987

Olinger, D. J., & Sreenivasan, K. R. (1988). Nonlinear dynamics of the wake of an oscillating cylinder. *Physical Review Letters*, 60(9), 797–800. doi:10.1103/PhysRevLett.60.797 PMID:10038655

Pettigrew, M.J., Taylor, C.E., Fisher, N.J., Yetisir, M., & Smith, B.A. (1998). Flow-induced vibration: recent findings and open questions. *Nuclear Engineering and Design*, 185, 249-276.

Shiels, D., Leonard, A., & Roshko, A. (2001). Flow-Induced Vibration of a Circular Cylinder at Limiting Structural Parameters. *Journal of Fluids and Structures*, 15(1), 3–21. doi:10.1006/jfls.2000.0330

Sreenivasan, K. R. (1985). On the Fine – Scale Intermittency of Turbulence. *Journal of Fluid Mechanics*, *151*(-1), 81–103. doi:10.1017/S0022112085000878

Sumner, D., Wong, S. S. T., Price, S. J., & Paidoussis, M. D. (1999). Fluid behavior of side-by-side circular cylinders in steady cross-flow. *Journal of Fluids and Structures*, *13*(3), 309–338. doi:10.1006/jfls.1999.0205

Valero-Lara, P., Igual, F. D., Prieto-Matías, M., Pinelli, A., & Favier, J. (2015). Accelerating fluid–solid simulations (Lattice-Boltzmann & Immersed-Boundary) on heterogeneous architectures. *Journal of Computational Science*, *10*, 249–261. doi:10.1016/j.jocs.2015.07.002

Van Atta, C. W., & Gharib, M. (1987). Ordered and chaotic vortex streets behind circular cylinders at low Reynolds number. *Journal of Fluid Mechanics*, *174*(-1), 113–133. doi:10.1017/S0022112087000065

Williamson, C. H. K. (1996). Vortex dynamics in the cylinder wake. *Annual Review of Fluid Mechanics*, *28*(1), 477–539. doi:10.1146/annurev.fl.28.010196.002401

Zhou, Y., So, R. M. C., Liu, M. H., & Zhang, H. J. (2000). Complex turbulent wakes generated by two and three side-by-side cylinders. *International Journal of Heat and Fluid Flow*, *21*(2), 125–133. doi:10.1016/S0142-727X(99)00077-6

KEY TERMS AND DEFINITIONS

Anti-Phase: If the phase difference is 180 degrees (π radians), then the two oscillators are said to be in antiphase. If two interacting waves meet at a point where they are in antiphase, then destructive interference will occur.

In-Phase: Two oscillators that have the same frequency and no phase difference are said to be in-phase.

Lattice Boltzmann Method (LBM): The lattice Boltzmann method is a powerful technique for the computational modeling of a wide variety of complex fluid flow problems including single and multiphase flow in complex geometries. It is a discrete computational method based upon the Boltzmann equation.

Reynolds (Re) Number: A dimensionless quantity used in fluid mechanics to predict flow patterns in fluid flow simulations.

RMS: RMS is the root-mean-square value of a signal. For a digitized signal, you can calculate it by squaring each value, finding the arithmetic mean of those squared values, and taking the square root of the result.

Side-by-Side Arrangement: The arrangement of bluff bodies in side-by-side manner is known as tandem configuration/arrangement.

Staggered Arrangement: The arrangement of bluff bodies in a zigzag/overlapping manner is known as tandem configuration/arrangement.

Strouhal Number (St): In dimensional analysis, the Strouhal number (St) is a dimensionless number describing oscillating flow mechanisms.

Tandem Arrangement: The arrangement of bluff bodies one behind another in a sequence is known as tandem configuration/arrangement.

Von Kármán Vortex Street: In fluid dynamics, a Kármán vortex street (or a von Kármán vortex street) is a repeating pattern of swirling vortices caused by the unsteady separation of flow of a fluid around blunt bodies.

Vortex Shedding: In fluid dynamics, vortex shedding is an oscillating flow that takes place when a fluid such as air or water flows past a bluff (as opposed to streamlined) body at certain velocities, depending on the size and shape of the body.

Wake: The trail left by a moving body (such as a ship) in a fluid (such as water).

APPENDIX

A Standard Two Dimensional Lattice Boltzmann (D2Q9 lattice) Program With Periodic Boundary Conditions were as follows,

```
#include <stdio.h>
#include <stdlib.h>
#include <string.h>
#include <unistd.h> /* for the sleep function. this may not be
standard */
#include <math.h>
#include <mygraph.h>
#define xdim 31
#define ydim 21
#define DEBUG
double f0[xdim][ydim],
f1[xdim][ydim],f2[xdim][ydim],f3[xdim][ydim],f4[xdim][ydim],
f5[xdim][ydim],f6[xdim][ydim],f7[xdim][ydim],f8[xdim][ydim];
#ifdef DEBUG
double b1[xdim][ydim],b3[xdim][ydim],b5[xdim][ydim],b6[xdim]
[ydim],
bb[xdim][ydim];
#endif
double omega=1;
/* Some constants that appear often and don't need to be
calculated
 over and over again. So we calculate them just once here. */
double
fourOnine=4.0/9.0,
oneOnine=1.0/9.0,
oneOthirtysix=1.0/36.0;
/* Some variables for the suspended particle */
typedef double *doublep;
typedef doublep pair[2];
pair *Bf1=NULL,*Bf3=NULL,*Bf5=NULL,*Bf6=NULL;
int Bf1c,Bf1m=0,Bf3c,Bf3m=0,Bf5c,Bf5m=0,Bf6c,Bf6m=0;
double Cx=15,Cy=10,Mx=0,My=0,Zxx=0,Zxy=0,Zyy=0,Ux=0,Uy=0,R=5
,M=100;
int Repeat=1,iterations=0,FrequencyMeasure=100,Graphics=1;
int Pause=1,sstep=0,done=0;
```

```
double Amp=0.001,Amp2=0.1,Width=10;
/* Some special data types that are required to view the
graphics */
int Xdim=xdim,Ydim=ydim,noreq;
double rho[xdim][ydim];
int rhoreq=0;
double u[xdim][ydim][2];
int ureq=0;
void BCmem(pair **p, int c, int *cm){
if (c<*cm-2) return;
*cm+=100;
*p=(pair *) realloc(*p,*cm*sizeof(pair));
}
void circleBC(){
/* Sets up the links that are cut by a circular object. */
int x,y,Px,Py,Pxp,Pyp,R2;
double dx,dy;
#ifdef DEBUG
for (x=0;x<xdim;x++) for (y=0;y<ydim;y++)
 b1[x][y]=b3[x][y]=b5[x][y]=b6[x][y]=bb[x][y]=0;
#endif
Bf1c=Bf3c=Bf5c=Bf6c=0;
R2=R*R;
for (x=Cx-R-2;x<Cx+R+2;x++){
 Px=(x+xdim)%xdim;
 Pxp=(x+1+xdim)%xdim;
 dx=x-Cx;
 for (y=Cy-R-2;y<Cy+R+2;y++){
 Py=(y+ydim)%ydim;
 Pyp=(y+1+ydim)%ydim;
 dy=y-Cy;
#ifdef DEBUG
 if ((dx*dx+dy*dy-R2)<=0) bb[Px][Py]=1;else bb[Px][Py]=-1;
#endif
 if ((dx*dx+dy*dy-R2)*((dx+1)*(dx+1)+dy*dy-R2)<=0){
BCmem(&Bf1,Bf1c,&Bf1m);
Bf1[Bf1c][0]=&(f2[Px][Py]);
Bf1[Bf1c++][1]=&(f1[(Pxp)][Py]);
#ifdef DEBUG
b1[Px][Py]=1;
```

```
 } else {
b1[Px][Py]=-1;
#endif
 }
 if ((dx*dx+dy*dy-R2)*((dx)*(dx)+(dy+1)*(dy+1)-R2)<=0){
BCmem(&Bf3,Bf3c,&Bf3m);
Bf3[Bf3c][0]=&(f4[Px][Py]);
Bf3[Bf3c++][1]=&(f3[Px][Pyp]);
#ifdef DEBUG
b3[Px][Py]=1;
 } else {
b3[Px][Py]=-1;
#endif
 }
 if ((dx*dx+dy*dy-R2)*((dx+1)*(dx+1)+(dy+1)*(dy+1)-R2)<=0){
BCmem(&Bf5,Bf5c,&Bf5m);
Bf5[Bf5c][0]=&(f7[Px][Py]);
Bf5[Bf5c++][1]=&(f5[Pxp][Pyp]);
#ifdef DEBUG
b5[Px][Py]=1;
 } else {
b5[Px][Py]=-1;
#endif
 }
 if (((dx)*(dx)+(dy+1)*(dy+1)-R2)*((dx+1)*(dx+1)+(dy)*(dy)
-R2)<=0){
BCmem(&Bf6,Bf6c,&Bf6m);
Bf6[Bf6c][0]=&(f8[Pxp][Py]);
Bf6[Bf6c++][1]=&(f6[Px][Pyp]);
#ifdef DEBUG
b6[Px][Py]=1;
 } else {
b6[Px][Py]=-1;
#endif
 }
 }
}
}
void initParticle(){
Cx=10;Cy=10;Mx=0;My=0;Ux=0;Uy=0;R=5;M=100;
```

```
}
void init(){
int x,y;
double n,ux,uy,uxx,uyy,uxy,usq;
printf("initialize\n");
iterations=0;
for (x=0;x<xdim;x++)
 for (y=0;y<ydim;y++){
 /* here we can define the macroscopic properties of the
initial condition. */
 n=1+Amp2*exp(-(pow(x-xdim/2,2)+pow(y-ydim/2,2))/Width);
 ux=0/*.05*sin((y-ydim/2)*2*M_PI/xdim)*/;
 uy=0;
 /*n=1;ux=0;uy=0;*/
 /* The following code initializes the f to be the local
equilibrium
values associated with the density and velocity defined
above.*/
 uxx=ux*ux;
 uyy=uy*uy;
 uxy=2*ux*uy;
 usq=uxx+uyy;
 f0[x][y]=fourOnine*n*(1-1.5*usq);
 f1[x][y]=oneOnine*n*(1+3*ux+4.5*uxx-1.5*usq);
 f2[x][y]=oneOnine*n*(1-3*ux+4.5*uxx-1.5*usq);
 f3[x][y]=oneOnine*n*(1+3*uy+4.5*uyy-1.5*usq);
 f4[x][y]=oneOnine*n*(1-3*uy+4.5*uyy-1.5*usq);
 f5[x][y]=oneOthirtysix*n*(1+3*(ux+uy)+4.5*(uxx+uxy+uyy)-
1.5*usq);
 f6[x][y]=oneOthirtysix*n*(1+3*(-ux+uy)+4.5*(uxx-uxy+uyy)-
1.5*usq);
 f7[x][y]=oneOthirtysix*n*(1+3*(-ux-uy)+4.5*(uxx+uxy+uyy)-
1.5*usq);
 f8[x][y]=oneOthirtysix*n*(1+3*(ux-uy)+4.5*(uxx-uxy+uyy)-
1.5*usq);

 }
}
void TotMomentum(){
int x,y;
```

```
double Momx,Momy;
Momx=Momy=0;
for (x=0;x<xdim;x++)
  for (y=0;y<ydim;y++){
Momx+=f1[x][y]-f2[x][y]+f5[x][y]-f6[x][y]-f7[x][y]+f8[x][y];
Momy+=f3[x][y]-f4[x][y]+f5[x][y]+f6[x][y]-f7[x][y]-f8[x][y];
  }
printf("MomF = (%e,%e), MomP = (%e,%e), MomT = (%e,%e)\n",
Momx,Momy,M*Ux,M*Uy,Momx+M*Ux,Momy+M*Uy);
}
void iterationColloid(){
#define alp 1 /* the degree of implicitness. See */
double zxx,zxy,zyy; /* The inverse Z tensor */
Cx+=Ux+xdim;
Cx=fmod(Cx,xdim);
Cy+=Uy+ydim;
Cy=fmod(Cy,ydim);
zxx=(M+alp*Zyy)/((M+alp*Zxx)*(M+alp*Zyy)+alp*alp*Zxy*Zxy);
zxy= alp*Zxy /((M+alp*Zxx)*(M+alp*Zyy)+alp*alp*Zxy*Zxy);
zyy=(M+alp*Zxx)/((M+alp*Zxx)*(M+alp*Zyy)+alp*alp*Zxy*Zxy);
Ux+=zxx*(Mx-Zxx*Ux-Zxy*Uy)+zxy*(My-Zxy*Ux-Zyy*Uy);
Uy+=zxy*(Mx-Zxx*Ux-Zxy*Uy)+zyy*(My-Zxy*Ux-Zyy*Uy);
#undef alp
}
void iteration(){
int x,y,i;
register double tmp1,tmp2;
register double n,ux,uy,uxx,uyy,uxy,usq,Fx,Fy,Fxx,Fyy,Fxy,Fsq;
double f1y[ydim],f2y[ydim],f5y[ydim],f6y[ydim],f7y[ydim],f8y[yd
im];
double f3x[xdim],f4x[xdim],f5x[xdim],f6x[xdim],f7x[xdim],f8x[xd
im];
/* first we perform the collision step */
for (x=0;x<xdim;x++)
  for (y=0;y<ydim;y++){
  n=f0[x][y]+f1[x][y]+f2[x][y]+f3[x][y]+f4[x][y]
+f5[x][y]+f6[x][y]+f7[x][y]+f8[x][y];
  ux=f1[x][y]-f2[x][y]+f5[x][y]-f6[x][y]-f7[x][y]+f8[x][y];
  uy=f3[x][y]-f4[x][y]+f5[x][y]+f6[x][y]-f7[x][y]-f8[x][y];
  ux/=n;
```

```
uy/=n;
uxx=ux*ux;
uyy=uy*uy;
uxy=2*ux*uy;
usq=uxx+uyy;
/* We now need to implement any forcing terms. The term
included
here is just an example. You should not calculate a constant
force term in the integration routine, but outside where it
only
gets calculated once.*/
Fx=Amp*sin(y*2*M_PI/ydim);
Fy=0;
Fxx=2*n*Fx*ux;
Fyy=2*n*Fy*uy;
Fxy=2*n*(Fx*uy+Fy*ux);
Fsq=Fxx+Fyy;
Fx*=n;
Fy*=n;
f0[x][y]+=omega*(fourOnine*n*(1-1.5*usq)-f0[x][y])
-fourOnine*1.5*Fsq;
f1[x][y]+=omega*(oneOnine*n*(1+3*ux+4.5*uxx -1.5*usq)-f1[x]
[y])
+oneOnine*(3*Fx+4.5*Fxx-1.5*Fsq);
f2[x][y]+=omega*(oneOnine*n*(1-3*ux+4.5*uxx -1.5*usq)-f2[x]
[y])
+oneOnine*(-3*Fx+4.5*Fxx-1.5*Fsq);
f3[x][y]+=omega*(oneOnine*n*(1+3*uy+4.5*uyy -1.5*usq)-f3[x]
[y])
+oneOnine*(3*Fy+4.5*Fyy-1.5*Fsq);
f4[x][y]+=omega*(oneOnine*n*(1-3*uy+4.5*uyy -1.5*usq)-f4[x]
[y])
+oneOnine*(-3*Fy+4.5*Fyy-1.5*Fsq);
f5[x][y]+=omega*(oneOthirtysix*n*(1+3*(ux+uy)+4.5*(uxx+uxy+u
yy)
   -1.5*usq)-f5[x][y])
+oneOthirtysix*(3*(Fx+Fy)+4.5*(Fxx+Fxy+Fyy)-1.5*Fsq);
f6[x][y]+=omega*(oneOthirtysix*n*(1+3*(-ux+uy)+4.5*(uxx-
uxy+uyy)
   -1.5*usq)-f6[x][y])
```

```
+oneOthirtysix*(3*(-Fx+Fy)+4.5*(Fxx-Fxy+Fyy)-1.5*Fsq);
 f7[x][y]+=omega*(oneOthirtysix*n*(1+3*(-ux-
uy)+4.5*(uxx+uxy+uyy)
   -1.5*usq)-f7[x][y])
+oneOthirtysix*(3*(-Fx-Fy)+4.5*(Fxx+Fxy+Fyy)-1.5*Fsq);
 f8[x][y]+=omega*(oneOthirtysix*n*(1+3*(ux-uy)+4.5*(uxx-
uxy+uyy)
   -1.5*usq)-f8[x][y])
+oneOthirtysix*(3*(Fx-Fy)+4.5*(Fxx-Fxy+Fyy)-1.5*Fsq);
 }
/* now we need to move the densities according to their
velocities
 we are using periodic boundary conditions */
/* since we are only using one lattice, we need to save some
data on
 the boundaries so that it does not get overwritten */
for (y=0;y<ydim;y++){
 f1y[y]=f1[xdim-1][y];
 f2y[y]=f2[0][y];
 f5y[y]=f5[xdim-1][y];
 f6y[y]=f6[0][y];
 f7y[y]=f7[0][y];
 f8y[y]=f8[xdim-1][y];
}
for (x=0;x<xdim;x++){
 f3x[x]=f3[x][ydim-1];
 f4x[x]=f4[x][0];
 f5x[x]=f5[x][ydim-1];
 f6x[x]=f6[x][ydim-1];
 f7x[x]=f7[x][0];
 f8x[x]=f8[x][0];
}
/* Now we can move the densities along the lattice.
 You can also do this using loops, but that is actually
 more complicated */
memmove(&f1[1][0],&f1[0][0],(xdim-1)*ydim*sizeof(double));
memmove(&f2[0][0],&f2[1][0],(xdim-1)*ydim*sizeof(double));
memmove(&f3[0][1],&f3[0][0],(xdim*ydim-1)*sizeof(double));
memmove(&f4[0][0],&f4[0][1],(xdim*ydim-1)*sizeof(double));
memmove(&f5[1][1],&f5[0][0],((xdim-1)*ydim-1)*sizeof(double));
```

```
memmove(&f7[0][0],&f7[1][1],((xdim-1)*ydim-1)*sizeof(double));
memmove(&f6[0][1],&f6[1][0],((xdim-1)*ydim)*sizeof(double));
memmove(&f8[1][0],&f8[0][1],((xdim-1)*ydim)*sizeof(double));
/* Now we need to fix the boundaries that have not yet been
correctly
 updated */
for (y=0;y<ydim;y++){
 f1[0][y] =f1y[y];
 f2[xdim-1][y] =f2y[y];
 f5[0][(y+1)%ydim] =f5y[y];
 f6[xdim-1][(y+1)%ydim]=f6y[y];
 f7[xdim-1][y] =f7y[(y+1)%ydim];
 f8[0][y] =f8y[(y+1)%ydim];
}
for (x=0;x<xdim;x++){
 f3[x][0] =f3x[x];
 f4[x][ydim-1] =f4x[x];
 f5[(x+1)%xdim][0] =f5x[x];
 f6[x][0] =f6x[(x+1)%xdim];
 f7[x][ydim-1] =f7x[(x+1)%xdim];
 f8[(x+1)%xdim][ydim-1]=f8x[x];
}
/* Objects in flow */
Mx=My=Zxx=Zxy=Zyy=0;
/* Really I am missing a factor of n here for the velocity
corrections */
for (i=0;i<Bf1c;i++){
 tmp1=*(Bf1[i][0]);
 tmp2=*(Bf1[i][1]);
 *(Bf1[i][0])=tmp2-2./3.*Ux;
 *(Bf1[i][1])=tmp1+2./3.*Ux;
 Mx+=2*(tmp2-tmp1);
 Zxx+= 2*2./3.;
}
for (i=0;i<Bf3c;i++){
 tmp1=*(Bf3[i][0]);
 tmp2=*(Bf3[i][1]);
 *(Bf3[i][0])=tmp2-2./3.*Uy;
 *(Bf3[i][1])=tmp1+2./3.*Uy;
 My+=2*(tmp2-tmp1);
```

```
 Zyy+= 2*2./3.;
}
for (i=0;i<Bf5c;i++){
 tmp1=*(Bf5[i][0]);
 tmp2=*(Bf5[i][1]);
 *(Bf5[i][0])=tmp2-1./6.*(Ux+Uy);
 *(Bf5[i][1])=tmp1+1./6.*(Ux+Uy);
 Mx+=2*(tmp2-tmp1);
 My+=2*(tmp2-tmp1);
 Zxx+= 2*1./6.;
 Zxy+= 2*1./6.;
 Zyy+= 2*1./6.;
}
for (i=0;i<Bf6c;i++){
 tmp1=*(Bf6[i][0]);
 tmp2=*(Bf6[i][1]);
 *(Bf6[i][0])=tmp2-1./6.*(-Ux+Uy);
 *(Bf6[i][1])=tmp1+1./6.*(-Ux+Uy);
 Mx+=-2*(tmp2-tmp1);
 My+= 2*(tmp2-tmp1);
 Zxx+= 2*1./6.;
 Zxy+=-2*1./6.;
 Zyy+= 2*1./6.;
}
}
void analysis(int iterations){
if (FrequencyMeasure%iterations==0){
}
}
void GetGraphics(){
double n;
int x,y;
if (rhoreq){
 rhoreq=0;
 for (x=0;x<xdim;x++)
 for (y=0;y<ydim;y++){
rho[x][y]=f0[x][y]+f1[x][y]+f2[x][y]+f3[x][y]+f4[x][y]
 +f5[x][y]+f6[x][y]+f7[x][y]+f8[x][y];
 }
}
```

```
if (ureq){
 ureq=0;
 for (x=0;x<xdim;x++)
 for (y=0;y<ydim;y++){
n=f0[x][y]+f1[x][y]+f2[x][y]+f3[x][y]+f4[x][y]
 +f5[x][y]+f6[x][y]+f7[x][y]+f8[x][y];
u[x][y][0]=f1[x][y]-f2[x][y]+f5[x][y]-f6[x][y]-f7[x][y]+f8[x]
[y];
u[x][y][1]=f3[x][y]-f4[x][y]+f5[x][y]+f6[x][y]-f7[x][y]-f8[x]
[y];
u[x][y][0]/=n;
u[x][y][1]/=n;
 }
}
}
void GUI(){
DefineGraphNxN_R("rho",&rho[0][0],&Xdim,&Ydim,&rhoreq);
#ifdef DEBUG
DefineGraphNxN_R("bb",&bb[0][0],&Xdim,&Ydim,&noreq);
DefineGraphNxN_R("b1",&b1[0][0],&Xdim,&Ydim,&noreq);
DefineGraphNxN_R("b3",&b3[0][0],&Xdim,&Ydim,&noreq);
DefineGraphNxN_R("b5",&b5[0][0],&Xdim,&Ydim,&noreq);
DefineGraphNxN_R("b6",&b6[0][0],&Xdim,&Ydim,&noreq);
#endif
DefineGraphNxN_RxR("u",&u[0][0][0],&Xdim,&Ydim,&ureq);
StartMenu("Lattice Boltzmann",1);
DefineDouble("1/tau",&omega);
DefineInt("Measurement freq.",&FrequencyMeasure);
StartMenu("Reinitialize",0);
DefineDouble("Amplitude",&Amp2);
DefineDouble("Width",&Width);
DefineFunction("reinitialize",&init);
DefineFunction("Particle init",&initParticle);
EndMenu();
DefineDouble("Velocity amplitude",&Amp);
StartMenu("Particle",0);
DefineDouble("R",&R);
DefineDouble("M",&M);
DefineDouble("Ux",&Ux);
DefineDouble("Uy",&Uy);
```

```
DefineDouble("Cx",&Cx);
DefineDouble("Cy",&Cy);
DefineDouble("Mx",&Mx);
DefineDouble("My",&My);
EndMenu();
DefineGraph(contour2d_,"Density&Vector plots");
DefineInt("Repeat",&Repeat);
DefineBool("Pause",&Pause);
DefineBool("Single Step",&sstep);
DefineBool("Done",&done);
EndMenu();
}
int main(){
int i,newdata;
if (Graphics) GUI();
init();
while (!done){
 if (Graphics){
 Events(newdata);
 GetGraphics();
 DrawGraphs();
 } else {done=1;Pause=0;}
 if (!Pause||sstep){
 sstep=0;
 newdata=1;
 for (i=0;i<Repeat;i++){
iterations++;
circleBC();
iteration();
iterationColloid();
TotMomentum();
analysis(iterations);
 }
 } else sleep(1);
}
return 0;
}
------------------------------------------------------------
------------------------------------------------------------
-
```

Chapter 8
Fluid–Structure Interaction Using Lattice Boltzmann Method Coupled With Finite Element Method

Zhe Li
Ecole Centrale de Nantes, France

Julien Favier
Aix-Marseille University, France

ABSTRACT

This chapter presents several partitioned algorithms to couple lattice Boltzmann method (LBM) and finite element method (FEM) for numerical simulation of transient fluid-structure interaction (FSI) problems with large interface motion. Partitioned coupling strategies allow one to solve separately the fluid and solid subdomains using adapted or optimized numerical schemes, which provides a considerable flexibility for FSI simulation, especially for more realistic and industrial applications. However, partitioned coupling procedures often encounter numerical instabilities due to the fact that the time integrations of the two subdomains are usually carried out in a staggered way. As a consequence, the energy transfer across the fluid-solid interface is usually not correctly simulated, which means numerical energy injection or dissipation might occur at the interface with partitioned methods. The focus of the present chapter is given to the energy conservation property of different partitioned coupling strategies for FSI simulation.

DOI: 10.4018/978-1-5225-4760-0.ch008

INTRODUCTION

Fluid-Structure Interaction (FSI) can be usually observed in nature and engineering processes. Well-known examples include wind-induced oscillations of tall buildings, collapse of bridges caused by wind gusts, flow-induced vibrations of airfoils and dynamics of blood flow through valves in veins etc. The FSI effects are interesting and of great importance, because in some cases they are the key points to understand well the underlying physical phenomenon.

Although experimental results may offer the most straightforward and effective conclusions on some FSI problems, the experimentations are often limited by some constraints, such as the choice of dominant dimensionless number, the high cost of the materials and the long period of test etc. With the development of High Performance Computation (HPC), numerical simulation becomes a useful tool which is more and more efficient and powerful for analyzing the FSI problems. Thus, the robustness and accuracy of the numerical methods for their simulations are of primary importance.

Due to the different material's characteristics of fluid and solid media, FSI simulations are often carried out with different numerical methods for the two individual sub-domains, i.e. fluid and solid. In such circumstance, a partitioned coupling procedure is often preferred, comparing with a monolithic coupling procedure. Because partitioned coupling procedures allow one to carry out separately the time integration of each sub-domain, unlike the monolithic ones which treat computationally the fluid and solid sub-domains as an entity (Felippa, Park, & Farhat, 2001). This is particularly convenient when one prefers to solve the fluid and solid equations using different numerical methods or existing softwares, which are already designed and optimized for each individual sub-domain (Farhat, van der Zee, & Geuzaine, 2006).

However, partitioned coupling procedures often suffer from numerical instabilities, if no special synchronization techniques, such as sub-iterative methods (Farhat, Rallu, Wang, & Belytschko, 2010) or structural predictors (Piperno, & Farhat, 2001), are applied. This is because in this kind of partitioned coupling procedure, the time integrations of the fluid and solid sub-domains are carried out in a staggered way, which means that one updates separately the fluid and solid status to the next time-instant, by introducing some approximations. For example, when updating the solid status, a usual approximation is to assume that the flow-induced pressure loading is constant during one time-step and it is equal to the pressure at the previous time-instant t^n. With this kind of partitioned coupling scheme, named as Ordinary Staggered Coupling Scheme (OSCS) hereafter, the FSI computations may diverge rapidly, even though the individual schemes used in the fluid and solid sub-domains are both numerically stable. This is mainly due to the time-lag between the time integrations of the fluid and solid sub-domains (Michler, Hulshoff, van Brummelen, & de Borst, 2004). From the energy point of view, this OSCS algorithmically injects or dissipates energy at the fluid-solid interface. When too much algorithmic interface energy is injected to the system, the coupling simulation will be interrupted due to the numerical instability. Hence this chapter will give the focus on the interface-energy-conserving property of different partitioned coupling algorithms for FSI simulations by coupling Lattice Boltzmann Method (LBM) for fluid and Finite Element Method (FEM) for solid.

The fluid sub-domain is simulated with the LBM, which is gaining more and more attention over the past two decades. As an alternative to conventional numerical solvers based on the resolution of Navier-Stokes (NS) equations, LBM consists in solving the discrete Boltzmann equation with collision and streaming processes, which can be proven to fully recover the macroscopic NS equations through the Chapman-Enskog analysis (Chapman, & Cowling, 1970). Recently, Shan et al. (Shan, Yuan, & Chen, 2006) have shown that the LBM can be systematically derived from the kinetic theory of hydrodynamics. In this chapter, a single-component isothermal LBM model is applied for the simulation of a weakly compressible laminar fluid flow interacted with a deformable solid structure which is simulated by means of FEM.

Based on the total Lagrangian formulation (Belytschko, Liu, Moran, & Elkhodary, 2013), the adopted FEM solver can be used to handle geometrical non-linearities, such as moderate deformation-large rotation cases. For time integration of the solid sub-domain, the Newmark scheme is used, which enjoys great popularity due to its 'single-step, single-solve' feature in linear as well as in non-linear dynamic analysis. Besides, the Newmark time integrator also features controllable energy dissipation with two coefficients of the scheme (Krenk, 2006). More details of the chosen Newmark scheme will be discussed subsequently.

The Immersed Boundary (IB) method is applied to couple the two numerical methods for FSI problems. In the literature, there exist many previous publications on the use of IB scheme in LBM for numerical simulations of FSI. In this chapter, the focus has been given to the FSI problems where the solid sub-domain is a deformable structure that is modelled by means of FEM. A brief review of this kind of FEM-LBM coupling will be given subsequently.

ISSUES FOR COUPLING FEM AND LBM

Given two different numerical simulation methods, FEM and LBM, one has several issues to handle for the coupling of the two methods.

How to Combine the Lagrangian and Eulerian Formulations?

Since the FEM is based on the Lagrangian formulation and the LBM is based on the Eulerian formulation, the first problem is how to communicate between the two formulations. Here, the Immersed Boundary (IB) method has been chosen to handle this difficulty. Initially proposed by Peskin (Peskin, 2002) for simulating blood flows in the hearts, IB method is particularly useful for introducing moving solid objects in the fluid domain modelled with a fixed Eulerian mesh, which is the case for LBM. Since its appearance, IB method has many variants (Mittal, & Iaccarino, 2005). Recently, several IB-LBM coupled schemes have been presented for simulating FSI problems: Wu and Shu (Wu, & Shu, 2009) proposed an implicit velocity correction-based IB-LBM for one-way (stationary solid boundary) FSI simulations; Favier et al. (Favier, Revell, & Pinelli, 2014) proposed an IB-LBM coupling scheme based on a prediction-correction sub-stage within each time-step, which was applied to simulate the fluid interaction with moving and slender flexible objects; de Rosis (de Rosis, Ubertini, & Ubertini, 2014) proposed an iterative strong IB-LBM coupling method for simulating two-way FSI problems in the presence of slender deformable solid. In the present chapter, the direct-forcing IB method proposed in (Li, Favier, D'Ortona, & Poncet, 2014) is adopted, which can enforce the no-slip condition at the immersed boundaries by using an appropriate local width for each Lagrangian point.

Notice that the adopted IB method can be categorized as diffuse interface IB method. The key word 'diffuse interface' means that the fluid-solid interface effects are smoothly diffused from the interface onto the lattice nodes by means of the kernel function in the spreading sub-stage. The other category is the sharp interface IB method, in which ghost fluid points are usually used to precisely impose the solid boundary condition, based on the geometrical information of the fluid-solid interface. Here the diffuse interface IB method is adopted, majorly because of the following reasons: (1) no special updating treatment for the newly appeared real fluid lattice node; (2) no pressure oscillation when the moving fluid-solid interface pass by a lattice node; (3) it is easy and straightforward to handle the moving solid geometry. Nevertheless, the diffuse interface IB method usually has a lower order of accuracy, compared to the sharp interface IB method.

How to Handle the Geometrical Non-Linearity for the Solid Structure?

When the deformation of the solid structure becomes relatively large, one can no more assume that the stiffness matrix is constant or time-independent in the FEM computation. In other words, the internal nodal force is a non-linear function of the displacement field. In this case, if one uses an implicit time integrator, such as the implicit Newmark scheme, to update the solid status, the final system of equations for the FSI simulation will be non-linear. Although it can be solved using some non-linear iterative algorithms, it is often costly and sometimes does not have a converged solution.

In order to avoid the sub-iterations, one can use explicit Newmark scheme, which is choice in the present chapter for the FEM simulation. This is because the explicit Newmark scheme allows one to calculate first the displacement field u_s^{n+1}, and then calculate the internal nodal force $F_{int}^{n+1}(u_s^{n+1})$ with material model. After this, the internal nodal force can be considered as known, which can linearize the final coupling equation system. Obviously, one drawback of this choice is that one should pay attention to the choice of the time-step, because of the use of an explicit time scheme.

How to Choose an Appropriate Common Time-Step for FEM and LBM Solvers?

As stated previously, with explicit Newmark time scheme, one needs to pay attention when choosing the time-step for the sake of numerical stability. In the frame of FEM-LBM coupling, choosing an appropriate common time-step is even more difficult, since in LBM, the time-step Δt and the spacing Δx are tied up, due to the intrinsic feature of LBM.

There are at least three constraint conditions to respect when choosing the common time-step:

- **Numerical Stability of the Explicit Newmark Scheme:** In FEM solvers, the critical or maximal time-step is usually evaluated as:

$$\Delta t < \Delta t_c = \min_e \left(\frac{l_e}{c_e} \right) \tag{1}$$

where l_e and c_e are the characteristic length and the wave speed of eth element. The wave speed is often estimated with the speed of sound in the solid structure.

- **Numerical Stability of the LBM Solver:** Since the fluid flow is simulated with LBM, the typical stability condition must be satisfied in order to have a numerically stable simulation. This condition is on the relaxation time:

$$\tau = 3v^{lat} + 0.5 > \tau_c \tag{2}$$

where τ is the relaxation time, υ^{lat} is the kinematic viscosity in lattice unit, which is related to the desired Reynolds number, and finally τ_c is a critical value, for example, one can choose a big enough value for this critical value $\tau_c = 0.53$. Since the Reynolds number is defined as:

$$\mathrm{Re} = \frac{U^{lat} L^{lat}}{\upsilon^{lat}} \tag{3}$$

where U^{lat} and L^{lat} denote the characteristic velocity and length in lattice unit. L^{lat} is the number of discretization segments of the physical characteristic length. Hence, its value needs to be kept moderate for having an efficient simulation. This is OK for low Reynolds number cases. When Reynolds number increases, and L^{lat} (or the number of discretization points) is small, then υ^{lat} should be small. However, υ^{lat} cannot be too small because of Equation 2. As a result, the choice of L^{lat} could affect the numerical stability of LBM calculation. In addition, in LBM framework, one has:

$$L^{lat} = \frac{L^{phy}}{\Delta x^{phy}} \text{ and } U^{phy} = \frac{\Delta x^{phy}}{\Delta t^{phy}} U^{lat} \tag{4}$$

hence, one can obtain the physical time-step:

$$\Delta t^{phy} = \frac{L^{phy}}{U^{phy}} \frac{U^{lat}}{L^{lat}} = \frac{L^{phy}}{U^{phy}} \frac{(U^{lat})^2}{\mathrm{Re}} \frac{1}{\upsilon^{lat}} \tag{5}$$

from which one can see that the physical time-step is related with the kinematic viscosity in lattice unit.

- **Weak Compressibility of the LBM Solver:** In Equation 5, one does not have many variables to modify. Once given a physical problem, one cannot modify physical characteristic velocity, length and the Reynolds number. Consequently, the only things that one can change are U^{lat} and υ^{lat}. As presented previously, υ^{lat} will influence the numerical stability of LBM computation, so cannot be too small. The last thing is U^{lat}, which cannot be freely chosen either. This is due to the weakly-compressible hypothesis for LBM solver. When the Mach number becomes too high in the LBM simulation, the error terms are then unneglectable, which means this standard LBM scheme can no more recover the NS equations with enough precision.

As a result, one should ensure that the Mach number is sufficiently small in LBM simulation. In a LBM solver, e.g. with the standard D2Q9 lattice, the speed of sound in lattice unit is $c_s^{lat} = 1/\sqrt{3}$. This means that U^{lat} should be small enough to keep a small Mach number which is defined as:

$$Ma = \frac{U^{lat}}{c_s^{lat}} \qquad (6)$$

Here, a simple strategy for choosing an appropriate common time-step is proposed: first, one fixes the U^{lat} which should be sufficiently small compared to $c_s^{lat} = 1/\sqrt{3}$, e.g. $U^{lat} = 0.05$. This choice gives us a Mach number equaling $Ma \approx 0.0866$, which is small enough for the sake of weakly-compressible hypothesis; second, based on the Reynolds number and discretization points, one choose a kinematic viscosity v^{lat}, which should be big enough due to Equation 2; third, determine the physical time-step for LBM solver using Equation 5; finally, verify if this time-step satisfy the stability condition for FEM solver with Equation 1.

How to Reduce the Time-Lag Between the Two Time Integrations?

As presented previously, when coupling two different numerical simulation methods with a partitioned coupling algorithm, it is possible and easy to introduce a time-lag between the time integrations of the two sub-domains. In order to reduce such time-lag, one can apply several synchronization techniques, e.g. structure predictor, sub-iterations in each time-step, or solving implicitly the coupling equations at the fluid-solid interface etc. However, even using a structure predictor, the FSI coupling is still staggered in time, since one can never exactly predict the real value of solid velocity at the next time instant without knowing the fluid-induced loading at the next time instant. The only thing that one can do is to try to estimate a new velocity field using the information from the previous time instant. Hence, such prediction may fail in some extreme cases. The sub-iteration-based technique does enhance the synchronization or reduce the time-lag between the two time integrations. Nevertheless, they are usually very costly, since several sub-iterations are needed within each physical time-step, especially with a stricter convergence criterion. In strong FSI cases, sub-iteration-based coupling method might even fail. The implicit method is a good choice, since it can eliminate, by construction, the time-lag, and is not too much costly, compared to sub-iteration-based methods. One drawback of this kind of method is that one needs to modify the fluid and solid codes in order to extract the information for constructing the system of coupling equations.

The objective of the present chapter is to compare several different strategies for coupling FEM and LBM via a diffuse interface IB method for the numerical simulation of FSI problems in the presence of large interface motion and structural deformation. The capability of retaining the numerical stability of each coupling method will be assessed with a well-known 2D test-case. The focus will be put on the interface-energy-conserving property of each method.

MATHEMATICAL FORMULATIONS AND NUMERICAL SCHEMES FOR FLUID AND SOLID SUB-DOMAINS

Lattice Boltzmann Method for Single-Component Fluid Flow

In the lattice Boltzmann method the fluid state is updated by resolving the discrete Boltzmann equation:

$$f_\alpha\left(x + e_\alpha \Delta t, t + \Delta t\right) - f_\alpha\left(x, t\right) = -\frac{\Delta t}{\tau}\left(f_\alpha\left(x, t\right) - f_\alpha^{(eq)}\left(x, t\right)\right) + "tG_\alpha \tag{7}$$

where $f_\alpha\left(x, t\right)$ denotes the distribution function at the site x and the time t, in the αth direction of the used D2Q9 (Qian, D'Humières, & Lallemand, 1992) lattice for 2D cases, as shown in Figure 1, and e_α is the αth discrete velocity vector.

Figure 1. The D2Q9 lattice used for 2D LBM simulations

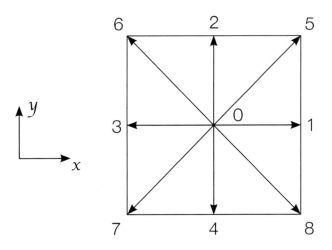

In Equation 7, the single-relaxation-time Bhatnagar-Gross-Krook (BGK) collision model is adopted and τ denotes the relaxation time. Here, $f_\alpha^{(eq)}(x,t)$ is referred to as the discrete equilibrium distribution function, which can be obtained by Hermite series expansion of the Maxwell-Boltzmann equilibrium distribution (Shan, Yuan, & Chen, 2006):

$$f_\alpha^{(eq)} = \rho \omega_\alpha \left[1 + \frac{e_\alpha \cdot u}{c_s^2} + \frac{(e_\alpha \cdot u)^2}{2c_s^4} - \frac{u^2}{2c_s^2} \right] \tag{8}$$

where $\rho = \rho(x,t)$ and $u = u(x,t)$ denote the macroscopic fluid density and velocity, $c_s = 1/\sqrt{3}$ representing the speed of sound, and ω_α the weight coefficient equaling $\omega_0 = 4/9$, $\omega_{1-4} = 1/9$ and $\omega_{5-8} = 1/36$ for D2Q9 lattice. In this isothermal single-component LBM model, the fluid pressure is calculated as $p = \rho c_s^2$ and the kinematic viscosity is related to the relaxation time by $\upsilon = c_s^2 (\tau - 0.5\Delta t)$.

Additionally, a body force scheme of Guo et al. (Guo, Zheng, & Shi, 2002) is adopted in the LBM simulation:

$$G_\alpha = \left(1 - \frac{\Delta t}{2\tau} \right) \omega_\alpha \left[\frac{e_\alpha - u}{c_s^2} + \frac{e_\alpha \cdot u}{c_s^4} e_\alpha \right] \cdot F^{IB} \tag{9}$$

in which F^{IB} represents the IB-related body force, which will be obtained from the solid structural effects simulated by means of a diffuse interface IB method.

Finally, once one calculates all the distribution functions $f_\alpha(x, t+\Delta t)$ with Equation 7, one can update the macroscopic fluid status by the definition (Guo, Zheng, & Shi, 2002):

$$\begin{cases} \rho(x, t+\Delta t) = \sum_\alpha f_\alpha(x, t+\Delta t) \\ \rho(x, t+\Delta t) u(x, t+\Delta t) = \sum_\alpha e_\alpha f_\alpha(x, t+\Delta t) + \frac{\Delta t}{2} F^{IB} \end{cases} \tag{10}$$

Note that this definition of the macroscopic fluid velocity should be used at each time instant in order to make the LBM scheme fully recover the Navier-Stokes equations.

Finite Element Method for Solid Structure

As presented in (Belytschko, Liu, Moran, & Elkhodary, 2013), the weak total Lagrangian formulation for solid can be obtained by integrating the momentum equation multiplied by a virtual displacement field over the initial configuration:

$$\int_{\Omega_s^0} \delta u_s \left(\rho_s^0 \frac{\partial^2 u_s}{\partial t^2} - \nabla_0 \cdot P_s - \rho_s^0 b_s \right) d\Omega_s^0 = 0 \tag{11}$$

where $\Omega_s^0(X_s)$ denotes the solid initial configuration, as shown in Figure 2, with X_s being the time-independent Lagrangian or material coordinate. In addition, $\delta u_s(X_s)$ denotes the virtual displacement field, $\rho_s^0(X_s)$ the initial solid density, $u_s(X_s,t)$ the solid displacement field defined as $u_s(X_s,t) = x_s(X_s,t) - X_s$ where $x_s(X_s,t)$ denotes the Eulerian or spatial coordinate of the material point X_s in the current solid configuration. $P_s(X_s,t)$ is the nominal stress tensor and $\nabla_0 \cdot$ is the divergence operator with respect to the material coordinate X_s. Finally, $b_s(X_s,t)$ is the body force vector per unit mass such as the gravity.

Figure 2. Initial and current solid configurations

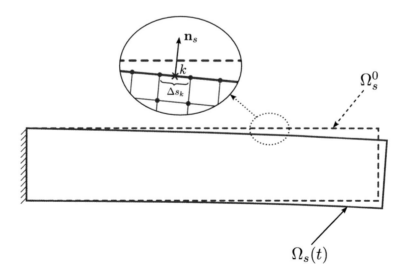

271

Equation 11 is also referred to as the virtual work principle that can give us the semi-discrete solid equations in matrix form:

$$M_s a_s = f_{ext} - f_{int} \tag{12}$$

where $a_s\left(X_s, t\right)$ denotes the acceleration field defined as:

$$
\left\{
\begin{aligned}
a_s\left(X_s, t\right) &= \left.\frac{\partial v_s\left(X_s, t\right)}{\partial t}\right|_{X_s} \\
v_s\left(X_s, t\right) &= \left.\frac{\partial u_s\left(X_s, t\right)}{\partial t}\right|_{X_s}
\end{aligned}
\right. \tag{13}
$$

with the displacement field $u_s = \left[u_s^1, u_s^2, \cdots, u_s^N\right]^{\mathrm{T}}$, the velocity field $v_s = \left[v_s^1, v_s^2, \cdots, v_s^N\right]^{\mathrm{T}}$ and the acceleration field $a_s = \left[a_s^1, a_s^2, \cdots, a_s^N\right]^{\mathrm{T}}$, in which $u_s^I = \left[u_s^{I,x}\left(t\right), u_s^{I,y}\left(t\right)\right]$, $v_s^I = \left[v_s^{I,x}\left(t\right), v_s^{I,y}\left(t\right)\right]$ and $a_s^I = \left[a_s^{I,x}\left(t\right), a_s^{I,y}\left(t\right)\right]$ are the displacement, velocity and acceleration in x and y directions of the Ith FEM node in 2D cases.

Additionally, M_s, f_{int} and f_{ext} are the mass matrix, the internal and external nodal forces, respectively. Moreover, the nominal stress tensor P_s is calculated by $P_s = S \cdot F^{\mathrm{T}}$ with S being the second Piola-Kirchhoff (PK2) stress and $F = \partial x_s / \partial X_s$ denoting the deformation gradient. In the present chapter, an elastic solid structure is considered, hence the PK2 stress is linearly related to the Green-Lagrange strain E by means of a constant fourth-order tensor C, i.e. $S = C \cdot E$ where $E = 1/2\left(F^{\mathrm{T}} \cdot F - I\right)$, which is reffered to as the Saint Venant-Kirchhoff material model. For more details, the reader may refer to (Belytschkos, Liu, Moran, & Elkhodary, 2013).

The Newmark scheme (Newmark, 1959) is chosen to integrate in time this semi-discrete system of equations:

$$
\left\{
\begin{aligned}
u_s^{n+1} &= u_s^n + \Delta t v_s^n + \frac{\Delta t^2}{2}\left(\left(1 - 2\beta\right)a_s^n + 2\beta a_s^{n+1}\right) \\
v_s^{n+1} &= v_s^n + \Delta t\left(\left(1 - \gamma\right)a_s^n + \gamma a_s^{n+1}\right)
\end{aligned}
\right. \tag{14}
$$

where the superscripts n and $n+1$ indicate the time instants t^n and t^{n+1} for the displacement u_s, velocity v_s and the acceleration a_s. In addition, Δt denotes the constant time-step, which is the same for both the solid and fluid subdomains. Finally, β and γ are the two coefficients of the Newmark scheme. In the present work, we choose $\beta = 0$ and $\gamma = 0.5$ for the solid simulations, with which the Newmark time integrator is essentially an explicit central difference scheme possessing second-order accuracy in time and conditional stability. The time-step Δt should be smaller than the critical time-step determined by Equation 1.

In the present work, the FSI happens only at the fluid-solid interface. For the FEM solver, the velocity boundary condition is tackled with the elimination method, and the time-varying force boundary condition is imposed by using a geometric operator L_p that relates the external nodal force f_{ext} with the flow-induced force Λ as $f_{ext} = -L_p \Lambda$. For more details about how to generate this geometrical operator, the reader may refer to (Li, & Favier, 2017).

A Diffuse Interface Immersed Boundary Method

In this work, we apply the IB method proposed by the authors in the previous work (Li, Favier, D'Ortona, & Poncet, 2016), in which the IB method was used to impose moving solid boundary conditions in the fluid flow. This IB method is based on the interpolated definition of the macroscopic fluid velocity from the Eulerian (fluid) nodes to the Lagrangian (solid) points:

$$I\left[\rho_f\right]_k v_{f,k} = I\left[\sum_\alpha e_\alpha f_\alpha\right]_k + \frac{\Delta t}{2} F_k^{IB} \tag{15}$$

where $v_{f,k}$ and F_k^{IB} denote the fluid velocity and the IB-related force at the kth interface element, respectively. $I\left[\bullet\right]_k$ represents the interpolation operator defined as:

$$\begin{aligned}\varphi\left(x_k, t\right) &= I\left[\varphi\left(x, t\right)\right]_k \\ &= \int \varphi\left(x, t\right) \delta\left(x - x_k\right) dx \approx \sum_{j \in D_k} \varphi\left(x_j, t\right) \tilde{\delta}\left(x_j - x_k\right) \triangle x \triangle y\end{aligned} \tag{16}$$

which provides an interpolated value of a given variable at solid point. This form of the interpolation operator makes use of the sampling property of the Dirac delta function. In Equation 16, $\varphi\left(x_j, t\right)$ is the value of any function at the jth Eulerian (fluid) node located inside the support domain D_k of the Lagrangian (solid) point, as shown in Figure 3. Finally, $\tilde{\delta}\left(x_j - x_k\right)$ is a mollifier or a smooth approximation to the Dirac delta function. In the present work, we adopt the mollifier proposed by Roma et al. (Roma, Peskin, & Berger, 1999):

$$\tilde{\delta}\left(\vec{x}_j - \vec{x}_k\right) = \frac{1}{\Delta x}\tilde{\delta}\left(\frac{\left|x_j - x_k\right|}{\Delta x}\right)\frac{1}{\Delta y}\tilde{\delta}\left(\frac{\left|y_j - y_k\right|}{\Delta y}\right) \tag{17}$$

with:

$$\tilde{\delta}\left(r\right) = \begin{cases} \dfrac{1}{3}\left(1 + \sqrt{1 - 3r^2}\right) & 0 \leq r < 0.5 \\ \dfrac{1}{6}\left[5 - 3r - \sqrt{1 - 3\left(r - 1\right)^2}\right] & 0.5 \leq r < 1.5 \\ 0 & else \end{cases} \tag{18}$$

Supposing that at the instant t^n all variables are already known, and we will resolve the LBM equation in order to update the fluid state to the instant t^{n+1}. After calculating the new distribution functions with Equation 7, we can update the fluid

Figure 3. The fluid lattice and the support domain of the interface point for IB method

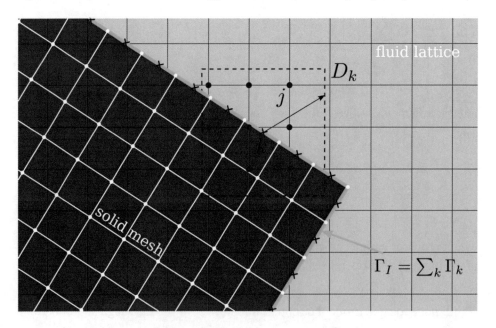

density, but we cannot update the fluid velocity, since the IB-related body force is not known yet. To clarify this point, let us rewrite Equation 15 at t^{n+1}:

$$I\left[\rho_f^{n+1}\right]_k v_{f,k}^{n+1} = I\left[\sum_\alpha e_\alpha f_\alpha^{n+1}\right]_k + \frac{\Delta t}{2} F_k^{n+1} \tag{19}$$

In one-way FSI problems, such as the ones presented in (Li, Favier, D'Ortona, & Poncet, 2016), the fluid velocity at the solid point $v_{f,k}^{n+1}$ is equal to the solid velocity under the no-slip condition, which is usually preset or imposed by the applied solid-motion law. As a result, one can directly calculate the IB-related force F_k^{n+1} at solid points. However, in two-way FSI simulations, the velocity $v_{f,k}^{n+1}$ can only be known after resolving the system of coupling equations, since the solid velocity at the instant t^{n+1} also depends on F_k^{n+1}. That is why it is referred to as the two-way coupled problem.

COUPLING STRATEGIES

In the previous publications (Clausen, Reasor, & Aidun, 2010), (Kollmannsberger, Geller, Düster, Tölke, Sorger, Krafczyk, & Rank, 2009) and (Krüger, Varnik, & Raabe, 2011), different FEM-LBM coupling strategies have been proposed for the simulation of FSI problems in the presence of deformable solid structure. However, all of them be classified as staggered coupling procedures, in which there always exists a lag between the time integrations of fluid and solid subdomains. For example, in (Clausen, Reasor, & Aidun, 2010), the force vector for the FEM solver needed to be guessed with a force predictor, because the fluid-structure coupling determines the effective force. In (Krüger, Varnik, & Raabe, 2011), one takes the interface at the moment t^n to compute the fluid velocity at the next moment t^{n+1}, which actually depends on F^{n+1}. In order to reduce the time lag, structural predictors have been used in (Kollmannsberger, Geller, Düster, Tölke, Sorger, Krafczyk, & Rank, 2009) to obtain a numerically stable simulation. This time-lag may sometimes degrade the stability or convergence order of the numerical schemes. In spite of the staggered feature, the advantage of these coupling strategies is that one does not need to significantly modify the existing codes or softwares for the FSI implementation.

This subsection starts with a brief presentation of several staggered coupling algorithms, and then will present a non-staggered FEM-LBM coupling scheme proposed in (Li, & Favier, 2017).

Ordinary Staggered Coupling Scheme

The first coupling strategy is the ordinary staggered coupling scheme based on the assumption that the fluid-induced force is constant during one time-step for the solid structure, which is very straightforward to be implemented. The procedure of this staggered algorithm is illustrated in Figure 4 and can be briefly summarized as:

Step 1: The interface force field Λ^n is sent to the solid solver, considered as the flow-induced force acted on the structure at t^{n+1}

Step 2: Using this force boundary condition, the solid solver makes use of the Newmark time integrator to update the solid status to the next time instant

Step 3: Meanwhile, the fluid solver calculates the new distribution functions

Step 4: The newly obtained structural geometry and velocity condition are sent to the fluid solver as a preset solid boundary condition, with which one will determine the new IB-related force so as to fully update the macroscopic fluid status to the next time instant

Figure 4. The ordinary staggered coupling scheme

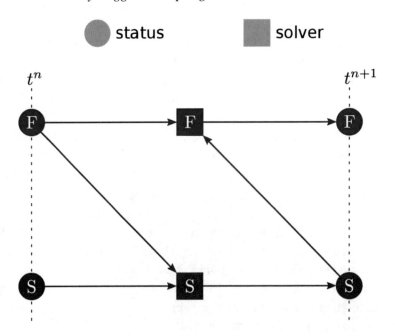

As one can observe, there is a time-lag in this staggered coupling procedure, because the solid solver takes the interface force Λ^n as the force boundary condition at the instant t^{n+1}. Such assumption ruins the force continuity at the fluid-solid interface, which is the main reason why such staggered coupling method suffers sometimes from numerical instabilities.

One possible way for evaluating the incremental interface energy is to use the following equation:

$$\Delta E_I = \sum_{k \in \Gamma_I} \Delta t \overline{F}_{s,k} \cdot \overline{v}_{s,k} + \sum_{k \in \Gamma_I} \Delta t \overline{F}_{f,k} \cdot \overline{v}_{f,k} \tag{20}$$

where $\overline{F}_{s,k} = \left(F_{s,k}^n + F_{s,k}^{n+1} \right) / 2$ and $\overline{F}_{f,k} = \left(F_{f,k}^n + F_{f,k}^{n+1} \right) / 2$ denote the mean values of the interface forces at each interface element, which act on the solid and the fluid, respectively. Since the force continuity is not ensured in this staggered coupling scheme, this incremental interface energy is normally not zero.

Staggered Coupling Scheme With a Structural Predictor

Piperno and Farhat (Piperno, & Farhat, 2001) concluded that a conventional sequential staggered procedure, with or without structural predictor, generally cannot conserve energy at the fluid-solid interface. However, the structural predictor can be carefully adjusted to control the imbalance of energy at the interface, and reduce it as much as possible.

In the present chapter, since the explicit Newmark scheme is adopted, the solid displacement can be correctly calculated for the next time-instant. So, instead of predicting solid displacement (Piperno, & Farhat, 2001), we adopt a structural velocity predictor in the ordinary staggered coupling scheme, as shown in Figure 5.

The coupling algorithm is summarized as follows:

Step 1: The solid solver uses the explicit Newmark time integrator to update the new displacement filed and then the new geometry at t^{n+1}. Meanwhile, a predicted solid velocity field $v_s^{p+1} = v_s^n + \Delta t a_s^n$ is prepared for the fluid solver

Step 2: The fluid solver uses the new solid geometry and the predicted solid velocity as the prescribed boundary condition to update the fluid state, density and velocity to the next time instant

Step 3: The solid solver receives the IB-related interface force Λ^{n+1} from the fluid solver, and then update the solid acceleration field a_s^{n+1} and the real velocity field v_s^{n+1}

Figure 5. The staggered coupling scheme with a structural predictor

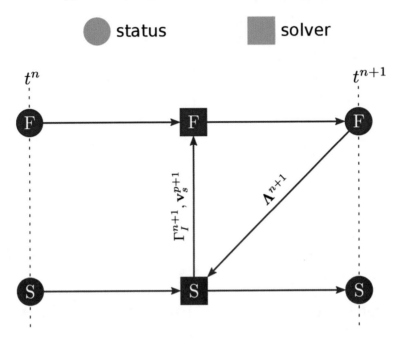

Figure 5 shows that, intead of taking the previous solid velocity v_s^n, the fluid solver uses a predicted velocity field v_s^{p+1} in order to finish one time-step. In this coupling scheme, the mean interface forces in Equation 20 are equal and opposite for solid and fluid, since the fluid and solid solvers share the same Λ at each time-step. However, the mean interface velocities are still different, because:

$$
\begin{cases}
\overline{v}_{s,k} = \dfrac{1}{2}\left(v_{s,k}^{n+1} + v_{s,k}^{n} \right) \\
\overline{v}_{f,k} = \dfrac{1}{2}\left[\left(v_{s,k}^{n} + \Delta ta_{s,k}^{n} \right) + \left(v_{s,k}^{n-1} + \Delta ta_{s,k}^{n-1} \right) \right]
\end{cases}
\tag{21}
$$

The difference between these two mean velocities will generate an error term for the interface energy evaluated by mean of Equation 20, which means that using a structural predictor cannot eliminate the time-lag.

Staggered Coupling Scheme Based on Sub-Iterations Within Each Time-Step

The major steps of such kind of coupling scheme are given as follows:

Step 1: The solid solver sends an interface state $\Gamma_I \left(u_s^{n+1}, \tilde{v}_s \right)$ to the fluid solver, where $\tilde{v}_s$ denotes an estimated solid velocity field. For the first sub-iteration step, one can set $\tilde{v}_s = v_s^n$

Step 2: With this interface state, the fluid solver updates the fluid state to the next instant and then sends back to the solid solver the interface force field Λ^{n+1}

Step 3: Using this interface force field Λ^{n+1}, the solid solver calculates a new solid velocity field v_s^{n+1} and the relative difference between v_s^{n+1} and $\tilde{v}_s$ by:

$$r = \frac{\sqrt{\left(v_s^{n+1} - \tilde{v}_s \right)^2 / N_s}}{U^0} \tag{22}$$

where U^0 is the characteristic fluid velocity and N_s is the total number of solid nodes.

Step 4: Compare r with the prescribed critical value r_c: if $r < r_c$, then break the sub-iteration loop and proceed the next physical time-step of the FSI simulation; else, set $\tilde{v}_s = v_s^{n+1}$ and goto Step 1

Sub-iteration-based coupling algorithms are widely applied because of the simplicity of implementation. More importantly, the sub-iteration steps help to reduce the interface energy so as to stabilize the FSI simulation and improve the accuracy. However, the sub-iterations are often costly and sometimes might diverge in strong fluid-structure coupling (Heil, 2004).

A Non-Staggered FEM-LBM Coupling Scheme

This non-staggered coupling algorithm was proposed by Li and Faiver (Li, & Favier, 2017). The basic idea is to construct a coupling system of equations as:

$$\begin{bmatrix} K_s^c & 0 & L_p \\ 0 & K_f^c & I \\ L_s & I & 0 \end{bmatrix} \begin{bmatrix} v_s^{n+1} \\ v_f^{n+1} \\ \Lambda^{n+1} \end{bmatrix} = \begin{bmatrix} g_s \\ g_f \\ 0 \end{bmatrix} \tag{23}$$

For more details about this coupling system of equations, the reader may refer to (Li, & Faiver, 2017). Following the proposed resolution procedure, one can efficiently calculate v_s^{n+1}, v_f^{n+1} and Λ^{n+1}. Once they are updated, the solid solver will calculate the new acceleration field. Meanwhile, the fluid solver will spread this newly obtained interface force field from the solid points onto the neighboring fluid nodes in order to accomplish the calculation of the macroscopic fluid velocity.

The coupling algorithm is illustrated in Figure 6 and can be briefly reviewed as follows:

Step 1: The solid and fluid solvers carry out independently and simultaneously the first-stage calculation: the solid solver calculates the new displacement field using the explicit Newmark scheme and then update the structural geometry; the fluid solver carries out the collision and streaming steps of LBM so that one can update the fluid

Step 2: The coupler interpolates the fluid information from the fluid nodes to the newly updated solid points so as to prepare the matrix in the coupling system of equations in order to obtain the new interface state

Step 3: The solid solver receives new velocity and the fluid solver receives new interface force field from the coupler and then accomplish the individual integrations of one entire time-step

Figure 6. The non-staggered coupling algorithm

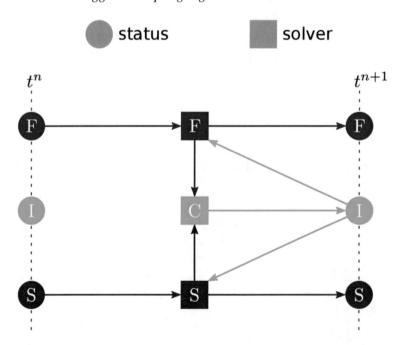

NUMERICAL EXAMPLES

This well-known test case was firstly proposed by Turek and Hron (Turek, & Hron, 2006) for the numerical benchmarking of laminar flow-elastic structure FSI simulations. As shown in Figure 7, we consider an elastic solid bar immersed in a rectangular fluid flow channel. The deformable solid bar is attached to a fixed rigid cylinder, of which the geometric center is located near the inlet and slightly deviated from the horizontal center line of the channel. The geometric and material parameters are provided in (Li, & Favier, 2017).

Results With the Staggered FEM-LBM Coupling Schemes

The ordinary staggered coupling algorithm is very straightforward and simple to be implemented for FSI simulations, especially when using two existing computation softwares. The drawback of such staggered algorithm is that it cannot ensure the zero-interface-energy condition, and then sometimes encounters numerical instability. In Figure 8, one can find that this staggered coupling algorithm cannot provide a numerically stable simulation for the chosen test case. The calculation diverged quickly after several hundred time-steps, as shown in Figure 8. The quickly increasing interface energy shows that this staggered coupling algorithm cannot ensure a zero interface energy, i.e. too much algorithmic energy has been injected into the coupled system at the interface, which finally interrupted the simulation.

Figure 7. Configuration of the validation test-case

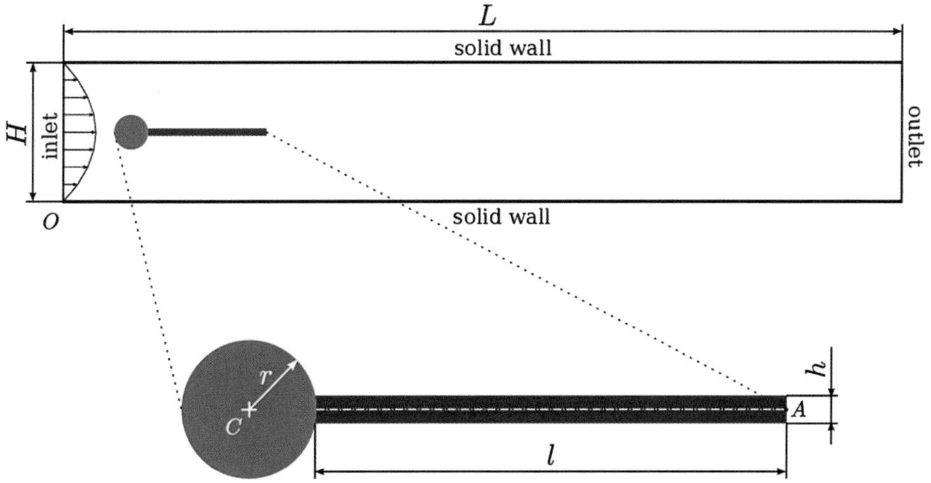

Figure 8. Comparison of the interface energy between the ordinary staggered and non-staggered coupling algorithms

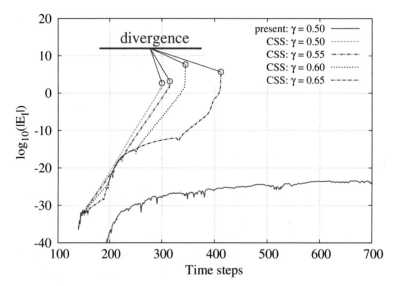

In this circumstance, one of the usual solutions is to choose a larger Newmark coefficient $\gamma > 0.5$, which introduces numerical dissipation in the solid simulation, and might probably stabilize the FSI simulation. However, such solution does not work all the time and it decreases the order of accuracy of the Newmark time integrator, and more inconveniently one can never know beforehand how big this coefficient needs to be in order to get a stable simulation. As shown in Figure 8, choosing a larger γ cannot stabilize the FSI simulation, even though it can slightly defer the divergence moment. In fact, this coefficient cannot be too much big either, for the sake of stability for the Newmark scheme.

Figure 9 shows the evolutions in time of the interface energy of the staggered algorithms with and without a structural predictor. In these numerical experimentations, we observe that: (1) both the two simulations diverged after several hundreds of time-steps, which means that applying a structural predictor in the staggered coupling procedure did not stabilize the simulation; (2) in this numerical example, the structural predictor accelerates the divergence of the simulation. This is possible, because when using a staggered coupling procedure, the continuity conditions at the interface are generally not satisfied, which might introduce errors in the numerical results. Since the predictor is based on $v_{s,k}^n$ and $a_{s,k}^n$, if they are not correctly calculated, $v_{s,k}^{p+1}$ cannot be properly predicted, i.e. not too far from the real solid $v_{s,k}^{n+1}$.

Figure 9. Interface energies using the ordinary staggered scheme with and without a structural predictor

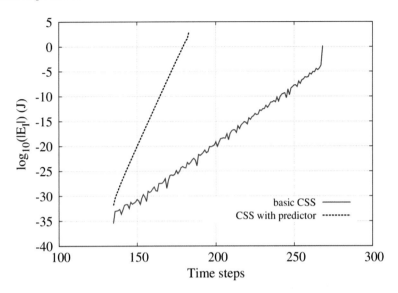

Figure 10. The simulation results of the sub-iteration-based coupling scheme

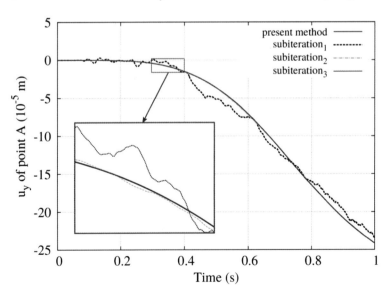

Figure 11. Velocity field of the deformable solid bar

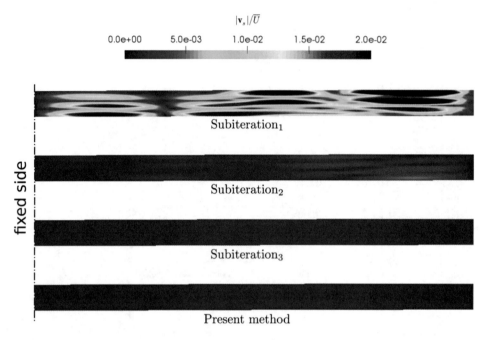

Figure 10 shows the numerical results obtained with the sub-iteration-based coupling algorithms using three different critical relative differences. In this comparison, one can observe that the staggered FSI simulations have been stabilized with the help of the sub-iterations at every time-step. In addition, as shown in 10, when the convergence criteria of sub-iteration is less strict, numerical oscillation occurs around the result obtained with the proposed non-staggered coupling method. This numerical oscillation can also be observed in the velocity magnitude field of the deformable solid bar, as shown in Figure 11. Too much energy has been injected to the solid subdomain. Finally, the accumulated interface energy is given in Figure 12, where one can observe that the level of interface energy is higher with a less strict convergence criteria for the sub-iterations, and the interface energy is strictly zero with the proposed non-staggered algorithm.

Results With the Non-Staggered FEM-LBM Coupling Algorithm

Figure 13 shows the vorticity in the fluid flow and the stress in the solid bar at different instants. Figure 14 gives the time history of the vertical displacement of the point A, from which one can observe that such flow-induced vibration begins to get stabilized after 10 seconds, and it can be considered as periodic after 12 seconds.

Figure 12. Time history of the absolute accumulated interface energy introduced with the sub-iteration-based staggered coupling method

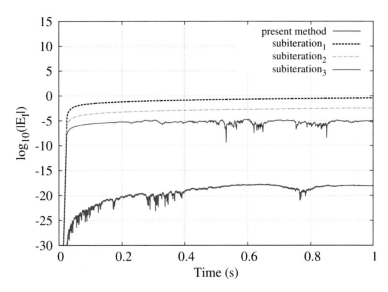

Figure 13. The vorticity field in the fluid flow and the stress component in the solid bar at four different instants

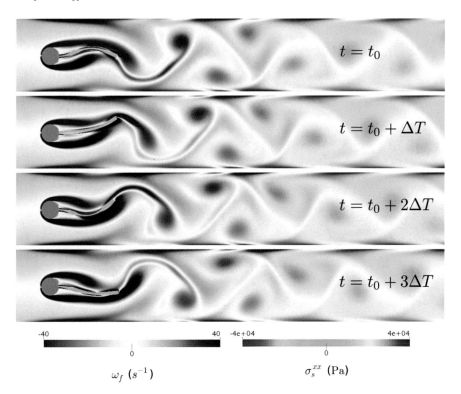

Figure 14. Tim evolution of the vertical displacement of the point A

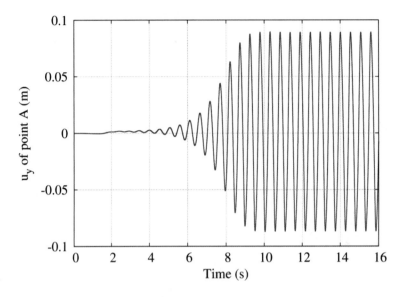

Figure 15. Comparison with the references in the literature

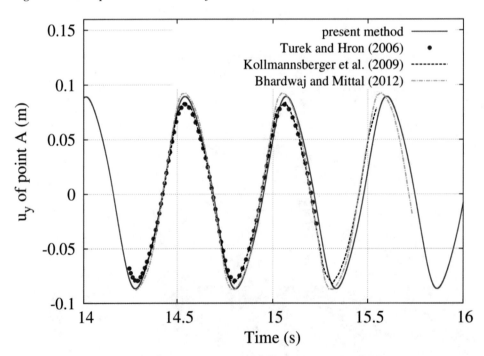

Figure 15 shows good agreements with the results of Turek and Hron (Turek, & Hron, 2006), Kollmannsberger et al. (Kollmannsberger, Geller, Düster, Tölke, Sorger, Krafczyk, & Rank, 2009) and Bhardwaj and Mittal (Bhardwaj, & Mittal, 2012).

In the present simulation, there are 257,706 lattice nodes for LBM, 1,936 mesh nodes for FEM, and 507 Lagrangian points for IB method. Two Xeon E5520 2.27 GHz cores were used: one for the LBM solver, one for the FEM solver. 16 seconds of physical time (160,000 time-steps) took 52 hours of CPU time. The time needed to compute each time-step of the FSI simulation is approximately 1.2 seconds.

Figure 16 shows the time history of the accumulated or total interface energy. Since the velocity and force continuities can be ensured at the interface at each time-step, the incremental interface energy is ensured to be zero by construction with this non-staggered coupling method. As one can observe that the absolute value of the accumulated interface energy is rigorously zero.

Figure 16. Time history of the absolute accumulated interface energy introduced with the non-staggered coupling scheme

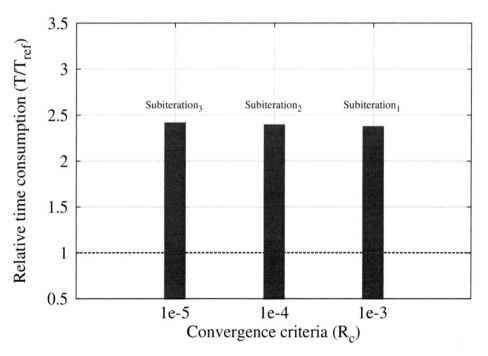

CONCLUSION

In the present chapter, several coupling procedures are presented for simulating fluid-structure interaction problems, which is based on the coupling of finite element method for solid and lattice Boltzmann method for fluid via an immersed boundary scheme. The most important feature of the non-staggered coupling method is that the fluid and solid sub-domains are coupled in a synchronous way, which means that there is no time lag between the two time integrations, so that the non-staggered coupling method can rigorously ensure a zero algorithmic energy at the fluid-solid interface. In the adopted validation test case, the present result is found to be in good agreement with the reference ones. Additionally, a comparison with the conventional serial staggered coupling procedure has also been carried out, with a structural predictor, or sub-iterations with each time-step. The result shows that, in this specific numerical framework, the staggered methods, with or without a structural predictor, cannot give a stable simulation, even if one uses a relatively large numerical dissipation coefficient of Newmark time integrator. The sub-iteration-based staggered coupling did stabilize the FSI simulation, but is much costly. On the contrary, the sub-iteration-free non-staggered coupling method can retain the numerical stability during the whole period of numerical simulation.

The advantage of this non-staggered coupling method is that it provides a stable sub-iteration-free numerical framework that couples two very different numerical methods for simulating fluid-structure interaction problems. The continuity conditions at fluid-solid interface are satisfied so that the incremental interface energy can be ensured to be zero by means of an implicit treatment of interface status. Nevertheless, some possible improvements could be (1) use of incompatible time-steps: in the present framework, the time-step must be the same for the fluid and solid solver, which might limit the efficiency of the coupling method; (2) use of implicit Newmark time integrator for solid: the present coupling is based on the use of explicit Newmark scheme that allows us to handle the geometrical nonlinearity without sub-iteration within each time-step; (3) coupling via a higher-order immersed boundary method: the 1st-order accuracy of the adopted immersed boundary method might limit the accuracy of the FSI simulations. In the future, the next step of the present work is to use incompatible time-steps for fluid and solid, while still preserving the interface energy.

REFERENCES

Belytschko, T., Liu, W. K., Moran, B., & Elkhodary, K. (2013). *Nonlinear finite elements for continua and structures*. John Wiley & Sons.

Bhardwaj, R., & Mittal, R. (2012). Benchmarking a Coupled Immersed-Boundary-Finite-Element Solver for Large-Scale Flow-Induced Deformation. *AIAA Journal*, *50*(7), 1638–1642. doi:10.2514/1.J051621

Chapman, S., & Cowling, T. G. (1970). *The Mathematical Theory of Non-uniform Gases: An Account of the Kinetic Theory of Viscosity, Thermal Conduction and Diffusion in Gases. Cambridge Mathematical Library.* Cambridge University Press.

Clausen, J. R., Reasor, D. A. Jr, & Aidun, C. K. (2010). Parallel performance of a lattice Boltzmann/finite element cellular blood flow solver on the IBM Blue Gene/P architecture. *Computer Physics Communications*, *181*(6), 1013–1020. doi:10.1016/j.cpc.2010.02.005

Combescure, A., & Gravouil, A. (2002). A numerical scheme to couple subdomains with different time-steps for predominantly linear transient analysis. *Computer Methods in Applied Mechanics and Engineering*, *191*(11-12), 1129–1157. doi:10.1016/S0045-7825(01)00190-6

Combescure, A., Gravouil, A., & Herry, B. (2003). An algorithm to solve transient structural non-linear problems for non-matching time-space domains. *Computers & Structures*, *81*(12), 1211–1222. doi:10.1016/S0045-7949(03)00037-3

De Rosis, A., Ubertini, S., & Ubertini, F. (2014). A partitioned approach for two-dimensional fluid structure interaction problems by a coupled lattice Boltzmann-finite element method with immersed boundary. *Journal of Fluids and Structures*, *45*, 202–215. doi:10.1016/j.jfluidstructs.2013.12.009

Farhat, C., Crivelli, L., & Géradin, M. (1993). On the spectral stability of time integration algorithms for a class of constrained dynamics problems. AIAA 34th Structural Dynamics Meeting. doi:10.2514/6.1993-1306

Farhat, C., & Lesoinne, M. (2000). Two efficient staggered algorithms for the serial and parallel solution of three-dimensional nonlinear transient aeroelastic problems. *Computer Methods in Applied Mechanics and Engineering*, *182*(3-4), 499–515. doi:10.1016/S0045-7825(99)00206-6

Farhat, C., Rallu, A., Wang, K., & Belytschko, T. (2010). Robust and provably second-order explicit-explicit and implicit-explicit staggered time integrators for highly non-linear compressible fluid-structure interaction problems. *International Journal for Numerical Methods in Engineering*, *84*(1), 73–107. doi:10.1002/nme.2883

Farhat, C., van der Zee, K. G., & Geuzaine, P. (2006). *Provably second-order time-accurate loosely-coupled solution algorithms for transient nonlinear computational aeroelasticity*. Academic Press.

Favier, J., Revell, A., & Pinelli, A. (2014). A Lattice Boltzmann – Immersed Boundary method to simulate the fluid interaction with moving and slender flexible objects. *Journal of Computational Physics*, *261*, 145–161. doi:10.1016/j.jcp.2013.12.052

Felippa, C. A., Park, K. C., & Farhat, C. (2001). Partitioned analysis of coupled mechanical systems. *Computer Methods in Applied Mechanics and Engineering*, *190*(24), 3247–3270. doi:10.1016/S0045-7825(00)00391-1

Gravouil, A., & Combescure, A. (2003). Multi-time-step and two-scale domain decomposition method for non-linear structural dynamics. *International Journal for Numerical Methods in Engineering*, *58*(10), 1545–1569. doi:10.1002/nme.826

Gravouil, A., Combescure, A., & Brun, M. (2015). Heterogeneous asynchronous time integrators for computational structural dynamics. *International Journal for Numerical Methods in Engineering*, *102*(3-4), 202–232. doi:10.1002/nme.4818

Guo, Z., Zheng, C., & Shi, B. (2002). Discrete lattice effects on the forcing term in the lattice Boltzmann method. *Physical Review. E*, *65*(4), 046308. doi:10.1103/PhysRevE.65.046308 PMID:12006014

Heil, M. (2004). An efficient solver for the fully coupled solution of large displacement fluid-structure interaction problems. *Computer Methods in Applied Mechanics and Engineering*, *193*(1-2), 1–23. doi:10.1016/j.cma.2003.09.006

Hughes, T. J. R. (2012). *The finite element method: linear static and dynamic finite element analysis*. Courier Corporation.

Kollmannsberger, S., Geller, S., Düster, A., Tölke, J., Sorger, C., Krafczyk, M., & Rank, E. (2009). Fixed-grid fluidstructure interaction in two dimensions based on a partitioned lattice Boltzmann and p-FEM approach. *International Journal for Numerical Methods in Engineering*, *79*(7), 817–845. doi:10.1002/nme.2581

Krenk, S. (2006). *Energy conservation in newmark based time integration algorithms*. Academic Press.

Krüger, T., Varnik, F., & Raabe, D. (2011). Efficient and accurate simulations of deformable particles immersed in a fluid using a combined immersed boundary lattice Boltzmann finite element method. *Computers & Mathematics with Applications (Oxford, England)*, *61*(12), 3485–3505. doi:10.1016/j.camwa.2010.03.057

Li, Z., Favier, J., D'Ortona, U., & Poncet, S. (2016). An immersed boundary-lattice Boltzmann method for single- and multi-component fluid flows. *Journal of Computational Physics*, *304*, 424–440. doi:10.1016/j.jcp.2015.10.026

Michler, C., Hulshoff, S. J., van Brummelen, E. H., & de Borst, R. (2004). A monolithic approach to fluid-structure interaction. *Computers & Fluids, 33*(5 – 6):839 – 848.

Newmark, N. M. (1959). A method of computation for structural dynamics. *Journal of the Engineering Mechanics Division*, 85.

Peskin, C. S. (2002). The immersed boundary method. *Acta Numerica, 11*, 1–39. doi:10.1017/S0962492902000077

Piperno, S., & Farhat, C. (2001). Partitioned procedures for the transient solution of coupled aeroelastic problems - Part II: Energy transfer analysis and three-dimensional applications. *Computer Methods in Applied Mechanics and Engineering, 190*(24-25), 3147–3170. doi:10.1016/S0045-7825(00)00386-8

Qian, Y. H., D'Humières, D., & Lallemand, P. (1992). Lattice BGK Models for Navier-Stokes equation. *Europhysics Letters, 17*(6), 479–484. doi:10.1209/0295-5075/17/6/001

Roma, A. M., Peskin, C. S., & Berger, M. J. (1999). An adaptive version of the immersed boundary method. *Journal of Computational Physics, 153*(2), 509–534. doi:10.1006/jcph.1999.6293

Shan, X., Yuan, X. F., & Chen, H. (2006). Kinetic theory representation of hydrodynamics: A way beyond the Navier-Stokes equation. *Journal of Fluid Mechanics, 550*(-1), 413–441. doi:10.1017/S0022112005008153

Soti, A. K., Bhardwaj, R., & Sheridan, J. (2015). Flow-induced deformation of a flexible thin structure as manifestation of heat transfer enhancement. *International Journal of Heat and Mass Transfer, 84*, 1070–1081. doi:10.1016/j.ijheatmasstransfer.2015.01.048

Turek, S., & Hron, J. (2006). Proposal for Numerical Benchmarking of Fluid-Structure Interaction between an Elastic Object and Laminar Incompressible Flow. In *Lecture Notes in Computational Science and Engineering: Vol. 53*. Springer Berlin Heidelberg.

Wu, J., & Shu, C. (2009). Implicit velocity correction-based immersed boundary lattice Boltzmann method and its applications. *Journal of Computational Physics, 228*(6), 1963–1979. doi:10.1016/j.jcp.2008.11.019

KEY TERMS AND DEFINITIONS

Interface Energy: In order to measure the quantity of energy that is lost or gained at the fluid-solid interface, one can calculate a net energy transfer, which is not unique, at the interface. When this interface energy is positive, it means that a quantity of energy is artificially injected into the whole coupled system, which might induce numerical instabilities.

Monolithic Coupling Strategy: In this kind of coupling algorithm, the two numerical computations are carried out in one unique solver. The equations of the two sub-domains are solved simultaneously by the same computation code.

Partitioned Coupling Strategy: In this kind of coupling algorithm, the two numerical computations are carried out separately.

Staggered Coupling: In numerical simulation of fluid-structure interaction problems, a staggered coupling scheme does not ensure that the force and velocity are both from the same time instants. Staggered coupling usually suffers numerical instabilities due to some assumptions for the sake of simplicity.

Sub-Iteration: A purely numerical communication procedure between two solvers, which is used to ensure certain equality or condition.

Time Integrator: A numerical scheme that is used to update the state of solid/ fluid in time.

Weakly-Compressible Solver: In this kind of numerical solver, the variation of density is allowed but limited to a small account, which is usually verified by a small enough Mach number (Ma < 0.1).

Chapter 9
Lattice Boltzmann Shallow Water Simulation With Surface Pressure

Iñaki Zabala
SENER Ingeniería y Sistemas S.A., Spain

Jesús M. Blanco
Universidad del País Vasco, Spain

ABSTRACT

Shallow water conditions are produced in coastal and river areas and allow the simplification of fluid solving by integrating in height to the fluid equations, discarding vertical flow so a 3D problem is solved with a set of 2D equations. Usually the boundary conditions defined by the surface pressure are discarded, as it is considered that the difference in atmospheric pressure in simulation domain is irrelevant in most hydraulic and coastal engineering scenarios. However, anticyclones and depressions produce noticeable pressure gradients that may affect the consequences of phenomena like tides and tsunamis. This chapter demonstrates how to remove this weakness from the LBM-SW by incorporating pressure into the LBM for this kind of scenario in a consistent manner. Other small-scale effects like buoyancy may be solved using this approach.

INTRODUCTION

Shallow Water Equations (SWEs) are part of computational fluid dynamics where instability often arises. The shallow water and mass transport equations have wide applications in ocean, coastal, and hydraulic engineering, which can benefit from

DOI: 10.4018/978-1-5225-4760-0.ch009

the advantages of the LBM. The LBM has recently become an attractive numerical method to solve various fluid dynamics phenomena (Tubbs & Tsai, 2011). The water depth in flows existing in rivers, channels, coastal areas, estuaries and harbors is usually much smaller than the horizontal scale. In such flows the horizontal motions are much more relevant than the vertical (Zhou, 2003). Due to the fact that the horizontal length scale is much greater than the vertical length scale, it is possible to consider that the vertical velocity and acceleration are irrelevant, and the pressure only depends on the water depth (Allen et al., 1990; Sterling & Chen, 1996). In this way the pressure is considered as hydrostatic (Shan et al., 2006). However, it is assumed that the surface elevation is single-valued, hence, waves do not break or overturn.

The shallow water equations are derived by depth-integrating the continuity equation and the Navier-Stokes equations. The depth integration of the mass transport equation leads to the shallow water transport equation. The shallow water equations can include forcing terms of wind, bottom friction, bed slope and the term representing the so called Coriolis effect. Most of the schemes, for example, finite difference method (FDM) when applied on SWEs, suffer from numerical instability. They produce non-physical oscillations mainly because discretization of the flux and source terms are not well balanced in their reconstructions. Lattice Boltzmann (LB) method was developed to model fluids under such flow regimes (Tumelo, 2011).

This chapter will introduce all these components as developed mainly by (Zhou, 2011) adding surface pressure influence and focuses on shallow water equation with the aim of applying the proposed method for numerical simulation of shallow water equations. The mathematical theoretical accounts can be very useful to understand the dynamics of water flows (Zergani, *et al.*, 2016).

GOVERNING EQUATIONS

Navier-Stokes

The conservation of mass (Ghia, *et al.*, 1982). at a volume element $dV = dx \cdot dy \cdot dz$ is represented by the continuity equation:

$$\frac{\partial \rho}{\partial t} + \frac{\partial (\rho u)}{\partial x} + \frac{\partial (\rho v)}{\partial y} + \frac{\partial (\rho w)}{\partial z} = 0 \tag{1}$$

with velocity components *u*, *v* and *w*.

This represents that the rate of change of mass in a volume element is equal to the mass flow into the volume and the variation of mass due to change on density.

For an incompressible flow density ρ is constant so this simplifies to:

$$\frac{\partial u}{\partial x} + \frac{\partial v}{\partial y} + \frac{\partial w}{\partial z} = 0 \tag{2}$$

Using vector notation and the nabla operator, these equations in a general coordinate system read:

$$\nabla v = 0 \tag{3}$$

The conservation of momentum at a volume element dV is represented by the following momentum equations:

$$\frac{\partial(\rho u)}{\partial t} + \frac{\partial(\rho uu)}{\partial x} + \frac{\partial(\rho uv)}{\partial y} + \frac{\partial(\rho uw)}{\partial z} = F_x + \frac{\partial \tau_{xx}}{\partial x} + \frac{\partial \tau_{yx}}{\partial y} + \frac{\partial \tau_{zx}}{\partial z}$$
$$\frac{\partial(\rho v)}{\partial t} + \frac{\partial(\rho vu)}{\partial x} + \frac{\partial(\rho vv)}{\partial y} + \frac{\partial(\rho vw)}{\partial z} = F_y + \frac{\partial \tau_{xy}}{\partial x} + \frac{\partial \tau_{yy}}{\partial y} + \frac{\partial \tau_{zy}}{\partial z} \tag{4}$$
$$\frac{\partial(\rho w)}{\partial t} + \frac{\partial(\rho wu)}{\partial x} + \frac{\partial(\rho wv)}{\partial y} + \frac{\partial(\rho ww)}{\partial z} = F_z + \frac{\partial \tau_{xz}}{\partial x} + \frac{\partial \tau_{yz}}{\partial y} + \frac{\partial \tau_{zz}}{\partial z}$$

They consider the rate of change of momentum in such a volume element that is the momentum flux (Bouzidi *et al.*, 2001), into the volume plus the shear and normal stresses acting on the volume element plus the forces acting on the mass of the volume.

The forces acting on the volume mass include the gravity and coriolis as well as the electric and magnetic forces that act on a flow, and are denoted by $F = \left(F_x, F_y, F_z\right)^T$

The pressure p can be written as the trace of the stress tensor:

$$p = -\frac{\tau_{xx} + \tau_{yy} + \tau_{zz}}{3} \tag{5}$$

The minus sign takes into account the fact that the pressure acts as a negative normal stress.

The three normal stresses τ_{xx}, τ_{yy} and τ_{zz} can each be split up into two parts, the pressure p and the contributions due to the friction of the fluid σ_{xx}, σ_{yy} and σ_{zz}:

$$
\begin{aligned}
\tau_{xx} &= \sigma_{xx} - p \\
\tau_{yy} &= \sigma_{yy} - p \\
\tau_{zz} &= \sigma_{zz} - p
\end{aligned}
$$

(6)

Inserting τ_{xx}, τ_{yy} and τ_{zz} we obtain:

$$
\frac{\partial(\rho u)}{\partial t} + \frac{\partial(\rho u u)}{\partial x} + \frac{\partial(\rho u v)}{\partial y} + \frac{\partial(\rho u w)}{\partial z} = F_x - \frac{\partial p}{\partial x} + \frac{\partial \sigma_{xx}}{\partial x} + \frac{\partial \tau_{yx}}{\partial y} + \frac{\partial \tau_{zx}}{\partial z}
$$

$$
\frac{\partial(\rho v)}{\partial t} + \frac{\partial(\rho v u)}{\partial x} + \frac{\partial(\rho v v)}{\partial y} + \frac{\partial(\rho v w)}{\partial z} = F_y - \frac{\partial p}{\partial y} + \frac{\partial \tau_{xy}}{\partial x} + \frac{\partial \sigma_{yy}}{\partial y} + \frac{\partial \tau_{zy}}{\partial z}
$$

$$
\frac{\partial(\rho w)}{\partial t} + \frac{\partial(\rho w u)}{\partial x} + \frac{\partial(\rho w v)}{\partial y} + \frac{\partial(\rho w w)}{\partial z} = F_z - \frac{\partial p}{\partial z} + \frac{\partial \tau_{xz}}{\partial x} + \frac{\partial \tau_{yz}}{\partial y} + \frac{\partial \sigma_{zz}}{\partial z}
$$

(7)

For Newtonian fluids the following relations hold:

$$
\begin{aligned}
\sigma_{xx} &= 2\mu \frac{\partial u}{\partial x} - \frac{2}{3}\mu\left(\frac{\partial u}{\partial x} + \frac{\partial v}{\partial y} + \frac{\partial w}{\partial z}\right) \\
\sigma_{yy} &= 2\mu \frac{\partial v}{\partial x} - \frac{2}{3}\mu\left(\frac{\partial u}{\partial x} + \frac{\partial v}{\partial y} + \frac{\partial w}{\partial z}\right) \\
\sigma_{zz} &= 2\mu \frac{\partial w}{\partial x} - \frac{2}{3}\mu\left(\frac{\partial u}{\partial x} + \frac{\partial v}{\partial y} + \frac{\partial w}{\partial z}\right)
\end{aligned}
$$

(8)

And with the symmetry condition:

$$
\begin{aligned}
\tau_{yx} &= \tau_{xy} = \mu\left(\frac{\partial v}{\partial x} + \frac{\partial u}{\partial y}\right) \\
\tau_{yz} &= \tau_{zy} = \mu\left(\frac{\partial w}{\partial y} + \frac{\partial v}{\partial z}\right) \\
\tau_{zx} &= \tau_{xz} = \mu\left(\frac{\partial u}{\partial z} + \frac{\partial w}{\partial x}\right)
\end{aligned}
$$

(9)

Inserting the normal stresses and shear stresses according to Equation (8) into the conservation of momentum equations Equation (7), we obtain the equations:

$$\frac{\partial(\rho u)}{\partial t} + \frac{\partial(\rho uu)}{\partial x} + \frac{\partial(\rho uv)}{\partial y} + \frac{\partial(\rho uw)}{\partial z} = F_x$$

$$-\frac{\partial p}{\partial x} + \frac{\partial}{\partial x}\left\{\mu\left[2\frac{\partial u}{\partial x} - \frac{2}{3}(\nabla v)\right]\right\} + \frac{\partial}{\partial y}\left[\mu\left(\frac{\partial v}{\partial x} + \frac{\partial u}{\partial y}\right)\right] + \frac{\partial}{\partial z}\left[\mu\left(\frac{\partial u}{\partial z} + \frac{\partial w}{\partial x}\right)\right]$$

$$\frac{\partial(\rho v)}{\partial t} + \frac{\partial(\rho vu)}{\partial x} + \frac{\partial(\rho vv)}{\partial y} + \frac{\partial(\rho vw)}{\partial z} = F_y$$

$$-\frac{\partial p}{\partial y} + \frac{\partial}{\partial x}\left[\mu\left(\frac{\partial v}{\partial x} + \frac{\partial u}{\partial y}\right)\right] + \frac{\partial}{\partial y}\left\{\mu\left[2\frac{\partial v}{\partial x} - \frac{2}{3}(\nabla v)\right]\right\} + \frac{\partial}{\partial z}\left[\mu\left(\frac{\partial w}{\partial y} + \frac{\partial v}{\partial z}\right)\right]$$

$$\frac{\partial(\rho w)}{\partial t} + \frac{\partial(\rho wu)}{\partial x} + \frac{\partial(\rho wv)}{\partial y} + \frac{\partial(\rho ww)}{\partial z} = F_z$$

$$-\frac{\partial p}{\partial z} + \frac{\partial}{\partial x}\left[\mu\left(\frac{\partial u}{\partial z} + \frac{\partial w}{\partial x}\right)\right] + \frac{\partial}{\partial y}\left[\mu\left(\frac{\partial w}{\partial y} + \frac{\partial v}{\partial z}\right)\right] + \frac{\partial}{\partial z}\left\{\mu\left[2\frac{\partial w}{\partial x} - \frac{2}{3}\mu(\nabla v)\right]\right\}$$

$$(10)$$

For incompressible flows, we can use the continuity equation $\nabla v = 0$ to obtain:

$$\rho\left(\frac{\partial u}{\partial t} + \frac{\partial(uu)}{\partial x} + \frac{\partial(uv)}{\partial y} + \frac{\partial(uw)}{\partial z}\right) = F_x$$

$$-\frac{\partial p}{\partial x} + \frac{\partial}{\partial x}\left(2\mu\frac{\partial u}{\partial x}\right) + \frac{\partial}{\partial y}\left[\mu\left(\frac{\partial v}{\partial x} + \frac{\partial u}{\partial y}\right)\right] + \frac{\partial}{\partial z}\left[\mu\left(\frac{\partial u}{\partial z} + \frac{\partial w}{\partial x}\right)\right]$$

$$\rho\left(\frac{\partial v}{\partial t} + \frac{\partial(vu)}{\partial x} + \frac{\partial(vv)}{\partial y} + \frac{\partial(vw)}{\partial z}\right) = F_y$$

$$(11)$$

$$-\frac{\partial p}{\partial y} + \frac{\partial}{\partial x}\left[\mu\left(\frac{\partial v}{\partial x} + \frac{\partial u}{\partial y}\right)\right] + \frac{\partial}{\partial y}\left(2\mu\frac{\partial v}{\partial x}\right) + \frac{\partial}{\partial z}\left[\mu\left(\frac{\partial w}{\partial y} + \frac{\partial v}{\partial z}\right)\right]$$

$$\rho\left(\frac{\partial w}{\partial t} + \frac{\partial(wu)}{\partial x} + \frac{\partial(wv)}{\partial y} + \frac{\partial(ww)}{\partial z}\right) = F_z$$

$$-\frac{\partial p}{\partial z} + \frac{\partial}{\partial x}\left[\mu\left(\frac{\partial u}{\partial z} + \frac{\partial w}{\partial x}\right)\right] + \frac{\partial}{\partial y}\left[\mu\left(\frac{\partial w}{\partial y} + \frac{\partial v}{\partial z}\right)\right] + \frac{\partial}{\partial z}\left(2\mu\frac{\partial w}{\partial x}\right)$$

Using the continuity equation Equation (11), and assuming constant viscosity these may be rewritten in nonconservative form:

$$\rho\left(\frac{\partial u}{\partial t} + \frac{\partial(uu)}{\partial x} + \frac{\partial(uv)}{\partial y} + \frac{\partial(uw)}{\partial z}\right) = F_x - \frac{\partial p}{\partial x} + \mu\left(\frac{\partial^2 u}{\partial x^2} + \frac{\partial^2 u}{\partial y^2} + \frac{\partial^2 u}{\partial z^2}\right)$$

$$\rho\left(\frac{\partial v}{\partial t} + \frac{\partial(vu)}{\partial x} + \frac{\partial(vv)}{\partial y} + \frac{\partial(vw)}{\partial z}\right) = F_y - \frac{\partial p}{\partial y} + \mu\left(\frac{\partial^2 v}{\partial x^2} + \frac{\partial^2 v}{\partial y^2} + \frac{\partial^2 v}{\partial z^2}\right)$$

$$\rho\left(\frac{\partial w}{\partial t} + \frac{\partial(wu)}{\partial x} + \frac{\partial(wv)}{\partial y} + \frac{\partial(ww)}{\partial z}\right) = F_z - \frac{\partial p}{\partial z} + \mu\left(\frac{\partial^2 w}{\partial x^2} + \frac{\partial^2 w}{\partial y^2} + \frac{\partial^2 w}{\partial z^2}\right)$$

$$(12)$$

or, in more compact Einstein notation:

$$\rho\left(\frac{\partial u_i}{\partial t} + \frac{\partial(u_i u_j)}{\partial x_j}\right) = F_i - \frac{\partial p}{\partial x_i} + \mu\frac{\partial}{\partial x_j}\left(\frac{\partial u_i}{\partial x_j} + \frac{\partial u_j}{\partial x_i}\right) \tag{13}$$

Shallow Water Equations

The general 2D governing equations for shallow water flows can be derived based on the general flow continuity and momentum equations Equation (3) and Equation (12). Let's consider h as the water depth and b as the bathymetry (bottom height) measured from $Z = 0$ as shown in Figure 1.

In order to determine the continuity equation ∇v in terms of depth-averaged quantities, we integrate Equation (3) over depth from the bottom $z = b$ to the free surface $z = h + b$ including atmospheric pressure effect:

$$\int_b^{h+b}\left(\frac{\partial u}{\partial x} + \frac{\partial v}{\partial y} + \frac{\partial w}{\partial z}\right)dz = 0 \tag{14}$$

which leads to:

$$\int_b^{h+b}\frac{\partial u}{\partial x}dz + \int_b^{h+b}\frac{\partial v}{\partial y}dz + w_s - w_b = 0 \tag{15}$$

Figure 1. Shallow water environment

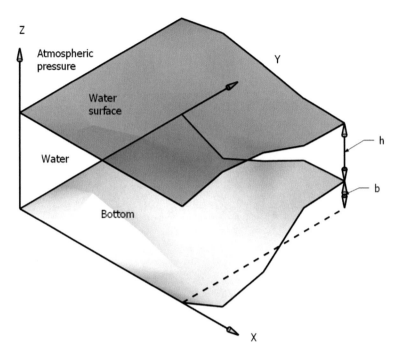

where w_s and w_b are the vertical velocities at the free surface and bottom, respectively.

Since both b and h depend on t, x and y, we can apply the Leibniz integral rule to the first and second terms:

$$\int_{b}^{h+b} \frac{\partial u}{\partial x} dz = \frac{\partial}{\partial x} \int_{b}^{h+b} u dz - u_s \frac{\partial(h+b)}{\partial x} + u_b \frac{\partial b}{\partial x}$$
$$\int_{b}^{h+b} \frac{\partial v}{\partial x} dz = \frac{\partial}{\partial y} \int_{b}^{h+b} v dz - v_s \frac{\partial(h+b)}{\partial y} + v_b \frac{\partial b}{\partial y}$$

(16)

Substituting Equation (16) into Equation (15) gives:

$$\frac{\partial}{\partial x} \int_{b}^{h+b} u dz + \frac{\partial}{\partial y} \int_{b}^{h+b} v dz + \left[w_s - u_s \frac{\partial(h+b)}{\partial x} - v_s \frac{\partial(h+b)}{\partial y} \right] - \left[w_b - u_b \frac{\partial b}{\partial x} - v_b \frac{\partial b}{\partial y} \right] = 0$$

(17)

The kinematic conditions at the water surface are given by:

$$w_s = \frac{\partial(h+b)}{\partial t} + u_s \frac{\partial(h+b)}{\partial x} + v_s \frac{\partial(h+b)}{\partial y} \tag{18}$$

and at the channel bed:

$$w_b = \frac{\partial b}{\partial t} + u_b \frac{\partial b}{\partial x} + v_b \frac{\partial b}{\partial y} \tag{19}$$

Applying the conditions to equation we get:

$$\frac{\partial}{\partial x}\int_b^{h+b} u\,dz + \frac{\partial}{\partial y}\int_b^{h+b} v\,dz + \left[\frac{\partial(h+b)}{\partial t} + u_s\frac{\partial(h+b)}{\partial x} + v_s\frac{\partial(h+b)}{\partial y} - u_s\frac{\partial(h+b)}{\partial x} - v_s\frac{\partial(h+b)}{\partial y}\right]$$
$$-\left[\frac{\partial b}{\partial t} + u_b\frac{\partial b}{\partial x} + v_b\frac{\partial b}{\partial y} - u_b\frac{\partial b}{\partial x} - v_b\frac{\partial b}{\partial y}\right] = 0 \tag{20}$$

Removing terms the expression is:

$$\frac{\partial}{\partial x}\int_b^{h+b} u\,dz + \frac{\partial}{\partial y}\int_b^{h+b} v\,dz + \frac{\partial h}{\partial t} = 0 \tag{21}$$

Defining depth-averaged velocities as:

$$\bar{u} = \frac{1}{h}\int_b^{h+b} u\,dz$$

$$\bar{v} = \frac{1}{h}\int_b^{h+b} v\,dz \tag{22}$$

We can apply them to previous equation. So the depth averaged continuity equation is:

$$\frac{\partial h}{\partial t} + \frac{\partial(h\bar{u})}{\partial x} + \frac{\partial(h\bar{v})}{\partial y} = 0 \tag{23}$$

or in Einstein notation:

$$\frac{\partial h}{\partial t} + \frac{\partial \left(h u_j \right)}{\partial x_j} = 0 \tag{24}$$

Integrating the component x of the momentum over depth and including $\nu = \mu / \rho$, we get:

$$\int_b^{h+b} \left[\frac{\partial u}{\partial t} + \frac{\partial \left(uu \right)}{\partial x} + \frac{\partial \left(vu \right)}{\partial y} + \frac{\partial \left(wu \right)}{\partial z} \right] dz = \int_b^{h+b} f_c v dz + \int_b^{h+b} \left[\frac{-1}{\rho} \frac{\partial p}{\partial x} + \nu \left(\frac{\partial^2 u}{\partial x^2} + \frac{\partial^2 u}{\partial y^2} + \frac{\partial^2 u}{\partial z^2} \right) \right] dz \tag{25}$$

Using the Leibniz rule for the first three terms of the left side gives:

$$\int_b^{h+b} \frac{\partial u}{\partial t} dz = \frac{\partial}{\partial t} \int_b^{h+b} u dz - u_s \frac{\partial \left(h+b \right)}{\partial t} + u_b \frac{\partial b}{\partial t}$$
$$\int_b^{h+b} \frac{\partial u^2}{\partial x} dz = \frac{\partial}{\partial x} \int_b^{h+b} u^2 dz - u_s^2 \frac{\partial \left(h+b \right)}{\partial x} + u_b^2 \frac{\partial b}{\partial x} \tag{26}$$
$$\int_b^{h+b} \frac{\partial \left(vu \right)}{\partial y} dz = \frac{\partial}{\partial y} \int_b^{h+b} vu dz - v_s u_s \frac{\partial \left(h+b \right)}{\partial y} + v_b u_b \frac{\partial b}{\partial y}$$

The last term on the left side of Equation (25) can be integrated directly as:

$$\int_b^{h+b} \frac{\partial \left(wu \right)}{\partial x} dz = w_s u_s - w_b u_b \tag{27}$$

Then Equation (26) are put together and rearranged to obtain:

$$\int_b^{h+b} \left[\frac{\partial u}{\partial t} + \frac{\partial \left(uu \right)}{\partial x} + \frac{\partial \left(vu \right)}{\partial y} + \frac{\partial \left(wu \right)}{\partial z} \right] dz = \frac{\partial}{\partial t} \int_b^{h+b} u dz + \frac{\partial}{\partial x} \int_b^{h+b} u^2 dz + \frac{\partial}{\partial y} \int_b^{h+b} vu dz$$
$$+ u_s \left[w_s - \frac{\partial \left(h+b \right)}{\partial t} - u_s \frac{\partial \left(h+b \right)}{\partial x} - v_s \frac{\partial \left(h+b \right)}{\partial y} \right] - u_b \left[w_b - \frac{\partial b}{\partial t} - u_b \frac{\partial b}{\partial x} - v_b \frac{\partial b}{\partial y} \right] \tag{28}$$

Using the kinematic conditions Equation (18) and (19) together with Equation (22), then Equation (28) can be simplified as:

$$\int\limits_{b}^{h+b} \left[\frac{\partial u}{\partial t} + \frac{\partial \left(uu\right)}{\partial x} + \frac{\partial \left(vu\right)}{\partial y} + \frac{\partial \left(wu\right)}{\partial z} \right] dz = \frac{\partial \left(h\overline{u}\right)}{\partial t} + \frac{\partial}{\partial x} \int\limits_{b}^{h+b} u^2 dz + \frac{\partial}{\partial y} \int\limits_{b}^{h+b} vu dz$$

$$(29)$$

By using the second mean value theorem for integrals:

$$\int\limits_{a}^{b} f\left(x\right)g\left(x\right)dx = f\left(\varsigma\right)\int\limits_{a}^{b} g\left(x\right)dx \tag{30}$$

The following terms can be expressed as:

$$\int\limits_{b}^{h+b} u^2 dz = u_1 \int\limits_{b}^{h+b} u dz = u_1 h\overline{u} \tag{31}$$

and:

$$\int\limits_{b}^{h+b} vu dz = u_2 \int\limits_{b}^{h+b} v dz = u_2 h\overline{v} \tag{32}$$

where $u_1 = \theta_1 \overline{u}$ and $u_2 = \theta_2 \overline{u}$, θ_1 and θ_2 are momentum correction factors which can be determined based on Equation (31) and Equation (32):

$$\theta_1 = \frac{1}{h\overline{u}^2} \int\limits_{b}^{h+b} u^2 dz$$

$$\theta_2 = \frac{1}{h\overline{v}\,\overline{u}} \int\limits_{b}^{h+b} vu dz \tag{33}$$

It is observed that using the second mean value theorem Equation (30) implies no change of directions for $u\left(x,y,z,t\right)$ and $v\left(x,y,z,t\right)$ over the water depth at time t. The velocities are assumed to satisfy u >= 0 or u < 0 from channel bed to free surface at the horizontal location (x, y), and v is treated similarly (Zhou, 2002). This gives the reason why a model based on two-dimensional SWEs cannot be applied to flow separations in the vertical direction. Inserting Equation (31) and (32) into Equation (29) leads to:

$$\int\limits_{b}^{h+b} \left(\frac{\partial u}{\partial t} + u\frac{\partial u}{\partial x} + v\frac{\partial u}{\partial y} + w\frac{\partial u}{\partial z} \right) dz = \frac{\partial \left(\overline{hu} \right)}{\partial t} + \frac{\partial \left(h\theta_1 \overline{u}^{\,2} \right)}{\partial x} + \frac{\partial \left(h\theta_2 \overline{vu} \right)}{\partial y} \tag{34}$$

In a similar way, when using the y-component of the momentum Equation (12), the following equation is obtained:

$$\int\limits_{b}^{h+b} \left(\frac{\partial u}{\partial t} + u\frac{\partial v}{\partial x} + v\frac{\partial v}{\partial y} + w\frac{\partial v}{\partial z} \right) dz = \frac{\partial \left(\overline{hv} \right)}{\partial t} + \frac{\partial \left(h\theta_2 \overline{vu} \right)}{\partial x} + \frac{\partial \left(h\theta_3 \overline{v}^{\,2} \right)}{\partial y} \tag{35}$$

with θ_3 defined by:

$$\theta_3 = \frac{1}{h\overline{v}^{-2}} \int\limits_{b}^{h+b} v^2 dz \tag{36}$$

Integrating the last term on the right side of Equation (25) gives:

$$\int\limits_{b}^{h+b} f_c v \, dz = f_c h\overline{v} \tag{37}$$

Since the vertical acceleration is insignificant compared to the horizontal effect, the z-component of the momentum equation Equation (12), is reduced with $w = 0$ to:

$$\frac{\partial p}{\partial z} = -\rho g \tag{38}$$

Integrating, gives:

$$p = -\rho gz + C_0 \tag{39}$$

where C_0 is the integration constant. Knowing that the pressure at the free surface is p_s, then using boundary conditions $p = p_s$ when $z = h + b$ yields:

$$C_0 = \rho g \left(h + b \right) + p_s \tag{40}$$

Substituting Equation (40) into Equation (39) gives:

$$p = \rho g \left(h + b - z \right) + p_s \tag{41}$$

Calling h_s the effective water height considering air pressure on water surface:

$$h_s = h + \frac{p_s}{\rho g} \tag{42}$$

we get:

$$p = \rho g \left(h_s + b - z \right) \tag{43}$$

Differentiating Equation (43) with respect to x leads to:

$$\frac{\partial p}{\partial x} = \rho g \frac{\partial \left(h_s + b \right)}{\partial x} \tag{44}$$

Since h and b are independent of z then, they should be dependent on x and y. As integrating from bottom to free surface implies to consider air pressure:

$$\int_b^{h+b} \frac{1}{\rho} \frac{\partial p}{\partial x} dz = \frac{h_s}{\rho} \frac{\partial p}{\partial x} \tag{45}$$

Substituting Equation (44) into Equation (45) gives:

$$\int_b^{h+b} \frac{1}{\rho} \frac{\partial p}{\partial x} dz = \frac{h_s}{\rho} \left(\rho g \frac{\partial \left(h_s + b \right)}{\partial x} \right) = g h_s \frac{\partial \left(h_s + b \right)}{\partial x} \tag{46}$$

Introducing h_s inside differential term and separating differential terms we get:

$$\int_b^{h+b} \frac{1}{\rho} \frac{\partial p}{\partial x} dz = g \frac{\partial}{\partial x} \left(\frac{h_s^2}{2} \right) + g h_s \frac{\partial b}{\partial x} \qquad (47)$$

The following approximations are introduced for the second and third terms on the right side of Equation (25), respectively, since the acceleration in the z direction is small and $\overline{u}$ (the average of component u along the z direction) is taken:

$$\int_b^{h+b} \nu \frac{\partial^2 u}{\partial x^2} dz \approx \nu \frac{\partial^2 \left(h\overline{u} \right)}{\partial x^2}$$
$$\int_b^{h+b} \nu \frac{\partial^2 u}{\partial y^2} dz \approx \nu \frac{\partial^2 \left(h\overline{u} \right)}{\partial y^2} \qquad (48)$$

The forth term on the right side of Equation (25) may be calculated as:

$$\int_b^{h+b} \nu \frac{\partial^2 u}{\partial z^2} dz = \left(\nu \frac{\partial u}{\partial z} \right)_s - \left(\nu \frac{\partial u}{\partial z} \right)_b \qquad (49)$$

The right side terms of Equation (49) can be approximated with the wind shear stress and the bed shear stress, respectively, in the x direction, giving:

$$\left(\nu \frac{\partial u}{\partial z} \right)_s = \frac{\tau_{wx}}{\rho}$$
$$\left(\nu \frac{\partial u}{\partial z} \right)_b = \frac{\tau_{bx}}{\rho} \qquad (50)$$

By substituting Equation (50) into Equation (49) leads to:

$$\int_b^{h+b} \nu \frac{\partial^2 u}{\partial z^2} dz = \frac{\tau_{wx}}{\rho} - \frac{\tau_{bx}}{\rho} \qquad (51)$$

Substitution of Equation (34), (37), (46), (48) and (51) into Equation (25) leads to the x momentum equation in the x-direction for the shallow water flows:

$$\frac{\partial\left(\overline{hu}\right)}{\partial t}+\frac{\partial\left(h\theta_1\overline{u}^{-2}\right)}{\partial x}+\frac{\partial\left(h\theta_2\overline{vu}\right)}{\partial y}=-g\frac{\partial}{\partial x}\left(\frac{h_s^{\,2}}{2}\right)+\nu\frac{\partial^2\left(\overline{hu}\right)}{\partial x^2}+\nu\frac{\partial^2\left(\overline{hu}\right)}{\partial y^2}-gh_s\frac{\partial b}{\partial x}-f_c\overline{hv}+\frac{\tau_{wx}}{\rho}-\frac{\tau_{bx}}{\rho}$$

$$(52)$$

The momentum equation in the y-direction can be derived in a similar way:

$$\frac{\partial\left(\overline{hv}\right)}{\partial t}+\frac{\partial\left(h\theta_2\overline{vu}\right)}{\partial x}+\frac{\partial\left(h\theta_3\overline{v}^{-2}\right)}{\partial y}=-g\frac{\partial}{\partial y}\left(\frac{h_s^{\,2}}{2}\right)+\nu\frac{\partial^2\left(\overline{hv}\right)}{\partial x^2}+\nu\frac{\partial^2\left(\overline{hv}\right)}{\partial y^2}-gh_s\frac{\partial b}{\partial y}-F_c\overline{hu}+\frac{\tau_{wy}}{\rho}-\frac{\tau_{by}}{\rho}$$

$$(53)$$

If velocity profiles for u and v are assumed or already known, the momentum factors θ_1, θ_2 and θ_3 can be calculated by Equation (33) and (36) theoretically. In most situations, however there are no valid universal velocity profiles. It is difficult to estimate the momentum correlation forces θ_1, θ_2 and θ_3 in circulation or separation flow, or in channels with complex geometry (Caiazzo & Junk, 2008). Therefore θ_1 = 1, θ_2 = 1 and θ_3 = 1 are adopted for shallow water flow, which give a good approximation in most situations. Substituting θ_1 = 1, θ_2 = 1 and θ_3 = 1 in Equation (52) and (53) leads to:

$$\frac{\partial\left(\overline{hu}\right)}{\partial t}+\frac{\partial\left(h\overline{u}^{-2}\right)}{\partial x}+\frac{\partial\left(\overline{hvu}\right)}{\partial y}=-g\frac{\partial}{\partial x}\left(\frac{h_s^{\,2}}{2}\right)+\nu\frac{\partial^2\left(\overline{hu}\right)}{\partial x^2}+\nu\frac{\partial^2\left(\overline{hu}\right)}{\partial y^2}-gh_s\frac{\partial b}{\partial x}-F_c\overline{hv}+\frac{\tau_{wx}}{\rho}-\frac{\tau_{bx}}{\rho}\quad(54)$$

and:

$$\frac{\partial\left(\overline{hv}\right)}{\partial t}+\frac{\partial\left(\overline{hvu}\right)}{\partial x}+\frac{\partial\left(h\overline{v}^{-2}\right)}{\partial y}=-g\frac{\partial}{\partial y}\left(\frac{h_s^{\,2}}{2}\right)+\nu\frac{\partial^2\left(\overline{hv}\right)}{\partial x^2}+\nu\frac{\partial^2\left(\overline{hv}\right)}{\partial y^2}-gh_s\frac{\partial b}{\partial y}-F_c\overline{hu}+\frac{\tau_{wy}}{\rho}-\frac{\tau_{by}}{\rho}$$

$$(55)$$

or in Einstein notation:

$$\frac{\partial\left(hu_i\right)}{\partial t}+\frac{\partial\left(hu_iu_j\right)}{\partial x_j}=-g\frac{\partial}{\partial x_i}\left(\frac{h_s^{\,2}}{2}\right)+\nu\frac{\partial^2\left(\overline{hu_i}\right)}{\partial x_j\partial x_j}+F_i$$

$$(56)$$

We can set the external forces in new term called F defined as:

$$F_i = -gh_s \frac{\partial b}{\partial x} + \frac{\tau_{wi}}{\rho} - \frac{\tau_{bi}}{\rho} + f_c h \left(u_y \delta_{ix} - u_x \delta_{iy} \right) \tag{57}$$

where δ_{ij} is the Kronecker delta function:

$$\delta_{ij} = \begin{cases} 0, & i \neq j \\ 1, & i = j \end{cases} \tag{58}$$

so the x and y equations are:

$$\begin{aligned} F_x &= -gh_s \frac{\partial b}{\partial x} + f_c h \bar{v} + \frac{\tau_{wx}}{\rho} - \frac{\tau_{bx}}{\rho} \\ F_y &= -gh_s \frac{\partial b}{\partial y} - f_c h \bar{u} + \frac{\tau_{wy}}{\rho} - \frac{\tau_{by}}{\rho} \end{aligned} \tag{59}$$

where f_c is the Coriolis coefficient that can be calculated as:

$$f_c = 2\Omega \sin \varphi \tag{60}$$

where φ is the latitude and Ω is rotation rate of the Earth that is around $7.2921 \cdot 10^{-5}$ rad/s. The bed shear stress τ_{bi} in i direction is given by the depth-averaged velocities:

$$\tau_{bi} = \rho C_b u_i \sqrt{u_j u_j} \tag{61}$$

in which C_b is the bed friction coefficient which may be either constant or estimated from:

$$C_b = \frac{g}{C_z^2} \tag{62}$$

where C_z is the Chezy coefficient given with either Manning equation:

$$C_z = \frac{h^{\frac{1}{6}}}{n_b}$$

(63)

where n_b is the Manning coefficient at bed.

The wind shear stress τ_{wi} is usually expressed as:

$$\tau_{wy} = \rho_a C_w u_{wi} \sqrt{u_{wj} u_{wj}}$$

(64)

where ρ_a is the density of air, C_w is the resistance coefficient, and u_{wi} the component of the wind velocity in i direction.

SHALLOW WATER LATTICE BOLTZMANN EQUATIONS

Introduction

LBM is a computational method based on the lattice gas automata that consists of three basic tasks: lattice Boltzmann equation, lattice pattern and local equilibrium distribution function. The first two are standard. The last determines how flow equations are solved by the lattice Boltzmann model. This section will demonstrate how to calculate the local equilibrium distribution function for shallow water flows. In addition the rest of forces like underlying terrain and wind, will be included in LBM method.

Lattice Boltzmann Equation

The lattice Boltzmann method (LBM) is originally evolved from the LGA (Lattice Gas Automata), i.e. the equation for the LGA (Hou et al. 1996), is replaced with the lattice Boltzmann equation (LBE). The LBM was initially developed to solve the equations of hydrodynamics governed by the Navier-Stokes equation based on the kinetic theory of gases described by the Boltzmann equation (McNamara & Zanetti 1988).

As will be shown later, the LBE can effectively be derived from the continuum Boltzmann equation, leading it to be self-explanatory in statistical physics. It is generally valid for fluid flows. According to the origin of the lattice Boltzmann method, it consists of two steps: a streaming step and a collision step. In the streaming step, the particles move to the neighboring lattice points in their directions of their velocities, which is governed by:

$$f_\alpha\left(x + e_\alpha \Delta t, t + \Delta t\right) = f_\alpha'\left(x, t\right) + \frac{\Delta t}{N_\alpha e^2} e_{\alpha i} F_i\left(x, t\right) \tag{65}$$

where f_α is the distribution function of particles; f_α' is the value of f_α before the streaming; $e = \Delta x / \Delta t$; Δx is the lattice size; Δt is the time step; F_i is the component of the force in i direction; e_α is the velocity vector of a particle in the α link and N_α is a constant, which is decided by the lattice pattern as:

$$N_\alpha = \frac{1}{e^2} \sum_\alpha e_{\alpha i} e_{\alpha i} \tag{66}$$

In the collision step, the arriving particles at the points interact one another and change their velocity directions according to scattering rules, which is expressed as:

$$f_\alpha'\left(x, t\right) = f_\alpha\left(x, t\right) + \Omega_\alpha\left[f\left(x, t\right)\right] \tag{67}$$

in which Ω_α is the collision operator which controls the speed of change in f_α during collision.

Theoretically, Ω_α is generally a matrix, which is decided by the microscopic dynamics (Higuera & Jimenez, 1989) first introduced an idea to linearize the collision operator around its local equilibrium state. This greatly simplifies the collision operator. Based on this idea, Ω_α can be expanded about its equilibrium value:

$$\Omega_\alpha\left(f\right) = \Omega_\alpha\left(f^{eq}\right) + \frac{\partial \Omega_\alpha\left(f^{eq}\right)}{\partial f_\beta}\left(f_\beta - f_\beta^{eq}\right) + O\left[\left(f_\beta - f_\beta^{eq}\right)^2\right] \tag{68}$$

where f_β^{eq} is the local equilibrium distribution function.

The solution process of the lattice Boltzmann equation is characterized by $f_\beta \rightarrow f_\beta^{eq}$, implying $\Omega_\alpha\left(f^{eq}\right) \approx 0$. After the higher-order terms in Equation (68) are neglected, we obtain a linearized collision operator:

$$\Omega_\alpha\left(f\right) \approx \frac{\partial \Omega_\alpha\left(f^{eq}\right)}{\partial f_\beta}\left(f_\beta - f_\beta^{eq}\right) \tag{69}$$

If assuming the local particle distribution relaxes to an equilibrium state at a single rate τ :

$$\frac{\partial \Omega_\alpha\left(f^{eq}\right)}{\partial f_\beta} = -\frac{1}{\tau}\delta_{\alpha\beta} \tag{70}$$

where $\delta_{\alpha\beta}$ is the Kronecker delta function:

$$\delta_{\alpha\beta} = \begin{cases} 0, & \alpha \neq \beta \\ 1, & \alpha = \beta \end{cases} \tag{71}$$

We can write Equation (69) as:

$$\Omega_\alpha\left(f\right) = \frac{1}{\tau}\delta_{\alpha\beta}\left(f_\alpha - f_\alpha^{eq}\right) \tag{72}$$

resulting in the Bhatnagar-Gross-Krook (BGK) collision operator (Bhatnagar *et al.* 1954) which represents changes in f_α due to particle collisions:

$$\Omega_\alpha\left(f\right) = -\frac{1}{\tau}\left(f_\alpha - f_\alpha^{eq}\right) \tag{73}$$

and τ is called as the single relaxation time. This makes the lattice Boltzmann equation extremely simple and efficient; hence it is widely used in a lattice Boltzmann model for fluid flows. With reference to Equation (67), the streaming and collision steps are usually combined into the following lattice Boltzmann equation:

$$f_\alpha\left(x + e_\alpha \Delta t, t + \Delta t\right) - f_\alpha\left(x, t\right) = -\frac{1}{\tau}\left(f_\alpha - f_\alpha^{eq}\right) + \frac{\Delta t}{N_\alpha e^2}e_{\alpha i}F_i\left(x, t\right) \tag{74}$$

which is the most popular form of the lattice Boltzmann equation in use today.

Lattice Pattern

Lattice pattern in the lattice Boltzmann method has two functions: representing grid points and determining particles' motions. The former plays a similar role to that in the traditional numerical methods. The latter defines a microscopic model for molecular dynamics. In addition, the constant N_α in Equation (74) is determined by the lattice pattern.

In 2D and 3D situations, generally square and cubic lattice patterns are preferred in the literature. Studies have shown that square lattices usually give more accurate results than that based on hexagonal lattice. Furthermore, the use of the square lattice provides an easy way to implement different boundary conditions, e.g. only by using the square lattice, the force term associated with a gradient and boundary conditions can be accurately and easily determined.

Depending to the number of particle speed at lattice node, the square lattice can have 4-speed, 5-speed, 8-speed or 9-speed models. Not all of these models have sufficient lattice symmetry which is a dominant requirement for recovery of the correct flow equations. Theoretical analysis and numerical studies indicate that 9-speed square lattice (D2Q9 model) have such property and satisfactory performance in 2D numerical simulations.

The fluid movement through every lattice is defined by 9 directions as can be seen in Figure 2.

On the 9-speed square lattice shown in Figure 2 each particle moves one lattice unit at its velocity only along the eight links indicated with 1 - 8, in which 0 indicates the particle with zero speed. The velocity vector of particles is defined by:

$$e_\alpha = e \begin{Bmatrix} 0 & 1 & -1 & 0 & 0 & 1 & -1 & 1 & -1 \\ 0 & 0 & 0 & 1 & -1 & 1 & -1 & -1 & 1 \end{Bmatrix} \qquad (75)$$

As it is done in lattice Boltzmann D2Q9 model, in LBM for shallow water the simulation area is discretized with a set of rectangular lattices as are shown in Figure 3.

It is easy to show that the 9-speed square lattice has the following basic features:

$$\sum_\alpha e_{\alpha i} = \sum_\alpha e_{\alpha i} e_{\alpha j} e_{\alpha k} = 0 \qquad (76)$$

$$\sum_\alpha e_{\alpha i} e_{\alpha j} = 6e^2 \delta_{ij} \qquad (77)$$

Figure 2. D2Q9 Lattice Boltzmann fluid directions

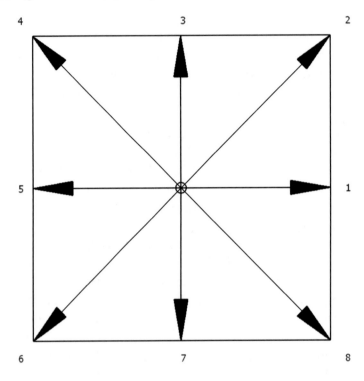

$$\sum_{\alpha} e_{\alpha i} e_{\alpha j} e_{\alpha k} e_{\alpha l} = 4e^2 \left(\delta_{ij}\delta_{kl} + \delta_{ik}\delta_{jl} + \delta_{il}\delta_{jk} \right) - 6e^4 \Delta_{ijkl} \tag{78}$$

where $\Delta_{ijkl} = 1$ if $i = j = k = l$, otherwise $\Delta_{ijkl} = 0$.

Using Equation (75) to evaluate the terms in Equation (66), we have:

$$N_{\alpha} = \frac{1}{e^2} \sum_{\alpha} e_{\alpha x} e_{\alpha x} = \frac{1}{e^2} \sum_{\alpha} e_{\alpha y} e_{\alpha y} = 6 \tag{79}$$

The substitution of the above equation into Equation (74) leads to:

$$f_{\alpha}\left(x + e_{\alpha}\Delta t, t + \Delta t \right) - f_{\alpha}\left(x, t \right) = -\frac{1}{\tau}\left(f_{\alpha} - f_{\alpha}^{eq} \right) + \frac{\Delta t}{6e^2} e_{\alpha i} F_i \left(x, t \right) \tag{80}$$

which is the most common form of a lattice Boltzmann model used for simulating fluid flows.

Figure 3. D2Q9 Area discretization

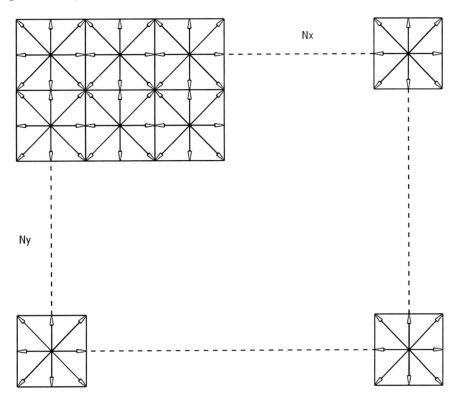

Underlying Terrain Solving

Force term F_i is:

$$F_i = -gh_s \frac{\partial b}{\partial x} + \frac{\tau_{wi}}{\rho} - \frac{\tau_{bi}}{\rho} + f_c h \left(u_y \delta_{ix} - u_x \delta_{iy} \right) \tag{81}$$

F_i equation contains a differential term. Including it in equation (80) it is $\frac{\Delta t}{6e^2} e_{\alpha j} \left(gh_s \frac{\partial b}{\partial x} \right)$.

Following a second order scheme (Zhou 2011) it may be integrated as:

$$\frac{\Delta t}{6e^2} e_{\alpha j} \left(gh_s \frac{\partial b}{\partial x} \right) = \frac{g\bar{h}_s}{6e^2} \left[b \left(x + e_\alpha \Delta t \right) - b \left(x \right) \right] \tag{82}$$

where:

$$\overline{h_s} = \frac{h_s\left(x + e_\alpha \Delta t\right) + h_s\left(x\right)}{2} \tag{83}$$

So the complete LBM expression would be:

$$f_\alpha\left(x + e_\alpha \Delta t, t + \Delta t\right) - f_\alpha\left(x, t\right) = \frac{1}{\tau}\left(f_\alpha^{eq} - f_\alpha\right) - \frac{g\overline{h_s}}{6e^2}\left[b\left(x + e_\alpha \Delta t\right) - b\left(x\right)\right] + \frac{\Delta t}{6e^2}e_{\alpha j}F_j \tag{84}$$

We will later demonstrate with Chapman-Enskog expansion how this approach complies with NS equations.

Local Equilibrium Distribution Function

Determining a suitable local equilibrium function plays an essential role in the lattice Boltzmann method. This function decides which flow equations are solved by means of the lattice Boltzmann Equation (80). In order to apply the Equation (80) for solution of the 2D shallow water Equation (24) and (56), we derive a suitable local equilibrium function f_α^{eq} in this section.

According to the theory of the lattice gas automata, an equilibrium function is the Maxwell-Boltzmann equilibrium distribution function, which is often expanded as a Taylor series in macroscopic velocity to its second order. However, the use of such equilibrium function in the lattice Boltzmann equation can recover the Navier-Stokes equation only. This severely limits the capability of the method to solve flow equations. Thus an alternative and powerful way is to assume that an equilibrium function can be expressed as a power series in macroscopic velocity as proposed by Rothman and Zaleski (1994), i.e.:

$$f_\alpha^{eq} = A_\alpha + B_\alpha e_{\alpha i} u_i + C_\alpha e_{\alpha i} e_{\alpha j} u_i u_j + D_\alpha u_i u_i \tag{85}$$

This turns out to be a general approach, which is successfully used for solution of various flow problems, demonstrating its accuracy and suitability. Since the equilibrium function has the same symmetry as the lattice (see Figure 2), there must be:

$$A_1 = A_3 = A_5 = A_7 = \overline{A}, \tag{86}$$

$$A_2 = A_4 = A_6 = A_8 = \overline{A}, \tag{87}$$

and similar expressions for B_α, C_α and D_α. Accordingly, it is convenient to write Equation (85) in the following form:

$$f_\alpha^{eq} = \begin{cases} A_0 + D_o u_i u_i & \alpha = 0 \\ \overline{A} + \overline{B} e_{\alpha i} u_i + \overline{C} e_{\alpha i} e_{\alpha j} u_i u_j + \overline{D} u_i u_i & \alpha = 1,3,5,7 \\ A + B e_{\alpha i} u_i + C e_{\alpha i} e_{\alpha j} u_i u_j + D u_i u_i & \alpha = 2,4,6,8 \end{cases} \tag{88}$$

The coefficients such as A_0, $\overline{A}$ and A can be determined based on the constraints on the equilibrium distribution function, i.e. it must obey the conservation relations such as mass and momentum conservations. For the shallow water equations, the local equilibrium distribution function Equation (88) must satisfy the following three conditions:

$$\sum_\alpha f_\alpha^{eq}(x,t) = h(x,t) \tag{89}$$

$$\sum_\alpha e_{\alpha i} f_\alpha^{eq}(x,t) = h(x,t) u_i(x,t) \tag{90}$$

$$\sum_\alpha e_{\alpha i} e_{\alpha j} f_\alpha^{eq}(x,t) = \frac{1}{2} g h_s^2(x,t) \delta_{ij} + h(x,t) u_i(x,t) u_j(x,t) \tag{91}$$

Once the local equilibrium function Equation (85) is determined under the above constraints, the calculation of the lattice Boltzmann Equation (80) leads to the solution of the 2D shallow water Equation (24) and (56). Substituting Equation (88) into Equation (89) yields:

$$\begin{aligned} & A_0 + D_o u_i u_i \\ & +4\overline{A} + \sum_{\alpha=1,3,5,7} \overline{B} e_{\alpha i} u_i + \sum_{\alpha=1,3,5,7} \overline{C} e_{\alpha i} e_{\alpha j} u_i u_j + 4\overline{D} u_i u_i \\ & +4A + \sum_{\alpha=2,4,6,8} B e_{\alpha i} u_i + \sum_{\alpha=2,4,6,8} C e_{\alpha i} e_{\alpha j} u_i u_j + 4D u_i u_i = h(x,t) \end{aligned} \tag{92}$$

After evaluating the terms in the above equation with Equation (75) and equating the coefficients of h and $u_i u_i$, respectively, we have:

$$A_0 + 4\overline{A} + 4A = h \tag{93}$$

and:

$$D_0 + 2e^2 \overline{C} + 4e^2 C + 4\overline{D} + 4D = 0 \tag{94}$$

Inserting Equation (88) to Equation (90) leads to:

$$
\begin{aligned}
&A_0 e_{\alpha i} + D_o e_{\alpha i} u_j u_j \\
&+ \sum_{\alpha=1,3,5,7} \left(\overline{A} + \overline{B} e_{\alpha i} u_i + \overline{C} e_{\alpha i} e_{\alpha j} u_i u_j + \overline{D} u_i u_i \right) \\
&+ \sum_{\alpha=2,4,6,8} \left(A + B e_{\alpha i} u_i + C e_{\alpha i} e_{\alpha j} u_i u_j + D u_i u_i \right) = h(x,t) u_i
\end{aligned}
\tag{95}
$$

from which we can obtain:

$$2e^2 \overline{B} + 4e^2 B = h \tag{96}$$

Substituting Equation (88) into Equation (91) results in:

$$
\begin{aligned}
&\sum_{\alpha=1,3,5,7} \left(\overline{A} e_{\alpha i} e_{\alpha j} + \overline{B} e_{\alpha i} e_{\alpha j} e_{\alpha k} u_k + \overline{C} e_{\alpha i} e_{\alpha j} e_{\alpha k} e_{\alpha l} u_k u_l + \overline{D} e_{\alpha i} e_{\alpha j} u_k u_k \right) \\
&+ \sum_{\alpha=2,4,6,8} \left(A e_{\alpha i} e_{\alpha j} + B e_{\alpha i} e_{\alpha j} e_{\alpha k} u_k + C e_{\alpha i} e_{\alpha j} e_{\alpha k} e_{\alpha l} u_k u_l + D e_{\alpha i} e_{\alpha j} u_k u_k \right) = \frac{1}{2} g h_s^2(x,t) \delta_{ij} \\
&+ h(x,t) u_i(x,t) u_j(x,t)
\end{aligned}
\tag{97}
$$

Use of Equation (75) to simplify the above equation leads to:

$$2\overline{A}e^2 \delta_{ij} + 2\overline{C}e^4 u_i u_i + 2\overline{D}e^2 u_i u_i + 4A e^2 \delta_{ij} + 8Ce^4 u_i u_j + 4Ce^4 u_i u_i + 4De^2 u_i u_i = \frac{1}{2} g h_s^2 \delta_{ij} + h u_i u_j \tag{98}$$

which provides the following four relations:

$$2\overline{A}e^2 + 4Ae^2 = \frac{1}{2}gh_s^{\;2} \tag{99}$$

$$8Ce^4 = h \tag{100}$$

$$2\overline{C}e^4 = h \tag{101}$$

$$2\overline{D}e^2 + 4De^2 + 4Ce^4 = 0 \tag{102}$$

Combining of Equation (100) and (101) gives:

$$\overline{C} = 4C \tag{103}$$

From the symmetry of the lattice, based on Equation (103), we have good reason to assume the three additional relations as follows:

$$\overline{A} = 4A \tag{104}$$

$$\overline{B} = 4B \tag{105}$$

$$\overline{D} = 4D \tag{106}$$

Solution of Equations. (93), (94), (96) and (99) - (106) results in:

$$A_0 = h - \frac{5gh_s^{\;2}}{6e^2} \tag{107}$$

$$D_0 = \frac{2h}{3e^2} \tag{108}$$

$$\overline{A} = \frac{gh_s^{\;2}}{6e^2} \tag{109}$$

$$\overline{B} = \frac{h}{3e^2} \tag{110}$$

$$\overline{C} = \frac{h}{2e^4} \tag{111}$$

$$\overline{D} = -\frac{h}{6e^2} \tag{112}$$

$$A = \frac{gh_s^2}{24e^2} \tag{113}$$

$$B = \frac{h}{12e^2} \tag{114}$$

$$C = \frac{h}{8e^4} \tag{115}$$

$$D = -\frac{h}{24e^2} \tag{116}$$

Substitution of the above equations (107) - (116) into Equation (88) leads to the following local equilibrium function:

$$f_\alpha^{eq} = \left\{ h - \frac{5gh_s^2}{6e^2} - \frac{2h}{3e^2} u_i u_i \atop \lambda_\alpha \left(\frac{gh_s^2}{6e^2} + \frac{h}{3e^2} e_{\alpha i} u_i + \frac{h}{2e^4} e_{\alpha i} e_{\alpha j} u_i u_j - \frac{h}{6e^2} u_i u_i \right) \right. \tag{117}$$

in which $\lambda_\alpha = 1$ when $\alpha = 1, 3, 5, 7$ and $\lambda_\alpha = 1/4$ when $\alpha = 2, 4, 6, 8$ which is used in the lattice Boltzmann Equation (80) for solution of the shallow water Equation (24) and (56).

MACROSCOPIC PROPERTIES

The lattice Boltzmann Equation (80) with the local equilibrium function Equation (117) form a lattice Boltzmann model for shallow water flows on the square lattices, which is described by Zhou (2003). The remaining task is how to determine the physical quantities, water depth h and velocity, u_i as the solution to the shallow water Equation (24) and (56). For this purpose, we examine the macroscopic properties of the lattice Boltzmann Equation (80). Taking the sum of the zeroth moment of the distribution function in Equation (80) over the lattice velocities leads to:

$$\sum_{\alpha}\left[f_{\alpha}\left(x + e_{\alpha}\Delta t, t + \Delta t\right) - f_{\alpha}\left(x, t\right)\right] = -\frac{1}{\tau}\sum_{\alpha}\left[f_{\alpha}\left(x, t\right) - f_{\alpha}^{eq}\left(x, t\right)\right] + \frac{\Delta t}{6e^2}\sum_{\alpha}e_{\alpha i}F_{i}\left(x, t\right)$$

(118)

Notice $\sum_{\alpha}e_{\alpha i}F_{i}\left(x, t\right)$, Equation (118) becomes:

$$\sum_{\alpha}\left[f_{\alpha}\left(x + e_{\alpha}\Delta t, t + \Delta t\right) - f_{\alpha}\left(x, t\right)\right] = -\frac{1}{\tau}\sum_{\alpha}\left[f_{\alpha}\left(x, t\right) - f_{\alpha}^{eq}\left(x, t\right)\right]$$

(119)

In the lattice Boltzmann method, we have an explicit constraint to preserve conservative property, i.e. the cumulative mass and momentum which are the corresponding summations of the microdynamic mass and momentum are conserved. The mass conservation requires the following identity:

$$\sum_{\alpha}f_{\alpha}\left(x + e_{\alpha}\Delta t, t + \Delta t\right) \equiv \sum_{\alpha}f_{\alpha}\left(x, t\right)$$

(120)

which is the continuity equation with microdynamic variables.

Substitution of the above equation into Equation (119) leads to:

$$\sum_{\alpha}f_{\alpha}\left(x, t\right) = \sum_{\alpha}f_{\alpha}^{eq}\left(x, t\right)$$

(121)

With reference to Equation (89), the above expression in fact results in the definition for the physical quantity, water depth h, as:

$$h\left(x, t\right) = \sum_{\alpha}f_{\alpha}\left(x, t\right)$$

(122)

Now, in order to find the expression for the velocity, we take the sum of the first moment of the distribution function in Equation (80) over the lattice velocities:

$$\sum_\alpha e_{\alpha i}\left[f_\alpha\left(x+e_\alpha\Delta t,t+\Delta t\right)-f_\alpha\left(x,t\right)\right]=-\frac{1}{\tau}\sum_\alpha e_{\alpha i}\left[f_\alpha\left(x,t\right)-f_\alpha^{eq}\left(x,t\right)\right]+\frac{\Delta t}{6e^2}\sum_\alpha e_{\alpha i}e_{\alpha j}F_i\left(x,t\right)$$

(123)

which can be simplified with Equation (77) and rearranged as:

$$\sum_\alpha e_{\alpha i}\left[f_\alpha\left(x+e_\alpha\Delta t,t+\Delta t\right)-f_\alpha\left(x,t\right)\right]=F_i\left(x,t\right)\Delta t-\frac{1}{\tau}\sum_\alpha e_{\alpha i}\left[f_\alpha\left(x,t\right)-f_\alpha^{eq}\left(x,t\right)\right]$$

(124)

which reflects the evolution of cumulative momentum in the distribution function. Again, the momentum conservation requires the following identity:

$$\sum_\alpha e_{\alpha i}\left[f_\alpha\left(x+e_\alpha\Delta t,t+\Delta t\right)-f_\alpha\left(x,t\right)\right]\equiv F_i\left(x,t\right)\Delta t$$

(125)

which is the momentum equation with microdynamic variables, representing the Newton's second law.

Substitution of Equation (125) into Equation (124) provides:

$$\sum_\alpha e_{\alpha i}f_\alpha\left(x,t\right)=\sum_\alpha e_{\alpha i}f_\alpha^{eq}\left(x,t\right)$$

(126)

The use of Equation (90) in the above equation leads to the definition for another physical variable, velocity u_i, as:

$$u_i\left(x,t\right)=\frac{1}{h\left(x,t\right)}\sum_\alpha e_{\alpha i}f_\alpha\left(x,t\right)$$

(127)

As can be seen from Equation (89), (90), (122) and (127), it seems that there are redundant definitions for the physical variables h and u_i. However, a careful examination indicates that this is just an important feature which is peculiar to the lattice Boltzmann method. First of all, the local equilibrium function f_α^{eq} given by Equation (117) satisfy Equation (89) and (90). Secondly, the distribution function f_α relaxes to its local equilibrium function f_α^{eq} via the lattice Boltzmann Equation (80). Finally, the physical variables determined from Equation (122) and (127) will guarantee that both Equation (121) and (126) hold true, (Germano, *et al.* 1991) hence preserving the two identities Equation (120) and (125) during the numerical procedure. This makes the lattice Boltzmann method very elegant and effectively explains why the method is accurate and conservative.

RECOVERY OF THE SWE

To ensure that the LBGK model solves the shallow water equations with proper LB parameters, the moments in Equation (122) and (127) are used to show the recovery of the shallow water Equation (80) up to second order by Chapman-Enskog multiscale analysis. Similar recovery work for single-layer shallow water equations can be found in (Zhou, 2004). Assuming Δt is small and is equal to ε:

$$\Delta t = \varepsilon \tag{128}$$

we have the Equation (80) expressed as:

$$f_\alpha \left(x + e_\alpha \varepsilon, t + \varepsilon \right) - f_\alpha \left(x, t \right) = -\frac{1}{\tau_t} \left(f_\alpha^{eq} - f_\alpha \right) - \frac{g\overline{h_s}}{6e^2} \left[b \left(x + e_\alpha \varepsilon \right) - b \left(x \right) \right] + \frac{\varepsilon}{6e^2} e_{\alpha j} F_j \tag{129}$$

Taking a Taylor expansion to the first term on the left-hand side of the above equation in time and space around point (**x**, t) leads to:

$$\varepsilon \left(\frac{\partial}{\partial t} + e_{\alpha j} \frac{\partial}{\partial x_j} \right) f_\alpha + \frac{1}{2} \varepsilon^2 \left(\frac{\partial}{\partial t} + e_{\alpha j} \frac{\partial}{\partial x_j} \right)^2 f_\alpha + O\left(\varepsilon^3 \right) \tag{130}$$

According to Chapman-Enskog procedure, we can also expand f_α around $f_\alpha^{(0)}$:

$$f_\alpha = f_\alpha^{(0)} + \varepsilon f_\alpha^{(1)} + \varepsilon^2 f_\alpha^{(2)} + O\left(\varepsilon^2 \right) \tag{131}$$

The second term on the right hand side of Equation (129) can also be expressed via the Taylor expansion:

$$\frac{g}{6e^2} \left[h_s + \frac{\varepsilon}{2} \left(\frac{\partial h_s}{\partial t} + e_{\alpha j} \frac{\partial h_s}{\partial x_j} \right) \right] \left(\varepsilon e_{\alpha j} \frac{\partial b}{\partial x_j} + \frac{\varepsilon^2}{2} e_{\alpha i} e_{\alpha j} \frac{\partial^2 b}{\partial x_i \partial x_j} \right) + O\left(\varepsilon^3 \right) \tag{132}$$

The centered scheme is used for force term F_j :

$$F_j = F_j\left(x + \frac{1}{2}\varepsilon e_\alpha, t + \frac{1}{2}\varepsilon\right) \tag{133}$$

which can again be written, via a Taylor expansion, as:

$$F_j\left(x + \frac{1}{2}\varepsilon e_\alpha, t + \frac{1}{2}\varepsilon\right) = F_j + \frac{1}{2}\varepsilon\left(\frac{\partial F_j}{\partial t} + e_{\alpha i}\frac{\partial F_j}{\partial x_i}\right) + O\left(\varepsilon^3\right) \tag{134}$$

After inserting Equation (130), (131), (132) and (134) into Equation (129), the equation to order ε^0 is $f_\alpha^{(0)} = f_\alpha^{eq}$ .To order ε is:

$$\left(\frac{\partial}{\partial t} + e_{\alpha j}\frac{\partial}{\partial x_j}\right)f_\alpha^{(0)} = \frac{-1}{\tau_t}f_\alpha^{(1)} - \frac{gh_s}{6e^2}e_{\alpha j}\frac{\partial b}{\partial x_j} + \frac{1}{6e^2}e_{\alpha j}F_j \tag{135}$$

And to order ε^2 is:

$$\left(\frac{\partial}{\partial t} + e_{\alpha j}\frac{\partial}{\partial x_j}\right)f_\alpha^{(1)} + \frac{1}{2}\left(\frac{\partial}{\partial t} + e_{\alpha j}\frac{\partial}{\partial x_j}\right)^2 f_\alpha^{(0)} = -\frac{1}{\tau_t}f_\alpha^{(2)}$$
$$-\frac{ge_{\alpha j}}{12e^2}\left(\frac{\partial h_s}{\partial t} + e_{\alpha i}\frac{\partial h_s}{\partial x_i}\right)\frac{\partial b}{\partial x_j} - \frac{gh_s}{12e^2}e_{\alpha i}e_{\alpha j}\frac{\partial^2 b}{\partial x_i \partial x_j} + \frac{e_{\alpha j}}{12e^2}\left(\frac{\partial F_j}{\partial t} + e_{\alpha i}\frac{\partial F_j}{\partial x_i}\right) \tag{136}$$

Substitution of Equation (135) into Equation (136), after rearranged, gives:

$$\left(1 - \frac{1}{2\tau}\right)\left(\frac{\partial}{\partial t} + e_{\alpha j}\frac{\partial}{\partial x_j}\right)f_\alpha^{(1)} = -\frac{1}{\tau}f_\alpha^{(2)} - \frac{1}{2}\left(\frac{\partial}{\partial t} + e_{\alpha j}\frac{\partial}{\partial x_j}\right)\left(\frac{1}{6e^2}e_{\alpha k}F_k\right) \tag{137}$$

Taking $\sum$ [(135) $+\varepsilon$ x (137)] about α provides:

$$\frac{\partial}{\partial t}\left(\sum_\alpha f_\alpha^{(0)}\right) + \frac{\partial}{\partial x_j}\left(\sum_\alpha e_{\alpha j}f_\alpha^{(0)}\right) = 0 \tag{138}$$

If the first-order accuracy for the force term is applied, evaluation of the other terms in the above equation using Equations. (75) and (117) results in:

$$\frac{\partial h}{\partial t} + \frac{\partial \left(h u_j\right)}{\partial x_j} = 0 \tag{139}$$

which is the continuity equation (24) for shallow water flows. Taking $\sum e_{\alpha i}$ [(135) $+ \varepsilon$ x (137)] about α provides:

$$\frac{\partial}{\partial t}\left(\sum_\alpha e_{\alpha i} f_\alpha^{(0)}\right) + \frac{\partial}{\partial x_j}\left(\sum_\alpha e_{\alpha i} e_{\alpha j} f_\alpha^{(0)}\right) + \varepsilon\left(1 - \frac{1}{2\tau_t}\right)\frac{\partial}{\partial x_j}\left(\sum_\alpha e_{\alpha i} e_{\alpha j} f_\alpha^{(1)}\right) = -gh_s\frac{\partial b}{\partial x_j} + F_j \tag{140}$$

Again, if the first-order accuracy for the force term is used, after the other terms is simplified with Equations. (75) and (117), the above equation becomes:

$$\frac{\partial \left(h u_i\right)}{\partial t} + \frac{\partial \left(h u_i u_j\right)}{\partial x_j} = -g\frac{\partial}{\partial x_i}\left(\frac{h_s^2}{2}\right) - \frac{\partial}{\partial x_j}\Lambda_{ij} + F_i \tag{141}$$

with:

$$\Lambda_{ij} = \frac{\varepsilon}{2\tau_t}\left(2\tau - 1\right)\sum_\alpha e_{\alpha i} e_{\alpha j} f_\alpha^{(1)} \tag{142}$$

With reference to Equation (135), using Equations. (75) and (117), after some algebra, we obtain:

$$\Lambda_{ij} \approx -\nu\left[\frac{\partial \left(h u_i\right)}{\partial x_j} + \frac{\partial \left(h u_j\right)}{\partial x_i}\right] \tag{143}$$

Substitution of Equation (143) into Equation (141) leads to:

$$\frac{\partial \left(h u_i\right)}{\partial t} + \frac{\partial \left(h u_i u_j\right)}{\partial x_j} = g\frac{\partial}{\partial x_i}\left(\frac{h_s^2}{2}\right) + \nu\frac{\partial^2 \left(h u_i\right)}{\partial x_j \partial x_j} + F_i \tag{144}$$

323

with the kinematic viscosity defined by:

$$\nu = \frac{e^2 \Delta t}{6} \left(2\tau - 1 \right) \tag{145}$$

and the force term F_i expressed as:

$$F_i = -gh_s \frac{\partial b}{\partial x} + \frac{\tau_{wi}}{\rho} - \frac{\tau_{bi}}{\rho} + E_i \tag{146}$$

The Equation (144) is just the momentum equation Equation (56) for the shallow water equations. It should be pointed that the above proof shows that the lattice Boltzmann equation Equation (80) is only first-order accurate for the recovered macroscopic continuity and momentum equations. We can prove that the use of a suitable form for the force term can make Equation (80) second-order accurate for the recovered macroscopic continuity and momentum equations.

STABILITY CONDITIONS

The lattice Boltzmann equation Equation (80) is a discrete form of a numerical method. It may suffer from a numerical instability like any other numerical methods. Theoretically, the stability conditions are not generally known for the method. In practice, a lot of computations have shown that the method is often stable if some basic conditions are satisfied. They are described now.

First of all, if a solution from the lattice Boltzmann equation Equation (80) represents a physical water flow, there must be diffusion phenomena. This implies that the kinematic viscosity ν should be positive, i.e. from Equation (145) we must have:

$$\nu = \frac{e^2 \Delta t}{6} \left(2\tau - 1 \right) > 0 \tag{147}$$

Thus an apparent constraint on the relaxation time is:

$$\tau > \frac{1}{2} \tag{148}$$

Secondly, the magnitude of the resultant velocity is smaller than the speed calculated with the lattice size divided by the time step:

$$\frac{u_j u_j}{e^2} < 1 \tag{149}$$

and so is the celerity:

$$\frac{gh}{e^2} < 1 \tag{150}$$

These equations would be equivalent to the Courant number and the requisites would be comparable to the Courant Friedrichs Lewy (CFL) condition. As the solving method is explicit, it is advised that the CFL number be much less than 1.

Finally, since the lattice Boltzmann method is limited to low speed flows, this suggests that the current lattice Boltzmann method is suitable for subcritical shallow water flows, which brings the final constraint on the method as:

$$\frac{u_j u_j}{gh} < 1 \tag{151}$$

because the term on the left hand side of the above expression is equivalent to the definition of the Froude number:

$$F_r = \frac{\sqrt{u_j u_j}}{\sqrt{gh}} \tag{152}$$

in hydraulics. The Froude number can be used to decide a flow state for flows with free surface, i.e. it is a subcritical flow if $F_r < 1$, a critical flow if $F_r = 1$, and a supercritical flow if $F_r > 1$. Consequently, the condition Equation (151) indicates that the lattice Boltzmann method is suitable for subcritical flows. Since such flows are the most scenarios in coastal areas, estuaries and harbors, the condition Equation (151) is normally satisfied.

It should be pointed out that the first three conditions Equation (148)-(150) can be easily satisfied by using suitable values for the relaxation time, the lattice size and the time step. Thus, in general, the lattice Boltzmann method is stable as long as these four stability conditions are satisfied.

DRY SECTIONS

The LBMSW described so far interacts with an arbitrary bed surface. However in dry areas like beaches, height is zero so because of equation Equation (127), macroscopic velocities u and v could not be obtained.

In order to allow the dynamic drying and wetting of the bed topography and thus having a moving shoreline, we have to extend the LBMSW algorithm to account for these new dry sections and how they behave with regard to the rest of the fluid. Probably the most popular algorithm to comply with these conditions is the thin film method. In this technique every cell is considered to be dry if the water level is under certain safety threshold h_{min}. In this case, the dry cell height is set to h_{min} and the velocities are set to zero. This algorithm is used in every iteration after calculating h using Equation (122). To set the velocities u and v to zero and to comply with Equation (122) and (127), it is necessary in addition to set the distributions functions to an appropriate value, so:

$$f_\alpha = 0, \quad \alpha = 1, 2, 3, 4, 5, 6, 7, 8 \tag{153}$$

and:

$$f_\alpha = h_{min}, \quad \alpha = 0 \tag{154}$$

BOUNDARY CONDITIONS

Introduction

In this section suitable boundary for shallow water will be provided. Boundary conditions (Chen, et al., 1996) in the LBM formulation rely on connecting the macroscopic boundary conditions in the physical problem to mesoscopic boundary conditions like water height and velocities on the distributions function. Different boundary conditions from periodic, inflows and outflows will be demonstrated.

Periodic Boundary Conditions

In some cases, periodic boundary conditions may be necessary. One such case is when a flow region consists of a number of same sub regions where the flow pattern repeats itself. In this case, only one sub region is actually required to be modeled using a periodic boundary condition. Implementing periodic boundary conditions in the lattice Boltzmann formulation is achieved by setting the unknown distribution functions, f_1, f_5 and f_8 at the inflow boundary to the corresponding known distribution functions at the outflow boundary:

$$f_\alpha\left(i = 1, j, t\right) = f_\alpha\left(i = N_x, j, t\right), \quad \alpha = 1, 5, 8 \tag{155}$$

and the unknown distribution functions, f_3, f_6 and f_7 at the inflow boundary:

$$f_\alpha\left(i = N_x, j, t\right) = f_\alpha\left(i = 1, j, t\right), \quad \alpha = 3, 6, 7 \tag{156}$$

Similarly, a periodic boundary condition in the y direction can be formulated. Boundary conditions for solid boundaries such as impermeable boundaries or structures in the flow region are prescribed by applying no-slip or free-slip at these boundaries to prescribe zero velocity or zero normal velocity at the boundary, respectively. Implementing no-slip and free-slip boundary conditions in the lattice Boltzmann formulation is simple using bounce-back scheme (Chen & Doolen, 1998). The basic idea behind the bounce-back scheme is that unknown distribution functions are a function of the known distribution functions incident on the boundary, defined by symmetry conditions.

A no-slip boundary condition is achieved by setting the unknown distribution functions, f_2, f_5 and f_6 at the south boundary to the known distributions f_4, f_7 and f_8 corresponding to the opposite directions;

$$f_2 = f_4, \quad f_5 = f_7, \quad f_6 = f_8 \tag{157}$$

This ensures a zero flux across the boundary in both the normal and tangential directions. A free slip boundary condition is achieved in a similar way; however, it results in a zero flux across the normal direction and non-zero flux along the tangential direction. This is achieved by setting the unknown distribution functions, f_2, f_5 and f_6 at the south boundary to the known distributions, f_4, f_7 and f_8 corresponding to the opposite direction along the normal direction and reflected direction along the tangential direction:

$$f_2 = f_4, \quad f_5 = f_8, \quad f_6 = f_7 \tag{158}$$

Following the same bounce back scheme, no-slip and free-slip boundary conditions can be implemented on the east and west boundaries.

Open Boundary Conditions

Boundary conditions for open boundaries such as inflow, outflow and seaward boundary conditions are prescribed by giving the macroscopic boundary values or functions at the boundary, i.e., constant water depth, water depth defined by tidal function, discharge, etc. If the velocity and depth are known, the unknown distribution functions, f_α, can be computed using Equation (122) and (127) following the method described by Zou and He (1997). At the inflow boundary, Equation (122) and (127) lead to three equations:

$$f_0 + f_1 + f_2 + f_3 + f_4 + f_5 + f_6 + f_7 + f_8 = h \tag{159}$$

$$e\left(f_1 + f_5 + f_8\right) - e\left(f_3 + f_6 + f_7\right) = hu_x \tag{160}$$

$$e\left(f_2 + f_5 + f_6\right) - e\left(f_4 + f_7 + f_8\right) = hu_y \tag{161}$$

If $u_y = 0$ is assumed, solving the above three equations for the unknown distribution functions:

$$f_1 = f_3 + \frac{2hu_x}{3c} \tag{162}$$

$$f_5 = f_7 + \frac{f_4 - f_2}{2} + \frac{hu_x}{6e} \tag{163}$$

$$f_8 = f_6 - \frac{f_4 - f_2}{2} + \frac{hu_x}{6e} \tag{164}$$

Following the same procedure, the unknown distribution functions, f_3, f_6 and f_7 for the outflow boundary can be determined using:

$$f_3 = f_1 - \frac{2hu_x}{3e} \tag{165}$$

$$f_6 = f_8 - \frac{f_4 - f_2}{2} - \frac{hu_x}{6e}$$

(166)

$$f_7 = f_5 + \frac{f_4 - f_2}{2} + \frac{hu_x}{6e}$$

(167)

Shallow Water Algorithm Pseudocode

The lattice Boltzmann method consists of two steps: a streaming step and a collision step. In the streaming step, the particles move to the neighboring lattice points in their directions of their velocities and in the collision step, the arriving particles at the points interact one another and change their velocity directions according to scattering rules. Both steps can be joined in just one as defined in equation (74). Following it will defined the pseudocode of this basic equation, implementing it in a pseudocode similar to C or BASIC like language, we would consider the next constants:

e is the lattice speed.
tau is the single relaxation time.
rho is the fluid density.
g is the gravity.

We have also the next variables in matrices:

fnew[width,height,9] is the distribution function of particles obtained in this iteration.
f[width,height,9] is the distribution function of particles from previous iteration.
xb[width,height] is the bathymetry.
ps[width,height] is the pressure in the water surface.

For every lattice cell defined by its coordinates x and y:

h_p = ps(x,y)/rho/g is the extra water column height considered due to surface pressure.

The new distribution function of particles for this iteration is obtained like this:

fnew(x+1,y, 1) = f(x,y,1) - (f(x,y,1) - feq(x,y,1))/tau

-g*((h(x,y)+h(x+1, y))/2 + h_p)*(zb(x+1,y) - zb(x,y))/(6*e^2)

fnew(x+1,y+1,2) = f(x,y,2) - (f(x,y,2) - feq(x,y,2))/tau

-g*((h(x,y)+h(x+1,y+1))/2 + h_p)*(zb(x+1,y+1) - zb(x,y))/(6*e^2)

fnew(x, y+1,3) = f(x,y,3) - (f(x,y,3) - feq(x,y,3))/tau

-g*((h(x,y)+h(x, y+1))/2 + h_p)*(zb(x, y+1) - zb(x,y))/(6*e^2)

fnew(x-1,y+1,4) = f(x,y,4) - (f(x,y,4) - feq(x,y,4))/tau

-g*((h(x,y)+h(x-1,y+1))/2 + h_p)*(zb(x-1,y+1) - zb(x,y))/(6*e^2)

fnew(x-1,y, 5) = f(x,y,5) - (f(x,y,5) - feq(x,y,5))/tau

-g*((h(x,y)+h(x-1,y))/2 + h_p)*(zb(x-1,y) - zb(x,y))/(6*e^2)

fnew(x-1,y-1,6) = f(x,y,6) - (f(x,y,6)-feq(x,y,6))/tau

-g*((h(x,y)+h(x-1,y-1))/2 + h_p)*(zb(x-1,y-1) - zb(x,y))/(6*e^2)

fnew(x, y-1,7) = f(x,y,7) - (f(x,y,7)-feq(x,y,7))/tau

-g*((h(x,y)+h(x, y-1))/2 + h_p)*(zb(x, y-1) - zb(x,y))/(6*e^2)

fnew(x+1,y-1,8) = f(x,y,8) - (f(x,y,8)-feq(x,y,8))/tau

-g*((h(x,y)+h(x+1,y-1))/2 + h_p)*(zb(x+1,y-1) - zb(x,y))/(6*e^2)

fnew(x, y, 0) = f(x,y,0) - (f(x,y,0)-feq(x,y,0))/tau

CASE STUDY

Background

Here a couple of examples are presented and studied.

Flow Near Spur-Dike

A spur-dike is a hydraulic structure with one end adjacent to the river bank and the other end projecting into the main flow. Experimental data obtained by (Rajaratnam & Nwachukwu, 1983) as depicted by (Molls & Chaudhry, 1995) was used to validate the numerical model. For this case, tests were conducted in a straight rectangular flume 37 m long and 0.9 m wide.

The spur-dike consisted of an aluminum plate, 3 mm thick and 152 mm long, projecting well above the water surface. The flow velocities were measured from 0.92 upstream of the spur-dike to 1.22 m downstream of the dike using a pitot-static tube in the regions where the flow was undisturbed and a three-tube yaw probe in the skewed regions.

Considering the Y axis as the tank width, these measurements were taken at different y/b distances, b being the length of the spur-dyke. A no-slip boundary condition is used for the dyke and a slip boundary condition is used for the channel walls. Following Zhou, et al. (2010), a reduced 9 m long numerical tank was considered, where 900 x 90 lattices were used; $\Delta t = 0.005s$, $\Delta x = 0.01m$ and $\tau = 0.62$. The flow is considered to be laminar, therefore $C_s = 0$.

The agreement is satisfactory, except at y/b = 2 similarly to other results reported in the literature for different numerical methods as Perkins & Richmond, (2004).

Bed Slope and Surface Pressure

This is a stationary case with bed slope proposed by LeVeque, (1998) and Zhou, (2011), having a bed topography defined as:

$$z_b\left(x\right) = \begin{cases} \dfrac{1}{4}\left[\cos\dfrac{\pi\left(x-0.5\right)}{0.1}+1\right] & if\left(x-0.5\right) < 0.1 \\ 0 & otherwise \end{cases} \tag{168}$$

Figure 4. Spur-dike test layout

Figure 5. Spur-dike test results for y/b locations from 1 to 4

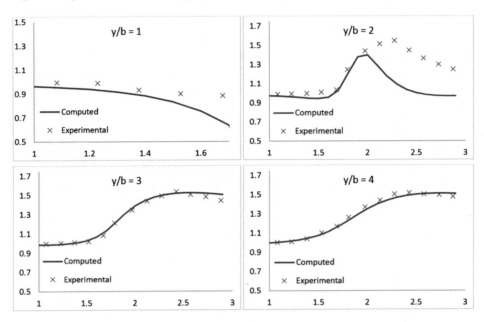

Figure 6. Stationary tank with surface pressure and bed slope

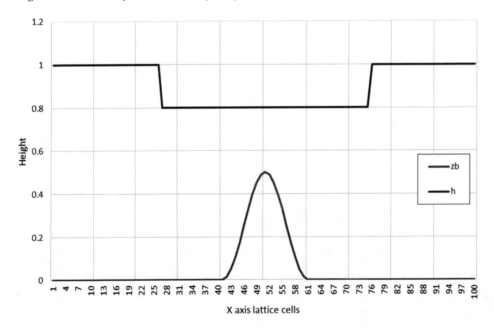

The channel length is 1 m and the numerical computation uses 100 lattices, $\Delta t = 0.005s$, $\Delta x = 0.01m$ and $\tau = 0.5000195$. The initial conditions are u = v = 0 and $h + z_b = 1$.

As the conditions are static, defined values of u, v and h have to remain static. In addition, the area in the middle from 0.25 to 0.75 m has a surface pressure of $P_s = \rho g \cdot 0.2$, so it is expected that water height will be reduced in that area in 0.2 m.

Simulation results in Figure. 3 demonstrate an accuracy until 10^{-15} (the order of magnitude of machine floating point precision) in agreement with expected u, v and h respectively.

REFERENCES

Allen, J. S., Barth, J. A., & Newberger, P. A. (1990). On Intermediate Models for Barotropic Continental Shelf and Slope Flow Fields. Part 1: Formulation and Comparison of Exact Solutions. *Journal of Physical Oceanography*, *20*(7), 1017–1042. doi:10.1175/1520-0485(1990)020<1017:OIMFBC>2.0.CO;2

Bhatnagar, P. L., Gross, E. P., & Krook, M. (1954). A model for collision processes in gases. I: Small amplitude processes in charged and neutral one-component system. *Physical Review*, *94*(3), 511–525. doi:10.1103/PhysRev.94.511

Bouzidi, M., Firdaouss, M., & Lallemand, P. (2001). Momentum transfer of a Boltzmann lattice fluid with boundaries. *Physics of Fluids*, *13*(11), 3452–3459. doi:10.1063/1.1399290

Brackbill, J. U., Kothe, D. B., & Zemach, C. (1992). A continuum method for modeling surface tension. *Journal of Computational Physics*, *100*(2), 335–354. doi:10.1016/0021-9991(92)90240-Y

Caiazzo, A., & Junk, M. (2008). Boundary forces in lattice Boltzmann: Analysis of momentum exchange algorithm. *Computers & Mathematics with Applications (Oxford, England)*, *55*(7), 1415–1423. doi:10.1016/j.camwa.2007.08.004

Chen, S., & Doolen, G. (1998). Lattice Boltzmann method for fluid flows. *Annual Review of Fluid Mechanics*, *30*(1), 329–364. doi:10.1146/annurev.fluid.30.1.329

Chen, S., Martinez, D., & Mei, R. (1996). On boundary conditions in lattice Boltzmann methods. *Physics of Fluids*, *8*(9), 2527–2536. doi:10.1063/1.869035

Germano, M., Piomeelli, U., Moin, P., & ... . (1991). A dynamic subgrid-scale eddy viscosity model. *Physics of Fluids. A, Fluid Dynamics*, *3*(7), 1760–1765. doi:10.1063/1.857955

Ghia, U., Ghia, K. N., & Shin, C. T. (1982). High-Re solutions for incompressible flow using the Navier-Stokes equations and a multigrid method. *Journal of Computational Physics*, *48*(3), 387–410. doi:10.1016/0021-9991(82)90058-4

Higuera, F. J., & Jiménez, J. (1989). Boltzmann Approach to Lattice Gas Simulations. *Europhysics Letters*, *9*(7), 663–654. doi:10.1209/0295-5075/9/7/009

Hou, S., Sterling, J., Chen, S., & ... . (1996). A lattice Boltzmann subgrid model for high Reynolds number flows. In R. Kapral (Ed.), *Pattern formation and lattice gas automata* (Vol. 6, pp. 151–166). Providence, RI: American Mathematical Society.

LeVeque, R. J. (1998). Balancing source terms and flux gradients in high-resolution Godunov methods: The quasi-steady wave-propagation algorithm. *Journal of Computational Physics*, *146*(1), 346–365. doi:10.1006/jcph.1998.6058

McNamara, G., & Zanetti, G. (1988). Use of the Boltzmann Equation to Simulate Lattice-Gas Automata. *Physical Review Letters*, *61*(20), 2332–2335. doi:10.1103/PhysRevLett.61.2332 PMID:10039085

Mohamad, A. A. (2011). *Lattice Boltzmann Method Fundamentals and Engineering Applications with Computer Codes*. London: Springer.

Molls, T., & Chaudhry, M. H. (1995). Depth-averaged open-channel flow model. *Journal of Hydraulic Engineering*, *121*(6), 133–149. doi:10.1061/(ASCE)0733-9429(1995)121:6(453)

Perkins, W. A., & Richmond, M. C. (2004). *MASS2 Modular Aquatic Simulation System in Two Dimensions, Theory and Numerical Methods*. Pacific Northwest National Laboratory.

Rajaratnam, N., & Nwachukwu, B. (1983). Flow near groin-like structures. *Journal of Hydraulic Engineering*, *109*(3), 256–267. doi:10.1061/(ASCE)0733-9429(1983)109:3(463)

Rothman, D. H., & Zaleski, S. (1994). Lattice-gas models of phase separation: Interfaces, phase transitions and multiphase flow. *Reviews of Modern Physics*, *66*(4), 1417–1479. doi:10.1103/RevModPhys.66.1417

Shan, X., Yuan, X. F., & Chen, H. (2006). Kinetic theory representation of hydrodynamics: A way beyond the Navier Stokes equation. *Journal of Fluid Mechanics*, *550*(-1), 413–441. doi:10.1017/S0022112005008153

Smagorinsky, J. (1963). General Circulation Experiments with the Primitive Equations. *Monthly Weather Review*, *91*(3), 99–164. doi:10.1175/1520-0493(1963)091<0099:GCEWTP>2.3.CO;2

Sterling, J. D., & Chen, S. (1996). Stability analysis of lattice Boltzmann methods. *Journal of Computational Physics*, *123*(1), 196–206. doi:10.1006/jcph.1996.0016

Tubbs, K., & Tsai, F. (2011). GPU accelerated lattice Boltzmann model for shallow water flow. *International Journal for Numerical Methods in Engineering*, *86*(3), 316–334. doi:10.1002/nme.3066

Tumelo, R. A. (2011). *Lattice Boltzmann methods for shallow water flow applications* (Master's dissertation). University of the Witwatersrand, Johannesburg, South Africa.

Zergani, S., Aziz, Z. A., & Viswanathan, K. K. (2016). Exact Solutions and Lattice Boltzmann Method Modelling for Shallow Water Equations. *Global Journal of Pure and Applied Mathematics*, *12*(3), 2243–2266.

Zhou, J. G. (2002). A Lattice Boltzmann Model for the Shallow Water Equations. *Methods in Applied Mechanics and Engineering*, *191*(32), 3527–3539. doi:10.1016/S0045-7825(02)00291-8

Zhou, J. G. (2003). *Lattice Boltzmann Methods for Shallow Water Flows*. Berlin: Springer-Verlag.

Zhou, J. G. (2004). *Lattice Boltzmann Methods for Shallow Water Flows*. Springer. doi:10.1007/978-3-662-08276-8

Zhou, J. G. (2011). Enhancement of the LABSWE for shallow water flows. *Journal of Computational Physics*, *230*(2), 394–401. doi:10.1016/j.jcp.2010.09.027

Zhou, J. G., Liu, H., Shafiai, S., Peng, Y., & Burrows, R. (2010). Lattice Boltzmann method for open-channel flows. *Engineering and Computational Mechanics*, *163*(4), 243–249.

Zou, Q., & He, X. (1997). On pressure and velocity boundary conditions for the lattice Boltzmann BGK model. *Physics of Fluids*, *9*(6), 1591–1598. doi:10.1063/1.869307

KEY TERMS AND DEFINITIONS

BGK: Bhatnagar, Gross, and Krook.

CFD: Computational fluid dynamics.

Coriolis Force: An effect whereby a mass moving in a rotating system experiences a force acting perpendicular to the direction of motion and to the axis of rotation.

DNS: Direct numerical simulation.

FDM: Finite difference method.

LBM: Lattice Boltzmann method.

LGA: Lattice gas automata.

N-S: Navier-Stokes.

RANS: Reynolds-averaged Navier-Stokes.

SWE: Shallow water equations.

δ_{ij} **:** Kronecker delta function.

Chapter 10
Large Eddy Simulation Turbulence Model Applied to the Lattice Boltzmann Method

Iñaki Zabala
SENER Ingeniería y Sistemas S.A., Spain

Jesús M. Blanco
Universidad del País Vasco, Spain

ABSTRACT

The lattice Boltzmann method (LBM) is a novel approach for simulating convection-diffusion problems. It can be easily parallelized and hence can be used to simulate fluid flow in multi-core computers using parallel computing. LES (large eddy simulation) is widely used in simulating turbulent flows because of its lower computational needs compared to others such as direct numerical simulation (DNS), where the Kolmogorov scales need to be solved. The aim of this chapter consists of introducing the reader to the treatment of turbulence in fluid dynamics through an LES approach applied to LBM. This allows increasing the robustness of LBM with lower computational costs without increasing the mesh density in a prohibitive way. It is applied to a standard D2Q9 structure using a unified formulation.

INTRODUCTION

Background

The LBM, an innovative numerical method based on kinetic theory is a reasonable candidate for simulating turbulence apart from other phenomena, such as flow-induced noise, and sound propagation. It is well known that the LBM is often used as a direct

DOI: 10.4018/978-1-5225-4760-0.ch010

numerical simulation tool without any assumptions for the relationship between the turbulence stress tensor and the mean strain tensor. Thus, the smallest captured scale in the LBM is the lattice unit, and the largest scale depends on the characteristic length scale in the simulation. These scales are often determined by the available computer memory. Consequently, the LBM is able to resolve relatively low Reynolds number flows (Haiqing & Yan 2015). Unlike the traditional Computational fluid dynamics (CFD) methods, which solve the conservation equations of macroscopic properties (i.e., mass, momentum, and energy) numerically, in LBM models the fluid is modelled as fictive particles, and such particles perform consecutive propagation and collision processes over a discrete lattice mesh. Due to its particulate nature and local dynamics, LBM has several advantages over other conventional CFD methods, especially in dealing with complex boundaries.

Numerical studies have shown that LBM can result in the numerical instability for simulating high Reynolds number flows if unresolved small-scale effects on large-scale dynamics are not considered. A better option is to combine the LBM and large eddy simulation (LES) model in order to solve the problem at high Reynolds numbers. A sub grid model is often used as LES model in the numerical simulation for traditional Navier–Stokes equation (Nieuwstadt & Keller 1973), (Dennis & Chang 1970), (Ghia, Ghia & Shin 1982). Anyway, this novel approach has some limitations. High-Mach number flows in aerodynamics are still difficult for LBM, and a consistent thermo-hydrodynamic scheme is absent. However, as with Navier–Stokes based CFD, LBM methods have been successfully coupled to thermal-specific solutions to enable heat transfer (solids-based conduction, convection and radiation) simulation capability. Simulating multiphase/multicomponent flows has always been a challenge to conventional CFD because of the moving and deformable interfaces. More fundamentally, the interfaces between different phases (liquid and vapor) or components (e.g., oil and water) originate from the specific interactions among fluid molecules.

Therefore, it is difficult to implement such microscopic interactions into the macroscopic Navier–Stokes equation. However, in LBM, the particulate kinetics provides a relatively easy and consistent way to incorporate the underlying microscopic interactions by modifying the collision operator. Several LBM multiphase/multicomponent models have been developed. Here phase separations are generated automatically from the particle dynamics and no special treatment is needed to manipulate the interfaces as in traditional CFD methods. Successful applications of multiphase/multicomponent LBM models can be found in various complex fluid systems, including interface instability, bubble/droplet dynamics, wetting on solid surfaces, interfacial slip, and droplet electrohydrodynamic deformations.

Large eddy simulation (LES) is a mathematical model for turbulence used in computational fluid dynamics. It was initially proposed in 1963 by Joseph

Smagorinsky to simulate atmospheric air currents, (Smagorinsky, 1963) and first explored by Deardorff, later in 1970 for engineering applications (Deardorff, 1970). LES is currently applied in a wide variety of engineering applications, including combustion (Pitsch, 2006), acoustics (Wagner, Hüttl & Sagaut, 2007), and simulations of the atmospheric boundary layer (Sullivan, McWilliams & Moeng, 1994).

The principal idea behind LES is to reduce the computational cost by ignoring the smallest length scales, which are the most computationally expensive to resolve, via low-pass filtering of the Navier–Stokes equations. Such a low-pass filtering, which can be viewed as a time- and spatial-averaging, effectively removes small-scale information from the numerical solution. This information is not irrelevant, however, and its effect on the flow field must be modeled, a task which is an active area of research for problems in which small-scales can play an important role, such as near-wall flows (Piomelli & Elias, 2002), Spalart, 2009), reacting flows (Pitsch, 2006), and multiphase flows (Fox, 2012).

The simulation of turbulent flows by numerically solving the Navier–Stokes (N-S) equations requires resolving a very wide range of time and length scales, all of which affect the flow field. Such a resolution can be achieved with direct numerical simulation (DNS), but DNS is computationally expensive, and its cost prohibits simulation of practical engineering systems with high Reynolds numbers and complex geometry or flow configurations, such as turbulent jets. The treatment of the turbulence will be shown next.

Treatment of Turbulence

Turbulence is a flow regime in fluid dynamics characterized by chaotic changes in pressure and flow velocity. It is in contrast to a laminar flow regime, which occurs when a fluid flows in parallel layers, with no disruption between those layers. Turbulence can be a natural or an artificial event in fluids that occurs when velocity gradients are high, resulting in instabilities in the flow domain as a function of space and time. Although turbulence is a subject of intensive study, it appears that many problems still remain unanswered, particularly in flows with high Mach and Reynolds numbers. Turbulence is commonly observed in everyday phenomena such as surf, fast flowing rivers, billowing storm clouds, or smoke from a chimney, and most fluid flows occurring in nature and created in engineering applications are turbulent (Ting, & Kirby, 1996), (Tennekes & Lumley, 1972). Turbulence is caused by excessive kinetic energy in parts of a fluid flow, which overcomes the damping effect of the fluid's viscosity. For this reason turbulence is easier to create in low viscosity fluids, but more difficult in highly viscous fluids. In general terms, in turbulent flow, unsteady vortices appear of many sizes which interact with each other, consequently drag due to friction effects increases. This would increase the energy needed to pump fluid through a pipe, for instance. However this effect can also be exploited by such as aerodynamic spoilers on aircraft, which deliberately "spoil" the laminar flow to increase drag and reduce lift.

Most flows encountered in engineering practice are turbulent and consequently require special treatment. Turbulent flow appears in a fluid in contact with walls or in between two adjacent layers of different velocities. They result from unsteady waves generated from laminar flows as the Reynolds number increases downstream. With velocity gradients increasing, the flow becomes rotational, leading to a strong stretching of vortex lines (Guo, Zheng & Shi, 2002), (Shan, Yuan & Chen, 2006).

Turbulent flows are distinguished by the following properties:

- Turbulent flows are highly unstable. A plot of the velocity as a function of time at most points in the flow would appear random to a spectator unaccustomed with these flows.
- They are three-dimensional. The instantaneous velocity field oscillates rapidly in all three spatial dimensions.
- They contain a great deal of vorticity. Indeed, vortex stretching is one of the principal mechanisms by which the intensity of turbulence is increased.
- Turbulence rises the mixing rate of conserved quantities.
- Fluid mixing is a dissipative process. By means of the turbulence fluids of different momentum set its content into contact. The reduction of the velocity gradients due to the action of viscosity reduces the kinetic energy of the flow. The energy lost is converted into internal energy of the fluid.
- Turbulent flows oscillate on a broad range of length and time scales. Large and small scales of continuous energy spectrum, which are proportional to the size of eddy motions, are mixed. Here, eddies are coinciding in space, with large ones carrying small ones. In this process, the turbulent kinetic energy transfers from larger eddies to smaller ones, with the smallest eddies eventually dissipating into heat through molecular viscosity (Chen & Doolen, 1998), (Adam, Ricot, Dubief, *et al.*, 2008), (Balasubramanian, Crouse, & Freed, 2009), (Keating, Dethioux, Satti, *et al.*, 2009).

The effects produced by turbulence may or may not be desirable, depending on the application. Strong mixing is useful when chemical mixing or heat transfer is needed; both of these may be increased by orders of magnitude by turbulence. However, increased mixing results in increased frictional forces, therefore increasing the power required for example to drive a vehicle; again, an increase by an order of magnitude is not unusual.

Turbulence Solving

There are different ways to model turbulence:

- In direct numerical simulation (DNS), an extremely refined mesh is used so that all of these scales, large and small, are resolved. Although some simple problems have been solved using DNS, it is not possible to assume industrial problems of practical interest due to the prohibitive computer cost. It is a simulation in computational fluid dynamics in which the flow equations are numerically solved without any turbulence model. This means that the whole range of spatial and temporal scales of the turbulence must be resolved. All the spatial scales of the turbulence must be resolved in the computational mesh, from the smallest dissipative scales (Kolmogorov microscales), up to the integral scale. Therefore, the computational cost of DNS is very high, even at low Reynolds numbers. For the Reynolds numbers encountered in most industrial applications, the computational resources required by a DNS would exceed the capacity of the most powerful computers currently available. However, direct numerical simulation is a useful tool in fundamental research in turbulence. Using DNS it is possible to perform "numerical experiments", and extract from them information difficult or impossible to obtain in the laboratory, allowing a better understanding of the physics of turbulence.
- Since turbulence is characterized by random fluctuations, statistical methods rather than deterministic methods have been studied extensively. In this approach, time averaging of variables is carried out in order to separate the mean quantities from fluctuations. These results in new unknown variables appearing in the governing equations so new equations are introduced to close the system. This process is known as Reynolds Averaged Navier-Stokes (RANS) methods. There are many options in providing the closure process (Sterling & Chen, 1996):
  - Zero-equation models (Prandtl mixing length)
  - One-equation models
  - Two-equation models (k-ε, k-ω, wall functions)
  - Second order closure models (Reynolds stress), and
  - Algebraic stress models

Similar to this approach all large and small scales of turbulence are modeled, mesh refinements as needed for DNS are not required.

- A compromise between DNS and RANS is the Large Eddy Simulation (LES). As its name suggests, large-scale eddies are computed (solved-simulated) and small scales are modeled. Small-scale eddies are associated with the dissipation range of isotropic turbulence, in which modeling is simpler than in RANS. Since the large scale turbulence is to be computed, the mesh refinements are required much more than in RANS, but not as much as in DNS because the small-scale turbulence is modeled (Hou, Sterling, Chen, *et al.,* 1996), (Hou, Sterling, Chen & Doolen, 1996), (Germano, Piomeelli, Moin, *et al.*, 1991). This approach results of special interest and will be then carefully described next.

LARGE EDDY SIMULATION (LES) METHOD

LES General Description

Large eddy simulation involves the solution to the discrete filtered governing equations using computational fluid dynamics. LES resolves scales from the domain size down to the filter size, and as such a substantial portion of high wave number turbulent fluctuations must be resolved. This requires either high-order numerical schemes, or fine grid resolution if low-order numerical schemes are used. (Pope, 2000) addresses the question of how fine a grid resolution is needed to resolve a filtered velocity field. (Ghosal, 1996) found that for low-order discretization schemes, such as those used in finite volume methods, the truncation error can be the same order as the sub filter scale contributions, unless the filter widths considerably larger than the grid spacing. While even-order schemes have truncation error, they are non-dissipative, (Randall & Leveque, 1992) and because sub filter scale models are dissipative, even-order schemes will not affect the sub filter scale model contributions as strongly as dissipative schemes.

The filtering operation in large eddy simulation can be implicit or explicit. Implicit filtering recognizes that the sub filter scale model will dissipate in the same manner as many numerical schemes. In this way, the grid, or the numerical discretization scheme, can be assumed to be the LES low-pass filter. While this takes full advantage of the grid resolution, and eliminates the computational cost of calculating a sub filter scale model term, it is difficult to determine the shape of the LES filter that is associated with some numerical issues. Additionally, truncation error can also become an issue (Grinstein, Margolin & Rider, 2007), (Meneveau & Katz, 2000).

Turbulent flows contain a wide range of length and time scales. The large scale motions are generally much more energetic than the small scale ones; their size and strength make them by far the most effective carriers of the conserved properties. The small scales are usually much weaker and provide little transport of these properties. In this way it is worth a simulation which treats the large eddies more exactly than the small ones; large eddy simulation is just such an approach that low-pass filters the fluid equations to remove small scale information. Large eddy simulations are three dimensional, time dependent and expensive but much less costly than DNS of the same flow. There are two major steps involved in the LES analysis: small eddy filtering and subgrid scale (SGS) modelling.

The co-existence of strongly coupled fluctuations at many scales makes turbulence modeling one of the most challenging unsolved problems in science and engineering. Still, turbulence modeling and prediction is of primary importance to many flow processes and applications ranging from aerodynamics, environmental, geophysical and astrophysical fluid dynamics, energy production and transportation, etc. The eliminated scales are called subfilter or subgrid-scale (SGS) motions. The spectrally sharp filter, the Gaussian filter and the box or top-hat filter are often used.

Small scale components filtering is best produced by analyzing the velocity field; in this approach, the large or resolved scale field, the one to be simulated, is essentially a local average of the complete field. It is essential to filter small scale components. This is best produced by filtering the velocity field (Leonard, 1974). In this approach, the large or resolved scale field, the one to be simulated, is essentially a local average of the complete field. There are other approaches to separate between large and small scales, such as expanding the velocity field using orthonormal basis functions. Truncating the summation can be used to define the large-scale field (a projection) and the discarded modes represent the range of subgrid-scale motions. For Fourier modes, the projection is equivalent to applying a spectral cutoff filter. The filtered velocity $\bar{u}(x, y, z, t)$ is defined by:

$$\bar{u}(x, y, z, t) = \iiint\limits_{\Delta x \Delta y \Delta z} u(x, y, z, t) G(x, y, z, x', y', z') dx' dy' dz' \tag{1}$$

where $G(x, y, z, x', y', z')$, the filter kernel, is a localized function. Filter kernels which have been applied in LES include Gaussian, box filter (a simple local average) and a cutoff (a filter which eliminates all Fourier coefficients belonging to wavenumbers above a cutoff). Every filter has a cutoff length scale Δ. Roughly, eddies of size larger than Δ are large eddies while those smaller than Δ are small eddies, the ones that need to be modeled.

When the Navier-Stokes equations are filtered the set of equations are:

$$\frac{\partial \bar{u}_j}{\partial x_j} = 0 \tag{2}$$

$$\rho \left(\frac{\partial \bar{u}_i}{\partial t} + \frac{\partial \left(\overline{u_i u_j} \right)}{\partial x_j} \right) = f_i - \frac{\partial \bar{p}}{\partial x_i} + \mu \frac{\partial}{\partial x_j} \left(\frac{\partial \bar{u}_i}{\partial x_j} + \frac{\partial \bar{u}_j}{\partial x_i} \right) \tag{3}$$

It is important to note that, since $\overline{u_i u_j} \neq \bar{u}_i \bar{u}_j$ and the quantity on the left side of this inequality is not easily computed, a modeling approximation for the difference between the two sides of this inequality was proposed by Leonard:

$$\tau_{ij}^s = \overline{u_i u_j} - \bar{u}_i \bar{u}_j \tag{4}$$

where τ_{ij}^s is the subgrid-scale residual or Reynolds stress tensor. The name 'stress' stems from the way in which it is treated rather than its physical nature. Physically, the SGS stress determines the dynamical coupling between large and small scales in turbulence. Dimensionally, it scales quadratically with turbulent velocity differences at scales of order Δ. It is in fact the large scale momentum flux caused by the action of the small or unresolved scales. The name 'subgrid scale' is also somewhat of a misnomer. The width of the filter, Δ, need not have anything to do with the grid size, h, other than the obvious condition that $\Delta > h$. The models used to approximate the SGS Reynolds stress are called subgrid-scale (SGS) or subfilter-scale models. The subgrid-scale Reynolds stress contains local averages of the small scale field so models for it should be based on the local velocity field or, perhaps, on the past history of the local fluid. The latter can be accomplished by using a model that solves partial differential equations to obtain the parameters needed to determine the SGS Reynolds stress. It shows that the two-point correlation between SGS stress elements and velocity increments, and the rate of dissipation, must be predicted correctly for resolved third-order moments of velocity to be realistic.

So that the filtered Navier Stokes equations become:

$$\frac{\partial \bar{u}_i}{\partial t} + \frac{\partial \left(\bar{u}_i \bar{u}_j \right)}{\partial x_j} = f_i - \frac{1}{\rho} \frac{\partial \bar{p}}{\partial x_i} + 2\nu \frac{\partial \bar{S}_{ij}}{\partial x_j} - \frac{\partial \tau_{ij}^s}{\partial x_j} \tag{5}$$

where:

$$\overline{S}_{ij} = \frac{1}{2}\left(\frac{\partial \overline{u}_i}{\partial x_j} + \frac{\partial \overline{u}_j}{\partial x_i}\right) \tag{6}$$

The earliest and most commonly used subgrid scale model is one proposed by Smagorinsky (1963). Traditionally, the effects of SGS motions upon resolved scales are modeled in analogy with molecular degrees of freedom like in kinetic theory of gases, in which the momentum fluxes are linearly dependent upon the rate of strain of the large scales. The averaging is usually performed over directions of statistical homogeneity in the flow. The dynamic Smagorinsky model has been applied to a large variety of flows. The model can also be applied with averaging over more localized regions, such as volumes containing a few neighboring grid points, temporal domains along the time evolution of fluid particles. All such models are based on the notion that the principal effects of the SGS Reynolds stress are increased transport and dissipation. As these phenomena are due to the viscosity in laminar flows, it seems reasonable to assume that the effective eddy viscosity ν_t is the fluid viscosity plus the turbulent or artificial SGS viscosity:

$$\nu_t = \nu + \nu_e \tag{7}$$

The Smagorinsky-Lilly equations serves to obtain the turbulent viscosity ν_e:

$$\nu_e = \left(C_s l_s\right)^2 \sqrt{\overline{S}_{ij}\overline{S}_{ij}} \tag{8}$$

where ν_e is the turbulent eddy viscosity, C_s is a model parameter to be determined and l_s is the filter length scale.

This model can be derived in a number of ways including heuristic methods, for example, by equating production and dissipation of subgrid-scale turbulent kinetic energy, or via turbulence theories.

Theories provide estimates of the parameter. Most of these methods apply only to isotropic turbulence for which they all agree that $C_s \approx 0.2$. Unfortunately testing has demonstrated that a constant C_s overestimates the amount of energy dissipation. Near walls, boundary layers introduce large amounts of dissipation that prevents eddy formation and can eliminate turbulence. Thus the value of the parameter C_s has to be reduced near boundary layers. Changes of this magnitude are required in all shear flows. To overcome this problem Van Driest proposed to reduce C_s to 0 as the boundary is approached. The van Driest scaling is:

$$C_s = C_{s0} \left(1 - e^{-y^+/A^+} \right)^2 \tag{9}$$

where $C_{s0} = 0.17$ is the Lilly-Smagorinsky constant, y^+ is the nondimensional distance to the wall and A^+ is the van Driest constant usually taken to be approximately 25.

Although this modification produces the desired results, it is difficult to justify in the context of LES. A SGS model should depend solely on the local properties of the flow and it is difficult to see how the distance from the wall qualifies in this regard.

By following the Bussinesq approach for turbulent stresses, we may represent the subgrid-scale stress with a SGS eddy viscosity ν_e as:

$$\tau_{ij}^s = -\nu_e \left(\frac{\partial \overline{u_i}}{\partial x_j} + \frac{\partial \overline{u_j}}{\partial x_i} \right) \tag{10}$$

Applying Equation (10) into Equation (5) leads to this momentum equation:

$$\frac{\partial \overline{u_i}}{\partial t} + \frac{\partial \left(\overline{u_i}\,\overline{u_j} \right)}{\partial x_j} = f_i - \frac{1}{\rho}\frac{\partial \overline{p}}{\partial x_i} + \left(\nu + \nu_e \right) \frac{\partial^2 \overline{u_i}}{\partial x_j \partial x_j} \tag{11}$$

LES Extension to Shallow Water Model

In the shallow water model the equations are derived from depth-integrating the Navier–Stokes equations, in the case where the horizontal length scale is much greater than the vertical length scale. Under this condition, conservation of mass implies that the vertical velocity of the fluid is small. It can be shown from the momentum equation that vertical pressure gradients are nearly hydrostatic, and that horizontal pressure gradients are due to the displacement of the pressure surface, implying that the horizontal velocity field is constant throughout the depth of the fluid.

By using the similar procedure to that given in (Zabala, 2017), based on the depth averaged continuity equation shown next:

$$\frac{\partial h}{\partial t} + \frac{\partial \left(h\overline{u} \right)}{\partial x} + \frac{\partial \left(h\overline{v} \right)}{\partial y} = 0 \tag{12}$$

The momentum equation is given by:

$$\frac{\partial \left(h u_i \right)}{\partial t} + \frac{\partial \left(h u_i u_j \right)}{\partial x_j} = -g \frac{\partial}{\partial x_i} \left(\frac{h_s^2}{2} \right) + \nu \frac{\partial^2 \left(\overline{h u_i} \right)}{\partial x_j \partial x_j} + F_i \tag{13}$$

where from Equation (2) and (11), the shallow water equations with the effect of the flow turbulence can be derived as:

$$\frac{\partial h}{\partial t} + \frac{\partial \left(\overline{h u_j} \right)}{\partial x_j} = 0 \tag{14}$$

$$\frac{\partial \left(\overline{h u_i} \right)}{\partial t} + \frac{\partial \left(\overline{h u_i} \, \overline{u_j} \right)}{\partial x_j} = -g \frac{\partial}{\partial x_i} \left(\frac{h_s^2}{2} \right) + \left(\nu + \nu_e \right) \frac{\partial^2 \left(\overline{h u_i} \right)}{\partial x_j \partial x_j} + F_i \tag{15}$$

The depth-averaged subgrid-scale stress τ_{ij}^s with eddy viscosity is defined by:

$$\tau_{ij}^s = -\nu_e \left[\frac{\partial \left(\overline{h u_i} \right)}{\partial x_j} + \frac{\partial \left(\overline{h u_j} \right)}{\partial x_i} \right] \tag{16}$$

The eddy viscosity ν_e retains the same form as Equation (8).

And $\overline{S}_{ij}$ is replaced with:

$$\overline{S}_{ij} = \frac{1}{2h} \left[\frac{\partial \left(\overline{h u_i} \right)}{\partial x_j} + \frac{\partial \left(\overline{h u_j} \right)}{\partial x_i} \right] \tag{17}$$

LES Applied to D2Q9

Lattice Boltzmann models can be operated on a number of different lattices, both cubic and triangular, and with or without rest particles in the discrete distribution function. A popular way of classifying the different methods by lattice is the DnQm scheme. Here "Dn" stands for "n dimensions", while "Qm" stands for "m speeds".

Due to the similitude between the standard D2Q9 model and the D2Q9 shallow water model proposed by (Zhou, 2014), this explanation will be common for both and the formulation will be shared.

As indicated previously, the subgrid-scale stress model is used for modelling flow turbulence. In order to consider the turbulence, the effect of the flow turbulence must be taken into account in the flow equations.

Now, we describe a lattice Boltzmann model with turbulence modelling by extending the standard LBM D2Q9 model. Mathematically, if we compare the turbulent Equation (2) and (11) with the standard Navier-Stokes mass and momentum equations or shallow water Equation (14) and (15) with the Equation (12) and (13) without flow turbulence, we will notice that the only difference between them lies in the momentum equations, or more specifically, the eddy viscosity ν_e. Since in the lattice Boltzmann method, the kinematic viscosity of the fluid is governed by the relaxation time:

$$\nu = \frac{e^2 \Delta t}{6} \left(2\tau - 1 \right) \tag{18}$$

the Smagorinsky subgrid model can be implemented by locally adjusting the relaxation time τ_t in the LBE as:

$$\tau_t = \tau + \tau_e \tag{19}$$

which gives a total viscosity ν_t:

$$\nu_t = \nu + \nu_e \tag{20}$$

The solution of the Bhatnagar, Gross and Krook (BGK) single relaxation time collision operator lattice Boltzmann equation:

$$f_\alpha \left(x + e_\alpha \Delta t, t + \Delta t \right) - f_\alpha \left(x, t \right) = -\frac{1}{\tau_t} \left(f_\alpha - f_\alpha^{eq} \right) + f_i \tag{21}$$

can generate the solution to the Equation (2) and (11), and shallow water equations Equation (14) and (15). f_i represents the influence of different force terms that are not affected by turbulence modelling. This is the basic idea behind the lattice Boltzmann subgrid-scale stress model proposed by (Germano, Piomeelli, Moin, *et al.* 1991). In this way, the flow turbulence is modelled in the standard lattice Boltzmann equation with the total relaxation time τ_t which includes the eddy relaxation time $\ddot{A}_e$ via Equation (17). In order to decide the total relaxation time τ_t, first of all, we need to determine the strain-rate tensor $\overline{S}_{ij}$. Since the lattice Boltzmann method is characterized by simplicity and efficiency, $\overline{S}_{ij}$ defined by Equation (17) involves calculation of derivatives and hence is not a suitable form in use. To keep the consistent feature with the lattice gas dynamics, it is natural to calculate $\overline{S}_{ij}$ in terms of the distribution function. By using the Chapman-Enskog expansion, it can be found that the strain-rate tensor $\overline{S}_{ij}$ is related to the non-equilibrium momentum flux tensor. This provides a simple and efficient way to calculate $\overline{S}_{ij}$:

$$\overline{S}_{ij} = -\frac{3}{2e^2 A \tau_t \Delta t} \sum_\alpha e_{\alpha i} e_{\alpha j} \left(f_\alpha - f_\alpha^{eq} \right) \tag{22}$$

where A term has to be replaced by ρ in normal 2D equations and by h in shallow water equations.

Contrary to the finite volume, Navier-Stokes solvers that require finite difference schemes to compute S_{ij}, the lattice Boltzmann model allows direct computation of the strain tensor using the nonequilibrium properties of the filtered particle distribution that are local variables. This simple procedure should save considerable computational time.

Then, if assuming ν_t and τ_t also satisfy the relation Equation (18), we have:

$$\tau_t = \frac{1}{2} + \frac{3\nu_t}{e^2 \Delta t} \tag{23}$$

Substitution of Equation (19) and (20) into (23) equation gives:

$$\tau_e + \tau = \frac{1}{2} + \frac{3\left(\nu_e + \nu\right)}{e^2 \Delta t} \tag{24}$$

With reference to Equation (18), this is simplified as:

$$\tau_e = \frac{3}{e^2 \Delta t} \nu_e \tag{25}$$

Now, replacing ν_e in the above equation with Equation (8) leads to:

$$\tau_e = \frac{3}{e^2 \Delta t} \left(C_s l_s \right)^2 \sqrt{\overline{S_{ij} S_{ij}}} \tag{26}$$

Considering that:

$$\Pi_{ij} = \sum_\alpha e_{\alpha i} e_{\alpha j} \left(f_\alpha - f_\alpha^{eq} \right) \tag{27}$$

and defining:

$$Q_{ij}^{1/2} = \sqrt{\Pi_{ij} \Pi_{ij}} \tag{28}$$

Substituting Equation (22) into Equation (26) we obtain:

$$\tau_e = \frac{3}{e^2 \Delta t} \left(C_s l_s \right)^2 \frac{3}{2e^2 A \tau_t \Delta t} Q_{ij}^{1/2} \tag{29}$$

Using relation (19), if $l_s = \Delta x$ is adopted, we can further write the Equation (29) as:

$$\tau_e = \frac{9}{2} \frac{C_s^2}{e^2 h \left(\tau_e + \tau \right)} Q_{ij}^{1/2} \tag{30}$$

Finally, solution of the above equation results in the eddy relaxation time:

$$\tau_e = \frac{-\tau + \sqrt{\tau^2 + \dfrac{18 C_s^2}{e^2 A} Q_{ij}^{1/2}}}{2} \tag{31}$$

hence giving the following total relaxation time τ_t through Equation (19):

$$\tau_t = \frac{\tau + \sqrt{\tau^2 + \dfrac{18 C_s^2}{e^2 A} Q_{ij}^{1/2}}}{2} \tag{32}$$

LES Algorithm Pseudocode

Following single relaxation time BGK model as defined in Equation (21), the Large Eddy Simulation model is implemented by adjusting the relaxation time as in Equation (19) in every lattice cell, so $\tau_t = \tau + \tau_e$ equation could be expressed better as:

$$\tau_{tij} = \tau + \tau_{eij} \tag{33}$$

and the added algorithmic effort is just devoted to calculate the τ_{tij} in each lattice cell to replace constant τ prior computing Equation (21). Equation (32) including cell indexing would look:

$$\tau_{tij} = \frac{\tau + \sqrt{\tau^2 + \dfrac{18C_s^2}{e^2 A_{ij}} Q_{ij}^{1/2}}}{2} \tag{34}$$

where all components are known but $Q_{ij}^{1/2}$ that is obtained from Equation (28), where Π_{ij} term is obtained from Equation (27). Implementing this in a pseudocode similar to C or BASIC like language, we would consider the next constants:

e is the lattice speed
C_s is the Smagorinsky constant
tau is the single relaxation time

The velocity vector of particles in i and j direction is:

ei[9] = {e, e, 0,-e,-e,-e, 0, e, 0}

ej[9] = {0, e, e, e, 0,-e,-e,-e, 0}

where the directions are defined according to (Figure 1), where central value is the ninth index.
We have also the next variables in matrices:
A[i, j] is the density ρ_{ij} in normal 2D flow and water level h_{ij} in shallow water simulation

f[i, j, a] is the distribution function of particles

Figure 1. Lattice direction numbering as used in the code

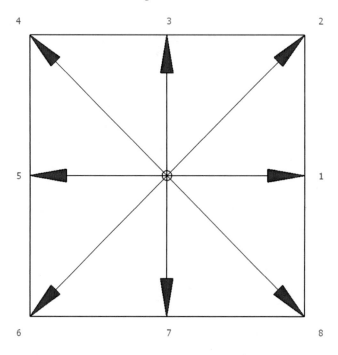

feq[i, j, a] is the local equilibrium distribution function

where index "a" indicates the 9 lattice directions.

Based on this, $\Pi_{ij}\Pi_{ij}$ components product is calculated like this:

pii = pij = pjj = 0

for (a = 1; a < 9; a++) {

As ei[9] == ej[9] == 0, it is not necessary to compute ninth element

pii = pii + ei[a]*ei[a]*(f[i, j, a] – feq[i, j, a])

pij = pij + ei[a]*ej[a]*(f[i, j, a] – feq[i, j, a])

pjj = pjj + ej[a]*ej[a]*(f[i, j, a] – feq[i, j, a])

}

pij_pij = pii^2 + 2*pij^2 + pjj^2

And $Q_{ij}^{1/2}$ is just a square root:

Q1_2_ij = sqrt(pij_pij)

So the total relaxation time τ_{tij} for i, j cell is calculated as Equation (34) as:

tau_t_ij = (tau + sqrt(tau^2 + 18*Cs^2*Q1_2_ij/e^2/(A[i, j])))/2.

tau_t_ij does not need to be saved into a tau_t[i, j] matrix as it may be directly used to calculate new iteration f[i, j, a] particles distribution function matrix cells.

CASE STUDY

Flow Around a Square Cylinder

The next set-up is based in the experiments by (Lyn and Rodi, 1994). It represents an open channel with a vertical cylinder in the central axis of square shape (Figure 2). The height of the cylinder is enough to avoid the fluid overtopping. The fluid

Figure 2. Case study geometry

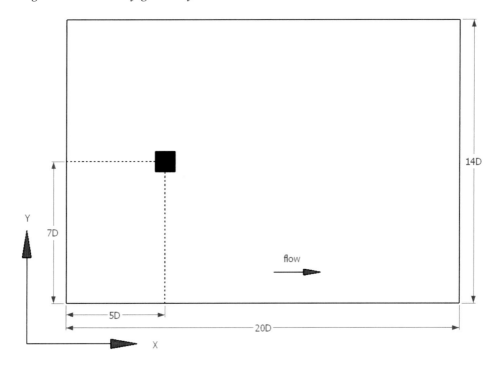

flow goes from the left to the right. The dimensions of the domain are defined by the side of the square D = 1 m as 20D in length and 14D in width, standing the middle of the cylinder at 5D in length and 7D in width. Slip boundary conditions are defined in all walls. Constant discharge flow of 0.1 m/s and fixed channel height of 4D are defined in left and right boundaries. Simulation is performed on 300x210, time step $\Delta t = 0.01$ s and Smagorinsky constant $C_s = 0.9$ is defined. Base relaxation time τ is set so that to obtain a Reynolds of 21400.

The results shown in Figure 3 present a good match with the experimental data behind the square cylinder in the recirculating region where turbulent vortex shedding occurs is properly simulated, illustrating the benefits of using the Smagorinsky LES model to capture the turbulent flow characteristics. The wake recovery region was poorly represented and additional parametrizations and the full three-dimensionality of the problem may need to be considered to properly represent the wake.

Figure 3. Case study results

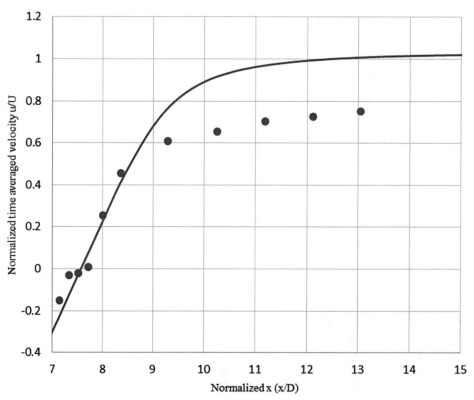

CONCLUSION

Compared with the other methods, the present method combining the LBM and LES model could solve the problem at high Reynolds numbers' flows. Some comparisons demonstrate that the present calculated results could obtain good agreement with the experimental ones.

DNS (direct numerical simulations) are useful in the development of turbulence models for practical applications, such as sub-grid scale models for large eddy simulation (LES) and models for methods that solve the Reynolds-averaged Navier–Stokes equations (RANS). This is done by means of "a priori" tests, in which the input data for the model is taken from a DNS simulation, or by "a posteriori" tests, in which the results produced by the model are compared with those obtained by DNS.

Other classes of SGS models have been proposed, such as solving additional transport equations for the full SGS stress tensor, solving equations for the probability density function, so called Filtered Density Function (FDF) methods, see, or explicitly constructing subgrid velocity fields based, e.g., on small-scale vortices or one-dimensional models of turbulence. The FDF transport equation is solved numerically via a Lagrangian Monte Carlo scheme in which the solutions of the equivalent Stochastic Differential Equations (SDE) are obtained. Closures employed in the FDF transport equation are assessed by comparisons with results obtained by DNS (Colucci, Jaberi, Givi & Pope, 1998).

There have been recently various attempts to develop LES approaches based not on coarse-graining the Navier-Stokes equations, but starting from slightly different momentum equations that have more benign mathematical properties. Examples include the so-called Leray regularization or the Lagrangian-averaged Navier-Stokes (LANS- α) model. The equations are an ensemble average of the Navier–Stokes equations over initial data in an α–radius phase–space ball, and converge to the Navier–Stokes equations as $\alpha \to 0$. Near a solid wall, the length scale α is seen to depend on the distance from the wall with a vanishing value at the wall (Zhao & Kamran, 2005). Careful tests in decaying isotropic 3D turbulence show diminishing accuracy at high grid Reynolds numbers.

A case study has been successfully applied here to a D2Q9 model and shallow water. The Smagorinsky subgrid model can be implemented by locally adjusting the relaxation time, and it can be found that the strain-rate tensor $\overline{S}_{ij}$ is related to the non-equilibrium momentum flux tensor. This provides a simple and efficient way to calculate $\overline{S}_{ij}$ in shallow water equations.

REFERENCES

Adam, J. L., Ricot, D., Dubief, F., & Guy, C. (2008). Aeroacoustic simulation of automobile ventilation outlets. *Journal of Acoustics of the American Society, 123*(5), 3250–3257. doi:10.1121/1.2933531

Balasubramanian, G., Crouse, B., & Freed, D. (2009). Numerical simulation of real world effects on sunroof buffeting of an idealized generic vehicle. In *15th AIAA/ CEAS aeroacoustics conference (30th AIAA aeroacoustics conference).* AIAA Paper 2009-3348.

Chen, S., & Doolen, G. (1998). Lattice Boltzmann method for fluid flows. *Annual Review of Fluid Mechanics, 30*(1), 329–364. doi:10.1146/annurev.fluid.30.1.329

Colucci, P. J., Jaberi, F. A., Givi, P., & Pope, S. B. (1998). Filtered density function for large eddy simulation of turbulent reacting flows. *Physics of Fluids, 10*(2), 499–515. doi:10.1063/1.869537

Deardorff, J. (1970). A numerical study of three-dimensional turbulent channel flow at large Reynolds numbers. *Journal of Fluid Mechanics, 41*(2), 453–480. doi:10.1017/S0022112070000691

Dennis, S. C. R., & Chang, G. Z. (1970). Numerical solutions for steady flow past a circular cylinder at Reynolds number up to 100. *Journal of Fluid Mechanics, 42*(03), 471–489. doi:10.1017/S0022112070001428

Fox, R. O. (2012). Large-eddy-simulation tools for multiphase flows. *Annual Review of Fluid Mechanics, 44*(1), 47–76. doi:10.1146/annurev-fluid-120710-101118

Germano, M., Piomeelli, U., & Moin, P. (1991). A dynamic subgrid-scale eddy viscosity model. *Physics of Fluids. A, Fluid Dynamics, 3*(7), 1760–1765. doi:10.1063/1.857955

Ghia, U., Ghia, K. N., & Shin, C. T. (1982). High-Re solutions for incompressible flow using the Navier-Stokes equations and a multigrid method. *Journal of Computational Physics, 48*(3), 387–410. doi:10.1016/0021-9991(82)90058-4

Ghosal, S. (1996). An analysis of numerical errors in large-eddy simulations of turbulence. *Journal of Computational Physics, 125*(1), 187–206. doi:10.1006/jcph.1996.0088

Grinstein, F., Margolin, L., & Rider, W. (2007). *Implicit large eddy simulation.* Cambridge University Press. doi:10.1017/CBO9780511618604

Guo, Z. L., Zheng, C. G., & Shi, B. C. (2002). Non-equilibrium extrapolation method for velocity and boundary conditions in the lattice Boltzmann method. *Chinese Physics*, *11*(4), 366–374. doi:10.1088/1009-1963/11/4/310

Haiqing, S., & Yan, S. (2015). Study on lattice Boltzmann method/ large eddy simulation and its application at high Reynolds number flow. *Advances in Mechanical Engineering*, *1*, 1–8.

Hou, S., Sterling, J., & Chen, S. (1996). A lattice Boltzmann subgrid model for high Reynolds number flows. In R. Kapral (Ed.), *Pattern formation and lattice gas automata* (Vol. 6, pp. 151–166). Providence, RI: American Mathematical Society.

Hou, S., Sterling, J., Chen, S., & Doolen, G. D. (1996). A lattice Boltzmann subgrid model for high Reynolds number flows. *Fields Institute Communications*, *6*, 151–166.

Keating, A., Dethioux, P., & Satti, R. (2009). Computational aeroacoustics validation and analysis of a nose landing gear. In *15th AIAA/CEAS aeroacoustics conference (30th AIAA aeroacoustics conference)*. AIAA Paper 2009-3154.

Leonard, A. (1974). Energy cascade in large eddy simulations of turbulent fluid flows. *Advances in Geophysics*, *18A*, 237–239.

Lyn, D. A., & Rodi, W. (1994). The flapping shear layer formed by flow separation from the forward corner of a square cylinder. *Journal of Fluid Mechanics*, *267*(-1), 353–376. doi:10.1017/S0022112094001217

Meneveau, C., & Katz, J. (2000). Scale-Invariance and Turbulence Models for Large-Eddy Simulation. *Annual Review of Fluid Mechanics*, *32*(1), 1–32. doi:10.1146/annurev.fluid.32.1.1

Nieuwstadt, F., & Keller, H. B. (1973). Viscous flow past circular cylinder. *Computers & Fluids*, *42*, 471–489.

Piomelli, U., & Elias, B. (2002). Wall-layer models for large-eddy simulations. *Annual Review of Fluid Mechanics*, *34*(1), 181–202. doi:10.1146/annurev.fluid.34.082901.144919

Pitsch, H. (2006). Large-Eddy Simulation of Turbulent Combustion. *Annual Review of Fluid Mechanics*, *38*(1), 453–482. doi:10.1146/annurev.fluid.38.050304.092133

Pope, S. B. (2000). *Turbulent Flows*. Cambridge University Press. doi:10.1017/CBO9780511840531

Randall, J., & Leveque, L. (1992). *Numerical Methods for Conservation Laws* (2nd ed.). Birkhäuser Basel.

Shan, X., Yuan, X. F., & Chen, H. (2006). Kinetic theory representation of hydrodynamics: A way beyond the Navier Stokes equation. *Journal of Fluid Mechanics, 550*(-1), 413–441. doi:10.1017/S0022112005008153

Smagorinsky, J. (1963). General Circulation Experiments with the Primitive Equations. *Monthly Weather Review, 91*(3), 99–164. doi:10.1175/1520-0493(1963)091<0099:GCEWTP>2.3.CO;2

Spalart, P. R. (2009). Detached-eddy simulation. *Annual Review of Fluid Mechanics, 41*(1), 181–202. doi:10.1146/annurev.fluid.010908.165130

Sterling, J. D., & Chen, S. (1996). Stability analysis of lattice Boltzmann methods. *Journal of Computational Physics, 123*(1), 196–206. doi:10.1006/jcph.1996.0016

Sullivan, P., McWilliams, J. C., & Moeng, C. H. (1994). A subgrid-scale model for large-eddy simulation of planetary boundary-layer flows. *Boundary-Layer Meteorology, 71*(3), 247–276. doi:10.1007/BF00713741

Tennekes, H., & Lumley, J. L. (1972). *A First Course in Turbulence*. MIT Press.

Ting, F. C. K., & Kirby, J. T. (1996). Dynamics of surf-zone turbulence in a spilling breaker. *Coastal Engineering, 27*(3-4), 131–160. doi:10.1016/0378-3839(95)00037-2

Wagner, C., Hüttl, T., & Sagaut, P. (2007). *Large-Eddy Simulation for Acoustics*. Cambridge University Press. doi:10.1017/CBO9780511546143

Zhao, H., & Kamran, M. (2005). A dynamic model for the Lagrangian-averaged Navier-Stokes-α equations. *Physics of Fluids, 17*(7), 236–297. doi:10.1063/1.1965166

Zhou, J. G. (2014). *Lattice Boltzmann Methods for Shallow Water Flows*. Springer.

KEY TERMS AND DEFINITIONS

BGK: Bhatnagar, Gross, and Krook.
CFD: Computational fluid dynamics.
DNS: Direct numerical simulation.
DnQm: System with "n" dimensions and "m" speeds.
FDF: Filtered density function.
LANS: Lagrangian-averaged Navier-Stokes.

LBM: Lattice Boltzmann method.

LES: Large eddy simulation.

N-S: Navier-Stokes.

RANS: Reynolds-averaged Navier-Stokes.

SDE: Stochastic differential equations.

SGS: Sub-grid scale.

APPENDIX: NOMENCLATURE

y^+ : The nondimensional distance to the wall.

A^+ : The van Driest constant usually taken to be approximately 25.

Δ: Incremental.

τ_{ij}^s : The subgrid-scale residual or Reynolds stress tensor.

$\overline{u}\left(x, y, z, t\right)$: Filtered velocity.

$\overline{S}_{ij}$: The strain-rate tensor.

f_i : The influence of different force terms.

τ_e : Eddy relaxation time.

ν_t : Eddy viscosity.

ν : Fluid viscosity.

ν_e : Artificial SGS viscosity.

Related References

To continue our tradition of advancing academic research, we have compiled a list of recommended IGI Global readings. These references will provide additional information and guidance to further enrich your knowledge and assist you with your own research and future publications.

Adeyemo, O. (2013). The nationwide health information network: A biometric approach to prevent medical identity theft. In *User-driven healthcare: Concepts, methodologies, tools, and applications* (pp. 1636–1649). Hershey, PA: IGI Global. doi:10.4018/978-1-4666-2770-3.ch081

Adler, M., & Henman, P. (2009). Justice beyond the courts: The implications of computerisation for procedural justice in social security. In A. Martínez & P. Abat (Eds.), *E-justice: Using information communication technologies in the court system* (pp. 65–86). Hershey, PA: IGI Global. doi:10.4018/978-1-59904-998-4.ch005

Aflalo, E., & Gabay, E. (2013). An information system for coping with student dropout. In L. Tomei (Ed.), *Learning tools and teaching approaches through ICT advancements* (pp. 176–187). Hershey, PA: IGI Global. doi:10.4018/978-1-4666-2017-9.ch016

Ahmed, M. A., Janssen, M., & van den Hoven, J. (2012). Value sensitive transfer (VST) of systems among countries: Towards a framework. *International Journal of Electronic Government Research*, 8(1), 26–42. doi:10.4018/jegr.2012010102

Aikins, S. K. (2008). Issues and trends in internet-based citizen participation. In G. Garson & M. Khosrow-Pour (Eds.), *Handbook of research on public information technology* (pp. 31–40). Hershey, PA: IGI Global. doi:10.4018/978-1-59904-857-4.ch004

Aikins, S. K. (2009). A comparative study of municipal adoption of internet-based citizen participation. In C. Reddick (Ed.), *Handbook of research on strategies for local e-government adoption and implementation: Comparative studies* (pp. 206–230). Hershey, PA: IGI Global. doi:10.4018/978-1-60566-282-4.ch011

Aikins, S. K. (2012). Improving e-government project management: Best practices and critical success factors. In *Digital democracy: Concepts, methodologies, tools, and applications* (pp. 1314–1332). Hershey, PA: IGI Global. doi:10.4018/978-1-4666-1740-7.ch065

Akabawi, M. S. (2011). Ghabbour group ERP deployment: Learning from past technology failures. In E. Business Research and Case Center (Ed.), Cases on business and management in the MENA region: New trends and opportunities (pp. 177–203). Hershey, PA: IGI Global. doi:10.4018/978-1-60960-583-4.ch012

Akabawi, M. S. (2013). Ghabbour group ERP deployment: Learning from past technology failures. In *Industrial engineering: Concepts, methodologies, tools, and applications* (pp. 933–958). Hershey, PA: IGI Global. doi:10.4018/978-1-4666-1945-6.ch051

Akbulut, A. Y., & Motwani, J. (2008). Integration and information sharing in e-government. In G. Putnik & M. Cruz-Cunha (Eds.), *Encyclopedia of networked and virtual organizations* (pp. 729–734). Hershey, PA: IGI Global. doi:10.4018/978-1-59904-885-7.ch096

Akers, E. J. (2008). Technology diffusion in public administration. In G. Garson & M. Khosrow-Pour (Eds.), *Handbook of research on public information technology* (pp. 339–348). Hershey, PA: IGI Global. doi:10.4018/978-1-59904-857-4.ch033

Al-Shafi, S. (2008). Free wireless internet park services: An investigation of technology adoption in Qatar from a citizens' perspective. *Journal of Cases on Information Technology*, *10*(3), 21–34. doi:10.4018/jcit.2008070103

Al-Shafi, S., & Weerakkody, V. (2009). Implementing free wi-fi in public parks: An empirical study in Qatar. *International Journal of Electronic Government Research*, *5*(3), 21–35. doi:10.4018/jegr.2009070102

Aladwani, A. M. (2002). Organizational actions, computer attitudes and end-user satisfaction in public organizations: An empirical study. In C. Snodgrass & E. Szewczak (Eds.), *Human factors in information systems* (pp. 153–168). Hershey, PA: IGI Global. doi:10.4018/978-1-931777-10-0.ch012

Aladwani, A. M. (2002). Organizational actions, computer attitudes, and end-user satisfaction in public organizations: An empirical study. *Journal of Organizational and End User Computing, 14*(1), 42–49. doi:10.4018/joeuc.2002010104

Allen, B., Juillet, L., Paquet, G., & Roy, J. (2005). E-government and private-public partnerships: Relational challenges and strategic directions. In M. Khosrow-Pour (Ed.), *Practicing e-government: A global perspective* (pp. 364–382). Hershey, PA: IGI Global. doi:10.4018/978-1-59140-637-2.ch016

Alshawaf, A., & Knalil, O. E. (2008). IS success factors and IS organizational impact: Does ownership type matter in Kuwait? *International Journal of Enterprise Information Systems, 4*(2), 13–33. doi:10.4018/jeis.2008040102

Ambali, A. R. (2009). Digital divide and its implication on Malaysian e-government: Policy initiatives. In H. Rahman (Ed.), *Social and political implications of data mining: Knowledge management in e-government* (pp. 267–287). Hershey, PA: IGI Global. doi:10.4018/978-1-60566-230-5.ch016

Amoretti, F. (2007). Digital international governance. In A. Anttiroiko & M. Malkia (Eds.), *Encyclopedia of digital government* (pp. 365–370). Hershey, PA: IGI Global. doi:10.4018/978-1-59140-789-8.ch056

Amoretti, F. (2008). Digital international governance. In A. Anttiroiko (Ed.), *Electronic government: Concepts, methodologies, tools, and applications* (pp. 688–696). Hershey, PA: IGI Global. doi:10.4018/978-1-59904-947-2.ch058

Amoretti, F. (2008). E-government at supranational level in the European Union. In A. Anttiroiko (Ed.), *Electronic government: Concepts, methodologies, tools, and applications* (pp. 1047–1055). Hershey, PA: IGI Global. doi:10.4018/978-1-59904-947-2.ch079

Amoretti, F. (2008). E-government regimes. In A. Anttiroiko (Ed.), *Electronic government: Concepts, methodologies, tools, and applications* (pp. 3846–3856). Hershey, PA: IGI Global. doi:10.4018/978-1-59904-947-2.ch280

Amoretti, F. (2009). Electronic constitution: A Braudelian perspective. In F. Amoretti (Ed.), *Electronic constitution: Social, cultural, and political implications* (pp. 1–19). Hershey, PA: IGI Global. doi:10.4018/978-1-60566-254-1.ch001

Amoretti, F., & Musella, F. (2009). Institutional isomorphism and new technologies. In M. Khosrow-Pour (Ed.), *Encyclopedia of information science and technology* (2nd ed.; pp. 2066–2071). Hershey, PA: IGI Global. doi:10.4018/978-1-60566-026-4.ch325

Andersen, K. V., & Henriksen, H. Z. (2007). E-government research: Capabilities, interaction, orientation, and values. In D. Norris (Ed.), *Current issues and trends in e-government research* (pp. 269–288). Hershey, PA: IGI Global. doi:10.4018/978-1-59904-283-1.ch013

Anderson, K. V., & Henriksen, H. Z. (2005). The first leg of e-government research: Domains and application areas 1998-2003. *International Journal of Electronic Government Research, 1*(4), 26–44. doi:10.4018/jegr.2005100102

Anttiroiko, A. (2009). Democratic e-governance. In M. Khosrow-Pour (Ed.), *Encyclopedia of information science and technology* (2nd ed.; pp. 990–995). Hershey, PA: IGI Global. doi:10.4018/978-1-60566-026-4.ch158

Association, I. R. (2010). *Networking and telecommunications: Concepts, methodologies, tools and applications* (Vols. 1–3). Hershey, PA: IGI Global. doi:10.4018/978-1-60566-986-1

Association, I. R. (2010). *Web-based education: Concepts, methodologies, tools and applications* (Vols. 1–3). Hershey, PA: IGI Global. doi:10.4018/978-1-61520-963-7

Baker, P. M., Bell, A., & Moon, N. W. (2009). Accessibility issues in municipal wireless networks. In C. Reddick (Ed.), *Handbook of research on strategies for local e-government adoption and implementation: Comparative studies* (pp. 569–588). Hershey, PA: IGI Global. doi:10.4018/978-1-60566-282-4.ch030

Becker, S. A., Keimer, R., & Muth, T. (2010). A case on university and community collaboration: The sci-tech entrepreneurial training services (ETS) program. In S. Becker & R. Niebuhr (Eds.), *Cases on technology innovation: Entrepreneurial successes and pitfalls* (pp. 68–90). Hershey, PA: IGI Global. doi:10.4018/978-1-61520-609-4.ch003

Becker, S. A., Keimer, R., & Muth, T. (2012). A case on university and community collaboration: The sci-tech entrepreneurial training services (ETS) program. In Regional development: Concepts, methodologies, tools, and applications (pp. 947-969). Hershey, PA: IGI Global. doi:10.4018/978-1-4666-0882-5.ch507

Bernardi, R. (2012). Information technology and resistance to public sector reforms: A case study in Kenya. In T. Papadopoulos & P. Kanellis (Eds.), *Public sector reform using information technologies: Transforming policy into practice* (pp. 59–78). Hershey, PA: IGI Global. doi:10.4018/978-1-60960-839-2.ch004

Bernardi, R. (2013). Information technology and resistance to public sector reforms: A case study in Kenya. In *User-driven healthcare: Concepts, methodologies, tools, and applications* (pp. 14–33). Hershey, PA: IGI Global. doi:10.4018/978-1-4666-2770-3.ch002

Bolívar, M. P., Pérez, M. D., & Hernández, A. M. (2012). Municipal e-government services in emerging economies: The Latin-American and Caribbean experiences. In Y. Chen & P. Chu (Eds.), *Electronic governance and cross-boundary collaboration: Innovations and advancing tools* (pp. 198–226). Hershey, PA: IGI Global. doi:10.4018/978-1-60960-753-1.ch011

Borycki, E. M., & Kushniruk, A. W. (2010). Use of clinical simulations to evaluate the impact of health information systems and ubiquitous computing devices upon health professional work. In S. Mohammed & J. Fiaidhi (Eds.), *Ubiquitous health and medical informatics: The ubiquity 2.0 trend and beyond* (pp. 552–573). Hershey, PA: IGI Global. doi:10.4018/978-1-61520-777-0.ch026

Borycki, E. M., & Kushniruk, A. W. (2011). Use of clinical simulations to evaluate the impact of health information systems and ubiquitous computing devices upon health professional work. In *Clinical technologies: Concepts, methodologies, tools and applications* (pp. 532–553). Hershey, PA: IGI Global. doi:10.4018/978-1-60960-561-2.ch220

Buchan, J. (2011). Developing a dynamic and responsive online learning environment: A case study of a large Australian university. In B. Czerkawski (Ed.), *Free and open source software for e-learning: Issues, successes and challenges* (pp. 92–109). Hershey, PA: IGI Global. doi:10.4018/978-1-61520-917-0.ch006

Buenger, A. W. (2008). Digital convergence and cybersecurity policy. In G. Garson & M. Khosrow-Pour (Eds.), *Handbook of research on public information technology* (pp. 395–405). Hershey, PA: IGI Global. doi:10.4018/978-1-59904-857-4.ch038

Burn, J. M., & Loch, K. D. (2002). The societal impact of world wide web - Key challenges for the 21st century. In A. Salehnia (Ed.), *Ethical issues of information systems* (pp. 88–106). Hershey, PA: IGI Global. doi:10.4018/978-1-931777-15-5.ch007

Burn, J. M., & Loch, K. D. (2003). The societal impact of the world wide web-Key challenges for the 21st century. In M. Khosrow-Pour (Ed.), *Advanced topics in information resources management* (Vol. 2, pp. 32–51). Hershey, PA: IGI Global. doi:10.4018/978-1-59140-062-2.ch002

Bwalya, K. J., Du Plessis, T., & Rensleigh, C. (2012). The "quicksilver initiatives" as a framework for e-government strategy design in developing economies. In K. Bwalya & S. Zulu (Eds.), *Handbook of research on e-government in emerging economies: Adoption, e-participation, and legal frameworks* (pp. 605–623). Hershey, PA: IGI Global. doi:10.4018/978-1-4666-0324-0.ch031

Cabotaje, C. E., & Alampay, E. A. (2013). Social media and citizen engagement: Two cases from the Philippines. In S. Saeed & C. Reddick (Eds.), *Human-centered system design for electronic governance* (pp. 225–238). Hershey, PA: IGI Global. doi:10.4018/978-1-4666-3640-8.ch013

Camillo, A., Di Pietro, L., Di Virgilio, F., & Franco, M. (2013). Work-groups conflict at PetroTech-Italy, S.R.L.: The influence of culture on conflict dynamics. In B. Christiansen, E. Turkina, & N. Williams (Eds.), *Cultural and technological influences on global business* (pp. 272–289). Hershey, PA: IGI Global. doi:10.4018/978-1-4666-3966-9.ch015

Capra, E., Francalanci, C., & Marinoni, C. (2008). Soft success factors for m-government. In A. Anttiroiko (Ed.), *Electronic government: Concepts, methodologies, tools, and applications* (pp. 1213–1233). Hershey, PA: IGI Global. doi:10.4018/978-1-59904-947-2.ch089

Cartelli, A. (2009). The implementation of practices with ICT as a new teaching-learning paradigm. In A. Cartelli & M. Palma (Eds.), *Encyclopedia of information communication technology* (pp. 413–417). Hershey, PA: IGI Global. doi:10.4018/978-1-59904-845-1.ch055

Charalabidis, Y., Lampathaki, F., & Askounis, D. (2010). Investigating the landscape in national interoperability frameworks. *International Journal of E-Services and Mobile Applications*, 2(4), 28–41. doi:10.4018/jesma.2010100103

Charalabidis, Y., Lampathaki, F., & Askounis, D. (2012). Investigating the landscape in national interoperability frameworks. In A. Scupola (Ed.), *Innovative mobile platform developments for electronic services design and delivery* (pp. 218–231). Hershey, PA: IGI Global. doi:10.4018/978-1-4666-1568-7.ch013

Chen, I. (2005). Distance education associations. In C. Howard, J. Boettcher, L. Justice, K. Schenk, P. Rogers, & G. Berg (Eds.), *Encyclopedia of distance learning* (pp. 599–612). Hershey, PA: IGI Global. doi:10.4018/978-1-59140-555-9.ch087

Chen, I. (2008). Distance education associations. In L. Tomei (Ed.), *Online and distance learning: Concepts, methodologies, tools, and applications* (pp. 562–579). Hershey, PA: IGI Global. doi:10.4018/978-1-59904-935-9.ch048

Chen, Y. (2008). Managing IT outsourcing for digital government. In A. Anttiroiko (Ed.), *Electronic government: Concepts, methodologies, tools, and applications* (pp. 3107–3114). Hershey, PA: IGI Global. doi:10.4018/978-1-59904-947-2.ch229

Chen, Y., & Dimitrova, D. V. (2006). Electronic government and online engagement: Citizen interaction with government via web portals. *International Journal of Electronic Government Research*, 2(1), 54–76. doi:10.4018/jegr.2006010104

Chen, Y., & Knepper, R. (2005). Digital government development strategies: Lessons for policy makers from a comparative perspective. In W. Huang, K. Siau, & K. Wei (Eds.), *Electronic government strategies and implementation* (pp. 394–420). Hershey, PA: IGI Global. doi:10.4018/978-1-59140-348-7.ch017

Chen, Y., & Knepper, R. (2008). Digital government development strategies: Lessons for policy makers from a comparative perspective. In H. Rahman (Ed.), *Developing successful ICT strategies: Competitive advantages in a global knowledge-driven society* (pp. 334–356). Hershey, PA: IGI Global. doi:10.4018/978-1-59904-654-9. ch017

Cherian, E. J., & Ryan, T. W. (2014). Incongruent needs: Why differences in the iron-triangle of priorities make health information technology adoption and use difficult. In C. El Morr (Ed.), *Research perspectives on the role of informatics in health policy and management* (pp. 209–221). Hershey, PA: IGI Global. doi:10.4018/978-1-4666-4321-5.ch012

Cho, H. J., & Hwang, S. (2010). Government 2.0 in Korea: Focusing on e-participation services. In C. Reddick (Ed.), *Politics, democracy and e-government: Participation and service delivery* (pp. 94–114). Hershey, PA: IGI Global. doi:10.4018/978-1-61520-933-0.ch006

Chorus, C., & Timmermans, H. (2010). Ubiquitous travel environments and travel control strategies: Prospects and challenges. In M. Wachowicz (Ed.), *Movement-aware applications for sustainable mobility: Technologies and approaches* (pp. 30–51). Hershey, PA: IGI Global. doi:10.4018/978-1-61520-769-5.ch003

Chuanshen, R. (2007). E-government construction and China's administrative litigation act. In A. Anttiroiko & M. Malkia (Eds.), *Encyclopedia of digital government* (pp. 507–510). Hershey, PA: IGI Global. doi:10.4018/978-1-59140-789-8.ch077

Ciaghi, A., & Villafiorita, A. (2012). Law modeling and BPR for public administration improvement. In K. Bwalya & S. Zulu (Eds.), *Handbook of research on e-government in emerging economies: Adoption, e-participation, and legal frameworks* (pp. 391–410). Hershey, PA: IGI Global. doi:10.4018/978-1-4666-0324-0.ch019

Ciaramitaro, B. L., & Skrocki, M. (2012). mHealth: Mobile healthcare. In B. Ciaramitaro (Ed.), Mobile technology consumption: Opportunities and challenges (pp. 99-109). Hershey, PA: IGI Global. doi:10.4018/978-1-61350-150-4.ch007

Comite, U. (2012). Innovative processes and managerial effectiveness of e-procurement in healthcare. In A. Manoharan & M. Holzer (Eds.), *Active citizen participation in e-government: A global perspective* (pp. 206–229). Hershey, PA: IGI Global. doi:10.4018/978-1-4666-0116-1.ch011

Cordella, A. (2013). E-government success: How to account for ICT, administrative rationalization, and institutional change. In J. Gil-Garcia (Ed.), *E-government success factors and measures: Theories, concepts, and methodologies* (pp. 40–51). Hershey, PA: IGI Global. doi:10.4018/978-1-4666-4058-0.ch003

Cropf, R. A. (2009). ICT and e-democracy. In M. Khosrow-Pour (Ed.), *Encyclopedia of information science and technology* (2nd ed.; pp. 1789–1793). Hershey, PA: IGI Global. doi:10.4018/978-1-60566-026-4.ch281

Cropf, R. A. (2009). The virtual public sphere. In M. Pagani (Ed.), *Encyclopedia of multimedia technology and networking* (2nd ed.; pp. 1525–1530). Hershey, PA: IGI Global. doi:10.4018/978-1-60566-014-1.ch206

D'Abundo, M. L. (2013). Electronic health record implementation in the United States healthcare industry: Making the process of change manageable. In V. Wang (Ed.), *Handbook of research on technologies for improving the 21st century workforce: Tools for lifelong learning* (pp. 272–286). Hershey, PA: IGI Global. doi:10.4018/978-1-4666-2181-7.ch018

Damurski, L. (2012). E-participation in urban planning: Online tools for citizen engagement in Poland and in Germany. *International Journal of E-Planning Research*, *1*(3), 40–67. doi:10.4018/ijepr.2012070103

de Almeida, M. O. (2007). E-government strategy in Brazil: Increasing transparency and efficiency through e-government procurement. In M. Gascó-Hernandez (Ed.), *Latin America online: Cases, successes and pitfalls* (pp. 34–82). Hershey, PA: IGI Global. doi:10.4018/978-1-59140-974-8.ch002

de Juana Espinosa, S. (2008). Empirical study of the municipalitites' motivations for adopting online presence. In A. Anttiroiko (Ed.), *Electronic government: Concepts, methodologies, tools, and applications* (pp. 3593–3608). Hershey, PA: IGI Global. doi:10.4018/978-1-59904-947-2.ch262 de Souza Dias, D. (2002). Motivation for using information technology. In C. Snodgrass & E. Szewczak (Eds.), *Human factors in information systems* (pp. 55–60). Hershey, PA: IGI Global. doi:10.4018/978-1-931777-10-0.ch005

Demediuk, P. (2006). Government procurement ICT's impact on the sustainability of SMEs and regional communities. In S. Marshall, W. Taylor, & X. Yu (Eds.), *Encyclopedia of developing regional communities with information and communication technology* (pp. 321–324). Hershey, PA: IGI Global. doi:10.4018/978-1-59140-575-7.ch056

Devonshire, E., Forsyth, H., Reid, S., & Simpson, J. M. (2013). The challenges and opportunities of online postgraduate coursework programs in a traditional university context. In B. Tynan, J. Willems, & R. James (Eds.), *Outlooks and opportunities in blended and distance learning* (pp. 353–368). Hershey, PA: IGI Global. doi:10.4018/978-1-4666-4205-8.ch026

Di Cerbo, F., Scotto, M., Sillitti, A., Succi, G., & Vernazza, T. (2007). Toward a GNU/Linux distribution for corporate environments. In S. Sowe, I. Stamelos, & I. Samoladas (Eds.), *Emerging free and open source software practices* (pp. 215–236). Hershey, PA: IGI Global. doi:10.4018/978-1-59904-210-7.ch010

Diesner, J., & Carley, K. M. (2005). Revealing social structure from texts: Meta-matrix text analysis as a novel method for network text analysis. In V. Narayanan & D. Armstrong (Eds.), *Causal mapping for research in information technology* (pp. 81–108). Hershey, PA: IGI Global. doi:10.4018/978-1-59140-396-8.ch004

Dologite, D. G., Mockler, R. J., Bai, Q., & Viszhanyo, P. F. (2006). IS change agents in practice in a US-Chinese joint venture. In M. Hunter & F. Tan (Eds.), *Advanced topics in global information management* (Vol. 5, pp. 331–352). Hershey, PA: IGI Global. doi:10.4018/978-1-59140-923-6.ch015

Drnevich, P., Brush, T. H., & Luckock, G. T. (2011). Process and structural implications for IT-enabled outsourcing. *International Journal of Strategic Information Technology and Applications*, 2(4), 30–43. doi:10.4018/jsita.2011100103

Dwivedi, A. N. (2009). *Handbook of research on information technology management and clinical data administration in healthcare* (Vols. 1–2). Hershey, PA: IGI Global. doi:10.4018/978-1-60566-356-2

Elbeltagi, I., McBride, N., & Hardaker, G. (2006). Evaluating the factors affecting DSS usage by senior managers in local authorities in Egypt. In M. Hunter & F. Tan (Eds.), *Advanced topics in global information management* (Vol. 5, pp. 283–307). Hershey, PA: IGI Global. doi:10.4018/978-1-59140-923-6.ch013

Eom, S., & Fountain, J. E. (2013). Enhancing information services through public-private partnerships: Information technology knowledge transfer underlying structures to develop shared services in the U.S. and Korea. In J. Gil-Garcia (Ed.), *E-government success around the world: Cases, empirical studies, and practical recommendations* (pp. 15–40). Hershey, PA: IGI Global. doi:10.4018/978-1-4666-4173-0.ch002

Esteves, T., Leuenberger, D., & Van Leuven, N. (2012). Reaching citizen 2.0: How government uses social media to send public messages during times of calm and times of crisis. In K. Kloby & M. D'Agostino (Eds.), *Citizen 2.0: Public and governmental interaction through web 2.0 technologies* (pp. 250–268). Hershey, PA: IGI Global. doi:10.4018/978-1-4666-0318-9.ch013

Estevez, E., Fillottrani, P., Janowski, T., & Ojo, A. (2012). Government information sharing: A framework for policy formulation. In Y. Chen & P. Chu (Eds.), *Electronic governance and cross-boundary collaboration: Innovations and advancing tools* (pp. 23–55). Hershey, PA: IGI Global. doi:10.4018/978-1-60960-753-1.ch002

Ezz, I. E. (2008). E-governement emerging trends: Organizational challenges. In A. Anttiroiko (Ed.), *Electronic government: Concepts, methodologies, tools, and applications* (pp. 3721–3737). Hershey, PA: IGI Global. doi:10.4018/978-1-59904-947-2.ch269

Fabri, M. (2009). The Italian style of e-justice in a comparative perspective. In A. Martínez & P. Abat (Eds.), *E-justice: Using information communication technologies in the court system* (pp. 1–19). Hershey, PA: IGI Global. doi:10.4018/978-1-59904-998-4.ch001

Fagbe, T., & Adekola, O. D. (2010). Workplace safety and personnel well-being: The impact of information technology. *International Journal of Green Computing*, *1*(1), 28–33. doi:10.4018/jgc.2010010103

Fagbe, T., & Adekola, O. D. (2011). Workplace safety and personnel well-being: The impact of information technology. In *Global business: Concepts, methodologies, tools and applications* (pp. 1438–1444). Hershey, PA: IGI Global. doi:10.4018/978-1-60960-587-2.ch509

Farmer, L. (2008). Affective collaborative instruction with librarians. In S. Kelsey & K. St.Amant (Eds.), *Handbook of research on computer mediated communication* (pp. 15–24). Hershey, PA: IGI Global. doi:10.4018/978-1-59904-863-5.ch002

Favier, L., & Mekhantar, J. (2007). Use of OSS by local e-administration: The French situation. In K. St.Amant & B. Still (Eds.), *Handbook of research on open source software: Technological, economic, and social perspectives* (pp. 428–444). Hershey, PA: IGI Global. doi:10.4018/978-1-59140-999-1.ch033

Fernando, S. (2009). Issues of e-learning in third world countries. In M. Khosrow-Pour (Ed.), *Encyclopedia of information science and technology* (2nd ed.; pp. 2273–2277). Hershey, PA: IGI Global. doi:10.4018/978-1-60566-026-4.ch360

Filho, J. R., & dos Santos, J. R. Jr. (2009). Local e-government in Brazil: Poor interaction and local politics as usual. In C. Reddick (Ed.), *Handbook of research on strategies for local e-government adoption and implementation: Comparative studies* (pp. 863–878). Hershey, PA: IGI Global. doi:10.4018/978-1-60566-282-4.ch045

Fletcher, P. D. (2004). Portals and policy: Implications of electronic access to U.S. federal government information services. In A. Pavlichev & G. Garson (Eds.), *Digital government: Principles and best practices* (pp. 52–62). Hershey, PA: IGI Global. doi:10.4018/978-1-59140-122-3.ch004

Fletcher, P. D. (2008). Portals and policy: Implications of electronic access to U.S. federal government information services. In A. Anttiroiko (Ed.), *Electronic government: Concepts, methodologies, tools, and applications* (pp. 3970–3979). Hershey, PA: IGI Global. doi:10.4018/978-1-59904-947-2.ch289

Forlano, L. (2004). The emergence of digital government: International perspectives. In A. Pavlichev & G. Garson (Eds.), *Digital government: Principles and best practices* (pp. 34–51). Hershey, PA: IGI Global. doi:10.4018/978-1-59140-122-3.ch003

Franzel, J. M., & Coursey, D. H. (2004). Government web portals: Management issues and the approaches of five states. In A. Pavlichev & G. Garson (Eds.), *Digital government: Principles and best practices* (pp. 63–77). Hershey, PA: IGI Global. doi:10.4018/978-1-59140-122-3.ch005

Gaivéo, J. M. (2013). Security of ICTs supporting healthcare activities. In M. Cruz-Cunha, I. Miranda, & P. Gonçalves (Eds.), *Handbook of research on ICTs for human-centered healthcare and social care services* (pp. 208–228). Hershey, PA: IGI Global. doi:10.4018/978-1-4666-3986-7.ch011

Garson, G. D. (1999). *Information technology and computer applications in public administration: Issues and trends*. Hershey, PA: IGI Global. doi:10.4018/978-1-87828-952-0

Garson, G. D. (2003). Toward an information technology research agenda for public administration. In G. Garson (Ed.), *Public information technology: Policy and management issues* (pp. 331–357). Hershey, PA: IGI Global. doi:10.4018/978-1-59140-060-8.ch014

Garson, G. D. (2004). The promise of digital government. In A. Pavlichev & G. Garson (Eds.), *Digital government: Principles and best practices* (pp. 2–15). Hershey, PA: IGI Global. doi:10.4018/978-1-59140-122-3.ch001

Garson, G. D. (2007). An information technology research agenda for public administration. In G. Garson (Ed.), *Modern public information technology systems: Issues and challenges* (pp. 365–392). Hershey, PA: IGI Global. doi:10.4018/978-1-59904-051-6.ch018

Gasco, M. (2007). Civil servants' resistance towards e-government development. In A. Anttiroiko & M. Malkia (Eds.), *Encyclopedia of digital government* (pp. 190–195). Hershey, PA: IGI Global. doi:10.4018/978-1-59140-789-8.ch028

Gasco, M. (2008). Civil servants' resistance towards e-government development. In A. Anttiroiko (Ed.), *Electronic government: Concepts, methodologies, tools, and applications* (pp. 2580–2588). Hershey, PA: IGI Global. doi:10.4018/978-1-59904-947-2.ch190

Ghere, R. K. (2010). Accountability and information technology enactment: Implications for social empowerment. In E. Ferro, Y. Dwivedi, J. Gil-Garcia, & M. Williams (Eds.), *Handbook of research on overcoming digital divides: Constructing an equitable and competitive information society* (pp. 515–532). Hershey, PA: IGI Global. doi:10.4018/978-1-60566-699-0.ch028

Gibson, I. W. (2012). Simulation modeling of healthcare delivery. In A. Kolker & P. Story (Eds.), *Management engineering for effective healthcare delivery: Principles and applications* (pp. 69–89). Hershey, PA: IGI Global. doi:10.4018/978-1-60960-872-9.ch003

Gil-Garcia, J. R. (2007). Exploring e-government benefits and success factors. In A. Anttiroiko & M. Malkia (Eds.), *Encyclopedia of digital government* (pp. 803–811). Hershey, PA: IGI Global. doi:10.4018/978-1-59140-789-8.ch122

Gil-Garcia, J. R., & González Miranda, F. (2010). E-government and opportunities for participation: The case of the Mexican state web portals. In C. Reddick (Ed.), *Politics, democracy and e-government: Participation and service delivery* (pp. 56–74). Hershey, PA: IGI Global. doi:10.4018/978-1-61520-933-0.ch004

Goldfinch, S. (2012). Public trust in government, trust in e-government, and use of e-government. In Z. Yan (Ed.), *Encyclopedia of cyber behavior* (pp. 987–995). Hershey, PA: IGI Global. doi:10.4018/978-1-4666-0315-8.ch081

Goodyear, M. (2012). Organizational change contributions to e-government project transitions. In S. Aikins (Ed.), *Managing e-government projects: Concepts, issues, and best practices* (pp. 1–21). Hershey, PA: IGI Global. doi:10.4018/978-1-4666-0086-7.ch001

Gordon, S., & Mulligan, P. (2003). Strategic models for the delivery of personal financial services: The role of infocracy. In S. Gordon (Ed.), *Computing information technology: The human side* (pp. 220–232). Hershey, PA: IGI Global. doi:10.4018/978-1-93177-752-0.ch014

Gordon, T. F. (2007). Legal knowledge systems. In A. Anttiroiko & M. Malkia (Eds.), *Encyclopedia of digital government* (pp. 1161–1166). Hershey, PA: IGI Global. doi:10.4018/978-1-59140-789-8.ch175

Graham, J. E., & Semich, G. W. (2008). Integrating technology to transform pedagogy: Revisiting the progress of the three phase TUI model for faculty development. In L. Tomei (Ed.), *Adapting information and communication technologies for effective education* (pp. 1–12). Hershey, PA: IGI Global. doi:10.4018/978-1-59904-922-9.ch001

Grandinetti, L., & Pisacane, O. (2012). Web services for healthcare management. In D. Prakash Vidyarthi (Ed.), *Technologies and protocols for the future of internet design: Reinventing the web* (pp. 60–94). Hershey, PA: IGI Global. doi:10.4018/978-1-4666-0203-8.ch004

Groenewegen, P., & Wagenaar, F. P. (2008). VO as an alternative to hierarchy in the Dutch police sector. In G. Putnik & M. Cruz-Cunha (Eds.), *Encyclopedia of networked and virtual organizations* (pp. 1851–1857). Hershey, PA: IGI Global. doi:10.4018/978-1-59904-885-7.ch245

Gronlund, A. (2001). Building an infrastructure to manage electronic services. In S. Dasgupta (Ed.), *Managing internet and intranet technologies in organizations: Challenges and opportunities* (pp. 71–103). Hershey, PA: IGI Global. doi:10.4018/978-1-878289-95-7.ch006

Gronlund, A. (2002). Introduction to electronic government: Design, applications and management. In Å. Grönlund (Ed.), *Electronic government: Design, applications and management* (pp. 1–21). Hershey, PA: IGI Global. doi:10.4018/978-1-930708-19-8.ch001

Gupta, A., Woosley, R., Crk, I., & Sarnikar, S. (2009). An information technology architecture for drug effectiveness reporting and post-marketing surveillance. In J. Tan (Ed.), *Medical informatics: Concepts, methodologies, tools, and applications* (pp. 631–646). Hershey, PA: IGI Global. doi:10.4018/978-1-60566-050-9.ch047

Hallin, A., & Lundevall, K. (2007). mCity: User focused development of mobile services within the city of Stockholm. In I. Kushchu (Ed.), Mobile government: An emerging direction in e-government (pp. 12-29). Hershey, PA: IGI Global. doi:10.4018/978-1-59140-884-0.ch002

Hallin, A., & Lundevall, K. (2009). mCity: User focused development of mobile services within the city of Stockholm. In S. Clarke (Ed.), Evolutionary concepts in end user productivity and performance: Applications for organizational progress (pp. 268-280). Hershey, PA: IGI Global. doi:10.4018/978-1-60566-136-0.ch017

Hallin, A., & Lundevall, K. (2009). mCity: User focused development of mobile services within the city of Stockholm. In D. Taniar (Ed.), Mobile computing: Concepts, methodologies, tools, and applications (pp. 3455-3467). Hershey, PA: IGI Global. doi:10.4018/978-1-60566-054-7.ch253

Hanson, A. (2005). Overcoming barriers in the planning of a virtual library. In M. Khosrow-Pour (Ed.), *Encyclopedia of information science and technology* (pp. 2255–2259). Hershey, PA: IGI Global. doi:10.4018/978-1-59140-553-5.ch397

Haque, A. (2008). Information technology and surveillance: Implications for public administration in a new word order. In T. Loendorf & G. Garson (Eds.), *Patriotic information systems* (pp. 177–185). Hershey, PA: IGI Global. doi:10.4018/978-1-59904-594-8.ch008

Hauck, R. V., Thatcher, S. M., & Weisband, S. P. (2012). Temporal aspects of information technology use: Increasing shift work effectiveness. In J. Wang (Ed.), *Advancing the service sector with evolving technologies: Techniques and principles* (pp. 87–104). Hershey, PA: IGI Global. doi:10.4018/978-1-4666-0044-7.ch006

Hawk, S., & Witt, T. (2006). Telecommunications courses in information systems programs. *International Journal of Information and Communication Technology Education*, 2(1), 79–92. doi:10.4018/jicte.2006010107

Helms, M. M., Moore, R., & Ahmadi, M. (2009). Information technology (IT) and the healthcare industry: A SWOT analysis. In J. Tan (Ed.), *Medical informatics: Concepts, methodologies, tools, and applications* (pp. 134–152). Hershey, PA: IGI Global. doi:10.4018/978-1-60566-050-9.ch012

Hendrickson, S. M., & Young, M. E. (2014). Electronic records management at a federally funded research and development center. In J. Krueger (Ed.), *Cases on electronic records and resource management implementation in diverse environments* (pp. 334–350). Hershey, PA: IGI Global. doi:10.4018/978-1-4666-4466-3.ch020

Henman, P. (2010). Social policy and information communication technologies. In J. Martin & L. Hawkins (Eds.), *Information communication technologies for human services education and delivery: Concepts and cases* (pp. 215–229). Hershey, PA: IGI Global. doi:10.4018/978-1-60566-735-5.ch014

Hismanoglu, M. (2011). Important issues in online education: E-pedagogy and marketing. In U. Demiray & S. Sever (Eds.), *Marketing online education programs: Frameworks for promotion and communication* (pp. 184–209). Hershey, PA: IGI Global. doi:10.4018/978-1-60960-074-7.ch012

Ho, K. K. (2008). The e-government development, IT strategies, and portals of the Hong Kong SAR government. In A. Anttiroiko (Ed.), *Electronic government: Concepts, methodologies, tools, and applications* (pp. 715–733). Hershey, PA: IGI Global. doi:10.4018/978-1-59904-947-2.ch060

Holden, S. H. (2003). The evolution of information technology management at the federal level: Implications for public administration. In G. Garson (Ed.), *Public information technology: Policy and management issues* (pp. 53–73). Hershey, PA: IGI Global. doi:10.4018/978-1-59140-060-8.ch003

Holden, S. H. (2007). The evolution of federal information technology management literature: Does IT finally matter? In G. Garson (Ed.), *Modern public information technology systems: Issues and challenges* (pp. 17–34). Hershey, PA: IGI Global. doi:10.4018/978-1-59904-051-6.ch002

Holland, J. W. (2009). Automation of American criminal justice. In M. Khosrow-Pour (Ed.), *Encyclopedia of information science and technology* (2nd ed.; pp. 300–302). Hershey, PA: IGI Global. doi:10.4018/978-1-60566-026-4.ch051

Holloway, K. (2013). Fair use, copyright, and academic integrity in an online academic environment. In *Digital rights management: Concepts, methodologies, tools, and applications* (pp. 917–928). Hershey, PA: IGI Global. doi:10.4018/978-1-4666-2136-7.ch044

Horiuchi, C. (2005). E-government databases. In L. Rivero, J. Doorn, & V. Ferraggine (Eds.), *Encyclopedia of database technologies and applications* (pp. 206–210). Hershey, PA: IGI Global. doi:10.4018/978-1-59140-560-3.ch035

Horiuchi, C. (2006). Creating IS quality in government settings. In E. Duggan & J. Reichgelt (Eds.), *Measuring information systems delivery quality* (pp. 311–327). Hershey, PA: IGI Global. doi:10.4018/978-1-59140-857-4.ch014

Hsiao, N., Chu, P., & Lee, C. (2012). Impact of e-governance on businesses: Model development and case study. In *Digital democracy: Concepts, methodologies, tools, and applications* (pp. 1407–1425). Hershey, PA: IGI Global. doi:10.4018/978-1-4666-1740-7.ch070

Huang, T., & Lee, C. (2010). Evaluating the impact of e-government on citizens: Cost-benefit analysis. In C. Reddick (Ed.), *Citizens and e-government: Evaluating policy and management* (pp. 37–52). Hershey, PA: IGI Global. doi:10.4018/978-1-61520-931-6.ch003

Hunter, M. G., Diochon, M., Pugsley, D., & Wright, B. (2002). Unique challenges for small business adoption of information technology: The case of the Nova Scotia ten. In S. Burgess (Ed.), *Managing information technology in small business: Challenges and solutions* (pp. 98–117). Hershey, PA: IGI Global. doi:10.4018/978-1-930708-35-8.ch006

Hurskainen, J. (2003). Integration of business systems and applications in merger and alliance: Case metso automation. In T. Reponen (Ed.), *Information technology enabled global customer service* (pp. 207–225). Hershey, PA: IGI Global. doi:10.4018/978-1-59140-048-6.ch012

Iazzolino, G., & Pietrantonio, R. (2011). The soveria.it project: A best practice of e-government in southern Italy. In D. Piaggesi, K. Sund, & W. Castelnovo (Eds.), *Global strategy and practice of e-governance: Examples from around the world* (pp. 34–56). Hershey, PA: IGI Global. doi:10.4018/978-1-60960-489-9.ch003

Imran, A., & Gregor, S. (2012). A process model for successful e-government adoption in the least developed countries: A case of Bangladesh. In F. Tan (Ed.), *International comparisons of information communication technologies: Advancing applications* (pp. 321–350). Hershey, PA: IGI Global. doi:10.4018/978-1-61350-480-2.ch014

Inoue, Y., & Bell, S. T. (2005). Electronic/digital government innovation, and publishing trends with IT. In M. Khosrow-Pour (Ed.), *Encyclopedia of information science and technology* (pp. 1018–1023). Hershey, PA: IGI Global. doi:10.4018/978-1-59140-553-5.ch180

Islam, M. M., & Ehsan, M. (2013). Understanding e-governance: A theoretical approach. In M. Islam & M. Ehsan (Eds.), *From government to e-governance: Public administration in the digital age* (pp. 38–49). Hershey, PA: IGI Global. doi:10.4018/978-1-4666-1909-8.ch003

Jaeger, B. (2009). E-government and e-democracy in the making. In M. Khosrow-Pour (Ed.), *Encyclopedia of information science and technology* (2nd ed.; pp. 1318–1322). Hershey, PA: IGI Global. doi:10.4018/978-1-60566-026-4.ch208

Jain, R. B. (2007). Revamping the administrative structure and processes in India for online diplomacy. In A. Anttiroiko & M. Malkia (Eds.), *Encyclopedia of digital government* (pp. 1418–1423). Hershey, PA: IGI Global. doi:10.4018/978-1-59140-789-8.ch217

Jain, R. B. (2008). Revamping the administrative structure and processes in India for online diplomacy. In A. Anttiroiko (Ed.), *Electronic government: Concepts, methodologies, tools, and applications* (pp. 3142–3149). Hershey, PA: IGI Global. doi:10.4018/978-1-59904-947-2.ch233

Jauhiainen, J. S., & Inkinen, T. (2009). E-governance and the information society in periphery. In C. Reddick (Ed.), *Handbook of research on strategies for local e-government adoption and implementation: Comparative studies* (pp. 497–514). Hershey, PA: IGI Global. doi:10.4018/978-1-60566-282-4.ch026

Jensen, M. J. (2009). Electronic democracy and citizen influence in government. In C. Reddick (Ed.), *Handbook of research on strategies for local e-government adoption and implementation: Comparative studies* (pp. 288–305). Hershey, PA: IGI Global. doi:10.4018/978-1-60566-282-4.ch015

Jiao, Y., Hurson, A. R., Potok, T. E., & Beckerman, B. G. (2009). Integrating mobile-based systems with healthcare databases. In J. Erickson (Ed.), *Database technologies: Concepts, methodologies, tools, and applications* (pp. 484–504). Hershey, PA: IGI Global. doi:10.4018/978-1-60566-058-5.ch031

Joia, L. A. (2002). A systematic model to integrate information technology into metabusinesses: A case study in the engineering realms. In F. Tan (Ed.), *Advanced topics in global information management* (Vol. 1, pp. 250–267). Hershey, PA: IGI Global. doi:10.4018/978-1-930708-43-3.ch016

Jones, T. H., & Song, I. (2000). Binary equivalents of ternary relationships in entity-relationship modeling: A logical decomposition approach. *Journal of Database Management*, *11*(2), 12–19. doi:10.4018/jdm.2000040102

Juana-Espinosa, S. D. (2007). Empirical study of the municipalitites' motivations for adopting online presence. In L. Al-Hakim (Ed.), *Global e-government: Theory, applications and benchmarking* (pp. 261–279). Hershey, PA: IGI Global. doi:10.4018/978-1-59904-027-1.ch015

Jun, K., & Weare, C. (2012). Bridging from e-government practice to e-government research: Past trends and future directions. In K. Bwalya & S. Zulu (Eds.), *Handbook of research on e-government in emerging economies: Adoption, e-participation, and legal frameworks* (pp. 263–289). Hershey, PA: IGI Global. doi:10.4018/978-1-4666-0324-0.ch013

Junqueira, A., Diniz, E. H., & Fernandez, M. (2010). Electronic government implementation projects with multiple agencies: Analysis of the electronic invoice project under PMBOK framework. In J. Cordoba-Pachon & A. Ochoa-Arias (Eds.), *Systems thinking and e-participation: ICT in the governance of society* (pp. 135–153). Hershey, PA: IGI Global. doi:10.4018/978-1-60566-860-4.ch009

Juntunen, A. (2009). Joint service development with the local authorities. In C. Reddick (Ed.), *Handbook of research on strategies for local e-government adoption and implementation: Comparative studies* (pp. 902–920). Hershey, PA: IGI Global. doi:10.4018/978-1-60566-282-4.ch047

Kamel, S. (2001). *Using DSS for crisis management*. Hershey, PA: IGI Global. doi:10.4018/978-1-87828-961-2.ch020

Kamel, S. (2006). DSS for strategic decision making. In M. Khosrow-Pour (Ed.), *Cases on information technology and organizational politics & culture* (pp. 230–246). Hershey, PA: IGI Global. doi:10.4018/978-1-59904-411-8.ch015

Kamel, S. (2009). The software industry in Egypt as a potential contributor to economic growth. In M. Khosrow-Pour (Ed.), *Encyclopedia of information science and technology* (2nd ed.; pp. 3531–3537). Hershey, PA: IGI Global. doi:10.4018/978-1-60566-026-4.ch562

Kamel, S., & Hussein, M. (2008). Xceed: Pioneering the contact center industry in Egypt. *Journal of Cases on Information Technology*, *10*(1), 67–91. doi:10.4018/jcit.2008010105

Kamel, S., & Wahba, K. (2003). The use of a hybrid model in web-based education: "The Global campus project. In A. Aggarwal (Ed.), *Web-based education: Learning from experience* (pp. 331–346). Hershey, PA: IGI Global. doi:10.4018/978-1-59140-102-5.ch020

Kardaras, D. K., & Papathanassiou, E. A. (2008). An exploratory study of the e-government services in Greece. In G. Garson & M. Khosrow-Pour (Eds.), *Handbook of research on public information technology* (pp. 162–174). Hershey, PA: IGI Global. doi:10.4018/978-1-59904-857-4.ch016

Kassahun, A. E., Molla, A., & Sarkar, P. (2012). Government process reengineering: What we know and what we need to know. In *Digital democracy: Concepts, methodologies, tools, and applications* (pp. 1730–1752). Hershey, PA: IGI Global. doi:10.4018/978-1-4666-1740-7.ch086

Khan, B. (2005). Technological issues. In B. Khan (Ed.), *Managing e-learning strategies: Design, delivery, implementation and evaluation* (pp. 154–180). Hershey, PA: IGI Global. doi:10.4018/978-1-59140-634-1.ch004

Khasawneh, A., Bsoul, M., Obeidat, I., & Al Azzam, I. (2012). Technology fears: A study of e-commerce loyalty perception by Jordanian customers. In J. Wang (Ed.), *Advancing the service sector with evolving technologies: Techniques and principles* (pp. 158–165). Hershey, PA: IGI Global. doi:10.4018/978-1-4666-0044-7.ch010

Khatibi, V., & Montazer, G. A. (2012). E-research methodology. In A. Juan, T. Daradoumis, M. Roca, S. Grasman, & J. Faulin (Eds.), *Collaborative and distributed e-research: Innovations in technologies, strategies and applications* (pp. 62–81). Hershey, PA: IGI Global. doi:10.4018/978-1-4666-0125-3.ch003

Kidd, T. (2011). The dragon in the school's backyard: A review of literature on the uses of technology in urban schools. In L. Tomei (Ed.), *Online courses and ICT in education: Emerging practices and applications* (pp. 242–257). Hershey, PA: IGI Global. doi:10.4018/978-1-60960-150-8.ch019

Kidd, T. T. (2010). My experience tells the story: Exploring technology adoption from a qualitative perspective - A pilot study. In H. Song & T. Kidd (Eds.), *Handbook of research on human performance and instructional technology* (pp. 247–262). Hershey, PA: IGI Global. doi:10.4018/978-1-60566-782-9.ch015

Kieley, B., Lane, G., Paquet, G., & Roy, J. (2002). e-Government in Canada: Services online or public service renewal? In Å. Grönlund (Ed.), Electronic government: Design, applications and management (pp. 340-355). Hershey, PA: IGI Global. doi:10.4018/978-1-930708-19-8.ch016

Kim, P. (2012). "Stay out of the way! My kid is video blogging through a phone!": A lesson learned from math tutoring social media for children in underserved communities. In *Wireless technologies: Concepts, methodologies, tools and applications* (pp. 1415–1428). Hershey, PA: IGI Global. doi:10.4018/978-1-61350-101-6.ch517

Kirlidog, M. (2010). Financial aspects of national ICT strategies. In S. Kamel (Ed.), *E-strategies for technological diffusion and adoption: National ICT approaches for socioeconomic development* (pp. 277–292). Hershey, PA: IGI Global. doi:10.4018/978-1-60566-388-3.ch016

Kisielnicki, J. (2006). Transfer of information and knowledge in the project management. In E. Coakes & S. Clarke (Eds.), *Encyclopedia of communities of practice in information and knowledge management* (pp. 544–551). Hershey, PA: IGI Global. doi:10.4018/978-1-59140-556-6.ch091

Kittner, M., & Van Slyke, C. (2006). Reorganizing information technology services in an academic environment. In M. Khosrow-Pour (Ed.), *Cases on the human side of information technology* (pp. 49–66). Hershey, PA: IGI Global. doi:10.4018/978-1-59904-405-7.ch004

Knoell, H. D. (2008). Semi virtual workplaces in German financial service enterprises. In P. Zemliansky & K. St. Amant (Eds.), *Handbook of research on virtual workplaces and the new nature of business practices* (pp. 570–581). Hershey, PA: IGI Global. doi:10.4018/978-1-59904-893-2.ch041

Koh, S. L., & Maguire, S. (2009). Competing in the age of information technology in a developing economy: Experiences of an Indian bank. In S. Koh & S. Maguire (Eds.), *Information and communication technologies management in turbulent business environments* (pp. 326–350). Hershey, PA: IGI Global. doi:10.4018/978-1-60566-424-8.ch018

Kollmann, T., & Häsel, M. (2009). Competence of information technology professionals in internet-based ventures. In I. Lee (Ed.), *Electronic business: Concepts, methodologies, tools, and applications* (pp. 1905–1919). Hershey, PA: IGI Global. doi:10.4018/978-1-60566-056-1.ch118

Kollmann, T., & Häsel, M. (2009). Competence of information technology professionals in internet-based ventures. In A. Cater-Steel (Ed.), *Information technology governance and service management: Frameworks and adaptations* (pp. 239–253). Hershey, PA: IGI Global. doi:10.4018/978-1-60566-008-0.ch013

Kollmann, T., & Häsel, M. (2010). Competence of information technology professionals in internet-based ventures. In *Electronic services: Concepts, methodologies, tools and applications* (pp. 1551–1565). Hershey, PA: IGI Global. doi:10.4018/978-1-61520-967-5.ch094

Kraemer, K., & King, J. L. (2006). Information technology and administrative reform: Will e-government be different? *International Journal of Electronic Government Research*, 2(1), 1–20. doi:10.4018/jegr.2006010101

Kraemer, K., & King, J. L. (2008). Information technology and administrative reform: Will e-government be different? In D. Norris (Ed.), *E-government research: Policy and management* (pp. 1–20). Hershey, PA: IGI Global. doi:10.4018/978-1-59904-913-7.ch001

Lampathaki, F., Tsiakaliaris, C., Stasis, A., & Charalabidis, Y. (2011). National interoperability frameworks: The way forward. In Y. Charalabidis (Ed.), *Interoperability in digital public services and administration: Bridging e-government and e-business* (pp. 1–24). Hershey, PA: IGI Global. doi:10.4018/978-1-61520-887-6.ch001

Lan, Z., & Scott, C. R. (1996). The relative importance of computer-mediated information versus conventional non-computer-mediated information in public managerial decision making. *Information Resources Management Journal*, *9*(1), 27–0. doi:10.4018/irmj.1996010103

Law, W. (2004). *Public sector data management in a developing economy.* Hershey, PA: IGI Global. doi:10.4018/978-1-59140-259-6.ch034

Law, W. K. (2005). Information resources development challenges in a cross-cultural environment. In M. Khosrow-Pour (Ed.), *Encyclopedia of information science and technology* (pp. 1476–1481). Hershey, PA: IGI Global. doi:10.4018/978-1-59140-553-5.ch259

Law, W. K. (2009). Cross-cultural challenges for information resources management. In M. Khosrow-Pour (Ed.), *Encyclopedia of information science and technology* (2nd ed.; pp. 840–846). Hershey, PA: IGI Global. doi:10.4018/978-1-60566-026-4.ch136

Law, W. K. (2011). Cross-cultural challenges for information resources management. In *Global business: Concepts, methodologies, tools and applications* (pp. 1924–1932). Hershey, PA: IGI Global. doi:10.4018/978-1-60960-587-2.ch704

Malkia, M., & Savolainen, R. (2004). eTransformation in government, politics and society: Conceptual framework and introduction. In M. Malkia, A. Anttiroiko, & R. Savolainen (Eds.), eTransformation in governance: New directions in government and politics (pp. 1-21). Hershey, PA: IGI Global. doi:10.4018/978-1-59140-130-8.ch001

Mandujano, S. (2011). Network manageability security. In D. Kar & M. Syed (Eds.), *Network security, administration and management: Advancing technology and practice* (pp. 158–181). Hershey, PA: IGI Global. doi:10.4018/978-1-60960-777-7.ch009

Marich, M. J., Schooley, B. L., & Horan, T. A. (2012). A normative enterprise architecture for guiding end-to-end emergency response decision support. In M. Jennex (Ed.), *Managing crises and disasters with emerging technologies: Advancements* (pp. 71–87). Hershey, PA: IGI Global. doi:10.4018/978-1-4666-0167-3.ch006

Markov, R., & Okujava, S. (2008). Costs, benefits, and risks of e-government portals. In G. Putnik & M. Cruz-Cunha (Eds.), *Encyclopedia of networked and virtual organizations* (pp. 354–363). Hershey, PA: IGI Global. doi:10.4018/978-1-59904-885-7.ch047

Martin, N., & Rice, J. (2013). Evaluating and designing electronic government for the future: Observations and insights from Australia. In V. Weerakkody (Ed.), *E-government services design, adoption, and evaluation* (pp. 238–258). Hershey, PA: IGI Global. doi:10.4018/978-1-4666-2458-0.ch014

i.   Martinez, A. C. (2008). Accessing administration's information via internet in Spain. In F. Tan (Ed.), *Global information technologies: Concepts, methodologies, tools, and applications* (pp. 2558–2573). Hershey, PA: IGI Global. doi:10.4018/978-1-59904-939-7.ch186

Mbarika, V. W., Meso, P. N., & Musa, P. F. (2006). A disconnect in stakeholders' perceptions from emerging realities of teledensity growth in Africa's least developed countries. In M. Hunter & F. Tan (Eds.), *Advanced topics in global information management* (Vol. 5, pp. 263–282). Hershey, PA: IGI Global. doi:10.4018/978-1-59140-923-6.ch012

Mbarika, V. W., Meso, P. N., & Musa, P. F. (2008). A disconnect in stakeholders' perceptions from emerging realities of teledensity growth in Africa's least developed countries. In F. Tan (Ed.), *Global information technologies: Concepts, methodologies, tools, and applications* (pp. 2948–2962). Hershey, PA: IGI Global. doi:10.4018/978-1-59904-939-7.ch209

Means, T., Olson, E., & Spooner, J. (2013). Discovering ways that don't work on the road to success: Strengths and weaknesses revealed by an active learning studio classroom project. In A. Benson, J. Moore, & S. Williams van Rooij (Eds.), *Cases on educational technology planning, design, and implementation: A project management perspective* (pp. 94–113). Hershey, PA: IGI Global. doi:10.4018/978-1-4666-4237-9.ch006

Melitski, J., Holzer, M., Kim, S., Kim, C., & Rho, S. (2008). Digital government worldwide: An e-government assessment of municipal web sites. In G. Garson & M. Khosrow-Pour (Eds.), *Handbook of research on public information technology* (pp. 790–804). Hershey, PA: IGI Global. doi:10.4018/978-1-59904-857-4.ch069

Memmola, M., Palumbo, G., & Rossini, M. (2009). Web & RFID technology: New frontiers in costing and process management for rehabilitation medicine. In L. Al-Hakim & M. Memmola (Eds.), *Business web strategy: Design, alignment, and application* (pp. 145–169). Hershey, PA: IGI Global. doi:10.4018/978-1-60566-024-0.ch008

Meng, Z., Fahong, Z., & Lei, L. (2008). Information technology and environment. In Y. Kurihara, S. Takaya, H. Harui, & H. Kamae (Eds.), *Information technology and economic development* (pp. 201–212). Hershey, PA: IGI Global. doi:10.4018/978-1-59904-579-5.ch014

Mentzingen de Moraes, A. J., Ferneda, E., Costa, I., & Spinola, M. D. (2011). Practical approach for implementation of governance process in IT: Information technology areas. In N. Shi & G. Silvius (Eds.), *Enterprise IT governance, business value and performance measurement* (pp. 19–40). Hershey, PA: IGI Global. doi:10.4018/978-1-60566-346-3.ch002

Merwin, G. A. Jr, McDonald, J. S., & Odera, L. C. (2008). Economic development: Government's cutting edge in IT. In M. Raisinghani (Ed.), *Handbook of research on global information technology management in the digital economy* (pp. 1–37). Hershey, PA: IGI Global. doi:10.4018/978-1-59904-875-8.ch001

Meso, P., & Duncan, N. (2002). Can national information infrastructures enhance social development in the least developed countries? An empirical investigation. In M. Dadashzadeh (Ed.), *Information technology management in developing countries* (pp. 23–51). Hershey, PA: IGI Global. doi:10.4018/978-1-931777-03-2.ch002

Meso, P. N., & Duncan, N. B. (2002). Can national information infrastructures enhance social development in the least developed countries? In F. Tan (Ed.), *Advanced topics in global information management* (Vol. 1, pp. 207–226). Hershey, PA: IGI Global. doi:10.4018/978-1-930708-43-3.ch014

Middleton, M. (2008). Evaluation of e-government web sites. In G. Garson & M. Khosrow-Pour (Eds.), *Handbook of research on public information technology* (pp. 699–710). Hershey, PA: IGI Global. doi:10.4018/978-1-59904-857-4.ch063

Mingers, J. (2010). Pluralism, realism, and truth: The keys to knowledge in information systems research. In D. Paradice (Ed.), *Emerging systems approaches in information technologies: Concepts, theories, and applications* (pp. 86–98). Hershey, PA: IGI Global. doi:10.4018/978-1-60566-976-2.ch006

Mital, K. M. (2012). ICT, unique identity and inclusive growth: An Indian perspective. In A. Manoharan & M. Holzer (Eds.), *E-governance and civic engagement: Factors and determinants of e-democracy* (pp. 584–612). Hershey, PA: IGI Global. doi:10.4018/978-1-61350-083-5.ch029

Mizell, A. P. (2008). Helping close the digital divide for financially disadvantaged seniors. In F. Tan (Ed.), *Global information technologies: Concepts, methodologies, tools, and applications* (pp. 2396–2402). Hershey, PA: IGI Global. doi:10.4018/978-1-59904-939-7.ch173

Molinari, F., Wills, C., Koumpis, A., & Moumtzi, V. (2011). A citizen-centric platform to support networking in the area of e-democracy. In H. Rahman (Ed.), *Cases on adoption, diffusion and evaluation of global e-governance systems: Impact at the grass roots* (pp. 282–302). Hershey, PA: IGI Global. doi:10.4018/978-1-61692-814-8.ch014

Molinari, F., Wills, C., Koumpis, A., & Moumtzi, V. (2013). A citizen-centric platform to support networking in the area of e-democracy. In H. Rahman (Ed.), *Cases on progressions and challenges in ICT utilization for citizen-centric governance* (pp. 265–297). Hershey, PA: IGI Global. doi:10.4018/978-1-4666-2071-1.ch013

Monteverde, F. (2010). The process of e-government public policy inclusion in the governmental agenda: A framework for assessment and case study. In J. Cordoba-Pachon & A. Ochoa-Arias (Eds.), *Systems thinking and e-participation: ICT in the governance of society* (pp. 233–245). Hershey, PA: IGI Global. doi:10.4018/978-1-60566-860-4.ch015

Moodley, S. (2008). Deconstructing the South African government's ICT for development discourse. In A. Anttiroiko (Ed.), *Electronic government: Concepts, methodologies, tools, and applications* (pp. 622–631). Hershey, PA: IGI Global. doi:10.4018/978-1-59904-947-2.ch053

Moodley, S. (2008). Deconstructing the South African government's ICT for development discourse. In C. Van Slyke (Ed.), *Information communication technologies: Concepts, methodologies, tools, and applications* (pp. 816–825). Hershey, PA: IGI Global. doi:10.4018/978-1-59904-949-6.ch052

Mora, M., Cervantes-Perez, F., Gelman-Muravchik, O., Forgionne, G. A., & Mejia-Olvera, M. (2003). DMSS implementation research: A conceptual analysis of the contributions and limitations of the factor-based and stage-based streams. In G. Forgionne, J. Gupta, & M. Mora (Eds.), *Decision-making support systems: Achievements and challenges for the new decade* (pp. 331–356). Hershey, PA: IGI Global. doi:10.4018/978-1-59140-045-5.ch020

Mörtberg, C., & Elovaara, P. (2010). Attaching people and technology: Between e and government. In S. Booth, S. Goodman, & G. Kirkup (Eds.), *Gender issues in learning and working with information technology: Social constructs and cultural contexts* (pp. 83–98). Hershey, PA: IGI Global. doi:10.4018/978-1-61520-813-5. ch005

Murphy, J., Harper, E., Devine, E. C., Burke, L. J., & Hook, M. L. (2011). Case study: Lessons learned when embedding evidence-based knowledge in a nurse care planning and documentation system. In A. Cashin & R. Cook (Eds.), *Evidence-based practice in nursing informatics: Concepts and applications* (pp. 174–190). Hershey, PA: IGI Global. doi:10.4018/978-1-60960-034-1.ch014

Mutula, S. M. (2013). E-government's role in poverty alleviation: Case study of South Africa. In H. Rahman (Ed.), *Cases on progressions and challenges in ICT utilization for citizen-centric governance* (pp. 44–68). Hershey, PA: IGI Global. doi:10.4018/978-1-4666-2071-1.ch003

Nath, R., & Angeles, R. (2005). Relationships between supply characteristics and buyer-supplier coupling in e-procurement: An empirical analysis. *International Journal of E-Business Research*, *1*(2), 40–55. doi:10.4018/jebr.2005040103

Nissen, M. E. (2006). Application cases in government. In M. Nissen (Ed.), *Harnessing knowledge dynamics: Principled organizational knowing & learning* (pp. 152–181). Hershey, PA: IGI Global. doi:10.4018/978-1-59140-773-7.ch008

Norris, D. F. (2003). Leading-edge information technologies and American local governments. In G. Garson (Ed.), *Public information technology: Policy and management issues* (pp. 139–169). Hershey, PA: IGI Global. doi:10.4018/978-1-59140-060-8.ch007

Norris, D. F. (2008). Information technology among U.S. local governments. In G. Garson & M. Khosrow-Pour (Eds.), *Handbook of research on public information technology* (pp. 132–144). Hershey, PA: IGI Global. doi:10.4018/978-1-59904-857-4.ch013

Northrop, A. (1999). The challenge of teaching information technology in public administration graduate programs. In G. Garson (Ed.), *Information technology and computer applications in public administration: Issues and trends* (pp. 1–22). Hershey, PA: IGI Global. doi:10.4018/978-1-87828-952-0.ch001

Northrop, A. (2003). Information technology and public administration: The view from the profession. In G. Garson (Ed.), *Public information technology: Policy and management issues* (pp. 1–19). Hershey, PA: IGI Global. doi:10.4018/978-1-59140-060-8.ch001

Northrop, A. (2007). Lip service? How PA journals and textbooks view information technology. In G. Garson (Ed.), *Modern public information technology systems: Issues and challenges* (pp. 1–16). Hershey, PA: IGI Global. doi:10.4018/978-1-59904-051-6.ch001

Null, E. (2013). Legal and political barriers to municipal networks in the United States. In A. Abdelaal (Ed.), *Social and economic effects of community wireless networks and infrastructures* (pp. 27–56). Hershey, PA: IGI Global. doi:10.4018/978-1-4666-2997-4.ch003

Okunoye, A., Frolick, M., & Crable, E. (2006). ERP implementation in higher education: An account of pre-implementation and implementation phases. *Journal of Cases on Information Technology, 8*(2), 110–132. doi:10.4018/jcit.2006040106

Olasina, G. (2012). A review of egovernment services in Nigeria. In A. Tella & A. Issa (Eds.), *Library and information science in developing countries: Contemporary issues* (pp. 205–221). Hershey, PA: IGI Global. doi:10.4018/978-1-61350-335-5.ch015

Orgeron, C. P. (2008). A model for reengineering IT job classes in state government. In G. Garson & M. Khosrow-Pour (Eds.), *Handbook of research on public information technology* (pp. 735–746). Hershey, PA: IGI Global. doi:10.4018/978-1-59904-857-4.ch066

Owsinski, J. W., & Pielak, A. M. (2011). Local authority websites in rural areas: Measuring quality and functionality, and assessing the role. In Z. Andreopoulou, B. Manos, N. Polman, & D. Viaggi (Eds.), *Agricultural and environmental informatics, governance and management: Emerging research applications* (pp. 39–60). Hershey, PA: IGI Global. doi:10.4018/978-1-60960-621-3.ch003

Owsiński, J. W., Pielak, A. M., Sęp, K., & Stańczak, J. (2014). Local web-based networks in rural municipalities: Extension, density, and meaning. In Z. Andreopoulou, V. Samathrakis, S. Louca, & M. Vlachopoulou (Eds.), *E-innovation for sustainable development of rural resources during global economic crisis* (pp. 126–151). Hershey, PA: IGI Global. doi:10.4018/978-1-4666-4550-9.ch011

Pagani, M., & Pasinetti, C. (2008). Technical and functional quality in the development of t-government services. In A. Anttiroiko (Ed.), *Electronic government: Concepts, methodologies, tools, and applications* (pp. 2943–2965). Hershey, PA: IGI Global. doi:10.4018/978-1-59904-947-2.ch220

Pani, A. K., & Agrahari, A. (2005). On e-markets in emerging economy: An Indian experience. In M. Khosrow-Pour (Ed.), *Advanced topics in electronic commerce* (Vol. 1, pp. 287–299). Hershey, PA: IGI Global. doi:10.4018/978-1-59140-819-2.ch015

Related References

Papadopoulos, T., Angelopoulos, S., & Kitsios, F. (2011). A strategic approach to e-health interoperability using e-government frameworks. In A. Lazakidou, K. Siassiakos, & K. Ioannou (Eds.), *Wireless technologies for ambient assisted living and healthcare: Systems and applications* (pp. 213–229). Hershey, PA: IGI Global. doi:10.4018/978-1-61520-805-0.ch012

Papadopoulos, T., Angelopoulos, S., & Kitsios, F. (2013). A strategic approach to e-health interoperability using e-government frameworks. In *User-driven healthcare: Concepts, methodologies, tools, and applications* (pp. 791–807). Hershey, PA: IGI Global. doi:10.4018/978-1-4666-2770-3.ch039

Papaleo, G., Chiarella, D., Aiello, M., & Caviglione, L. (2012). Analysis, development and deployment of statistical anomaly detection techniques for real e-mail traffic. In T. Chou (Ed.), *Information assurance and security technologies for risk assessment and threat management: Advances* (pp. 47–71). Hershey, PA: IGI Global. doi:10.4018/978-1-61350-507-6.ch003

Papp, R. (2003). Information technology & FDA compliance in the pharmaceutical industry. In M. Khosrow-Pour (Ed.), *Annals of cases on information technology* (Vol. 5, pp. 262–273). Hershey, PA: IGI Global. doi:10.4018/978-1-59140-061-5.ch017

Parsons, T. W. (2007). Developing a knowledge management portal. In A. Tatnall (Ed.), *Encyclopedia of portal technologies and applications* (pp. 223–227). Hershey, PA: IGI Global. doi:10.4018/978-1-59140-989-2.ch039

Passaris, C. E. (2007). Immigration and digital government. In A. Anttiroiko & M. Malkia (Eds.), *Encyclopedia of digital government* (pp. 988–994). Hershey, PA: IGI Global. doi:10.4018/978-1-59140-789-8.ch148

Pavlichev, A. (2004). The e-government challenge for public administration. In A. Pavlichev & G. Garson (Eds.), *Digital government: Principles and best practices* (pp. 276–290). Hershey, PA: IGI Global. doi:10.4018/978-1-59140-122-3.ch018

Penrod, J. I., & Harbor, A. F. (2000). Designing and implementing a learning organization-oriented information technology planning and management process. In L. Petrides (Ed.), *Case studies on information technology in higher education: Implications for policy and practice* (pp. 7–19). Hershey, PA: IGI Global. doi:10.4018/978-1-878289-74-2.ch001

Planas-Silva, M. D., & Joseph, R. C. (2011). Perspectives on the adoption of electronic resources for use in clinical trials. In M. Guah (Ed.), *Healthcare delivery reform and new technologies: Organizational initiatives* (pp. 19–28). Hershey, PA: IGI Global. doi:10.4018/978-1-60960-183-6.ch002

Pomazalová, N., & Rejman, S. (2013). The rationale behind implementation of new electronic tools for electronic public procurement. In N. Pomazalová (Ed.), *Public sector transformation processes and internet public procurement: Decision support systems* (pp. 85–117). Hershey, PA: IGI Global. doi:10.4018/978-1-4666-2665-2. ch006

Postorino, M. N. (2012). City competitiveness and airport: Information science perspective. In M. Bulu (Ed.), *City competitiveness and improving urban subsystems: Technologies and applications* (pp. 61–83). Hershey, PA: IGI Global. doi:10.4018/978-1-61350-174-0.ch004

Poupa, C. (2002). Electronic government in Switzerland: Priorities for 2001-2005 - Electronic voting and federal portal. In Å. Grönlund (Ed.), *Electronic government: Design, applications and management* (pp. 356–369). Hershey, PA: IGI Global. doi:10.4018/978-1-930708-19-8.ch017

Powell, S. R. (2010). Interdisciplinarity in telecommunications and networking. In *Networking and telecommunications: Concepts, methodologies, tools and applications* (pp. 33–40). Hershey, PA: IGI Global. doi:10.4018/978-1-60566-986-1.ch004

Priya, P. S., & Mathiyalagan, N. (2011). A study of the implementation status of two e-governance projects in land revenue administration in India. In M. Shareef, V. Kumar, U. Kumar, & Y. Dwivedi (Eds.), *Stakeholder adoption of e-government services: Driving and resisting factors* (pp. 214–230). Hershey, PA: IGI Global. doi:10.4018/978-1-60960-601-5.ch011

Prysby, C., & Prysby, N. (2000). Electronic mail, employee privacy and the workplace. In L. Janczewski (Ed.), *Internet and intranet security management: Risks and solutions* (pp. 251–270). Hershey, PA: IGI Global. doi:10.4018/978-1-878289-71-1.ch009

Prysby, C. L., & Prysby, N. D. (2003). Electronic mail in the public workplace: Issues of privacy and public disclosure. In G. Garson (Ed.), *Public information technology: Policy and management issues* (pp. 271–298). Hershey, PA: IGI Global. doi:10.4018/978-1-59140-060-8.ch012

Prysby, C. L., & Prysby, N. D. (2007). You have mail, but who is reading it? Issues of e-mail in the public workplace. In G. Garson (Ed.), *Modern public information technology systems: Issues and challenges* (pp. 312–336). Hershey, PA: IGI Global. doi:10.4018/978-1-59904-051-6.ch016

Radl, A., & Chen, Y. (2005). Computer security in electronic government: A state-local education information system. *International Journal of Electronic Government Research, 1*(1), 79–99. doi:10.4018/jegr.2005010105

Rahman, H. (2008). Information dynamics in developing countries. In C. Van Slyke (Ed.), *Information communication technologies: Concepts, methodologies, tools, and applications* (pp. 104–114). Hershey, PA: IGI Global. doi:10.4018/978-1-59904-949-6.ch008

Ramanathan, J. (2009). Adaptive IT architecture as a catalyst for network capability in government. In P. Saha (Ed.), *Advances in government enterprise architecture* (pp. 149–172). Hershey, PA: IGI Global. doi:10.4018/978-1-60566-068-4.ch007

Ramos, I., & Berry, D. M. (2006). Social construction of information technology supporting work. In M. Khosrow-Pour (Ed.), *Cases on information technology: Lessons learned* (Vol. 7, pp. 36–52). Hershey, PA: IGI Global. doi:10.4018/978-1-59140-673-0.ch003

Ray, D., Gulla, U., Gupta, M. P., & Dash, S. S. (2009). Interoperability and constituents of interoperable systems in public sector. In V. Weerakkody, M. Janssen, & Y. Dwivedi (Eds.), *Handbook of research on ICT-enabled transformational government: A global perspective* (pp. 175–195). Hershey, PA: IGI Global. doi:10.4018/978-1-60566-390-6.ch010

Reddick, C. G. (2007). E-government and creating a citizen-centric government: A study of federal government CIOs. In G. Garson (Ed.), *Modern public information technology systems: Issues and challenges* (pp. 143–165). Hershey, PA: IGI Global. doi:10.4018/978-1-59904-051-6.ch008

Reddick, C. G. (2010). Citizen-centric e-government. In C. Reddick (Ed.), *Homeland security preparedness and information systems: Strategies for managing public policy* (pp. 45–75). Hershey, PA: IGI Global. doi:10.4018/978-1-60566-834-5.ch002

Reddick, C. G. (2010). E-government and creating a citizen-centric government: A study of federal government CIOs. In C. Reddick (Ed.), *Homeland security preparedness and information systems: Strategies for managing public policy* (pp. 230–250). Hershey, PA: IGI Global. doi:10.4018/978-1-60566-834-5.ch012

Reddick, C. G. (2010). Perceived effectiveness of e-government and its usage in city governments: Survey evidence from information technology directors. In C. Reddick (Ed.), *Homeland security preparedness and information systems: Strategies for managing public policy* (pp. 213–229). Hershey, PA: IGI Global. doi:10.4018/978-1-60566-834-5.ch011

Reddick, C. G. (2012). Customer relationship management adoption in local governments in the United States. In S. Chhabra & M. Kumar (Eds.), *Strategic enterprise resource planning models for e-government: Applications and methodologies* (pp. 111–124). Hershey, PA: IGI Global. doi:10.4018/978-1-60960-863-7.ch008

Reeder, F. S., & Pandy, S. M. (2008). Identifying effective funding models for e-government. In A. Anttiroiko (Ed.), *Electronic government: Concepts, methodologies, tools, and applications* (pp. 1108–1138). Hershey, PA: IGI Global. doi:10.4018/978-1-59904-947-2.ch083

Riesco, D., Acosta, E., & Montejano, G. (2003). An extension to a UML activity graph from workflow. In L. Favre (Ed.), *UML and the unified process* (pp. 294–314). Hershey, PA: IGI Global. doi:10.4018/978-1-93177-744-5.ch015

Ritzhaupt, A. D., & Gill, T. G. (2008). A hybrid and novel approach to teaching computer programming in MIS curriculum. In S. Negash, M. Whitman, A. Woszczynski, K. Hoganson, & H. Mattord (Eds.), *Handbook of distance learning for real-time and asynchronous information technology education* (pp. 259–281). Hershey, PA: IGI Global. doi:10.4018/978-1-59904-964-9.ch014

Roche, E. M. (1993). International computing and the international regime. *Journal of Global Information Management, 1*(2), 33–44. doi:10.4018/jgim.1993040103

Rocheleau, B. (2007). Politics, accountability, and information management. In G. Garson (Ed.), *Modern public information technology systems: Issues and challenges* (pp. 35–71). Hershey, PA: IGI Global. doi:10.4018/978-1-59904-051-6.ch003

Rodrigues Filho, J. (2010). E-government in Brazil: Reinforcing dominant institutions or reducing citizenship? In C. Reddick (Ed.), *Politics, democracy and e-government: Participation and service delivery* (pp. 347–362). Hershey, PA: IGI Global. doi:10.4018/978-1-61520-933-0.ch021

Rodriguez, S. R., & Thorp, D. A. (2013). eLearning for industry: A case study of the project management process. In A. Benson, J. Moore, & S. Williams van Rooij (Eds.), Cases on educational technology planning, design, and implementation: A project management perspective (pp. 319-342). Hershey, PA: IGI Global. doi:10.4018/978-1-4666-4237-9.ch017

Roman, A. V. (2013). Delineating three dimensions of e-government success: Security, functionality, and transformation. In J. Gil-Garcia (Ed.), *E-government success factors and measures: Theories, concepts, and methodologies* (pp. 171–192). Hershey, PA: IGI Global. doi:10.4018/978-1-4666-4058-0.ch010

Ross, S. C., Tyran, C. K., & Auer, D. J. (2008). Up in smoke: Rebuilding after an IT disaster. In H. Nemati (Ed.), *Information security and ethics: Concepts, methodologies, tools, and applications* (pp. 3659–3675). Hershey, PA: IGI Global. doi:10.4018/978-1-59904-937-3.ch248

Ross, S. C., Tyran, C. K., Auer, D. J., Junell, J. M., & Williams, T. G. (2005). Up in smoke: Rebuilding after an IT disaster. *Journal of Cases on Information Technology*, 7(2), 31–49. doi:10.4018/jcit.2005040103

Roy, J. (2008). Security, sovereignty, and continental interoperability: Canada's elusive balance. In T. Loendorf & G. Garson (Eds.), *Patriotic information systems* (pp. 153–176). Hershey, PA: IGI Global. doi:10.4018/978-1-59904-594-8.ch007

Rubeck, R. F., & Miller, G. A. (2009). vGOV: Remote video access to government services. In A. Scupola (Ed.), Cases on managing e-services (pp. 253-268). Hershey, PA: IGI Global. doi:10.4018/978-1-60566-064-6.ch017

Saekow, A., & Boonmee, C. (2011). The challenges of implementing e-government interoperability in Thailand: Case of official electronic correspondence letters exchange across government departments. In Y. Charalabidis (Ed.), *Interoperability in digital public services and administration: Bridging e-government and e-business* (pp. 40–61). Hershey, PA: IGI Global. doi:10.4018/978-1-61520-887-6.ch003

Saekow, A., & Boonmee, C. (2012). The challenges of implementing e-government interoperability in Thailand: Case of official electronic correspondence letters exchange across government departments. In *Digital democracy: Concepts, methodologies, tools, and applications* (pp. 1883–1905). Hershey, PA: IGI Global. doi:10.4018/978-1-4666-1740-7.ch094

Sagsan, M., & Medeni, T. (2012). Understanding "knowledge management (KM) paradigms" from social media perspective: An empirical study on discussion group for KM at professional networking site. In M. Cruz-Cunha, P. Gonçalves, N. Lopes, E. Miranda, & G. Putnik (Eds.), *Handbook of research on business social networking: Organizational, managerial, and technological dimensions* (pp. 738–755). Hershey, PA: IGI Global. doi:10.4018/978-1-61350-168-9.ch039

Sahi, G., & Madan, S. (2013). Information security threats in ERP enabled e-governance: Challenges and solutions. In *Enterprise resource planning: Concepts, methodologies, tools, and applications* (pp. 825–837). Hershey, PA: IGI Global. doi:10.4018/978-1-4666-4153-2.ch048

Sanford, C., & Bhattacherjee, A. (2008). IT implementation in a developing country municipality: A sociocognitive analysis. *International Journal of Technology and Human Interaction*, 4(3), 68–93. doi:10.4018/jthi.2008070104

Schelin, S. H. (2003). E-government: An overview. In G. Garson (Ed.), *Public information technology: Policy and management issues* (pp. 120–138). Hershey, PA: IGI Global. doi:10.4018/978-1-59140-060-8.ch006

Schelin, S. H. (2004). Training for digital government. In A. Pavlichev & G. Garson (Eds.), *Digital government: Principles and best practices* (pp. 263–275). Hershey, PA: IGI Global. doi:10.4018/978-1-59140-122-3.ch017

Schelin, S. H. (2007). E-government: An overview. In G. Garson (Ed.), *Modern public information technology systems: Issues and challenges* (pp. 110–126). Hershey, PA: IGI Global. doi:10.4018/978-1-59904-051-6.ch006

Schelin, S. H., & Garson, G. (2004). Theoretical justification of critical success factors. In G. Garson & S. Schelin (Eds.), *IT solutions series: Humanizing information technology: Advice from experts* (pp. 4–15). Hershey, PA: IGI Global. doi:10.4018/978-1-59140-245-9.ch002

Scime, A. (2002). Information systems and computer science model curricula: A comparative look. In M. Dadashzadeh, A. Saber, & S. Saber (Eds.), *Information technology education in the new millennium* (pp. 146–158). Hershey, PA: IGI Global. doi:10.4018/978-1-931777-05-6.ch018

Scime, A. (2009). Computing curriculum analysis and development. In M. Khosrow-Pour (Ed.), *Encyclopedia of information science and technology* (2nd ed.; pp. 667–671). Hershey, PA: IGI Global. doi:10.4018/978-1-60566-026-4.ch108

Scime, A., & Wania, C. (2008). Computing curricula: A comparison of models. In C. Van Slyke (Ed.), *Information communication technologies: Concepts, methodologies, tools, and applications* (pp. 1270–1283). Hershey, PA: IGI Global. doi:10.4018/978-1-59904-949-6.ch088

Seidman, S. B. (2009). An international perspective on professional software engineering credentials. In H. Ellis, S. Demurjian, & J. Naveda (Eds.), *Software engineering: Effective teaching and learning approaches and practices* (pp. 351–361). Hershey, PA: IGI Global. doi:10.4018/978-1-60566-102-5.ch018

Seifert, J. W. (2007). E-government act of 2002 in the United States. In A. Anttiroiko & M. Malkia (Eds.), *Encyclopedia of digital government* (pp. 476–481). Hershey, PA: IGI Global. doi:10.4018/978-1-59140-789-8.ch072

Seifert, J. W., & Relyea, H. C. (2008). E-government act of 2002 in the United States. In A. Anttiroiko (Ed.), *Electronic government: Concepts, methodologies, tools, and applications* (pp. 154–161). Hershey, PA: IGI Global. doi:10.4018/978-1-59904-947-2.ch013

Seufert, S. (2002). E-learning business models: Framework and best practice examples. In M. Raisinghani (Ed.), *Cases on worldwide e-commerce: Theory in action* (pp. 70–94). Hershey, PA: IGI Global. doi:10.4018/978-1-930708-27-3.ch004

Shareef, M. A., & Archer, N. (2012). E-government service development. In M. Shareef, N. Archer, & S. Dutta (Eds.), *E-government service maturity and development: Cultural, organizational and technological perspectives* (pp. 1–14). Hershey, PA: IGI Global. doi:10.4018/978-1-60960-848-4.ch001

Shareef, M. A., & Archer, N. (2012). E-government initiatives: Review studies on different countries. In M. Shareef, N. Archer, & S. Dutta (Eds.), *E-government service maturity and development: Cultural, organizational and technological perspectives* (pp. 40–76). Hershey, PA: IGI Global. doi:10.4018/978-1-60960-848-4.ch003

Shareef, M. A., Kumar, U., & Kumar, V. (2011). E-government development: Performance evaluation parameters. In M. Shareef, V. Kumar, U. Kumar, & Y. Dwivedi (Eds.), *Stakeholder adoption of e-government services: Driving and resisting factors* (pp. 197–213). Hershey, PA: IGI Global. doi:10.4018/978-1-60960-601-5.ch010

Shareef, M. A., Kumar, U., Kumar, V., & Niktash, M. (2012). Electronic-government vision: Case studies for objectives, strategies, and initiatives. In M. Shareef, N. Archer, & S. Dutta (Eds.), *E-government service maturity and development: Cultural, organizational and technological perspectives* (pp. 15–39). Hershey, PA: IGI Global. doi:10.4018/978-1-60960-848-4.ch002

Shukla, P., Kumar, A., & Anu Kumar, P. B. (2013). Impact of national culture on business continuity management system implementation. *International Journal of Risk and Contingency Management*, 2(3), 23–36. doi:10.4018/ijrcm.2013070102

Shulman, S. W. (2007). The federal docket management system and the prospect for digital democracy in U S rulemaking. In G. Garson (Ed.), *Modern public information technology systems: Issues and challenges* (pp. 166–184). Hershey, PA: IGI Global. doi:10.4018/978-1-59904-051-6.ch009

Simonovic, S. (2007). Problems of offline government in e-Serbia. In A. Anttiroiko & M. Malkia (Eds.), *Encyclopedia of digital government* (pp. 1342–1351). Hershey, PA: IGI Global. doi:10.4018/978-1-59140-789-8.ch205

Simonovic, S. (2008). Problems of offline government in e-Serbia. In A. Anttiroiko (Ed.), *Electronic government: Concepts, methodologies, tools, and applications* (pp. 2929–2942). Hershey, PA: IGI Global. doi:10.4018/978-1-59904-947-2.ch219

Singh, A. M. (2005). Information systems and technology in South Africa. In M. Khosrow-Pour (Ed.), *Encyclopedia of information science and technology* (pp. 1497–1502). Hershey, PA: IGI Global. doi:10.4018/978-1-59140-553-5.ch263

Singh, S., & Naidoo, G. (2005). Towards an e-government solution: A South African perspective. In W. Huang, K. Siau, & K. Wei (Eds.), *Electronic government strategies and implementation* (pp. 325–353). Hershey, PA: IGI Global. doi:10.4018/978-1-59140-348-7.ch014

Snoke, R., & Underwood, A. (2002). Generic attributes of IS graduates: An analysis of Australian views. In F. Tan (Ed.), *Advanced topics in global information management* (Vol. 1, pp. 370–384). Hershey, PA: IGI Global. doi:10.4018/978-1-930708-43-3.ch023

Sommer, L. (2006). Revealing unseen organizations in higher education: A study framework and application example. In A. Metcalfe (Ed.), *Knowledge management and higher education: A critical analysis* (pp. 115–146). Hershey, PA: IGI Global. doi:10.4018/978-1-59140-509-2.ch007

Song, H., Kidd, T., & Owens, E. (2011). Examining technological disparities and instructional practices in English language arts classroom: Implications for school leadership and teacher training. In L. Tomei (Ed.), *Online courses and ICT in education: Emerging practices and applications* (pp. 258–274). Hershey, PA: IGI Global. doi:10.4018/978-1-60960-150-8.ch020

Speaker, P. J., & Kleist, V. F. (2003). Using information technology to meet electronic commerce and MIS education demands. In A. Aggarwal (Ed.), *Web-based education: Learning from experience* (pp. 280–291). Hershey, PA: IGI Global. doi:10.4018/978-1-59140-102-5.ch017

Spitler, V. K. (2007). Learning to use IT in the workplace: Mechanisms and masters. In M. Mahmood (Ed.), *Contemporary issues in end user computing* (pp. 292–323). Hershey, PA: IGI Global. doi:10.4018/978-1-59140-926-7.ch013

Stellefson, M. (2011). Considerations for marketing distance education courses in health education: Five important questions to examine before development. In U. Demiray & S. Sever (Eds.), *Marketing online education programs: Frameworks for promotion and communication* (pp. 222–234). Hershey, PA: IGI Global. doi:10.4018/978-1-60960-074-7.ch014

Straub, D. W., & Loch, K. D. (2006). Creating and developing a program of global research. *Journal of Global Information Management, 14*(2), 1–28. doi:10.4018/jgim.2006040101

Straub, D. W., Loch, K. D., & Hill, C. E. (2002). Transfer of information technology to the Arab world: A test of cultural influence modeling. In M. Dadashzadeh (Ed.), *Information technology management in developing countries* (pp. 92–134). Hershey, PA: IGI Global. doi:10.4018/978-1-931777-03-2.ch005

Straub, D. W., Loch, K. D., & Hill, C. E. (2003). Transfer of information technology to the Arab world: A test of cultural influence modeling. In F. Tan (Ed.), *Advanced topics in global information management* (Vol. 2, pp. 141–172). Hershey, PA: IGI Global. doi:10.4018/978-1-59140-064-6.ch009

Suki, N. M., Ramayah, T., Ming, M. K., & Suki, N. M. (2013). Factors enhancing employed job seekers intentions to use social networking sites as a job search tool. In A. Mesquita (Ed.), *User perception and influencing factors of technology in everyday life* (pp. 265–281). Hershey, PA: IGI Global. doi:10.4018/978-1-4666-1954-8.ch018

Suomi, R. (2006). Introducing electronic patient records to hospitals: Innovation adoption paths. In T. Spil & R. Schuring (Eds.), *E-health systems diffusion and use: The innovation, the user and the use IT model* (pp. 128–146). Hershey, PA: IGI Global. doi:10.4018/978-1-59140-423-1.ch008

Swim, J., & Barker, L. (2012). Pathways into a gendered occupation: Brazilian women in IT. *International Journal of Social and Organizational Dynamics in IT*, *2*(4), 34–51. doi:10.4018/ijsodit.2012100103

Tarafdar, M., & Vaidya, S. D. (2006). Adoption and implementation of IT in developing nations: Experiences from two public sector enterprises in India. In M. Khosrow-Pour (Ed.), *Cases on information technology planning, design and implementation* (pp. 208–233). Hershey, PA: IGI Global. doi:10.4018/978-1-59904-408-8.ch013

Tarafdar, M., & Vaidya, S. D. (2008). Adoption and implementation of IT in developing nations: Experiences from two public sector enterprises in India. In G. Garson & M. Khosrow-Pour (Eds.), *Handbook of research on public information technology* (pp. 905–924). Hershey, PA: IGI Global. doi:10.4018/978-1-59904-857-4.ch076

Thesing, Z. (2007). Zarina thesing, pumpkin patch. In M. Hunter (Ed.), *Contemporary chief information officers: Management experiences* (pp. 83–94). Hershey, PA: IGI Global. doi:10.4018/978-1-59904-078-3.ch007

Thomas, J. C. (2004). Public involvement in public administration in the information age: Speculations on the effects of technology. In M. Malkia, A. Anttiroiko, & R. Savolainen (Eds.), *eTransformation in governance: New directions in government and politics* (pp. 67–84). Hershey, PA: IGI Global. doi:10.4018/978-1-59140-130-8.ch004

Treiblmaier, H., & Chong, S. (2013). Trust and perceived risk of personal information as antecedents of online information disclosure: Results from three countries. In F. Tan (Ed.), *Global diffusion and adoption of technologies for knowledge and information sharing* (pp. 341–361). Hershey, PA: IGI Global. doi:10.4018/978-1-4666-2142-8.ch015

van Grembergen, W., & de Haes, S. (2008). IT governance in practice: Six case studies. In W. van Grembergen & S. De Haes (Eds.), *Implementing information technology governance: Models, practices and cases* (pp. 125–237). Hershey, PA: IGI Global. doi:10.4018/978-1-59904-924-3.ch004

van Os, G., Homburg, V., & Bekkers, V. (2013). Contingencies and convergence in European social security: ICT coordination in the back office of the welfare state. In M. Cruz-Cunha, I. Miranda, & P. Gonçalves (Eds.), *Handbook of research on ICTs and management systems for improving efficiency in healthcare and social care* (pp. 268–287). Hershey, PA: IGI Global. doi:10.4018/978-1-4666-3990-4.ch013

Velloso, A. B., Gassenferth, W., & Machado, M. A. (2012). Evaluating IBMEC-RJ's intranet usability using fuzzy logic. In M. Cruz-Cunha, P. Gonçalves, N. Lopes, E. Miranda, & G. Putnik (Eds.), *Handbook of research on business social networking: Organizational, managerial, and technological dimensions* (pp. 185–205). Hershey, PA: IGI Global. doi:10.4018/978-1-61350-168-9.ch010

Villablanca, A. C., Baxi, H., & Anderson, K. (2009). Novel data interface for evaluating cardiovascular outcomes in women. In A. Dwivedi (Ed.), *Handbook of research on information technology management and clinical data administration in healthcare* (pp. 34–53). Hershey, PA: IGI Global. doi:10.4018/978-1-60566-356-2.ch003

Villablanca, A. C., Baxi, H., & Anderson, K. (2011). Novel data interface for evaluating cardiovascular outcomes in women. In *Clinical technologies: Concepts, methodologies, tools and applications* (pp. 2094–2113). Hershey, PA: IGI Global. doi:10.4018/978-1-60960-561-2.ch806

Virkar, S. (2011). Information and communication technologies in administrative reform for development: Exploring the case of property tax systems in Karnataka, India. In J. Steyn, J. Van Belle, & E. Mansilla (Eds.), *ICTs for global development and sustainability: Practice and applications* (pp. 127–149). Hershey, PA: IGI Global. doi:10.4018/978-1-61520-997-2.ch006

Virkar, S. (2013). Designing and implementing e-government projects: Actors, influences, and fields of play. In S. Saeed & C. Reddick (Eds.), *Human-centered system design for electronic governance* (pp. 88–110). Hershey, PA: IGI Global. doi:10.4018/978-1-4666-3640-8.ch007

Wallace, A. (2009). E-justice: An Australian perspective. In A. Martínez & P. Abat (Eds.), *E-justice: Using information communication technologies in the court system* (pp. 204–228). Hershey, PA: IGI Global. doi:10.4018/978-1-59904-998-4.ch014

Wang, G. (2012). E-democratic administration and bureaucratic responsiveness: A primary study of bureaucrats' perceptions of the civil service e-mail box in Taiwan. In K. Kloby & M. D'Agostino (Eds.), *Citizen 2.0: Public and governmental interaction through web 2.0 technologies* (pp. 146–173). Hershey, PA: IGI Global. doi:10.4018/978-1-4666-0318-9.ch009

Wangpipatwong, S., Chutimaskul, W., & Papasratorn, B. (2011). Quality enhancing the continued use of e-government web sites: Evidence from e-citizens of Thailand. In V. Weerakkody (Ed.), *Applied technology integration in governmental organizations: New e-government research* (pp. 20–36). Hershey, PA: IGI Global. doi:10.4018/978-1-60960-162-1.ch002

Wedemeijer, L. (2006). Long-term evolution of a conceptual schema at a life insurance company. In M. Khosrow-Pour (Ed.), *Cases on database technologies and applications* (pp. 202–226). Hershey, PA: IGI Global. doi:10.4018/978-1-59904-399-9.ch012

Whybrow, E. (2008). Digital access, ICT fluency, and the economically disadvantages: Approaches to minimize the digital divide. In F. Tan (Ed.), *Global information technologies: Concepts, methodologies, tools, and applications* (pp. 1409–1422). Hershey, PA: IGI Global. doi:10.4018/978-1-59904-939-7.ch102

Whybrow, E. (2008). Digital access, ICT fluency, and the economically disadvantages: Approaches to minimize the digital divide. In C. Van Slyke (Ed.), *Information communication technologies: Concepts, methodologies, tools, and applications* (pp. 764–777). Hershey, PA: IGI Global. doi:10.4018/978-1-59904-949-6.ch049

Wickramasinghe, N., & Geisler, E. (2010). Key considerations for the adoption and implementation of knowledge management in healthcare operations. In M. Saito, N. Wickramasinghe, M. Fuji, & E. Geisler (Eds.), *Redesigning innovative healthcare operation and the role of knowledge management* (pp. 125–142). Hershey, PA: IGI Global. doi:10.4018/978-1-60566-284-8.ch009

Wickramasinghe, N., & Geisler, E. (2012). Key considerations for the adoption and implementation of knowledge management in healthcare operations. In *Organizational learning and knowledge: Concepts, methodologies, tools and applications* (pp. 1316–1328). Hershey, PA: IGI Global. doi:10.4018/978-1-60960-783-8.ch405

Wickramasinghe, N., & Goldberg, S. (2007). A framework for delivering m-health excellence. In L. Al-Hakim (Ed.), *Web mobile-based applications for healthcare management* (pp. 36–61). Hershey, PA: IGI Global. doi:10.4018/978-1-59140-658-7.ch002

Wickramasinghe, N., & Goldberg, S. (2008). Critical success factors for delivering m-health excellence. In N. Wickramasinghe & E. Geisler (Eds.), *Encyclopedia of healthcare information systems* (pp. 339–351). Hershey, PA: IGI Global. doi:10.4018/978-1-59904-889-5.ch045

Wyld, D. (2009). Radio frequency identification (RFID) technology. In J. Symonds, J. Ayoade, & D. Parry (Eds.), *Auto-identification and ubiquitous computing applications* (pp. 279–293). Hershey, PA: IGI Global. doi:10.4018/978-1-60566-298-5.ch017

Yaghmaei, F. (2010). Understanding computerised information systems usage in community health. In J. Rodrigues (Ed.), *Health information systems: Concepts, methodologies, tools, and applications* (pp. 1388–1399). Hershey, PA: IGI Global. doi:10.4018/978-1-60566-988-5.ch088

Yee, G., El-Khatib, K., Korba, L., Patrick, A. S., Song, R., & Xu, Y. (2005). Privacy and trust in e-government. In W. Huang, K. Siau, & K. Wei (Eds.), *Electronic government strategies and implementation* (pp. 145–190). Hershey, PA: IGI Global. doi:10.4018/978-1-59140-348-7.ch007

Yeh, S., & Chu, P. (2010). Evaluation of e-government services: A citizen-centric approach to citizen e-complaint services. In C. Reddick (Ed.), *Citizens and e-government: Evaluating policy and management* (pp. 400–417). Hershey, PA: IGI Global. doi:10.4018/978-1-61520-931-6.ch022

Young-Jin, S., & Seang-tae, K. (2008). E-government concepts, measures, and best practices. In A. Anttiroiko (Ed.), *Electronic government: Concepts, methodologies, tools, and applications* (pp. 32–57). Hershey, PA: IGI Global. doi:10.4018/978-1-59904-947-2.ch004

Yun, H. J., & Opheim, C. (2012). New technology communication in American state governments: The impact on citizen participation. In K. Bwalya & S. Zulu (Eds.), *Handbook of research on e-government in emerging economies: Adoption, e-participation, and legal frameworks* (pp. 573–590). Hershey, PA: IGI Global. doi:10.4018/978-1-4666-0324-0.ch029

Zhang, N., Guo, X., Chen, G., & Chau, P. Y. (2011). User evaluation of e-government systems: A Chinese cultural perspective. In F. Tan (Ed.), *International enterprises and global information technologies: Advancing management practices* (pp. 63–84). Hershey, PA: IGI Global. doi:10.4018/978-1-60960-605-3.ch004

Related References

Zuo, Y., & Hu, W. (2011). Trust-based information risk management in a supply chain network. In J. Wang (Ed.), *Supply chain optimization, management and integration: Emerging applications* (pp. 181–196). Hershey, PA: IGI Global. doi:10.4018/978-1-60960-135-5.ch013

Compilation of References

Adam, J. L., Ricot, D., Dubief, F., & Guy, C. (2008). Aeroacoustic simulation of automobile ventilation outlets. *Journal of Acoustics of the American Society*, *123*(5), 3250–3257. doi:10.1121/1.2933531

Adrover, A., & Giona, M. (1996). A predictive model for permeability of correlated porous media. *The Chemical Engineering Journal and the Biochemical Engineering Journal*, *64*(1), 7–19. doi:10.1016/S0923-0467(96)03084-9

Agarwal, A., Djenidi, L., & Antonia, R. A. (2006). Investigation of flow around of a pair of side-by-side square cylinders using the lattice Boltzmann method. *Computers & Fluids*, *35*(10), 1093–1107. doi:10.1016/j.compfluid.2005.05.008

Aharonov, E., & Rothman, D. H. (1993). Non-Newtonian flow (through porous media): A lattice-Boltzmann method. *Geophysical Research Letters*, *20*(8), 679–682. doi:10.1029/93GL00473

Alexander, F. J., Chen, S., & Sterling, J. D. (1993). Lattice Boltzmann Thermohydrodynamics. *Physical Review E: Statistical Physics, Plasmas, Fluids, and Related Interdisciplinary Topics*, *47*(4), R2249–R2252. doi:10.1103/PhysRevE.47.R2249 PMID:9960345

Alexandrov, V., Lees, M., Krzhizhanovskaya, V., Dongarra, J., Sloot, P., Crimi, G., ... Tripiccione, R. (2013). Early Experience on Porting and Running a Lattice Boltzmann Code on the Xeon-phi Co-Processor. *Procedia Computer Science*, *18*, 551–560. doi:10.1016/j.procs.2013.05.219

Allen, J. S., Barth, J. A., & Newberger, P. A. (1990). On Intermediate Models for Barotropic Continental Shelf and Slope Flow Fields. Part 1: Formulation and Comparison of Exact Solutions. *Journal of Physical Oceanography*, *20*(7), 1017–1042. doi:10.1175/1520-0485(1990)020<1017:OIMFBC>2.0.CO;2

Amati, G., Succi, S., & Piva, R. (1997). Massively parallel lattice-Boltzmann simulation of turbulent channel flow. *International Journal of Modern Physics C*, *08*(04), 869–877. doi:10.1142/S0129183197000746

Anderson, J. D., Menter, F. R., Dick, E., Degrez, G., & Vierendeels, J. (2013). *Introduction to Computational Fluid Dynamics*. von Karman Institute for Fluid Dynamics.

Anderson, J. D. (1995). *Computational fluid dynamics - the basics with applications*. McGraw-Hill.

Compilation of References

Anderson, J. D., Menter, F. R., Dick, E., Degrez, G., & Vierendeels, J. (2013). *Introduction to computational fluid dynamics*. Von Karman Institute for Fluid Dynamics.

Anzt, H., Haugen, B., Kurzak, J., Luszczek, P., & Dongarra, J. (2015). Experiences in autotuning matrix multiplication for energy minimization on GPUs. *Concurrency and Computation, 27*(17), 5096–5113. doi:10.1002/cpe.3516

Artoli, A. M., Hoekstra, A. G., & Sloot, P. M. A. (2003). Simulation of a systolic cycle in a realistic artery with the lattice Boltzmann BGK method. *International Journal of Modern Physics B, 17*(1-2), 95-98.

Artoli, A., Hoekstra, A., & Sloot, P. (2006). Mesoscopic simulations of systolic flow in the human abdominal aorta. *Journal of Biomechanics, 39*(5), 873–884. doi:10.1016/j.jbiomech.2005.01.033 PMID:16488226

Artoli, A., Kandhai, D., Hoefsloot, H., Hoekstra, A., & Sloot, P. (2004). Lattice BGK simulations of flow in a symmetric bifurcation. *Future Generation Computer Systems, 20*(6), 909–916. doi:10.1016/j.future.2003.12.002

Asinari, P., Quaglia, M. C., von Spakovsky, M. R., & Kasula, B. V. (2007). Direct numerical calculation of the kinematic tortuosity of reactive mixture flow in the anode layer of solid oxide fuel cells by the lattice Boltzmann method. *Journal of Power Sources, 170*(2), 359–375. doi:10.1016/j.jpowsour.2007.03.074

Astorino, M., Sagredo, J., & Quarteroni, A. (2012). A modular lattice Boltzmann solver for GPU computing processors. *SeMA Journal, 59*(1), 53–78. doi:10.1007/BF03322610

Axner, L., Bernsdorf, J., Zeiser, T., Lammers, P., Linxweiler, J., & Hoekstra, A. (2008). Performance evaluation of a parallel sparse lattice Boltzmann solver. *Journal of Computational Physics, 227*(10), 4895–4911. doi:10.1016/j.jcp.2008.01.013

Axner, L., Hoekstra, A. G., Jeays, A., Lawford, P., Hose, R., & Sloot, P. M. (2009). Simulations of time harmonic blood flow in the mesenteric artery: Comparing finite element and lattice Boltzmann methods. *Biomedical Engineering Online, 8*(1), 23. doi:10.1186/1475-925X-8-23 PMID:19799782

Axner, L., Hoekstra, A., Jeays, A., Lawford, P., Hose, P., & Sloot, P. (2000). Simulations of time harmonic blood flow in the mesenteric artery: Comparing finite element and lattice boltzmann methods. *Biomedical Engineering Online*. PMID:19799782

Ayguadé, E., Badia, R. M., Bellens, P., Cabrera, D., Duran, A., Ferrer, R., & Quintana-Ortí, E. S. (2010). Extending OpenMP to Survive the Heterogeneous Multi-Core Era. *International Journal of Parallel Programming, 38*(5-6), 440–459. doi:10.1007/s10766-010-0135-4

Bailey, P., Myre, J., Walsh, S., Lilja, D., & Saar, M. (2009). Accelerating lattice Boltzmann fluid flow simulations using graphics processors. In *Proceedings of International Conference on Parallel Processing* (pp. 550-557). Academic Press. doi:10.1109/ICPP.2009.38

Balasubramanian, G., Crouse, B., & Freed, D. (2009). Numerical simulation of real world effects on sunroof buffeting of an idealized generic vehicle. In *15th AIAA/CEAS aeroacoustics conference (30th AIAA aeroacoustics conference)*. AIAA Paper 2009-3348.

Balasubramanian, K., Hayot, F., & Saam, W. F. (1987). Darcy's law from lattice-gas hydrodynamics. *Physical Review A.*, *36*(5), 2248–2253. doi:10.1103/PhysRevA.36.2248 PMID:9899116

Bao, J., Yuan, P., & Schaefer, L. (2008). A mass conserving boundary condition for the lattice Boltzmann equation method. *Journal of Computational Physics*, *227*(18), 8472–8487. doi:10.1016/j.jcp.2008.06.003

Bardow, A., Karlin, I., & Gusev, A. (2006). General characteristic-based algorithm for off-lattice Boltzmann simulations. *Europhysics Letters*, *75*(3), 434–440. doi:10.1209/epl/i2006-10138-1

Bearman, P. W., & Wadcock, A. J. (1973). The interaction between a pair of circular cylinders normal to a stream. *Journal of Fluid Mechanics*, *61*(03), 499–511. doi:10.1017/S0022112073000832

Begum, R., & Basit, M. A. (2008). Lattice Boltzmann Method and its Applications to Fluid Flow Problems. *European Journal of Science & Research*, *22*, 216–231.

Belytschko, T., Liu, W. K., Moran, B., & Elkhodary, K. (2013). *Nonlinear finite elements for continua and structures*. John Wiley & Sons.

Belytschko, T., Lu, Y. Y., & Gu, L. (1994). Element-free galerkin methods. *International Journal for Numerical Methods in Engineering*, *37*(2), 229–256. doi:10.1002/nme.1620370205

Benzi, R., Succi, S., & Vergassola, M. (1992). The lattice Boltzmann equation: Theory and applications. *Physics Reports*, *222*(3), 145–197. doi:10.1016/0370-1573(92)90090-M

Bernard, C., Christ, N., Gottlieb, S., Jansen, K., Kenway, R., Lippert, T., ... Wittig, H. (2002). Panel discussion on the cost of dynamical quark simulations. *Nuclear Physics B - Proceedings Supplement*, *106*(Supplement C), 199–205. doi:10.1016/S0920-5632(01)01664-4

Bernaschi, M., Bisson, M., Fatica, M., & Melchionna, S. (2013). 20 petaflops simulation of proteins suspensions in crowding conditions. In *SC'13 - International conference for high performance computing, networking, storage and analysis* (pp. 1-11). Academic Press.

Bernaschi, M., Matsuoka, S., Bisson, M., Fatica, M., Endo, T., & Melchionna, S. (2011, Nov). Petaflop biofluidics simulations on a two million-core system. In *SC'11 International conference for high performance computing, networking, storage and analysis* (pp. 1-12). Academic Press. doi:10.1145/2063384.2063389

Bernaschi, M., Bisson, M., Fatica, M., Melchionna, S., & Succi, S. (2013). Petaflop hydrokinetic simulations of complex flows on massive GPU clusters. *Computer Physics Communications*, *184*(2), 329–341. doi:10.1016/j.cpc.2012.09.016

Bernaschi, M., Fatica, M., Melchiona, S., Succi, S., & Kaxiras, E. (2010). A flexible high-performance lattice boltzmann gpu code for the simulations of fluid flows in complex geometries. *Concurrency Computa.: Pract. Exper.*, *22*(1), 1–14. doi:10.1002/cpe.1466

Bernaschi, M., Melchionna, S., Succi, S., Fyta, M., Kaxiras, E., & Sircar, J. (2009). Muphy: A parallel MUlti PHYsics/scale code for high performance bio-fluidic simulations. *Computer Physics Communications*, *180*(9), 1495–1502. doi:10.1016/j.cpc.2009.04.001

Bernsdorf, J., Durst, F., & Schäfer, M. (1999). Comparison of cellular automata and finite volume techniques for simulation of incompressible flows in complex geometries. *International Journal for Numerical Methods in Fluids*, *29*(3), 251–264. doi:10.1002/(SICI)1097-0363(19990215)29:3<251::AID-FLD783>3.0.CO;2-L

Bhardwaj, R., & Mittal, R. (2012). Benchmarking a Coupled Immersed-Boundary-Finite-Element Solver for Large-Scale Flow-Induced Deformation. *AIAA Journal*, *50*(7), 1638–1642. doi:10.2514/1.J051621

Bhatnagar, P. L., Gross, E. P., & Krook, M. (1954). A model for collision processes in gases. I. Small amplitude processes in charged and neutral one-component systems. *Physical Review Letters*, *94*(3), 511–525. doi:10.1103/PhysRev.94.511

Biferale, L., Mantovani, F., Pivanti, M., Pozzati, F., Sbragaglia, M., Scagliarini, A., & Tripiccione, R. (2012). A Multi-GPU implementation of a D2Q37 Lattice Boltzmann code. In R. Wyrzykowski, J. Dongarra, K. Karczewski, & J. Waśniewski (Eds.), *Parallel processing and applied mathematics: 9th international conference, PPAM 2011, Torun, Poland, September 11-14, 2011. revised selected papers, part i* (pp. 640-650). Berlin: Springer Berlin Heidelberg. doi:10.1007/978-3-642-31464-3_65

Biferale, L., Mantovani, F., Pivanti, M., Pozzati, F., Sbragaglia, M., Scagliarini, A., & Tripiccione, R. (2013). An optimized D2Q37 Lattice Boltzmann code on GP-GPUs. *Computers & Fluids*, *80*, 55–62. doi:10.1016/j.compfluid.2012.06.003

Biferale, L., Mantovani, F., Pivanti, M., Sbragaglia, M., Scagliarini, A., Schifano, S. F., & Tripiccione, R. (2010). Lattice Boltzmann fluid-dynamics on the QPACE supercomputer. *Procedia Computer Science*, *1*(1), 1075–1082. doi:10.1016/j.procs.2010.04.119

Bilardi, G., Pietracaprina, A., Pucci, G., Schifano, F., & Tripiccione, R. (2005). The potential of on-chip multiprocessing for QCD machines. *Lecture Notes in Computer Science*, *3769*, 386–397. doi:10.1007/11602569_41

Bisson, M., Bernaschi, M., Melchionna, S., Succi, S., & Kaxiras, E. (2012). Multiscale hemodynamics using GPU clusters. *Communications in Computational Physics*, *11*(1), 48–64. doi:10.4208/cicp.210910.250311a

Blair, S., Albing, C., Grund, A., & Jocksch, A. (2015). Accelerating an MPI Lattice Boltzmann code using OpenACC. In *Proceedings of the second workshop on accelerator programming using directives* (pp. 3:1-3:9). New York: ACM. doi:10.1145/2832105.2832111

Boek, E. S., Chin, J., & Coveney, P. V. (2003). Lattice Boltzmann simulation of the flow of non-Newtonian fluids in porous media. *International Journal of Modern Physics B*, *17*(1-2), 99-102.

Boek, E. S., & Venturoli, M. (2010). Lattice-Boltzmann studies of fluid flow in porous media with realistic rock geometries. *Computers & Mathematics with Applications (Oxford, England)*, *59*(7), 2305–2314. doi:10.1016/j.camwa.2009.08.063

Bonati, C., Calore, E., Coscetti, S., D'Elia, M., Mesiti, M., Negro, F., & Tripiccione, R. (2015). Development of scientific software for HPC architectures using OpenACC: The case of LQCD. In The 2015 international workshop on software engineering for high performance computing in science (sE4HPCS) (pp. 9-15). Academic Press. doi:10.1109/SE4HPCS.2015.9

Bonati, C., Coscetti, S., D'Elia, M., Mesiti, M., Negro, F., Calore, E., & Tripiccione, R. (2017). Design and optimization of a portable LQCD monte carlo code using OpenACC. *International Journal of Modern Physics C*, *28*(5), 1750063. doi:10.1142/S0129183117500632

Bonati, C., Cossu, G., D'Elia, M., & Incardona, P. (2012). QCD simulations with staggered fermions on GPUs. *Computer Physics Communications*, *183*(4), 853–863. doi:10.1016/j.cpc.2011.12.011

Bortolotti, G., Caberletti, M., Crimi, G., Ferraro, A., Giacomini, F., Manzali, M., & Zanella, M. (2014). Computing on Knights and Kepler architectures. *Journal of Physics: Conference Series*, *513*(5), 052032. doi:10.1088/1742-6596/513/5/052032

Bouzidi, M., Firdaouss, M., & Lallemand, P. (2001). Momentum transfer of a Boltzmann lattice fluid with boundaries. *Physics of Fluids*, *13*(11), 3452–3459. doi:10.1063/1.1399290

Brackbill, J. U., Kothe, D. B., & Zemach, C. (1992). A continuum method for modeling surface tension. *Journal of Computational Physics*, *100*(2), 335–354. doi:10.1016/0021-9991(92)90240-Y

Caiazzo, A., & Junk, M. (2008). Boundary forces in lattice Boltzmann: Analysis of momentum exchange algorithm. *Computers & Mathematics with Applications (Oxford, England)*, *55*(7), 1415–1423. doi:10.1016/j.camwa.2007.08.004

Calore, E. (2016). *PAPI-power-reader*. Retrieved from https://baltig.infn.it/COKA/PAPI-power-reader

Calore, E., Demo, N., Schifano, S. F., & Tripiccione, R. (2016a). Experience on vectorizing Lattice Boltzmann kernels for multi- and many-core architectures. In *Parallel processing and applied mathematics: 11th international conference, PPAM 2015, Krakow, Poland, September 6-9, 2015. revised selected papers, part i* (pp. 53-62). Cham: Springer International Publishing. doi:10.1007/978-3-319-32149-3_6

Calore, E., Schifano, S. F., & Tripiccione, R. (2014b). On portability, performance and scalability of an MPI OpenCL Lattice Boltzmann code. In L. Lopes, J. Žilinskas, A. Costan, R. G. Cascella, G. Kecskemeti, E. Jeannot, & M. Alexander (Eds.), *Euro-par 2014: Parallel processing workshops: Euro-par 2014 international workshops, Porto, Portugal, August 25-26, 2014, revised selected papers, part II* (pp. 438-449). Cham: Springer International Publishing. doi:10.1007/978-3-319-14313-2_37

Compilation of References

Calore, E., Gabbana, A., Kraus, J., Schifano, S. F., & Tripiccione, R. (2016b). Performance and portability of accelerated Lattice Boltzmann applications with OpenACC. *Concurrency and Computation, 28*(12), 3485–3502. doi:10.1002/cpe.3862

Calore, E., Gabbana, A., Schifano, S. F., & Tripiccione, R. (2017a). *Early experience on using Knights Landing processors for Lattice Boltzmann applications.* (in press)

Calore, E., Gabbana, A., Schifano, S. F., & Tripiccione, R. (2017b). Evaluation of DVFS techniques on modern HPC processors and accelerators for energy-aware applications. *Concurrency and Computation, 29*(12), e4143. doi:10.1002/cpe.4143

Calore, E., Gabbana, A., Schifano, S. F., & Tripiccione, R. (2017c). Optimization of Lattice Boltzmann simulations on heterogeneous computers. *International Journal of High Performance Computing Applications*, 1–16. doi:10.1177/1094342017703771

Calore, E., Schifano, S. F., & Tripiccione, R. (2014a). A Portable OpenCL Lattice Boltzmann Code for Multi-and Many-core Processor Architectures. *Procedia Computer Science, 29*, 40–49. doi:10.1016/j.procs.2014.05.004

Cancelliere, A., Chang, C., Foti, E., Rothman, D. H., & Succi, S. (1990). The permeability of a random medium: Comparison of simulation with theory. *Physics of Fluids. A, Fluid Dynamics, 2*(12), 2085–2088. doi:10.1063/1.857793

Cao, N., Chen, S., Jin, S., & Martinez, D. (1997). Physical symmetry and lattice symmetry in the lattice Boltzmann method. *Physical Review. E, 55*(1), R21–R24. doi:10.1103/PhysRevE.55.R21

Chai, Z., Shi, B., Lu, J., & Guo, Z. (2010). Non-Darcy flow in disordered porous media: A lattice Boltzmann study. *Computers & Fluids, 39*(10), 2069–2077. doi:10.1016/j.compfluid.2010.07.012

Chapman, B., Jost, G., & Van Der Pas, R. (2008). *Portable Shared Memory Parallel Programming* (Vol. 10). MIT Press.

Chapman, S., & Cowling, T. G. (1970). *The Mathematical Theory of Non-uniform Gases: An Account of the Kinetic Theory of Viscosity, Thermal Conduction and Diffusion in Gases. Cambridge Mathematical Library.* Cambridge University Press.

Chapman, S., & Cowling, T. G. (1991). *The mathematical theory of non-uniform gases.* Cambridge University Press.

Chen, F., Flatken, M., Basermann, A., Gerndt, A., Hetheringthon, J., Krüger, T., et al. (2012). Enabling in situ pre- and post-processing for exascale hemodynamic simulations - A co-design study with the sparse geometry lattice-Boltzmann code HemeLB. *2012 SC companion: High performance computing, networking storage and analysis*, 662-668.

Cheng, M., & Morreti, M. (1988). Experimental study of the flow field downstream of a single tube row. *Experimental Thermal and Fluid Science, 1*(1), 69–74. doi:10.1016/0894-1777(88)90049-0

Chen, H. (1998). Volumetric formulation of the lattice Boltzmann method for fluid dynamics: Basic concept. *Physical Review. E, 58*(3), 3955–3963. doi:10.1103/PhysRevE.58.3955

Chen, S., Chen, H., Martnez, D., & Matthaeus, W. (1991). Lattice Boltzmann model for simulation of magnetohydrodynamics. *Physical Review Letters, 67*(27), 3776–3779. doi:10.1103/PhysRevLett.67.3776 PMID:10044823

Chen, S., & Doolen, C. D. (1998). Lattice Boltzmann Method for Fluid Flows. *Annual Review of Fluid Mechanics, 30*(1), 329–364. doi:10.1146/annurev.fluid.30.1.329

Chen, S., Martinez, D., & Mei, R. (1996). On boundary conditions in lattice Boltzmann methods. *Physics of Fluids, 8*(9), 2527–2536. doi:10.1063/1.869035

Chen, Y., Ohashi, H., & Akiyama, M. (1994). Thermal lattice Bhatnagar-Gross-Krook model without nonlinear deviations in macrodynamic equations. *Physical Review E: Statistical Physics, Plasmas, Fluids, and Related Interdisciplinary Topics, 50*(4), 2776–2783. doi:10.1103/PhysRevE.50.2776 PMID:9962315

Chevalier, C., & Pellegrini, F. (2008). PT-SCOTCH: A tool for efficient parallel graph ordering. *Parallel Computing, 34*(6-8), 318–331. doi:10.1016/j.parco.2007.12.001

Chun, B., & Ladd, A. (2007). Interpolated boundary condition for lattice Boltzmann sim- ulations of flows in narrow gaps. *Physical Review. E, 75*(6), 066705. doi:10.1103/PhysRevE.75.066705 PMID:17677387

Chung, T. J. (2010). *Computational Fluid Dynamics*. Cambridge, MA: Cambridge University Press. doi:10.1017/CBO9780511780066

Clausen, J. R., Reasor, D. A. Jr, & Aidun, C. K. (2010). Parallel performance of a lattice Boltzmann/finite element cellular blood flow solver on the IBM Blue Gene/P architecture. *Computer Physics Communications, 181*(6), 1013–1020. doi:10.1016/j.cpc.2010.02.005

Colucci, P. J., Jaberi, F. A., Givi, P., & Pope, S. B. (1998). Filtered density function for large eddy simulation of turbulent reacting flows. *Physics of Fluids, 10*(2), 499–515. doi:10.1063/1.869537

Combescure, A., & Gravouil, A. (2002). A numerical scheme to couple subdomains with different time-steps for predominantly linear transient analysis. *Computer Methods in Applied Mechanics and Engineering, 191*(11-12), 1129–1157. doi:10.1016/S0045-7825(01)00190-6

Combescure, A., Gravouil, A., & Herry, B. (2003). An algorithm to solve transient structural non-linear problems for non-matching time-space domains. *Computers & Structures, 81*(12), 1211–1222. doi:10.1016/S0045-7949(03)00037-3

Coplin, J., & Burtscher, M. (2016). Energy, Power, and Performance Characterization of GPGPU Benchmark Programs. *12th IEEE Workshop on High-Performance, Power-Aware Computing (HPPAC'16)*. doi:10.1109/IPDPSW.2016.164

Davide Rossetti. (2014). *Benchmarking GPU Direct RDMA on modern server platforms*. Retrieved from http://devblogs.nvidia.com/parallelforall/benchmarking-gpudirect-rdma-on-modern-server-platforms

Compilation of References

De Rosis, A., Ubertini, S., & Ubertini, F. (2014). A partitioned approach for two-dimensional fluid structure interaction problems by a coupled lattice Boltzmann-finite element method with immersed boundary. *Journal of Fluids and Structures*, *45*, 202–215. doi:10.1016/j.jfluidstructs.2013.12.009

Deardorff, J. (1970). A numerical study of three-dimensional turbulent channel flow at large Reynolds numbers. *Journal of Fluid Mechanics*, *41*(2), 453–480. doi:10.1017/S0022112070000691

Dennis, S. C. R., & Chang, G. Z. (1970). Numerical solutions for steady flow past a circular cylinder at Reynolds numbers up to 100. *Journal of Fluid Mechanics*, *42*(3), 471–489. doi:10.1017/S0022112070001428

Desplat, J.-C., Pagonabarraga, I., & Bladon, P. (2001). Ludwig: A parallel lattice-Boltzmann code for complex fluids. *Computer Physics Communications*, *134*(3), 273–290. doi:10.1016/S0010-4655(00)00205-8

Donath, S., Zeiser, T., Hager, G., Habich, J., & Wellein, G. (2005). Optimizing performance of the lattice Boltzmann method for complex structures on cache-based architectures. In Proceedings Simulationstechnique ASIM (pp. 728-735). Academic Press.

Dong, H. (2008). *Micro-CT imaging and pore network extraction* (Doctoral dissertation). Department of Earth Science and Engineering, Imperial College London.

Doolen, G. (1990). *Lattice gas methods for partial differential equations*. Addison-Wesley.

Dupuis, A., & Chopard, B. (1999). Lattice gas: An efficient and reusable parallel library based on a graph partitioning technique. In P. Sloot, M. Bubak, A. Hoekstra, & B. Hertzberger (Eds.), *High-performance computing and networking: 7th International conference, HPCN Europe 1999, Amsterdam, The Netherlands* (pp. 319-328). Berlin: Springer Berlin Heidelberg.

Dupuis, A., & Chopard, B. (2003). Theory and applications of an alternative lattice Boltzmann grid refinement algorithm. *Physical Review. E*, *67*(6), 066707. doi:10.1103/PhysRevE.67.066707 PMID:16241380

Duster, A., Demkowicz, L., & Rank, E. (2006). High order finite elements applied to the discrete Boltzmann equations. *International Journal for Numerical Methods in Engineering*, *67*(8), 1094–1121. doi:10.1002/nme.1657

Etinski, M., Corbalán, J., Labarta, J., & Valero, M. (2012). Understanding the future of energy-performance trade-off via DVFS in HPC environments. *Journal of Parallel and Distributed Computing*, *72*(4), 579–590. doi:10.1016/j.jpdc.2012.01.006

Fakhari, A., & Lee, T. (2014). Finite-difference lattice boltzmann method with a block-structured adaptive-mesh-refinement technique. *Physical Review*, *89*(033310). PMID:24730970

Farhat, C., Crivelli, L., & Géradin, M. (1993). On the spectral stability of time integration algorithms for a class of constrained dynamics problems. AIAA 34th Structural Dynamics Meeting. doi:10.2514/6.1993-1306

Farhat, C., van der Zee, K. G., & Geuzaine, P. (2006). *Provably second-order time-accurate loosely-coupled solution algorithms for transient nonlinear computational aeroelasticity.* Academic Press.

Farhat, C., & Lesoinne, M. (2000). Two efficient staggered algorithms for the serial and parallel solution of three-dimensional nonlinear transient aeroelastic problems. *Computer Methods in Applied Mechanics and Engineering, 182*(3-4), 499–515. doi:10.1016/S0045-7825(99)00206-6

Farhat, C., Rallu, A., Wang, K., & Belytschko, T. (2010). Robust and provably second-order explicit-explicit and implicit-explicit staggered time integrators for highly non-linear compressible fluid-structure interaction problems. *International Journal for Numerical Methods in Engineering, 84*(1), 73–107. doi:10.1002/nme.2883

Favier, J., Revell, A., & Pinelli, A. (2014). A Lattice Boltzmann–Immersed Boundary method to simulate the fluid interaction with moving and slender flexible object. *Journal of Computational Physics, 261*(0), 145–161. doi:10.1016/j.jcp.2013.12.052

Feichtinger, C., Donath, S., Köstler, H., Götz, J., & Rüde, U. (2011). WaLBerla: HPC software design for computational engineering simulations. *Journal of Computational Science, 2*(2), 105–112. doi:10.1016/j.jocs.2011.01.004

Feichtinger, C., Götz, J., Donath, S., Iglberger, K., & Rüde, U. (2009). WaLBerla: Exploiting massively parallel systems for lattice Boltzmann simulations. In R. Trobec, M. Vajtersic, & P. Zinterhof (Eds.), *Parallel computing: Numerics, applications, and trends* (pp. 241–260). London: Springer London. doi:10.1007/978-1-84882-409-6_8

Feichtinger, C., Habich, J., Kstler, H., Rude, U., & Aoki, T. (2015). Performance modeling and analysis of heterogeneous lattice boltzmann simulations on cpugpu clusters. *Parallel Computing, 46*(0), 1–13. doi:10.1016/j.parco.2014.12.003

Felippa, C. A., Park, K. C., & Farhat, C. (2001). Partitioned analysis of coupled mechanical systems. *Computer Methods in Applied Mechanics and Engineering, 190*(24), 3247–3270. doi:10.1016/S0045-7825(00)00391-1

Fietz, J., Krause, M. J., Schulz, C., Sanders, P., & Heuveline, V. (2012). Optimized hybrid parallel lattice Boltzmann fluid flow simulations on complex geometries. In C. Kaklamanis, T. Papatheodorou, & P. G. Spirakis (Eds.), *Euro-Par 2012 parallel processing: 18th International conference, Euro-Par 2012, Rhodes Island, Greece* (pp. 818-829). Berlin: Springer Berlin Heidelberg. doi:10.1007/978-3-642-32820-6_81

Filippova, O., & Hänel, D. (1998). Grid refinement for lattice-BGK models. *Journal of Computational Physics, 147*(1), 219–228. doi:10.1006/jcph.1998.6089

Flekkøy, E. G. (1993). Lattice Bhatnagar-Gross-Krook models for miscible fluids. *Physical Review E: Statistical Physics, Plasmas, Fluids, and Related Interdisciplinary Topics, 47*(6), 4247–4257. doi:10.1103/PhysRevE.47.4247 PMID:9960501

Fox, R. O. (2012). Large-eddy-simulation tools for multiphase flows. *Annual Review of Fluid Mechanics, 44*(1), 47–76. doi:10.1146/annurev-fluid-120710-101118

Freund, H., Zeiser, T., Huber, F., Klemm, E., Brenner, G., Durst, F., & Emig, G. (2003). Numerical simulations of single phase reacting flows in randomly packed fixed-bed reactors and experimental validation. *Chemical Engineering Science*, *58*(3-6), 903–910. doi:10.1016/S0009-2509(02)00622-X

Frisch, U., d' Humieres, D., Hasslacher, B., Lallemand, P., Pomeau, Y., & Rivet, J. (1986). *Lattice gas hydrodynamics in two and three dimensions.* Retrieved from http://www.osti.gov/scitech/servlets/purl/6063731

Frish, U., Hasslacher, B., & Pomeau, Y. (1986). Lattice gas automata for the Navier-Stokes equation. *Physical Review Letters*, *56*(14), 1505–1508. doi:10.1103/PhysRevLett.56.1505 PMID:10032689

Gao, Y., Zhang, X., Rama, P., Chen, R., Ostadi, H., & Jiang, K. (2013). Lattice Boltzmann simulation of water and gas flow in porous gas diffusion layers in fuel cells reconstructed from micro-tomography. *Computers & Mathematics with Applications (Oxford, England)*, *65*(6), 891–900. doi:10.1016/j.camwa.2012.08.006

Geller, S., Krafczyk, M., Tölke, J., Turek, S., & Hron, J. (2006). Benchmark computations based on lattice-Boltzmann, finite element and finite volume methods for laminar flows. *Computers & Fluids*, *35*(8-9), 888–897. doi:10.1016/j.compfluid.2005.08.009

Ge, R., Vogt, R., Majumder, J., Alam, A., Burtscher, M., & Zong, Z. (2013). Effects of Dynamic Voltage and Frequency Scaling on a K20 GPU. In *Proceedings of the 2013 42nd international conference on parallel processing* (pp. 826-833). Washington, DC: IEEE Computer Society. doi:10.1109/ICPP.2013.98

Germano, M., Piomeelli, U., Moin, P., & ... . (1991). A dynamic subgrid-scale eddy viscosity model. *Physics of Fluids. A, Fluid Dynamics*, *3*(7), 1760–1765. doi:10.1063/1.857955

Ghia, U., Ghia, K. N., & Shin, C. T. (1982). High-Re solutions for incompressible flow using the Navier-Stokes equations and a multigrid method. *Journal of Computational Physics*, *48*(3), 387–410. doi:10.1016/0021-9991(82)90058-4

Ghosal, S. (1996). An analysis of numerical errors in large-eddy simulations of turbulence. *Journal of Computational Physics*, *125*(1), 187–206. doi:10.1006/jcph.1996.0088

Godenschwager, C., Schornbaum, F., Bauer, M., Köstler, H., & Rüde, U. (2013). A framework for hybrid parallel flow simulations with a trillion cells in complex geometries. In *Proceedings of the international conference on high performance computing, networking, storage and analysis* (pp. 35:1-35:12). New York: ACM. doi:10.1145/2503210.2503273

Gravouil, A., & Combescure, A. (2003). Multi-time-step and two-scale domain decomposition method for non-linear structural dynamics. *International Journal for Numerical Methods in Engineering*, *58*(10), 1545–1569. doi:10.1002/nme.826

Gravouil, A., Combescure, A., & Brun, M. (2015). Heterogeneous asynchronous time integrators for computational structural dynamics. *International Journal for Numerical Methods in Engineering*, *102*(3-4), 202–232. doi:10.1002/nme.4818

Grew, K. N., Joshi, A. S., Peracchio, A. A., & Chiu, W. K. (2010). Pore-scale investigation of mass transport and electrochemistry in a solid oxide fuel cell anode. *Journal of Power Sources, 195*(8), 2331–2345. doi:10.1016/j.jpowsour.2009.10.067

Grew, K. N., Peracchio, A. A., & Chiu, W. K. (2010). Characterization and analysis methods for the examination of the heterogeneous solid oxide fuel cell electrode microstructure: Part 2. Quantitative measurement of the microstructure and contributions to transport losses. *Journal of Power Sources, 195*(24), 7943–7958. doi:10.1016/j.jpowsour.2010.07.006

Grinstein, F., Margolin, L., & Rider, W. (2007). *Implicit large eddy simulation*. Cambridge University Press. doi:10.1017/CBO9780511618604

Groen, D., Chacra, D. A., Nash, R. W., Jaros, J., Bernabeu, M. O., & Coveney, P. V. (2015). Weighted decomposition in high-performance lattice-Boltzmann simulations: Are some lattice sites more equal than others? In S. Markidis & E. Laure (Eds.), *Solving software challenges for exascale: International Conference on Exascale Applications and Software, EASC 2014, Stockholm, Sweden, April 2-3, 2014, revised selected papers* (pp. 28-38). Cham: Springer International Publishing. doi:10.1007/978-3-319-15976-8_2

Groen, D., Hetherington, J., Carver, H. B., Nash, R. W., Bernabeu, M. O., & Coveney, P. V. (2013). Analysing and modelling the performance of the HemeLB lattice-Boltzmann simulation environment. *Journal of Computational Science, 4*(5), 412–422. doi:10.1016/j.jocs.2013.03.002

Grucelski, A., & Pozorski, J. (2013). Lattice Boltzmann Simulations of flow past a circular cylinder and in a simple porous media. *Computers & Fluids, 71*, 406–416. doi:10.1016/j.compfluid.2012.11.006

Guillaume, D. W., & LaRue, J. C. (1999). Investigation of the flopping regime with two-, three- and four-cylinder arrays. *Experiments in Fluids, 27*(2), 145–156. doi:10.1007/s003480050339

Guo, Z. L., Zheng, C. G., & Shi, B. C. (2002). Non-equilibrium extrapolation method for velocity and boundary conditions in the lattice Boltzmann method. *Chinese Physics, 11*(4), 366–374. doi:10.1088/1009-1963/11/4/310

Guo, Z., Shi, B., & Wang, N. (2000). Lattice BGK Model for Incompressible Navier-Stokes Equation. *Journal of Computational Physics, 165*(1), 288–306. doi:10.1006/jcph.2000.6616

Guo, Z., Zheng, C., & Shi, B. (2002). Discrete lattice effects on the forcing term in the lattice Boltzmann method. *Physical Review. E, 65*(4), 046308. doi:10.1103/PhysRevE.65.046308 PMID:12006014

Habich, J., Feichtinger, C., Kstler, H., Hager, G., & Wellein, G. (2013). Performance engineering for the lattice Boltzmann method on GPGPUs: Architectural requirements and performance results. *Computers & Fluids, 80*(0), 276–282. doi:10.1016/j.compfluid.2012.02.013

Haiqing, S., & Yan, S. (2015). Study on lattice Boltzmann method/ large eddy simulation and its application at high Reynolds number flow. *Advances in Mechanical Engineering, 1*, 1–8.

Han, B., & Meng, H. (2013). Numerical studies of interfacial phenomena in liquid water transport in polymer electrolyte membrane fuel cells using the lattice Boltzmann method. *International Journal of Hydrogen Energy*, *38*(12), 5053–5059. doi:10.1016/j.ijhydene.2013.02.055

Han, T., & Abdelrahman, T. (2011). hiCUDA: High-Level GPGPU Programming. *Parallel and Distributed Systems. IEEE Transactions on*, *22*(1), 78–90. doi:10.1109/TPDS.2010.62

Hao, L., & Cheng, P. (2009). Lattice Boltzmann simulations of anisotropic permeabilities in carbon paper gas diffusion layers. *Journal of Power Sources*, *186*(1), 104–114. doi:10.1016/j.jpowsour.2008.09.086

Hao, L., & Cheng, P. (2010). Pore-scale simulations on relative permeabilities of porous media by lattice Boltzmann method. *International Journal of Heat and Mass Transfer*, *53*(9-10), 1908–1913. doi:10.1016/j.ijheatmasstransfer.2009.12.066

Hart, A., Ansaloni, R., & Gray, A. (2012). Porting and scaling OpenACC applications on massively-parallel, GPU-accelerated supercomputers. *The European Physical Journal. Special Topics*, *210*(1), 5–16. doi:10.1140/epjst/e2012-01634-y

Hasert, M., Bernsdorf, J., & Roller, S. (2011). Lattice Boltzmann simulation of non-Darcy flow in porous media. *Procedia Computer Science*, *4*, 1048–1057. doi:10.1016/j.procs.2011.04.111

Hasert, M., Masilamani, K., Zimny, S., Klimach, H., Qi, J., Bernsdorf, J., & Roller, S. (2014). Complex fluid simulations with the parallel tree-based lattice Boltzmann solver Musubi. *Journal of Computational Science*, *5*(5), 784–794. doi:10.1016/j.jocs.2013.11.001

Heil, M. (2004). An efficient solver for the fully coupled solution of large displacement fluid-structure interaction problems. *Computer Methods in Applied Mechanics and Engineering*, *193*(1-2), 1–23. doi:10.1016/j.cma.2003.09.006

Herdman, J., Gaudin, W., McIntosh-Smith, S., Boulton, M., Beckingsale, D., Mallinson, A., & Jarvis, S. A. (2012). Accelerating hydrocodes with OpenACC, OpenCL and CUDA. In High Performance Computing, Networking, Storage and Analysis (SCC), 2012 SC Companion: (pp. 465-471). IEEE. doi:10.1109/SC.Companion.2012.66

He, X., & Luo, L. S. (1997). A priori derivation of the lattice boltzmann equation. *Physical Review*, 55.

He, X., Luo, L. S., & Dembo, M. (1996). Some progress in lattice Boltzmann method. Part I. Nonuniform mesh grids. *Journal of Computational Physics*, *129*(2), 357–363. doi:10.1006/jcph.1996.0255

He, X., & Luo, L.-S. (1997). A priori derivation of the lattice boltzmann equation. *Physical Review E: Statistical Physics, Plasmas, Fluids, and Related Interdisciplinary Topics*, *55*(6), 6333–6336. doi:10.1103/PhysRevE.55.R6333

He, X., & Luo, L.-S. (1997). Theory of the Lattice Boltzmann method: From the Boltzmann equation to the Lattice Boltzmann equation. *Physical Review E: Statistical Physics, Plasmas, Fluids, and Related Interdisciplinary Topics*, *56*(6), 6811–6817. doi:10.1103/PhysRevE.56.6811

Higuera, F. J., & Jiménez, J. (1989). Boltzmann Approach to Lattice Gas Simulations. *Europhysics Letters*, *9*(7), 663–654. doi:10.1209/0295-5075/9/7/009

Higuera, F. J., Succi, S., & Benzi, R. (1989). Lattice gas dynamics with enhanced collisions. *Europhysics Letters*, *9*(4), 345–349. doi:10.1209/0295-5075/9/4/008

Hirabayashi, M., Ohta, M., Rüfenacht, D. A., & Chopard, B. (2003). Characterization of flow reduction properties in an aneurysm due to a stent. *Phys. Rev. E*, *68*(2), 021918. doi:10.1103/PhysRevE.68.021918 PMID:14525017

Holewinski, J., Pouchet, L.-N., & Sadayappan, P. (2012). High-performance code generation for stencil computations on GPU architectures. In *Proceedings of the 26th aCM international conference on supercomputing* (pp. 311-320). New York: ACM. doi:10.1145/2304576.2304619

Hou, S., Sterling, J., Chen, S., & ... . (1996). A lattice Boltzmann subgrid model for high Reynolds number flows. In R. Kapral (Ed.), *Pattern formation and lattice gas automata* (Vol. 6, pp. 151–166). Providence, RI: American Mathematical Society.

Hou, S., Sterling, J., Chen, S., & Doolen, G. D. (1996). A lattice Boltzmann subgrid model for high Reynolds number flows. *Fields Institute Communications*, *6*, 151–166.

Huang, C., Shi, B., Guo, Z., & Chai, Z. (2015). Multi-GPU based lattice Boltzmann method for hemodynamic simulation in patient-specific cerebral aneurysm. *Communications in Computational Physics*, *17*(04), 960–974. doi:10.4208/cicp.2014.m342

Hughes, T. J. R. (2012). *The finite element method: linear static and dynamic finite element analysis*. Courier Corporation.

Inoue, G., Yoshimoto, T., Matsukuma, Y., & Minemoto, M. (2008). Development of simulated gas diffusion layer of polymer electrolyte fuel cells and evaluation of its structure. *Journal of Power Sources*, *175*(1), 145–158. doi:10.1016/j.jpowsour.2007.09.014

Ishigai, S., & Nishikawa, E. (1975). Experimental study of structure of gas flow in tube banks with tube axes normal to flow. Part II: On the structure of gas flow in single-column, single-row, and double-rows tube banks. *Bulletin of Japan Society of Mechanical Engineering*, *18*(119), 528–535. doi:10.1299/jsme1958.18.528

Iwai, H., Shikazono, N., Matsui, T., Teshima, H., Kishimoto, M., Kishida, R., ... Yoshida, H. (2010). Quantification of SOFC anode microstructure based on dual beam FIB-SEM technique. *Journal of Power Sources*, *195*(4), 955–961. doi:10.1016/j.jpowsour.2009.09.005

Januszewski, M., & Kostur, M. (2014). Sailfish: A flexible multi-GPU implementation of the lattice Boltzmann method. *Computer Physics Communications*, *185*(9), 2350–2368. doi:10.1016/j.cpc.2014.04.018

Jeffers, J., & Reinders, J. (2013). *Intel Xeon Phi Coprocessor High Performance Programming*. San Francisco, CA: Morgan Kaufmann.

Jiri Kraus. (2013). *An introduction to CUDA-aware MPI*. Retrieved from http://developer.nvidia. com/content/introduction-cuda-aware-mpi

Jonas, L. (2007). *How to implement your ddqq dynamics with only q variables per node (instead of 2q). (Technical report)*. Tufts University.

Joshi, A. S., Grew, K. N., Peracchio, A. A., & Chiu, W. K. (2007). Lattice Boltzmann modeling of 2D gas transport in a solid oxide fuel cell anode. *Journal of Power Sources, 164*(2), 631–638. doi:10.1016/j.jpowsour.2006.10.101

Kandhai, D., Koponen, A., Hoekstra, A., Kataja, M., Timonen, J., & Sloot, P. (1998). Lattice-Boltzmann hydrodynamics on parallel systems. *Computer Physics Communications, 111*(1), 14–26. doi:10.1016/S0010-4655(98)00025-3

Kandhai, D., Vidal, D. J. E., Hoekstra, A. G., Hoefsloot, H., Iedema, P., & Sloot, P. M. A. (1998). A comparison between lattice-boltzmann and finite-element simulations of fluid flow in static mixer reactors. *International Journal of Modern Physics, 09*(08), 1123–1128. doi:10.1142/ S0129183198001035

Kandhai, D., Vidal, D.-E., Hoekstra, A., Hoefsloot, H., Iedema, P., & Sloot, P. (1999). Lattice-Boltzmann and finite element simulations of fluid flow in a SMRX static mixer reactor. *International Journal for Numerical Methods in Fluids, 31*(6), 1019–1033. doi:10.1002/ (SICI)1097-0363(19991130)31:6<1019::AID-FLD915>3.0.CO;2-I

Kanno, D., Shikazono, N., Takagi, N., Matsuzaki, K., & Kasagi, N. (2011). Evaluation of SOFC anode polarization simulation using three-dimensional microstructures reconstructed by FIB tomography. *Electrochimica Acta, 56*(11), 4015–4021. doi:10.1016/j.electacta.2011.02.010

Karthik Selva Kumar, K., & Kumaraswamidhas, L. A. (2014). Numerical Study on Fluid Flow Characteristics Over the Side-By-Side Square Cylinders at Different Spacing Ratio. *International Review of Mechanical Engineering, 8*(5), 962–969. doi:10.15866/ireme.v8i5.3709

Karthik Selva Kumar, K., & Kumaraswamidhas, L. A. (2015a). Experimental investigation on flow induced vibration excitation in the elastically mounted circular cylinder in cylinder arrays. *Fluid Dynamics Research, 47*(1), 015508. doi:10.1088/0169-5983/47/1/015508

Karthik Selva Kumar, K., & Kumaraswamidhas, L. A. (2015b). Experimental investigation on flow induced vibration excitation in the elastically mounted square cylinders. *Journal of Vibroengineering, 17*, 468–477.

Karthik Selva Kumar, K., & Kumaraswamidhas, L. A. (2015c). Experimental and Numerical Investigation on Flow Induced Vibration Excitation in Engineering Structures: A Review. *International Journal of Applied Engineering Research, 10*(15), 35971–35991.

Karypis, G., & Kumar, V. (1998). A fast and high quality multilevel scheme for partitioning irregular graphs. *SIAM Journal on Scientific Computing, 20*(1), 359–392. doi:10.1137/S1064827595287997

Kawashima, N., & Kawamura, H. (1997). Numerical analysis of les of flow past a long square cylinder. In *Direct and Large-Eddy Simulation II*. Springer. doi:10.1007/978-94-011-5624-0_40

Keating, A., Dethioux, P., & Satti, R. (2009). Computational aeroacoustics validation and analysis of a nose landing gear. In *15th AIAA/CEAS aeroacoustics conference (30th AIAA aeroacoustics conference)*. AIAA Paper 2009-3154.

Khan, W. A., Culham, J. R., & Yovanovich, M. M. (2005). Fluid Flow Around and Heat Transfer from an Infinite Circular Cylinder, *ASME. Journal of Heat Transfer, 127*(7), 785–790. doi:10.1115/1.1924629

Kim, H. J., & Durbin, P. A. (1988). Investigation of the flow between a pair of circular cylinders in the flopping regime. *Journal of Fluid Mechanics, 196*(-1), 431–448. doi:10.1017/S0022112088002769

Knutson, C. E., Werth, C. J., & Valocchi, A. J. (2001). Pore-scale modeling of dissolution from variably distributed nonaqueous phase liquid blobs. *Water Resources Research, 37*(12), 2951–2963. doi:10.1029/2001WR000587

Kobel, S., Valero, A., Latt, J., Renaud, P., & Lutolf, M. (2010). Optimization of microfluidic single cell trapping for long-term on-chip culture. *Lab on a Chip, 10*(7), 857–863. doi:10.1039/b918055a PMID:20300672

Koido, T., Furusawa, T., & Moriyama, K. (2008). An approach to modeling two-phase transport in the gas diffusion layer of a proton exchange membrane fuel cell. *Journal of Power Sources, 175*(1), 127–136. doi:10.1016/j.jpowsour.2007.09.029

Kollmannsberger S., Geller S., Dster A., Tlke J., Sorger C., Krafczyk M., Rank E. (2009). *Fixed-grid fluid-structure interaction in two dimensions based on a partitioned lattice Boltzmann and p-fem approach*. Academic Press.

Kollmannsberger, S., Geller, S., Dster, A., Tlke, J., Sorger, C., Krafczyk, M., & Rank, E. (2009). Fixed-grid fluid-structure interaction in two dimensions based on a partitioned lattice boltzmann and p-fem approach. *International Journal for Numerical Methods in Engineering, 79*(7), 817–845. doi:10.1002/nme.2581

Kopal, Z. (1947). *Tables of supersonic flow around cones*. Cambridge University Press.

Koponen, A., Kataja, M., & Timonen, J. (1997). Permeability and effective porosity of porous media. *Physical Review E: Statistical Physics, Plasmas, Fluids, and Related Interdisciplinary Topics, 56*(3), 3319–3325. doi:10.1103/PhysRevE.56.3319

Koponen, A., Kataja, M., Timonen, J., & Kandhai, D. (1998). Simulations of single-fluid flow in porous media. *International Journal of Modern Physics C, 09*(08), 1505–1521. doi:10.1142/S0129183198001369

Kraus, J., Schlottke, M., Adinetz, A., & Pleiter, D. (2014). Accelerating a C++ CFD code with OpenACC. In *Accelerator programming using directives (WACCPD), 2014 first workshop on* (pp. 47-54). Academic Press. doi:10.1109/WACCPD.2014.11

Krause, M. J., Gengenbach, T., & Heuveline, V. (2011). Hybrid parallel simulations of fluid flows in complex geometries: Application to the human lungs. In M. R. Guarracino & ... (Eds.), *Euro-Par 2010 Parallel processing workshops* (pp. 209–216). Berlin: Springer Berlin Heidelberg. doi:10.1007/978-3-642-21878-1_26

Kraus, J., Pivanti, M., Schifano, S., Tripiccione, R., & Zanella, M. (2013). Benchmarking GPUs with a Parallel Lattice-Boltzmann Code. In *Proceeding of the 25th SBAC-PAD* (pp. 160-167). Porto de Galinhas, Brazil: IEEE. doi:10.1109/SBAC-PAD.2013.37

Krenk, S. (2006). *Energy conservation in newmark based time integration algorithms.* Academic Press.

Krivovichev, G. V. (2014). On the Finite-Element-Based Lattice Boltzmann Scheme. *Applied Mathematical Sciences*, *8*(33), 1605–1620. doi:10.12988/ams.2014.4138

Krüger, T., Varnik, F., & Raabe, D. (2011). Efficient and accurate simulations of deformable particles immersed in a fluid using a combined immersed boundary lattice Boltzmann finite element method. *Computers & Mathematics with Applications (Oxford, England)*, *61*(12), 3485–3505. doi:10.1016/j.camwa.2010.03.057

Kupershtokh, A. L. (2014). Three-dimensional LBE simulations of a decay of liquid dielectrics with a solute gas into the system of gas-vapor channels under the action of strong electric fields. *Computers & Mathematics with Applications (Oxford, England)*, *67*(2), 340–349. doi:10.1016/j.camwa.2013.08.030

Kwon, Y. W. (2006). Development of coupling technique for LBM and FEM for FSI application. *Engineering Computations*, *23*(8), 860–875. doi:10.1108/02644400610707766

Lagrava, D., Malaspinas, O., Latt, J., & Chopard, B. (2012). Advances in multi-domain lattice boltzmann grid refinement. *Journal of Computational Physics*, *231*(14), 4808–4822. doi:10.1016/j.jcp.2012.03.015

Laurence, S. J., Deiterding, R., & Hornung, H. G. (2007). Proximal bodies in hypersonic flows. *Journal of Fluid Mechanics*, *590*, 209–237. doi:10.1017/S0022112007007987

Lee, S., & Eigenmann, R. (2010). OpenMPC: Extended OpenMP Programming and Tuning for GPUs. In *Proceedings of the 2010 ACM/IEEE International Conference for High Performance Computing, Networking, Storage and Analysis* (pp. 1-11). Washington, DC: IEEE Computer Society. doi:10.1109/SC.2010.36

Lee, T., & Lin, C. L. (2001). A characteristic Galerkin method for discrete Boltzmann equation. *Journal of Computational Physics*, *171*(1), 336–356. doi:10.1006/jcph.2001.6791

Lee, T., & Lin, C. L. (2003). An Eulerian description of the streaming process in the lattice Boltzmann equation. *Journal of Computational Physics*, *185*(2), 445–471. doi:10.1016/S0021-9991(02)00065-7

Leonard, A. (1974). Energy cascade in large eddy simulations of turbulent fluid flows. *Advances in Geophysics*, *18A*, 237–239.

LeVeque, R. J. (1998). Balancing source terms and flux gradients in high-resolution Godunov methods: The quasi-steady wave-propagation algorithm. *Journal of Computational Physics*, *146*(1), 346–365. doi:10.1006/jcph.1998.6058

Li, K., Yang, W., & Li, K. (2016). A hybrid parallel solving algorithm on gpu for quasi-tridiagonal system of linear equations. *IEEE Transactions on Parallel and Distributed Systems*, *27*(10), 2795–2808. doi:10.1109/TPDS.2016.2516988

Lima, J. V. F., Broquedis, F., Gautier, T., & Raffin, B. (2013). Preliminary Experiments with XKaapi on Intel Xeon Phi Coprocessor. In *Proceedings of the 25th SBAC-PAD*. Porto de Galinhas, Brazil: IEEE. doi:10.1109/SBAC-PAD.2013.28

Liu, G. R. (2003). *Meshfree methods-moving beyond the finite element method*. London: CRC press.

Li, X., Zhang, Y., Wang, X., & Ge, W. (2013). GPU-based numerical simulation of multi-phase flow in porous media using multiple-relaxation-time lattice Boltzmann method. *Chemical Engineering Science*, *102*, 209–219. doi:10.1016/j.ces.2013.06.037

Li, Y., LeBoeuf, E. J., & Basu, P. K. (2005). Least-squares finite-element scheme for the lattice Boltzmann method on an unstructured mesh. *Physical Review. E*, *72*(4), 046711. doi:10.1103/PhysRevE.72.046711 PMID:16383571

Li, Z., Favier, J., D'Ortona, U., & Poncet, S. (2016). An immersed boundary-lattice Boltzmann method for single- and multi-component fluid flows. *Journal of Computational Physics*, *304*, 424–440. doi:10.1016/j.jcp.2015.10.026

Lu, Y. Y., Belytschko, T., & Gu, L. (1994). A new implementation of element free galerkin methods. *Computer Methods in Applied Mechanics and Engineering*, *113*(3-4), 397–414. doi:10.1016/0045-7825(94)90056-6

Lyn, D. A., & Rodi, W. (1994). The flapping shear layer formed by flow separation from the forward corner of a square cylinder. *Journal of Fluid Mechanics*, *5*(267), 353–376. doi:10.1017/S0022112094001217

Maier, R. S., Kroll, D. M., Bernard, R. S., Howington, S. E., Peters, J. F., & Davis, H. T. (2000). Pore-scale simulation of dispersion. *Physics of Fluids*, *12*(8), 2065–2079. doi:10.1063/1.870452

Maier, R. S., Kroll, D. M., Kutsovsky, Y. E., Davis, H. T., & Bernard, R. S. (1998). Simulation of flow through bead packs using the lattice Boltzmann method. *Physics of Fluids*, *10*(1), 60–74. doi:10.1063/1.869550

Malaspinas, O., & Sagaut, P. (2012). Consistent subgrid scale modelling for lattice boltzmann methods. *Journal of Fluid Mechanics*, *700*, 514–542. doi:10.1017/jfm.2012.155

Mantovani, F., Pivanti, M., Schifano, S. F., & Tripiccione, R. (2013a). Exploiting parallelism in many-core architectures: Lattice Boltzmann models as a test case. *Journal of Physics: Conference Series*, *454*(1). doi:10.1088/1742-6596/454/1/012015

Mantovani, F., Pivanti, M., Schifano, S. F., & Tripiccione, R. (2013b). Performance issues on many-core processors: A D2Q37 Lattice Boltzmann scheme as a test-case. *Computers & Fluids*, *88*, 743–752. doi:10.1016/j.compfluid.2013.05.014

Manz, B., Gladden, L. F., & Warren, P. B. (1999). Flow and dispersion in porous media: Lattice-Boltzmann and NMR studies. *AIChE Journal. American Institute of Chemical Engineers*, *45*(9), 1845–1854. doi:10.1002/aic.690450902

Marié, S., Ricot, D., & Sagaut, P. (2009). Comparison between lattice boltzmann method and navier-stokes high order schemes for computational aeroacoustics. *Journal of Computational Physics*, *228*(4), 1056–1070. doi:10.1016/j.jcp.2008.10.021

Martys, N. S., & Hagedorn, J. G. (2002). Multiscale modeling of fluid transport in heterogeneous materials using discrete Boltzmann methods. *Materials and Structures*, *35*(10), 650–658. doi:10.1007/BF02480358

Maruyama, N., & Aoki, T. (2014). Optimizing stencil computations for NVIDIA kepler GPUs. In *International workshop on high-performance stencil computations* (pp. 1-7). Vienna, Austria: Academic Press.

Matsuzaki, K., Shikazono, N., & Kasagi, N. (2011). Three-dimensional numerical analysis of mixed ionic and electronic conducting cathode reconstructed by focused ion beam scanning electron microscope. *Journal of Power Sources*, *196*(6), 3073–3082. doi:10.1016/j.jpowsour.2010.11.142

Mattila, K., Hyväluoma, J., Rossi, T., Aspnäs, M., & Westerholm, J. (2007). An efficient swap algorithm for the lattice Boltzmann method. *Computer Physics Communications*, *176*(3), 200–210. doi:10.1016/j.cpc.2006.09.005

Mattila, K., Hyväluoma, J., Timonen, J., & Rossi, T. (2008). Comparison of implementations of the lattice-Boltzmann method. *Computers & Mathematics with Applications (Oxford, England)*, *55*(7), 1514–1524. doi:10.1016/j.camwa.2007.08.001

Mazzeo, M., & Coveney, P. (2008). HemeLB: A high performance parallel lattice-Boltzmann code for large scale fluid flow in complex geometries. *Computer Physics Communications*, *178*(12), 894–914. doi:10.1016/j.cpc.2008.02.013

McNamara, G. R., Garcia, A. L., & Alder, B. J. (1995). Stabilisation of thermal lattice Boltzmann models. *Journal of Statistical Physics*, *81*(1-2), 395–408. doi:10.1007/BF02179986

McNamara, G. R., & Zanetti, G. (1988). Use of the Boltzmann equation to simulate lattice-gas automata. *Physical Review Letters*, *61*(20), 2332–2335. doi:10.1103/PhysRevLett.61.2332 PMID:10039085

Mei, R., & Shyy, W. (1998). On the Finite Difference-Based Lattice Boltzmann Method in Curvilinear Coordinates. *Journal of Computational Physics*, *143*(2), 426–448. doi:10.1006/jcph.1998.5984

Mendoza, M., Boghosian, B. M., Herrmann, H. J., & Succi, S. (2010). Fast lattice Boltzmann solver for relativistic hydrodynamics. *Physical Review Letters, 105*(1), 014502. doi:10.1103/PhysRevLett.105.014502 PMID:20867451

Meneveau, C., & Katz, J. (2000). Scale-Invariance and Turbulence Models for Large-Eddy Simulation. *Annual Review of Fluid Mechanics, 32*(1), 1–32. doi:10.1146/annurev.fluid.32.1.1

Michler, C., Hulshoff, S. J., van Brummelen, E. H., & de Borst, R. (2004). A monolithic approach to fluid-structure interaction. *Computers & Fluids, 33*(5 – 6):839 – 848.

Min, M., & Lee, T. (2011). A spectral-element discontinuous Galerkin lattice Boltzmann method for nearly incompressible flows. *Journal of Computational Physics, 230*(1), 245–259. doi:10.1016/j.jcp.2010.09.024

Mohamad, A. A. (2011). *Lattice Boltzmann Method Fundamentals and Engineering Applications with Computer Codes*. London: Springer.

Mohamad, A. A. (2011). *The lattice boltzmann method–fundamental and engineering applications with computer codes*. Springer.

Mohamad, A. A. (2011). *The lattice Boltzmann method–fundamental and engineering applications with computer codes*. Springer.

Mohamad, A. A. (2011). *The lattice Boltzmann method–Fundamental and engineering applications with computer codes*. Springer.

Mohamad, A. A., & Succi, S. (2009). A note on equilibrium boundary conditions in lattice Boltzmann fluid dynamic simulations. *The European Physical Journal. Special Topics, 171*(1), 213–221. doi:10.1140/epjst/e2009-01031-9

Molls, T., & Chaudhry, M. H. (1995). Depth-averaged open-channel flow model. *Journal of Hydraulic Engineering, 121*(6), 133–149. doi:10.1061/(ASCE)0733-9429(1995)121:6(453)

Murakami, S., & Mochida, A. (1995). On turbulent vortex shedding flow past 2d square cylinder predicted by CFD. *Journal of Wind Engineering and Industrial Aerodynamics, 54-55*(0), 191–211. doi:10.1016/0167-6105(94)00043-D

Musavi, S. H., & Ashrafizaadeh, M. (2016). A mesh-free lattice Boltzmann solver for flows in complex geometries. *International Journal of Heat and Fluid Flow, 59*, 10–19. doi:10.1016/j.ijheatfluidflow.2016.01.006

Nabovati, A., & Sousa, A. C. (2015). LBM mesoscale modeling of porous media. *International Journal on Heat and Mass Transfer - Theory and Applications, 3*(4).

Nabovati, A., & Sousa, A. C. M. (2007). Fluid flow simulation in random porous media at pore level using lattice Boltzmann method. In F. G. Zhuang & J. C. Li (Eds.), *New trends in fluid mechanics research: Proceedings of the fifth international conference on fluid mechanics* (pp. 518-521). Berlin: Springer Berlin Heidelberg. doi:10.1007/978-3-540-75995-9_172

Nabovati, A., Llewellin, E. W., & Sousa, A. C. (2009). A general model for the permeability of fibrous porous media based on fluid flow simulations using the lattice Boltzmann method. *Composites. Part A, Applied Science and Manufacturing, 40*(6-7), 860–869. doi:10.1016/j. compositesa.2009.04.009

Nabovati, A., & Sousa, A. C. M. (2008). Fluid flow simulation at open–porous medium interface using the lattice Boltzmann method. *International Journal for Numerical Methods in Fluids, 56*(8), 1449–1456. doi:10.1002/fld.1614

Nannelli, F., & Succi, S. (1992). The lattice Boltzmann equation on irregular lattices. *Journal of Statistical Physics, 68*(3-4), 401–407. doi:10.1007/BF01341755

Nejat, A., Abdollahi, V., & Vahidkhah, K. (2011). Lattice Boltzmann simulation of non-Newtonian flows past confined cylinders. *Journal of Non-Newtonian Fluid Mechanics, 166*(12-13), 689–697. doi:10.1016/j.jnnfm.2011.03.006

Newmark, N. M. (1959). A method of computation for structural dynamics. *Journal of the Engineering Mechanics Division, 85.*

Nickolls, J., Buck, I., Garland, M., & Skadron, K. (2008). Scalable Parallel Programming with CUDA. *Queue, 6*(2), 40–53. doi:10.1145/1365490.1365500

Nieuwstadt, F., & Keller, H. B. (1973). Viscous flow past circular cylinder. *Computers & Fluids, 42,* 471–489.

Nita, C., Itu, L., Suciu, C., & Suciu, C. (2013). GPU Accelerated Blood Flow Computation Using the Lattice Boltzmann Method. In *Proceedings of the IEEE 2013 HPEC* (pp. 1-6). IEEE. doi:10.1109/HPEC.2013.6670324

Niu, X.-D., Munekata, T., Hyodo, S.-A., & Suga, K. (2007). An investigation of water-gas transport processes in the gas-diffusion-layer of a PEM fuel cell by a multiphase multiple-relaxation-time lattice Boltzmann model. *Journal of Power Sources, 172*(2), 542–552. doi:10.1016/j. jpowsour.2007.05.081

Nozawa, K., & Tamura, T. (1997). Les of flow past a square cylinder using embedded meshes. In *Direct and Large-Eddy Simulation II.* Springer. doi:10.1007/978-94-011-5624-0_39

NVIDIA Fermi. (2009). Retrieved from http://www.nvidia.com/content/PDF/fermi_white_papers/ NVIDIA_Fermi_Compute_Architecture_Whitepaper.pdf

NVIDIA Kepler GK110. (2012). Retrieved from http://www.nvidia.com/content/PDF/kepler/ NVIDIA-Kepler-GK110-Architecture-Whitepaper.pdf

NVIDIA Pascal P100. (2016). Retrieved from https://images.nvidia.com/content/pdf/tesla/ whitepaper/pascal-architecture-whitepaper.pdf

NVIDIA Volta V100. (2017). Retrieved from https://images.nvidia.com/content/volta-architecture/ pdf/Volta-Architecture-Whitepaper-v1.0.pdf

O'Brien, G., Bean, C., & McDermott, F. (2002). A comparison of published experimental data with a coupled lattice Boltzmann-analytic advection-diffusion method for reactive transport in porous media. *Journal of Hydrology (Amsterdam)*, *268*(1-4), 143–157. doi:10.1016/S0022-1694(02)00173-7

O'Brien, G., Bean, C., & McDermott, F. (2003). Numerical investigations of passive and reactive flow through generic single fractures with heterogeneous permeability. *Earth and Planetary Science Letters*, *213*(3-4), 271–284. doi:10.1016/S0012-821X(03)00342-X

O'Connor, R., & Fredrich, J. (1999). Microscale flow modelling in geologic materials. *Physics and Chemistry of the Earth. Part A: Solid Earth and Geodesy*, *24*(7), 611–616. doi:10.1016/S1464-1895(99)00088-5

Obrecht, C., Kuznik, F., Tourancheau, B., & Roux, J.-J. (2011). A New Approach to the Lattice Boltzmann Method for Graphics Processing Units. *Computers & Mathematics with Applications (Oxford, England)*, *61*(12), 3628–3638. doi:10.1016/j.camwa.2010.01.054

Obrecht, C., Kuznik, F., Tourancheau, B., & Roux, J.-J. (2013). Scalable lattice Boltzmann solvers for CUDA GPU clusters. *Parallel Computing*, *39*(6-7), 259–270. doi:10.1016/j.parco.2013.04.001

Ohta, M., Nakamura, T., Yoshida, Y., & Matsukuma, Y. (2011). Lattice Boltzmann simulations of viscoplastic fluid flows through complex flow channels. *Journal of Non-Newtonian Fluid Mechanics*, *166*(7–8), 404–412. doi:10.1016/j.jnnfm.2011.01.011

Olinger, D. J., & Sreenivasan, K. R. (1988). Nonlinear dynamics of the wake of an oscillating cylinder. *Physical Review Letters*, *60*(9), 797–800. doi:10.1103/PhysRevLett.60.797 PMID:10038655

OpenACC. (2016). *OpenACC directives for accelerators*. Retrieved from http://www.openacc-standard.org

OpenMP. (2016). *OpenMP application program interface version 4.0*. Retrieved from http://www.openmp.org/mp-documents/OpenMP4.0.0.pdf

Owens, J. D., Houston, M., Luebke, D., Green, S., Stone, J. E., & Phillips, J. C. (2008). GPU Computing. *Proceedings of the IEEE*, *96*(5), 879–899. doi:10.1109/JPROC.2008.917757

Pan, C., Hilpert, M., & Miller, C. T. (2004). Lattice-Boltzmann simulation of two-phase flow in porous media. *Water Resources Research*, *40*(1). doi:10.1029/2003WR002120

Pan, C., Luo, L.-S., & Miller, C. T. (2006). An evaluation of lattice Boltzmann schemes for porous medium flow simulation. *Computers & Fluids*, *35*(8), 898–909. doi:10.1016/j.compfluid.2005.03.008

Pan, C., Prins, J. F., & Miller, C. T. (2004). A high-performance lattice Boltzmann implementation to model flow in porous media. *Computer Physics Communications*, *158*(2), 89–105. doi:10.1016/j.cpc.2003.12.003

Park, J., & Li, X. (2008). Multi-phase micro-scale flow simulation in the electrodes of a PEM fuel cell by lattice Boltzmann method. *Journal of Power Sources, 178*(1), 248–257. doi:10.1016/j. jpowsour.2007.12.008

Park, J., Matsubara, M., & Li, X. (2007). Application of lattice Boltzmann method to a micro-scale flow simulation in the porous electrode of a PEM fuel cell. *Journal of Power Sources, 173*(1), 404–414. doi:10.1016/j.jpowsour.2007.04.021

Parmigiani, A., Huber, C., Bachmann, O., & Chopard, B. (2011). Pore-scale mass and reactant transport in multiphase porous media flows. *Journal of Fluid Mechanics, 686*, 40–76. doi:10.1017/ jfm.2011.268

Patil, D. V., & Lakshmisha, K. (2009). Finite volume TVD formulation of lattice Boltzmann simulation on unstructured mesh. *Journal of Computational Physics, 228*(14), 5262–5279. doi:10.1016/j.jcp.2009.04.008

Perkins, W. A., & Richmond, M. C. (2004). *MASS2 Modular Aquatic Simulation System in Two Dimensions, Theory and Numerical Methods.* Pacific Northwest National Laboratory.

Peskin, C. S. (2002). The immersed boundary method. *Acta Numerica, 11*, 479–517. doi:10.1017/ S0962492902000077

Peters, A., Melchionna, S., Kaxiras, E., Lätt, J., Sircar, J., Bernaschi, M., ... Succi, S. (2010. Multiscale simulation of cardiovascular flows on the IBM BlueGene/P: Full heart-circulation system at red-blood cell resolution. In *2010 ACM/IEEE International conference for high performance computing, networking, storage and analysis* (pp. 1-10). IEEE. doi:10.1109/SC.2010.33

Pettigrew, M.J., Taylor, C.E., Fisher, N.J., Yetisir, M., & Smith, B.A. (1998). Flow-induced vibration: recent findings and open questions. *Nuclear Engineering and Design, 185*, 249-276.

Piomelli, U., & Elias, B. (2002). Wall-layer models for large-eddy simulations. *Annual Review of Fluid Mechanics, 34*(1), 181–202. doi:10.1146/annurev.fluid.34.082901.144919

Piperno, S., & Farhat, C. (2001). Partitioned procedures for the transient solution of coupled aeroelastic problems - Part II: Energy transfer analysis and three-dimensional applications. *Computer Methods in Applied Mechanics and Engineering, 190*(24-25), 3147–3170. doi:10.1016/ S0045-7825(00)00386-8

Pitsch, H. (2006). Large-Eddy Simulation of Turbulent Combustion. *Annual Review of Fluid Mechanics, 38*(1), 453–482. doi:10.1146/annurev.fluid.38.050304.092133

Pohl, T., Deserno, F., Thurey, N., Rüde, U., Lammers, P., Wellein, G., & Zeiser, T. (2004). Performance evaluation of parallel large-scale lattice Boltzmann applications on three supercomputing architectures. In *Supercomputing, 2004. Proceedings of the ACM/IEEE SC2004 conference* (pp. 21-21). IEEE. doi:10.1109/SC.2004.37

Pohl, T., Kowarchik, M., Wilke, J., Rüde, U., & Iglberger, K. (2003). Optimization and profiling of the cache performance of parallel lattice boltzmann codes. *Parallel Processing Letters, 13*(4), 549–560. doi:10.1142/S0129626403001501

Pope, S. B. (2000). *Turbulent Flows*. Cambridge University Press. doi:10.1017/CBO9780511840531

Pourquie, M., Breuer, M., & Rodi, W. (1997). Computed test case: Square cylinder. In *Direct and Large-Eddy Simulation II*. Springer. doi:10.1007/978-94-011-5624-0_34

Qian, Y. H., D'Humires, D., & Lallemand, P. (1992). Lattice bgk models for navier-stokes equation. *Europhysics Letters*, *17*(6), 479–484. doi:10.1209/0295-5075/17/6/001

Rajaratnam, N., & Nwachukwu, B. (1983). Flow near groin-like structures. *Journal of Hydraulic Engineering*, *109*(3), 256–267. doi:10.1061/(ASCE)0733-9429(1983)109:3(463)

Randall, J., & Leveque, L. (1992). *Numerical Methods for Conservation Laws* (2nd ed.). Birkhäuser Basel.

Randles, A. P., Kale, V., Hammond, J., Gropp, W., & Kaxiras, E. (2013). Performance Analysis of the Lattice Boltzmann Model beyond Navier-Stokes. In *IEEE 27th International Symposium on Parallel & Distributed Processing* (pp. 1063-1074). Boston: IEEE.

Rapaka, S., Mansi, T., Georgescu, B., Pop, M., Wright, G. A., Kamen, A., & Comaniciu, D. (2012). Lbm-ep: Lattice-boltzmann method for fast cardiac electrophysiology simulation from 3d images. In *Proceedings of the Medical Image Computing and Computer-Assisted Intervention* (pp. 33–40). Academic Press. doi:10.1007/978-3-642-33418-4_5

Regulski, W., Szumbarski, J., Łaniewski-Wołłk, L., Gumowski, K., Skibiński, J., Wichrowski, M., & Wejrzanowski, T. (2015). Pressure drop in flow across ceramic foams - a numerical and experimental study. *Chemical Engineering Science*, *137*, 320–337. doi:10.1016/j.ces.2015.06.043

Reinders, J., Jeffers, J., & Sodani, A. (2016). *Intel Xeon Phi Processor High Performance Programming, Knights Landing Edition*. Cambridge, MA: Morgan Kaufmann.

Reyes, R., López, I., Fumero, J. J., & de Sande, F. (2013). A preliminary evaluation of OpenACC implementations. *The Journal of Supercomputing*, *65*(3), 1063–1075. doi:10.1007/s11227-012-0853-z

Rinaldi, P. R., Dari, E. A., Vénere, M. J., & Clausse, A. (2012). A Lattice-Boltzmann solver for 3D fluid simulation on GPU. *Simulation Modelling Practice and Theory*, *25*, 163–171. doi:10.1016/j.simpat.2012.03.004

Ripesi, P., Biferale, L., Schifano, S. F., & Tripiccione, R. (2014). Evolution of a double-front Rayleigh-Taylor system using a graphics-processing-unit-based high-resolution thermal Lattice Boltzmann model. *Phys. Rev. E*, *89*(4), 043022. doi:10.1103/PhysRevE.89.043022 PMID:24827347

Roma, A. M., Peskin, C. S., & Berger, M. J. (1999). An adaptive version of the immersed boundary method. *Journal of Computational Physics*, *153*(2), 509–534. doi:10.1006/jcph.1999.6293

Rong, L., Dong, K., & Yu, A. (2014). Lattice-Boltzmann simulation of fluid flow through packed beds of spheres: Effect of particle size distribution. *Chemical Engineering Science*, *116*, 508–523. doi:10.1016/j.ces.2014.05.025

Rothman, D. H. (1988). Cellular-automaton fluids: A model for flow in porous media. *Geophysics*, *53*(4), 509–518. doi:10.1190/1.1442482

Rothman, D. H., & Zaleski, S. (1994). Lattice-gas models of phase separation: Interfaces, phase transitions and multiphase flow. *Reviews of Modern Physics*, *66*(4), 1417–1479. doi:10.1103/RevModPhys.66.1417

Sanders, P., & Schulz, C. (2011). Engineering multilevel graph partitioning algorithms. In C. Demetrescu & M. M. Halldorsson (Eds.), *Algorithms - ESA 2011: 19th Annual European symposium, Saarbrücken, Germany* (pp. 469–480). Berlin: Springer Berlin Heidelberg.

Sbragaglia, M., Benzi, R., Biferale, L., Chen, H., Shan, X., & Succi, S. (2009). Lattice Boltzmann method with self-consistent thermo-hydrodynamic equilibria. *Journal of Fluid Mechanics*, *628*, 299–309. doi:10.1017/S002211200900665X

Scagliarini, A., Biferale, L., Sbragaglia, M., Sugiyama, K., & Toschi, F. (2010). Lattice Boltzmann methods for thermal flows: Continuum limit and applications to compressible Rayleigh-Taylor systems. *Physics of Fluids*, *22*(5), 055101. doi:10.1063/1.3392774

Schepke, C., Maillard, N., & Navaux, P. O. A. (2009). Parallel Lattice Boltzmann Method with Blocked Partitioning. *International Journal of Parallel Programming*, *37*(6), 593–611. doi:10.1007/s10766-009-0113-x

Schnherr, M., Kucher, K., Geier, M., Stiebler, M., Freudiger, S., & Krafczyk, M. (2011). Multi-thread implementations of the lattice boltzmann method on non-uniform grids for CPUs and GPUs. *Computers & Mathematics with Applications (Oxford, England)*, *61*(12), 3730–3743. doi:10.1016/j.camwa.2011.04.012

Schönherr, M., Geier, M., & Krafczyk, M. (2011). 3D GPGPU LBM implementation on non-uniform grids. *International conference on parallel computational fluid dynamics ParCFD*.

Schornbaum, F., & Rüde, U. (2016). Massively parallel algorithms for the lattice Boltzmann method on nonuniform grids. *SIAM Journal on Scientific Computing*, *38*(2), C96–C126. doi:10.1137/15M1035240

Schulz, M., Krafczyk, M., Tölke, J., & Rank, E. (2002). Parallelization strategies and efficiency of CFD computations in complex geometries using lattice Boltzmann methods on high-performance computers. In M. Breuer, F. Durst, & C. Zenger (Eds.), *High Performance Scientific and Engineering Computing: Proceedings of the 3rd International FORTWIHR Conference on HPSEC, Erlangen* (pp. 115-122). Berlin: Springer Berlin Heidelberg. doi:10.1007/978-3-642-55919-8_13

Schure, M. R., Maier, R. S., Kroll, D. M., & Davis, H. T. (2002). Simulation of packed-bed chromatography utilizing high-resolution flow fields: Comparison with models. *Analytical Chemistry*, *74*(23), 6006–6016. doi:10.1021/ac0204101 PMID:12498196

Shan, X. (2016). The mathematical structure of the lattices of the Lattice Boltzmann method. *Journal of Computational Science*, *17*, 475–481. doi:10.1016/j.jocs.2016.03.002

Shan, X., & Chen, H. (1993). Lattice Boltzmann model for simulating flows with multiple phases and components. *Physical Review. E*, *47*(3), 1815–1819. doi:10.1103/PhysRevE.47.1815 PMID:9960203

Shan, X., Yuan, X. F., & Chen, H. (2006). Kinetic theory representation of hydrodynamics: A way beyond the Navier-Stokes equation. *Journal of Fluid Mechanics*, *550*(-1), 413–441. doi:10.1017/S0022112005008153

Shet A. G., Siddharth K., Sorathiya S. H., Deshpande A. M., Sher-lekar S. D., Kaul B., & Ansumali S. (2013). On Vectorization for Lattice Based Simulations. *International Journal of Modern Physics*.

Shet, A. G., Siddharth, K., Sorathiya, S. H., Deshpande, A. M., Sherlekar, S. D., Kaul, B., & Ansumali, S. (2013a). On vectorization for lattice based simulations. *International Journal of Modern Physics C*, *24*(12), 1340011. doi:10.1142/S0129183113400111

Shet, A. G., Sorathiya, S. H., Krithivasan, S., Deshpande, A. M., Kaul, B., Sherlekar, S. D., & Ansumali, S. (2013b). Data structure and movement for lattice-based simulations. *Phys. Rev. E*, *88*(1), 013314. doi:10.1103/PhysRevE.88.013314 PMID:23944590

Shiels, D., Leonard, A., & Roshko, A. (2001). Flow-Induced Vibration of a Circular Cylinder at Limiting Structural Parameters. *Journal of Fluids and Structures*, *15*(1), 3–21. doi:10.1006/jfls.2000.0330

Shikazono, N., Kanno, D., Matsuzaki, K., Teshima, H., Sumino, S., & Kasagi, N. (2010). Numerical assessment of SOFC anode polarization based on three-dimensional model microstructure reconstructed from FIB-SEM images. *Journal of the Electrochemical Society*, *157*(5), B665–B672. doi:10.1149/1.3330568

Shi, X. I, Lin, J., & Yu, Z. (2003). Discontinuous Galerkin spectral element lattice Boltzmann method on triangular element. *International Journal for Numerical Methods in Fluids*, *42*(11), 1249–1261. doi:10.1002/fld.594

Singh, S. & Bhargava, R. (2014). Simulation of phase transition during cryosurgical treatment of a tumor tissue loaded with nano-particles using meshfree approach. *ASME Journal of Heat Transfer*, *136*(12). DOI: .10.1115/1.4028730

Singh, A., Singh, I. V., & Prakash, R. (2007). Numerical analysis of fluid squeezed between two parallel plates by meshless method. *Computers & Fluids*, *36*(9), 1460–1480. doi:10.1016/j.compfluid.2006.12.005

Singh, M., & Mohanty, K. (2000). Permeability of spatially correlated porous media. *Chemical Engineering Science*, *55*(22), 5393–5403. doi:10.1016/S0009-2509(00)00157-3

Singh, S., & Bhargava, R. (2015). Numerical simulation of a phase transition problem with natural convection using hybrid FEM / EFGM technique. *International Journal of Numerical Methods for Heat & Fluid Flow*, *25*(3), 570–592. doi:10.1108/HFF-06-2013-0201

Smagorinsky, J. (1963). General Circulation Experiments with the Primitive Equations. *Monthly Weather Review*, *91*(3), 99–164. doi:10.1175/1520-0493(1963)091<0099:GCEWTP>2.3.CO;2

Sodani, A., Gramunt, R., Corbal, J., Kim, H., Vinod, K., Chinthamani, S., ... Liu, Y. (2016). Knights Landing: Second-Generation Intel Xeon Phi Product. *IEEE Micro*, *36*(2), 34–46. doi:10.1109/MM.2016.25

Sofonea, V., & Sekerka, R. F. (2003). Viscosity of finite difference lattice Boltzmann models. *Journal of Computational Physics*, *184*(2), 422–434. doi:10.1016/S0021-9991(02)00026-8

Sone, Y. (2002). *Kinetic theory and fluid dynamics*. Birkhäuser. doi:10.1007/978-1-4612-0061-1

Soti, A. K., Bhardwaj, R., & Sheridan, J. (2015). Flow-induced deformation of a flexible thin structure as manifestation of heat transfer enhancement. *International Journal of Heat and Mass Transfer*, *84*, 1070–1081. doi:10.1016/j.ijheatmasstransfer.2015.01.048

Spalart, P. R. (2009). Detached-eddy simulation. *Annual Review of Fluid Mechanics*, *41*(1), 181–202. doi:10.1146/annurev.fluid.010908.165130

Sreenivasan, K. R. (1985). On the Fine – Scale Intermittency of Turbulence. *Journal of Fluid Mechanics*, *151*(-1), 81–103. doi:10.1017/S0022112085000878

Stahl, B., Chopard, B., & Latt, J. (2010). Measurements of wall shear stress with the lattice Boltzmann method and staircase approximation of boundaries. *Computers & Fluids*, *39*(9), 1625–1633. doi:10.1016/j.compfluid.2010.05.015

Sterling, J. D., & Chen, S. (1996). Stability Analysis of Lattice Boltzmann Methods. *Journal of Computational Physics*, *123*(1), 196–206. doi:10.1006/jcph.1996.0016

Stiebler, M., Tolke, J., & Krafczyk, M. (2006). An upwind discretization scheme for the finite volume lattice boltzamnn method. *Computers & Fluids*, *35*(8-9), 814–819. doi:10.1016/j.compfluid.2005.09.002

Straka, R. (2016). Numerical simulation of heat transfer in packed beds by two population thermal lattice Boltzmann method. *Mechanics & Industry*, *17*(2), 203. doi:10.1051/meca/2015071

Strohmaier, E. (2006). Top500 supercomputer. In *Proceedings of the 2006 ACM/IEEE conference on supercomputing*. New York: ACM.

Stürmer, M., Götz, J., Richter, G., Dörfler, A., & Rüde, U. (2009). Fluid flow simulation on the Cell broadband engine using the lattice Boltzmann method. *Computers & Mathematics with Applications (Oxford, England)*, *58*(5), 1062–1070. doi:10.1016/j.camwa.2009.04.006

Succi, S. (2001). *The Lattice Boltzmann Equation for Fluid Dynamics and Beyond*. New York: Oxford University Press.

Succi, S. (2001). *The lattice Boltzmann Equation for Fluid Dynamics and Beyond*. Oxford University Press.

Succi, S. (2001). *The lattice Boltzmann equation: for fluid dynamics and beyond*. New York: Oxford university press.

Succi, S. (2001). *The lattice Boltzmann equation: For fluid dynamics and beyond*. New York: Oxford university press.

Succi, S. (2001). *The Lattice-Boltzmann Equation*. Oxford, UK: Oxford University Press.

Succi, S., Foti, E., & Higuera, F. (1989). Three-dimensional flows in complex geometries with the lattice Boltzmann method. *EPL*, *10*(5), 433–438. doi:10.1209/0295-5075/10/5/008

Sukop, M., & Thorne, D. T. (2006). *Lattice Boltzmann Modeling: an introduction for geoscientists and engineers* (1st ed.). Springer Verlag.

Sullivan, P., McWilliams, J. C., & Moeng, C. H. (1994). A subgrid-scale model for large-eddy simulation of planetary boundary-layer flows. *Boundary-Layer Meteorology*, *71*(3), 247–276. doi:10.1007/BF00713741

Sullivan, S. P., Gladden, L. F., & Johns, M. L. (2006). 3D chemical reactor LB simulations. *Mathematics and Computers in Simulation*, *72*(2-6), 206–211. doi:10.1016/j.matcom.2006.05.023

Sullivan, S., Gladden, L., & Johns, M. (2006). Simulation of power-law fluid flow through porous media using lattice Bboltzmann techniques. *Journal of Non-Newtonian Fluid Mechanics*, *133*(2–3), 91–98. doi:10.1016/j.jnnfm.2005.11.003

Sullivan, S., Sani, F., Johns, M., & Gladden, L. (2005). Simulation of packed bed reactors using lattice Boltzmann methods. *Chemical Engineering Science*, *60*(12), 3405–3418. doi:10.1016/j.ces.2005.01.038

Sullivan, S., Sederman, A., Johns, M., & Gladden, L. (2007). Verification of shear-thinning LB simulations in complex geometries. *Journal of Non-Newtonian Fluid Mechanics*, *143*(2-3), 59–63. doi:10.1016/j.jnnfm.2006.12.008

Sumner, D., Wong, S. S. T., Price, S. J., & Paidoussis, M. D. (1999). Fluid behavior of side-by-side circular cylinders in steady cross-flow. *Journal of Fluids and Structures*, *13*(3), 309–338. doi:10.1006/jfls.1999.0205

Suzue, Y., Shikazono, N., & Kasagi, N. (2008). Micro modeling of solid oxide fuel cell anode based on stochastic reconstruction. *Journal of Power Sources*, *184*(1), 52–59. doi:10.1016/j.jpowsour.2008.06.029

Swarztrauber, P. N. (1974). A direct Method for the Discrete Solution of Separable Elliptic Equations. *SIAM Journal on Numerical Analysis*, *11*(6), 1136–1150. doi:10.1137/0711086

Tennekes, H., & Lumley, J. L. (1972). *A First Course in Turbulence*. MIT Press.

Ting, F. C. K., & Kirby, J. T. (1996). Dynamics of surf-zone turbulence in a spilling breaker. *Coastal Engineering*, *27*(3-4), 131–160. doi:10.1016/0378-3839(95)00037-2

Tölke, J. (2010). Implementation of a Lattice Boltzmann kernel Using the Compute Unified Device Architecture Developed by nVIDIA. *Computing and Visualization in Science, 13*(1), 29–39. doi:10.1007/s00791-008-0120-2

Tölke, J., & Krafczyk, M. (2008). TeraFLOP Computing on a Desktop PC with GPUs for 3D CFD. *International Journal of Computational Fluid Dynamics, 22*(7), 443–456. doi:10.1080/10618560802238275

Tomczak, T., & Szafran, R. G. (2016). *Memory layout in GPU implementation of lattice Boltzmann method for sparse 3D geometries.* CoRR, abs/1611.02445

Tomczak, T., & Szafran, R. G. (2017). *Sparse geometries handling in lattice-Boltzmann method implementation for graphic processors.* CoRR, abs/1703.08015

Tubbs, K., & Tsai, F. (2011). GPU accelerated lattice Boltzmann model for shallow water flow. *International Journal for Numerical Methods in Engineering, 86*(3), 316–334. doi:10.1002/nme.3066

Tumelo, R. A. (2011). *Lattice Boltzmann methods for shallow water flow applications* (Master's dissertation). University of the Witwatersrand, Johannesburg, South Africa.

Turek, S., & Hron, J. (2006). Proposal for Numerical Benchmarking of Fluid-Structure Interaction between an Elastic Object and Laminar Incompressible Flow. In *Lecture Notes in Computational Science and Engineering: Vol. 53.* Springer Berlin Heidelberg.

Ubertini, S., Bella, G., & Succi, S. (2003). Lattice Boltzmann method on unstructured grids: Further developments. *Physical Review. E, 68*(1), 016701. doi:10.1103/PhysRevE.68.016701 PMID:12935281

Uribe-Paredes, R., Valero-Lara, P., Arias, E., Sánchez, J. L., & Cazorla, D. (2011). A GPU-Based Implementation for Range Queries on Spaghettis Data Structure. In *International Conference on Computational Science and Its Applications - ICCSA 2011* (pp. 615-629). Springer. doi:10.1007/978-3-642-21928-3_45

Valero-Lara, P. (2014b). A fast multi-domain lattice-boltzmann solver on heterogeneous (multicore-gpu) architectures. In *Proceedings of 14th International Conference Computational and Mathematical Methods in Science and Engineering* (pp. 1239-1250). Academic Press.

Valero-Lara, P. (2014c). A fast multi-domain lattice-boltzmann solver on heterogeneous (multicore-gpu) architectures. In *Proceedings of 14th International Conference Computational and Mathematical Methods in Science and Engineering* (pp. 1239-1250). Academic Press.

Valero-Lara, P., & Jansson, J. (2017). Heterogeneous CPU+GPU approaches for mesh refinement over lattice-Boltzmann simulations. *Concurrency and Computation: Practice and Experience, 29*(7).

Valero-Lara, P., Pinelli, A., & Prieto-Matías, M. (2014). Accelerating Solid-fluid Interaction using Lattice-boltzmann and Immersed Boundary Coupled Simulations on Heterogeneous Platforms. In *Proceedings of the International Conference on Computational Science* (pp. 50-61). Academic Press. doi:10.1016/j.procs.2014.05.005

Valero-Lara, P. (2014a). Accelerating solid-fluid interaction based on the immersed boundary method on multicore and GPU architectures. *The Journal of Supercomputing, 70*(2), 799–815. doi:10.1007/s11227-014-1262-2

Valero-Lara, P. (2016). Leveraging the performance of LBM-HPC for Large sizes on GPUs using ghost cells. In J. Carretero, J. Garcia-Blas, R. Ko, P. Mueller, & K. Nakano (Eds.), Lecture Notes in Computer Science: Vol. 10048. *Algorithms and Architectures for Parallel Processing. ICA3PP 2016* (pp. 417–430). Cham: Springer. doi:10.1007/978-3-319-49583-5_31

Valero-Lara, P., Igual, F. D., Prieto-Matías, M., Pinelli, A., & Favier, J. (2015). Accelerating fluid-solid simulations (Lattice-Boltzmann & Immersed-Boundary) on heterogeneous architectures. *Journal of Computational Science, 10*, 249–261. doi:10.1016/j.jocs.2015.07.002

Valero-Lara, P., Igual, F. D., Prieto-Matías, M., Pinelli, A., & Favier, J. (2015). Accelerating fluid–solid simulations (Lattice-Boltzmann & Immersed-Boundary) on heterogeneous architectures. *Journal of Computational Science, 39*(67), 259–270.

Valero-Lara, P., & Jansson, J. (2015). A non-uniform staggered cartesian grid approach for lattice-boltzmann method. *Procedia Computer Science, 51*, 296–305. doi:10.1016/j.procs.2015.05.245

Valero-Lara, P., & Jansson, J. (2015). LBM-HPC An open-source tool for fluid simulations. case study: Unified parallel C (UPC-PGAS). In *2015 IEEE International Conference on Cluster Computing* (pp 318-321). IEEE. doi:10.1109/CLUSTER.2015.52

Valero-Lara, P., & Jansson, J. (2017). Heterogeneous cpu+gpu approaches for mesh refinement over lattice- boltzmann simulations. *Concurrency and Computation, 29*(7), e3919. doi:10.1002/cpe.3919

Valero-Lara, P., Pinelli, A., Favier, J., & Prieto-Matías, M. (2012). Block Tridiagonal Solvers on Heterogeneous Architectures. In *Proceedings of 10th IEEE International Symposium on Parallel and Distributed Processing with Applications Workshop* (pp. 609-616). IEEE.

Valero-Lara, P., Pinelli, A., & Prieto-Matías, M. (2014). Fast finite difference Poisson solvers on heterogeneous architectures. *Computer Physics Communications, 185*(4), 1265–1272. doi:10.1016/j.cpc.2013.12.026

Van Atta, C. W., & Gharib, M. (1987). Ordered and chaotic vortex streets behind circular cylinders at low Reynolds number. *Journal of Fluid Mechanics, 174*(-1), 113–133. doi:10.1017/S0022112087000065

Verstappen, R. W. C. P., & Veldman, A. E. P. (1997). Fourth-order dns of flow past a square cylinder: First results. In *Direct and Large-Eddy Simulation II*. Springer. doi:10.1007/978-94-011-5624-0_35

Vidal, D., Roy, R., & Bertrand, F. (2010a). On improving the performance of large parallel lattice Boltzmann flow simulations in heterogeneous porous media. *Computers & Fluids, 39*(2), 324–337. doi:10.1016/j.compfluid.2009.09.011

Vidal, D., Roy, R., & Bertrand, F. (2010b). A parallel workload balanced and memory efficient lattice-Boltzmann algorithm with single unit BGK relaxation time for laminar Newtonian flows. *Computers & Fluids, 39*(8), 1411–1423. doi:10.1016/j.compfluid.2010.04.011

Vizitiu, A., Itu, L., Lazar, L., & Suciu, C. (2014). Double precision stencil computations on kepler GPUs. In *System theory, control and computing (iCSTCC), 2014 18th international conference* (pp. 123-127). Academic Press. doi:10.1109/ICSTCC.2014.6982402

Vizitiu, A., Itu, L., Niţă, C., & Suciu, C. (2014). Optimized three-dimensional stencil computation on fermi and kepler GPUs. In *High performance extreme computing conference (HPEC), 2014* (pp. 1–6). IEEE. doi:10.1109/HPEC.2014.7040968

Wagner, C., Hüttl, T., & Sagaut, P. (2007). *Large-Eddy Simulation for Acoustics*. Cambridge University Press. doi:10.1017/CBO9780511546143

Wang, G., & Vanka, S. P. (1997). Les of flow over a square cylinder. In *Direct and Large-Eddy Simulation II*. Springer. doi:10.1007/978-94-011-5624-0_37

Wang, J., Zhang, X., Bengough, A. G., & Crawford, J. W. (2005). Domain- decomposition method for parallel lattice Boltzmann simulation of incompressible flow in porous media. *Phys. Rev. E, 72*(1), 016706. doi:10.1103/PhysRevE.72.016706 PMID:16090133

Wang, L.-P., & Afsharpoya, B. (2006). Modeling fluid flow in fuel cells using the lattice-Boltzmann approach. *Mathematics and Computers in Simulation, 72*(2-6), 242–248. doi:10.1016/j.matcom.2006.05.038

Weaver, V., Johnson, M., Kasichayanula, K., Ralph, J., Luszczek, P., Terpstra, D., & Moore, S. (2012). Measuring energy and power with PAPI. In *Parallel processing workshops (iCPPW), 2012 41st international conference on* (pp. 262-268). Academic Press. doi:10.1109/ICPPW.2012.39

Wellein, G., Zeiser, T., Hager, G., & Donath, S. (2006). On the single processor performance of simple lattice boltzmann kernels. *Computers & Fluids, 35*(8-9), 910–919. doi:10.1016/j.compfluid.2005.02.008

Wendt, J. F., & Anderson, J. D. (2008). *Computational fluid dynamics: An introduction*. Springer.

Wendt, J. F., & Anderson, J. D. (2008). *Computational Fluid Dynamics: An Introduction*. Springer.

Wienke, S., Springer, P., Terboven, C., & an Mey, D. (2012). OpenACC-first experiences with real-world applications. In Euro-Par 2012 Parallel Processing (pp. 859-870). Springer Berlin Heidelberg. doi:10.1007/978-3-642-32820-6_85

Wienke, S., Terboven, C., Beyer, J. C., & Müller, M. S. (2014). A pattern-based comparison of OpenACC and OpenMP for accelerator computing. In F. Silva, I. Dutra, & V. Santos Costa (Eds.), *Euro-par 2014 parallel processing: 20th international conference, Porto, Portugal, August 25-29, 2014. proceedings* (pp. 812-823). Cham: Springer International Publishing. doi:10.1007/978-3-319-09873-9_68

Williamson, C. H. K. (1996). Vortex dynamics in the cylinder wake. *Annual Review of Fluid Mechanics*, *28*(1), 477–539. doi:10.1146/annurev.fl.28.010196.002401

Wittmann, M., Zeiser, T., Hager, G., & Wellein, G. (2011). *Comparison of different propagation steps for the lattice Boltzmann method.* CoRR, abs/1111.0922

Wittmann, M., Zeiser, T., Hager, G., & Wellein, G. (2013). Comparison of different propagation steps for lattice Boltzmann methods. *Computers & Mathematics with Applications (Oxford, England)*, *65*(6), 924–935. doi:10.1016/j.camwa.2012.05.002

Wittmann, M., Zeiser, T., Hager, G., & Wellein, G. (2013b). Domain decomposition and locality optimization for large-scale lattice Boltzmann simulations. *Computers & Fluids*, *80*, 283–289. doi:10.1016/j.compfluid.2012.02.007

Wu Z., Xu Z., Kim O., & Alber M. (2014). Three-dimensional multi-scale model of deformable platelets adhesion to vessel wall in blood flow. Philosophical Transactions of the Royal Society of London A: Mathematical. *Physical and Engineering Sciences, 372*(2021).

Wu, J., & Shu, C. (2009). Implicit velocity correction-based immersed boundary lattice Boltzmann method and its applications. *Journal of Computational Physics*, *228*(6), 1963–1979. doi:10.1016/j.jcp.2008.11.019

Xian, W., & Takayuki, A. (2011). Multi-GPU performance of incompressible flow computation by lattice Boltzmann method on GPU cluster. *Parallel Computing*, *37*(9), 521–535. doi:10.1016/j.parco.2011.02.007

Xi, H., Peng, G., & Chou, S. H. (1999). Finite-volume lattice Boltzmann method. *Physical Review. E*, *59*(5), 6202–6205. doi:10.1103/PhysRevE.59.6202 PMID:11969609

Xiong, Q., Li, B., Xu, J., Fang, X. J., Wang, X. W., Wang, L. M., ... Ge, W. (2012). Efficient parallel implementation of the lattice Boltzmann method on large clusters of graphic processing units. *Chinese Science Bulletin*, *57*(7), 707–715. doi:10.1007/s11434-011-4908-y

Yang, A., Miller, C. T., & Turcoliver, L. D. (1996). Simulation of correlated and uncorrelated packing of random size spheres. *Physical Review E: Statistical Physics, Plasmas, Fluids, and Related Interdisciplinary Topics*, *53*(2), 1516–1524. doi:10.1103/PhysRevE.53.1516 PMID:9964415

Yang, W., Li, K., Mo, Z., & Li, K. (2015). Performance optimization using partitioned spmv on gpus and multicore cpus. *IEEE Transactions on Computers*, *64*(9), 2623–2636. doi:10.1109/TC.2014.2366731

Yoon, D. H., Yang, K. S., & Choi, C. B. (1994). Flow past a square cylinder with an angle of incidence. *Physics of Fluids*, *22*(4).

Yoshino, M., Hotta, Y., Hirozane, T., & Endo, M. (2007). A numerical method for incompressible non-Newtonian fluid flows based on the lattice Boltzmann method. *Journal of Non-Newtonian Fluid Mechanics*, *147*(1–2), 69–78. doi:10.1016/j.jnnfm.2007.07.007

Yu, D., Mei, R., Luo, L., & Shyy, W. (2003). Viscous flow computations with the method of lattice Boltzmann equation. *Progress in Aerospace Sciences*, *39*(5), 329–367. doi:10.1016/S0376-0421(03)00003-4

Yuen, E., Sederman, A., Sani, F., Alexander, P., & Gladden, L. (2003). Correlations between local conversion and hydrodynamics in a 3-D fixed-bed esterification process: An MRI and lattice-Boltzmann study. *Chemical Engineering Science*, *58*(3-6), 613–619. doi:10.1016/S0009-2509(02)00586-9

Zeiser, T., Hager, G., & Wellein, G. (2009a). Benchmark analysis and application results for lattice Boltzmann simulations on NEC SX vector and Intel Nehalem systems. *Parallel Processing Letters*, *19*(04), 491–511. doi:10.1142/S0129626409000389

Zeiser, T., Hager, G., & Wellein, G. (2009b). Vector computers in a world of commodity clusters, massively parallel systems and many-core many-threaded CPUs: Recent experience based on an advanced lattice Boltzmann flow solver. In W. E. Nagel, D. B. Kröner, & M. M. Resch (Eds.), *High performance computing in science and engineering: Transactions of the high performance computing center, Stuttgart (HLRS)* (pp. 333–347). Berlin: Springer Berlin Heidelberg. doi:10.1007/978-3-540-88303-6_24

Zergani, S., Aziz, Z. A., & Viswanathan, K. K. (2016). Exact Solutions and Lattice Boltzmann Method Modelling for Shallow Water Equations. *Global Journal of Pure and Applied Mathematics*, *12*(3), 2243–2266.

Zhang, X., Bengough, A. G., Deeks, L. K., Crawford, J. W., & Young, I. M. (2002). A novel three-dimensional lattice Boltzmann model for solute transport in variably saturated porous media. *Water Resources Research*, *38*(9), 6-1-6-10.

Zhang, X., Deeks, L. K., Bengough, A. G., Crawford, J. W., & Young, I. M. (2005). Determination of soil hydraulic conductivity with the lattice Boltzmann method and soil thin-section technique. *Journal of Hydrology (Amsterdam)*, *306*(1-4), 59–70. doi:10.1016/j.jhydrol.2004.08.039

Zhang, X., & Ren, L. (2003). Lattice Boltzmann model for agrochemical transport in soils. *Journal of Contaminant Hydrology*, *67*(1-4), 27–42. doi:10.1016/S0169-7722(03)00086-X PMID:14607468

Zhao, H., & Kamran, M. (2005). A dynamic model for the Lagrangian-averaged Navier-Stokes-α equations. *Physics of Fluids*, *17*(7), 236–297. doi:10.1063/1.1965166

Zhou, H., Mo, G., Wu, F., Zhao, J., Rui, M., & Cen, K. (2012). GPU implementation of lattice boltzmann method for flows with curved boundaries. *Computer Methods in Applied Mechanics and Engineering*, *225228*(0), 65–73. doi:10.1016/j.cma.2012.03.011

Zhou, J. G. (2002). A Lattice Boltzmann Model for the Shallow Water Equations. *Methods in Applied Mechanics and Engineering, 191*(32), 3527–3539. doi:10.1016/S0045-7825(02)00291-8

Zhou, J. G. (2003). *Lattice Boltzmann Methods for Shallow Water Flows*. Berlin: Springer-Verlag.

Zhou, J. G. (2011). Enhancement of the LABSWE for shallow water flows. *Journal of Computational Physics, 230*(2), 394–401. doi:10.1016/j.jcp.2010.09.027

Zhou, J. G., Liu, H., Shafiai, S., Peng, Y., & Burrows, R. (2010). Lattice Boltzmann method for open-channel flows. *Engineering and Computational Mechanics, 163*(4), 243–249.

Zhou, Y., So, R. M. C., Liu, M. H., & Zhang, H. J. (2000). Complex turbulent wakes generated by two and three side-by-side cylinders. *International Journal of Heat and Fluid Flow, 21*(2), 125–133. doi:10.1016/S0142-727X(99)00077-6

Zhu, T., & Atluri, S. N. (1998). A modified collocation method and a penalty formulation for enforcing the essential boundary conditions in element free Galerkin method. *Computational Mechanics, 21*(3), 211–222. doi:10.1007/s004660050296

Zienkiewicz, O. C. (1989). *The finite element method, 4th edItion*. London: Mc.Graw-Hill.

O. Zikanov (Ed.). (2010). *Essential computational fluid dynamics*. John Wiley & Sons.

Zimny, S., Chopard, B., Malaspinas, O., Lorenz, E., Jain, K., Roller, S., & Bernsdorf, J. (2013). A multiscale approach for the coupled simulation of blood flow and thrombus formation in intracranial aneurysms. *Procedia Computer Science, 18*, 1006–1015. doi:10.1016/j.procs.2013.05.266

Zou, Q., & He, X. (1997). Pressure and velocity boundary conditions for the lattice Boltzmann. *Journal of Physics of Fluids, 9*(6), 1591–1598. doi:10.1063/1.869307

About the Contributors

Jesus M. Blanco is Associate professor of the Nuclear Engineering and Fluid Mechanics Department at the University of the Basque Country. He became PhD in industrial engineering in 1998 and MSc by Research in 2009 (Cranfield University. U.K.). He is now supervising two PhD candidates in this field and has published 26 papers in international peer reviewed journals (JCR) and 45 conferences in the field of CFD optimization. Author of 6 books and 5 book chapters and co-author of an active patent from 1998 related to a fluid mixture optimization device. He has leaded several local Research Projects based in the field of CFD. He has participated in two regional research projects related to CFD surfaces optimization (SHILAM and HIDROLAM). He is habitual referee of journals and member of the scientific committee of the Spanish Society for Numerical Methods in Engineering since 2008. He is Programme coordinator of the Erasmus Mundus Master in Renewable Energy in the Marine environment (REM).

Enrico Calore received his BSc and MSc Degree in Computer Engineering from Università degli Studi di Padova (Italy) in 2006 and 2010 respectively. In the meanwhile he worked at INFN (Italian National Institute of Nuclear Physics) thanks to technical and later research fellowship programs. He received his PhD in Computer Science form Università degli Studi di Milano in 2014 and is now a Postdoctoral Researcher at Università degli Studi di Ferrara and INFN Ferrara Associate. His main interests are in the fields of HPC, parallel and distributed computing, scientific computing, code optimization and energy-efficient computing.

Alessandro Gabbana graduated from the University of Ferrara (Italy), with a bachelor degree in computer science. He continued his studies at the University of Ume\r{a} (Sweden) with a Master in computational science and engineering. In his Master thesis he has been working on a multi-GPU implementation of the D3Q19 Lattice Boltzmann Model. His current research interests lie in the field of High-performance computing, in particular in the evaluation of new highly parallel computing architectures for the solution of computational physics problems. He is enrolled in a European joint doctorate (HPC-LEAP project), with joint degree awarding institutions Universit`a degli Studi di Ferrara (UNIFE) and Bergische Universitaet Wuppertal (BUW). The project entitled "Optimized implementations of the Lattice Boltzmann Method in 2 and 3 dimensions on highly parallel computing devices" is supervised by Prof. Raffaele Tripiccione and Prof. Matthias Ehrhardt.

K. Karthik Selva Kumar obtained his Bachelor Degree in Mechanical Engineering from Anna University. Subsequently, he obtained his M.E. in Production Engineering from Thiagarajar College of Engineering/ Anna University. Besides having a strong technical expertise and analytical skills, he acquired his Ph.D. degree from Indian Institute of Technology IIT(ISM), Dhanbad, He started his career to satisfy his passion for teaching and research by Joining National Institute of Technology (NIT)-Jamshedpur from 2016. In addition to teaching at engineering colleges, he has been also working as an administrator/coordinator for student associations and laboratories. As an active researcher, Dr. K. Karthik Selva Kumar is associated with many foreign Universities, along with that he is a reviewer of 8 International Peer-Reviewed Journals. Consecutively he has contributed to the areas of Automobiles, Vibration, Engineering Design and Computational Fluid Dynamics with his research publications. A technical and education management expert, Dr. K. Karthik Selva Kumar believes that Science, Engineering, and Technology are advancing at a fast pace and obsolescence of physical infrastructure, skills, and competence take place rapidly. He is keen on taking steps to improve the existing infrastructure, investment, and intellectual strength wherever they exist and network them so as to utilize them effectively and optimally for meeting the changing needs.

L. A. Kumaraswamidhas obtained his Bachelor Degree in Mechanical Engineering from Bharathiar University, in 1999. Subsequently, he obtained his M.E. in Engineering Design from PSG Tech/ Bharathiar University, Coimbatore, in 2002. Besides having a strong technical expertise and analytical skills, he acquired his Ph.D degree from Anna University, Chennai, in 2008. He started his career from 2002 as a Teaching Research Associate in Madras Institute of Technology, Chennai, to satisfy his passion for teaching and research and then he joined National Institute of Technology (NIT)-Trichy as an Assistant Professor from 2006. Besides having a strong technical expertise and analytical skills, he acquired his Ph.D degree from Anna University, Chennai, in 2008. Before he was posted as Associated in Indian School of Mines, Dr. L. A. Kumaraswamidhas served as an Assistant Professor at National Institute of Technology, Tiruchirappalli in Tamil Nadu during 2006-2012. In addition to teaching at engineering colleges, he had also worked as an administrator/coordinator for student associations and laboratories. By virtue of working for a considerable number of years in the academic arena, he reached the position of the Mining-Machinery Coordinator at Indian School of Mines. During his stint as MME Coordinator, Dr. L. A. Kumaraswamidhas became known for his contribution of value-creation and value-addition to various sectors such as overall administration, academic affairs, education and research of the University. He was reputed for the timely conduct of examinations in University Departments and always ensured prompt release of results. As an active researcher, Dr. L. A. Kumaraswamidhas is associated with many foreign Universities, along with that he is an Editorial Board Member of 5 Reputed Journals and also a reviewer of 8 International journal. Consecutively he has contributed to the areas of Automobiles, Vibration, Tribology, Engineering Design and Computational Fluid Dynamics with his 35 research publications. As a research guide, Dr. L. A. Kumaraswamidhas produced 1 Ph.D and 10 M.S. scholars in various fields. At present, 10 research scholars are pursuing their Ph.D. under his direct supervision. A technical and education management expert, Dr. L. A. Kumaraswamidhas, believes that Science, Engineering and Technology are advancing at a fast pace and obsolescence of physical infrastructure, skills and competence takes place rapidly. He is keen on taking steps to improve the existing infrastructure, investment and intellectual strength wherever they exist and network them so as to utilize them effectively and optimally for meeting the changing needs.

João V. F. Lima is Associate Professor (Professor Adjunto I) at the Federal University of Santa Maria (UFSM) in Santa Maria, Brazil. He received a Ph.D. in Computer Science from the Federal University of Rio Grande do Sul (UFRGS), Brazil and the MSTII Grenoble University, France, in 2014 by cotutelle agreement. He received a Master in Computer Science from UFRGS, Brazil and a Bachelor in Computer Science from the Federal University of Santa Maria (UFSM), Brazil. He has experience in computer science with emphasis in High Performance Processing, He research especially high performance computing and parallel applications. Since the bachelor, he woks with parallel programming interfaces. In the last years he was one of the developer of the XKaapi tool for parallel programming.

Claudio Schepke is a professor at the Federal University of Pampa since 2012. He holds a degree in Computer Science at Federal University of Santa Maria (2005) and master's (2007) and doctorate degree (2012) in Computer Science from the Federal University of Rio Grande do Sul, in sandwich mode at the Technische Universität Berlin, Germany (2010-2011). He has experience in computer science, with emphasis on Parallel and Distributed Processing, acting on the following topics: high performance computing, parallel programming and cloud computing. He has interest in High Performance Computing applications.

Sebastiano Fabio Schifano is graduated in Computer Science from University of Pisa (Italy). He spent his early scientific carrier at IEI-CNR and at INFN, as researcher and senior researcher, and from 2006 he is assistant professor at University of Ferrara (Italy). He had a major role in several projects for the development of parallel systems optimized for scientific applications, like Lattice Gauge Theory (LQCD), fluid dynamics and spin-glasses. In 2007 he was a co-author of the proposal for the QPACE project, a German project to develop a massively parallel system based on IBM Cell-BE processors, interconnected by a custom 3D-mesh network, awarded as best Green500 system in Nov'09 and Jun'10. More recently, his research activities are focused on the design and optimization of LQCD and Lattice-Boltzmann applications for multi- and many-core processor architectures. He is author of 90+ articles and conference papers.

Matheus Serpa is graduated in Computer Science by Unipampa in 2015. He is currently a master student of Computer Science at Informatics Institute of UFRGS and supported by Intel in a project for teaching programming skills for multi and many core systems. Matheus has experience in optimizations and parallel programming techniques for scientific applications. He develop parallel codes using different interfaces like Pthreads, OpenMP, Cilk, MPI, CUDA, OpenACC and OpenCL and participate and many competitions of sequential and parallel programing marathons.

Sonam Singh is working as an assistant professor at Cluster Innovation Center, University of Delhi, India. She has completed her Ph.D in computational Fluid Dynamics in 2014 and M.Sc. in applied mathematics in 2009 from I.I.T. Roorkee, India. The author has immense interest in advanced numerical techniques and she has a number of international research publications in this field.

Tadeusz Tomczak received M.S. and Ph.D. degrees in computer science all from the Institute of Computers, Control, and Robotics, Wroclaw University of Technology, Poland, in 2002 and 2007 respectively. His research interests include residue number systems, fast computational hardware and parallel computing.

Raffaele Tripiccione was born in Florence (Italy) in 1956. He graduated in physics (summa cum laude) in 1980 and then then attended the graduate school at the Scuola Normale Superiore, Pisa. He is a Professor of Physics at Universita' di Ferrara (Italy). His early scientific interests were in the areas of quantum field theory and the phenomenology of elementary particle physics. More recently, he has focused mainly on several facets of computational theoretical physics such as lattice gauge theories (LGT), computational fluid dynamics and spin systems. Over the years, he has worked on large simulations in LGT, on the study of the statistical properties and scaling laws of fluids in the turbulent regime, on the simulation, with Monte Carlo techniques, of spin glasses and on the development of Lattice Boltzmann computational methods. He his author/co-author of approximately 200 scientific papers, conference proceedings and reports.

Iñaki Zabala is a research engineer in SENER Ingeniería y Sistemas, S.A. working in marine renewable energy technologies assessment.

Index

A

Accelerator Architectures 50
Anti-Phase 230, 241, 251, 254
AoS 10-11, 14, 29, 69-71, 108-110

B

BGK 5, 27, 39, 63, 124, 153, 162, 178,
190, 197-198, 214, 228, 230-231, 275,
296, 315, 340-341, 353, 356, 363
Burst Memory Transfer 191

C

CFD 1, 61, 115, 117, 119-121, 153, 188,
341, 343, 363
Chaotic Flow 230, 241-242, 244, 250, 252
Complex Geometries 25, 37, 112, 151,
157-158, 160, 175, 179, 181, 184-185,
188-189, 193, 195, 200-201, 212,
215, 254
Computational Fluid Dynamics 1, 25, 28-
29, 55, 117, 119-120, 151, 155, 187,
211, 229, 298, 341-343, 346-347, 363
Connectivity Matrix 157, 159, 169-171,
174, 177
Coprocessors 37, 43, 50-53, 58, 192
Coriolis Force 341
CPU 19, 22, 28-29, 47, 57, 61, 66-69, 74,
80-81, 98-99, 102, 104-105, 110, 119-
120, 122, 136-137, 141-142, 145-150,
154-155, 169-170, 172, 175, 189,
191-192, 292

CUDA 16, 43, 45-56, 61, 67-69, 73-75,
80-81, 83, 95-96, 110, 115-116, 119,
129, 135, 212

D

D3Q19 35, 37, 40, 48, 53, 55, 71, 98
Directive-Based Programming 119
DnQm 352, 363
DNS 154, 341-342, 344, 346-348, 360, 363
Domain Decomposition 77, 98, 157, 160,
173, 175-177, 190, 295
Drag Coefficient 155, 211, 228, 234, 238,
244-246, 251

E

Eddy Viscosity 339, 350-353, 361, 365
Element free Galerkin method 193, 195,
205, 210-211, 217-218, 222, 225
Energy Efficiency 59, 105-106, 110-111
Exascale Computing 36, 57, 176

F

FDF 360, 363
FDM 211, 299, 341
FEM 161, 168, 193, 195, 202, 208, 211-
212, 214, 216, 225, 267, 269-271,
273-274, 277-278, 280, 292
Finite Element Method 161, 215, 217-218,
267, 269, 276, 293, 295
Fluid Index Array 157, 160, 169, 171, 177
Fluid-Structure Interaction 26, 152, 194,
201, 267-268, 293-297

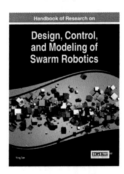

Stay Current on the Latest Emerging Research Developments

Become an IGI Global Reviewer for Authored Book Projects

Premier Reference Source

Emerging GIS Applications for Emergency and Disaster Management

Premier Reference Source

Managerial Strategies and Green Solutions for Project Sustainability

Premier Reference Source

Comparative Approaches to Using R and Python for Statistical Data Analysis

Premier Reference Source

Solutions for High-Touch Communications in a High-Tech World

The overall success of an authored book project is dependent on quality and timely reviews.

In this competitive age of scholarly publishing, constructive and timely feedback significantly decreases the turnaround time of manuscripts from submission to acceptance, allowing the publication and discovery of progressive research at a much more expeditious rate. Several IGI Global authored book projects are currently seeking highly qualified experts in the field to fill vacancies on their respective editorial review boards:

Applications may be sent to:
development@igi-global.com

Applicants must have a doctorate (or an equivalent degree) as well as publishing and reviewing experience. Reviewers are asked to write reviews in a timely, collegial, and constructive manner. All reviewers will begin their role on an ad-hoc basis for a period of one year, and upon successful completion of this term can be considered for full editorial review board status, with the potential for a subsequent promotion to Associate Editor.

If you have a colleague that may be interested in this opportunity, we encourage you to share this information with them.

Information Resources Management Association

Advancing the Concepts & Practices of Information Resources Management in Modern Organizations

Become an IRMA Member

Members of the **Information Resources Management Association (IRMA)** understand the importance of community within their field of study. The Information Resources Management Association is an ideal venue through which professionals, students, and academicians can convene and share the latest industry innovations and scholarly research that is changing the field of information science and technology. Become a member today and enjoy the benefits of membership as well as the opportunity to collaborate and network with fellow experts in the field.

IRMA Membership Benefits:

- **One FREE Journal Subscription**
- **30% Off Additional Journal Subscriptions**
- **20% Off Book Purchases**
- Updates on the latest events and research on Information Resources Management through the IRMA-L listserv.
- Updates on new open access and downloadable content added to Research IRM.
- A copy of the Information Technology Management Newsletter twice a year.
- A certificate of membership.

IRMA Membership $195

Scan code or visit **irma-international.org** and begin by selecting your free journal subscription.

Membership is good for one full year.

Printed in the United States
By Bookmasters